Lecture Notes in Computer Science 15648

Founding Editors

Gerhard Goos
Juris Hartmanis

The series Lecture Notes in Computer Science (LNCS), including its subseries Lecture Notes in Artificial Intelligence (LNAI) and Lecture Notes in Bioinformatics (LNBI), has established itself as a medium for the publication of new developments in computer science and information technology research, teaching, and education.

LNCS enjoys close cooperation with the computer science R & D community, the series counts many renowned academics among its volume editors and paper authors, and collaborates with prestigious societies. Its mission is to serve this international community by providing an invaluable service, mainly focused on the publication of conference and workshop proceedings and postproceedings. LNCS commenced publication in 1973.

Osvaldo Gervasi · Beniamino Murgante ·
Chiara Garau · Yeliz Karaca · David Taniar ·
Ana Maria A. C. Rocha · Bernady O. Apduhan
Editors

Computational Science and Its Applications – ICCSA 2025

25th International Conference
Istanbul, Turkey, June 30 – July 3, 2025
Proceedings, Part I

 Springer

Editors

Osvaldo Gervasi 🔟
University of Perugia
Perugia, Italy

Beniamino Murgante 🔟
University of Basilicata
Potenza, Italy

Chiara Garau 🔟
University of Cagliari
Cagliari, Italy

Yeliz Karaca 🔟
University of Massachusetts Chan Medical
Worcester, MA, USA

David Taniar 🔟
Monash University
Clayton, VIC, Australia

Ana Maria A. C. Rocha 🔟
University of Minho
Braga, Portugal

Bernady O. Apduhan
Kyushu Sangyo University
Fukuoka, Japan

ISSN 0302-9743   ISSN 1611-3349 (electronic)
Lecture Notes in Computer Science
ISBN 978-3-031-96999-7   ISBN 978-3-031-97000-9 (eBook)
https://doi.org/10.1007/978-3-031-97000-9

Preface

The compiled 3 volumes (LNCS volumes 15648–15650) consist of the peer-reviewed papers from the 6 Main Conference Tracks of the 2025 International Conference on Computational Science and Its Applications (ICCSA 2025), which was held between June 30 – July 3, 2025 in Istanbul (Türkiye). The peer-reviewed papers of the 68 Workshops are published in a separate set made up of fourteen volumes (LNCS 15886–15899).

The conference was held in a hybrid form, with the large majority of participants in presence, hosted by Galatasaray University, Istanbul, Türkiye. We enabled virtual participation for those who did not attend the event in person due to logistical, political and economic problems, by adopting a technological infrastructure via open-source software (jitsi + riot) and a commercial Cloud infrastructure.

With the 2025 edition, ICCSA celebrated its 25th anniversary, a quarter of a century as a memorable moment that is harmoniously aligned with Istanbul, an extraordinary city located at the crossroads and acting as a bridge connecting Asia and Europe, representing different cultures, beliefs as well as lifestyles, which highlights its intercultural fabric.

ICCSA 2025 marked another fruitful and thought-provoking academic event in the International Conferences on Computational Science and Its Applications (ICCSA) conference series, previously held in Hanoi, Vietnam (2024), Athens, Greece (2023), Málaga, Spain (2022), Cagliari, Italy (hybrid with a few participants in presence in 2021 and completely online in 2020), whilst earlier editions took place in Saint Petersburg, Russia (2019), Melbourne, Australia (2018), Trieste, Italy (2017), Beijing, China (2016), Banff, Canada (2015), Guimaraes, Portugal (2014), Ho Chi Minh City, Vietnam (2013), Salvador, Brazil (2012), Santander, Spain (2011), Fukuoka, Japan (2010), Suwon, South Korea (2009), Perugia, Italy (2008), Kuala Lumpur, Malaysia (2007), Glasgow, UK (2006), Singapore (2005), Assisi, Italy (2004), Montreal, Canada (2003), and (as ICCS) Amsterdam, the Netherlands (2002) and San Francisco, USA (2001).

Computational Science constitutes the main pillar of most present research, industrial and commercial applications, and plays a unique role in exploiting ICT innovative technologies, and the ICCSA conference series has, accordingly, provided ample opportunities to researchers and industry practitioners to discuss new ideas, to share complex problems and their solutions, and to shape new trends in Computational Science. As the conference mirrors society from a scientific point of view, this year's undoubtedly dominant theme was large language models, machine learning and Artificial Intelligence (AI) and their applications in the most diverse technological, economic and industrial fields, amongst the others.

The ICCSA 2025 conference was structured in six general tracks covering the fields of computational science and its applications: Computational Methods, Algorithms and Scientific Applications – High Performance Computing and Networks – Geometric Modeling, Graphics and Visualization – Advanced and Emerging Applications – Information Systems and Technologies – Urban and Regional Planning. In addition, the conference consisted of 68 workshops, focusing on topical issues of utmost importance to science, technology and society: from new computational approaches for earth science, to mathematical methods for image processing, new statistical and optimization methods, several Artificial Intelligence approaches, sustainability issues, smart cities and related technologies, to name some.

In the Main Conference Proceedings, we accepted 71 full papers, 6 short papers and 1 Ph.D. Showcase paper from 269 submissions to the General Tracks of the Conference (with an acceptance rate of 29.9%). In the Workshops proceedings, we accepted 362 full papers, 37 short papers and 2 Ph.D. Showcase papers from a total of 1043 submissions (Acceptance rate 38.4%). We would like to convey our sincere appreciation to the workshops' chairs and co-chairs and program committee members for their diligent work, commitment and dedication.

The success and consistent maintenance of the ICCSA conference series in general, and of ICCSA 2025 in particular, rely upon the support of many people: authors, presenters, participants, keynote speakers, workshop chairs, session chairs, organizing committee members, student volunteers, Program Committee members, Advisory Committee members, International Liaison chairs, reviewers and other individuals in various roles. Thus, we take this opportunity to wholehartedly thank each and everyone.

We additionally wish to thank publisher Springer for their agreement to publish the proceedings, besides sponsoring part of the best papers awards and for their kind assistance and cooperation during the editing process.

We would cordially like to invite you to refer to the ICCSA website https://iccsa.org, where you can find the relevant details regarding this academic endeavor and event of ours.

June 2025

Osvaldo Gervasi
Yeliz Karaca
Beniamino Murgante
Chiara Garau

A Welcome Message from the Organizers

The International Conference on Computational Science and Its Applications (ICCSA) reflects a culmination of meticulous and dedicated efforts and academic endeavors toward the progress of science and technology.

One of the most noteworthy aspects of ICCSA is its fostering of a collective spirit, bringing together a plethora of participants from all over the world. Correspondingly, this merging power manifests itself in the 25th anniversary of ICCSA, which is a quarter of a century, in Istanbul, Türkiye, which connects and acts as a bridge between two continents, namely Asia and Europe. This unique location in the world hosts the 25th year of ICCSA at Galatasaray University, located on Çırağan Avenue by Istanbul's Bosphorus, which is an established international university bestowed with a distinctive past of teaching tradition, research and education exceeding five centuries.

Istanbul, having served as the capital city of four empires, namely the Roman Empire (330–395), the Byzantine Empire (395–1204 and 1261–1453), the Latin Empire (1204–1261) and the Ottoman Empire (1453–1922), is an exceptional city of the Republic of Türkiye founded by Mustafa Kemal Atatürk.

Situated at a strategic location along the historic Silk Road, Istanbul is at the core of extending rail networks which span across Europe and West Asia along with the only sea route between the Black Sea and the Mediterranean.

The cultural, historical and economic pulses of the country are evident in Istanbul whose rooted origins have embraced varying beliefs, lifestyles and populace, which highlights the city's mosaic quality with blended fabric in a constant harmonious flow. This has enabled cultures to grow and be nurtured, which is profoundly rooted in its urban culture.

Computational Science constitutes the main pillar of most present research, industrial and commercial activities besides manifesting a unique role in exploiting and addressing innovative Information and Communication Technologies. Thus, the 25-year-old ICCSA conference series provides remarkable opportunities to get acquainted with leading researchers, scientists, scholars, practitioners and many more while exchanging innovative ideas and initiating new partnerships, associations and bonds.

With the hosting of Galatasaray University, I would personally and on behalf of the Local Organizing Committee, with the members Emre Alptekin, Gülfem Işıklar Alptekin, Cengiz Kahraman, Abdullah Çağrı Tolga and Ayberk Zeytin, like to convey our sincere gratitude and thanks to everyone who exerted their efforts in and contributed to the realization of ICCSA 2025. With these notes and remarks, welcome to Istanbul!

Cordially yours,

On behalf of the Local Organizing Committee.

June 2025 Yeliz Karaca

Organization

Honorary General Chairs

Bernady O. Apduhan   Kyushu Sangyo University, Japan
Kenneth C. J. Tan   Sardina Systems, UK

General Chairs

Yeliz Karaca   University of Massachusetts, USA
Osvaldo Gervasi   University of Perugia, Italy
David Taniar   Monash University, Australia

Program Committee Chairs

Beniamino Murgante   University of Basilicata, Italy
Chiara Garau   University of Cagliari, Italy
Ana Maria A. C. Rocha   University of Minho, Portugal
A. Çağrı Tolga   Galatasaray University, Türkiye

International Advisory Committee

Jemal Abawajy   Deakin University, Australia
Dharma P. Agarwal   University of Cincinnati, USA
Rajkumar Buyya   Melbourne University, Australia
Claudia Bauzer Medeiros   University of Campinas, Brazil
Manfred M. Fisher   Vienna University of Economics and Business, Austria
Pierre Frankhauser   University of Franche-Comté/CNRS, France
Marina L. Gavrilova   University of Calgary, Canada
Sumi Helal   University of Florida, USA & Lancaster University, UK
Bin Jiang   University of Gävle, Sweden
Yee Leung   Chinese University of Hong Kong, China

International Liaison Chairs

Ivan Blečić	University of Cagliari, Italy
Giuseppe Borruso	University of Trieste, Italy
Elise De Donker	Western Michigan University, USA
Maria Noelia Faginas Lago	University of Perugia, Italy
Maria Irene Falcão	University of Minho, Portugal
Robert C. H. Hsu	Chung Hua University, Taiwan
Yeliz Karaca	University of Massachusetts Chan Medical School, USA
Tae-Hoon Kim	Zhejiang University of Science and Technology, China
Vladimir Korkhov	Saint Petersburg University, Russia
Takashi Naka	Kyushu Sangyo University, Japan
Rafael D. C. Santos	National Institute for Space Research, Brazil
Maribel Yasmina Santos	University of Minho, Portugal
Anastasia Stratigea	National Technical University of Athens, Greece

Workshop and Session Organizing Chairs

Beniamino Murgante	University of Basilicata, Italy
Chiara Garau	University of Cagliari, Italy

Award Chair

Wenny Rahayu	La Trobe University, Australia

Publicity Committee Chairs

Elmer Dadios	De La Salle University, Philippines
Nataliia Kulabukhova	Saint Petersburg University, Russia
Daisuke Takahashi	Tsukuba University, Japan
Shangwang Wang	Beijing University of Posts and Telecommunications, China

Local Organizing Committee Chairs

Emre Alptekin	Galatasaray University, Türkiye
Gülfem Işıklar Alptekin	Galatasaray University, Türkiye
Cengiz Kahraman	İstanbul Technical University, Türkiye
A. Çağrı Tolga	Galatasaray University, Türkiye
Ayberk Zeytin	Galatasaray University, Türkiye

Technology Chair

Damiano Perri	University of Perugia, Italy

Program Committee

Vera Afreixo	University of Aveiro, Portugal
Vladimir Alarcon	Northern Gulf Institute, USA
Filipe Alvelos	University of Minho, Portugal
Debora Anelli	Polytechnic University of Bari, Italy
Hartmut Asche	Hasso-Plattner-Institut für Digital Engineering Ggmbh, Germany
Nizamettin Aydın,	İstanbul Technical University, Türkiye
Ginevra Balletto	University of Cagliari, Italy
Nadia Balucani	University of Perugia, Italy
Socrates Basbas	Aristotle University of Thessaloniki, Greece
David Berti	ART SpA, Italy
Michela Bertolotto	University College Dublin, Ireland
Sandro Bimonte	CEMAGREF, TSCF, France
Ana Cristina Braga	University of Minho, Portugal
Tiziana Campisi	Kore University of Enna, Italy
Yves Caniou	Université Claude Bernard Lyon 1, France
Alessandra Capolupo	Polytechnic University of Bari, Italy
José A. Cardoso e Cunha	Universidade Nova de Lisboa, Portugal
Rui Cardoso	University of Beira Interior, Portugal
Leocadio G. Casado	University of Almería, Spain
Mete Celik	Erciyes University, Turkey
Maria Cerreta	University of Naples Federico II, Italy
Ta Quang Chieu	Thuyloi University, Vietnam
Rachel Chien-Sing Lee	Sunway University, Malaysia
Birol Ciloglugil	Ege University, Turkey
Mauro Coni	University of Cagliari, Italy

Suzan Obaiys	University of Malaya, Malaysia
Marcin Paprzycki	Polish Academy of Sciences, Poland
Eric Pardede	La Trobe University, Australia
Ana Isabel Pereira	Polytechnic Institute of Bragança, Portugal
Damiano Perri	University of Perugia, Italy
Massimiliano Petri	University of Pisa, Italy
Telmo Pinto	University of Coimbra, Portugal
Alessandro Plaisant	University of Sassari, Italy
Maurizio Pollino	ENEA, Italy
Alenka Poplin	Iowa State University, USA
Marcos Quiles	Federal University of São Paulo, Brazil
Nguyen Huu Quynh	Thuyloi University, Vietnam
Albert Rimola	Universitat Autònoma de Barcelona, Spain
Humberto Rocha	University of Coimbra, Portugal
Marzio Rosi	University of Perugia, Italy
Lucia Saganeiti	University of L'Aquila, Italy
Francesco Scorza	University of Basilicata, Italy
Marco Paulo Seabra dos Reis	University of Coimbra, Portugal
Jie Shen	University of Michigan, USA
Francesco Tajani	Sapienza University of Rome, Italy
Rodrigo Tapia Mcclung	Centro de Investigación en Ciencias de Información Geoespacial, Mexico
Eufemia Tarantino	Polytechnic University of Bari, Italy
Sergio Tasso	University of Perugia, Italy
Ana Paula Teixeira	Universidade do Minho, Portugal
Yiota Theodora	National Technical University of Athens, Greece
Giuseppe A. Trunfio	University of Sassari, Italy
Toshihiro Uchibayashi	Kyushu University, Japan
Marco Vizzari	University of Perugia, Italy
Frank Westad	Norwegian University of Science and Technology, Norway
Fukuko Yuasa	High Energy Accelerator Research Organization, Japan
Ljiljana Zivkovic	Republic Geodetic Authority, Serbia

General Tracks

1. Computational Methods, Algorithms and Scientific Applications

Computational Biology
Computational Combustion
Computational Chemistry

Computational Fluid Dynamics
Computational Physics
Computational Geometry
Computational Mathematics
Computational Mechanics
Computational Electro-magnetics
Numerical Methods and Algorithms

2. High Performance Computing and Networks

Parallel and Distributed Computing
Cluster Computing
Supercomputing
Cloud Computing
Autonomic Computing
P2P Computing
Mobile Computing
Edge Computing
Workflow Design and Practice
Computer and Network Architecture

3. Geometric Modeling, Graphics and Visualization

Scientific Visualization
Computer Graphics
Geometric Modeling
Pattern Recognition
Image Processing
CAD/CAM
Web3D, Virtual and Augmented Reality

4. Advanced and Emerging Applications

Biochemistry
Bioinformatics
Astrophysics
Biometric Modeling
Environmental, Climate and Weather Modeling
Geology and Geophysics
Nuclear Physics
Financial and Economical Modeling
Computational Journalism

5. Information Systems and Technologies

Information Retrieval
Scientific Databases
Security Engineering
Risk Analysis
Reliability Engineering

Software Engineering
Data Mining
Artificial Intelligence
Machine Learning
Learning Technologies
Web-Based Computing
Web 2.0
Blockchain

6. Urban and Regional Planning

Urban and Regional Growth
Sustainable Urban and Regional Development
Socio-ecological Systems
Open Data/Big Data
Cultural Heritage
Smart and Sustainable Cities
Mobility and Intelligent Transport Systems
Geographical Information Systems
Decision Support Systems
Complexity Assessment and Mapping
Logistics

Sponsoring Organizations

ICCSA 2025 would not have been possible without the tremendous support of many organizations and institutions, for which all organizers and participants of ICCSA 2025 express their sincere gratitude:

Galatasaray University, Istanbul, Türkiye
(https://gsu.edu.tr/en)

African Mathematical Union
(https://www.africanmathunion.org/)

Springer Nature Switzerland AG, Switzerland
(https://www.springer.com)

The University of Massachusetts, USA
(https://www.umass.edu/)

University of Perugia, Italy
(https://www.unipg.it)

University of Basilicata, Italy (http://www.unibas.it)

Monash University, Australia
(https://www.monash.edu/)

Kyushu Sangyo University, Japan
(https://www.kyusan-u.ac.jp/)

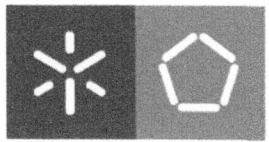

Universidade do Minho
Escola de Engenharia

University of Minho, Portugal
(https://www.uminho.pt/)
Venue
ICCSA 2025 took place in: **Galatasaray University, Istanbul, Türkiye**

Additional Reviewers

Reviewers
The review tasks for each workshop have been carried out by the workshop Organizers and the members of the workshop Program Committee.

Plenary Lectures

Sky Safe with GAI and Post-quantum Computing

Elizabeth Chang

Professor of the Cyber Security and Head of Discipline, University of Sunshine Coast, Australia

Abstract. Professor Chang's talk in this presentation has two distinct parts. To start, she will introduce the landscape of cybersecurity development, attacks, threats, and vulnerabilities, as well as state-of-the-art cyber protection, cyber defence, and cyber incident prevention. This is followed by a discussion of the impact of Generative AI (GAI) and quantum-safe cryptographic computing, highlighting the major issues and challenges in research, education, and training. In conclusion, she will present a vision for Sky Safe solutions, aiming to achieve cyber resilience that supports business and economic stability, enhances human capabilities, and promotes environmental sustainability.

Disaster Preparedness and Risk Profiling in the Digital Era from Earth Observation Lens

Jagannath Aryal

Department of Infrastructure Engineering, University of Melbourne, Australia

Abstract. Natural hazards which turn into disasters result in severe losses of lives, infrastructure, and property. Disasters such as earthquakes and landslides and their impacts on transportation safety, infrastructure resilience, and displacement of people to new places are challenges. To address such challenges, earth observation data and intelligent methods can provide potential solutions in developing decision support systems. This talk will present the state of the in Earth observation for disaster resilience using intelligent methods. In the earth observation space, digitalisation has revolutionised the way we map, monitor, and develop decision support systems. Global case study examples covering earthquake-induced landslides from the Himalayan region will cover the digital capabilities. The digital capabilities will embrace object recognition, interpretation, and their accurate and precise capture to integrate into digital models. The developed digital models from representative case studies can be leveraged in other jurisdictions in profiling risks to protect lives and infrastructure and creating disaster preparedness in the era of digital age and digital economy.

Intelligent Image Enhancement for Real-World Applications in Adverse Atmospheric Conditions

Khan Muhammad

Department of Global Convergence, Sungkyunkwan University, South Korea

Abstract. The adverse impacts of atmospheric conditions such as haze, fog, and low-light environments pose significant challenges for real-world applications reliant on computer vision, including autonomous driving, surveillance, and remote sensing. This keynote explores cutting-edge advancements in intelligent image enhancement, drawing insights from two pivotal studies. The first introduces HazeSpace2M, a comprehensive dataset and novel classification-guided dehazing framework that improves image clarity across diverse atmospheric conditions, addressing the gap between synthetic and real-world dehazing performance. The second focuses on LoLI-Street, a benchmark for low-light image enhancement tailored to urban environments, extending beyond enhancement to enable robust object detection and scene understanding. Taken together, these contributions demonstrate how integrating domain-specific datasets, advanced algorithms, and performance benchmarks can significantly elevate the reliability of computer vision systems under challenging weather and lighting conditions. Attendees will gain valuable insights into the methodologies, datasets, and practical applications driving innovation in this field, with implications for research and industry alike.

In Memory of Carmelo Torre

Unfortunately, Professor Carmelo Torre, one of the cornerstones of the ICCSA Conference, passed away last December, leaving everyone stunned and deeply saddened. His loss has created a profound void within our academic community. Carmelo was not only a respected scholar and dedicated contributor to the success and growth of ICCSA, but also a generous colleague, mentor, and friend to many. His intellectual rigor, warm personality, and unwavering commitment to advancing research will be remembered with great admiration. As we continue the work he helped shape, we honor his legacy and the indelible mark he left on all of us. 'Carmelo Torre graduated in engineering at the Polytechnic of Bari with a thesis on urban planning under Dino Borri's guidance. He began his research career by collaborating with Franco Selicato. During his PhD at the University of Naples Federico II under Luigi Fusco Girard, he specialized in real estate market analysis and multi-criteria evaluation methods. He explored the social impacts of urban transformations with his lifelong friend Maria Cerreta. His first ICCSA participation was in Perugia in 2008, in the session Geographical Analysis, Urban Modeling, Spatial Statistics. Instantly captivated by the conference, his charisma enabled him to involve various Italian scientific communities, including those in real estate and statistics. ICCSA became a yearly commitment for him, where he valued the high editorial quality of the proceedings and the dynamic post-presentation discussions and debates he passionately and expertly enriched. In 2012, alongside Maria Cerreta and Paola Perchinunno, he organized the workshop Econometrics and Multidimensional Evaluation in the Urban Environment (EMEUE), fostering dialogue on critical topics. His influence steadily grew, drawing numerous research groups to ICCSA and establishing real estate and assessment as one of the conference's leading fields. A pillar of ICCSA, he was involved across all facets of the event. Torre's contributions to academic discourse were marked by intellectual rigor and innovative thinking. His conference interventions consistently challenged conventional wisdom, offering insights transcending disciplinary boundaries. Beyond the conference, he passionately advocated for equity and social justice. His left-leaning ideology, though firm, earned respect from those with differing views, thanks to his sincerity and loyalty. He was creative, generous, and always willing to help, even at a personal cost. Despite battling illness, he maintained his characteristic optimism, warmth, cheerfulness, and commitment, supported by his partner, Caterina Rinaldo. His legacy lives on in his ideas, dedication, and unmatched generosity.

Contents – Part I

High Performance Computing and Networks

Geometric Modeling, Graphics and Visualization

Advanced and Emerging Applications

Contents – Part II

Contents – Part III

Urban and Regional Planning

PHD Showcase Papers

Short Papers

Computational Methods, Algorithms and Scientific Applications

Generation and Visualization of NURBS Surfaces Derived from Controlled NURBS Curves

Ruben Teodoro Urbina Guzman$^{(\boxtimes)}$ [iD], Yheff Alexander Castillo Maza[iD], and Ronald Paul Santamaria Silupu[iD]

Universidad Nacional de Piura, Urb. Miraflores s/n, Piura, Peru
rurbinag@unp.edu.pe, 1302018004@alumnos.unp.edu.pe,
rsantamarias@egresados.unp.edu.pe

Abstract. This study presents the generation and visualization of Non-Uniform Rational B-Spline surfaces derived from controlled curves, implemented in Python within the Jupyter Notebook environment. Three main approaches are examined: translation surfaces, revolution surfaces, and tensor product surfaces constructed from B-spline curves.

Matrix-based algorithms and object-oriented implementations enable the precise modeling of parametric surfaces through control points, weights, and knot vectors. Among the approaches, revolution surfaces exhibit the highest geometric accuracy and smoothness when applied to symmetric base curves, such as circles and ellipses. Translation surfaces are computationally efficient but limited to linear or parallel curve interactions, while tensor product surfaces demonstrate greater versatility for complex free-form modeling, albeit with increased computational cost.

Experimental results show that the methods achieve high visual fidelity and parametric continuity for both regular and irregular shapes, including cylinders, cones, hyperboloids, and user-defined geometries. In addition to its computational value, the study offers an educational perspective: the use of Python as a programming and visualization tool facilitates the comprehension of abstract mathematical concepts in undergraduate-level geometry and modeling courses. Its readable syntax and interactive environment foster experimentation, allowing students to engage with core ideas in computational geometry through practical implementations.

These findings highlight the adaptability and pedagogical potential of NURBS surfaces in both scientific applications and mathematics education.

Keywords: NURBS curves · NURBS surfaces · Surface generation · Python modeling · Geometric design

1 Introduction

The Non-Uniform Rational B-Spline (NURBS) representation constitutes a fundamental standard in computational geometry and is widely used in Computer-

O. Gervasi et al. (Eds.): ICCSA 2025, LNCS 15648, pp. 3–20, 2025.
https://doi.org/10.1007/978-3-031-97000-9_1

Aided Geometric Design (CAGD) for the precise modeling of curves and surfaces [1]. It supports the construction of both simple entities, such as lines and circles, and complex surfaces in $\mathbb{E}^2 \to \mathbb{E}^2$ and $\mathbb{E}^3 \to \mathbb{E}^3$. Advancements in NURBS have enhanced their generation, approximation, and manipulation in geometric modeling and CAD. Techniques based on curve reparameterization have enabled the construction of developable surfaces using algebraic formulations [1], while generalizations of NURBS provide improved control over complex geometries such as helicoids and ruled surfaces [2]. Algorithms for precise surface fitting, surface generation, distance calculations, and intersection detection have been proposed, especially for applications in digital manufacturing and computer graphics [3,4]. Tejada's study [5] demonstrated the construction of revolution spheres and tori by rotating base curves, though this approach is constrained to single-axis rotations. Meanwhile, Cuartas [6] optimized NURBS surfaces using 3D scanned data and the Levenberg-Marquardt algorithm, achieving high accuracy but requiring specialized acquisition hardware. Python, a high-level general-purpose programming language, is increasingly employed for its readable syntax and accessible learning curve [7]. Several libraries enable the manipulation and visualization of NURBS geometry, although they may lack low-level control for detailed modeling tasks. Recent research has expanded Python's capabilities in this area. For instance, [8] introduces algorithms that convert 3D images into CAD models through control networks and optimization, while [9] presents a GPU-accelerated differentiable module in PyTorch for computing derivatives and enhancing CAD-related operations.

In addition to its computational utility, Python also offers pedagogical advantages. Its flexible syntax and support for multiple paradigms—structured, object-oriented, functional, and imperative—foster student engagement in programming and promote deeper understanding of mathematical structures [10,11]. Interactive environments like Jupyter Notebook further support exploratory learning by enabling real-time manipulation of control points, weights, and knots.

This work proposes a computational framework for constructing and visualizing NURBS curves and surfaces using Python. The foundation is the mathematical definition of B-spline basis functions, implemented through a set of Python classes and functions. The methodology supports three construction strategies: (1) translation of a generating curve along a guiding curve; (2) generation of revolution surfaces via matrix products; and (3) formation of tensor product surfaces from two or more B-spline curves. These approaches have been optimized for compatibility across Python environments.

The resulting implementations validate the effectiveness of the proposed methods, yielding precise representations of NURBS geometries and extending the modeling capacity for complex surfaces via generalized matrix operations.

2   Mathematical Preliminaries

This section outlines the foundational mathematical tools used in constructing and visualizing NURBS surfaces, including B-spline basis functions, rational curves, and matrix transformations.

2.1   Bases B-Spline

Let $U = \{u_0, \ldots, u_m\}$ be a non-decreasing sequence of real numbers, i.e., $u_i \leq u_{i+1}$, $i = 0, \ldots, m-1$. The u_i are called *knots*, and U is the *knot vector*. The i-th B-spline basis function of degree p (order $p+1$), denoted as $N_{i,p}(u)$, is defined as:

$$N_{i,0}(u) = \begin{cases} 1, & \text{if } u_i \leq u < u_{i+1}, \\ 0, & \text{otherwise.} \end{cases}$$

$$N_{i,p}(u) = \frac{u - u_i}{u_{i+p} - u_i} N_{i,p-1}(u) + \frac{u_{i+p+1} - u}{u_{i+p+1} - u_{i+1}} N_{i+1,p-1}(u).$$

- $N_{i,0}(u)$ is a step function, equal to zero everywhere except in the half-open interval $u \in [u_i, u_{i+1})$.

2.2   NURBS Curves

A p-degree NURBS curve is defined by

$$C(u) = \frac{\sum_{i=0}^{n} N_{i,p}(u) w_i P_i}{\sum_{i=0}^{n} N_{i,p}(u) w_i}, \quad a \leq u \leq b,$$

where

- The P_i are the control points (forming a control polygon). These influence the shape of the curve, and not all points necessarily lie on the curve.
- The w_i are the weights, which are associated with each control point P_i.
- The $N_{i,p}(u)$ are the p-degree B-spline basis functions defined on a non-periodic (and non-uniform) knot vector.

$$U = \{a, \ldots, a, u_{p+1}, \ldots, u_{m-p-1}, b, \ldots, b\}$$

Unless otherwise stated, we assume that $a = 0$, $b = 1$, and that $w_i > 0$ for all i.

$$R_{i,p}(u) = \frac{N_{i,p}(u) w_i}{\sum_{j=0}^{n} N_{j,p}(u) w_j}$$

This allows us to rewrite the equation in the form:

$$C(u) = \sum_{i=0}^{n} R_{i,p}(u) P_i$$

The $R_{i,p}(u)$ are the rational basis functions; they are piecewise rational functions defined on $u \in [0, 1]$.

2.3   Superficies NURBS

The definitions stated in this subsection are taken from [10]. A NURBS surface of degree p in the u direction and degree q in the v direction is a piecewise rational bivariate and vector-valued function of the form:

$$S(u,v) = \frac{\sum_{i=0}^{n} \sum_{j=0}^{m} N_{i,p}(u) N_{j,q}(v) w_{i,j} P_{i,j}}{\sum_{i=0}^{n} \sum_{j=0}^{m} N_{i,p}(u) N_{j,q}(v) w_{i,j}}, \quad 0 \le u, v \le 1$$

The $P_{i,j}$ form a bidirectional control mesh, the $w_{i,j}$ are the weights, and the $N_{i,p}(u)$ and $N_{j,q}(v)$ are the non-rational B-spline basis functions.

Introducing the piecewise-defined rational basis functions.

$$R_{i,j}(u,v) = \frac{N_{i,p}(u) N_{j,q}(v) w_{i,j}}{\sum_{k=0}^{n} \sum_{l=0}^{m} N_{k,p}(u) N_{l,q}(v) w_{k,l}}$$

Thus, the equation of the surface can be written as follows:

$$S(u,v) = \sum_{i=0}^{n} \sum_{j=0}^{m} R_{i,j}(u,v) P_{i,j}$$

It is worth mentioning that the generation of the weights $w_{i,j}$ is derived from the weights w_i and w_j through an internal operation, which is generally convenient to use as the product. Similarly, the control points $P_{i,j}$ are generated from the control points P_i and P_j through an internal operation (such as addition, a cross product, among others).

2.4   Rotation Matrices in 2D and 3D

According to Dunn [19], there are two types of rotations. The first refers to transforming each point of the object embedded in a space to another point within the same space, while the second refers to transforming the coordinate space itself. The commonly known rotation matrices usually correspond to the first type of transformation, meaning they transform each point of the object.

When rotating in the two-dimensional plane by an angle θ, it is done with reference to a point, which for simplicity is taken as the origin of the system.

$$\mathbf{R}(\theta) = \begin{bmatrix} p' \\ q' \end{bmatrix} = \begin{bmatrix} \cos\theta & \sin\theta \\ -\sin\theta & \cos\theta \end{bmatrix} \begin{bmatrix} p \\ q \end{bmatrix}$$

When the rotation occurs in three-dimensional space, it is performed with reference to an axis. Thus, there are three fundamental rotation matrices, each corresponding to the coordinate axes (the x-axis, y-axis, and z-axis).

After constructing a matrix from the rotated basis vectors, we obtain:

$$\mathbf{R}_x(\theta) = \begin{bmatrix} p' \\ q' \\ r' \end{bmatrix} = \begin{bmatrix} 1 & 0 & 0 \\ 0 & \cos\theta & \sin\theta \\ 0 & -\sin\theta & \cos\theta \end{bmatrix}$$

$$\mathbf{R}_y(\theta) = \begin{bmatrix} p' \\ q' \\ r' \end{bmatrix} = \begin{bmatrix} \cos\theta & 0 & -\sin\theta \\ 0 & 1 & 0 \\ \sin\theta & 0 & \cos\theta \end{bmatrix}$$

$$\mathbf{R}_z(\theta) = \begin{bmatrix} p' \\ q' \\ r' \end{bmatrix} = \begin{bmatrix} \cos\theta & \sin\theta & 0 \\ -\sin\theta & \cos\theta & 0 \\ 0 & 0 & 1 \end{bmatrix}$$

2.5 Translation Surfaces

According to [20], translation surfaces are a method developed using a guiding curve $\Gamma_1 : \boldsymbol{R}(u) = (x(u), y(u), z(u))$ and a generating curve $\Gamma_2 : \boldsymbol{R}^*(v) = (x^*(v), y^*(v), z^*(v))$. These surfaces consist of all the curves obtained by translating the generating curve parallel to itself as a point $P_0 = (x_0, y_0, z_0)$ moves along the guiding curve. It is important to note that P_0 is a common point between the curves Γ_1 and Γ_2 (Fig. 1).

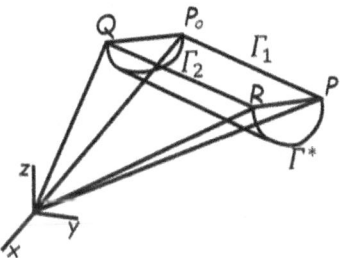

Fig. 1. Translation surfaces, obtained from [20].

The parametric equation of these translation surfaces is:

$$\begin{cases} x = x(u) + x^*(v) - x_0 \\ y = y(u) + y^*(v) - y_0 \\ z = z(u) + z^*(v) - z_0 \end{cases}$$

3 Construction of NURBS Circles

3.1 Generation of Control Points, Weights, and Knots on n-Sided Polygons

To generate NURBS circles inscribed in n-sided polygons, specific control points, weights, and parameters are used. For this purpose, a class is introduced that, given the parameter n (number of polygon sides) and r (radius of the inscribed circle), generates the NURBS circle using subcommands previously implemented within the class Construction:

- Polygon is an attribute of the Construction class and returns a list of two-dimensional points, which are the control points of the circle.

Code 1

```
A = Construccion(n=num_lado, r=radio)
A.polygon()
```

- Peso is another attribute of the Construction class and returns a list of numbers that represent the weights associated with each control point.

Code 2

```
A = Construccion(n=num_lado, r=radio)
A.peso()
```

- Lastly, open1 is an attribute that returns a list of numbers representing the nodes of the circle, i.e., the interval.

Code 3

```
A = Construccion(n=num_lado, r=radio)
A.open1()
```

3.2   NURBS Circles Through Control Points Obtained from Polygons

The construction of circles is initiated by inscribed within an n-sided polygon, using an approach based on strategically placed control points on the polygons. These control points define NURBS curves that allow precise modeling of the inscribed circle in the polygon. The following class enables the visualization of a circle with radius "r" inscribed in an "n"-sided polygon with "p" degrees of freedom.

Code 4

```
C3 = Nurbs_curve2D_graph(n=num_lados, r=radio, p=grado
     de la curva)
C3.grafica(puntos=True)
```

The implementation is carried out through the class Nurbs_curve2D_graph, which receives three parameters: number of sides (n), radius (r), and degree of freedom $(p = 2)$ corresponding to the circle. Additionally, the attribute gráfica includes a boolean parameter (puntos) that allows visualizing the circle with or without the control points used. This design ensures flexibility and clarity in the representation of the model.

4   Generation of NURBS Surfaces

Three approaches for surface generation are presented. The first focuses on translation surfaces. The second involves revolution surfaces based on matrix multiplication, described in 4.2. Finally, the third approach consists of tensor product surfaces, which are constructed using a set of points defined by two or more curves, allowing the formation of surfaces bounded by them.

4.1   Construction of Translation Surfaces

The following describes the class that constructs translation surfaces. This class is computationally similar to surfaces obtained through rotation, with the difference that only the generation of the control points P_{ij} has been modified, as described in Sect. 2.5.

Having the NURBS control points for both the generating and guiding curves, we construct the mesh for the points P_{ij} as follows.

$$P_{ij} = pdir_i + pgen_j - P_0$$

Here is the class that allows graphing this type of surface.

Code 5

```
mi_superficie = Nurbs_superficie3D_graph2(pts1=pdir,
    pts2=pgen, P=punto, pes1=w1, pes2=w2, nod1=x1,
    nod2=x2, p1=2, p2=2)
mi_superficie.grafica(pdir=False, pgen=False,
    c_pdir=True, c_pgen=True, enmaller=True,
    pts_ctrl=True, superficie=True)
```

As mentioned in previous lines, this class is very similar to the class for plotting revolution surfaces. The parameters do not change significantly; in fact, they remain the same, except for the addition of a single parameter $P = puntos$, which represents the common point of the two guiding and generating curves.

4.2   NURBS Revolution Surfaces

From 2D and 3D rotation, the concept is generalized to the rotation of points around other points.

Let the points P_{ij} of the generating curve in the XY plane be:

$$P_i = (P_{ix}, 0, P_{iz}) \quad \text{in plane } XZ$$
$$R_j = (R_{jx}, R_{jy}, 0) \quad \text{in plane } XY$$

Graphical representation of P_i and R_j in a three-dimensional space with coordinates x, y, z.

Generating Curve:

$$[P_{ix}, 0, P_{iz}]$$

Rotation matrix defined by R_j:

$$\begin{bmatrix} R_{ix} & R_{jy} & 0 \\ -R_{jy} & R_{jx} & 0 \\ 0 & 0 & 1 \end{bmatrix}$$

Generalized Rotation:

$$P_{ij} = \begin{bmatrix} P_{ix} & 0 & P_{iz} \end{bmatrix} \begin{bmatrix} R_{ix} & R_{jy} & 0 \\ -R_{jy} & R_{jx} & 0 \\ 0 & 0 & 1 \end{bmatrix}$$

Resulting:

$$P_{ij} = (P_{ix}R_{jx}, P_{ix}R_{jy}, P_{iz})$$

Based on the curve product described previously, we will incorporate the class, considering the following aspects:

- The guiding curve (circle) rests in the XY plane, while the generating curve (arbitrary curve) lies on the XZ plane. For example, taking the guiding curve as the circle inscribed in an equilateral triangle and the generating curve as a semicircle inscribed in a hexagon, the rotation results in a sphere.
- A NURBS circle is defined on the basis of the XY plane and a NURBS semicircle in the YZ plane. Using the control points that generate these circles, the matrix product is applied to generate described in Sect. 4.2 to obtain a list of points forming a mesh. From these generated points, the NURBS surface is constructed from the resulting mesh.

Code 6

```
mi_superficie = Nurbs_superficie3D_graph(pts1=dir,
   pts2=gen, pes1=w1, pes2=w2, nod1=n1, nod2=n2, p1=2,
   p2=2)
mi_superficie.grafica(pdir=True, pgen=True, c_pdir=True,
   c_pgen=True, enmaller=True, pts_ctrl=True,
      superficie=True)
```

The class Nurbs_superficie3D_graph allows plotting surfaces generated by the rotation of two curves: a generating curve and a guiding curve. In the first line, the instance is initialized where the arguments pts1 is a list of control points of the guiding curve; pts2 is a list of control points of the generating curve; pes1 and pes2 are the respective weights of the two curves; the nodes of the respective curves are represented by nod1 and nod2; and finally, the degrees of freedom of the curves, p1 and p2.

In the second line, it allows for plotting the surface where some "features" can be controlled. For example:

- `pdir=True` indicates that the line passing through the control point list of the guiding curve is drawn.
- `pgen=True` indicates that the generating curve is drawn.
- `c_pdir=True` indicates that the guiding curve is drawn.
- `enmaller=True` and `pts_ctrl=True` specify that the mesh will be added along with all control points.
- Finally, `superficie=True` specifies that the surface will be added to the plot.

4.3   Tensor Product Surfaces with NURBS Curves

In Python, the class `Nurbs_superficie3D_graph1` has been created to plot NURBS surfaces, which instead of taking two NURBS curves as input, receives a matrix where each column represents a list of control points of a curve. In the first line, the instance is initialized where the argument `data` is the input matrix; `pes1` and `pes2` are the respective weights, one at the row level and the other at the column level; `nod1` and `nod2` are the nodes associated with the curves at the row and column level; `p1` and `p2` are the degrees of freedom of the curves at the row and column level. Finally, the range for the parameters u and v of the surface to be plotted is specified.

Code 7

```
mi_superficie = Nurbs_superficie3D_graph1(data=mi_data,
    pes1=w1, pes2=w2, nod1=n1, nod2=n2, p1=2, p2=2,
    ran_u=(u1, u2, ran_v=(v1, v2))
mi_superficie.grafica(enmaller=True, pts_ctrl=True,
    superficie=True, curv=True)
```

In the second line, the method `grafica` allows:

- `enmaller=True`: Add the point mesh.
- `pts_ctrl=True`: Draw the control points.
- `superficie=True`: Add the surface to the plot.
- `curv=True`: Draw the generated curves.

5   Results

The curves and surfaces obtained are based on the classes mentioned in the development section. In Fig. 2, NURBS-type circles constructed through control points obtained from polygons are shown. These circles have been generated using the class `Nurbs_curve2D_graph`.

5.1   Translation Surfaces in Python

The first approach is visualized using the class to build NURBS translation surfaces `Nurbs_superficie3D_graph2`. In this case, the hyperbolic paraboloid was obtained, as shown in Fig. 3. This result was achieved using two NURBS parabolas, where one is translated along the other.

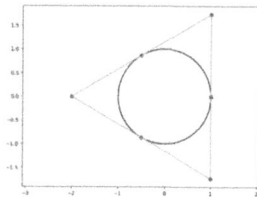 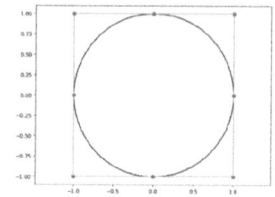 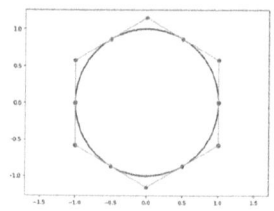

Fig. 2. Circles obtained from different polygons.

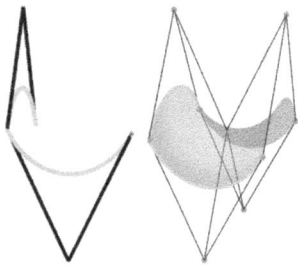

Fig. 3. Saddle surface

5.2   Revolution Surfaces in Python

In this approach, several NURBS surfaces are constructed based on rotational transformations.

In Fig. 4, a sphere is generated by rotating a semicircular NURBS curve, defined in the YZ plane, around a guiding NURBS curve inscribed in the XY plane.

Figure 5 illustrates the construction of a unit NURBS sphere using different base polygons. The resulting mesh configurations vary according to the selected polygon, confirming the dependency of surface topology on control geometry.

Figure 6 presents a dome formed by combining two semicircles inscribed in hexagons. The generated mesh demonstrates coherence and precision in the modeling process.

In Fig. 7, a similar procedure is applied; however, the resulting surface does not correspond to a dome, despite the similarity in the mesh structure. This suggests that the geometric outcome is sensitive to the specific combination of generating and guiding curves, enabling the construction of free-form surfaces through appropriate parametric selection.

Based on the overall modeling outcomes, additional surfaces are generated by systematically modifying the guiding and generating curves. Representative examples of these configurations are shown in Figs. 8, 9, 10, 11, 12, 13, 14 and 15.

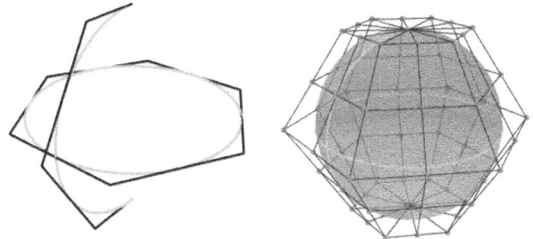

Fig. 4. GGenerating Curve: Circle inscribed in a hexagon and Guiding Curve: Semi-circle inscribed in a hexagon.

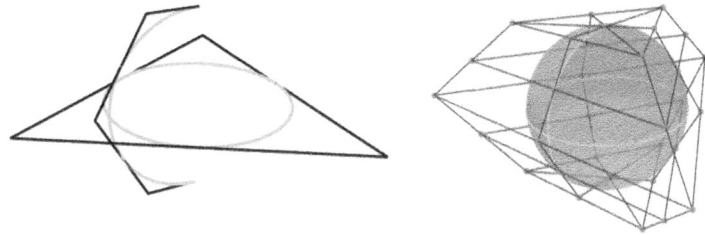

Fig. 5. Visualization of the unit NURBS sphere.

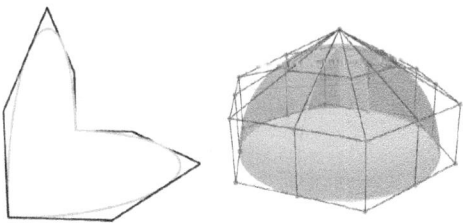

Fig. 6. Generating Curve: Semicircle with hexagon. Guiding Curve: Semicircle with hexagon.

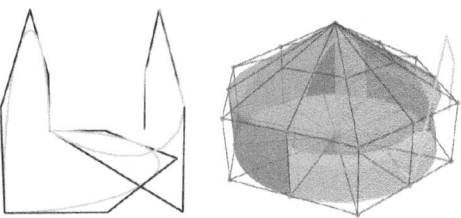

Fig. 7. Generation of Dome.

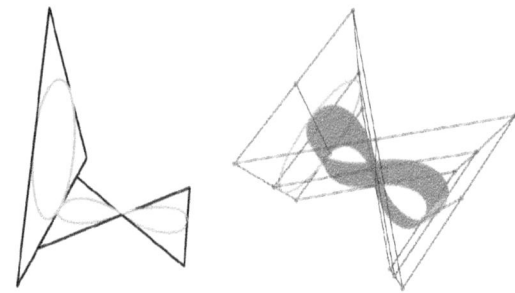

Fig. 8. Generating Curve: Lemniscate and Guiding Curve: Circle with Triangle.

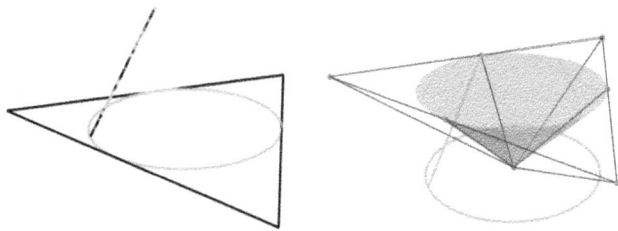

Fig. 9. Generating Curve: Circle Triangle and Guiding Curve: Line.

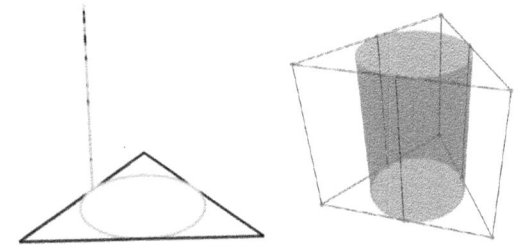

Fig. 10. Generating Curve: Circle Triangle and Guiding Curve: Line.

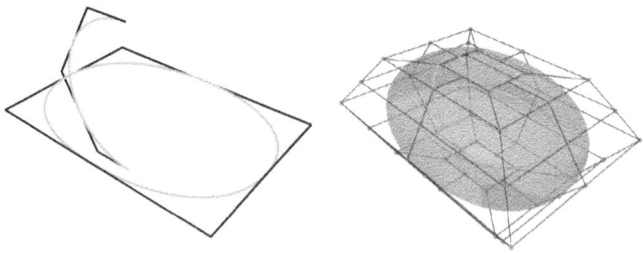

Fig. 11. Ellipsoid: Guiding Curve - an ellipse with 9 points. Generating Curve - a semi-ellipse from the hexagon.

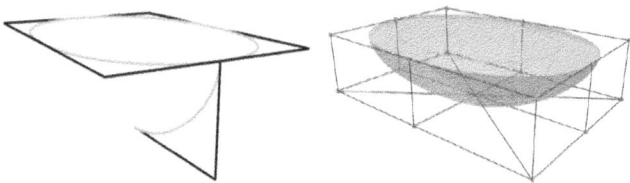

Fig. 12. Paraboloid: Guiding Curve - an ellipse. Generating Curve - a parabola with 3 control points.

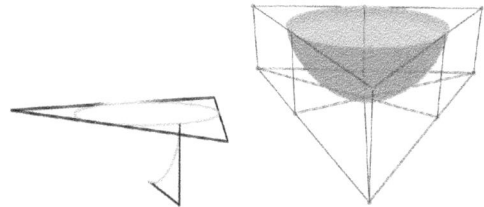

Fig. 13. Another Paraboloid: Same as the previous one, except the guiding curve is a circle derived from the triangle.

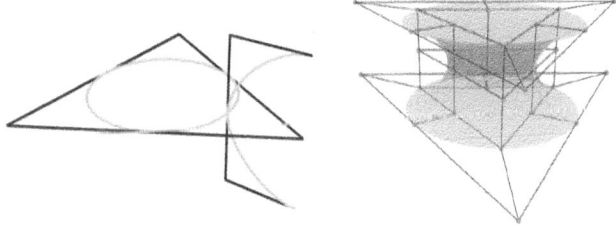

Fig. 14. Hyperboloid of one sheet.

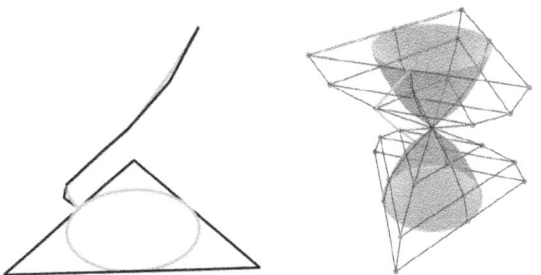

Fig. 15. Hourglass.

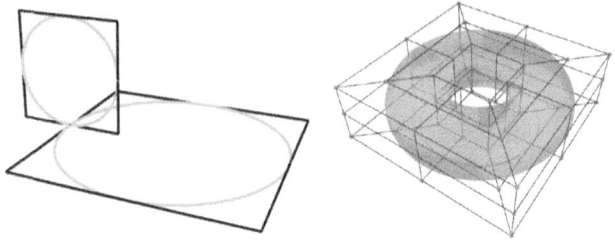

Fig. 16. Generating Curve: Circle with Square and Guiding Curve: Circle with Square.

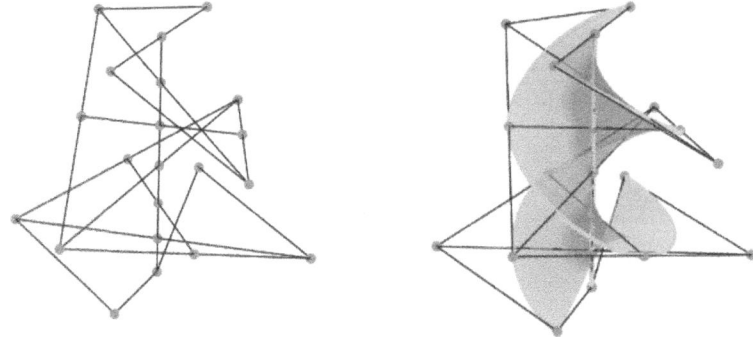

Fig. 17. Circular Helix.

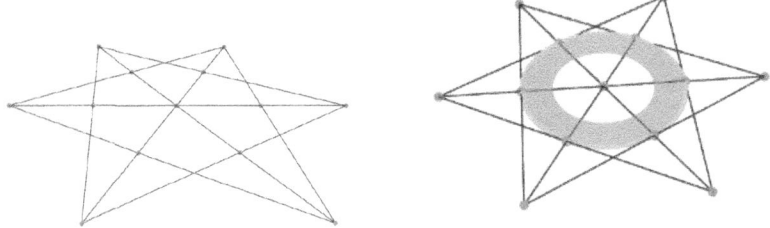

Fig. 18. Circle.

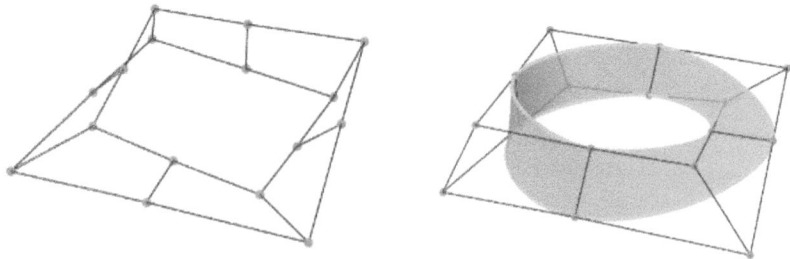

Fig. 19. Möbius Strip.

These results correspond to NURBS surfaces such as a cylinder, a cone, an ellipsoid, a paraboloid, and a hyperboloid of one sheet. From these constructions, most of the quadric surfaces have been generated.

Finally, a NURBS revolution torus will be visualized, based on its mathematical definition as the product of two circles. In this case, the construction process is similar to that of the previous NURBS surfaces. The result can be seen in Fig. 16.

5.3 Tensor Product Surfaces with NURBS Curves in Python

In this final approach, we will focus on surfaces bounded by NURBS curves, as explained in Sect. 4.3. This method allows for surface generation using the tensor product, creating a three-dimensional mesh of control points based on the base curve data. This ensures high precision and flexibility in geometric design. The implementation in Python, using the `Nurbs_superficie3D_graph1` class, facilitates the configuration of key parameters such as weights, nodes, and degrees of freedom of the curves. For this, a set of control points is needed to construct the NURBS surfaces, as shown in Figs. 17, 18 and 19.

6 Discussion and Perspectives

The results of this study demonstrate that Python, combined with a structured implementation of NURBS geometry, provides an effective environment for constructing, manipulating, and visualizing parametric surfaces. The three approaches explored—translation, revolution, and tensor product surfaces—offer distinct advantages depending on the geometric features of the problem.

From a performance standpoint, revolution surfaces yield the greatest precision and continuity when applied to symmetric and closed generating curves, making them suitable for classical geometries such as spheres, domes, and tori. Translation surfaces, though limited in variety, are computationally efficient and offer intuitive mesh control, making them especially appropriate for educational purposes and ruled surface generation. Tensor product surfaces, while more demanding computationally, enable the modeling of complex, free-form geometries, extending the versatility of the methodology.

A notable strength of this work lies in its pedagogical dimension. The Python-based implementation, integrated into interactive Jupyter Notebooks, supports conceptual understanding through real-time manipulation of control points, weights, and knot vectors. This fosters experiential learning and facilitates engagement with core topics in B-spline theory, linear algebra, and differential geometry. Additionally, the modular, object-oriented code structure encourages good programming practices consistent with contemporary computational mathematics instruction.

Looking ahead, this framework opens pathways for both educational innovation and further research. Potential extensions include the incorporation of real-time parameter tuning, integration with physical simulation engines, and quantitative evaluation of surface continuity. The methodology can also be adapted to early undergraduate or secondary education, introducing geometric modeling concepts through interactive environments. Furthermore, combining this framework with symbolic computation or machine learning could enhance applications in shape optimization and surface fitting.

In comparison with existing literature, this implementation stands out for its integration of computational generality and instructional clarity. Unlike prior studies such as Tejada (2021), which focused on fixed-axis revolution surfaces, this work generalizes surface generation by supporting arbitrary generating and guiding curves. Similarly, in contrast to Cuartas and Prieto (2015), whose approach relies on 3D scanned data and optimization routines, the present methodology remains independent of specialized hardware and is fully synthetic and customizable, broadening both its practical and educational utility.

All implementations run efficiently on standard personal computers with at least 4 GB RAM, using Python 3.10 and the Jupyter Notebook environment.

Overall, the proposed framework contributes to bridging the gap between theoretical geometry, computational modeling, and educational practice, in alignment with contemporary needs in mathematics, design, and interdisciplinary education.

7   Conclusions and Future Work

This study demonstrated the feasibility and effectiveness of generating and visualizing Non-Uniform Rational B-Spline (NURBS) surfaces using three construction methods—translation, revolution, and tensor product—implemented in Python through the Jupyter Notebook environment. The proposed object-oriented framework, grounded in matrix operations and B-spline basis functions, enables precise geometric control and supports the creation of both classical and free-form surfaces with high flexibility.

Among the techniques evaluated, revolution surfaces exhibited superior performance in terms of smoothness and geometric continuity, especially for closed and symmetric base curves. Translation surfaces offered computational simplicity and intuitive mesh structure, making them suitable for educational and ruled-surface contexts. Tensor product surfaces, while more computationally intensive, facilitated the construction of intricate and compound geometries. The comparative use of these methods highlights trade-offs among accuracy, adaptability, and computational demand, providing a versatile toolkit for surface modeling.

From a pedagogical standpoint, the Python-based implementation proved highly effective in supporting the teaching and learning of advanced mathematical concepts. Its visual and interactive nature encourages intuitive understanding of rational parametrization, matrix transformations, and spline theory. By promoting hands-on experimentation, the framework fosters an inquiry-based learning environment that bridges theoretical content with computational practice—particularly valuable in undergraduate courses in geometry, computer graphics, and applied mathematics.

As a continuation of this work, future research may focus on several directions:

- Quantitative evaluation of surface continuity (e.g., G1/G2 smoothness) and computational performance under varying curve configurations;
- Integration of optimization algorithms, such as energy minimization or least-squares fitting, to refine control point placement;
- Expansion of the pedagogical toolkit, including auto-evaluation modules, parameter sliders, and multilingual interfaces to support international educational contexts;
- Extension to higher-dimensional or time-varying surfaces, enabling applications in animation, scientific visualization, and real-time CAD environments.

References

1. Fernández-Jambrina, L., Pérez-Arribas, F.: Developable surface patches bounded by NURBS curves. J. Comput. Math. **38**(5), 693–709 (2020). https://doi.org/10.4208/JCM.1904-M2018-0209
2. Taheri, A.H., Suresh, K.: Surface approximations using generalized NURBS. Eng. Comput. 1–19 (2021). https://doi.org/10.1007/s00366-021-01483-8
3. Guo, Z., Sun, W.: Study on a NURBS surface fitting algorithm. 35–40 (2022). https://doi.org/10.1109/AHPCAI57455.2022.10087689
4. Watts, A.: Algorithms for geometrical operations with NURBS surfaces (2022). https://doi.org/10.48550/arxiv.2210.13160
5. Tejada, P.: Construcción de esferas y toros de revolución mediante el uso de superficies B-Spline racionales. Universidad Nacional de Piura, Facultad de Ciencias, Escuela Profesional de Matemática, Trabajo de investigación (2021)
6. Cuartas, E., Prieto, F.: Optimización de la representación con superficies NURBS de imágenes en tiempo real. Revista Energía y Computación **15**(2), 31–37 (2015)
7. Cuervo, L., Cuervo, N., Cuervo, J.: Iniciando a programar con Python: Guía básica de programación. Editorial de la Universidad Pedagógica y Tecnológica de Colombia - UPTC, Bogotá (2018)
8. Perney, A., Bordas, S., Kerfriden, P.: NURBS-based surface generation from 3D images: spectral construction and data-driven model selection. J. Comput. Des. Eng. **10**, 1856–1867 (2023). https://doi.org/10.1093/jcde/qwad082
9. Prasad, A., Balu, A., Shah, H.S., Sarkar, S., Hegde, C., Krishnamurthy, A.: NURBS-diff: a differentiable programming module for NURBS. Comput. Aided Des. **146**, 103199 (2021)
10. Johansson, R.: Introduction to Computing with Python, pp. 1–24. Apress, Berkeley (2015). https://doi.org/10.1007/978-1-4842-0553-2_1
11. Lvov, M., Kruglyk, V.: Teaching algorithmization and programming using Python language. **20**, 13–23 (2014). https://doi.org/10.14308/ITE000493
12. Piegl, L., Tiller, W.: The NURBS Book. 2nd edn. Springer, Berlin (1997). https://doi.org/10.1007/978-3-642-59223-2
13. Cordero, J., Cortés, J.: Curvas y superficies para modelado geométrico. Ed. ilustrada. Ra-Ma, Librería y Editorial Microinformática (2002)
14. Prautzsch, H., Paluszny, M., Böhm, W.: Métodos de Bézier y B-splines. KIT Scientific Publishing, Karlsruhe (2005)
15. Lancaster, P., Salkauskas, K.: Curve and Surface Fitting: An Introduction. Academic Press, New York (1986)

16. Farin, G.: Curves and Surfaces for Computer-Aided Geometric Design: A Practical Guide, 4th edn. Academic Press, San Diego (1996)
17. Salomon, D.: Curves and Surfaces for Computer Graphics. Springer-Verlag, London (2006). https://doi.org/10.1007/0-387-28452-4
18. Bingol, O.R., Krishnamurthy, A.: NURBS-python: an open-source object-oriented NURBS modeling framework in Python. SoftwareX **9**, 85–94 (2019). https://doi.org/10.1016/j.softx.2018.12.005
19. Dunn, F., Parberry, I.: 3D Math Primer for Graphics and Game Development. Wordware Publishing Inc, Plano (2002)
20. López, A., Villa, A.: Geometría Diferencial. Editorial Clásica, Madrid (1994)
21. Cordero, L.A., Fernández, M., Gray, A.: Geometría diferencial de curvas y superficies con matemática. Addison-Wesley Iberoamericana, Wilmington (1998)

Randomness from Deterministic Chaos: A Novel Algorithm for Random Number Generation

Sajad Ahmad Mir$^{(\boxtimes)}$ⒾD and Puneet SharmaⒾD

Indian Institute of Technology Jodhpur, Jodhpur 342030, India
{mir.1,puneet}@iitj.ac.in

Abstract. In this article, we address the problem of generation of pseudo-random sequences using deterministic chaotic maps. Using a set of three deterministic chaotic maps, we propose an algorithm for generation of pseudo-random sequences. We establish that the sequences generated through the algorithm are random in accordance with the criteria prescribed by the NIST 800-22 Test suite. We also establish the independence of output sequences with the sequences generated by any of the generator maps. The results indicate that the output sequence exhibits sufficiently high degree of randomness when the perturbations are non-dissipative.

Keywords: Random number generation · Chaotic Maps · Correlation and S Plots · Perturbation analysis · Time Series Analysis · NIST 800-22 Test suite

1 Introduction

In modern day world, the field of random number generation caters to a wide range of requirements arising across various state of the art applications. While true random number generators are computationally infeasible, pseudo-random number generators are capable of generating sufficiently long "nearly random" sequences that share many properties with truly random sequences and can be applied to address many modern-day technological challenges. The field has found applications in several areas, such as cryptography, communication, online gaming and many more. In particular, pseudo-random number generation has found applications in fields such as multimedia encryption schemes, system security, and generation of one-time passwords [2]. As instant generation of pseudo random sequences using algorithms of lower complexity can have a meaningful impact on current state of the art facilities, it is not only important to generate sequences with sufficient degree of randomness, it is critical to generate such sequences using algorithms with lower time complexity. While "randomness" broadly refers to the unpredictability of the system, chaos theory also investigates the unpredictability in a deterministic system over a long periods of time. It is interesting to determine whether chaotic maps can be used to generate a pseudo-random sequence [1].

It is worth noting that chaotic maps are aperiodic sensitive deterministic mathematical functions capable of generating arbitrary patterns and hence can be used to generate pseudo-random sequences with sufficient degree of unpredictability. In [3], the author provides an efficient way to combine two or more Multiplicative Linear Congruential Generators (MLCGs) to propose a class of more efficient and portable random number generators. In [4], the authors propose a discrete time chaotic system-based TRNG (true random number generator) using the Henon map and the logistic map. The design utilizes the two dimensional structure of the Henon map with the one dimensional logistic map to propose a true random number generator. The proposed algorithm produces high-entropy random bit sequences without post-processing and passed all NIST 800-22 statistical tests [5]. In [6], the authors describe a portable set of software utilities for uniform generation. The utilities describe for multiple generators (streams) running simultaneously with each generator having its numbers partitioned into many long disjoint contiguous substreams. In [7], the authors introduce a software library offering a collection of utilities for the empirical statistical testing of uniform random number generators (RNGs). The investigation provides tools to perform systematic studies of the interaction between a specific test and the structure of the point sets produced by a given family of RNGs and provides a survey and a classification of statistical tests for RNGs.

In [8], the authors proposed random number generators using the Linear congruential map. In [9], the authors present good parameter sets to combine parallel multiple recursive sequences to implement random number generators with long periods and good structural properties. The author investigated the problem to combine multiple recursive generators of different sizes and also provided a code faster than previous implementations of similar generators. In [10] the authors used Ikeda maps and XOR operations over Arduino platform to generate a sequence of random numbers. In [11], the authors propose a TRNG using zigzag map for random bit generation. They investigate key chaotic properties and attributes of the map under discussion. The authors show that with certain modifications, a TRNG based on the zigzag map passes all NIST 800-22 statistical randomness tests using simple post-processing of output data. In [12], Moysis et al. created a pseudo-random bit generator utilizing multiple-digit comparison. They employed several maps to create the pseudo-random bit after comparing the outcomes of each bit produced by each map. In [13], the authors discuss various algorithms to generate pseudo-random sequences using maps such as Logistic, sine, linked sine, Renyi, Chebyshev (and many more) for various applications.

In this article, we investigate the problem of random number generation using chaotic maps such as logistic map, sawtooth map and the baker map. Using this fixed set of chaotic maps, we propose a scheme to generate a pseudo-random sequence using a linear congruence map as the decision map. The algorithm was executed and implemented in python environment. The algorithm generates a pseudo random sequence using a simple deterministic mechanism and hence generates pseudo random sequences in a fast and efficient manner (with lower time complexity). As a result of simple mechanism and lower time complexity, the algorithm can be used in various applications such as neural networks, graphics and simulations, online gaming, OTP generation and encryption schemes. Further, as the algorithm utilizes a sufficiently long periodic sequence for map selection, the algorithm indicates a possible relation between chaotic orbits and pseudo random sequences. While some of the existing works use multidimensional chaotic maps to generate pseudo random sequences [4], the proposed algorithm uses a collection of one dimensional maps and hence provides a simple mechanism to generate the pseudo random sequences. Further, some of the works combine MLCGs to generate the desired sequences [3], such algorithms use integer keyspace and hence do not utilize the sensitivity of the underlying system. As the proposed algorithm utilizes a collection of maps with sensitive dependence on initial conditions, the generated sequences exhibit sensitivity to small changes in the keyspace.

The proposed scheme generates a pseudo-random sequence in accordance with the criteria prescribed by the NIST 800-22 Test suite. We also conduct a qualitative analysis of the sequences generated. The results indicate that if the sequence of perturbations in the generating parameters is non-dissipative ($\sum_{i=1}^{\infty} p_i = \infty$) the sequence generated exhibits sufficient degree of randomness. Further, the results indicate that if the sequence of perturbations in the generating parameters is dissipative ($\sum_{i=1}^{\infty} p_i < \infty$), the sequences generated fails to qualify the NIST 800-22 Test suite criteria for randomness. We also establish the independence of the sequence generated with sequences generated by any of the generator maps. As a result of this work, an R package **PRNG** was developed and published in the CRAN platform [14].

2   Basic Tools and Setup

2.1   Linear Congruence Map

Let $\mathbb{N}$ be the set of natural numbers $a, b \in \mathbb{N}$ and p be a **prime**. For any $z_0 \in \mathbb{N}$,

$$z_{n+1} = (az_n + b)mod(p) \tag{1}$$

generates a sequence of natural numbers. As any pseudo-random sequence generated using linear congruence is periodic in nature, we choose the values a, b and p so that the pseudo-random sequences generated are of sufficient large length. In this work, we use $a = 7^5$, $b = 0$, $p = 2^{31} - 1$(a large **prime**). In [8], Lehmer's method exemplifies the charm of simplicity to select the parameters of the linear congruence map to ensure sufficiently long sequences. The procedure involves the meticulous selection of two predetermined integer parameters a (the multiplier) and the prime p.

2.2   The Logistic Map

Let $I = [0, 1]$ be the unit interval,then for each $\mu \in [0, 4]$, $f : I \rightarrow I$ defined as

$$f_\mu(x) = \mu x(1 - x) \tag{2}$$

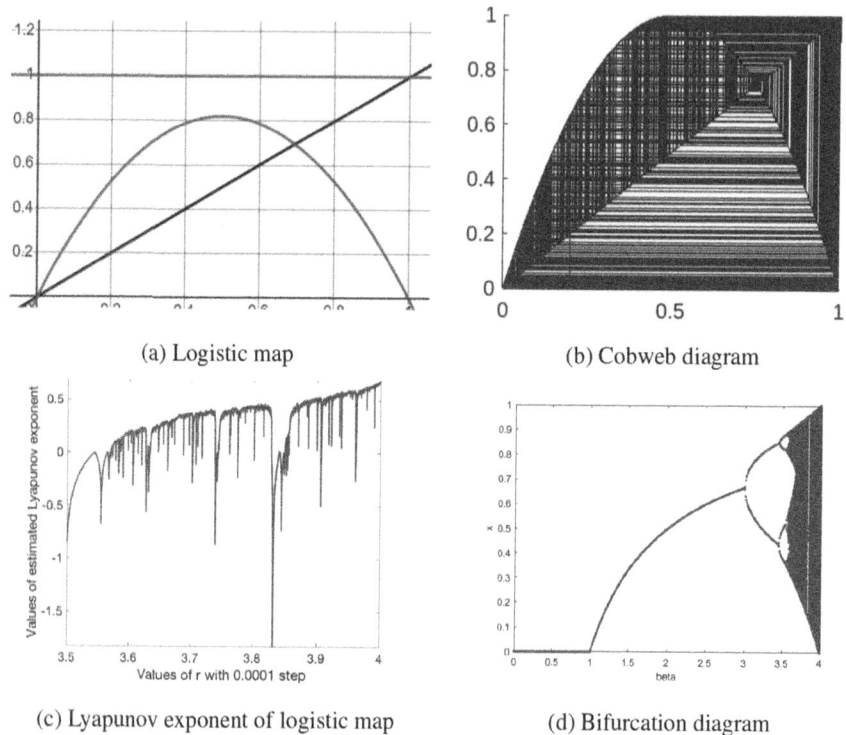

(a) Logistic map

(b) Cobweb diagram

(c) Lyapunov exponent of logistic map

(d) Bifurcation diagram

Fig. 1. Dynamical Analysis of Logistic Map.

is called the logistic map with parameter μ. The map is known to be chaotic for $\mu \in [3.57, 4]$. The map is known to exhibit sensitive dependence on the initial conditions, as assessed by the **Lyapunov exponent** λ and has periodic points of all orders [1]. The long-term behavior can be predicted through the cobweb diagram.(see Fig. 1)

2.3 Baker Map

Consider the unit interval $I = [0, 1]$. Then for each $\mu \in (0.5, 1)$, the map $B_\mu : I \to I$ defined as

$$B_\mu(x) = \begin{cases} 2\mu x, & \text{if } 0 \leq x \leq \frac{1}{2}, \\ \mu(2x - 1), & \text{if } \frac{1}{2} \leq x \leq 1. \end{cases} \tag{3}$$

is called the Baker map. In [1] the map is found to be sensitive to initial conditions for $\mu \in (0.5, 1)$. The map along with its cobweb diagram and bifurcation diagram are shown in Fig. 2.

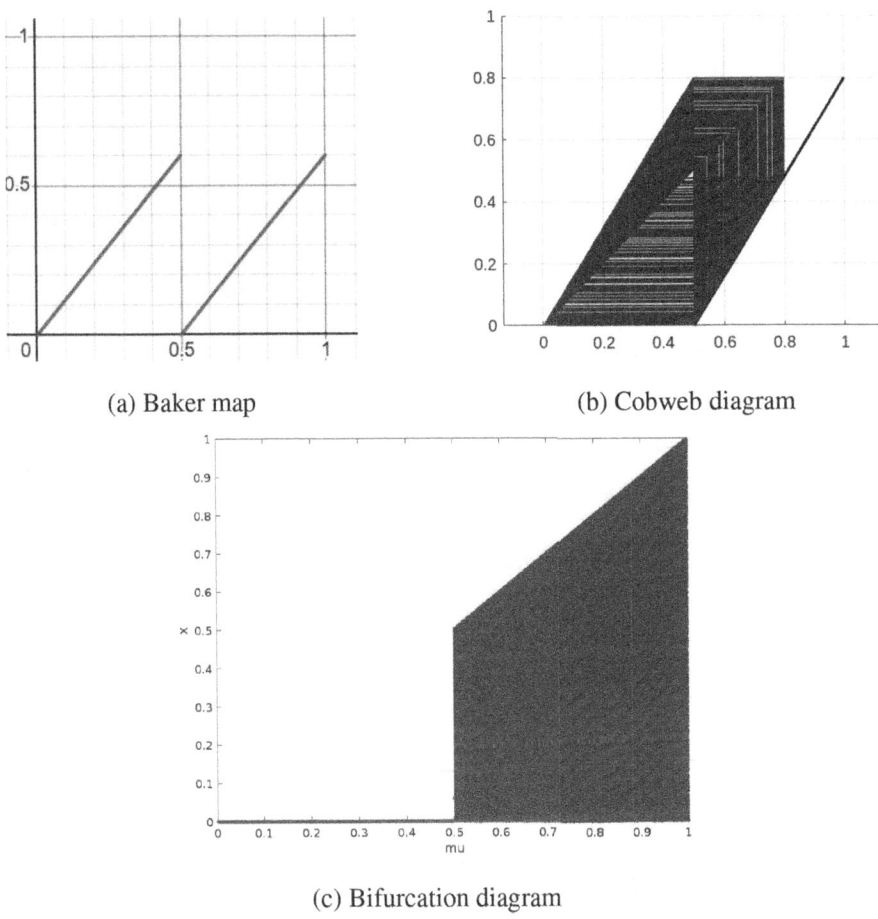

(a) Baker map

(b) Cobweb diagram

(c) Bifurcation diagram

Fig. 2. Dynamics of Baker Map.

2.4 The Sawtooth Map

Consider the function $h : I \to I$ defined by

$$h(x) = 3x (mod\ 1) \tag{4}$$

where $x \in (0, 1)$. The map is called the sawtooth map and is known to be sensitive to initial conditions [1]. The map is piecewise linear, consists of linear segments or "teeth" (where each tooth represents a linear map) and is known to be topologically mixing (see Fig. 3).

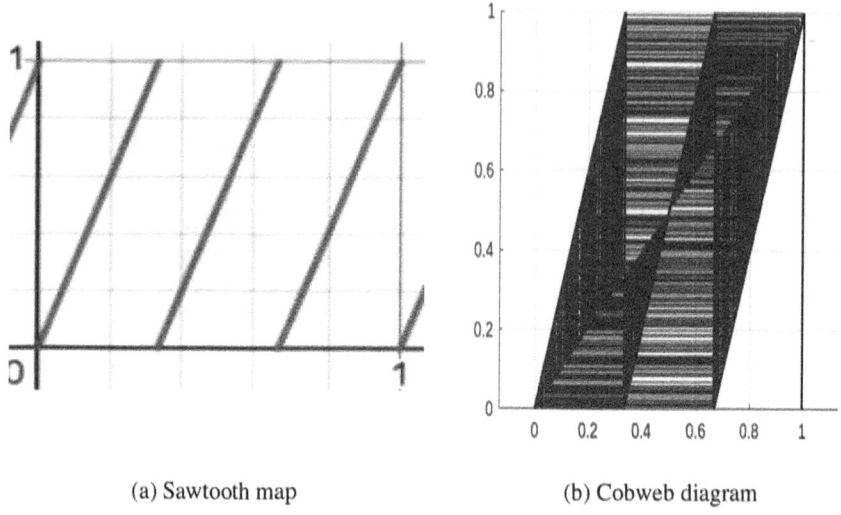

(a) Sawtooth map   (b) Cobweb diagram

Fig. 3. Dynamics of Sawtooth Map.

3   Proposed Algorithm

In this algorithm, we propose a pseudo-random generator using a set of three deterministic chaotic maps. We consider logistic map, Baker map and saw-tooth map as the generating maps for the proposed scheme. We use Linear congruence map as a decision map. Parameter Space:

n_0 = initial seed for the Linear congruence map
x_1 = the initial input for logistic map $0 < x_1 < 1$
a_1 = the initial value of the parameter of logistic map $3.57 \leq a_1 \leq 4$
x_2 = the initial input for baker map $0 < x_2 < 1$
a_2 = the initial value of the parameter of baker map $a_2 \geq 0.5$
x_3 = the initial input for saw-tooth map $0 < x_3 < 1$
N = the required length of random sequence

Algorithm

INPUT: **key** $[n_0, x_1, a_1, x_2, a_2, x_3, N]$
OUTPUT: Random sequence of length N

1:   $RanSeq \leftarrow [\,]$
2: **for** $i \in \{1 \cdots N\}$ **do**
3:     $n \leftarrow$ **Linear-con**(n_0)
4:     $n_1 \leftarrow n \mod 3$
5:     **if** $n_1 = 0$ **then**
6:        $x \leftarrow$ **logistic map**(x_1, a_1)
7:        $x_1 \leftarrow x$
8:        $a_1 \leftarrow a_1 + \frac{1}{\sqrt{i}}$ ▷ Update parameter a_1
9:     **else if** $n_1 = 1$ **then**
10:       $x \leftarrow$ **Baker map**(x_2, a_2)
11:       $x_2 \leftarrow x$
12:       $a_2 \leftarrow a_2 + \frac{1}{\sqrt{i}}$ ▷ Update parameter a_2
13:     **else**
14:       $x \leftarrow$ **saw-tooth**(x_3)
15:       $x_3 \leftarrow x$
16:     **end if**
17:     $RanSeq.$**append**(x)
18:     $n_0 \leftarrow n$
19: **end for**
20: **return** $RanSeq$

This sequence of x(i)'s$\in (0, 1)$ are the required random numbers returned as a list. Inorder to generate random bits we consider the decision $w_i = 1$ for $x_i > 0.5$ and 0 otherwise. The time complexity of the algorithm is $\mathcal{O}(N)$. Since we need to store the key only for reproducing the sequences. Therfore the space complexity of the algorithm is $\mathcal{O}(1)$

4   Testing and Analysis

4.1   Histogram Analysis

The purpose of the histogram test is to identify any bias that the algorithm may have towards a particular region in the output space. The analysis of the sequences generated by the proposed algorithm shows the uniformity in the bin heights and thus demonstrates the unbaisedness in the generated sequence. We observe that the generated sequences are uniformly distributed in the output region (Fig. 4).

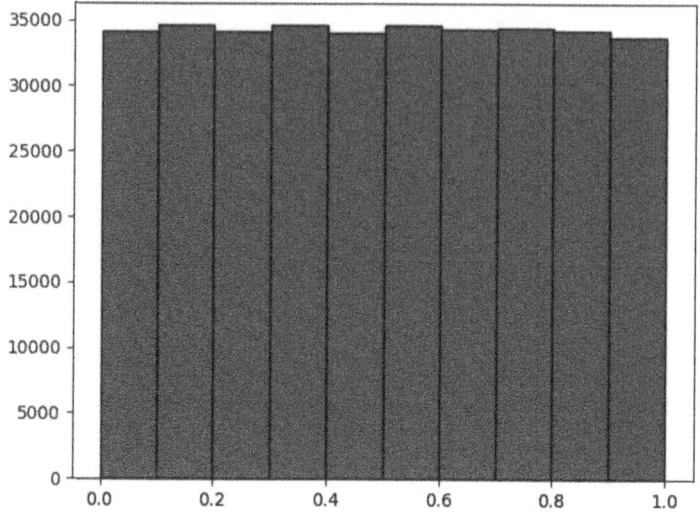

Fig. 4. Histogram analysis.

4.2 Autocorrelation Test

In order to assess the presence of any autocorrelation in the output sequences, the auto-correlation test for generated sequences of varying lengths was conducted. The analysis indicates that the sequences exhibit no significant autocorrelation, as depicted in the autocorrelation plot (see Fig. 5, conducted for sequences with a fixed length of 10^5).

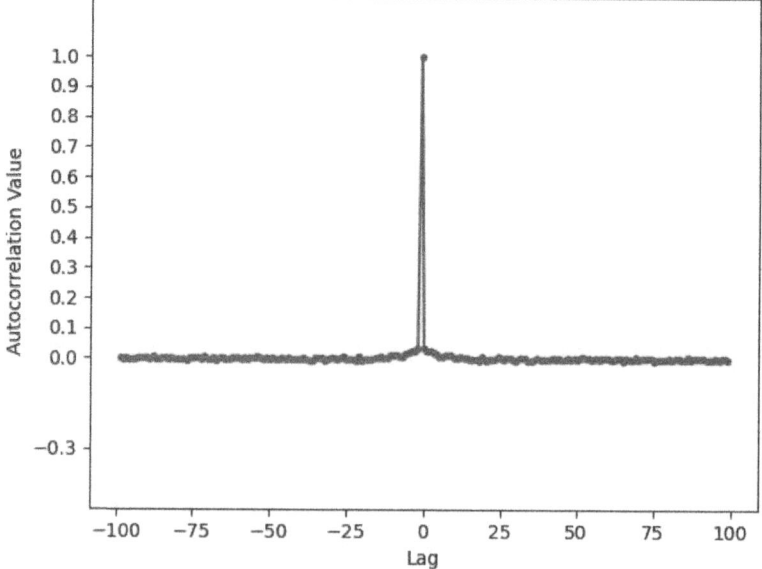

Fig. 5. Autocorrelation plot.

4.3 Time Series Analysis

The time series plots are used to determine the variations in the output sequence under small perturbations in the seed values or the parameter values. The plots for the proposed algorithm indicate a significant variation in the output sequence when seed values or parameter values (or both) are subject to small perturbations (Fig. 6). We also examine the variation between the originally generated sequence and the sequence generated under perturbed values using Granger causality test. We perform the Granger causality test for sequences of fixed length (10000 each) with up to 10 lags under a sufficiently small perturbation parameter ($\epsilon \in [0.0001, 0.001]$). The results for the Grager causality indicated for p-values exceeding 0.05 is shown in the Fig. 7. The test confirms that the perturbed sequences significantly differs from the original sequence and cannot be used to predict the original sequence.

4.4 Bits to Pixel Analysis

The generated sequence (of numbers) was converted in the binary form and was examined for any possible patterns present. The transformed image shows no apparent trends in the pixels, indicating a certain degree of randomness in the output sequence (Fig. 8).

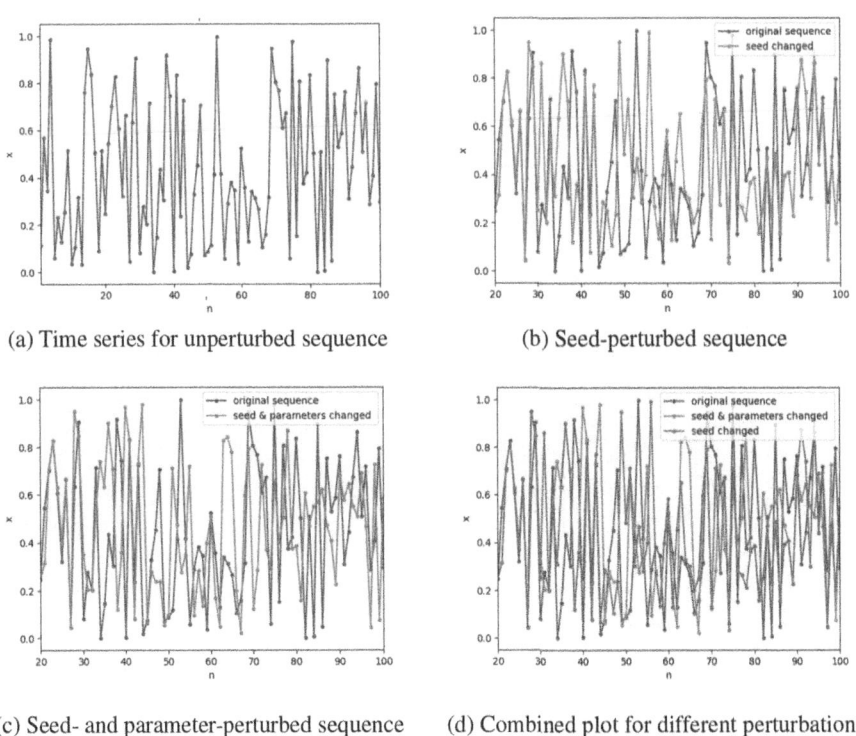

(a) Time series for unperturbed sequence

(b) Seed-perturbed sequence

(c) Seed- and parameter-perturbed sequence

(d) Combined plot for different perturbations

Fig. 6. Output sequences under various perturbations.

4.5 I.I.D Sequences

The proposed algorithm was used in conjunction with the Inversion Principle method to generate sequences using various distributions. The generated sequences were tested for independence and their distributions were examined for possible correlation using Ljung-Box test (conducted on 1000 sequences of 1000 length each). The results indicate that only 0.8% and 6.2% of the P-values are less than 0.01 for the normal distribution and uniform distribution respectively, thus providing a strong evidence that the sequences generated are indeed independent and identically distributed (are IID sequences). The distribution of the P-values obtained are plotted in Fig. 9.

4.6 Correlation and Scatter Plots

The sequences generated from each of the generators was examined for possible correlation with the output (pseudorandom) sequence generated using the heat map and scatter plots. If the generated sequence is of sufficiently large length, the plots are observed to be densely populated exhibiting no apparent patterns. The plots establish low levels of correlation between the sequences generated by each of the generating maps and the proposed algorithm (Fig. 10).

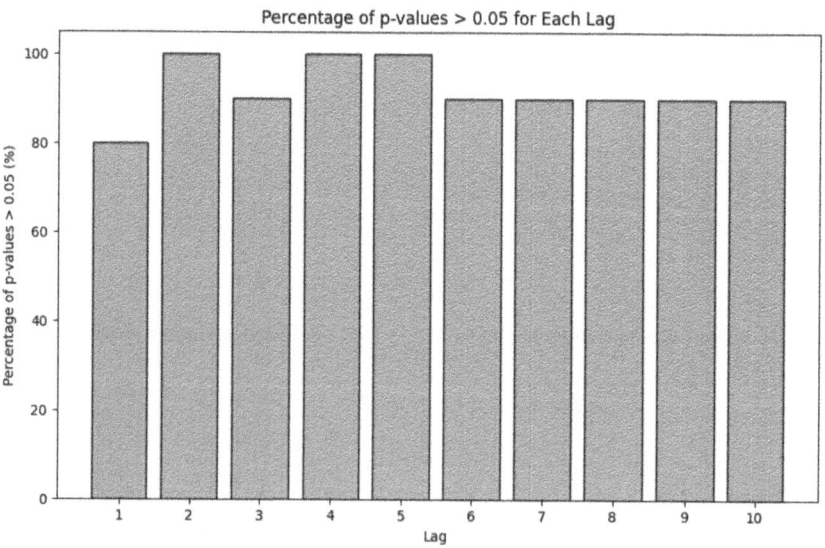

Fig. 7. Success plot for Granger causality test.

Fig. 8. Pixel analysis.

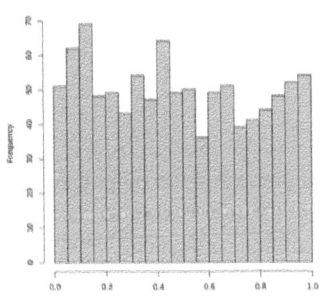

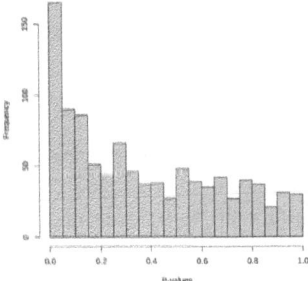

(a) P-values for normally distributed data   (b) P-values for uniformly distributed data

Fig. 9. Distribution of P-values from the Ljung-Box test.

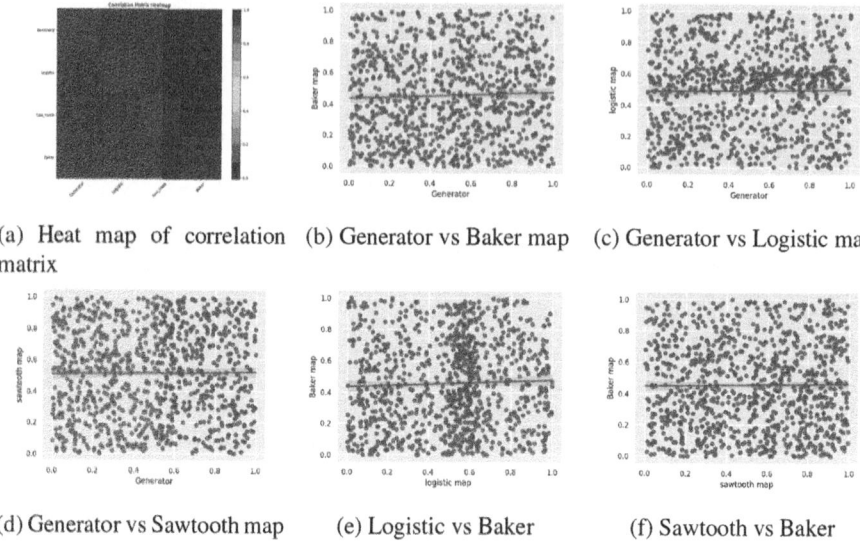

(a) Heat map of correlation matrix   (b) Generator vs Baker map   (c) Generator vs Logistic map

(d) Generator vs Sawtooth map   (e) Logistic vs Baker   (f) Sawtooth vs Baker

Fig. 10. Heat map and scatter plots.

4.7 NIST Test Suite Report

The NIST 800-22 test suite is used to examine the randomness in the output sequences. The tests determine existence of any possible patterns in the output sequence. The results establish high level of randomness in the output sequences produced(See Table 1).

Table 1. Results From The NIST Test Module

Statistical Test	Proportion	P-value	Result
Frequency	10/10	0.350485	Success
Block Frequency	10/10	0.534146	Success
Cumulative Sums	10/10	0.991468	Success
Runs	10/10	0.534146	Success
Longest Run	9/10	0.350485	Success
Rank	10/10	0.350485	Success
FFT	9/10	0.350485	Success
Nonoverlapping Template	10/10	0.911413	Success
Overlapping Template	9/10	0.534146	Success
Universal	10/10	0.447934	Success
Approximate Entropy	8/10	0.350485	Success
Random Excursions	2/2	—	Success
Random Excursions Variant	2/2	—	Success
Serial	10/10	0.534146	Success
Linear Complexity	10/10	0.911413	Success

5   Conclusions and Observations

The above work proposes an algorithm to generate pseudo random sequences with sufficiently high degree of randomness using a fixed set of chaotic maps. The algorithm uses the linear congruence map for map selection and hence provides a simple and robust mechanism with lower time complexity to generate arbitrarily long pseudo random sequences. The generated sequences passes all the tests in NIST 800-22 test suite. Consequently, chaotic maps can be used (in conjunction with sufficiently long periodic sequences) to generate sequences with sufficiently high degree of randomness. The generated sequences are observed to be independent of the sequences generated by any of the component maps. The sequences generated by any subset of proposed chaotic maps fail to qualify the standards of the NIST 800-22 test suite. The perturbation analysis and parameter dependence for the proposed algorithm was performed. It is observed that if the perturbations in the parameter are too small (dissipative), the algorithm fails to achieve sufficient degree of randomness in the generated sequences. It is interesting to investigate the nature of the sequences generated when the generating maps have positive entropy or possesses Li-Yorke sensitivity. It is also interesting to investigate randomness in the sequences generated using a smaller collection of generating maps (possibly with decision map of higher complexity). The pointwise summary of observations and results is included below to provide better understanding of the working and functionality of the algorithm.

1. The sequences generated by the decision map used (linear congruence modulo 3) or any of the generating maps fail to pass the NIST 800-22 test suite. However, the chaotic maps can be used in conjunction with linear congruence map (deterministic periodic sequences of sufficiently large length) to generate pseudo-random sequences with high degree of randomness (passes the NIST 800-22 test suite).
2. The pseudo-random sequence generated is independent of the sequence generated through any of the component generators and cannot be predicted using sequences generated by individual generator maps.
3. The sequence generated by any two maps taken from above collection fails to pass the NIST 800-22 test suite (with decision map being linear congruence modulus 2). The results thus indicate minimal level of complexity required for the proposed algorithm to produce sequences with sufficient degree pf randomness.
4. The results indicate that the degree of randomness in the output sequence depends on the perturbation in the parameter values. If the perturbations are dissipative ($\sum_{i=1}^{\infty} p_i < \infty$), the proposed algorithm fails to produce sequences with sufficient degree of randomness. However, if the perturbations are non-dissipative ($\sum_{i=1}^{\infty} p_i = \infty$), the output sequence generated by the proposed scheme passes all the tests in the NIST 800-22 test suite and hence indicate sufficient degree of randomness in the output sequence. The observations relating the perturbations and randomness of the generated sequence are given below:
   (a) if $p_i = \frac{1}{i}$ **passes all the tests**
   (b) if $p_i = \frac{1}{i^2}$ **fails the frequency monobit test which results failure in other tests**

(c) if $p_i = \frac{1}{\sqrt{i}}$ **passes all the tests**

(d) if $p_i = \frac{1}{i^3}$ **fails the frequency monobit test**

(e) if $p_i = \frac{1}{i^{1/3}}$ **passes all the tests**

6   PRNG R Package

As a conclusion to the results obtained in the article, we have developed PRNG R package for the proposed algorithm. The PRNG package [14] provides functions for generating pseudo-random numbers and random bits. The package can be found at https://doi.org/10.32614/CRAN.package.PRNG

Acknowledgments. The first author is thankful to Ministry of Education, India, for the financial support.

Disclosure of Interests. The authors have no competing interests to declare that are relevant to the content of this article.

References

1. Elaydi, S.N.: Discrete Chaos-With Applications in Science and Engineering. CRC Press, Hoboken, NJ, USA (2007)
2. Panagiotou, P., Sklavos, N., Darra, E., Zaharakis, I.D.: Cryptographic system for data applications, in the context of Internet of Things. Microprocess. Microsyst. **72**, 102921 (2020). https://doi.org/10.1016/j.micpro.2019.102921
3. L'Ecuyer, P.: Efficient and portable combined random number generators. Commun. ACM **31**(6), 742–749 (1988). https://doi.org/10.1145/62959.62969
4. Magfirawaty, Suryadi, M.T., Ramli, K.: On the design of Henon and logistic map-based random number generator. In: J. Phys. Conf. Ser. **893**(1), 012060 (2017). https://doi.org/10.1088/1742-6596/893/1/012060
5. Bassham, L., Rukhin, A., Soto, J., Nechvatal, J., Smid, M., et al.: A statistical test suite for random and pseudorandom number generators for cryptographic applications. NIST Special Publication **800-22r1a** (2010). https://doi.org/10.6028/NIST.SP.800-22r1a
6. L'Ecuyer, P., Simard, R., Chen, E.J., Kelton, W.D.: An object-oriented random-number package with many long streams and substreams. Oper. Res. **50**(6), 1073–1075 (2002). https://www.jstor.org/stable/3088626
7. L'Ecuyer, P., Simard, R.: TestU01: a C library for empirical testing of random number generators. ACM Trans. Math. Softw. **33**(4), 1–40 (2007). https://doi.org/10.1145/1268776.1268777
8. Park, S.K., Miller, K.W.: Random number generators: good ones are hard to find. Commun. ACM **31**(10), 1192–1201 (1988). https://doi.org/10.1145/63039.63042
9. L'Ecuyer, P.: Good parameters and implementations for combined multiple recursive random number generators. Oper. Res. **47**(1), 159–164 (1999). https://doi.org/10.1287/opre.47.1.159
10. Stoyanov, B., Ivanova, T.: CHAOSA: Chaotic map-based random number generator on Arduino platform. In: AIP Conf. Proc. **2172**(1), 090001 (2019). https://doi.org/10.1063/1.5133578

11. Nejati, H., Beirami, A., Ali, W.H.: Discrete-time chaotic-map truly random number generators: design, implementation, and variability analysis of the zigzag map. arXiv (2012). https://doi.org/10.48550/arXiv.1206.1039
12. Moysis, L., Tutueva, A., Volos, C., Butusov, D.: A chaos-based pseudo-random bit generator using multiple digits comparison. J. Comput. Eng. Inf. Technol. **2**, 58–68 (2020)
13. Naik, R.B., Singh, U.: A review on applications of chaotic maps in pseudo-random number generators and encryption. Ann. Data Sci. 1–26 (2021). https://doi.org/10.1007/s40745-021-00364-7
14. Mir, S.A., Sharma, P.: PRNG: Pseudo-random number generator. R Package Version 0.0.2.1.2 (2024). https://doi.org/10.32614/CRAN.package.PRNG

CFD Prediction of Tandem Water Columns Aerobreakup Using Open-Source Codes

F. Edoardo Taglialatela$^{(\boxtimes)}$ ⓘ and Giuliano De Stefano ⓘ

Engineering Department, University of Campania Luigi Vanvitelli, 81031 Aversa, Italy
feliceedoardo.taglialatela@unicampania.it

Abstract. The present study addresses the comparison of two different novel open-source computational fluid dynamics (CFD) codes for the numerical simulation of the deformation and breakup of tandem water columns subjected to high-speed air flow. The computations are conducted using the code ECOGEN and a customized version of Open-FOAM. Both codes employ a volume-of-fluid interface-tracking method coupled with a higher-order finite-volume approach. Unlike some similar studies, viscous and capillary effects are taken into account. As to the computational setup, a virtual shock tube environment is arranged to accurately replicate the experimental conditions. The well-defined post-shock air flow conditions allow to model the post-impact dynamics, capturing key phenomena such as interface deformation, leading edge drift, and incipient breakup. A comparative analysis of the results highlights the strengths and limitations of each solver. Comparison of results with experimental observations indicates that while both codes capture the primary mechanism of aerobreakup, differences arise in the formation of early-stage instabilities and ligament stripping dynamics. By validating open-source codes against experimental observations, this study aims to contribute to the ongoing refinement of multiphase flow modeling tools.

Keywords: Multiphase flow · compressible flow · aerobreakup · computational fluid dynamics

1 Introduction

Aerobreakup is a highly widespread phenomenon, frequently occurring in nature (e.g., in raindrops formation) as well as in industrial engineering applications. To name but a few, one can consider combustion and detonation of multiphase mixture [1], and erosion damage to structures [2,3]. Droplet *aerobreakup* happens when a high-velocity air stream impacts a liquid droplet. The liquid body, due to the surrounding gas flow, experiences significant deformation and subsequent fragmentation into a multitude of smaller sub-droplets, referred to as *daughter* droplets. During the interaction, the momentum transport from the high-speed air flow and the resistive forces, caused by both surface tension and viscosity,

© The Author(s), under exclusive license to Springer Nature Switzerland AG 2025
O. Gervasi et al. (Eds.): ICCSA 2025, LNCS 15648, pp. 36–50, 2025.
https://doi.org/10.1007/978-3-031-97000-9_3

oppose each other. The imbalance between the two determines the degree of deformation. For this reason, the physical mechanism can be cataloged in terms of two non-dimensional parameters, namely, the Weber number

$$\text{We} = \frac{\rho_g u_g^2 d_0}{\sigma} \tag{1}$$

that relates aerodynamic forces and surface tension forces, and the Ohnesorge number

$$\text{Oh} = \frac{\mu_\ell}{\sqrt{\rho_\ell \sigma d_0}} \tag{2}$$

that compares the viscosity of the liquid and surface tension effects. Here, ρ and u_g are the post shock density and velocity magnitude, d_0 is the initial droplet diameter, μ is the viscosity and σ is the surface tension coefficient between the two different fluids. The subscripts "ℓ" and "g" denote the liquid and gas phase, respectively.

The Weber number is a key parameter to catalog the breakup regimes, not only to embed the main physical features of the phenomenon, but also to determine the characteristics of the resultant droplet cloud. The original classification involved five distinct regimes: *vibrational breakup, bag breakup, multimode breakup, sheet thinning breakup* and *catastrophic breakup*. Each of them occurred in specific ranges of the Weber number. More recently, Theofanous and Li [4,5] provided a complete review of aerobreakup physics, and a new classification. In particular, it was recognized that the so-called *catastrophic breakup* regime was only a visual artifact observed in the experiments. The re-classification consists of only two distinct regimes: the Rayleigh-Taylor Piercing (RTP) is observed for $10 < \text{We} < 10^2$, and the Shear-Induced Entrainment (SIE) occurred for $\text{We} > 10^3$. At low Weber number, the primary factor inducing breakup are Rayleigh-Taylor instabilities, whereas at higher Weber number, the predominant mechanism for liquid filament stripping is attributed to the substantial shear effects exerted by the adjacent airflow. As the relative importance of viscous forces is expressed by the Ohnesorge number, it is that for low values of this parameter ($\text{Oh} < 0.1$), the viscosity plays a very marginal role, and can be neglected. On the other hand, at higher values ($\text{Oh} > 1$), the required forces for the breakup increase owing to viscous dissipation, e.g. [6].

The primary objective of the study is to set up a virtual shock tube environment using two different open-source codes based on the finite volume (FV) approach. The two codes employed are ECOGEN [7] and a custom version of OpenFOAM using the solver vofTwoPhaseCentralFoam [8]. The first was developed by Schmidmayer et al. [9], while the second was introduced by Kraposhin and co-workers [10]. Both solvers were successfully tested for multidimensional compressible single-phase and two-phase flows, e.g. 1D and 2D transport tests, surface tension tests to verify Laplace's law, gas-liquid shock tube and other significant problems [9,10]. Performance scalability tests have also been provided.

In this study, the tandem breakup phenomenon is investigated in order to effectively predict the post-shock droplet dynamics, in terms of leading edge drift and streamwise extent. Also, a qualitative view of the flow field and the overall interface deformation dynamics of the two cylinders is shown. Differently from previous droplet aerobreakup studies following the unsteady Reynolds-averaged Navier-Stokes (URANS) approach [11–13], where the mean flow was resolved, supplying the simulation with suitable turbulence closures, the present codes directly solve the original governing equations. However, in contrast to other scale-resolving simulations [14,15], the current methods do not utilize an explicit subgrid-scale model for approximating the effect of unresolved turbulent flow motions. Rather, they rely on the implicit numerical dissipation provided by the adopted numerical scheme, e.g. [16].

The residual of the paper is organized as follows. In Sect. 2, the physical model of the problem is introduced, including the governing equations for both solvers. The CFD models are described in Sect. 3, while the results of the numerical computations are presented and discussed in Sect. 4. Finally, some concluding remarks are drawn in Sect. 5.

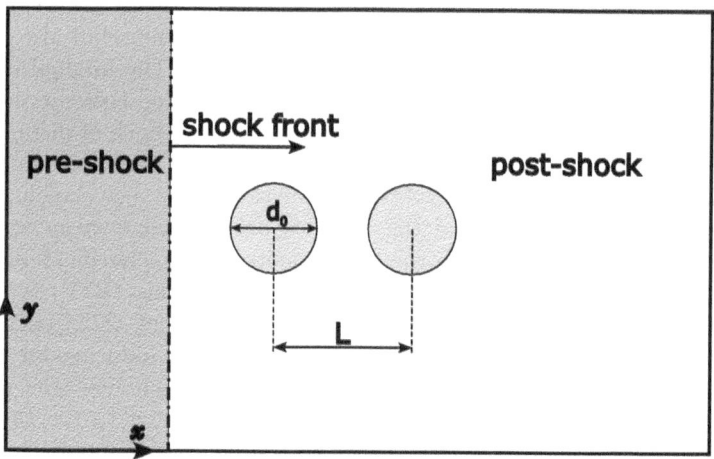

Fig. 1. Two-phase flow geometry (not in scale).

2   Physical Model

The shock/droplet interaction is often studied in two dimensions by simulating the shock wave passage over a water column, e.g. [11]. Pioneering experimental studies such as those by Igra and Takayama [17,18] are generally used to verify numerical results. A very common experimental setup is represented by a shock tube, where a physical diaphragm divides the enclosed tube into two distinct zones: a driver section with high-pressure air and a driven section at atmospheric conditions. Once the diaphragm is removed, a travelling shock is produced that impacts the column in the test zone. The described setup aims to produce very well-defined post-shock conditions for the water bodies. Figure 1 shows the domain of the problem, where two cylinders with diameter d_0 are situated in the driven section at the distance L.

In the following subsections, the systems of equations used by ECOGEN and vofTwoPhaseCentralFoam are presented, for the specific case of a liquid-gas mixture. Both methods are derived from the Baer-Nunziato 7-equation model [19] and combine a volume-of-fluid (VOF) interface-capturing scheme with a shock-capturing FV approach. Furthermore, both are influenced by a parameter represented as μ, referred to as pressure relaxation coefficient, which determines the speed at which the system attains mechanical equilibrium.

2.1 ECOGEN: Six-Equation Model

The six-equation model should not be considered as a physical model, but more as a step model to numerically solve the equations upon using a finite or infinite pressure relaxation. The better properties for the numerical approximation regard the preservation of the positivity for the volume fractions and the monotonicity of sound speed. The pressure- and temperature-disequilibrium, multicomponent system of equations employed by ECOGEN is the following [20]:

$$\frac{\partial \alpha_\ell}{\partial t} + \boldsymbol{u} \cdot \nabla \alpha_\ell = \mu(p_\ell - p_{\mathrm{g}}), \tag{3}$$

$$\frac{\partial \alpha_\ell \rho_\ell}{\partial t} + \nabla \cdot (\alpha_\ell \rho_\ell \boldsymbol{u}) - 0, \tag{4}$$

$$\frac{\partial \alpha_{\mathrm{g}} \rho_{\mathrm{g}}}{\partial t} + \nabla \cdot (\alpha_{\mathrm{g}} \rho_{\mathrm{g}} \boldsymbol{u}) = 0, \tag{5}$$

$$\frac{\partial \rho \boldsymbol{u}}{\partial t} + \nabla \cdot (\rho \boldsymbol{u} \otimes \boldsymbol{u} + p\boldsymbol{I} + \boldsymbol{\Omega} - \boldsymbol{\tau}) = \boldsymbol{0}, \tag{6}$$

$$\frac{\partial \alpha_\ell \rho_\ell e_\ell}{\partial t} + \nabla \cdot (\alpha_\ell \rho_\ell e_\ell \boldsymbol{u}) + \alpha_\ell p_\ell \nabla \cdot \boldsymbol{u} = -p_I \mu(p_\ell - p_{\mathrm{g}}) + \alpha_\ell \boldsymbol{\tau}_\ell : \nabla \boldsymbol{u}, \tag{7}$$

$$\frac{\partial \alpha_{\mathrm{g}} \rho_{\mathrm{g}} e_{\mathrm{g}}}{\partial t} + \nabla \cdot (\alpha_{\mathrm{g}} \rho_{\mathrm{g}} e_{\mathrm{g}} \boldsymbol{u}) + \alpha_{\mathrm{g}} p_{\mathrm{g}} \nabla \cdot \boldsymbol{u} = p_I \mu(p_\ell - p_{\mathrm{g}}) + \alpha_g \boldsymbol{\tau}_{\mathrm{g}} : \nabla \boldsymbol{u}. \tag{8}$$

In the above equations: μ represents the relaxation parameter; α_k, ρ_k, e_k, and p_k indicate volume fraction, density, internal energy, and pressure of one of the two components ($k = \ell$ or $k = g$); $\boldsymbol{I}$ stands for the identity tensor; the variable $p_I = \frac{Z_{\mathrm{g}} p_\ell + Z_\ell p_{\mathrm{g}}}{Z_\ell + Z_{\mathrm{g}}}$ denotes the interfacial pressure; $Z_k = \rho_k c_k$ the acoustic impedance; $\boldsymbol{\Omega}$ is the capillary tensor; $\boldsymbol{\tau}$ is the viscous stress tensor. In the VOF formulation, the mixture variables are given by

$$\rho = \alpha_\ell \rho_\ell + \alpha_{\mathrm{g}} \rho_{\mathrm{g}} \quad \text{and} \quad p = \alpha_\ell p_\ell + \alpha_{\mathrm{g}} p_{\mathrm{g}}. \tag{9}$$

In regular zones the model is self-consistent. However, in presence of shocks, the internal energy equations are inappropriate because of their non-conservative nature. Due to this reason, a redundant equation for the total energy of the mixture is necessary to correct the thermodynamic state predicted [21]. The equation reads:

$$\frac{\partial \rho E + \varepsilon_\sigma}{\partial t} + \nabla \cdot ((\rho E + \varepsilon_\sigma + p)\boldsymbol{u} + \boldsymbol{\Omega} \cdot \boldsymbol{u} - \boldsymbol{\tau} \cdot \boldsymbol{u}) = 0, \tag{10}$$

where $E = e + \frac{1}{2}\|\boldsymbol{u}\|^2$, and ε_σ is the capillary energy. The internal energy is given by

$$e = Y_\ell e_\ell + Y_g e_g. \tag{11}$$

In this equation, $Y_k = \frac{\alpha_k \rho_k}{\rho}$ are the mass fractions, and e_k is given by an appropriate equation of state.

In this case, finite relaxation is used and the value of 3.5 is selected for the parameter μ, which plays a crucial role [22].

2.2   vofTwoPhaseCentralFoam: Five-Equation Model

The infinite pressure relaxation hypothesis ($\mu \to +\infty$), meaning that the equilibrium state is reached instantly, makes the six-equation model converge to the mechanical-equilibrium model of Kapila et al. [23]. At the end of the asymptotic reduction process [21], there exists a single equilibrium pressure (and velocity), suppressing undesired spurious interfacial oscillations. The resulting hyperbolic model is thermodynamically consistent and particularly suitable for describing immiscible fluids. In the case of a water-air mixture, it reads [24]:

$$\frac{\partial \rho}{\partial t} + \nabla \cdot (\rho \boldsymbol{u}) = 0, \tag{12}$$

$$\frac{\partial (\rho \boldsymbol{u})}{\partial t} + \nabla \cdot (\rho \boldsymbol{u} \otimes \boldsymbol{u}) = -\nabla p + \nabla \cdot \boldsymbol{\tau}, \tag{13}$$

$$\frac{\partial (\rho E)}{\partial t} + \nabla \cdot [(\rho E + p)\boldsymbol{u}] = \nabla \cdot (\boldsymbol{\tau} \cdot \boldsymbol{u}), \tag{14}$$

$$\frac{\partial (\alpha_\ell \rho_\ell)}{\partial t} + \nabla \cdot (\alpha_\ell \rho_\ell \boldsymbol{u}) = 0, \tag{15}$$

$$\frac{\partial \alpha_\ell}{\partial t} + \nabla \cdot (\alpha_\ell \boldsymbol{u}) = \alpha_\ell \nabla \cdot \boldsymbol{u} + K \nabla \cdot \boldsymbol{u}, \tag{16}$$

where $K = \frac{\alpha_\ell \alpha_g (Z_\ell - Z_g)}{\alpha_\ell Z_\ell + \alpha_g Z_g}$ is the interface compression coefficient, while the other symbols represent the same quantities already defined in Sect. 2.1.

2.3   Thermodynamic Closure

As far as the thermodynamic closure is concerned, both CFD models treat the air phase as an ideal gas. By denoting $R_g = R/M_g$ the particular gas constant, with M_g the associated molar mass, and R the universal gas constant, the gas density is calculated as follows:

$$\rho_g = \frac{p_g}{R_g T}. \tag{17}$$

As for the water phase, ECOGEN uses the stiffened equation of state, thus the density is:

$$\rho_\ell = \frac{p_\ell + \pi_\infty}{(e_\ell - e_{\ell,\text{ref}})(\gamma_{\text{sg}} - 1)}, \tag{18}$$

where π_∞ and γ_{sg} are fitting parameters set according to [25]. Table 1 sums up the properties of the fluids used in the current simulations.

Table 1. Fluids properties.

Parameter	Description	Value	Unit
ρ_ℓ	Liquid density	1028	$kg \cdot m^{-3}$
π_∞	SG fitting parameter	343.44	MPa
γ_{sg}	SG fitting parameter	6.12	–
σ	Surface tension	0.0728	$N \cdot m^{-1}$
μ_ℓ	Liquid dynamic viscosity	1.0×10^{-3}	$Pa \cdot s$
μ_g	Gas dynamic viscosity	1.85×10^{-5}	$Pa \cdot s$

On the other hand, the equation of state for water in vofTwoPhaseCentral-Foam corresponds to the perfect fluid formulation, calculating the density as follows:

$$\rho_\ell = \rho_{\ell 0} + \frac{p}{RT}. \tag{19}$$

Following experimental studies, the initial diameter d_0 is set to 4.8mm and the center-to-center distance between the columns, L, is 30mm [18]. In addition, given the properties in Table 1, the non-dimensional numbers defined in Eq. 1 and Eq. 2 are: We $= 7.41 \times 10^3$ and Oh $= 1.70 \times 10^{-3}$. The Reynolds number is Re $= 1.07 \times 10^5$. These conditions place the phenomenon in the SIE regime, as confirmed by [4]. Lastly, owing to the low Oh number, capillary effects could be neglected, as in previous studies [25]. However, in the present simulations, those effects are included, as they become more important in the late stages of the interaction [26,27].

3   Computational Models

Using the initial column diameter d_0 as a reference length, the computational domain Ω is measured as a multiple of it. In both simulations, Ω is initialized to reproduce the experimental conditions of the shock tube and to simulate the interaction in its entirety, without enforcing any symmetry. Given the Mach number of the shock, the compression ratio $\beta = p_2/p_1$ is known and can be used to obtain p_4/p_1, where the subscripts "4" and "1" are used to denote driver and driven sections, respectively. The two sections, separated by a virtual diaphragm, are initialized with still air ($u_4 = u_1 = 0$) at the same temperature ($T_4 = T_1$) and very different pressure and density levels: $p_4 \gg p_1$, $\rho_4 \gg \rho_1$. The cell size of was chosen according to previous studies, decreasing it compared to [25, 28].

3.1   Code ECOGEN

In the above context, the physical domain shown in Fig. 1 is discretized using a structured grid made up entirely of square cells. The novel adaptive mesh refinement (AMR) technique presented in [29] is used, refining the grid twice based on the gradients of the field variables in the domain. The finest resolution is 128 cells per diameter (cpd). The non-reflective boundary conditions (NRBCs) are set to every boundary and allow to shrink the domain without unphysical reflections influencing the test zone. The final dimensions for Ω are $[0, 25d_0] \times [0, 10d_0]$.

The numerical solution of equations (3) to (8) is structured as follows, and it is based on a splitting procedure:

- the left-hand side of the equations are solved using an explicit Godunov-type method, where it is included the additional equation for the energy correction;
- the relaxation terms are integrated with a first-order explicit Euler scheme;
- a second-order monotonic upwind scheme for conservation laws (MUSCL) is used, where a monotonized central (MC) limiter is employed for the primitive variables;
- the timestep is automatically controlled to maintain the Courant-Friedrich-Levy (CFL) number below 0.6.

For further information regarding the model, the interested reader is encouraged to delve into the articles detailing the solution method, i.e. [20].

3.2   Code vofTwoPhaseCentralFoam

The computational domain used to obtain the solution in OpenFOAM is divided into a uniform square grid. In the absence of AMR, to obtain a higher resolution where needed, multiple nested refinement regions are programmed to gradually increase the local resolution. The finest region is made of 128 cpd. The domain itself is much larger, compared to the one used in ECOGEN, measuring $\Omega = [-24d_0, 96d_0] \times [-30d_0, 30d_0]$. With such an extent, the absence of NRBCs and the subsequent unphysical reflections do not interfere with the simulation, allowing for longer visualization times. The boundary conditions applied are shown in Table 2, using the OpenFOAM naming convention. Here, the solving procedure is as follows:

– fluxes are calculated using a hybrid Kurganov-Noelle-Petrova (KNP)/ PIMPLE algorithm, to ensure monotonicity of the primitive variables;
– the acoustically conservative interface discretization (ACID) technique helps suppress spurious oscillations near the interfaces;
– the multidimensional universal limiter for explicit solution (MULES) approach is used, where a Minmod limiter is employed;
– the equations are marched in time using a first-order explicit Euler scheme;
– the timestep is automatically controlled setting CFL < 0.15.

Figure 2 shows the comparison of both meshes in proximity to the water body. For further information on the numerical model, the interested reader is encouraged to consult [10]. In addition, more details on the implementation of this particular solver for the investigation of droplet aerobreakup can be found in [30].

Table 2. Summary of boundary conditions employed in the OpenFOAM solver.

Boundary	p	T	u	α_ℓ
Driver section side	zeroGradient	zeroGradient	fixedValue	fixedValue
Driven section side	zeroGradient	zeroGradient	zeroGradient	zeroGradient
Lateral sides	zeroGradient	zeroGradient	slip	zeroGradient

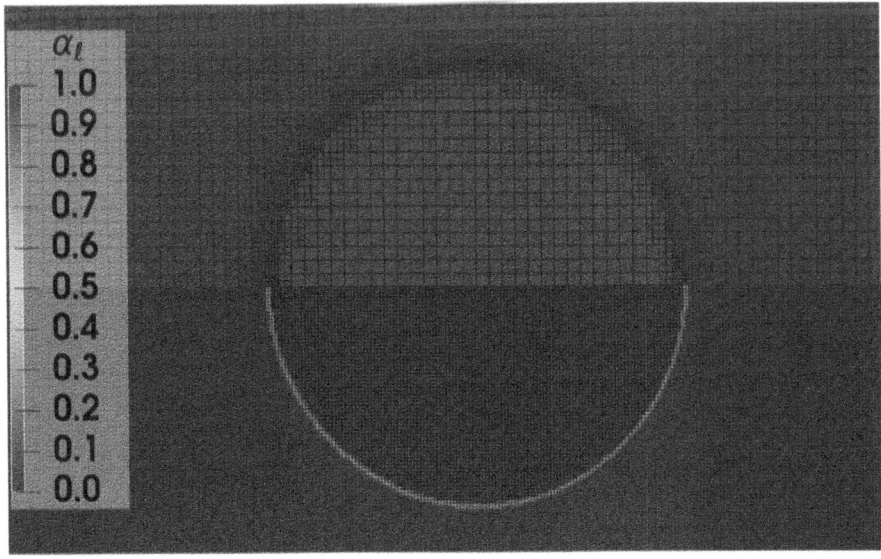

Fig. 2. Comparison between the meshes: ECOGEN (top) and vofTwoPhaseCentralFoam (bottom).

4   Results

Both solutions are analyzed from a qualitative point of view, depicting the velocity magnitude and the numerical Schlieren contours shown in Fig. 3. Herein, the numerical Schlieren is defined by:

$$\Phi = \exp\left(-k\frac{|\nabla\rho|}{\max(|\nabla\rho|)}\right),\tag{20}$$

where k is a user-defined constant.

Fig. 3. Velocity magnitude and Schlieren contours for ECOGEN (left) and vofTwoPhaseCentralFoam (right) at $t^* \approx 3.1$, 9, 15.1, and 17.9.

Notably, the calculated velocity magnitudes are different: ECOGEN predicts higher peak values, localized further from the interface. The pressure differential between the two sides of each cylinder is captured by both codes, which eventually causes flattening and peripheral elongation.

Figure 4 shows the time histories of the volume fraction contour of the liquid phase, sampled for both solvers. It can be seen that the time evolution of the captured interface is similar in the early stages, and as time passes, more differences arise. The aforementioned flattening shows itself in both simulations. However, a first difference can be seen on the front side, where vofTwoPhaseCentralFoam captures more instabilities, while the other solution appears to be more regular (details in Figs. 4 (a) and 4 (b)).

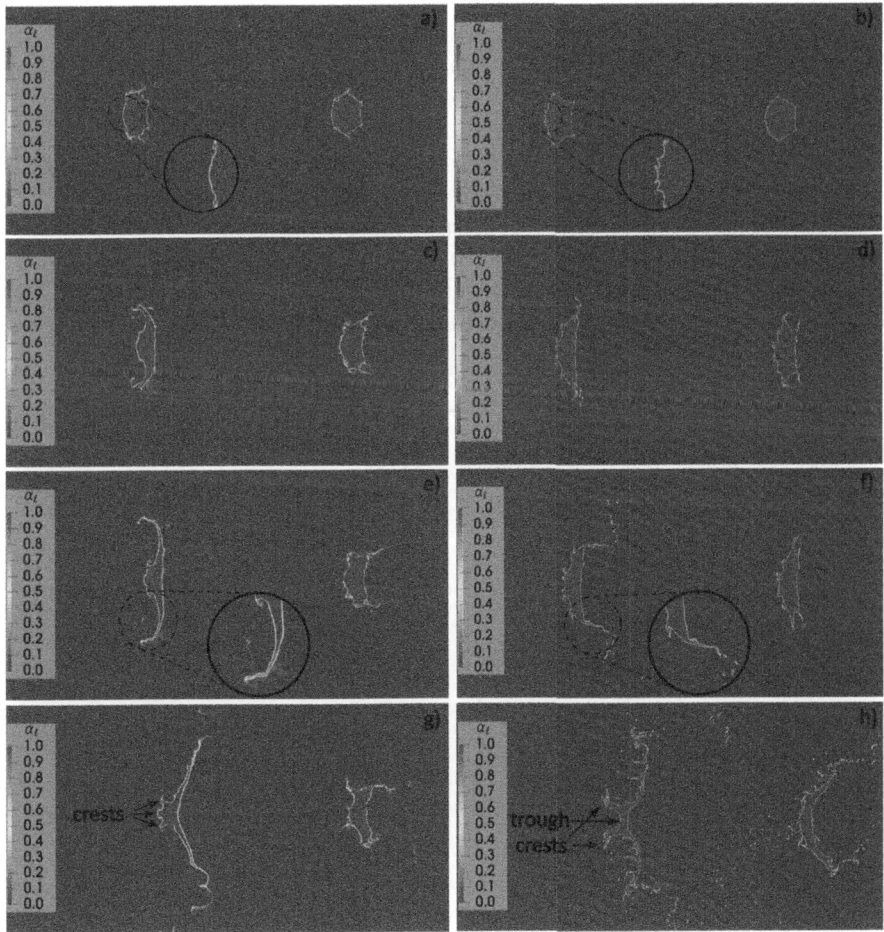

Fig. 4. Liquid volume fraction contours for ECOGEN (left) and vofTwoPhaseCentral-Foam (right) at $t^* \approx 9$, 15.1, 17.9 and 22.1 (from top to bottom row).

According to experimental findings, the early stages of the interaction show a closer match with what was calculated by ECOGEN. In fact, as mentioned by

Theofanous and Li in [4], a significant area surrounding the front stagnation point is smooth, while the radially redirected flow gives birth to surface instabilities that produce peripheral elongation and ultimately lips. This characteristic of mass redistribution from a cylinder to an elongated structure also aligns with what was observed in the SIE regime, where the stripping mechanism drives the fragmentation.

In the above context, the prediction of the lips highlights a different behavior. As shown in the particulars of Fig. 4 (e) and Fig. 4 (f), the ligaments predicted by vofTwoPhaseCentralFoam tend to go downstream, while the more peripheral and diffuse parts calculated by ECOGEN initially point in the opposite direction. As time passes, the vofTwoPhaseCentralFoam calculation resembles the formation of the ligaments and the overall shape of the cylinders more closely [4,27,31]. In the late stages, ECOGEN recovers the correct behavior, as the shedded lips are pushed by the air stream toward the leeward side (subfigures (g) and (h)), and the two captured surfaces appear similar. Connected with the late stages, the prediction of the front stagnation zone is similar: both simulations show that the surface instabilities previously created tend to drift less, when compared to the rest of the cylinder, which gets further pushed downstream.

With respect to the rear column, both solutions show similar behavior for the majority of the interaction. Nevertheless, in the late stages, vofTwoPhase-CentralFoam appears closer to the experimental findings. This behavior could indicate a different calculation of the vortical structures in the wake of the first cylinder.

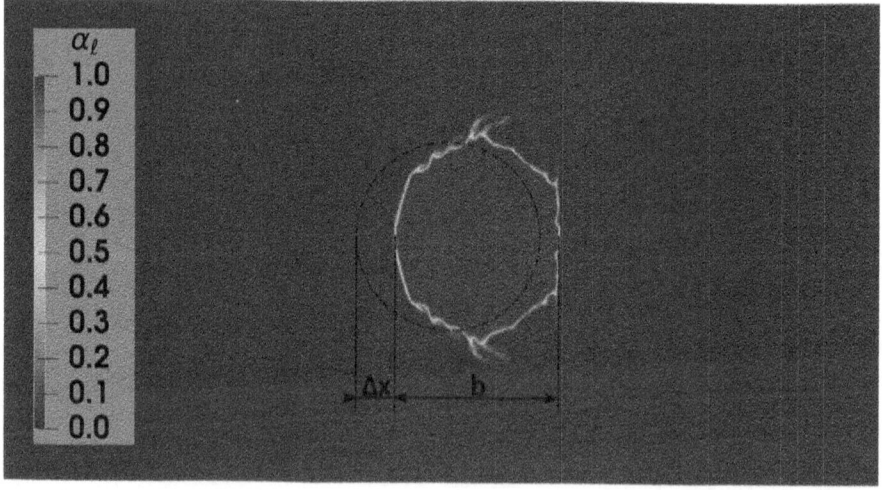

Fig. 5. Leading edge displacement and streamwise extent of the front column shown at $t^* \approx 4$ (ECOGEN).

The numerical results are further analyzed in terms of leading edge drift Δx_{LE} and streamwise deformation b, shown in Fig. 5. Both quantities are then non-dimensionalized by the characteristic length of this problem, namely d_0, and plotted with respect to the normalized time (using the so-called *inertial* time scale), defined as follows

$$t^* = \frac{u_2}{d_0}(t - t_0),$$ (21)

where t_0 is the instant of the impact between the shock and the front column. Figure 6 shows the time evolution of such quantities, sampled for both solvers and compared to experimental findings by Igra and Takayama [18].

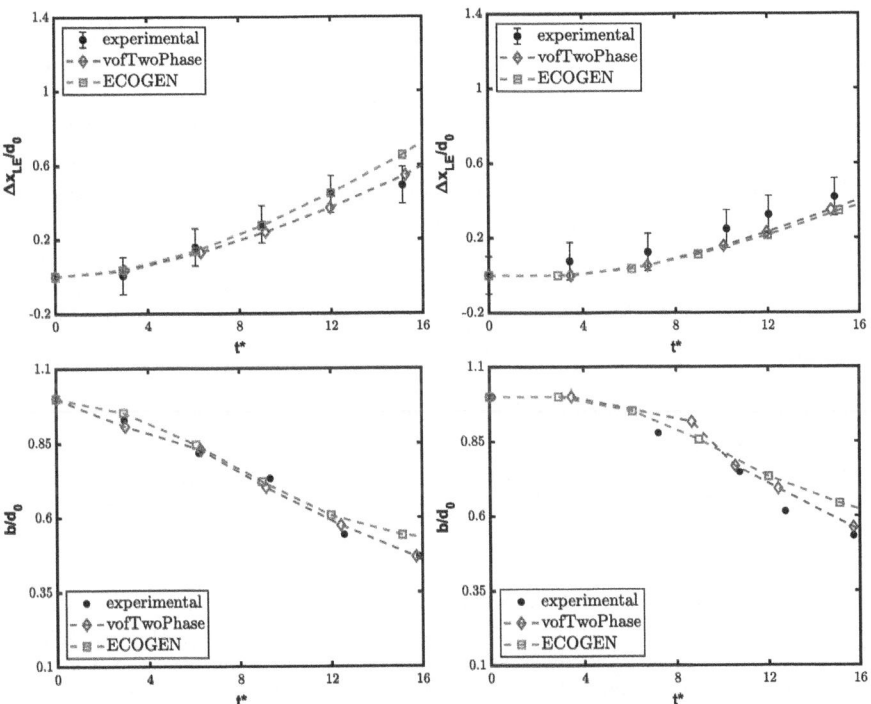

Fig. 6. Normalized leading edge displacement (top) and streamwise extent (bottom) for the front (left) and the rear column (right).

In particular, it is clear that the second column experiences less force from the air stream, as a result of the front column acting as an attenuator. As noted before, this qualitative observation is substantiated here: the surface crests on the front column, which do not undergo deformation in the late stages, make the streamwise extent less close to the experimental observations when it comes to ECOGEN. The prediction of vofTwoPhaseCentralFoam is closer as a consequence of the presence of the central trough between the two crests, as highlighted in Figs. 4 (g) and 4 (h).

5   Conclusions

Two novel open-source codes were compared, numerically reproducing the inter-action between a traveling shock wave and two water columns in tandem, while simulating a shock tube device. The system of partial differential equations that govern the physical phenomenon was solved by using the FV method, supplied with high-order numerical schemes. The inevitable numerical dissipation that comes as a counterpart showed in the time evolutions of the leading edge drift and streamwise displacement. However, the complex flow field was replicated with good agreement by both codes.

Unlike previous similar works, the current research employs non-commercial softwares that allow full code access. The results of the present simulations, taking into account capillary and viscous effects, highlight the importance of these effects in modeling the late stages of shock-induced liquid fragmentation, which can improve the predictive capability of numerical solvers in practical engi-neering applications, such as the detonation of air-fuel mixtures. Although both ECOGEN and vofTwoPhaseCentralFoam have been shown to effectively capture primary breakup mechanisms, differences in instability formation and ligament shedding are observed, which suggests further research. In fact, while early-stage accuracy benefits from numerical dissipation, late-stage accuracy requires a more balanced treatment of interface sharpening and numerical diffusion. In this very challenging context, where a very broad range of scales play an important role, computational efficiency remains a great challenge. The use of adaptive meshing refinement strategies and the correct implementation of non-reflective boundary conditions largely decreased computational costs in terms of simulation times.

The aerobreakup of liquid droplets is an active area of research. Future work could explore the inclusion of explicit subgrid-scale models to better resolve small-scale instabilities and phenomena associated with droplet breakup [15].

Acknowledgments. The authors acknowledge financial support under the National Recovery and Resilience Plan (NRRP), Mission 4, Component 2, Investment 1.1, Call for tender No. 104 published on 2.2.2022 by the Italian Ministry of University and Research (MUR), funded by the European Union - NextGenerationEU- Project 2022B2X937 Title "Next Generation Space Propulsion Design Techniques" - CUP E53D23003080006 - Grant Assignment Decree No. 961 adopted on 30.6.2023 by MUR.

Disclosure of Interests. The authors have no competing interests to declare that are relevant to the content of this article.

References

1. Redding, J.P., Khare, P.: A computational study on shock induced deformation, fragmentation and vaporization of volatile liquid fuel droplets. Int. J. Heat Mass Transf. **184**, 122345 (2022)
2. Villermaux, E.: Fragmentation. Annu. Rev. Fluid Mech. **39**, 419–446 (2007)
3. Villermaux, E., Bossa, B.: Single-drop fragmentation determines size distribution of raindrops. Nat. Phys. **5**, 697–702 (2009)

4. Theofanous, T.G., Li, G.J.: On the physics of aerobreakup. Phys. Fluids **20**, 052103 (2008)
5. Theofanous, T.G.: Aerobreakup of Newtonian and viscoelastic liquids. Annu. Rev. Fluid Mech. **43**, 661–690 (2011)
6. Sharma, S., Chandra, N.K., Basu, S., Kumar, A.: Advances in droplet aerobreakup. Eur. Phys. J. Spec. Top. **232**, 719–733 (2023)
7. https://code-mphi.github.io/ECOGEN/. Accessed 25 Feb 2025
8. https://github.com/mkraposhin/hybridCentralSolvers/tree/edo-problem. Accessed 18 Jan 2025
9. Schmidmayer, K., Petitpas, F., Le Martelot, S., Daniel, E.: ECOGEN: an opensource tool for multiphase, compressible, multiphysics flows. Comput. Phys. Commun. **251**, 107093 (2020)
10. Kraposhin, M.V., Kukharskii, A.V., Korchagova, V.N., Shevelev, A.A.: An extension of the all-Mach number pressure-based solution framework for numerical modelling of two-phase flows with interface. Ind. Processes Technol. **166**, 6–27 (2022)
11. Rossano, V., De Stefano, G.: Computational evaluation of shock wave interaction with a cylindrical water column. Appl. Sci. **11**, 4934 (2021)
12. Rossano, V., Cittadini, A., De Stefano, G.: Computational evaluation of shock wave interaction with a liquid droplet. Appl. Sci. **12**, 1349 (2022)
13. Rossano, V., De Stefano, G.: Hybrid VOF-lagrangian CFD modeling of droplet aerobreakup. Appl. Sci. **12**, 8302 (2022)
14. Rossano, V., De Stefano, G.: Scale-resolving simulation of shock-induced aerobreakup of water droplet. Computation **12**, 71 (2024)
15. Rossano, V., De Stefano, G.: Large-eddy simulation of droplet deformation and fragmentation under shock wave impact. Appl. Sci. **15**, 1233 (2025)
16. De Stefano, G.: Wavelet-based adaptive implicit large-eddy simulation of turbulent channel flow. Comput. Fluids **272**, 106190 (2024)
17. Igra, D., Takayama, K.: Investigation of aerodynamic breakup of a cylindrical water droplet. At. Sprays **11**, 167–185 (2001)
18. Igra, D., Takayama, K.: Experimental investigation of two cylindrical water columns subjected to planar shock wave loading. J. Fluids Eng. **125**, 325–331 (2003)
19. Baer, M.R., Nunziato, J.W.: A two-phase mixture theory for the deflagration-to-detonation transition (DDT) in reactive granular materials. Int. J. Multiph. Flow **12**, 861–889 (1986)
20. Schmidmayer, K., Cazé, J., Petitpas, F., Daniel, E., Favrie, N.: Modelling interactions between waves and diffused interfaces. Int. J. Numer. Meth. Fluids **95**, 215–241 (2023)
21. Saurel, R., Petitpas, F., Berry, R.A.: Simple and efficient relaxation methods for interfaces separating compressible fluids, cavitating flows and shocks in multiphase mixtures. J. Comput. Phys. **228**, 1678–1712 (2009)
22. Biasiori-Poulanges, L., Schmidmayer, K.: A phenomenological analysis of droplet shock-induced cavitation using a multiphase modeling approach. Phys. Fluids **35**, 013312 (2023)
23. Kapila, A.K., Menikoff, R., Bdzil, J.B., Son, S.F., Stewart, D.S.: Two-phase modeling of deflagration-to-detonation transition in granular materials: reduced equations. Phys. Fluids **13**, 3002–3024 (2001)
24. Saurel, R., Pantano, C.: Diffuse-interface capturing methods for compressible two-phase flows. Annu. Rev. Fluid Mech. **50**, 105–130 (2018)
25. Meng, J.C., Colonius, T.: Numerical simulations of the early stages of high-speed droplet breakup. Shock Waves **25**, 399–414 (2015)

26. Meng, J.C., Colonius, T.: Numerical simulation of the aerobreakup of a water droplet. J. Fluid Mech. **835**, 1108–1135 (2018)
27. Dorschner, B., Biasiori-Poulanges, L., Schmidmayer, K., El-Rabii, H., Colonius, T.: On the formation and recurrent shedding of ligaments in droplet aerobreakup. J. Fluid Mech. **904**, A20 (2020)
28. Hong, Z.Y., et al.: Deformation and mutual influence of two cylindrical water columns in tandem subjected to shock wave. Chinese Phys. B **33**, 084702 (2024)
29. Schmidmayer, K., Petitpas, F., Daniel, E.: Adaptive mesh refinement algorithm based on dual trees for cells and faces for multiphase compressible flows. J. Comput. Phys. **388**, 252–278 (2019)
30. Taglialatela, F.E., De Stefano, G.: Numerical investigation of cylindrical water droplets subjected to air shock loading at a high Weber number. Fluids **10**, 81 (2025)
31. Poplavski, S.V., Minakov, A.V., Shebeleva, A.A., Boyko, V.M.: On the interaction of water droplet with a shock wave: experiment and numerical simulation. Int. J. Multiph. Flow **127**, 103273 (2020)

The Impact of External Factors on Cardiac Parameters

Bianca-Alexandra Zîrnă[1]([✉]) [ID], Denis Mihailovschi[2] [ID], Evan Mathis[3] [ID],
Alin-Alexandru Şerban[2] [ID], and Mădălin-Corneliu Frunzete[2] [ID]

[1] Faculty of Medical Engineering, National University of Science and Technology
POLITEHNICA, Bucharest, Romania
bianca.zirna@upb.ro

[2] Applied Electronics and Information Technology, National University of Science and
Technology POLITEHNICA, Bucharest, Romania
{denis.mihailovschi,alin.serban0507,madalin.frunzete}@upb.ro

[3] École Polytechnique Universitaire de Lyon, Claude Bernard Lyon 1 University, Villeurbanne,
France
evan.mathis@etu.univ-lyon1.fr

Abstract. Life in urban areas that are busy and noisy includes factors that are
not usually taken into consideration when talking about a "healthy heart". Even
though factors like noise, stress, or negative thoughts are ignored, they can affect
vital parameters such as heart rate and heart rate variability in a bad way. At the
opposite point, art, music, and cognitive activities can positively influence these
parameters and improve both the well-being state and the health of a subject.
This is why it is critical to continuously monitor the parameters through wearable
devices. Thus, one of the goals of this paper is to observe the influence of the
external factors on two parameters, heart rate and heart rate variability, by developing and using an Arduino-based device that records electrocardiographic (ECG)
signals, that were first compared with the ones recorded with the Biopac system.
To record the changes in the ECG signals caused by the external factors, a presentation containing four distinct tasks, besides relaxation (to establish the baseline)
—visual variations, auditive variations, cognitive activities, and memories—was
used. Another goal is to design and implement a graphical user interface (GUI)
that is user-friendly and can help the subject to better visualize and understand the
outcomes of the recordings.

Keywords: Electrocardiogram · external factors · heart rate · heart rate
variability · Arduino and Matlab systems · signal acquisition and processing ·
statistics

1 Introduction

Unbalanced and excessive urban development degrades the quality of life in cities. The
level of noise pollution rises as a result of inhabitants' growing discomfort in tandem with
an increase in traffic [1]. Every day, millions of individuals endure elements including

© The Author(s), under exclusive license to Springer Nature Switzerland AG 2025
O. Gervasi et al. (Eds.): ICCSA 2025, LNCS 15648, pp. 51–70, 2025.
https://doi.org/10.1007/978-3-031-97000-9_4

traffic, noise, stress, and busy lives. While it is generally accepted that factors like smoking, drinking, and so on cause a significant increase in heart rate, this study proposes to present that other factors that do not directly affect the subject—like exposure to sounds, depression, or stress—can affect heart rate and the heart rate variability in both positive and negative ways [2]. For instance, according to the European Environment Agency [3], long-term exposure to ambient noise results in 48000 new cases of ischemic heart disease and 12000 early deaths in Europe each year, and stress also represents a well-known risk factor for cardiovascular diseases [4].

The electrocardiogram (ECG) can be utilized to differentiate between the traces left by each condition. An ECG is a method for assessing the cardiac muscle and electrical activity [5]. This provides both physiological and pathological information, forming the diagnosis of the disease. Heart rate (HR) is the number of heartbeats in one minute. The HR depends on the activity at that moment. Over time, the body modifies the HR in response to emotional states and its needs for energy. HR increases when a person is stressed or anxious and decreases when a person is happy and calm. These differences in HR change the time interval between each heartbeat, meaning heart rate variability (HRV). People with high HRV are usually happier and less stressed. In general, low HRV is considered a sign of current or future health problems because it shows that the body is less resilient and struggles to handle changing situations. HRV gets lower if a person is stressed, depressed, or exposed to noise [6]. Evaluating both parameters— HR and HRV—is necessary since they indicate unique characteristics and because two individuals with the same HR may have different HRVs.

The aim of this study is to observe the influence of external factors on the HR and the HRV and to offer a personalized graphical user interface (GUI), as well as demonstrate that an Arduino-based device can achieve results comparable to those of a more sophisticated, professional device, such as Biopac, the focus nowadays being on lowbudget, small, and lightweight, wearable devices.

As mentioned before and according to studies in the field, it has been observed that external factors influence the cardiac rhythm [2]. The paper [7] has the main objective of performing an analysis of specialized literature to obtain an overview of the factors that affect HR. The main categories that stand out from this study are physiological/pathological, neuropsychological, non-modifiable, lifestyle, and environmental factors; thus, it is observed that these factors are interdependent. The study [8] had 33 healthy subjects perform emotion regulation tasks, during which they were instructed to either passively view negative images or attempt to regulate the effect elicited by the images. During the test, ECG was recorded and HRV was measured. Thus, certain conclusions were drawn related to the increase or decrease in HR depending on the subject's emotional state. The paper [9] studies the influence of music on HR as it increases it. Paper [10] emphasized the idea that, according to a recognized neuroscience explanation of emotions [11], emotion-related signals are variations in a person's visceral state, such as HR, that show how that person emotionally reacts to certain situations.

Section 1 introduced the ECG signals, the necessity of this work, and previous studies in this field. The rest of the paper is divided into two main sections, both following two directions: signal acquisition and signal processing (Fig. 1). Section 2 consists of the signal acquisition with two different devices – Arduino and Biopac – followed by the offline signal processing and statistics based on the outcomes, and presents the materials and methods used, both hardware and software, the results of the experiment, statistics, and comparisons and discussions. In Section 3, based on the previous results, the Arduino device is developed, the signals are now analyzed in real-time, and the outcomes are displayed in a user-friendly GUI. The final conclusions of the paper are formulated in the end, and the limitations and perspectives of this study are presented.

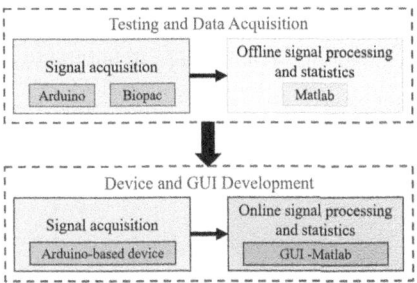

Fig. 1. The two main sections of the proposed work

2   Testing and Data Acquisition

2.1 Materials and Methods

In this stage, two different devices, Arduino and Biopac, are used to record the signals, which are then uploaded into Matlab for further analysis (offline). Subsequently, every phase will be described in detail.

Participants and Database
Ten volunteers, five of them male and five of them female, with ages ranging from 25 to 58 (Mean = 32.8, Standard Deviation = 12.43), participated in this study. They received instructions not to consume any food or coffee for two hours prior to the experiment, and they were also requested not to smoke right before the experiment because, as mentioned in other papers, quitting smoking can cause fluctuations in a smoker's heart rate. Rather, they should hydrate appropriately before.

Each participant in the study signed a written consent, agreeing to participate in this study, including the signal recording and the anonymous use of their responses and personal information, such as gender, age, pathologic history, and form responses. This form consists of 8 sections: the consent, some details about the subject relevant for the study (such as age or gender), the aforementioned protocol before the acquisition, and four paragraphs corresponding to the four tasks that will be later described, as well as the form. For each participant, an approximately 36-min signal is recorded, which will be split according to the protocol, as it will be further described.

Acquisition Devices and Protocol

Devices

Using two devices, an Arduino-based sensor (alongside the DataStreamer Toolbox from Excel) and the Biopac system, the signals are randomly acquired from the ten participants, storing them as .csv files for further processing in Matlab. The aim of this comparison, as we did in our previous work [12], is to see whether outcomes obtained with a less complex and less expensive device are comparable to those from a more advanced and expensive one. For a visual representation, Fig. 2 displays two signals of the same duration that were obtained using these two distinct devices; the Biopac signal has 10 times more samples than the Arduino signal, but the waveforms are similar.

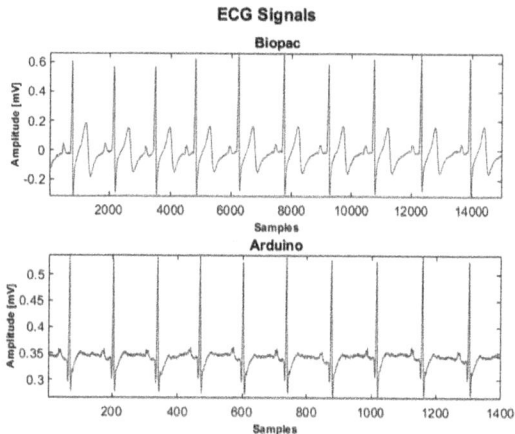

Fig. 2. A comparison between the two acquisition systems

Arduino. An Arduino Uno board, an AD8232 sensor, jumper wires, and a USB cable are the few materials required to conduct this experiment. Because it is less expensive and has enough memory and pins, the Arduino Uno board is adequate for this application. Also, the AD8232 sensor has been tested in previous studies, such as [12, 13], and it has been demonstrated to be an affordable, practical tool for recording high-quality ECG signals. Since it needs to be connected to power, ground, and an analog pin in order to read the signal, just three jumper wires are required. It is enough to use the USB cable because wireless data transfer is not required since the participants remain seated throughout the whole experiment. The sampling frequency is 200 Hz.

Biopac. The BioNomadix 2Ch Wireless ECG Amplifier (ECG2-R) module, which is a transmitter and receiver module with a simultaneous dual-channel recording feature, is used alongside the Biopac system. This feature might be helpful in other experiments, but since each participant has a unique set of answers, this experiment should be performed individually. Signals acquired with Biopac are transmitted wirelessly, with a 2000 Hz sample frequency, compared to the Arduino system.

Protocol

For better understanding, Fig. 3 illustrates all the details regarding the acquisition protocol. Since the recording is performed continuously, an automatic PowerPoint presentation is created, with a fixed duration for each slide. Every participant completes the acquisition procedure individually. The experiment is carried out in a room with a standard temperature, no external noise, and no distracting lights while the patient remains seated throughout. Additionally, the same electrode placement—Einthoven's triangle on the chest—and disposable gel electrodes are used, as well as the same acquisition protocol.

At first, during the device's calibration period, the participant receives an exhaustive description of the full process, including every task and break. The entire procedure includes an initial task (task 0) in which a 5-min signal is recorded while the patient is sitting calmly. This is followed by 4 main tasks (tasks 1-4), each of which has 2 separate 3-minute scenarios (a and b) separated by 10 seconds and a 1-minute break in between the main tasks. A ten-second introductory slide with task information is presented before each subsequent task.

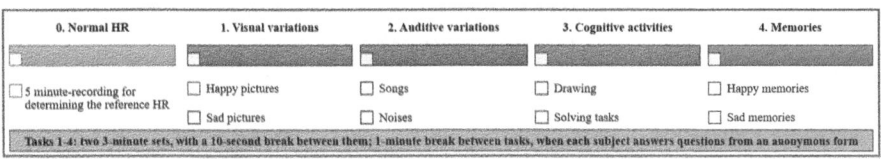

Fig. 3. The acquisition protocol with all the tasks

1. **Visual variations.** This task consists of 2 scenarios: happy pictures and sad pictures. Thirty pictures covering a variety of subjects are presented one after the other for each task (from landscapes, animals, and art, to war, pollution, and natural disasters).
2. **Auditive variations.** This task consists of 2 scenarios: songs and noises. Six distinct songs or noises (ranging from pop, rock, or classical music to alarms, sirens, and insects) are played for each task.
3. **Cognitive activities.** There are two primary objectives in this task: drawing and solving. First, the subject has to draw three distinct pictures in accordance with the term that is displayed on the slide (holiday, home, hobby). Then, he has to complete a few tasks on time, like computing, counting letters, numbers, and shapes, and responding to brief attention-getting questions.
4. **Memories.** There are two scenarios in this task: happy memories and sad memories. Three images accompanied by songs related to various themes are presented and played one after the other for every task. The images range from an airport, a beach, and a forest to a train station, a rainy day through a window, and a dark forest. The participant is required to recall six memories that bring these circumstances to mind.

Signal Processing

After the process of signal acquisition, the signals are uploaded into Matlab as .csv files for further analysis. Additional signal filtering is not required because the signals are already filtered when they are recorded, and only the R peaks (the highest amplitude peaks) need to be detected. The signals are first divided into the corresponding tasks based on the sampling frequency and task duration, obtaining 9 signals per subject. The R peaks are then identified as local maxima (percentage of the signal's mean amplitude) separated by a minimum number of samples. The RR intervals are calculated in samples and then converted to seconds based on the location of the R peaks. The outcomes are kept if they fall within the proper range for a healthy subject (0.6 to 1.2 s); if not, they are removed as considered artifacts. The process is demonstrated using a 3.2-second Arduino-recorded signal (Fig. 4). The four R-peaks are identified first, then the three RR intervals are computed, first in samples, then converted into seconds or milliseconds (by knowing the sampling frequency), and then HR and HRV are computed. Moreover, the experiment is not affected by the acquisition equipment because both systems recorded accurate ECG signals and accurate enough data to locate the R-peaks needed to calculate the HR and HRV.

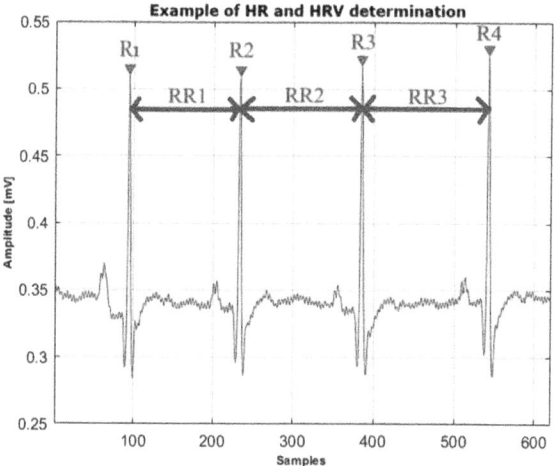

Fig. 4. An example of HR and HRV determination: R-peaks detection and RR intervals duration

Using the formula (1) and the correct RR intervals, one important parameter is computed: HR, with the mean value of the previously computed RR intervals.

$$HR = \frac{60}{RR\ intervals\ (s)} \tag{1}$$

Given that all the subjects are in good health with no history of cardiovascular diseases, the HR values are evaluated to ensure they fall within the appropriate range of 50 to 110 bpm. In the unlikely scenario that the values go outside of the range, the entire algorithm is retested with revised parameters after debugging. Then, another important parameter is HRV, computed with the method called RMSSD (Root Mean Square of

Successive Differences between each heartbeat), as Formula (2) describes. Given that all the subjects are in good health with no history of cardiovascular diseases, the HRV values are evaluated to ensure they fall within the appropriate range of 20 to 80 ms.

$$RMSSD = \sqrt{RR\ intervals^2\ (ms)} \tag{2}$$

The values are stored for every task for each participant if they fall within the proper range, and statistics are computed to provide a more comprehensive understanding of the variations in HR and HRV. The whole algorithm is synthesized in Fig. 5.

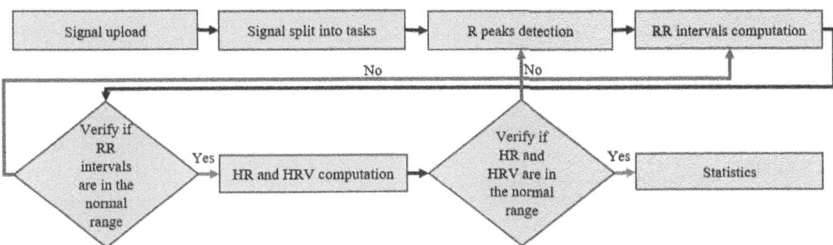

Fig. 5. The block diagram of the algorithm

2.2 Results

All the results are consolidated in Table 1, followed by separate discussions for each of the seven series of outcomes (in accordance with the procedure described previously). For the first three series, + denotes a good value and - a bad value. The notation + for differences above 0 and - for differences below 0 applies to the remaining four series and the rest of the differences in series 1-3.

Series 1: RR intervals duration. The first step is to verify if the RR interval duration is within the normal range. The RR interval lengths are determined, as was discussed in the previous section, and all participants' values, both during the relaxation state (0.66-1.09 s) and the whole experiment (0.68-1.07 s), fall within the normal range. These results were expected because the algorithm proved to be accurate, and no subjects reported having cardiovascular diseases.

Series 2: HR. Checking to determine if the HR is within the normal range is the second step. All of the individuals' computed HR values, both in the relaxation state (55-91 bpm) and during the experiment (56-89 bpm), fall within the normal range. These results were expected because the algorithm proved to be accurate, and no subject reported having any cardiovascular disease. Nevertheless, 60% of the participants had a greater HR in their relaxation state than throughout the experiment, indicating that overall, the experiment decreased their HR, as determined by calculating the difference between the HR in the relaxation state and the mean HR for the rest of the experiment.

Table 1. The outcomes of the first experiment

No.	State	Subjects				Values range	
		+		-		Range	Difference
1	**RR intervals (relaxation)**	10	100%	0	0%	0.66 - 1.09 s	0.43 s
	Mean RR intervals	10	100%	0	0%	0.68 - 1.07 s	0.39 s
2	**HR (relaxation)**	10	100%	0	0%	55 - 91 bpm	36 bpm
	Mean HR	10	100%	0	0%	56 - 89 bpm	33 bpm
	HR (relaxation vs. mean)	6	60%	4	40%	−1.25 - 2.32 bpm	3.57 bpm
3	**HRV (relaxation)**	10	100%	0	0%	29.87 - 64.92 ms	35.05 ms
	Mean HRV	10	100%	0	0%	27.03 - 53.45 ms	26.43 ms
	HRV (relaxation vs. mean)	6	60%	4	40%	−4.83 - 19.69 ms	24.53 ms
4	**HR (relaxation vs. task)**						
	relax - a1	7	70%	3	30%	−3.92 - 5.41 bpm	9.33 bpm
	relax - b1	6	60%	4	40%	−5.06 - 2.61 bpm	7.67 bpm
	relax - a2	5	50%	5	50%	−1.34 - 2.09 bpm	3.43 bpm
	relax - b2	5	50%	5	50%	−1.99 - 3.03 bpm	5.02 bpm
	relax - a3	4	40%	6	60%	−4.30 - 2.49 bpm	6.79 bpm
	relax - b3	6	60%	4	40%	−3.87 - 4.53 bpm	8.4 bpm
	relax - a4	9	90%	1	10%	−2.11 - 7.01 bpm	9.12 bpm
	relax - b4	9	90%	1	10%	−0.84 - 5.18 bpm	6.02 bpm
5	**HR (task a vs. b)**						
	task 1	3	30%	7	70%	−2.90 - 4.09 bpm	6.99 bpm
	task 2	4	40%	6	60%	−4.01 - 2.39 bpm	6.4 bpm
	task 3	6	60%	4	40%	−3.45 - 7.06 bpm	10.51 bpm
	task 4	4	40%	6	60%	−4.26 - 2.82 bpm	7.08 bpm
6	**HRV (relaxation vs. task)**						
	relax - a1	7	70%	3	30%	−14.55 - 37.69 ms	52.24 ms
	relax - b1	6	60%	4	40%	−14.36 - 30.10 ms	44.46 ms
	relax - a2	5	50%	5	50%	−29.44 - 29.99 ms	59.43 ms
	relax - b2	8	80%	2	20%	−5.52 - 12.63 ms	18.15 ms

(*continued*)

Table 1. (*continued*)

No.	State	Subjects				Values range	
		+		-		Range	Difference
	relax - a3	6	60%	4	40%	−34.53 - 28.79 ms	63.32 ms
	relax - b3	5	50%	5	50%	−21.42 - 3.97 ms	25.40 ms
	relax - a4	8	80%	2	20%	−19.51 - 23.78 ms	43.28 ms
	relax - b4	7	70%	3	30%	−6.68 - 32.20 ms	38.99 ms
7	**HRV (task a vs. b)**						
	task 1	4	40%	6	60%	−7.59 - 2.32 ms	9.91 ms
	task 2	6	60%	4	40%	−33.58 - 35.30 ms	68.88 ms
	task 3	2	20%	8	80%	−50.21 - 33.89 ms	84.10 ms
	task 4	7	70%	3	30%	−7.52 - 31.23 ms	38.75 ms

Series 3: HRV. Checking to see whether the HRV is within the normal range represents the next step. The HRV values are computed, as was explained in the previous section, and all participants had values within the normal range throughout the experiment (27.03 - 53.45 ms) and in the relaxation state (29.87 - 64.92 ms). Since none of the subjects reported having any cardiovascular disorders, these results were anticipated. Nevertheless, it can be observed that 60% of the participants had a greater HRV in their relaxation state than in the experiment, indicating that overall, the experiment decreased their HRV by computing the difference between the HRV in the relaxation state and the mean HRV for the rest of the experiment.

Series 4: HR variations between relaxation state and each scenario. In this series, the difference between HR in the relaxation state and HR in each scenario is computed. For task 1 (visual variations), 70% of the subjects had a lower HR when watching happy pictures and 60% when watching sad pictures. For task 2 (auditive variations), 50% experienced a lower HR in both scenarios (music and noise). For task 3 (cognitive activities), 40% of the subjects had a lower HR when drawing, and 60% of the subjects had a lower HR when resolving cognitive tasks. For task 4 (memories), 90% of the subjects had a lower HR in both scenarios (happy and sad memories). From these computations, it can be seen that the memories have the greatest influence over HR compared to the normal HR of a subject, decreasing it, followed by the happy pictures that also decrease the HR. Auditive factors do not follow a specific pattern, as half of the subjects experienced an increased HR and half of them decreased HR. The greatest range of values is obtained in task 1, scenario a, and task 4, scenario a (visual variations – happy pictures, cognitive activities - drawing): 9.33 bpm, 9.12 bpm, respectively.

Series 5: HR variations between tasks a and b. In this series, the difference between the HR in different scenarios of the same task is computed. For task 1 (visual variations), 70% of the subjects have higher HR when watching sad pictures. For task 2 (auditive variations), 60% of the subjects have higher HR when listening to noises. For task 3 (cognitive activities), 60% of the subjects have higher HR when drawing. For task 4 (memories), 60% of the subjects have a higher HR when thinking of sad memories. From these computations, it can be seen that the greatest difference between two scenarios of the same task is given by the visual variation, as 70% of the subjects have higher HR when watching sad pictures. Also, negative emotions (including watching sad pictures, listening to various noises, or thinking of sad memories) increase the HR, while positive emotions decrease it. Task 3 (cognitive activities) has the widest range of values, with a difference of 10.51 bpm between the maximum and the minimum values, since it is the most subjective task.

Series 6: HRV variations between relaxation state and each scenario. In this series, the difference between the HRV in the relaxation state and HRV in each scenario is computed. For task 1 (visual variations), 70% of the subjects had a lower HRV when watching happy pictures and 60% when watching sad pictures. For task b (auditive variations), 50% experienced a lower HRV when listening to music and 80% when listening to noises. For task 3 (cognitive activities), 60% of the subjects had a lower HRV when drawing, and 50% of the subjects had a lower HRV when resolving cognitive tasks. For task 4 (memories), 80% of the subjects had a lower HRV when thinking of happy memories and 70% when thinking of sad memories. From these computations, it can be seen that the noises have the greatest influence over HRV compared to the normal HRV of a subject, decreasing it, followed by the happy images and the sad memories, which also decrease the HRV. Music and cognitive activities do not follow a specific pattern, as half of the subjects experienced an increased HRV and half of them a decreased HRV. Task 3, scenario a (cognitive activities – drawing) has the widest range of values, with a difference of 63.32 ms between the maximum and the minimum values.

Series 7: HRV variations between tasks a and b. In this series, the difference between the HRV in different scenarios of the same task is computed. For task 1 (visual variations), 60% of the subjects have a higher HRV when watching sad pictures. For task 2 (auditive variations), 60% of the subjects have a higher HRV when listening to music. For task 3 (cognitive activities), 80% of the subjects have a higher HRV when solving cognitive tasks. For task 4 (memories), 70% of the subjects have a higher HRV when thinking of happy memories. From these computations, it can be seen that the greatest difference between two scenarios of the same task is given by the cognitive activities, as 80% of the subjects have a higher HRV when solving cognitive tasks. Also, music and happy memories increase HRV. Task 3, scenario a (cognitive activities), has the widest range of values, with a difference of 84.10 ms between the maximum and the minimum values.

Given that the HR and HRV have an inverse correlation, comparing the HR and HRV results indicates that happy memories cause the HR to decrease and the HRV to increase, along with other positive emotions, while negative emotions cause the HR to increase and the HRV to decrease. Because it depends on the subject, the cognitive activities do not provide a particularly accurate discrimination between them and relaxation; yet, performing cognitive tasks increases HRV values, even though the difference in HR values is not obvious. Although there is a greater differentiation between certain tasks than others, it is obvious that no pattern can be established since each subject should examine his personal results as the impact of external factors on HR or HRV in comparison with his regular HR or HRV is very subjective.

2.3 Form

In this section, the results of the form and the correlations of it with the signal outcomes will be discussed. The questionnaire has different types of questions: Yes / No, options, free answers, etc. The results are centralized in Tables 2 and 3.

The questions about consent, diseases, and conditions prior to the protocol (Table 2) must be completed before the experiment. As can be observed, every subject gave his consent (and also signed a written one) for the signal recording, did not eat, smoke, or drink coffee before the protocol, and hydrated properly. Ten participants, five female and five male, ages ranging from 25 to 58, took part in the study. Moreover, the subjects did not report any neurological, muscular, or cardiovascular disorders.

Table 2. Questions prior to the acquisition protocol

Question	Yes			No
Consent	10	100%	0	0%
Previous coffee consumption	0	0%	10	100%
Previously eaten	0	0%	10	100%
Previously smoked	0	0%	10	100%
Previously hydrated	10	100%	0	0%
Age	25–58			
Gender	5	50%	5	50%
Cardiovascular diseases	0	0%	10	100%
Neurological diseases	0	0%	10	100%
Muscular diseases	0	0%	10	100%

In accordance with the four tasks, the rest of the form is split into four separate sections (Table 3). For the first two tasks, 90% of the participants said that they enjoyed the happy images and the music more than the sad pictures and noises. As mentioned before, the HR and HRV values show that while negative emotions have the opposite effect, good emotions lead to an increase in HRV and a decrease in HR. Regarding the cognitive activities, as the text on the PowerPoint indicated, all the drawings covered the concepts of holidays, home, and hobbies. At least nine of the twelve questions were properly answered by every participant. Because 40% of the participants preferred the drawing activity, 40% preferred the cognitive tasks, and 20% enjoyed both activities, the preferences of the subjects could be relevant.

For this reason, Table 4 summarizes the correlation between different parameters. There is a strong inverse correlation between age and mean HR, as well as HR in the relaxation state. This means that the older a subject is, the lower the HR is. There is also a high correlation between age and HRV in the relaxation state and lower with mean HRV. This means that the older a subject is, the higher the HRV is. There is no correlation between gender and HR, and a low correlation between gender and HRV. Between HR and favourite images or favourite sounds, the correlation is high but significantly lower in the case of HRV. However, the favourite task and the HR or HRV are quite lowly correlated.

Table 3. Questions regarding the four tasks

Question	Task a		Task b		Both		None	
Favourite images	9	90%	0	0%	0	0%	1	10%
Favourite sounds	9	90%	1	10%	0	0%	0	0%
Favourite activity	4	40%	4	40%	2	20%	0	0%
Drawings	mountain, beach, travel, family, animals, sports, painting							
No. of correct answers	9–12 / 12							
Happy memories	holidays							
Sad memories	death, loneliness, sadness							

Table 4. Correlations between different parameters

Correlations	
Between age and mean HR	−0.67
Between age and mean HRV	0.35
Between age and HR in the relaxation state	−0.67
Between age and HRV in the relaxation state	0.57
Between gender and mean HR	0.06
Between gender and mean HRV	−0.22
Between gender and HR in the relaxation state	0.09
Between gender and HRV in the relaxation state	0.35
Between favourite images and HR variations between tasks	0.51
Between favourite images and HRV variations between tasks	−0.27
Between favourite sounds and HR variations between tasks	0.41
Between favourite sounds and HRV variations between tasks	0.27
Between favourite activity and HR variations between tasks	0.33
Between favourite activity and HRV variations between tasks	−0.20

3 Device and GUI Development

3.1 Device Development

The results obtained with the AD8328 sensor having proven to be conclusive, the AD8232 sensor was paired with a data recording system via Matlab, since this software was used for signal processing. Moreover, using DataStreamer could potentially alter the quality of the recordings, as its sampling frequency was not perfectly suited to the sensor's data transmission rate, and due to the fact that it implies offline processing, since it cannot connect directly to Matlab for online processing. This third acquisition method was therefore intended to deepen the study while further validating the effectiveness of the AD8328 sensor previously demonstrated in offline signal processing by developing an online signal acquisition and processing system.

After several promising preliminary tests, a complete and compact solution for HR and HRV analysis was developed, based on this acquisition method. The goal was to provide the user with a direct and autonomous evaluation of these two parameters by offering a PowerPoint presentation for recording stimuli, as well as a dedicated GUI, developed with Matlab App Designer and directly linked to this new acquisition method. The hardware specifications of this solution can be found in Table 5, as well as the circuit and the connections in Fig. 6.

Table 5. List of components of the developed ECG signal recording device

Component	Connection	Role
Arduino UNO	All	Controls all components
Resistors	Buzzer, Push Button	Regulate current
LEDs + 220 Ω Resistors	PB3, PB4, PB5	Indicates recording phases
Passive Buzzer	PB1	Emits sound signals
Push Button + 1kΩ Resistor	PD4	Initiates recording cycles
ECG AD8232	PC0	Records ECG signals

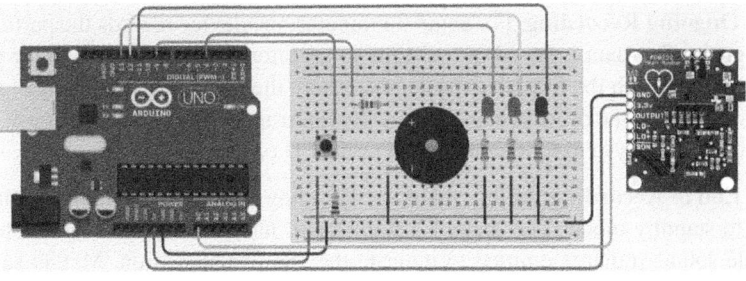

Fig. 6. Diagram (Tinkercad) of the implemented ECG signal recording device

The ECG sensor electrodes must be arranged in a triangular configuration (Einthoven's triangle) on the user, with two electrodes attached to the arms and the third on the right ankle or on the chest. The arms-and-ankle arrangement was finally chosen for this part after several successful tests, due to its practicality and showing similar results as the chest configuration [12, 13], avoiding the need for participants to undress or feel uncomfortable and enabling the recordings anywhere, anytime. Moreover, good contact between the electrodes and the skin is essential to ensure signal quality; that is why before each recording, the skin is disinfected with sanitary alcohol.

The implementation of auditory and visual alerts, such as LEDs and a buzzer, aims to guide the user throughout the recording process, as shown in Fig. 6. Additionally, the push button allows the users to switch between the different system states (Initialization, Visualization, and Recording) by following the instructions provided in the protocol displayed in the GUI. Integrating this button ensures complete user autonomy in controlling the recording, particularly by enabling navigation between the necessary windows for the recording process (Matlab application and PowerPoint presentation), allowing the user to start both the recording and the presentation simultaneously by pressing the button at the same time.

System Behaviour During a Recording Session

Step 1: Power-up and Standby Mode. The device is connected to its power source, usually through a USB cable to the computer. During this phase, the red LED is on, indicating that the system is in standby mode. No data is transmitted at this stage. The system is ready to receive instructions from the user via the push button.

Step 2: Sensor Placement and Initialization. Once the button is pressed, the yellow LED lights up. The device can send data in visualization mode to allow for sensor calibration and an initial check of the signal quality before starting the recording. Raw sensor data is continuously transmitted to the PC via the serial connection.

Step 3: Start of Recording. When the user presses the push button again, the system switches to recording mode, and the green LED lights up. The Arduino sends a specific frame to Matlab via the serial connection to indicate the beginning of data collection. From this point, the sensor data is continuously transmitted and recorded by Matlab. A sound signal·is emitted by the buzzer to confirm the start.

Step 4: Ongoing Recording. For about 36 minutes, the device records the participant's ECG signals. The data is saved in real-time in a vector. The user can monitor the live data display through the Matlab console and ensure the recording is running smoothly. If any issues arise, the process can be manually interrupted by pressing the push button, which returns the system to its initial state (red LED on).

Step 5: End of Recording. At the end of the recording period, the system automatically returns to standby mode. The green LED turns off, and the red LED lights up again. A double sound signal is emitted to indicate the end of the session. Matlab saves the collected data in a *.csv* file. The system returns to its initial state (red LED on).

Participants and Database

Since there was a high correlation between age and HR and HRV, especially HR, six participants of the same age (21-23 years, Mean = 22.17, Standard Deviation = 0.69) were chosen. However, there was no correlation between gender and HR and a lower correlation between gender and HRV, so both genders were chosen (three feminine, three masculine). There was not a high correlation between the answers from the form and the values, so the form was not included anymore in this part. As the previous participants, they also received instructions not to consume any food or coffee for two hours prior to the experiment, were requested not to smoke right before the experiment, and were advised to hydrate properly. All of them signed the written consent, agreeing to participate in this study, including the signal recording and the anonymous use of their personal information (gender and age). All the experiments were conducted in the same conditions as the previous ones. A 36-min signal was recorded from each participant, which was split according to the same protocol as the one described before.

3.2 GUI

The final step was to integrate everything into a GUI called *appECG*: the app is launched, the signals are recorded with the proposed Arduino-based device in real-time or have been recorded previously, and after the recording/uploading process, the outcomes are computed (following the same signal processing algorithm as previously described) and displayed. The entire app flow is presented in Fig. 7. As it can be seen, there are three pages containing buttons with different functions and a "Back" button available all the time. In the beginning, the first page has two buttons. If the user presses the "Start a new session" button, a new recording will start. The instructions for the hardware and software will be provided and displayed for the user. After that, he has to decide on a number for his upcoming recording. The next two buttons remain disabled until the recording is over. If the "Upload an old session" button is pressed or when the recording is over, the two other buttons appear. The user can choose any signal from the database by pressing the "Previous results" button, but if he presses the "Newest results" button, the most recent stored signal from the database is automatically uploaded. The last page is the main one, which contains several features and displays the outcomes immediately after the signal has been uploaded. In the upper left corner, a random section of the signal is plotted, alongside the mean HR of the recorded signal. Two tabs can be found in the upper right corner; in the "Relaxation vs. task" tab, the difference between the HR or HRV during the relaxation phase and the HR or HRV during a task is computed, while in the "Task a vs. task b" tab, the difference between the HR or HRV during both tasks of the same phase is computed. According to the scale below, the dot's colour represents the size of the difference. A switch button in the centre of the page enables the display of either the HR and HRV values' graphs or some essential HR and HRV information.

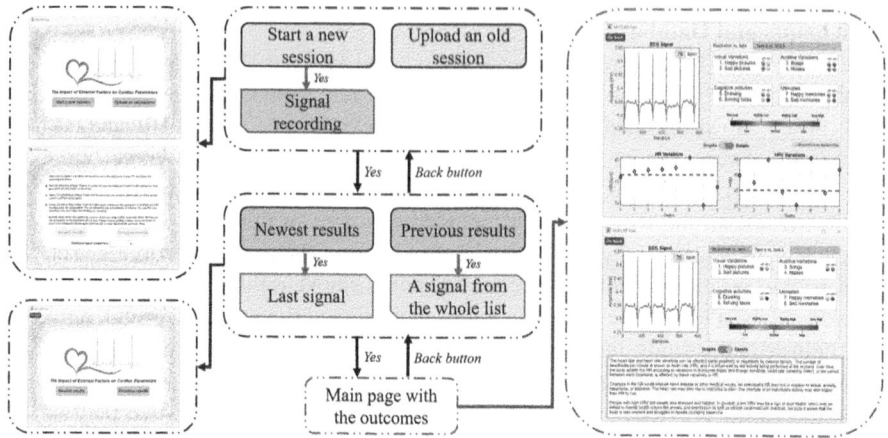

Fig. 7. Diagram of the designed GUI

3.3 Results

In this step, all the results are summarized from the *appECG*. In the same way as before, the outcomes are consolidated in a table (Table 6), and there will be separate discussions for each of the seven series of outcomes. For the first two series, + denotes a good value and - a bad value. For the rest of the five series, the notation + is for differences above 2, 0 is for the differences between -2 and 2, and – is for differences below -2. However, the results that are displayed to the subject are more specific, with a colour assigned to each interval, as presented in Fig. 8. Based on the colour, the subject can identify the problems and can also read some details that are written below. For the example presented in Fig. 7, The 1-5 tasks did not increase the HR compared to the relaxation HR. While task 6 increased the HR, tasks 7 and 8 decreased it in comparison with the HR in the relaxation state. Furthermore, there is a big change in HR when the subject is performing tasks 7-8 (the sad memories increase HR), and also the HR is higher when solving tasks than drawing. The HRV values vary more. When listening to songs or solving tasks, the HRV increases considerably, but it decreases when drawing. The most significant change appears between the 5-6 tasks.

Series 1: Mean HR. In the first series, the mean HR is checked to be within the normal range. All of the individuals' HR falls within the normal range (66-79 bpm). These results were expected because the algorithm proved to be accurate before, and no subject reported any cardiovascular disease.

Series 2: HR and HRV in the relaxation state. All of the individuals' HR and HRV fall within the normal range in the relaxation state, as can be also observed in the graphs (dotted lines).

Series 3: Overall values. In the case of variations between relaxation state and each task, the HR was the same in almost half of the cases (46%), and the other half was approximately split between lower and higher, while HRV varied in most of the cases (almost half lower (42%) and half higher (50%)). With 67% of the HR being the same

Table 6. The outcomes of the second experiment

No.	State	Subjects					
		+		0		-	
1	**Mean HR: 66–79 bpm**	6	100%			0	0%
2	**HR (relaxation)**	6	100%			0	0%
	HRV (relaxation)	6	100%			0	0%
3	**Overall HR (relaxation vs. task)**	16	33%	22	46%	10	21%
	Overall HRV (relaxation vs. task)	24	50%	4	8%	20	42%
	Overall HR (task a vs. b)	6	25%	16	67%	2	8%
	Overall HRV (task a vs. b)	10	42%	5	21%	9	38%
4	**HR (relaxation vs. task)**						
	relax - a1	3	50%	3	50%	0	0%
	relax - b1	2	33%	4	67%	0	0%
	relax - a2	2	33%	2	33%	2	33%
	relax - b2	2	33%	2	33%	2	33%
	relax - a3	1	17%	3	50%	2	33%
	relax - b3	1	17%	4	67%	1	17%
	relax - a4	2	33%	2	33%	2	33%
	relax b4	3	50%	2	33%	1	17%
5	**HR (task a vs. b)**						
	task 1	1	17%	4	67%	1	17%
	task 2	1	17%	5	83%	0	0%
	task 3	3	50%	2	33%	1	17%
	task 4	1	17%	5	83%	0	0%
6	**HRV (relaxation vs. task)**						
	relax - a1	4	67%	0	0%	2	33%
	relax - b1	3	50%	0	0%	3	50%
	relax - a2	1	17%	1	17%	4	67%
	relax - b2	2	33%	0	0%	4	67%
	relax - a3	2	33%	0	0%	4	67%
	relax - b3	4	67%	0	0%	2	33%
	relax - a4	4	67%	1	17%	1	17%
	relax - b4	4	67%	1	17%	1	17%

(continued)

Table 6. (*continued*)

No.	State	Subjects					
		+		0		-	
7	**HRV (task a vs. b)**						
	task 1	2	33%	1	17%	3	50%
	task 2	3	50%	1	17%	2	33%
	task 3	3	50%	1	17%	2	33%
	task 4	2	33%	2	33%	2	33%

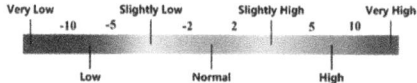

Fig. 8. Colour map and the corresponding values

and 25% being higher in task a, there was no greater HR variation between tasks a and b. However, the HRV variations were nearly evenly distributed between lower and higher, with less equal values across the two tasks (21%).

Series 4: HR variations between relaxation state and each scenario. In this series, the difference between HR in the relaxation state and HR in each scenario is computed. For task 1, no subject had a higher HR than in the relaxation state, just lower or the same, when watching happy pictures. No subject had a higher HR than in the relaxation state when watching sad pictures, but more than half had the same HR (67%). In task 2, in both cases, the values are evenly split. Task 3 shows the same HR values as in the relaxation state in half or more than half of the cases. In task 4, when thinking of sad memories, half of the subjects experienced a lower HR, but when thinking of happy memories, the values are evenly split.

Series 5: HRV variations between relaxation state and each scenario. In this series, the difference between HRV in the relaxation state and HRV in each scenario is computed. For task 1, no participant had the same HRV as in the relaxation state. More participants had a lower HRV when watching happy pictures (67%), but when watching sad pictures, the values are equally split between lower and higher values. For task 2, more than half of the participants had a higher HRV than in the relaxation state when listening to both songs and noises (67%). For task 3, more than half of the participants had a higher HRV than in the relaxation state when drawing (67%), and more than half lower when solving tasks. No participant had the same HRV as in the relaxation state. In both cases of task 4, the subjects had a lower HRV than in the relaxation state (67%).

Series 6: HR variations between tasks a and b. More than half of the subjects had the same HR values in both tasks (67%) when watching pictures, and half of them had a higher HR when drawing. Almost all of them (83%) had the same HR values in both tasks when listening to songs or noises and thinking of memories.

Series 7: HRV variations between tasks a and b. Half of the subjects had higher HRV values when watching sad pictures, listening to songs, and drawing. When thinking of memories, the values were equally split.

From these computations and from the previous results, it can still be seen that a pattern cannot be established, since the influence of external factors on HR or HRV compared to the normal HR or HRV of a person is very subjective. However, a difference between some tasks can be observed, so each subject should trace his individual variations, which is exactly the purpose of *appECG*.

4 Conclusions

In this paper, the design and development of an Arduino-based device that records ECG signals that are then analyzed in real-time is proposed, and the outcomes are displayed in the *appECG* GUI. The initial step was observing how external factors influence both HR and HRV, and in the end, it was proven that two individuals with nearly the same HRs have different HRVs, so it is important to consider both parameters. Even though some differences in HR and HRV were identified between certain tasks, it was concluded that these factors have different influences on the HR and HRV values depending on each individual, leading to the necessity of developing a user-friendly application that offers personalized outcomes for each user. At the same time, another primary purpose was to demonstrate that, given the current emphasis on low-cost, lightweight, wearable devices, an Arduino-based device could provide results that are as satisfactory as a more professional system—Biopac. The fact that both systems acquired qualitative ECG signals and accurate, adequate information to identify the R-peaks necessary for computing HR and HRV demonstrated that the experiment was not influenced by the acquisition equipment.

Both the Arduino device and GUI are very intuitive due to the features that guide the hardware part (LEDs, buzzer, button) and the instructions displayed in the GUI, colour maps and graphs. There are a few hardware resources at a relatively low cost, the connections are not complex, and the software requires little memory and runtime. The fact that everything is compatible with Matlab software is a big advantage since the whole process is straightforward and does not need to include other software.

The database dimension was one of the paper's limitations. In further research, the database should be expanded to include signals from groups of patients of different ages or other criteria that could be correlated with HR and HRV. It might also focus on particular aspects (e.g., if certain musical genres have an impact on HR and HRV). Furthermore, the development of a large database may offer better resources for ultimately identifying particular statistical patterns. Given that every subject is in good condition, this introduces another limitation. Different diseases can be investigated in the future to see how they affect HR and HRV. Evaluating additional factors such as caffeine or alcohol consumption, smoking, and physical activity offers a different perspective. The following goal is to turn the proposed method into a wearable, encapsulated, customized device that can monitor HR and HRV continuously and display the data in a mobile application, like the one presented in [14]. There will also be additional options for the device, such as fitness tracking, traffic flow estimation, and driving mode detection based on ECG signals. However, it is crucial to secure any application that stores medical information to prevent unauthorized access to that data [15, 16].

Acknowledgments. This work was supported by a grant from the National Program for Research of the National Association of Technical Universities - GNAC ARUT 2023.

References

1. Li, Z., Ba, M., Kang, J.: Physiological indicators and subjective restorativeness with audio-visual interactions in urban soundscapes. Sustain. Cities Soc. **75**, 103360 (2021). https://doi.org/10.1016/j.scs.2021.103360
2. Sammito, S., Böckelmann, I.: Factors influencing heart rate variability. International Cardiovascular Forum J. **6** (2016). https://doi.org/10.17987/icfj.v6i0.242
3. European Environment Agency. https://www.eea.europa.eu/publications/health-riskscaused-by-environmental. Accessed 7 Mar 2025
4. Dar, T., Radfar, A., Abohashem, S., Pitman, R.K., Tawakol, A., Osborne, M.T.: Psychosocial stress and cardiovascular disease. Current Treatment Options Cardio Med **21**(23), 117 (2019). https://doi.org/10.1007/s11936-019-0724-5
5. Li, W.: Wavelets for electrocardiogram: overview and taxonomy. IEEE Access **7**, 2562725649 (2018). https://doi.org/10.1109/ACCESS.2018.2877793
6. King, L.M.: What Is Heart Rate Variability? (2024). https://www.webmd.com/. Accessed 7 Mar 2025
7. Fatisson, J., Oswald, V., Lalonde, F.: Influence diagram of physiological and environmental factors affecting heart rate variability: an extended literature overview. Heart international **11**(1), heartint-5000232 (2016), https://doi.org/10.5301/heartint.5000232
8. Di Simplicio, M., Costoloni, M., Western, D., Hanson, B., Taggart, P., Harmer, C.J.: Decreased heart rate variability during emotion regulation in subjects at risk for psychopathology. Psychol. Med. **42**(8), 1775–1783 (2012). https://doi.org/10.1017/S0033291711002479
9. Mojtabavi, H., Saghazadeh, A., Valenti, V.E., Rezaei, N.: Can music influence cardiac autonomic system? a systematic review and narrative synthesis to evaluate its impact on heart rate variability. Complement. Ther. Clin. Pract. **39**, 101162 (2020). https://doi.org/10.1016/j.ctcp.2020.101162
10. LeBlanc, V.R., McConnell, M.M., Monteiro, S.D.: Predictable chaos: a review of the effects of emotions on attention, memory and decision making. Adv in Health Sci Educ **20**, 265–282 (2015). https://doi.org/10.1007/s10459-014-9516-6
11. Bechara, A., Damasio, A.R.: The somatic marker hypothesis: a neural theory of economic decision. Games Econom. Behav. **52**(2), 336–372 (2005). https://doi.org/10.1016/j.geb.2004.06.010
12. Mihailovschi, D., Zîrnă, B.A., Frunzete, M.C.: Development of a portable heart rate monitoring device. In: Costin, HN., Magjarević, R., Petroiu, G.G. (eds) Advances in Digital Health and Medical Bioengineering. EHB 2023. IFMBE Proceedings, vol 109. Springer, Cham. (2024). https://doi.org/10.1007/978-3-031-62502-2_22
13. Zîrnă, B.A., Mihailovschi, D., Şerban, A.A., Frunzete, M.C.: Design of a portable EMG and ECG signal-based system for upper limb recovery using data compression. In: 2024 Signal Processing: Algorithms, Architectures, Arrangements, and Applications (SPA), pp. 109–114. IEEE, Poznan, Poland (2024), https://doi.org/10.23919/SPA61993.2024.10715623
14. Popescu, A.L., Ionescu, R.T., Popescu, D.: Cardiowatch: a solution for monitoring the heart rate on a mobile device, university politehnica of bucharest scientific bulletin series c-electrical engineering and computer. Science **78**(3), 63–74 (2016)
15. Dinu, A., Frunzete, M.: Singularity, observability and statistical independence in the context of chaotic systems. Mathematics **11**(2), 305 (2023). https://doi.org/10.3390/math11020305
16. Dinu, A.: Singularity, observability, and independence: unveiling lorenz's cryptographic potential. Mathematics **12**(18), 2798 (2024). https://doi.org/10.3390/math12182798

Study Cases on Initial Solution and Searching for Tabu Search and Threshold Accepting Algorithms on Bin-Packing Problem

Vanesa Landero Nájera[1]([✉]), Ortega Joaquín Pérez[2], Laura Cruz Reyes[3],
Carlos Rodríguez Orta[1], and Carlos Collazos Morales[4]

[1] Universidad Politécnica de Apodaca, Nuevo León, México
vanesa.landero@upapnl.edu.mx
[2] Centro Nacional de Investigación y Desarrollo Tecnológico (CENIDET),
Departamento de Ciencias Computacionales, AP 5-164, Cuernavaca 62490, México
jperez@cenidet.edu.mx
[3] División de Estudios de Posgrado e Investigación, Instituto Tecnológico de Ciudad Madero
(ITCM), Cd. Madero, México
laura.cr@cdmadero.tecnm.mx
[4] Universidad Manuela Beltrán, Bogotá, Colombia

Abstract. The scientific community has identified four principal parts on approximation algorithm's logical structure (tuning parameter, generating initial solution, searching and generating neighbor solutions, stopping algorithm execution) and has performed improvements for solving problems such as sorting, forecasting, classification, clustering, constraint satisfaction, decision, optimization. A reviewing of state of art for algorithms Tabu Search (TS) and Threshold Accepting (TA) indicates that in most cases it has performed improvement on logical part for tuning parameter. A reflection about it shows that up to now there has not been an analysis about the other logical parts: initial solution and searching. Study cases for TS and TA over one dimension Bin Packing problem were configured for discovering knowledge of these parts on algorithm performance in terms of quality and time. The results for all configurations indicated that generate a deterministic initial solution and neighbor solutions from this using one method for searching permit to algorithms TA and TS perform better on very short time (reaching solutions with best, same quality and worst with a very minimal difference) than intensify the searching with several methods. It would be of interest if this found knowledge is like other algorithms for other problems, which could contribute to building self-adaptive algorithms that do not waste effort to give the best solution to complex problems.

1 Introduction and General Review

The scientific community of several areas of knowledge (computational complexity theory, graph theory, data mining, artificial intelligence, machine learning, combinatorial optimization, operations research) for solving problems such as decision, optimization, forecasting, classification, clustering, sorting, has identified four principal parts from the

© The Author(s), under exclusive license to Springer Nature Switzerland AG 2025
O. Gervasi et al. (Eds.): ICCSA 2025, LNCS 15648, pp. 71–87, 2025.
https://doi.org/10.1007/978-3-031-97000-9_5

logical internal structure of the solution algorithms, for developing improvements into them and giving the best solution. These logical parts are related to the methodology for: parameter tuning (PT) as temperature, size of tabu list, size of population, etc.; initial solution generating (IS); neighbor solutions searching (SM); algorithm execution stopping (SC). Table 1 presents a revision of literature consulted for Threshold Accepting (TA) and Tabu Search (TS) algorithms [1–11], which have become applied for solving some problems from some mentioned knowledge areas. No work was found that improved the logical part (SC) for these algorithms, but another work, for the k-means clustering algorithm is quoted for exemplifying this logical part [12].

Table 1. Reviewed Specialized Literature

Work	Algorithm Internal Logical Structure			
	PT	IS	SM	SC
[1]	✓			
[2]	✓			
[3]	✓		✓	
[4]			✓	
[5]	✓			
[6]	✓		✓	
[7]	✓	✓		
[8]	✓		✓	
[9]			✓	
[10]	✓			
[11]	✓		✓	
This paper		✓	✓	

As it can be observed in Table 1, the majority of the related works consulted have worked for tuning control parameters [1–3, 5–8, 10, 11]; some other also it is included work for searching in some way into the problem space, generating neighbor solutions and improving the algorithms performance [3, 4, 6, 8, 9, 11]. However, these related works develop improvements in some of these logical parts without analyzing the effects of different methodologies applied to logical parts and understand better the behavior and performance of algorithms. Only a few works perform such study in parameter tuning [2, 5]. In the case of TA algorithm for satisfiability problem (SAT) [2], the proposed geometric cooling function has the best execution time than exponential and logarithmic cooling proposed functions with a minimal difference (smaller than one percent) and similar results were in the case of best solution quality. In the case of TS algorithm for problems quadratic assignment (QAP) and maximum clique problem (MCP) [5], the TS performance is strongly dependent on the characteristics of the instances tackled for setting the best parameter configuration. It could be interpreted that the performance of both algorithms for those problems does not have a great improvement in the management of one or another proposed methodology for parameter tuning or there is a dependency on the features of problem instance in hand.

A reflection on the reviewed specialized literature shows that up to now there is no work that performs a thorough experimental analysis on the other logical parts, for example: generating of initial solution and performing a searching into the problem space. The analysis of these logical parts could allow the discovery of guidelines to direct the algorithm to not spend so much time in finding the best solution.

The algorithms have been seen as a partial black-box and therefore, it is necessary and important to open completely the box and identify logical parts relevant to the connection of the algorithm and problem during the solution process [13]. As well as identifying the algorithm domination region and delving into its performance, analyzing not only solution quality but also the execution time [14]. The above is due to scenarios existing with a minimal significant difference between solution qualities from two algorithms a_1 and a_2 in comparison but with a very big significant difference between solution times. It would be wrong to affirm that one algorithm outperforms to another only because solution quality is lightly better than another is.

Therefore, it would be interesting to analyze algorithm performance, considering these other logical parts and domination region in terms of solution quality and time, to discover relevant knowledge which could permit the designing of self-adaptive algorithms that do not waste effort to give the best solution to complex problems.

To be able to give small, but relevant steps according to all mentioned above, firstly, starting for a specific domain; in this paper, the focus and main contributions are next. In Sect. 2, a framework is proposed to perform an analysis on the algorithm logical parts in different scenarios of methodologies for: generating the initial solution; generating neighbor solutions and searching into the problem space. Therefore, scenarios and cases of study were configured on: the one-dimension Bin Packing problem, considering important repositories of problem instances [15, 16], which are known by scientific community; the Threshold Accepting and Tabu Search algorithms, which have become successful for solving hard combinatorial optimization problems [6, 7, 17]. In Sect. 3, an analysis of algorithms performance results is performed in terms of domination regions, considering solution quality and execution time for studies cases from configured scenarios. Graphical and statistical analyses were applied. In Sect. 4, a comparison and discussion of results is performed. Finally, in Sect. 5, conclusions about performed work are presented, as well as research future works.

2 Framework

2.1 Formal Nomenclature

$P = \{x_1, x_2,..., x_m\}$ a set instances of problem domain **P**, the space for analysis.
$A = \{a_1, a_2,..., a_n\}$ a set of n algorithms.
$Y =$ the performance space, it represents the mapping of each algorithm to a set of performance metrics (quality and time).

2.2 Problem (Set P) and Algorithms

The framework consists of study cases for analyzing the algorithm logical parts in different scenarios of methodologies for: generating the initial solution; generating neighbor solutions and searching into the problem space. The set P refers to the One Dimension Bin-Packing (BPP) problem and it contains 324 problem instances, which were selected randomly from repositories: Beasley's OR-Library [15], the Operational Research Library [16]. The algorithms for solving these problem instances are Tabu Search (TS) and Threshold Accepting (TA) algorithms. The size of Tabu list was fixed as 7 [18] for TS algorithm and the initial temperature was fixed 1 [19] for TA algorithm. The stop criterion happens after 4000 iterations (divergence) in both algorithms.

2.3 Algorithms Variants and Scenarios (Set A)

For specific purposes in this paper, the internal logical structure of algorithms Tabu Search algorithm and Threshold Accepting algorithm will be analyzed focusing on methodology for generating the initial solution, which can be generated randomly (R), commonly used by scientific community, or by means deterministic procedure (D), see Algorithms 1, 2.

Algorithm 1. Pseudocode for Generating a Random Initial Solution

	GenerateInitialSolution_Random
1	**Begin**
2	While objects exist to accommodate
3	Insert randomly an object into a new container
4	Do
5	Obtain a list of candidate objects that can enter to
6	container
7	If there are candidates, Then
8	Select randomly an object
9	Insert to container
10	While objects exist that can be entered into container
11	**End**

These two ways for generating the initial solution were analysing in two different scenarios. In the first scenario (see Table 2), the methodology for generating the neighborhoods, from the initial solution and after from generated solutions and so on, consisted in use one method (O). Unlike the second scenario (see Table 3), where it consisted in use several methods (M). These methods O and M were proposed in [20] and described in Algorithms 3, 4. The set A of algorithms for each study case of scenarios 1 and 2 is shown in Tables 2 and 3 respectively. More specifically, $A_1 = \{a_1, a_2\}, A_2 = \{a_3, a_4\}$ (scenario 1) and $A_1 = \{a_1, a_2\}, A_2 = \{a_3, a_4\}$ (scenario 2).

Algorithm 2. Pseudocode for Generating a Deterministic Initial Solution

	GenerateInitialSolution_Deterministic
1	**Begin**
2	While objects exist to accommodate
3	Insert randomly an object into a new container
4	Do
5	Obtain a list of candidate objects that can enter to
6	container
7	If there are candidates, Then
8	Calculate the probability distribution of candidates
9	Choice randomly a number r between (0, 1)
10	For each candidate object
11	If $r \leq$ to the object probability, Then
12	Choice the object
13	break
14	Insert selected object to container
15	While exists objects can be enter into container
16	**End**

Table 2. Scenario 1

set A	variants	Initial Solution Methodology		Neighborhood Methodology		Algorithm
		R	D	O	M	
A1	a_1	✓		✓		Threshold Accepting
	a_2		✓	✓		ThresholdAccepting
A_2	a_3	✓		✓		Tabu Search
	a_4		✓	✓		Tabu Search

Table 3. Scenario 2

set A	variants	Initial Solution Methodology		Neighborhood Methodology		Algorithm
		R	D	O	M	
A_1	a_1	✓			✓	Threshold Accepting
	a_2		✓		✓	Threshold Accepting
A_2	a_3	✓			✓	Tabu Search
	a_4		✓		✓	Tabu Search

Algorithm 3. Pseudocode for Generating a Neighbour Solution with One Method

GenerateNeighbourSolution_OneMethod
1	**Begin**
2	Choice randomly a source container and a destination container
3	Intent generates a neighbor solution with operator (1, 0)
4	If Neighbor solution could not be generated, Then
5	Exchange source and destination
6	Intent generates a neighbor solution with operator (1, 0)
7	If Neighbor solution could not be generated, Then
8	An infeasible solution is accounted
9	**End**

Algorithm 4. Pseudocode for Generating a Neighbour Solution with Several Methods

GenerateNeighbourSolution_SeveralMethods
1	**Begin**
2	Choice randomly a movement of: operator (1, 0), operator (1, 1), operator
3	(1, 2) and Operator (2, 2)
4	Choice randomly a source container and a destination container
5	For four kinds of movements
6	//It begins with a selected movement
7	Generate a neighbor solution
8	If Neighbor solution could be generated, Then
9	Break
10	If Neighbor solution could not be generated, Then
11	Exchange source and destination
12	Intent generates a neighbor solution with operator (1, 0)
13	If Neighbor solution could not be generated, Then
14	Intent generates a neighbor solution with operator (1, 2)
15	If Neighbor solution could not be generated, Then
16	An infeasible solution is accounted
17	**End**

2.4   Characterizing Algorithm Performance (Set Y) and Studies Cases

The algorithms in sets A_1 and A_2 for scenario 1 and scenario 2 were executed to solve the problem instances of set P. After execution of each problem instance $(1, 2, …, m)$, the algorithm performance is measured by performance metrics *time* and *quality*, described in expressions 1 and 2 respectively. The evaluations number of fitness function for feasible and infeasible solutions is considered for *time*. The *quality* is the ratio between the best solution found by algorithm Q_f (final number of containers) and theoretical solution Q_t (sum of object sizes divided by container capacity c), the lower the value, the better the quality.

$$time = feasibles + infeasibles \tag{1}$$

$$quality = \frac{Q_f}{Q_t} \tag{2}$$

$$Q_t = \frac{\sum_{i=1}^{k} s_i}{c} \tag{3}$$

The sets Y for scenario 1 (Y_1 and Y_2) and scenario 2 (Y_1 and Y_2) are being built, mapping these performance features to each algorithm with the specific order as Expression 4; where $n = 2$, is the total of algorithms executed for each set. The values of $quality_{11}$, $time_{11}$ meaning the performance of algorithm 1 for problem instance 1; the values of $quality_{12}$, $time_{12}$ meaning the performance of algorithm 2 for problem instance 1; the values of $quality_{m1}$, $time_{m1}$ meaning the performance of algorithm 1 for problem instance m; the values of $quality_{m2}$, $time_{m2}$ meaning the performance of algorithm 2 for problem instance m, and so on. Remembering, $m = 324$ problem instances of set P.

$$Y = \left\{ \begin{array}{c} \{\{quality_{11}, time_{11}\}, \{quality_{12}, time_{12}\}, \ldots, \{quality_{1n}, time_{1n}\}\} \\ \cdot \\ \cdot \\ \cdot \\ \{\{quality_{m1}, time_{m1}\}, \{quality_{m2}, time_{m2}\}, \ldots, \{quality_{mn}, time_{mn}\}\} \end{array} \right\} \tag{4}$$

The function $s(a_q, i)$ considers information of algorithm a_q from set Y (Y_1 and Y_2 - scenario 1, Y_1 and Y_2 - scenario 2) for one problem instance i (consider a_q as algorithm that will be object of study). Expression 5 describes the function $s(a_q, i)$. This function returns the performance scope of algorithm a_q compared to other algorithms for problem instance i. The set Sa_q contains the values of scope of algorithm a_q for all problem instances (see Expression 6). A value 1 means that algorithm a_q was the best to solve the problem instance in turn, in terms of performance metrics, $quality$ and $time$; otherwise, it has a value 0.

$$s(a_q, i) = \left\{ \begin{array}{c} 1, if\,(Y\left(quality_{iq}\right) = Y\left(quality_{i\alpha}\right) and Y\left(time_{iq}\right) > Y(time_{i\alpha})) \\ or \\ Y\left(quality_{iq}\right) > Y(quality_{i\alpha}), \forall\, \alpha \neq t; quality_{iq} \in Y; quality_{i\alpha} \in Y; \\ 0, otherwise. \end{array} \right\} \tag{5}$$

$$Saq = \{s(a_q, 1), s(a_q, 2), \ldots, s(a_q, m)\} \tag{6}$$

The function s applied to an algorithm a_q permits obtain the algorithm total scope TSa_q, by means Expression 7, so too, the domination region of algorithm, which is described by the sets C and W.

$$TSa_q = \sum_{i=1}^{m} s(a_q, i) \tag{7}$$

$C = \{C_1, C_2,...,C_n\}$ a partition of P, where $|A|=|C|$, and.

$W = \{(a_q \in A, C_q \in C) \mid s(a_q, x) = 1$ compared to $\alpha, \forall \alpha \in (A - \{a_q\}), \forall x \in C_q\}$, is a set of domination regions, ordered pairs (a_q, C_q), where each dominant algorithm $a_q \in A$ is associated with one element C_q of partition C, because this gives the best performance scope to partition C_q.

Each case of study (see Table 4) for the scenario 1 (one method for generating neighbor solutions), consists of comparing two variants of algorithms Thresholding and Tabu Search belonging to sets A_1 and A_2, which only are different by method for generating the initial solution (random, deterministic), so too, the total scope of performance of variants is calculated and also the sets of domination regions are analysed with more detail. The same procedure for cases of study of scenario 2 (several methods for generating neighbor solutions).

Table 4. Study cases

Scenario	Study case	set A	Algorithm	Variants Comparison	Algorithms Scope Total	Domination Regions (set W)
1	1	A_1	Threshold	a_1 vs. a_2	TSa_1, TSa_2	$(a_1, C_1), (a_2, C_2)$
	2	A_2	Tabu Search	a_3 vs. a_4	TSa_3, TSa_4	$(a_3, C_3), (a_4, C_4)$
2	3	A_1	Threshold	a_1 vs. a_2	TSa_1, TSa_2	$(a_1, C_1), (a_2, C_2)$
	4	A_2	Tabu Search	a_3 vs. a_4	TSa_3, TSa_4	$(a_3, C_3), (a_4, C_4)$

3   Results Analysis

3.1   Graphical and Statistical Analysis

Scenario 1. Analysing initial solution methodology on a searching with one method
Case of study 1 – Threshold Accepting (TA)

The Fig. 1 and Fig. 2 show the results of *quality* and *time*, at lower values, better *quality* and *time*, for the variants of Threshold Accepting algorithm (TA): a_1 performs the methodology of algorithm 1 for generating a random initial solution and a_2 performs the methodology of algorithm 2 for generating a deterministic initial solution. In this scenario 1, from the generated initial solution, whatever random or deterministic, the variants generate neighbour solutions with one method (see Algorithm 3) and perform the searching in this way. As it can see in the figures, there are big differences of time where variant a_2 seems to be better than a_1. So too, there are small differences of solution quality, where it is not possible to distinguish which of the two variants is better. The total scope of variants in terms of domination by means Expression 7, $TSa_1 = 147$, $TSa_2 = 177$; thereafter determining their total scope percentage $PTSa_1 = 147/324 = 45.37\%$ and $PTSa_2 = 177/324 = 54.62\%$.

Analysing the set W, specifically the regions of domination of variants a_1, (a_1, C_1) and a_2, (a_2, C_2) in more detail. In the partition C_1, a_1 wins 147 in *quality*, the *time*

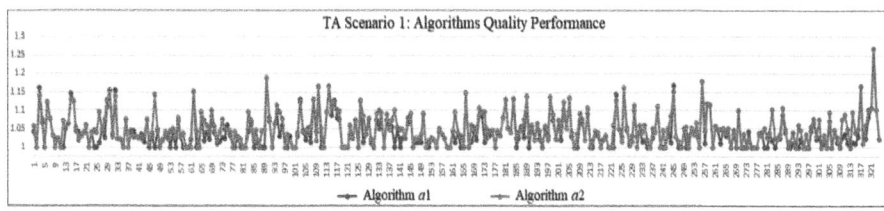

Fig. 1. Variants (algorithms a_1 and a_2) Quality Performance in Scenario 1 - Case of Study 1 for Threshold Accepting Algorithm

in these instances is bigger than algorithm a_2. The differences in *time* are too big (see Fig. 2), therefore it is not necessary to apply a statistical test. However, it is necessary to verify the values of *quality* metric (see Fig. 1), specifically when algorithm a_1 has the best *quality* C_1 (147 instances). The values of performance measures *quality* and *time* for each one of variants of all studies cases do not assume a normal distribution. Thus, a nonparametric statistical test of two independent samples is applied (the two sample two-side wilcoxon signed rank test) for significance levels 95% and 99%. The Dataplot statistical software (www.itl.nist.gov) was used for all tests.

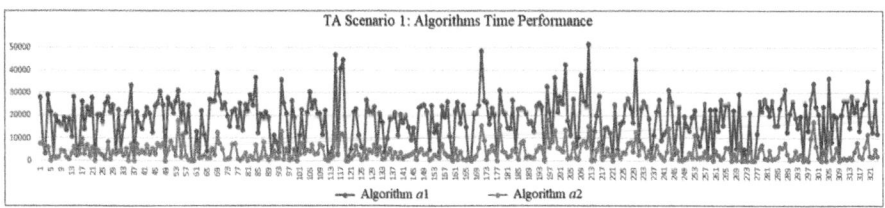

Fig. 2. Variants (algorithms a_1 and a_2) Time Performance in Scenario 1 - Case of Study 1 for Threshold Accepting Algorithm

The test statistic was -10.3383 and the critical values were 1.96, 2.5758 for significance levels 95% and 99%. The null hypothesis (**H$_0$**: equal means) is rejected and it means that there is a significant difference between qualities. The algorithm a_1 is better than a_2 in quality for these instances C_1 (147 instances); however, its time is greater than a_2.

Analyzing the partition C_2 (177 instances) of algorithm a_2, all instances have the best *time* (differences are too big), 33 instances have the best *quality* and 144 the same *quality* as algorithm a_1, but a_2 wins due its *time*.

Case of study 2 – Tabu Search Algorithm (TS).

The Fig. 3 and Fig. 4 show the results of *quality* and *time* for the variants of Tabu Search algorithm (TS): a_3 performs the methodology of algorithm 1 for generating a random initial solution and a_4 performs the methodology of algorithm 2 for generating a deterministic initial solution. In this scenario 1, from the generated initial solution, whatever random or deterministic, the variants generate neighbour solutions with one method (see Algorithm 3) and perform the searching in this way.

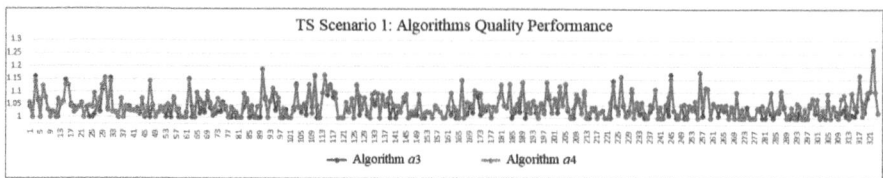

Fig. 3. Variants (algorithms a_3 and a_4) Quality Performance in Scenario 1 - Case of Study 2 for Tabu Search Algorithm

As it can see, there are big differences of time where variant a_4 seems to be better than a_3. So too, there are small differences of solution quality, where it is not possible to distinguish which of the two variants is better. The total scope of is $TSa_3 = 164$, $TSa_4 = 160$ and their total scope percentage $PTSa_3 = 164/324 = 50.62\%$, $PTSa_4 = 160/324 = 49.38\%$.

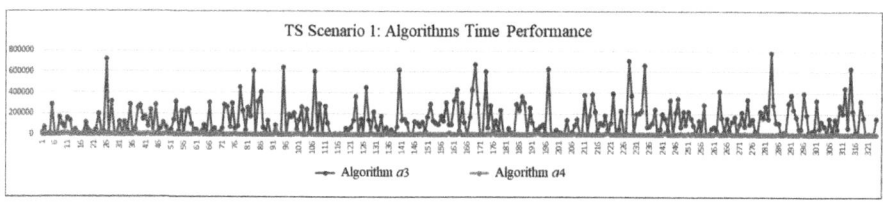

Fig. 4. Variants (algorithms a_3 and a_4) Time Performance in Scenario 1 - Case of Study 2 for Tabu Search Algorithm

Analysing the set W, the regions of domination of variants a_3, (a_3, C_3) and a_4, (a_4, C_4) in more detail, a_3 wins 164 in *quality*, partition C_3 (164 instances), the *time* in these instances is bigger than algorithm a_4. The differences in *time* are too big (Fig. 4), therefore it is not necessary to apply a statistical test for a second analysis. However, it is necessary to verify the values of *quality* metric (Fig. 3), specifically when algorithm a_3 has the best *quality* C_3 (164 instances). The test statistic was -11.1079 and the critical values were 1.96, 2.5758 for significance levels 95% and 99%. The null hypothesis (**H**$_0$: equal means) is rejected and it means that there is a significant difference between qualities. Analysing the partition C_4 (160 instances) of algorithm a_4, all instances have the best *time* (differences too big), 67 instances have the best *quality* and 93 the same *quality* as algorithm a_3, but a_4 wins due its *time*.

3.2   Graphical and Statistical Analysis

Scenario 2. Analysing the initial solution methodology on a searching with several methods

Case of study 3 – Threshold Accepting Algorithm (TA)

The Fig. 5 and 6 show the results of *quality* and *time* for the variants of Threshold Accepting algorithm (TA): a_1 performs the methodology of algorithm 1 for generating a random initial solution and a_2 performs the methodology of algorithm 2 for generating a deterministic initial solution. In this scenario 2, from the generated initial solution, whatever random or deterministic, the variants generate neighbour solutions with several methods (see Algorithm 4) and perform the searching in this way. As it can see, it is not possible to distinguish which of the two variants is better. The total scope of variants is $TSa_1 = 65$, $TSa_2 = 259$, and their total scope percentage $PTSa_1 = 65/324 = 20.06\%$, $PTSa_2 = 259/324 = 79.94\%$. Analysing the set W, the regions of domination of variants a_1, (a_1, C_1) and a_2, (a_2, C_2) in more detail. In the partition C_1 (65 instances), a_1 wins 65 in *quality*. The test statistic was -6.68 and the critical values were 1.96, 2.5758 for significance levels 95% and 99%. The null hypothesis ($\mathbf{H_0}$: equal means) is rejected and it means that there is a significant difference between qualities. The algorithm a_1 is better than a_2 in *quality* for those instances C_1 (65); however, its time is greater than a_2.

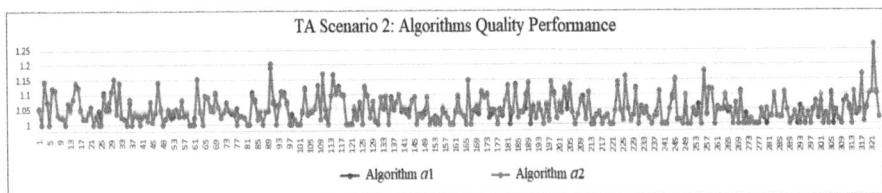

Fig. 5. Variants (algorithms a_1 and a_2) Quality Performance in Scenario 2 - Case of Study 3 for Threshold Accepting Algorithm

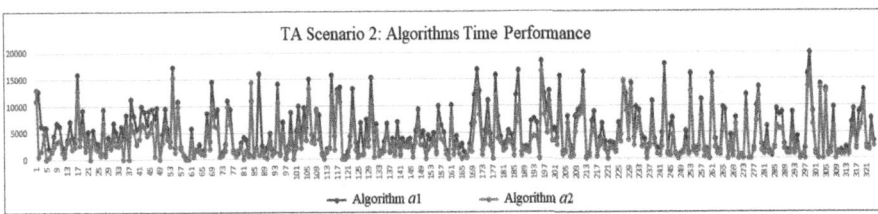

Fig. 6. Variants (algorithms a_1 and a_2) Time Performance in Scenario 2 - Case of Study 3 for Threshold Accepting Algorithm

Analysing the partition C_2 (259 instances) of algorithm a_2, all instances have the best *time*, 48 instances have the best *quality* and 211 the same *quality* as algorithm a_1, where a_2 wins due its *time*. However, it is necessary to verify these values of *time* metric. The test statistic was 11.9530 and the critical values were 1.96, 2.5758 for significance levels 95% and 99%. The null hypothesis ($\mathbf{H_0}$: equal means) is rejected and it means that there is a significant difference between times.

Case of study 4 – Tabu Search Algorithm (TS)

The Fig. 7 and Fig. 8 show the results of *quality* and *time* for the variants of Tabu Search algorithm (TS): a_3 performs the methodology of algorithm 1 for generating a random initial solution and a_4 performs the methodology of algorithm 2 for generating a deterministic initial solution. In this scenario 2, from the generated initial solution, whatever random or deterministic, the variants generate neighbour solutions with several methods (see Algorithm 4) and perform the searching in this way. As it can see, it is not possible to distinguish which of the two variants is better.

The total scope of variants is $TSa_3 = 132$, $TSa_4 = 192$ and their total scope percentage $PTSa_3 = 132/324 = 40.74\%$, $PTSa_4 = 192/324 = 59.26\%$. Analyzing the set **W**, the regions of domination of variants a_3, (a_3, C_3) and a_4, (a_4, C_4) in more detail. In the partition C_3 (132 instances) of algorithm a_3, indicates a_3 wins 38 instances in *quality*; where the time for these instances is bigger that algorithm a_4. So too, the algorithm a_3 wins 94 instances in *time* when the *quality* is the same. In the case of *quality* (38), the test statistic was -5.3734 and the critical values were 1.96, 2.5758 for significance levels 95% and 99%. The null hypothesis (**H₀**: equal means) is rejected and it means that there is a significant difference between qualities. In the case of *time* (94), when the quality is the same, the test statistic was -8.4146 and the critical values were 1.96, 2.5758 for significance levels 95% and 99%. The null hypothesis (**H₀**: equal means) is rejected and it means that there is a significant difference between times.

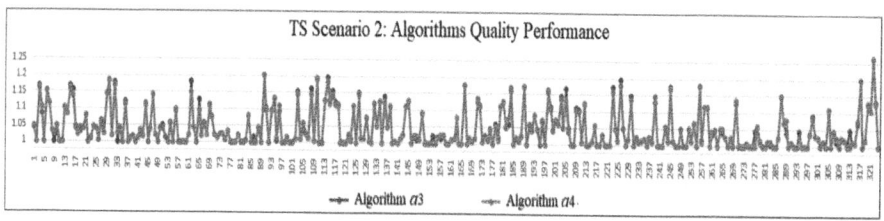

Fig. 7. Variants (algorithms a_3 and a_4) Quality Performance in Scenario 2 - Case of Study 4 for Tabu Search Algorithm

In the same context, but now, analyzing the region of domination of algorithm a_4 with more detail, (a_4, C_4), C_4 (192 instances), the algorithm a_4 wins in *time* 146 when the *quality* is the same and it wins 46 instances in *quality*, where in 20 instances has better *time* than a_3 and 26 instances has worse *time* than a_3. However, it is necessary to verify the values of *time* metric for these 146 instances. The test statistic was 10.482 and the critical values were 1.96, 2.5758 for significance levels 95% and 99%. The null hypothesis (**H₀**: equal means) is rejected and it means that there is a significant difference between times.

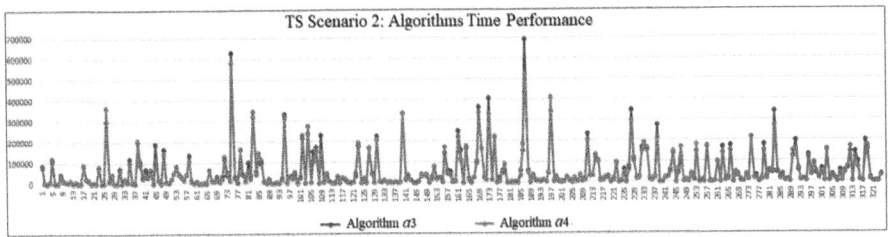

Fig. 8. Variants (algorithms a_3 and a_4) Time Performance in Scenario 2 - Case of Study 4 for Tabu Search Algorithm

4 Comparison and Discussion of Results

Table 5 shows case studies of scenarios 1 and 2: the domination region of algorithms in terms of performance total scope for the *Quality* and *Time* metrics; all values of test statistic and critical values from Wilcoxon statistical tests applied to differences between values *quality* and *time* from algorithm variants. The results of statistical test indicated that there is a significant difference between solutions qualities and times, the null hypothesis **H$_0$** is rejected in all studies cases from two scenarios.

Table 5. Domination Regions, Statistical Results and Observations

| | | | Domination Region (set W) | | Statistical Results* | | | Observations | | |
		variants	Quality	Time	Test Statistical *	Critical Value	Null Hypothesis **H$_0$** (means equal)	Same Quality		Worst Time
1	1 (TA)	a_1(147)	147*		-10.3383	1.96/2.58	Rejected			147$^+$
		a_2(177)		144$^+$				144		
			33*	33$^+$	5.0121	1.96/2.58	Rejected			
	2 (TS)	a_3(164)	164*		-11.1079	1.96/2.58	Rejected			164$^+$
		a_4(160)		93$^+$				93		
			67*	67$^+$	7.1151	1.96/2.58	Rejected			
2	3 (TA)	a_1(65)	65*		-6.68/6.8519	1.96/2.58	Rejected			65*
		a_2(259)		211*	11.9530	1.96/2.58	Rejected	211		
			48*	48*	6.03/5.24	1.96/2.58	Rejected			
	4 (TS)	a_3(132)		94*	-8.4146	1.96/2.58	Rejected	94		
			38*		-5.373/4.97	1.96/2.58	Rejected			38*
		a_4(146)	46*	20	5.9053	1.96/2.58	Rejected			26
			146*		10.482	1.96/2.58	Rejected	146		

+ The differences are too big (shown in Figs. 2, 4). There had not necessity to apply statistical test

The results are similar for the study cases 1 (Threshold Accepting algorithm - TA) and 2 (Tabu Search algorithm - TS) from scenario 1. Remembering, this scenario consists of generating an initial solution random (algorithm 1) or deterministic (algorithm 2) and from this generating neighbour solutions with one method (algorithm 3) and performs the searching in this way. Therefore, the results indicate that the domination region of variants of algorithms TA and TS that perform the methodology of algorithm 1 for generating a random initial solution (variants a_1 and a_3) have a great cost in *time*, their time is too big, for winning in *quality* to variants of algorithms TA and TS that perform the methodology of algorithm 2 for generating a deterministic initial solution (variants a_2 and a_4). It is to say, these variants (deterministic initial solution) finish faster than those variants a_1, a_3 (random initial solution), where their cost in *quality* (variants a_2 and a_4) is a mean difference 0.021 from 147 problem instances and 0.033 from 164 problem instances, respectively, which are too small. So too, the domination region of these variants (variants a_2 and a_4) always wins in *time* (time is too small) with the best or same *quality*.

The Fig. 9 shows scatter plots for study cases of scenarios 1 (Above) and 2 (Below). As it can see for scenario 1 (Above), the scatter plots help to reinforce what was mentioned before. It is to say, variants a_2 and a_4 (deterministic initial solution) in the scenario 1 seem to be a better alternative than variants a_1 and a_3 (random initial solution) when you are looking for the best *time* (time is too small) and can be reached in some cases with best *quality* or same *quality* or worst *quality* with a minimal difference.

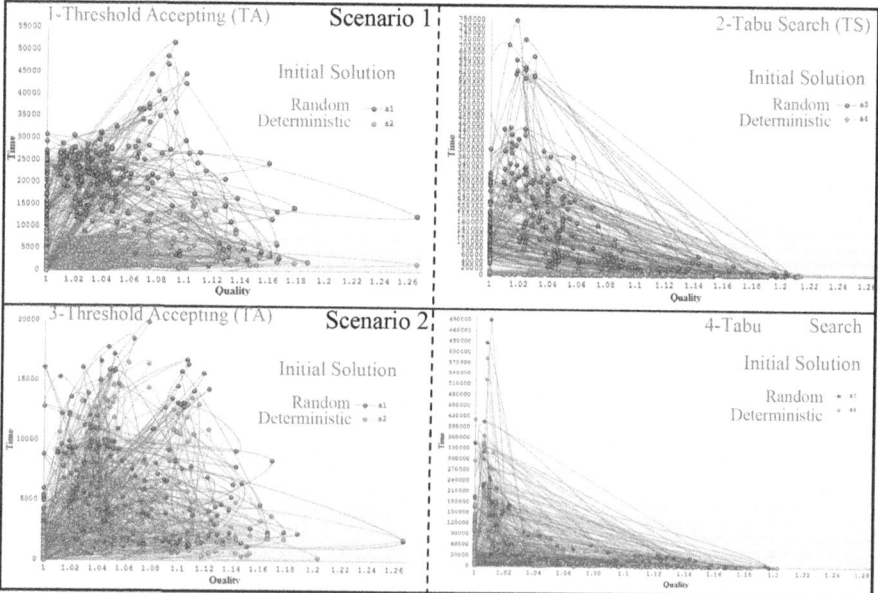

Fig. 9. Scatter plots for study cases 1,3 (TA) and 2,4 (TS) of scenarios 1-Searching with one method (Above) and 2-Searching with several methods (Below)

On the other hand, in the scenario 2, remembering that it consists of generating an initial solution random (algorithm 1) or deterministic (algorithm 2) and from this generating neighbour solutions with several methods (algorithm 4) and performs the searching in this way. The results in Table 5 of study case 3 indicate that variant a_2 (deterministic initial solution) of Threshold Accepting algorithm (TA) seem to be the better in time than variant a_1 (random initial solution) in all problem instances when it has better, same quality and worst quality with a very minimal difference 0.015 from 59 problem instances. So too, as it can see for this study case 3, the scatter plot (below left) of scenario 2 (Below) in Fig. 9 help to reinforce this result, which is some very similar for TA algorithm in scenario 1, with the difference of that it (scenario 1) has less source code in the program. Otherwise in the study case 4, the results in Table 5 indicate that variants a_3 (random initial solution) and a_4 (deterministic initial solution) of Tabu Search algorithm (TS) have a good time with better, same quality and worst quality. The scatter plot (below right) of Fig. 9 help to reinforce this, where there is no difference in *quality* and *time* between them.

5 Conclusions

There are four principal parts on logical internal structure of approximation algorithms: tuning parameter, generating initial solution, searching and generating neighbour solutions, stopping algorithm execution. The scientific community has performed improvements in some of these logical parts for solving problems as sorting, forecasting, classification, clustering, constraint satisfaction, decision, optimization. A reviewing of state of art indicates that in most cases it has performed improvement on logical part for tuning parameter. A reflection about it shows that up to now the algorithms have been seen as a partial black-box and it is necessary and important to open completely the box, analyse other logical parts relevant to the connection of the algorithm and problem during the solution process.

A framework is proposed to perform an analysis on the algorithm logical parts in different scenarios of methodologies for: generating the initial solution; generating neighbour solutions and searching into the problem space. Scenarios and cases of study were configured on: the one-dimension Bin Packing problem, considering important repositories of problem instances, which are known by scientific community; the Threshold Accepting and Tabu Search algorithms, which have become successful for solving hard combinatorial optimization problems. Graphical and statistical analysis were performed in terms of domination regions, considering solution quality and execution time. In general terms, the results indicated that an initial solution generated by deterministic methodology, either for Threshold Accepting algorithm or Tabu Search algorithm, is adjust better when from this, neighbour solutions are generated using one method for searching into the problem space. It is to say, a good initial seed could direct to a searching without intensify it (less source code in the program) and finish in much less time with solutions of better or same quality and in situations of worst quality but with a minimal difference, where the time is more important in a real situation than this minimal difference. As future work, continuing opening the black box of algorithms logical internal structure, it would be interesting to perform an analysis on initial solution methodology in conjunction with the searching methodology for other problems and approximation algorithms. The results could give formal guidelines in the development of self-adapting algorithms that do not waste effort to give the best solution to complex problems, depending on specific needs in various real-life situations.

References

1. Tarantilis, C.D., Kiranoudis, C.T., Vassiliadis, V.S.: A threshold accepting metaheuristic for the heterogeneous fixed fleet vehicle routing problem. Eur. J. Oper. Res. **152**(1), 148–158 (2004)
2. Martinez-Rios, F., Frausto-Solis, J.: An hybrid simulated annealing threshold accepting algorithm for satisfiability problems using dynamically cooling schemes. Electrical and Computer Engineering Series WSEAS, pp. 282–286 (2007)
3. Abdelaziz, A.Y., Mohamed, F.M., Mekhamer, S.F., Badr, M.A.L.: Distribution system reconfiguration using a modified Tabu Search algorithm. Electric Power Systems Res. **80**(8), 943–953 (2010)
4. Gnewuch, M., Wahlström, M., Winzen, C.: A new randomized algorithm to approximate the star discrepancy based on threshold accepting. SIAM J. Numer. Anal. **50**(2), 781–807 (2012)
5. Pellegrini, P., Mascia, F., Stützle, T., Birattari, M.: On the sensitivity of reactive tabu search to its meta-parameters. Soft. Comput. **18**, 2177–2190 (2014)
6. Adamczewski, K., Suh, Y., Mu Lee, K.: Discrete tabu search for graph matching. In Proceedings of the IEEE International Conference on Computer Vision, pp. 109–117 (2015)
7. Abyazi-Sani, R., Ghanbari, R.: An efficient tabu search for solving the uncapacitated single allocation hub location problem. Comput. Ind. Eng. **93**, 99–109 (2016)
8. Ansótegui, C., Heymann, B., Pon, J., Sellmann, M., Tierney, K.: Hyper-reactive tabu search for MaxSAT. In Learning and Intelligent Optimization: 12th International Conference, LION 12, Kalamata, Greece, June 10–15, 2018, Revised Selected Papers 12, pp. 309–325, Springer International Publishing (2019)
9. Leite, N., Melício, F., Rosa, A.C.: A fast threshold acceptance algorithm for the examination timetabling problem. Handbook of Operations Research and Management Science in Higher Education, pp. 323–363 (2021)
10. Awad, F.H., Al-Kubaisi, A., Mahmood, M.: Large-scale timetabling problems with adaptive tabu search. J. Intell. Syst. **31**(1), 168–176 (2022)
11. Wu, L., Lin, K., Lin, X., Lin, J.: List-based threshold accepting algorithm with improved neighbor operator for 0–1 knapsack problem. Algorithms **17**(11), 478 (2024)
12. Pérez, O.J., Pazos, R.R., Cruz, R.L., Reyes, S.G., Basave, T.R., Fraire, H.H.: Improving the efficiency and efficacy of the k-means clustering algorithm through a new convergence condition. In: Computational Science and Its Applications–ICCSA 2007: International Conference, Kuala Lumpur, Malaysia, August 26–29. Proceedings. Part III 7, pp. 674–682, Springer Berlin Heidelberg (2007)
13. Barr, R., Golden, B., Kelly, J., Resende, M., Stewart, W.: Designing and reporting on computational experiments with heuristic methods. Journal of Heuristics **1**(1), 9–32 (1995)
14. Weise, T., Wu, Y., Chiong, R., Tang, K., Lässig, J.: Global versus local search: the impact of population sizes on evolutionary algorithm performance. J. Global Optim. **66**, 511–534 (2016)
15. Beasley, J.E.: OR-Library. Brunel University (2006). http://people.brunel.ac.uk/~mastjjb/jeb/orlib/binpackinfo.html
16. Scholl, A., Klein, R.: http://www.wiwi.uni-jena.de/Entscheidung/binpp/ (2003)

17. Lin, C.K.Y., Haley, K.B., Sparks, C.: A comparative study of both standard and adaptive versions of threshold accepting and simulated annealing algorithms in three scheduling problems. Eur. J. Oper. Res. **83**, 330–346 (1995)
18. Glover, F.: Tabu search - part i, first comprehensive description of tabu search. ORSA-Journal on Computing **1**(3), 190–206 (1989)
19. Dueck, G., Scheuer, T.: Threshold accepting: a general purpose optimization algorithm appearing superior to simulated annealing. J. Computational Physics, pp.161–175 (1990)
20. Fleszar, K., Hindi, K.S.: New heuristics for one-dimensional bin packing. In: Computers and Operations Research, Elsevier Science Ltd, **29**, 821–839 (2002)

An Online Human-AI Collaborative Tool for Steering a Genetic Algorithm to Address the Maximum Clique Problem

Brynner Barbosa de Brito⬤, Thiago Sylas Antunes da Costa⬤,
Kevin Washington Azevedo da Cruz⬤, Natã Ferreira Lobato⬤,
Nelson Cruz Sampaio Neto⬤, and Carlos Gustavo Resque dos Santos$^{(\boxtimes)}$⬤

Universidade Federal do Pará, Belém, Brazil
carlosresque@ufpa.br

Abstract. This paper presents an online Human-AI collaborative tool designed to steer a genetic algorithm in solving the Maximum Clique Problem (MCP). By employing human-in-the-loop principles, the system enables users to dynamically adjust algorithmic parameters in real-time. We developed an interactive tool to investigate possible directions for these challenges, enabling an intense collaboration between human experts and artificial intelligence in addressing an NP-Hard problem. We assess the tool by conducting tests with DIMACS benchmark datasets to validate the effectiveness of the approach and gain insights about this form of Human-AI interaction. Additionally, a heuristic evaluation was carried out with domain experts, who interacted with the system to assess usability. Heuristic evaluation confirmed that the tool meets basic requirements, with 17.29% of observations highlighting areas for improvement, particularly in tool functionality and visualization enhancements. The experimental results indicate that the collaborative tool achieves competitive performance while enhancing user engagement and control over the optimization process. Additionally, the results showed interaction preferences, strengths, and weaknesses.

Keywords: Human-in-the-Loop · Genetic Algorithm · Maximum Clique Problem · Human-AI Collaboration

1 Introduction

The integration of human expertise and artificial intelligence (AI) systems has gained prominence to enhance optimization processes [26]. In particular, the human-in-the-loop (HITL) paradigm has emerged in machine learning and optimization tasks, allowing users to interact with algorithms to refine solutions, improve interpretability, and guide the decision-making process. By incorporating human intuition, experience, and contextual knowledge, AI systems become more adaptable, flexible, and transparent, mitigating the "black box" [1].

O. Gervasi et al. (Eds.): ICCSA 2025, LNCS 15648, pp. 88–105, 2025.
https://doi.org/10.1007/978-3-031-97000-9_6

In the field of combinatorial optimization, the Maximum Clique Problem (MCP) stands out as a challenge with applications in bioinformatics, social network analysis, artificial intelligence, and cryptography. In a graph G (V, E), with vertices set V and edges set E connecting pairs of vertices, a complete subgraph of G is one whose vertices are mutually adjacent. A clique is a maximal complete subgraph [3]. The MCP aims to determine a largest clique in a graph G. It is one of the NP-complete problems.

Optimization approaches often struggle due to the inherent complexity of the MCP and experts must settle for near-optimal solutions. In such scenarios, it is not just about the final solution but also about how an expert can interact with the optimization process, dynamically adjusting parameters, exploring alternative solutions, and refining constraints based on domain knowledge [29].

One of the greatest advantages of Human-AI collaboration is the ability of users to dynamically adjust parameters while the algorithm is running. This approach contrasts with conventional methods, where the parameters are predefined based on prior knowledge or determined through extensive and time-consuming parameter sweeps [2].

Dynamic parameter tuning, guided by human intuition, enables real-time adaptation of algorithms, making the search process more transparent. This approach allows users to adjust critical variables as they observe the results, optimizing the exploration of the solution space and improving the overall performance of the system [13].

In this study, we propose a tool to integrate human interaction into solving the MCP based on genetic algorithms. Our approach emphasizes user engagement throughout the evolutionary process, enabling dynamic parameter adjustments and real-time feedback and visualizations.

This paper is structured as follows: Sect. 2 provides an overview of related works. Section 3 presents the developed tool. Section 4 presents experimental results from pilot tests. Section 5 presents a heuristic evaluation conducted by experts in the field, and finally, Sect. 6 discusses future research directions and concludes with reflections on the broader implications of interactive optimization paradigms.

2   Related Works

Llorà et al. [20] introduced Active Interactive Genetic Algorithms (aiGA), where users rank solutions without altering selection or mutation. The tool tracks user interactions, updates preference models, and presents new solutions. Hettenhausen et al. [16] employed an interactive heatmap to guide particle swarm movement and applied a novel technique in using multiple visualizations, including parallel coordinates and scatter plots, with user interaction through the selection of value ranges to guide the algorithm.

Lutton and Fekete [21] evaluated visual analytics tools like ScatterDice and GeneaQuilts for complex Evolution Algorithm (EA) data sets. Farooq et al. [14] introduced Visualization of Genetic Algorithm on 2-D (VIGA-2D) Graph, which requires occasional human intervention to propose new solutions. Boukhelifa et al. [4] evaluated and analyzed a framework for Evolutionary Visual Exploration (EVE) created by them named EvoGraphDice, an interactive system interface that reflects the evolutionary process and user input in real time via a scatterplot matrix.

Cruz et al. [9] introduced tools for focusing generations and tracking lineages with options to select individuals, and manipulate visual details like fitness, genetic operators, and offspring information through tree and parallel coordinates, while Walker [33] used treemaps and 2D charts to visualize multi-objective data. Radhika and Velayutham [28] explored visual analysis of Differential Evolution (DE) search, using scatter plots and difference vectors to detect premature convergence and stagnation across six DE variants.

Vallerio et al. [32] presented a multi-objective framework where users select weights for Pareto front optimization, visualizing relationships with parallel coordinates. McPhee et al. [22] analyzed ancestry in evolutionary computation runs through visualizations of parent-child relationships. Medvet and Tušar [23] proposed a heatmap summarizing genotype diversity and gene contributions across different EAs.

Daneshpajouh and Zakaria [10] introduced a clustering-based visualization tool for Genetic Algorithm (GA) search refinement interactively in a 3D environment, while Mexicano-Santoyo et al. [25] provided a Differential Evolution (DE) analysis tool with interactive views through 2D and 3D graphics where users can manipulate data views by adjusting generations, individuals, and algorithm parameters like mutation factor and crossing probability. Sathyajit and Velayutham [30] investigated the visual analysis of Genetic Algorithms (GAs) applied to the simple 0–1 Knapsack problem[1] using heat maps.

Dolson and Ofria [12] developed a Virtual Reality (VR) framework to explore evolutionary history through 3D fitness landscapes and population lineages. Meiguins et al. [24] presented tools for exploring evolutionary processes in Auto-Clustering, providing various visualizations like scatterplots, heatmaps, and parallel coordinates. Chae et al. [7] explored the evolutionary process of neural networks through lineage views and fitness hyperparameter adjustments.

Vidaurre et al. [8] developed a system for visualizing and tuning genetic algorithms to generate software unit tests. Ivanov et al. [18] allowed to guide the algorithm by manipulating tiles, which represent evolving genomes on a hexagonal grid. Walter et al. [34] introduced a tool for visualizing algorithm search on discrete dual- and multi-objective knapsack problems, and Hakanen et al. [15] employed coordinated multiple views for optimization through user preferences via parallel coordinates and other views.

Although there are various tools and methods of interacting with optimization algorithms, in general, these tools do not allow online interaction, or do not provide visualizations that update at runtime, or are alternatives for very

---

[1] The 0/1 Knapsack Problem aims to maximize total value by selecting items within a weight and value limit without exceeding the knapsack's capacity, where each item can be either included (1) or excluded (0).

specific applications. The tool proposed in this article is innovative by applying these characteristics to a problem that can be used in a series of applications and can be adapted to other similar classical problems without much effort.

3   Proposed Tool

The proposed tool was developed primarily to support human-in-the-loop interactions. It was built using JavaScript to enable the creation of visualizations and interactive interfaces that update at runtime. The user also has control over the execution time by adjusting hyperparameters that make the execution slower or faster. Table 1 describes the hyperparameters that the user can adjust at runtime.

Table 1. GA hyperparameters that can be adjusted by the user during execution.

Variable Name	Description
$populationSize$	Size of the population
$survivalRate$	Rate of individuals that survive from the current to the next generation
$mutSelectionRate$	Mutation rate applied to selected individuals
$mutationRate$	Probability that a new individual undergoes mutation
$partialReset$	Performs a reset on $1 - survivalRate$ to the next generation
$1sProb$	Probability of generating a 1 in the bitstring of a randomly generated individual
$hasMaxAge$	When set to $true$, resets the fitness of individuals that survived more than $maxAge$ generations
$maxAge$	Maximum number of generations an individual can survive when $hasMaxAge = true$
$hasImprovement$	When set to $true$, performs local improvement on new individuals
$preventEqual$	Prevents the creation of duplicate individuals already present in the population
$calcUpperBound$	Computes a simple heuristic to estimate the chromatic number

This section is divided into two parts. The first explains the implementation details of the Genetic Algorithm. The second part explains the interfaces and visualizations that the user has to analyze and manipulate the GA.

3.1   GA Implementation

The Genetic Algorithm (GA) was selected due to its ease of understanding and widespread adoption, which reduces the tool's learning curve and enhances user familiarity. GA was also considered suitable for an initial implementation because of its large number of hyperparameters, providing users with extensive flexibility for algorithm tuning.

The algorithm design was inspired by the implementation of Huang [17] due to its simplicity and reasonable efficiency. Certain aspects were modified to prioritize speed over efficiency, as user interactions are required to occur in real time.

Each individual is represented by a binary mask, where each bit indicates the presence (1) or absence (0) of the vertices in a graph G, thus defining a subgraph. Since the binary mask can represent any subgraph, it is necessary to verify whether it forms a clique by checking if all selected vertices are pairwise connected. If the subgraph is a valid clique, its size is determined by counting the number of 1 s in the mask. Each new individual is generated in three steps. Initially, a zero-filled array is created; then, 1 s are randomly inserted with $1sProb$ probability; if $hasImprovement = true$ the extraction and improvement operations are applied (these operations are described next). This procedure is used both for initializing the population and during the partial reset operation [31], which can be triggered by the user.

The fitness[2] is calculated by summing the number of 1 s in the binary mask. If $hasImprovement = false$, individuals may represent a subgraph that is not a valid clique. In this case, the fitness is the negative number of missing edges required to obtain a valid clique. In the crossover[3], two parents are randomly selected from the population, and a single-point crossover is applied at a randomly chosen position. If $hasImprovement = true$, the extraction and improvement operations are applied.

The mutation[4] is applied only into offspring generated via crossover, with a probability $mutSelectionRate$. The operation consists of performing a bit swap on each bit of the binary mask with a probability defined by the $mutationRate$ parameter. In other words, the $mutSelectionRate$ controls how many offspring undergo mutation, and the $mutationRate$ controls the amount of bit swaps in a mutation.

The $survivalRate$ variable controls the percentage of the current population that is retained. Only the top-performing individuals from the previous population are preserved. The remaining individuals who will form the new population are generated through crossover followed by mutation. The extraction operation randomly removes vertices from the clique until it represents a valid clique. The improvement operation randomly adds vertices until the subgraph becomes a maximal clique. Together, these two operations ensure that the resulting individual represents a valid (after extraction) and maximal (after improvement) clique.

---

[2] In genetic algorithms, *fitness* quantifies how well a candidate solution satisfies the problem's objective.

[3] In genetic algorithms, *crossover* combines parts of two parent solutions to generate new offspring, promoting genetic diversity.

[4] In genetic algorithms, *mutation* introduces random alterations to a solution to maintain diversity and explore new regions of the search space.

The partial reset eliminates $1 - survivalRate$ individuals in the new population and replaces them by randomly generated individuals, following the same procedure used for initializing the original population.

Each individual has an age counter that is incremented every generation it survives. If $hasMaxAge = true$ and the individual has $age > maxAge$, its fitness becomes 0. This parameter allows the user to control when the population elite should be refreshed.

3.2   Interfaces and Visualizations

Figure 1 shows a screenshot of the interfaces available for user interaction with the GA. These interfaces are web pages that can be freely arranged by the user, with each operating independently. This allows users to customize their own dashboard layout.

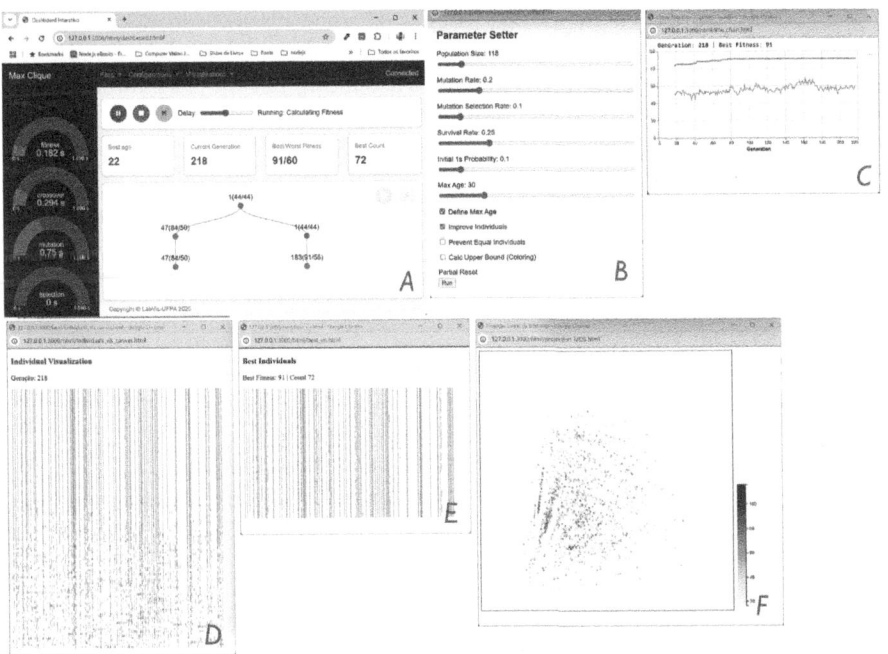

Fig. 1. Screenshot of the tool displaying all currently available interfaces.

The main dashboard provides a real-time overview of the algorithm's execution, displaying key metrics and interactive controls. In the menu bar, the user can upload and manage datasets and saves. The execution bar (below the menu bar) shows the current execution status, allowing the user to pause, restart, stop, process the next generation, and adjust the runtime speed. Performance gauges (on the left side) monitor the execution time of each core operation in the algorithm, enabling performance analysis throughout the evolutionary process.

The informational cards (bellow execution bar) summarize the algorithm's execution. It shows the current generation; the best and worst fitness of the current population; the best count card shows the number of different solutions encountered with the same best fitness; and the best age card provides the age of the best individual in the current population. During the GA execution, the user can save the current GA state (all hyperparameters and population) to be able to recover to this saved point. The dendrogram visualization documents the saves' history, where each node represents a specific state, similar to a breadcrumb idea. Users can click on any node to restore that specific execution state and run the algorithm from this point with distinct parameters.

The parameter configuration interface allows users to dynamically adjust key genetic algorithm hyperparameters, directly influencing its convergence and performance. The interface includes controls for tuning *populationSize*, *mult-SelectionRate*, *mutationRate*, *survivalRate*, *1sProb*, and the *maxAge* of individuals, as shown in Table 1. Below these controls, additional options allow toggling specific settings *maxAge*, *hasImprovement*, *preventEqual*, and *calcUpperBound*. A *partialReset* button triggers the partial reset into the next generation. All changes are applied immediately without interrupting the algorithm's execution, allowing for continuous and dynamic tuning throughout the evolutionary process.

The line chart visualization tracks the evolution of *fitness* across generations, enabling real-time monitoring of the genetic algorithm's performance. At the top, key information is displayed, including the current generation, the best fitness found, and the best upper bound found.

The individual visualization provides a grid visual representation of individuals in the population, where each line shows the individual binary mask (1 in black) and each column represents a vertice of the graph. The density and pattern of these markers indicate the population's diversity degree and convergence trends. Whenever a new individual with higher fitness is found, it is recorded in a separate visualization using the same format (Best Individuals window). The number of lines increases as different individuals with the same fitness are discovered.

In scatterplot visualization, each individual is represented as a point obtained by projecting its bits array into $\mathbb{R}^2$. The Multidimensional Scaling (MDS)[5] is used due to its proven effectiveness [11]. MDS is applied only to the initial generation to avoid computational overhead and ensure real-time updates. Being the initial population random, it provides good spatial dispersion. In subsequent generations, new points are projected using K Nearest Neighbor (KNN), ensuring plot stability and that identical individuals across different generations are

---

[5] Multidimensional Scaling (MDS) is a class of dimensionality reduction techniques that use proximities among any kind of objects to project high-dimensional data into a lower-dimensional space while preserving the pairwise distances between points as closely as possible.

plotted in the same position. K=5 is used because it empirically yielded good results, but this value can be configured and better evaluated in future works.

The purpose of this visualization is to illustrate the GA's trajectory through the search space over time. Hence, each generation's points are drawn on the canvas, with a fade-out effect applied to the previous points. This effect emphasizes recent generations without completely removing the previous ones, offering a continuous view of the population's trajectory on the search space.

4   Internal Validation Tests

This test aims to evaluate the efficiency of the tool developed to address the Maximum Clique Problem (MCP). Additionally, it seeks to identify possible bugs, making the heuristic evaluation with specialists less susceptible to such errors.

4.1   Test Setup

The tests were conducted by the tool's developers, who interacted with the application and recorded relevant impressions regarding its efficiency and functionality. Any bugs encountered in this phase were fixed.

The test was conducted in a dedicated room, equipped with air conditioning and an office chair. The tool was executed on a notebook with an Intel Core i7-10750H Comet Lake processor (6 cores, 2.6 GHz frequency), 64 GB of DDR4 RAM (2933MHz), an NVIDIA GeForce RTX 2070 GPU (8GB GDDR6), and PCIe SSD storage. The test setup included two screens for participant interaction: the notebook's built-in monitor, a 15.6" Full HD (1920×1080p) LED display with a 144 Hz refresh rate, and an external monitor with 27" UHD 4K (3840×2160) IPS display, 5ms response time, and a 60 Hz refresh rate.

The test utilized the Center for Discrete Mathematics and Theoretical Computer Science (DIMACS) benchmark [19], which includes datasets with the best known solutions for MCP[6]. The evaluators tested the tool with each of the available datasets. During execution, the evaluators have to adjust the hyperparameter in the GA and have support of real-time visualizations to perceive and analyze the impact of these changes. The evaluators could take note of suggestions about their interaction. The following metrics were recorded (system logs) during execution: (1) best clique found, (2) number of users interactions, and (3) total execution time.

The task consisted of finding the best known clique. For some datasets, the result was found quickly, but for others it was not found at all. There was no time limit to complete the task, but the evaluators were already tired after about 25 min, as showed in the results.

---

[6] A useful link of datasets: https://iridia.ulb.ac.be/~fmascia/maximum_clique/.

4.2   Results

Table 2 presents results from three Evaluators (Ev. 1, Ev. 2 and Ev. 3). The values in the Ev. column have the best clique found, the number of interactions (in parentheses), and the time taken in minutes [in brackets]. Bold clique values indicate that the evaluator found the best-known clique ($\omega(G)$).

The evaluators reached the best-known clique in 23 out of 37 datasets (62.16%), with an average execution time of 6.57 min and an average of 45.21 user interactions. This data suggests that, for some datasets, the GA—as designed—could solve the problem quickly by simply selecting appropriate hyperparameters from the start.

Thus, to conduct a more in-depth analysis, we filtered datasets that: (1) did not exceed 15 min of execution time, and (2) did not discover a new best clique after the 5-minute. This filtering resulted in a subset of 8 more challenging datasets. Under these conditions, the average execution time increased to 14.4 min and an average of 105.9 interactions.

Figure 2 presents user interactions across these 8 datasets for each evaluator. Each timeline represents the total execution time, where the black dot indicates when a new best clique was found. Colored dots represent user interactions throughout the run. A random jitter was applied to the y-axis for easier visualization.

Overall, a typical fitness curve behavior is observed—many better cliques are found early in the process, even with minimal user interaction. From approximately the 2-minute mark, the GA struggles to find the best clique with the same ease. After this stage, the visualization reveals user interactions until they find a new best. It also indicates that the most frequently adjusted parameters were: *populationSize*, *survivalRate*, *mutSelectionRate*, and *mutationRate*.

In a follow-up meeting after the tests, the evaluators discussed the strengths and weaknesses of the tool, as well as potential improvements. Strengths included the real-time visualizations, parameter controls for *populationSize*, *survivalRate*, *mutSelectionRate*, *mutationRate*, and *preventEqual*, and the ability to navigate the GA save history. The visualizations enabled real-time analysis of how hyperparameter adjustments influenced the GA's behavior. In particular, when manipulating the five mentioned parameters, evaluators identified an effective strategy: maintaining population diversity by reducing elitism (especially by lowering *survivalRate* and increasing *mutationRate*), while preserving a reasonable portion of the elite to ensure crossover operations produce solutions near high-performing individuals.

Weaknesses included the *partialReset* feature. Although its intended purpose was to increase population diversity when stuck in a local optimum, evaluators observed that when the population had already reached a favorable balance between diversity and elitism—and the fitness had significantly diverged from the initial random state—the new individuals generated by partial reset closely resembled the non-elite individuals and were replaced with ease, having no impact on the algorithm search process.

Table 2. Results of the internal evaluation. The first four columns are some dataset metadata, and the three last columns are evaluators results with $n/i/t$ mask. Where n is the best clique found (bold if benchmark found), i is the number of interactions, and t is the runtime in minutes.

Dataset	Nodes	Links	$\omega(G)$	Ev. 1 $(n/i/t)$	Ev. 2 $(n/i/t)$	Ev. 3 $(n/i/t)$
C125.9	125	6963	34	**34**/2/0	**34**/5/0	**34**/24/7
C250.9	250	27984	44	**44**/31/6	**44**/31/1	43/63/5
C500.9	500	112332	57	54/102/27	53/153/10	53/237/11
C1000.9	1000	450079	68	63/47/22	64/100/10	63/292/18
C2000.9	2000	1799532	80	66/41/20	70/96/13	66/102/3
DSJC1000_5	1000	499652	15	14/42/25	14/62/3	14/163/14
DSJC500_5	500	125248	13	**13**/16/41	12/34/3	**13**/132/8
C2000.5	2000	999836	16	**16**/8/3	**16**/41/8	14/58/14
C4000.5	4000	4000268	18	16/42/25	15/69/10	15/112/7
MANN_a27	378	70551	126	**126**/17/6	**126**/30/2	**126**/46/3
MANN_a45	1035	533115	345	342/49/17	342/123/15	342/142/3
MANN_a81	3321	5506380	1100	1096/48/20	1096/61/2	1096/99/7
brock200_2	200	9876	12	**12**/9/1	**12**/9/0	**12**/12/2
brock200_4	200	13089	17	**17**/7/1	**17**/12/1	**17**/35/3
brock400_2	400	59786	29	24/78/18	25/164/13	24/258/12
brock400_4	400	59765	33	25/40/13	**33**/68/3	24/191/23
brock800_2	800	208166	24	19/31/11	20/87/11	20/149/8
brock800_4	800	207643	26	20/41/20	20/84/10	20/120/8
gen200_p0.9_44	200	17910	44	**44**/27/4	**44**/28/1	40/55/7
gen200_p0.9_55	200	17910	55	**55**/3/1	**55**/6/0	**55**/6/1
gen400_p0.9_55	400	71820	55	50/16/6	50/67/8	50/98/4
gen400_p0.9_65	400	71820	65	**65**/6/2	**65**/8/1	**65**/8/1
gen400_p0.9_75	400	71820	75	**75**/0/0	**75**/1/1	**75**/2/1
hamming10-4	1024	434176	40	**40**/12/8	**40**/60/11	38/111/8
hamming8-4	256	20864	16	**16**/0/0	**16**/1/1	**16**/1/1
keller4	171	9435	11	**11**/0/0	**11**/0/0	**11**/0/1
keller5	776	225990	27	**27**/7/1	**27**/8/1	**27**/11/1
keller6	3361	4619898	59	52/11/19	52/59/25	55/66/3
p_hat300-1	300	10933	8	**8**/2/0	**8**/2/0	**8**/2/1
p_hat300-2	300	21928	25	**25**/0/0	**25**/1/0	**25**/1/1
p_hat300-3	300	33390	36	**36**/0/0	**36**/1/0	**36**/30/4
p_hat700-1	700	60999	11	**11**/8/3	**11**/9/1	**11**/45/4
p_hat700-2	700	121728	44	**44**/4/1	**44**/5/1	**44**/5/1
p_hat700-3	700	183010	62	**62**/0/0	**62**/1/1	61/47/4
p_hat1500-1	1500	284923	12	11/48/12	10/95/11	10/205/15
p_hat1500-2	1500	568960	65	**65**/3/1	**65**/13/4	**65**/39/5
p_hat1500-3	1500	847244	94	92/27/11	91/38/6	92/105/11

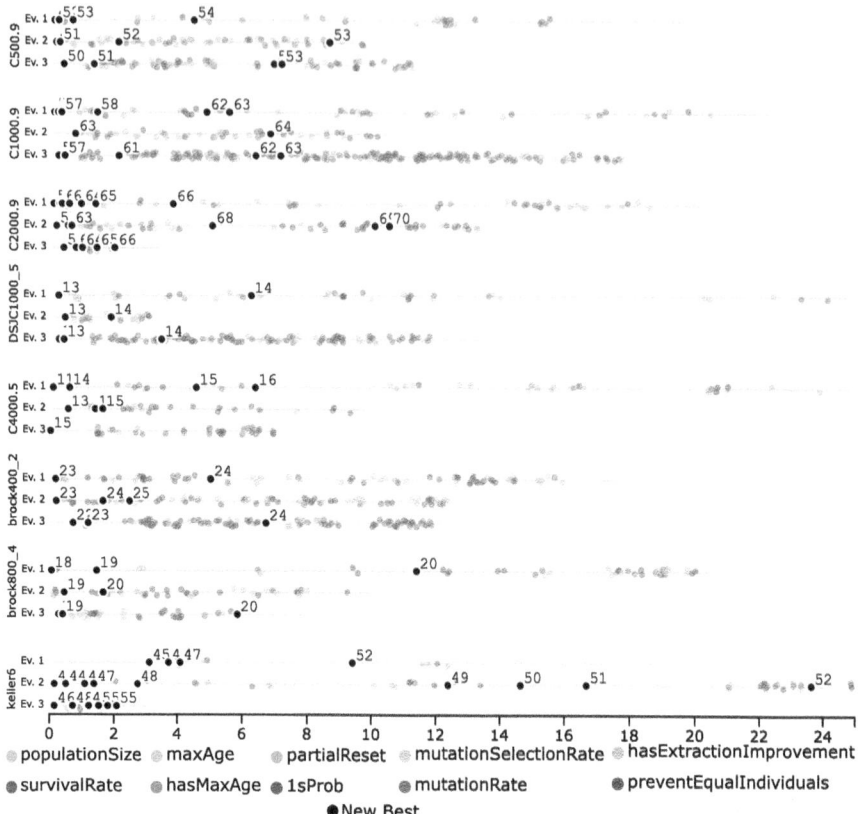

Fig. 2. Visualization of internal evaluation logs for selected challenging datasets. Each row represents the timeline of an evaluator for a specific dataset. Black dots indicate the moment a new best solution was found, while colored dots represent user interactions, as indicated in the legend. Over black dots is the number represents the best clique size. The x-axis is in minutes.

Proposed and documented improvements for the next development cycle include: making the best solution immortal (thus, it can be replaced if $hasMaxAge = true$) or reviving a subset of the best individuals ever found; plotting a fitness color gradient to Individual Visualization; displaying metadata of the running dataset; and providing a one-click option to open all visualizations and controls at once.

5   Heuristic Evaluation

The heuristic evaluation aims to analyze the usability and effectiveness of the tool based on the experience of experts in artificial intelligence and graph theory. The process was based on heuristic guidelines consolidated in the literature, allowing for a critical assessment of the interface quality and user experience. This evaluation used the same environment as the Internal Validation Tests.

5.1 Test Setup

Three experts were invited: professors who teach artificial intelligence and/or graph theory courses and have published research in the field.

First, the experiment facilitator briefly introduced the tool, explaining all available windows and options. A simple problem was solved as an example of how to use the tool.

The experts then used the tool, interacting with it and adjusting the GA parameters to attempt to find the maximum clique. After completing the tests, the experts participated in an interview in which the questions were structured based on heuristic evaluation proposed by [27] and on the guidelines proposed by [2]. The participants were allowed to interact freely with the tool if they needed to recall something during the interview.

The interviews were recorded and transcribed for later qualitative analysis. A thematic analysis was conducted to identify patterns in responses and create a mental map of the main positive and negative aspects and areas for improvement.

The specialists were informed about the goal of assessing the usability, efficiency, and effectiveness of the proposed tool through a heuristic evaluation based on predefined guidelines. The interviews were recorded in audio format for posterior transcription. Based on the guidelines, the following questions were asked:

- 1. How was your overall experience interacting with the tool?
- 2. Did you have any difficulty understanding the interface or commands?
- 3. Was the interaction flow intuitive, or were there moments of confusion?
- 4. Were the on-screen information clear and well-organized?
- 5. Was the visual feedback sufficient to understand what was happening?
- 6. Was it easy to learn how to use the tool?
- 7. Does the system communicate what it is capable of doing?
- 8. Does the system demonstrate that it can perform its intended tasks?
- 9. Does the system provide a good response time for executed actions?
- 10. Does the system display contextually relevant information?
- 11. Does the system help the user efficiently reject unnecessary commands?
- 12. Does the system record recent interactions?
- 13. Does the system prevent information overload?
- 14. Does the system inform users about the consequences of their actions?
- 15. Does the system provide global controls?
- 16. Does the system present changes in AI behavior?
- 17. Have you used any similar tools before? How does this one stand out?
- 18. What could be improved in the tool?
- 19. Could the tool benefit a broader audience?
- 20. Do you think this approach increases reliability in AI?

5.2   Thematic Analysis

After transcribing the interviews, two coders conducted the thematic analysis [6], following its six-phase approach. The coders didn't participate in the tool development or evaluation process. They began by thoroughly familiarizing themselves with the data, carefully reviewing all transcriptions to ensure consistency. During this initial phase, they shared their general impressions, identifying preliminary patterns and key aspects that would guide the subsequent coding and theme development. Next, an independent coding of all content was performed. Individually, each coder also generated themes by grouping similar codes. The independently generated themes were validated collaboratively, with both coders comparing differences and jointly deciding on the theme definition and naming.

After validating the themes, descriptions were extracted, and analyses were conducted to generate results that revealed key insights from the participants regarding the tool. To facilitate this thematic analysis, the QualCoder software [5] was utilized, allowing for the organization and examination of textual data. QualCoder enabled the identification of patterns and relationships within the dataset, enhancing the depth and clarity of the findings.

5.3   Results

Figure 3 shows the mind map that graphically organizes the main categories of feedback and suggestions for improvement. The structure of the map shows how the experts perceive the tool, highlighting areas for improvement and positive points of the system.

The results of the heuristic evaluation demonstrated that the expected objectives were achieved, highlighting that a significant portion of the assessments consisted of improvement suggestions. Based on the thematic analysis conducted using QualCoder software, approximately 17.29% of the observations were related to recommendations for enhancing the tool. These suggestions encompassed general system improvements and refinements in the presentation of visualizations. The percentages in parentheses represent the number of observations from participants relative to the total number of observations. An observation can be related to one or more codes.

- **Tool Improvement** (10.6%): General recommendations to improve the user experience and the functionality of the system. For instance, the Participant 2 (P2) stated, "Inclusion of new variation options and crossover techniques, as well as adaptive features to suggest hyperparameters and optimize the user experience [...]".
- **Improve Visualizations** (6.69%): Suggestions to optimize the presentation of data and the usability of graphical representations. For instance, Participant 3 (P3) suggests that "For the graph of the best and worst individual's fitness, show a curve representing the average fitness of the population [...]".

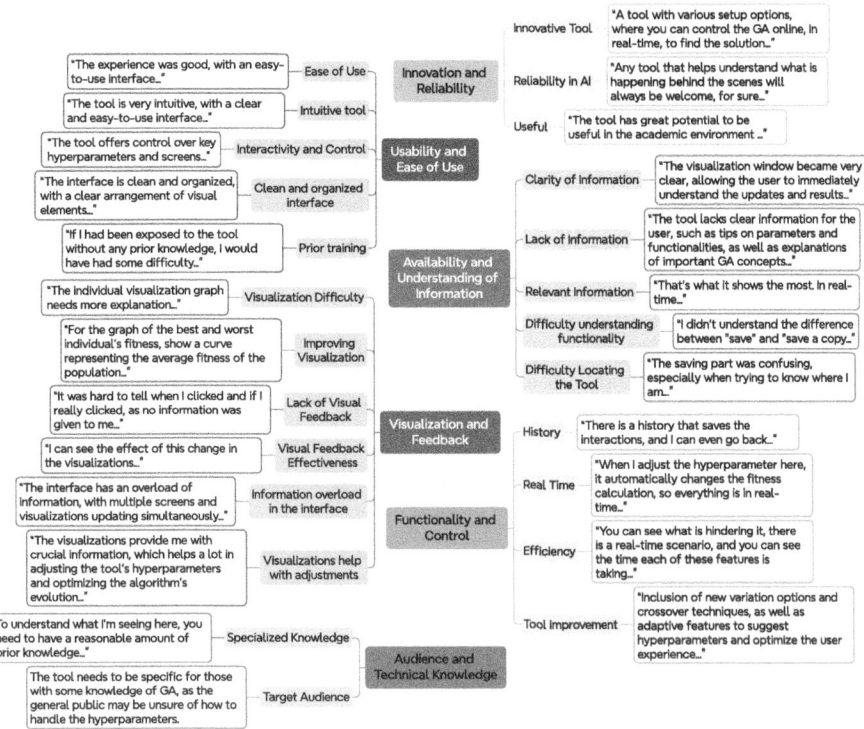

Fig. 3. Results of the thematic analysis. The figure provides a visual summary of the identified themes along with their respective codes

The feedback from the experts is the following:

Usability and Ease of Use: the codes about Clean and Organized Interface (3.15%) are illustrated by the P2 statement: "The interface is clean and organized, with a clear arrangement of visual elements [...]" and the Intuitive Tool (1.57%) codes are illustrated by the P1 statement: "The tool is very intuitive, with a clear and easy-to-use interface [...]". Indicate that the system already has a solid foundation in terms of usability, allowing the user to rearrange screens according to their needs. About Ease of Use (9.45%) the P2 stated that "the experience was good, with an easy-to-use interface [...]". The system has a learning curve that could be optimized. Although it is intuitive in some aspects, it could benefit from initial training to make it easier to handle the buttons and visualizations. About Interactivity and Control (5.51%) the P2 stated that "the tool offers control over key hyperparameters and screens [...]" and that there is the possibility of expanding functionalities to allow for greater customization.

Visualization and Feedback: in the code Information Overload on the Interface (3.15%) some users reported that the amount of information displayed simultaneously can create difficulties in understanding, especially for those without previous experience. P3 stated that "the interface has an overload of information, with multiple screens and visualizations updating simultaneously [...]". In the code Visualizations Help with Adjustments (5.12%), the visualizations used make it easier to understand and make adjustments to the tool. Suggestions include creating new visualizations, a curve of the best average fitness of the population, with the standard deviation behind it, in a very smooth way, so as not to pollute so much. The P2 stated that "the visualizations provide me with crucial information, which helps a lot in adjusting the tool's hyperparameters and optimizing the algorithm's evolution [...]".

Availability and Understanding of Information: Clarity of Information and Relevant Information (5.12%) codes reveals that the organization and terminology could be refined. Experts highlighted the importance of displaying data in a clear and accessible way within the system. P1 stated that "the visualization window became very clear, allowing the user to immediately understand the updates and results [...]" and P3 stated that "that's what it shows the most. In real-time [...]".

Functionality and Control: Real Time (5.12%) codes reveals that the experts emphasized the importance of updating data in real time. The system's response to changes in hyperparameters was considered efficient and useful for monitoring the process. P1 stated that "when I adjust the hyperparameter here, it updates everything in real-time".

Some participants felt they needed training to use the tool better, mentioning aspects such as Prior training (2.76%) and Specialized knowledge (2.76%). In addition, certain functionalities, such as dimensionality reduction and clustering, were perceived as complex, suggesting the need for additional explanatory materials. The P3 stated, "If I had been exposed to the tool without any prior knowledge, I would have had some difficulty [...]" and "to understand what I'm seeing here, you need to have a reasonable amount of prior knowledge".

The Lack of Information in some areas of the interface was also pointed out (7.09%), making interpretation of the results more difficult, especially for users unfamiliar with Genetic Algorithms (GA). The P1 stated that "The tool lacks clear information for the user, such as tips on parameters and functionalities, as well as explanations of important GA concepts [...]".

Among the challenges pointed out were Difficulty Understanding Functionality (4.72%) and Visualization Difficulty (4.33%). P1 stated, "I didn't understand the difference between save and save a copy [...]", and P2 stated that "The individual visualization graph needs more explanation [...]". Suggestions include adding tooltips to explain elements and adjusting the shapes and colors of elements in the visualizations for better understanding.

The Reliability in Artificial Intelligence (AI) code (2.76%) reflects that users consider the technology employed to be reliable, since they point out that a tool that helps to understand what is going on inside the algorithm is always welcome. P3 stated that "any tool that helps understand what is happening behind the scenes will always be welcome, for sure [...]". The Innovative Tool codes (2.76%) indicate that the system was recognized as innovative due to its visual approach and real-time integration with the optimization technique's hyperparameters. For instance, P2 stated that the proposed tool is a "[...] tool with various setup options, where you can control the GA online, in real-time [...]".

Therefore, the heuristic evaluation showed that the tool meets the fundamental requirements but has significant room for improvement. Suggestions for improvement focused on optimizing the system, and the presentation of visualizations can positively impact the user experience. In addition, the experts' feedback provides important direction for ongoing adjustments and refinements, ensuring that the solution effectively meets users' expectations and needs.

6   Conclusion and Future Works

We introduced a Human-AI collaborative system for addressing the Maximum Clique Problem (MCP) through a steerable genetic algorithm. The system allows users to guide the evolutionary process in real time, putting the human inside the optimization process and actively changing the algorithm behavior.

Internal testing on Center for Discrete Mathematics and Theoretical Computer Science (DIMACS) benchmark datasets demonstrated that the proposed method identifies acceptable solutions while encouraging the user to collaborate with the algorithm. The results reveal that user manipulations over population size, survival rate and mutation rates are more effective to address this problem compared with available interactions.

Furthermore, a heuristic evaluation conducted with domain experts analyzed the user experience, interaction quality, and perceived control within the system. The results indicated that the tool has a solid foundation in usability and interactivity, with strengths in interface clarity and real-time feedback. However, experts highlighted areas for improvement, such as information overload, the need for clearer explanations, and better onboarding resources. Enhancing visual clarity and expanding guidance materials were key suggestions to improve accessibility and user understanding, particularly for those without prior knowledge.

This tool represents our first investigation about this type of Human-AI interaction, opening up several insights for future directions. As future works, we will investigate new visualizations and interactions; make visualizations interactive, such as creating filters in the search space visualized in the projected scatter plot; investigate the use of different types of meta-heuristics; verify the feasibility of human-machine interaction with the best local searches developed specifically for MCP; compare this approach with adaptive meta-heuristics and include suggestions of interactions for the user based on the these algorithms strategies; and investigate the possibility of other styles of collaboration, such as many IA algorithms or many humans on the same objective.

Disclosure of Interests. The authors have no competing interests to declare that are relevant to the content of this article.

References

1. Adadi, A., Berrada, M.: Peeking inside the black-box: a survey on explainable artificial intelligence (XAI). IEEE Access **6**, 52138–52160 (2018)
2. Amershi, S., et al.: Guidelines for human-AI interaction. In: CHI Conference on Human Factors in Computing Systems. ACM (2019)
3. Balas, E., Yu, C.S.: Finding a maximum clique in an arbitrary graph. SIAM J. Comput. **15**(4), 1054–1068 (1986)
4. Boukhelifa, N., et al.: Evolutionary visual exploration: evaluation of an IEC framework for guided visual search. Evol. Comput. **25**(1), 55–86 (2017)
5. Brailas, A., Tragou, E., Papachristopoulos, K.: Introduction to qualitative data analysis and coding with QualCoder. Am. J. Qual. Res. **7**(3), 19–31 (2023)
6. Braun, V., Clarke, V.: Using thematic analysis in psychology. Qual. Res. Psychol. **3**(2), 77–101 (2006)
7. Chae, J., et al.: Visualization system for evolutionary neural networks for deep learning. In: 2019 IEEE International Conference on Big Data (Big Data), pp. 4498–4502. IEEE (2019)
8. Cota Vidaurre, A., et al.: TestEvoViz: visualizing genetically-based test coverage evolution. Empirical Softw. Eng. **27**(7) (2022)
9. Cruz, A., et al.: ELICIT: evolutionary computation visualization. In: Proceedings of the Companion Publication of the 2015 Annual Conference on Genetic and Evolutionary Computation, pp. 949–956. GECCO '15, ACM (2015)
10. Daneshpajouh, H., Zakaria, N.: A clustering-based visual analysis tool for genetic algorithm. In: Proceedings of the 12th International Joint Conference on Computer Vision, Imaging and Computer Graphics Theory and Applications, pp. 233–240. SCITEPRESS - Science and Technology Publications (2017)
11. De Lorenzo, A., et al.: An analysis of dimensionality reduction techniques for visualizing evolution. In: Genetic and Evolutionary Computation Conference Companion, pp. 1864–1872. GECCO '19, Association for Computing Machinery, New York, NY, USA (2019)
12. Dolson, E., Ofria, C.: Visualizing the tape of life: exploring evolutionary history with virtual reality. In: Genetic and Evolutionary Computation Conference Companion, pp. 1553–1559. ACM (2018)
13. Farhood, H., Saberi, M., Najafi, M.: Human-in-the-Loop Optimization for Artificial Intelligence Algorithms, pp. 92–102. Springer International Publishing (2022)
14. Farooq, H., et al.: An interactive visualization of genetic algorithm on 2-D graph. In: IEEE 10th International Conference on Cognitive Informatics and Cognitive Computing (ICCI-CC'11), pp. 144–151. IEEE (2011)
15. Hakanen, J., et al.: Interactivized: visual interaction for better decisions with interactive multiobjective optimization. IEEE Access **10**, 33661–33678 (2022)
16. Hettenhausen, J., et al.: Interactive multi-objective particle swarm optimisation using decision space interaction. In: 2013 IEEE Congress on Evolutionary Computation, pp. 3411–3418. IEEE (2013)
17. Huang, B.: Finding Maximum Clique With a Genetic Algorithm. Master's thesis, Penn. State Harrisburg (2002)
18. Ivanov, A., Willett, W., Jacob, C.: EvoIsland: interactive evolution via an island-inspired spatial user interface framework. In: Genetic and Evolutionary Computation Conference, pp. 1200–1208. ACM (2022)
19. Johnson, D.S., Trick, M.A.: Cliques, Coloring, and Satisfiability: Second DIMACS Implementation Challenge, October 11-13, 1993, vol. 26. American Mathematical Soc. (1996)

20. Llorà, X., et al.: Analyzing active interactive genetic algorithms using visual analytics. In: Proceedings of the 8th Annual Conference on Genetic and Evolutionary Computation. GECCO06, ACM (2006)
21. Lutton, E., Fekete, J.D.: Visual Analytics and Experimental Analysis of Evolutionary Algorithms. Tech. rep, INRIA (2011)
22. McPhee, N.F., et al.: Visualizing genetic programming ancestries. In: Proceedings of the 2016 on Genetic and Evolutionary Computation Conference Companion, pp. 1419–1426. GECCO '16, ACM (2016)
23. Medvet, E., et al.: Unveiling evolutionary algorithm representation with DU maps. Genet. Program Evolvable Mach. **19**(3), 351–389 (2018)
24. Meiguins, A., et al.: Visual analysis scenarios for understanding evolutionary computational techniques' behavior. Information **10**(3), 88 (2019)
25. Mexicano-Santoyo, A., et al.: Visual Analysis of Differential Evolution Algorithms, pp. 512–521. Springer International Publishing (2018)
26. Mosqueira-Rey, E., et al.: Human-in-the-loop machine learning: a state of the art. Artif. Intell. Rev. **56**(4), 3005–3054 (2022)
27. Nielsen, J., Molich, R.: Heuristic evaluation of user interfaces. In: SIGCHI Conference on Human Factors in Computing Systems Empowering People, pp. 249–256. ACM Press (1990)
28. Radhika, P.R., Velayutham, C.S.: Visualization – A Potential Alternative for Analyzing Differential Evolution Search, pp. 31–41. Springer International Publishing (2015)
29. Ramos, G., et al.: Interactive machine teaching: a human-centered approach to building machine-learned models. Hum. Comput. Interact. **35**(5–6), 413–451 (2020)
30. Sathyajit, B.P., Velayutham, C.S.: Visual Analysis of Genetic Algorithms While Solving 0-1 Knapsack Problem, pp. 68–78. Springer International Publishing (2018)
31. Tendresse, I.l., Gottlieb, J., Kao, O.: The effects of partial restarts in evolutionary search. In: International Conference on Artificial Evolution (Evolution Artificielle), pp. 117–127. Springer (2001)
32. Vallerio, M., et al.: An interactive decision-support system for multi-objective optimization of nonlinear dynamic processes with uncertainty. Expert Syst. Appl. **42**(21), 7710–7731 (2015)
33. Walker, D.J.: Visualising multi-objective populations with treemaps. In: Proceedings of the Companion Publication of the 2015 Annual Conference on Genetic and Evolutionary Computation, pp. 963–970. GECCO '15, ACM (2015)
34. Walter, M.J., Walker, D.J., Craven, M.J.: An Explainable visualisation of the evolutionary search process. In: Proceedings of the Genetic and Evolutionary Computation Conference Companion, pp. 1794–1802. GECCO '22, ACM (2022)

Predicting Sleep Disorders Using Machine Learning: A Comparative Analysis

Sarah Goodyear and Abdallah Alsammani$^{(\boxtimes)}$ (iD)

Department of Mathematics, Jacksonville University, Jacksonville, FL 32211, USA
`aalsamm@ju.edu`

Abstract. Insomnia and sleep apnea represent sleep disorders that profoundly affect human health and well-being. This study examines how different machine learning (ML) approaches can determine sleep disorder risks based on physiological measurements alongside lifestyle and demographic data. The analysis involved a complete dataset that included sleep duration and quality measurements, physical activity levels, stress levels, cardiovascular health factors, and demographic information. The study conducted a thorough evaluation of multiple supervised classification algorithms, such as logistic Regression, decision tree, random forest, k-nearest neighbors (kNN), Gaussian naïve Bayes, multinomial naïve Bayes, Bernoulli naïve Bayes, support vector machines (SVM), and linear Regression. Decision tree, random forest, and kNN algorithms showed better predictive performance after preprocessing data thoroughly and selecting features through correlation analysis and cross-validation. The random forest model produced the best results with an accuracy rate of 94.38%, a precision level of 0.96%, a recall rate of 0.98% for the no sleep disorder class, and an AUC score of 0.98%. The feature importance analysis identified age, BMI category, blood pressure, and occupation as essential predictors for sleep disorders. The findings of this study demonstrate how machine learning methods enable the precise and timely detection of sleep disorder risks within clinical settings.

Keywords: Machine Learning · Sleep Disorders · Random Forest · Decision Tree · Logistic Regression · Health Informatics

1 Introduction

Sleep disorders constitute a significant public health challenge worldwide, affecting millions by lowering life quality and productivity while increasing healthcare expenses [6]. Two common sleep disorders that can result in serious health problems when untreated are insomnia and sleep apnea [2,17]. Insomnia involves challenges with falling asleep and staying asleep and reduced sleep quality, while sleep apnea causes repeated breathing interruptions during sleep [17].

New developments in technology alongside data science research have created fresh techniques for identifying and treating sleep disorders. Machine learning

O. Gervasi et al. (Eds.): ICCSA 2025, LNCS 15648, pp. 106–121, 2025.
https://doi.org/10.1007/978-3-031-97000-9_7

(ML) enables systems to learn and self-improve from data through artificial intelligence techniques and has demonstrated significant potential in healthcare applications [7]. Machine learning methods provide potentially revolutionary new options for sleep disorder prediction and diagnosis beyond traditional diagnostic approaches [16].

While polysomnography (PSG) remains the primary diagnostic method for sleep disorders, it demands extensive resources alongside specialized laboratory facilities and trained technicians [12]. The diagnostic precision of PSG does not overcome its challenges, which include restricted accessibility, elevated costs, and scalability limitations [15]. The limitations of PSG can be overcome by combining machine learning techniques with accessible health metrics to create screening tools that identify at-risk individuals before needing extensive diagnostic tests [10].

Multiple research efforts have investigated different ML methods for classifying sleep disorders through support vector machines [11], neural networks [4], and decision tree models [19]. The latest findings demonstrate that machine learning algorithms successfully distinguish between various sleep disorders and typical sleep patterns by analyzing multiple physiological and behavioral datasets [3,9]. Despite recent advancements, performing comparative evaluations of ML algorithms is crucial to determine the best predictive methods for sleep disorders across various populations [14].

Our research focuses on creating several machine learning classification frameworks that predict sleep disorders by analyzing an extensive dataset containing health metrics like sleep duration and quality, physical activity, and cardiovascular indicators. Through the analysis of decision trees combined with random forests and k-nearest neighbors (kNN) algorithms, we determine which predictive models demonstrate the highest accuracy and which features impact classification performance [1,5,8].

The results of our study provide essential knowledge for medical practices and public health strategies. ML-driven tools that make detecting sleep disorders early and conducting screenings easier can enable faster interventions, which help decrease their harmful effects on personal health and healthcare systems [13]. Healthcare providers can develop personalized treatment plans and targeted prevention measures by identifying key predictive features.

2   Methods

2.1   Data Collection

The data used for this study is the Sleep Health and Lifestyle Dataset [18]. This dataset consists of synthetic data generated using algorithms to simulate results, allowing for unconstrained public analysis, and is stored in CSV format. There are 374 samples with data for 13 features relating to sleep, lifestyle, and physiological characteristics.

2.2   Data Exploration

Examining the contents of this dataset reveals that all samples are unique and contain no missing data. However, the Python data frame interprets the "None" in the "sleep disorder" column, representing no sleep disorder as clarified in the metadata, as a NaN value. Replacing these incorrectly labeled NaN values in the "sleep disorder" column with "No disorder" resolves this misinterpretation.

Boxplots were used to visualize the distribution of individual numeric features. This and individual statistical summaries reveal any possible skew or abnormalities. Age (Distribution 1) is spread approximately a bell curve from the minimum age 27 to the maximum age 59. Sleep duration (Distribution 2) is appropriately spread from 6.4 h to 8.5 h. Quality of sleep (Distribution 3) is left-skewed, ranging from a minimum of 4 to a maximum of 9, with the lower and upper quartiles falling between 6 and 8 and averaging 7. The physical activity level (Distribution 4) is evenly distributed, ranging from 30 to 90 min, with an average of 60 min. The stress level (Distribution 5) is relatively evenly spread from ratings 3 to 8, averaging 5, on a scale of 10. The heart rate (Distribution 6) is right-skewed, with a minimum of 65 to a maximum of 86, averaging 70 beats per minute. Daily steps (Distribution 7) are slightly left-skewed with a minimum of 3000, a maximum of 10000, a lower quartile of 5600, an upper quartile of 8000, and an average of 8000 steps daily. Person ID (Distribution 0) is an arbitrary label representing distinct subjects and is irrelevant to any numeric analysis. Of the other seven features, none of the distributions have any notable anomalies that could reasonably lead to deviated results.

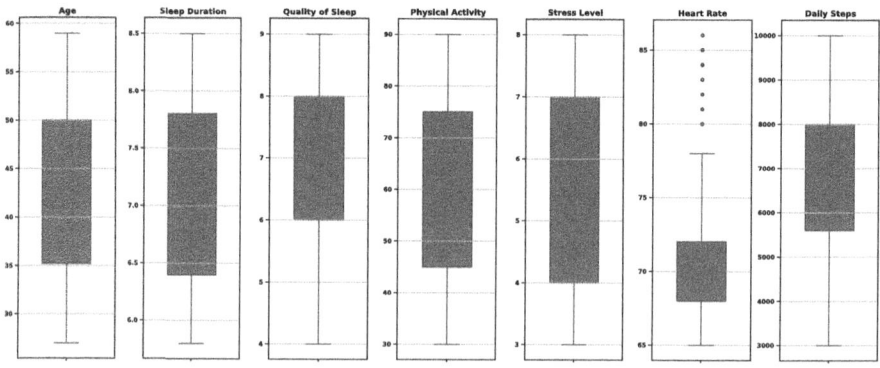

Fig. 1. Boxplots showing the distribution of seven health variables with median values (red lines), interquartile ranges (blue boxes), and outliers (red dots). The plots reveal typical values and variability for Age, Sleep Duration, Sleep Quality, Physical Activity, Stress Level, Heart Rate, and Daily Steps across the dataset. (Color figure online)

Similarly, bar plots were used to visualize the distribution of categorical features to examine possible anomalies. Gender (Distribution 8) is evenly distributed, with only four more male samples than female samples. Occupation

(Distribution 9) consists of nurses, doctors, engineers, lawyers, accountants, scientists, software engineers, sales representatives, and managers, in that order of prevalence. BMI category (Distribution 9) has the most occurrences of normal weight, followed by overweight, and then obese, making this most representative of a healthy-weighted population. However, normal weight is represented by both "Normal" and "Normal Weight," which can be combined to "Normal." Blood pressure (Distribution 11) has the most occurrences of 130/85, followed by 140/95, 125/80, and 120/80, accounting for most of these observations. This means the data is most representative of a population with slightly elevated blood pressure. Sleep disorder (Distribution 12) measures whether the subject has no disorder, sleep apnea, or insomnia, with no disorder being about three times as common in the population as either disorder. Combining "Sleep Apnea" and "Insomnia" to represent "Sleep Disorder" when a sleep disorder of any type is present allows for the prediction of the presence of a sleep disorder instead of focusing on specific types. Like the numeric features, no significant anomalies are present.

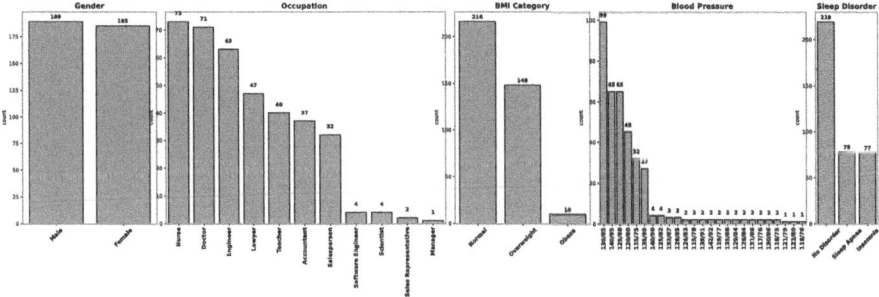

Fig. 2. The plots show count distributions Gendernder (balanced maleGendere representation), Occupation (dominated by healthcare and technical professions), BMI Category (mostly normal weight individuals), Blood Pressure (primarily clustering around 130/80 mmHg), and Sleep Disorder (majority with no disorder, with equal prevalence of sleep apnea and insomnia).

After cleaning the data, dummy variables were created for the categorical features so that numeric and categorical features could be normalized. They were normalized on a scale of 0 to 1. Normalization was more ideal than standardization for this study to limit the impact of the skew and any outliers present in the features by placing the values in a fixed range. Normalization also allows the data to be more easily interpreted by a wider audience and has the potential to perform better in a broader range of machine learning models. K-Nearest Neighbors (kNN) and many unsupervised techniques are more applicable when data is fixed on a bounded scale. Normalizing the data allows for a more thorough analysis of supervised techniques and prepares for a follow-up analysis and comparison with unsupervised techniques. With this data, several research goals can be identified. First, cross-validation can be used to explore which supervised machine learning models have the most potential to predict the presence of a sleep disorder most accurately. The three models with the highest potential can be selected using these results to train more robust models. This can be used to gauge better what machine learning model can most effectively predict the presence of a sleep disorder with lifestyle and physiological data. Next, a correlation matrix was developed to aid in feature selection. Person ID is included in the matrix, but these metrics should be disregarded in the analysis since this feature is an arbitrary value to distinguish uniqueness and holds no statistical significance. The warmer the tone, the more positive the correlation; the cooler the tone, the more negative the correlation. Age, occupation, physical activity level, stress level, BMI category, blood pressure, and heart rate are observed to have positive correlations with sleep disorders. ConverseGendernder, sleep gender derivation, quality of sleep, and daily steps are observed to have negative correlations with sleep disorders.

3   Machine Learning

3.1   Feature Selection

Correlation metrics 3 were compared with the target variable, sleep disorder, using the correlation matrix to determine which features to include. Any corre-

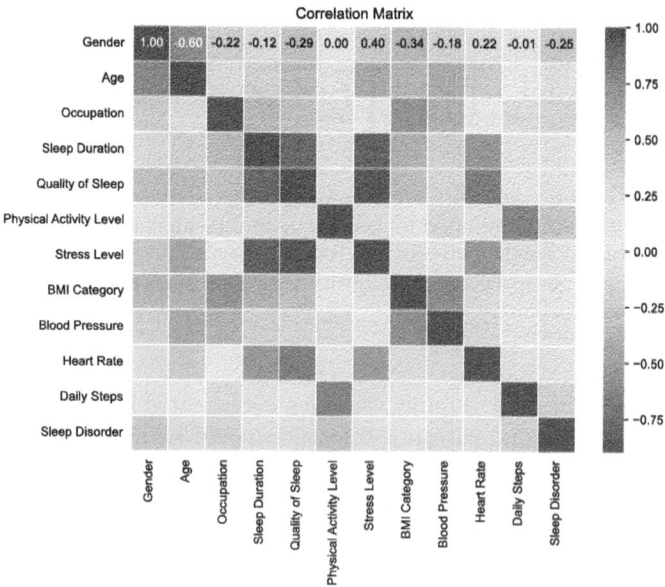

Fig. 3. The heatmap shows relationships between variables using color intensity (red for positive, blue for negative correlations). Notable relationships exist between sleep duration and quality, stress level and sleep metrics, BMI category, and blood pressure. (Color figure online)

lation with the person ID is disregarded. A threshold of 0.4 was selected, which accounts for the inclusion of four features: age, occupation, BMI category, and blood pressure.

3.2   5-Fold Cross Validation for Supervised Models

Nine supervised learning models were assessed using 5-fold cross-validation: decision tree, random forest, k-nearest-neighbors (kNN), Gaussian naïve bayes (GNB), multinomial naïve bayes (MNB), Bernoulli naïve bayes (BNB), logistic Regression, support vector machines (SVM), and linear regression model. Default parameters were set for each model before performing cross-validation. For the decision tree and random forest, the random state was set to 42. The number of neighbors for kNN was set to 5. The three naïve Bayes and the linear model types had no default feature set. Logistic Regression set the maximum iterations to 1000 and the random state to 42. SVM sets a linear kernel with an actual probability and a random state 42. For the cross-validation, a stratified k-fold was used, where there were five folds, shuffle was set to true, and random state was set to 42. A for loop was used to evaluate all nine models and store the accuracy, F1 score, and AUC-ROC, except the linear model, which only stored the correlation coefficient for later comparison. After evaluation, the models were ranked based on accuracy or correlation coefficient to determine the order of efficacy.

3.3   Models

The three models selected for training based on cross-validation results were the decision tree, random forest, and k-nearest neighbors (kNN). Parameter optimization was performed before training for each of these models. Each model was trained using the same four selected features and the same train-test split. The test size was 20% of the data, leaving 80% for training, and the random state was set to 42. After each model was trained, predictions were made using the test set, accuracy was computed, confusion matrices were produced, classification reports were printed, and auROC curves were created. These evaluation metrics were stored for each model for final comparison.

3.4   Logistic Regression

Logistic Regression is a statistical classification method that models binary outcome probabilities by examining the relationships between predictor variables and a binary response variable. The researchers used logistic Regression to differentiate between patients who have sleep disorders and those who do not based on specific physiological and demographic indicators.

The logistic regression model uses the logistic function to calculate the probability p that indicates whether a sleep disorder exists.

The probability p of having a sleep disorder is calculated using the logistic function as

$$p = \frac{1}{1 + e^{-(\beta_0 + \beta_1 X_1 + \beta_2 X_2 + \cdots + \beta_k X_k)}} \qquad (1)$$

p stands for the probability of the sleep disorder outcome with β_0 as the intercept and $\beta_1, \beta_2, \ldots, \beta_k$ as the coefficients for the predictor variables $X_1, X_2, \ldots, X_k$.

The logistic regression model transforms to a log-odds expression as follows:

The log-odds of the probability p equals the intercept β_0 added to the sum of products of regression coefficients β_i with predictor variables X_i for each i from 1 to k.

The left-hand side shows the logit transformation of probability p.

Demographic factors (age and sex) and physiological measurements (heart rate variability and sleep duration) were chosen as predictor variables for this study because previous sleep disorder research highlighted their significance. Model parameters ($\beta_0, \beta_1, \ldots, \beta_k$) were estimated through maximum likelihood estimation (MLE) using the training data subset after splitting the dataset into training and testing portions. The logistic regression model's performance was evaluated by applying the test dataset.

The classification accuracy and robustness of the logistic regression model were assessed through standard metrics, including accuracy, precision, recall (sensitivity), F1-score, and the receiver operating characteristic (ROC) curve with the area under the curve (AUC).

The logistic regression model showed excellent classification results by attaining high accuracy and maintaining balanced precision, recall, and F1-scores for both sleep disorder and no sleep disorder outcome classes. The detailed performance metrics will be discussed further in the Results section.

3.5   Decision Tree

The research team used a Decision Tree classifier to construct an interpretable model that classifies subjects according to their sleep disorder status. Decision Trees build hierarchical structures by recursively splitting data based on its feature values and producing decision nodes with leaf nodes representing classification results.

The dataset $\mathcal{D}$ comprises pairs (x_i, y_i) for $i = 1, \cdots, N$ where the feature vectors x_i belong to $\mathbb{R}^p$ and the class labels y_i are from the set $\{1, 2, \ldots, J\}$. The Decision Tree constructs distinct regions within the feature space $\mathbb{R}^p$ by implementing binary divisions at each node. The splits are chosen through impurity minimization to achieve the best separation between classes within each data subset.

The research applied the Classification and Regression Tree (CART) algorithm with the Gini impurity index for split evaluation. The mathematical definition of Gini impurity for a node dataset D is:

$$\text{Gini}(D) = 1 - \sum_{j=1}^{J} p_j^2, \qquad (2)$$

Within node D, the variable p_j indicates the ratio of data points that fall into class j, while J indicates the number of unique classes. The splitting criterion selects partitions that reduce the aggregate weighted Gini impurities between child nodes.

$$\text{Weighted Gini} = \frac{|D_L|}{|D|} \text{Gini}(D_L) + \frac{|D_R|}{|D|} \text{Gini}(D_R), \tag{3}$$

D and D refer to the left and right child nodes after splitting, while $|D|$ depicts the total data points within the parent node.

The data was divided into training and testing subsets in a 70%/30% ratio, providing a stringent assessment of model generalization capacity. Grid search with 5-fold cross-validation was utilized on training data for hyperparameter optimization of maximum depth, minimum samples per split, and minimum samples per leaf to prevent overfitting.

The model performance evaluation on the test dataset involved multiple metrics, including confusion matrix analysis and precision, recall, F1-score calculations, and Receiver Operating Characteristic (ROC) curve examination. The precision and recall metrics were evaluated separately for every class. The F1-score is calculated as the harmonic mean of precision and recall.

$$\text{F1-score} = 2 \cdot \frac{\text{Precision} \cdot \text{Recall}}{\text{Precision} + \text{Recall}}. \tag{4}$$

The ROC curve and the area under the Curve (AUC) were calculated to evaluate the model's classification performance across different classes.

The Decision Tree's interpretable structure enabled unambiguous identification of essential physiological and demographic predictors for accurate sleep disorder risk classification.

3.6 Random Forest

The ensemble learning Random Forest (RF) algorithm was the basis for classifying sleep disorders according to physiological and demographic data. The Random Forest method builds multiple decision trees during training before combining their results to improve accuracy while reducing overfitting.

The RF model consists of an ensemble that brings together multiple decision trees.

$$\{T_k(x, \Theta_k), k = 1, 2, \ldots, K\}, \tag{5}$$

The input feature vector is represented by x while Θ_k stands for independent, identically distributed random vectors that define each decision tree structure, and K denotes the total number of trees. The final classification output $\hat{y}$ results from:

$$\hat{y} = \arg\max_c \sum_{k=1}^{K} I(T_k(x, \Theta_k) = c), \tag{6}$$

The indicator function $I(\cdot)$ returns true when its argument matches the class label c.

The optimization of estimator number, maximum tree depth, and minimum samples per split and leaf was achieved through a grid search with 5-fold cross-validation during hyperparameter tuning. Predictive accuracy on the validation dataset determined the selection of optimal hyperparameters.

The machine learning pipeline started with feature selection, in which we identified key predictors from demographic data (age, sex, BMI), physiological parameters (heart rate variability, breathing rate, oxygen saturation), and lifestyle factors before proceeding to model training. The Gini impurity reduction criterion provided the mathematical definition to measure feature importance.

$$\text{Gini} = 1 - \sum_{i=1}^{J} p_i^2, \tag{7}$$

p_i indicates the fraction of samples from class i while J signifies the overall number of classes.

The model evaluation process used a hold-out test set to compute performance metrics, including confusion matrices, precision, recall, F1-score, and the AUC of the ROC curve. The interpretation of model performance became possible through confusion matrix analysis, which specified accurate favorable rates alongside true negatives and the amounts of false positives and negatives. The evaluation included precision and recall analysis for each class to achieve balanced prediction accuracy.

The RF model unified predictions from various decision trees through ensemble learning methods to produce reliable and stable classification outcomes. We implemented all analytical processes through Python's `scikit-learn` library.

4   Results

4.1   Cross Validation

A 5-fold cross-validation was performed to evaluate and compare the performance of nine supervised learning models. The models were ranked based on their classification accuracy, F1-score, and area under the receiver operating characteristic curve (ROC AUC), as shown in Table 1.

The top-performing models were the Random Forest and Decision Tree classifiers, both achieving an accuracy of 94.38%. The Random Forest model demonstrated superior discriminative performance with an ROC AUC of 98.00% and an F1-score of 91.5%, outperforming the Decision Tree, which had a slightly lower ROC AUC of 93.00% and an F1-score of 93.0%.

Logistic Regression also performed well, achieving an accuracy of 90.90%, an F1-score of 89.0%, and a high ROC AUC of 96.00%, indicating good overall classification ability despite its lower accuracy compared to the tree-based models.

Other models such as k-Nearest Neighbors (kNN), Support Vector Machines (SVM), and the various Naïve Bayes classifiers (Gaussian, Bernoulli, and Multinomial) showed moderate to strong performance. Still, they did not surpass the top three models. The kNN model achieved an accuracy of 93.30% and a ROC AUC of 92.22%, which were close but not competitive with the ensemble methods. Multinomial Naïve Bayes (MNB) had consistent scores around 86.90%, while Gaussian Naïve Bayes (GNB) and Bernoulli Naïve Bayes (BNB) hovered near 90.63% accuracy.

Linear Regression was the least effective model in this context. It did not output classification scores and was evaluated using the R^2 metric, which yielded a score of 64.36%, only marginally better than a random guess compared to classification-based models.

These results highlight the strength of ensemble learning and decision tree-based methods in classifying sleep disorders when trained on lifestyle and physiological data.

Table 1. Performance Comparison of Machine Learning Models for Sleep Disorder Classification and Regression

ML Model	Accuracy %	F1-score %	ROC AUC %	R2 score %
Random Forest	94.38	94.37	93.47	NaN
Decision Tree	94.38	94.37	93.91	NaN
kNN	93.30	93.30	92.22	NaN
Logistic Regression	90.90	90.91	93.38	NaN
SVM	90.63	90.65	92.70	NaN
BNB	90.63	90.65	90.34	NaN
GNB	90.37	93.80	93.36	NaN
MNB	86.90	86.91	86.03	NaN
Linear Regression	NaN	NaN	NaN	64.36

To evaluate the results of each model, a confusion matrix and area under the receiver operating characteristic curve (auROC) were developed. Classification reports showing precision, recall, and F1-scores were also created. These metrics give insight into how well each model can distinguish between classes and what classification types account for the error in predicting the test set.

4.2   Logistic Regression

The logistic regression classifier showed a strong ability to differentiate between patients with sleep disorders and those without. Figure 1 illustrates that the model attained high classification accuracy through various evaluation metrics. According to the confusion matrix in Fig. 1's left panel, the model demonstrated excellent predictive ability by accurately predicting 41 true negatives and 26 true positives alongside eight incorrect classifications (2 false negatives and six false positives). The classification metrics analysis from Fig. 1's middle panel shows the model produced close precision results for both categories, with values of 0.87 for no sleep disorder and 0.93 for sleep disorder classes. The no-sleep disorder class achieved a higher recall rate of 0.95 against the sleep disorder class's 0.81, yet both classes showed balanced F1-scores of 0.91 and 0.87, respectively. The model's strong discriminative ability is confirmed by the receiver operating characteristic curve showcased in Fig. 1's right panel, which produces an area under the curve (AUC) value of 0.96, indicating exceptional classification performance. The evidence points to logistic Regression as a dependable tool for evaluating sleep disorder risks using specific physiological and demographic indicators.

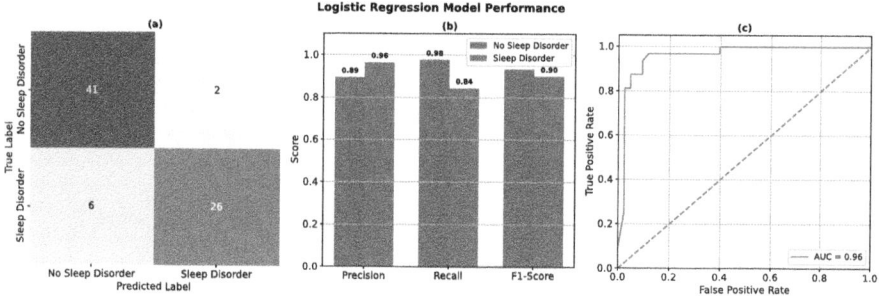

Fig. 4. Evaluation of Logistic Regression classifier. (a) Confusion Matrix; (b) Precision, Recall, F1-scores; (c) ROC Curve showing AUC = 0.96.

Figure 4 shows that logistic regression yields balanced performance across classes, with a particularly high AUC score of 0.96. The confusion matrix indicates a slight tendency toward false positives, while classification metrics suggest robust generalization capacity.

4.3   Decission Tree

The Decision Tree classifier demonstrated excellent predictive performance for sleep disorder classification, as illustrated in Fig. 2. he confusion matrix in the left panel displays how the model correctly recognized 41 subjects who do not have sleep disorders and 29 subjects with sleep disorders, while experiencing minimal errors with two false negatives and three false positives. According to the middle panel analysis, the precision metrics for both groups show excellent balanced classification performance between the no sleep disorder group at 0.93 and the sleep disorder group at 0.94. The model displayed excellent recall metrics for both class types, with scores of 0.95 for no sleep disorder and 0.91 for sleep disorder, which led to balanced F1-scores of 0.94 and 0.92, respectively. The ROC curve in the right panel demonstrates that the decision tree model has strong discriminative power with an AUC score of 0.93, significantly higher than random chance performance. The optimized decision tree algorithm offers a dependable and understandable method for assessing sleep disorder risk with selected physiological and demographic features.

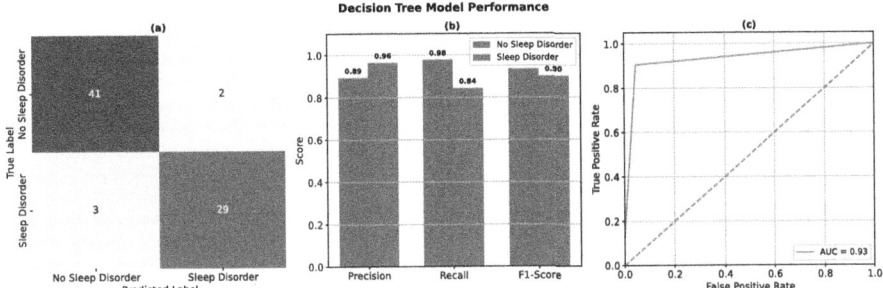

Fig. 5. Evaluation of Decision Tree classifier. (a) Confusion Matrix; (b) Class performance metrics; (c) ROC Curve with AUC = 0.93.

Figure 5 demonstrates the Decision Tree model's effectiveness in identifying sleep disorder status. he model shows excellent classification accuracy, with fewer misclassifications than logistic Regression. The AUC of 0.93 confirms reliable discriminative capacity.

4.4   Random Forest

The Random Forest algorithm demonstrated superior performance in sleep disorder classification. Figure 3 indicates that this ensemble learning approach delivered outstanding discriminative power across various evaluation metrics. The model has shown high accuracy through the confusion matrix in Fig. 3's left panel by correctly classifying 42 non-sleep disorder subjects and 27 sleep disorder subjects while maintaining minimal misclassification with one false negative and five false positives. The classification metrics analysis from Fig. 3, middle panel, demonstrates that different strengths complement each other across classes with a high precision of 0.96 in detecting sleep disorders and an excellent recall rate of 0.98 for the no sleep disorder class. The model achieved strong F1-scores of 0.93 and 0.90 for the two distinct classes. An AUC of 0.98 on the receiver operating characteristic curve (Fig. 3, right panel) demonstrates the model's outstanding capacity to separate classes, which approaches perfection in classification. The Random Forest ensemble method achieves dependable sleep disorder risk assessment by combining the predictive capabilities of numerous decision trees with selected physiological and demographic features.

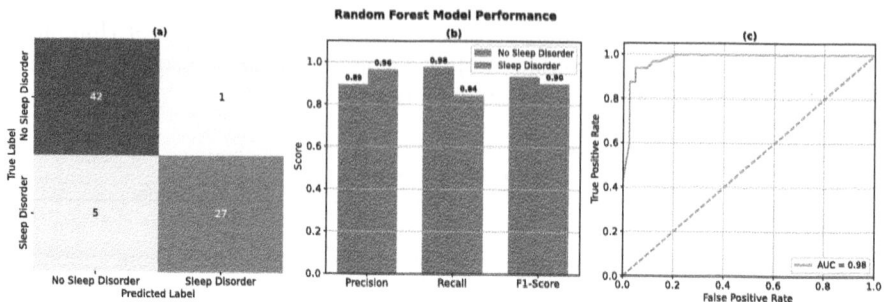

Fig. 6. Evaluation of Random Forest classifier. (a) Confusion Matrix; (b) Class-wise performance metrics; (c) ROC Curve with AUC = 0.98.

Figure 6 highlights the Random Forest model's superiority. It achieves the highest classification metrics across all models, with minimal false predictions. Its near-perfect AUC score of 0.98 confirms excellent reliability for clinical prediction use.

Table 2 presents the performance metrics of the three most effective models—Random Forest, Decision Tree, and Logistic Regression—after parameter tuning and final testing. All three models achieved high accuracy, F1-scores, and ROC AUC values, indicating strong predictive performance in classifying sleep disorder presence. The Random Forest model yielded the highest ROC AUC at 98.00%, demonstrating its superior ability to distinguish between classes. Although the Decision Tree and Logistic Regression models achieved the same accuracy of 94.38%, their F1-scores and ROC AUC values reveal nuanced differences: Decision Tree performed slightly better in F1-score (93.00%). At the same time, Logistic Regression showed stronger class separation with an ROC AUC of 96.00%. These findings confirm that ensemble methods and interpretable models can be effective, depending on the prioritized evaluation metric.

Table 2. Performance metrics of the top three optimized models

Model	Accuracy (%)	F1 Score (%)	ROC AUC (%)
Random Forest	94.38	91.5	98.0
Decision Tree	94.38	93.0	93.0
Logistic Regression	90.90	89.0	96.0

5   Discussion

This study examined the application of supervised machine learning algorithms to classify sleep disorders using the Sleep Health and Lifestyle Dataset. Through comprehensive data preprocessing, including cleaning, normalization, and feature selection via correlation analysis, we established a robust foundation for model training and evaluation. Three of the nine models assessed were selected for optimization based on their strong cross-validation performance: Random Forest, Decision Tree, and Logistic Regression.

The Random Forest classifier achieved the most reliable and accurate results, attaining an accuracy of 94.38%, an F1 score of 91.5%, and an outstanding ROC AUC of 98.0%. This ensemble learning architecture, which integrates multiple decision trees, allowed the model to maintain generalization capability while minimizing overfitting. These findings confirm the Random Forest's ability to be a dependable predictive model for sleep disorder risk in clinical screening contexts.

The Decision Tree model also demonstrated high predictive accuracy (94.38%) and a superior F1 score (93.0%), with a slightly lower ROC AUC score of 93.0%. Despite its performance being marginally behind that of Random Forest, its interpretable structure makes it highly suitable for healthcare applications that require transparency and explainability. The ability to visualize and trace decision paths based on key features (e.g., age, BMI category, and blood pressure) enhances the model's utility for practitioners.

Logistic Regression offered strong discriminative performance with an ROC AUC of 96.0%, though it trailed overall accuracy (90.90%) and F1 score (89.0%) compared to the tree-based models. However, its simplicity, interpretability, and efficiency make it a practical option for initial screenings or in settings where computational resources are limited.

Overall, our results reinforce the value of supervised machine learning in the early detection of sleep disorders using accessible physiological and lifestyle indicators. The ensemble-based Random Forest model stands out for its robustness and classification power, while Decision Tree and Logistic Regression remain valuable options depending on clinical and operational needs.

6   Conclusion

The study confirms that supervised machine learning techniques can accurately classify sleep disorders when applied to demographic and physiological information. The Random Forest algorithm achieved superior predictive accuracy and demonstrated strong performance metrics, making it the preferred choice for clinical implementation. Decision Trees provide a transparent option for situations that require clear interpretation, but Logistic Regression continues to be an applicable choice because of its strong classification power.

Future research plans should extend to include real-world clinical data in the dataset, assess more physiological indicators, and implement unsupervised analysis methods for detailed patient subgroup studies. Amm is conducting ongoing clinical study validations to demonstrate these predictive models' practical applicability and widespread relevance. s essential

Acknowledgments. The authors would like to thank the Department of Mathematics at Jacksonville University for their generous support and funding assistance for the conference registration. Their encouragement and resources made this research and its dissemination possible.

Conflict of Interest. The authors declare that there is no conflict of interest regarding the publication of this paper.

References

1. Aha, D.W., Kibler, D., Albert, M.K.: Instance-based learning algorithms. Mach. Learn. **6**(1), 37–66 (1991)
2. Alsammani, A., Gliske, S., Stacey, W.: Effect of sleep stage on high-frequency oscillations and artifacts. In: AES 2021 Annual Meeting Abstract Database. AESnet.org (2021), presented at the American Epilepsy Society Annual Meeting, November 22 (2021)
3. Alsammani, A., Stacey, W.C., Gliske, S.V.: Estimation of circular statistics in the presence of measurement bias. IEEE J. Biomed. Health Inform. **28**(2), 1089–1100 (2023)
4. Biswal, S., Sun, H., Goparaju, B., Westover, B.: An expert system for sleep apnea diagnosis using neural networks. J. Clin. Sleep Med. **14**(12), 2029–2040 (2018)
5. Breiman, L.: Random forests. Mach. Learn. **45**(1), 5–32 (2001)
6. Chattu, V.K., Manzar, M.D., Kumary, S., Burman, D., Spence, D.W., Pandi-Perumal, S.R.: The global problem of insufficient sleep and its serious public health implications. Healthcare **7**(1), 1 (2018)
7. Deo, R.C.: Machine learning in medicine. Circulation **132**(20), 1920–1930 (2015)
8. Diaz-Uriarte, R., Alvarez de Andres, S.: Gene selection and classification of microarray data using random forest. BMC Bioinform. **7**, 3 (2006)
9. Goldstein, C.A., Berry, R.B., Kent, D.T., Kristo, D.A., Seixas, A.A.: Artificial intelligence in sleep medicine: background and implications for clinicians. J. Clin. Sleep Med. **16**(4), 609–618 (2020)
10. Goldstein, C.A., et al.: Artificial intelligence in sleep medicine: background and implications for clinicians. J. Clin. Sleep Med. **16**(4), 609–618 (2020)
11. Kang, J., Kim, J., Lee, H.G., et al.: Support vector machines for the diagnosis of insomnia. Sensors **17**(7), 1502 (2017)
12. Kapur, V.K., et al.: Clinical practice guideline for diagnostic testing for adult obstructive sleep apnea: an American academy of sleep medicine clinical practice guideline. J. Clin. Sleep Med. **13**(3), 479–504 (2017)
13. Khosla, A., et al.: Automated detection of sleep disorders using machine learning algorithms. J. Clin. Sleep Med. **14**(8), 1423–1430 (2018)
14. Liu, Y., et al.: Systematic analysis of long non-coding RNAs and mRNAs in the ovaries of Duroc pigs during different follicular stages using rna sequencing. Int. J. Mol. Sci. **19**(6), 1722 (2018)
15. Malhotra, A., Ayappa, I., Ayas, N., et al.: Diagnostic accuracy and limitations of polysomnography. Chest **153**(2), 333–340 (2018)
16. Mostafa, S.S., Mendonça, F., G. Ravelo-García, A., Morgado-Dias, F.: A systematic review of detecting sleep apnea using deep learning. Sensors **19**(22), 4934 (2019)
17. Sateia, M.J.: International classification of sleep disorders-third edition: highlights and modifications. Chest **146**(5), 1387–1394 (2014)

18. Tharmalingam, L.: Sleep health and lifestyle dataset. Kaggle. https://www.kaggle. com/datasets/uom190346a/sleep-health-andlifestyle-dataset. Accessed 8 Feb 2024 (2023)
19. Ting, H., Mai, Y.T., Hsu, H.C., Wu, H.C., Tseng, M.H.: Decision tree based diagnostic system for moderate to severe obstructive sleep apnea. J. Med. Syst. **38**, 1–10 (2014)

Totally Greedy Sequences Defined by Second-Order Linear Recurrences With Constant Coefficients

Hebert Pérez-Rosés(✉) ⓘ

Department of Computer Science and Mathematics, Universitat Rovira i Virgili, Tarragona, Spain
hebert.perez@urv.cat

Abstract. The change-making problem consists of representing a certain amount of money with the least possible number of coins, from a given, pre-established set of denominations. The greedy algorithm works by choosing the coins of largest possible denomination first. This greedy strategy does not always produce the least number of coins, except when the set of denominations obeys certain properties. We call a set of denominations with these properties a greedy set. If the set of denominations is an infinite sequence, we call it totally greedy if every prefix subset is greedy. In this paper we investigate some totally greedy sequences arising from second-order linear recurrences with constant coefficients, as well as their subsequences, and we prove sufficient conditions under which these sequences are totally greedy.

Keywords: Change-making problem · greedy algorithm · greedy number sequences · linear recurrences

1 Greedy and Totally Greedy Sets

In the *money-changing problem*, or *change-making problem*, we have a set of coin denominations $S = \{s_1 = 1, s_2, \ldots, s_t\}$, with $s_1 < \ldots < s_t$. We also have a target amount k, and the goal is to make k using as few coins as possible. Mathematically, we are looking for a *payment vector* $(a_1, \ldots, a_t)$, such that

$$a_i \in \mathbb{N}_0 \quad \text{for all } i = 1, \ldots, t \tag{1}$$

$$\sum_{i=1}^{t} a_i s_i = k, \tag{2}$$

$$\sum_{i=1}^{t} a_i \text{ is minimal,} \tag{3}$$

where $\mathbb{N}_0$ denotes the set of nonnegative integers.

This problem has been extensively studied in recent years (see for instance [1–4,16]), and it bears some relationships to other Diophantine-like problems, such as the *Frobenius problem* and the *postage stamp problem* [14]. It is also a special case of the well known *knapsack problem* [7].

O. Gervasi et al. (Eds.): ICCSA 2025, LNCS 15648, pp. 122–139, 2025.
https://doi.org/10.1007/978-3-031-97000-9_8

In regard to its computational complexity, finding the optimal payment vector for a given k is NP-hard if the coins are large and represented in binary (or decimal). This result was stated by Lueker in a technical report [6], and it has been cited many times, although the report itself is not available on the Internet.

One approach for dealing with the problem is the *greedy algorithm*, which proceeds by always choosing in the first place the coin of the largest possible denomination. The pseudocode of the greedy method is given in Algorithm 1:

Algorithm 1: GREEDY PAYMENT METHOD

    Input   : The set of denominations $S = \{1, s_2, \ldots, s_t\}$, with
                  $1 < s_2 < \ldots < s_t$, and a target amount $k \geq 0$.
    Output: Payment vector $\mathbf{a} = (a_1, a_2, \ldots, a_t)$.

1 **for** $i := t$ **downto** 1 **do**
2      $a_i := k$ div s_i;
3      $k := k$ mod s_i;
4   **if** $k = 0$ **then**
5 | **return** a
6   **end**
7 **end**

Definition 1. *For a given set of denominations* $S = 1, s_2, \ldots, s_t$, *the* greedy payment vector *is the payment vector* $(a_1, a_2, \ldots, a_t)$ *produced by Algorithm 1, and* $\text{GREEDYCOST}_S(k) = \sum_{i=1}^{t} a_i$.

The greedy payment vector is not necessarily optimal ($\text{GREEDYCOST}_S(k)$ is not always minimal among all possible payment vectors) but there exist some sets of denominations S for which we can guarantee that the greedy payment vector is indeed optimal.

Example 1. Let $S_1 = \{1, 4, 6\}$ and $S_2 = \{1, 2, 5\}$ be two sets of denominations, and suppose that we want to represent the quantity $k = 8$. The greedy payment vector obtained by Algorithm 1 with S_1 is $(2, 0, 1)$, and $\text{GREEDYCOST}_{S_1}(8) = 3$. This is obviously not optimal, since we can easily find a better way to represent the quantity 8, namely $8 = 4 + 4$, which uses only two coins.

On the other hand, with the set S_2, the greedy payment vector is $(1, 1, 1)$, and $\text{GREEDYCOST}_{S_2}(8)$ is also equal to 3. However, in this case the greedy payment vector is optimal, i.e. it is impossible to find a representation of 8 using fewer coins of S_2. In fact, it can be proved that with the set S_2, the greedy payment vector is *always* optimal for *any* quantity k.

Definition 2. *If a set S of denominations* always *produces an* optimal payment vector *for* any *given amount k, then S is called* orderly, canonical, *or* greedy.

Besides being interesting in their own right, greedy sets have a variety of potential applications. They can be used, for instance, to construct circulant networks with efficient routing algorithms [10].

There is a polynomial-time algorithm that determines whether a given set of denominations is greedy [9,14], as well as plenty of necessary or sufficient conditions for special families of denomination sets [1,2,4,16]. The current paper proceeds precisely along the latter direction. The paper is an extension of [11], containing significant additions. We have omitted some of the proofs in order to comply with the page limits and other guidelines of the conference. The missing proofs can be consulted at [11]. A full version of the paper, including all the proofs, can be found in [12].

Obviously, a set S consisting of one or two denominations is always greedy. For sets of cardinal 3 we have the following characterization [1]:

Proposition 1. *The set $S = \{1, a, b\}$ (with $a < b$) is greedy if, and only if, $b - a$ belongs to the set*

$$\mathfrak{D}(a) = \{a - 1, a\} \cup \{2a - 2, 2a - 1, 2a\} \cup \ldots \{ma - m, \ldots ma\} \cup \ldots =$$
$$= \bigcup_{m=1}^{\infty} \bigcup_{s=0}^{m} \{ma - s\}$$

□

The most powerful necessary and sufficient condition is given by the so-called *one-point theorem* (see Theorem 2.1 [1]). Here we state it in a modified form:

Theorem 1. *Suppose that $S = \{1, s_2, \ldots, s_t\}$ is a greedy set of denominations, and $s_{t+1} > s_t$. Now let $m = \left\lceil \dfrac{s_{t+1}}{s_t} \right\rceil$. Then $\hat{S} = \{1, s_2, \ldots, s_t, s_{t+1}\}$ is greedy if, and only if, $\text{GREEDYCOST}_S(ms_t - s_{t+1}) < m$.*

□

Notice that

$$(m - 1)s_t + 1 \leq s_{t+1} \leq ms_t,$$

by the definition of m. A straightforward consequence of the one-point theorem is the following

Corollary 1. *[Lemma 7.4 of [1]] Suppose that $S = \{1, s_2, \ldots, s_t\}$ is a greedy set, and $s_{t+1} = us_t$, for some $u \in \mathbb{N}$. Then $\hat{S} = \{1, s_2, \ldots, s_t, s_{t+1}\}$ is also greedy.*

□

Definition 3. *A set $S = \{1, s_2, \ldots, s_t\}$ is totally greedy[1] if every prefix subset $\{1, s_2, \ldots, s_k\}$, with $k \leq t$ is greedy.*

Obviously, a totally greedy set is also greedy, but the converse is not true in general. Take, for instance, the greedy set $\{1, 2, 5, 6, 10\}$, whose prefix subset $\{1, 2, 5, 6\}$ is not greedy.

Definition 3 can be extended to infinite sequences in a straightforward way:

---

[1] Also called normal, or totally orderly.

Definition 4. *Let* $S = \{s_n\}_{n=1}^{\infty}$ *be an integer sequence, with* $s_1 = 1$ *and* $s_i < s_{i+1}$ *for all* $i \in \mathbb{N}$. *We say that* S *is* totally greedy *(or simply, greedy) if every prefix subset* $\{1, s_2, \ldots, s_k\}$ *is greedy.*

Totally greedy sequences are mentioned very briefly in [4], where some sufficient conditions are also given, that allow to construct greedy sequences from recurrence relations, although the conditions are a bit cumbersome (see Corollary 2.12 of [4]). In this paper we provide a simpler set of sufficient conditions that produce greedy sequences from second-order recurrences, and we also investigate some properties of these sequences and their sub-sequences. Unlike previous results, which are mainly based on combinatorial arguments, we will use a mix of analytic and combinatorial techniques that can be easily extended to other types of recurrences. We focus mainly on homogenous recurrences, though we also make some comments on the non-homogenous case.

2   Sequences of the Form $G_{n+2} = pG_{n+1} + qG_n$

In this section will consider sequences $\{G_n\}_{n=1}^{\infty}$ generated by the recurrence

$$G_n = \begin{cases} 1 & \text{if } n = 1, \\ a & \text{if } n = 2, \\ pG_{n-1} + qG_{n-2}, & \text{if } n > 2, \end{cases} \tag{4}$$

where a, p, q are positive integers, with $a > 1$, and some additional restrictions that we will see later on.

Note that the (shifted) Fibonacci sequence $\{F_n\}_{n=1}^{\infty}$, defined by $F_0 = 0$, $F_1 = 1$, and $F_n = F_{n-1} + F_{n-2}$, is a very special case of Eq. 4, namely, when $a = p = q = 1$. Equation 4 also generalizes the Lucas numbers (Sequence A000032 of [8]), the Pell numbers (Sequence A000129 of [8]), and other special cases of Horadam-type sequences.

The parameter a in Eq. 4 acts as a 'perturbation' with respect to the 'regular' sequence

$$H_n = \begin{cases} 1 & \text{if } n = 1, \\ p & \text{if } n = 2, \\ pH_{n-1} + qH_{n-2}, & \text{if } n > 2. \end{cases} \tag{5}$$

Albeit small, this perturbation has a significant impact on the greediness of $\{G_n\}_{n=1}^{\infty}$, and it also affects other properties of the sequence. We *need* to introduce the parameter a, for reasons that will become apparent in Sect. 4.

Anyway, the characteristic polynomial associated with Eq. 4 is $x^2 - px - q$, with roots

$$\lambda = \frac{1}{2} \left(p + \sqrt{p^2 + 4q} \right), \qquad \mu = \frac{1}{2} \left(p - \sqrt{p^2 + 4q} \right), \tag{6}$$

so that $\mu + \lambda = p$ and $\mu\lambda = -q$. Since the roots λ and μ are real and distinct, the general term of $\{G_n\}_{n=1}^{\infty}$ is

$$G_{n+1} = c_1\lambda^n + c_2\mu^n, \tag{7}$$

where $c_1 = \dfrac{a - \mu}{\lambda - \mu}$ and $c_2 = \dfrac{\lambda - a}{\lambda - \mu}$.

Obviously, $\{G_n\}_{n=1}^{\infty}$ is monotonically increasing and $|\lambda| > |\mu|$. Moreover, $\lambda > p$ and $\mu < 0$. If $q \le p$ we can bound the roots λ and μ with more precision.

Lemma 1. *If $\{G_n\}_{n=1}^{\infty}$ is a sequence defined by Eq. 4, with $q \le p$, and λ and μ are the roots of the characteristic polynomial, as defined in Eq. 6, then*

$$-1 < \mu < 0 \quad \text{and} \quad p < \lambda < p + 1.$$

□

Note that as a consequence of the above results, c_1 is always positive, while c_2 can be positive or negative, depending on a. In the rest of the paper, sequences that obey Eq. 4, with $q \le p$, will also be called *type-1-sequences*.

Type-1-sequences were already investigated in [11]. In this section we make a brief review of the results contained in [11], omitting the proofs for the sake of brevity.

Let's denote the prefix set $\{1, G_2, \ldots, G_k\}$ of $\{G_n\}_{n=1}^{\infty}$ by $G^{(k)}$. We know that $G^{(2)} = \{1, a\}$ is always greedy. Regarding $G^{(3)}$ we have:

Lemma 2. *Let $\{G_n\}_{n=1}^{\infty}$ be a type-1-sequence, then $G^{(3)} = \{1, a, pa + q\}$ is (totally) greedy if, and only if, $2 \le a \le p + q$.*

□

The main result of [11] (and this section) is:

Theorem 2. *Let $\{G_n\}_{n=1}^{\infty}$ be a type-1-sequence with $2 \le a \le p + q$. Then $\{G_n\}_{n=1}^{\infty}$ is totally greedy.*

□

The proof of Theorem 2 is done by induction, where the base case is provided by Lemma 2. Then we move from one prefix $G^{(k)}$ to $G^{(k+1)}$ with the aid of Theorem 1.

Theorem 2 can be applied to some known sequences, for instance:

Corollary 2. *Consider the following sequences:*

- $\{F_n\}_{n=1}^{\infty} = \{1, 2, 3, 5, 8, 13, \ldots\}$ *(shifted Fibonacci numbers)*
- $\{P_n\}_{n=1}^{\infty} = \{1, 2, 5, 12, 29, 70 \ldots\}$ *(shifted Pell numbers)*

Then, $\{F_n\}_{n=1}^{\infty}$ and $\{P_n\}_{n=1}^{\infty}$ are totally greedy.

□

If $q > p$ we can no longer guarantee that $\{G_n\}_{n=1}^{\infty}$ is totally greedy. Take for instance the (shifted) Jacobstahl numbers: $\{\mathcal{J}_n\}_{n=2}^{\infty} = \{1, 3, 5, 11, 21, 43, 85 \ldots\}$, defined by $\mathcal{J}_0 = 0$, $\mathcal{J}_1 = 1$, and $\mathcal{J}_n = \mathcal{J}_{n-1} + 2\mathcal{J}_{n-2}$. Indeed, $\left\lceil \dfrac{\mathcal{J}_7}{\mathcal{J}_6} \right\rceil = 3 = m$, but $3 \cdot 21 - 43 = 20$, and $\text{GREEDYCOST}_{\mathcal{J}^{(6)}}(20) = 4 > m$. Hence, $\mathcal{J}^{(7)} = \{1, 3, 5, 11, 21, 43\}$ is not greedy, and $\{\mathcal{J}_n\}_{n=2}^{\infty}$ is not totally greedy. Intuitively, the problem here seems to be the largest root $\lambda = 2$, which is an integer, while the ratio $\dfrac{\mathcal{J}_{k+1}}{\mathcal{J}_k}$ approaches λ from above and below, and hence sometimes $\left\lceil \dfrac{\mathcal{J}_{k+1}}{\mathcal{J}_k} \right\rceil = 3$.

2.1   The Non-homogenous Case

Let us now consider sequences $\{T_n\}_{n=1}^{\infty}$ defined by the non-homogenous recurrence relation

$$T_n = \begin{cases} 1 & \text{if } n = 1, \\ a & \text{if } n = 2, \\ pT_{n-1} + qT_{n-2} \pm r, & \text{if } n > 2, \end{cases} \tag{8}$$

where a, p, q, r are positive integers.

By subtracting $T_n = pT_{n-1} + qT_{n-2} \pm r$ from $T_{n+1} = pT_n + qT_{n-1} \pm r$, we get the homogenous third-order recurrence $T_{n+1} = (p+1)T_n + (q-p)T_{n-1} - qT_{n-2}$, with characteristic equation $x^3 - (p+1)x^2 + (p-q)x + q = 0$. The roots of this characteristic equation are the same λ and μ of Eq. 6, plus the additional root $\xi = 1$. Hence, the general term of the sequence is

$$T_n = c_1\lambda^n + c_2\mu^n + c_3, \tag{9}$$

for some constants c_1, c_2, c_3.

By proceeding as in the homogenous case, we get that

$$\lim_{n \to \infty} \frac{T_{n+1}}{T_n} = \lambda, \tag{10}$$

which lies in the interval $(p, p+1)$, provided that $q \leq p$. In [11] we have proved the following result (see Corollary 10 of [11]):

Lemma 3. Let $\{G_n\}_{n=1}^{\infty}$ be a type-1-sequence. Then there exists an integer $2 \leq K_0 \leq 3$ such that for all $n \geq K_0$ we have

$$\frac{G_{n+1}}{G_n} \in (p, p+1) \tag{11}$$

From this, we can prove the following result, as a weaker version of Theorem 2:

Proposition 2. Let $\{T_n\}_{n=1}^{\infty}$ be a sequence defined by Eq. 8, with $q \leq p$. Let K_0 be the integer described in Corollary 3, and suppose that $K_0 \geq 3$, and the set $\{1, T_2, \ldots, T_{K_0}\}$ is greedy. Then $\{T_n\}_{n=1}^{\infty}$ is totally greedy.

Proof: The proof is similar to that of Theorem 2.

□

In order to strengthen Proposition 2 we would have to make a detailed analysis of the sequence $\{T_n\}_{n=1}^{\infty}$, as we did for type-1 sequences. However, this will be deferred for future work.

3   Sequences of the Form $J_{n+2} = pJ_{n+1} - qJ_n$

We will now consider sequences $\{J_n\}_{n=1}^{\infty}$ generated by the recurrence

$$J_n = \begin{cases} 1 \text{ if } n = 1, \\ a \text{ if } n = 2, \\ pJ_{n-1} - qJ_{n-2}, \text{ if } n > 2, \end{cases} \tag{12}$$

where a, p, q are integers, with $p, q > 0$ and $a > 1$.

Recurrences defined by Eq. 12 are intimately related with the type-1 sequences that we have just seen in Sect. 2. This phenomenon was already noticed in the case of Fibonacci numbers in [13,15], and we will take a deeper look at it in Sect. 4. A special case of Eq. 12 is investigated in [5] under the name *d-sequences*.

The characteristic polynomial associated with this recurrence is $x^2 - px + q$, with roots

$$\lambda = \frac{1}{2}\left(p + \sqrt{p^2 - 4q}\right), \qquad \mu = \frac{1}{2}\left(p - \sqrt{p^2 - 4q}\right), \tag{13}$$

so that $p = \mu + \lambda$ and $q = \mu\lambda$.

If λ and μ are real and distinct, then the general term of $\{J_n\}_{n=1}^{\infty}$ is

$$J_n = c_1 \lambda^{n-1} + c_2 \mu^{n-1}, \tag{14}$$

where $c_1 = \dfrac{a - \mu}{\lambda - \mu}$ and $c_2 = \dfrac{\lambda - a}{\lambda - \mu}$.

The roots (13) are distinct and real if, and only if $q < \dfrac{p^2}{4}$.

As in Sect. 2, we are interested in a subclass of the sequences defined by Eq. 12, namely those with $1 \le q < p - 1$, which henceforth will be called *type-2-sequences*. The condition $1 \le q \le p - 2$ implies $q < \dfrac{p^2}{4}$, and it also implies that the dominant root $\lambda > 1$, so that the sequence $\{J_n\}_{n=1}^{\infty}$ is monotonically increasing. Additionally, we can see that $0 < \mu < 1$, which means that λ cannot be an integer.

In fact, we can bound the root λ even further:

Lemma 4. *If $\{J_n\}_{n=1}^{\infty}$ is a type-2-sequence, and λ and μ are the roots of the characteristic polynomial, as defined in Eq. 13, then $p - 1 < \lambda < p$.*

Proof: The proof is straightforward and is omitted here.

□

As before, in order to apply Theorem 1 we have to investigate the ratio

$$\frac{J_{n+1}}{J_n} = \frac{c_1 \lambda^n + c_2 \mu^n}{c_1 \lambda^{n-1} + c_2 \mu^{n-1}} \tag{15}$$

Dividing the numerator and the denominator by λ^n we get

$$\lim_{n \to \infty} \frac{J_{n+1}}{J_n} = \lambda \in (p-1, p). \tag{16}$$

In type-2 sequences we are also interested in the behaviour of the subsequences of $\left\{ \frac{J_{n+1}}{J_n} \right\}$, and how they approach the limit value λ.

Lemma 5. *Let* $\left\{ J_n \right\}_{n=1}^{\infty}$ *be a type-2-sequence. If* $a < \lambda$ *(respectively* $a > \lambda$*) then the sequence* $\left\{ \frac{J_{n+1}}{J_n} \right\}_{n=1}^{\infty}$ *is monotonically increasing (respectively decreasing).*

Proof: We will now investigate the difference

$$\frac{J_{n+1}}{J_n} - \frac{J_{n+2}}{J_{n+1}} = \frac{J_{n+1}^2 - J_n J_{n+2}}{J_n J_{n+1}}. \tag{17}$$

Since the denominator $J_n J_{n+1} > 0$, the sign of Eq. 17 depends on the numerator

$$J_{n+1}^2 - J_n J_{n+2} = c_1 c_2 \lambda^{n-1} \mu^{n-1} \left(2\lambda\mu - \lambda^2 - \mu^2 \right). \tag{18}$$

The factors $c_1, \lambda^{n-1}, \mu^{n-1}$ are positive, while $2\lambda\mu - \lambda^2 - \mu^2 = 4q - p^2$ is negative. Hence, the sign of (18) depends solely on $c_2 = \dfrac{\lambda - a}{\lambda - \mu}$. The rest is straightforward.

□

From Lemmas 4 and 5 we get

Lemma 6. *Let* $\left\{ J_n \right\}_{n=1}^{\infty}$ *be a type-2 sequence. Then there exists an integer* $1 < K_0 \leq 4$ *such that for all* $n \geq K_0$ *we have*

$$\frac{J_{n+1}}{J_n} \in (p-1, p). \tag{19}$$

In particular, if $a > \dfrac{q}{2}$ *then* $K_0 \leq 3$, *and if* $a > q$, *then* $K_0 = 2$.

Proof: The existence of K_0 follows directly from Lemmas 4 and 5, so we only have to verify the bounds.

In the case $a > q$ it is easy to verify that $\dfrac{J_3}{J_2} \in (p-1, p)$. In the case $a > \dfrac{q}{2}$ we have to check that $\dfrac{J_4}{J_3} \in (p-1, p)$, which is equivalent to $\dfrac{qa}{pa-q} < 1$, which in turn amounts to $pa - q - qa > 0$. But since $p \geq q + 2$ we get $pa - q - qa \geq 2a - q > 0$, as desired.

Consequently, we are left with the case $2 \leq a \leq \frac{q}{2}$, $4 \leq q \leq p - 2$, whence $p \geq 6$. In order to prove that $K_0 \leq 4$ in this case, we have to check that $\frac{J_5}{J_4} = p - q\frac{J_3}{J_4} \in (p - 1, p)$, which is tantamount to proving that $q\frac{J_3}{J_4} < 1$, which in turn amounts to $p^2 a - pq - qa - pqa + q^2 > 0$.

Now, to prove this inequality we can use standard techniques from multivariable Calculus. Let us fix p and investigate the (continuous) bivariate polynomial $F_p(q, a) = p^2 a - pq - qa - pqa + q^2$ in the triangular region $T = \{(q, a) \in \mathbb{R}^2 : 4 \leq q \leq p - 2, 2 \leq a \leq \frac{q}{2}\}$. Since T is closed and bounded, and $F_p(q, a)$ is continuous everywhere in $\mathbb{R}^2$, then by the Weierstrass extreme value theorem $F_p(q, a)$ achieves its maximum and minimum values in T. Then we only have to check that the minimum value is positive.

Let us first find the stationary points of $F_p(q, a)$ in $\mathbb{R}^2$. We compute the partial derivatives and equate them to zero:

$$\frac{\partial F_p}{\partial q} = -p - a - pa + 2q = 0$$

$$\frac{\partial F_p}{\partial a} = p^2 - q - pq = 0.$$

By solving the first equation for a we get $a = \frac{2q - p}{p + 1}$ (note that $p \neq -1$). By solving the second equation for q we get $q = \frac{p^2}{p + 1}$. We can then substitute $\frac{p^2}{p + 1}$ for q in the expression of a to get $a = \frac{p(p - 1)}{(p + 1)^2}$.

Hence, the only stationary point is $\left(\frac{p^2}{p + 1}, \frac{p(p - 1)}{(p + 1)^2}\right)$. However, it is not difficult to verify that this point does not belong to T, since $\frac{p^2}{p + 1} < p - 2$ implies $p \leq -2$.

So, let us now investigate the boundary of T (including its vertices as a special case). To begin with we can substitute $\frac{q}{2}$ for a in the expression of $F_p(q, a)$, and we get the function

$$\hat{F}_{p,1}(q) = \frac{1}{2}(1 - p)q^2 + \left(\frac{1}{2}p^2 - p\right)q,$$

which only depends on q. Solving

$$\hat{F}'_{p,1}(q) = (1 - p)q + \frac{1}{2}p^2 - p = 0,$$

we get $q = \frac{\frac{1}{2}p^2 - p}{p - 1}$. Instead of trying to find out if this point lies in T, we can check that $\hat{F}''_{p,1}(q) = (1 - p) < 0$, which means that this point is a local maximum, and therefore irrelevant for our purposes.

Next we check the side $q = p - 2$. After the substitution we get the function

$$\hat{F}_{p,2}(a) = pa - 2p + 2a + 4,$$

whose derivative is $\hat{F}'_{p,2}(a) = p + 2$, which means that $\hat{F}_{p,2}(a)$ does not have any stationary points.

On the side $a = 2$ we get the function

$$\hat{F}_{p,3}(q) = 2p^2 + q^2 - 3pq - 2q.$$

Solving

$$\hat{F}'_{p,3}(q) = 2q - 3p - 2 = 0,$$

we get $q = \dfrac{3}{2}p - 1$, which also falls without T.

Thus, we are only left with the vertices of T as potential minima. Namely,

$$F_p(p - 2, 2) = 8,$$

$$F_p\left(p - 2, \frac{p - 2}{2}\right) = \frac{1}{2}(p - 2)^2 = \frac{1}{2}q^2 > 0,$$

$$F_p(4, 2) = p^2 - 6p + 4 = \left(p - (3 - \sqrt{5})\right)\left(p - (3 + \sqrt{5})\right) > 0 \text{ for } p \geq 6.$$

Consequently, $\dfrac{J_5}{J_4} \in (p - 1, p)$ for $p \geq 6$, as desired.

□

The next lemma establishes the bounds for $\dfrac{J_4}{J_3}$ in the worst case of Lemma 6, i.e. when $K_0 = 4$, so that $\dfrac{J_5}{J_4} \in (p - 1, p)$ but $\dfrac{J_4}{J_3} \notin (p - 1, p)$.

Lemma 7. Let $\{J_n\}_{n=1}^{\infty}$ be a type-2 sequence. Suppose also that the number K_0 described in Lemma 6 is equal to 4. Then, $\dfrac{J_4}{J_3} \in (p - 2, p - 1]$.

Proof: Recall from Lemma 6 that, if $a > \dfrac{q}{2}$ then $K_0 \leq 3$, hence the condition $K_0 = 4$ implies $a \leq \dfrac{q}{2}$. That means our sequence $\left\{\dfrac{J_{n+1}}{J_n}\right\}$ is monotonically increasing, by Lemma 5.

Thus, we already know that $\dfrac{J_4}{J_3} < p$ but $\dfrac{J_4}{J_3} \notin (p - 1, p)$, so we only have to prove that $\dfrac{J_4}{J_3} > p - 2$. Now,

$$\frac{J_4}{J_3} = p - q\frac{J_2}{J_3} = p - \frac{qa}{pa - q},$$

and

$$p - \frac{qa}{pa - q} > p - 2 \quad \text{iff} \quad \frac{qa}{pa - q} < 2$$

$$\text{iff} \quad 2pa - 2q - pa > 0.$$

For proving the latter inequality we can use the same technique that we used in the proof of Lemma 6, i.e. we fix p and we define the two-variable function $F_p(q, a) = 2pa - 2q - pa$. Then we can look for the minimum value of $F_p(q, a)$ over the triangular region $T = \{(q, a) \in \mathbb{R}^2 : 4 \leq q \leq p - 2, 2 \leq a \leq \frac{q}{2}\}$. Finally we just have to check that this minimum is positive.

So, let us first find the stationary points of $F_p(q, a)$ in $\mathbb{R}^2$. We compute the partial derivatives and equate them to zero:

$$\frac{\partial F_p}{\partial q} = -2 - a = 0$$

$$\frac{\partial F_p}{\partial a} = 2p - q = 0.$$

The only solution of this system is the point $(2p, -2)$, which is not in T. Hence, we just need to look at the boundary of T (including its vertices as a special case).

To begin with we can substitute $\frac{q}{2}$ for a in the expression of $F_p(q, a)$, and we get the function

$$\hat{F}_{p,1}(q) = pq - 2q - \frac{1}{2}q^2,$$

which only depends on q. Then we set

$$\hat{F}'_{p,1}(q) = p - 2 - q = 0.$$

It turns out that the solution to the previous equation, the point $\left(p - 2, \frac{p - 2}{2}\right)$, is a vertex of T; we will check all the vertices at the end. Next we check the side $q = p - 2$. After the substitution we get the function

$$\hat{F}_{p,2}(a) = 2pa - 2p - ap + 2a + 4,$$

whose derivative is $\hat{F}'_{p,2}(a) = p + 2$, which can only be zero if $p = -2$.

On the side $a = 2$ we get the function

$$\hat{F}_{p,3}(q) = 4p - 4q,$$

with constant derivative $\hat{F}'_{p,3}(q) = -4$, which means that there are no stationary points on this side either.

Thus, we are only left with the vertices of T as potential minima. Namely,

$$F_p(p - 2, 2) = 8,$$

$$F_p\left(p - 2, \frac{p - 2}{2}\right) = \frac{1}{2}p^2 - 2p + 2 = \frac{1}{2}(p - 2)^2 = \frac{1}{2}q^2 > 0,$$

$$F_p(4, 2) = 4p - 16 > 0 \text{ for } p > 4.$$

Consequently, $\frac{J_4}{J_3} \in (p - 2, p - 1]$ as desired.

☐

The approach we have used in proving the inequalities of Lemmas 6 and 7 might not be as elegant as an ad hoc argument, and is probably not the shortest route to the proof, but on the other hand, it is easy to extend to other inequalities, and exhibits nicely the interplay between Analysis and Combinatorics.

Next we continue the study of the worst-case sequences, and in particular, we turn our attention to the prefix set $\{1, J_2, J_3, J_4\}$, whose quotients $\frac{J_{k+1}}{J_k}$ lie outside $(p-1, p)$.

As in Sect. 2, let's denote the prefix set $\{1, J_2, \ldots, J_k\}$ by $J^{(k)}$.

Lemma 8. *Let $\{J_n\}_{n=1}^{\infty}$ be a type-2 sequence. Then the prefix set $J^{(4)}$ is (totally) greedy.*

Proof: Let us first check that $J^{(3)}$ is greedy. By Proposition 1, the set $J^{(3)} = \{1, a, pa - q\}$ is greedy iff the difference $pa - q - a = (p-1)a - q$ belongs to the set

$$\mathfrak{D}(a) = \{a - 1, a\} \cup \{2a - 2, 2a - 1, 2a\} \cup \ldots \{ma - m, \ldots ma\} \cup \ldots,$$

i.e. iff $0 \le q \le p - 1$, but $0 < q \le p - 2$ by the assumptions.

By Lemma 6, either $K_0 \le 3$ or $K_0 = 4$. If $K_0 \le 3$, then $m = \left\lceil \frac{J_4}{J_3} \right\rceil = p$. Therefore,

$$pJ_3 - J_4 = pJ_3 - (pJ_3 - q.I_2) = qJ_2,$$

and $\text{GREEDYCOST}_{J^{(3)}}(qJ_2) = q < p - 1 < m$.

Now, in the case $K_0 = 4$ we know that $a \le \frac{q}{2}$. We also know, by Lemma 7, that $\frac{J_4}{J_3} \in (p - 2, p - 1]$, hence $\left\lceil \frac{J_4}{J_3} \right\rceil = p - 1$. It is trivial to check that the condition $\frac{J_4}{J_3} \le p - 1$ is equivalent to $qa - pa + q \ge 0$, which in turn implies $a \le \frac{q}{p - q} \le \frac{q}{2}$.

Coincidentally, in order to prove that $J^{(4)}$ is greedy we have to compute $\text{GREEDYCOST}_{J^{(3)}}((p-1)J_3 - J_4) = \text{GREEDYCOST}_{J^{(3)}}(qa - pa + q)$. There are two possible cases for $qa - pa + q$:

$$0 \le qa - pa + q < J_2 = a$$
$$a \le qa - pa + q < J_3 = pa - q,$$

which translate to

$$\frac{q}{p - q} \ge a > \frac{q}{p - q + 1} \quad \text{and} \quad \frac{q}{p - q + 1} \ge a > \frac{2q}{2p - q},$$

respectively. Note that a hypothetical third case, $pa - q \le qa - pa + q < J_4 = p^2 a - pq - qa$, is impossible, for it would imply $\frac{2q}{2p - q} \ge 2$, which would mean that $q \ge p$.

So, in the first case $\text{GREEDYCOST}_{J^{(3)}}(qa - pa + q) = qa - pa + q < a \leq \dfrac{q}{p-q} < p - 1$.

In the second case $qa - pa + q = qa - pa + q'a + r = (q - p + q')a + r$, where q' is the quotient of the integer division of q by a, and $0 \leq r < a$ is the remainder. So, $\text{GREEDYCOST}_{J^{(3)}}((q - p + q')a + r) = q - p + q' + r$. Now, recall that $a \geq 2$, hence $q' \leq \dfrac{q}{2}$. Additionally, $r < a \leq \dfrac{q}{2}$ (in fact, $a \leq \dfrac{q}{p-q+1} < \dfrac{q}{2}$) and $q \leq p - 2$. Combining these inequalities we get $q - p + q' + r < p - 4$.

$\square$

Now we are ready to prove the main result of this section:

Theorem 3. *Let $\{J_n\}_{n=1}^{\infty}$ be a type-2 sequence, i.e. a sequence defined by Eq. 12, with $q < p - 1$. Then $\{J_n\}_{n=1}^{\infty}$ is totally greedy.*

Proof: We prove the theorem by induction. The base case is guaranteed by Lemma 8, which states that $J^{(4)}$ is (totally) greedy. So, let's suppose that $J^{(k)}$ is totally greedy for some arbitrary $k \geq 4$, and let's prove that $J^{(k+1)}$ is also greedy (and hence totally greedy).

By Lemmas 4 – 6 we know that $p - 1 < \dfrac{J_{k+1}}{J_k} < p$, so $m = \left\lceil \dfrac{J_{k+1}}{J_k} \right\rceil = p$. Now,

$$pJ_k - J_{k+1} = pJ_k - (pJ_k - qJ_{k-1}) = qJ_{k-1}.$$

Finally, $\text{GREEDYCOST}_{J^{(k)}}(qJ_{k-1}) = q < p - 1 < m$.

$\square$

In summary, we have verified that type-2 sequences are totally greedy, regardless of a, although this fact is harder to prove than the corresponding property of type-1 sequences. In any case, this property of type-2 sequences will turn out to be very useful in Sect. 4, where we analyze the subsequences of both type-1 and type-2 sequences.

Unfortunately, Theorem 3 does not seem to have a straightforward generalization to the non-homogenous case, as Theorem 2 does. Take for instance the non-homogenous sequence $\{T_n\}_{n=1}^{\infty}$ defined by the equation

$$T_n = 3T_{n-1} - T_{n-2} + 2 \quad \text{for } n > 2, \quad \text{with } T_1 = 1 \text{ and } T_2 = 3. \qquad (20)$$

First note that the parameters $p = 3$ and $q = 1$ meet the condition $q < p - 1$ of Theorem 3. Note also that $\lambda \approx 2.618$, and for all $n \geq 3$, the ratio $\frac{T_{n+1}}{T_n}$ lies in the interval $(2, 3)$, hence $K_0 = 3$. Moreover, $\{1, T_2, T_3, T_4\}$ is totally greedy. However, neither $\{1, T_2, \ldots, T_5\}$ nor $\{1, T_2, \ldots, T_6\}$ are greedy.

Determining the exact conditions under which Theorem 3 can be generalized to the non-homogenous case remains an open problem.

4   Even and Odd Subsequences

Given a totally greedy type-1-sequence $\{G_n\}_{n=1}^{\infty}$, or a totally greedy type-2-sequence $\{J_n\}_{n=1}^{\infty}$, we now want to study the behaviour of the subsequence formed by the even terms, i.e. $\left\{G_{2k}\right\}_{k=1}^{\infty}$ and $\left\{J_{2k}\right\}_{k=1}^{\infty}$, and the subsequence formed by the odd terms, i.e. $\left\{G_{2k-1}\right\}_{k=1}^{\infty}$ and $\left\{J_{2k-1}\right\}_{k=1}^{\infty}$. For simplicity we may call them the *even* and *odd subsequences*, respectively.

Note in passing that starting the sequences at $G_1 = J_1 = 1$, rather than starting at $G_0 = J_0 = 1$, was a convenient choice from the point of view of notation, because now the even subsequence and the odd subsequence coincide with the even-indexed terms and the odd-indexed terms, respectively.

There is an interesting relationship between the subsequences of type-1 and type-2 sequences, which had already been noticed in the case of Fibonacci numbers [13, 15]:

Proposition 3. *Let* $\left\{G_n\right\}_{n=1}^{\infty}$ *be a type-1-sequence and* $\left\{J_n\right\}_{n=1}^{\infty}$ *a type-2-sequence. Then,*

1. *The odd and even subsequences of* $\left\{G_n\right\}_{n=1}^{\infty}$ *are of type 2.*
2. *The odd and even subsequences of* $\left\{J_n\right\}_{n=1}^{\infty}$ *are also of type 2.*

Proof: In order to obtain a recurrence equation for the odd and even subsequences we adapt a simple (yet clever) technique developed in [15] for the Fibonacci numbers.

1. Let's start with the subsequences of $\left\{G_n\right\}_{n=1}^{\infty}$. We have

$$qG_n = 2qG_n - qG_n \tag{21}$$

$$pG_{n+1} = p^2 G_n + pqG_{n-1}. \tag{22}$$

Adding (21) and (22) we get

$$pG_{n+1} + qG_n = (p^2 + 2q)G_n + pqG_{n-1} - qG_n$$
$$G_{n+2} = (p^2 + 2q)G_n + q(pG_{n-1} - G_n)$$
$$G_{n+2} = (p^2 + 2q)G_n - q^2 G_{n-2}. \tag{23}$$

The recurrence Eq. 23 applies to both the odd and even subsequences of $\left\{G_n\right\}_{n=1}^{\infty}$, and has the form of Eq. 12. To complete the proof of this case we just have to verify that $q \le p$ effectively implies $q^2 < p^2 + 2q - 1$.

2. Now we do the same for the subsequences of $\left\{J_n\right\}_{n=1}^{\infty}$. We have

$$qJ_n = 2qJ_n - qJ_n \tag{24}$$

$$pJ_{n+1} = p^2 J_n - pqJ_{n-1}. \tag{25}$$

Subtracting (24) from (25) we get

$$pJ_{n+1} - qJ_n = (p^2 - 2q)J_n + qJ_n - pqJ_{n-1}$$
$$J_{n+2} = (p^2 - 2q)J_n + q(J_n - pJ_{n-1})$$
$$J_{n+2} = (p^2 - 2q)J_n - q^2 J_{n-2}. \tag{26}$$

Again, note that Eq. 26 has the form of Eq. 12. To complete the proof we just have to verify that $q^2 < p^2 + 2q - 1$ is equivalent $q < p - 1$ when q and $p - 1$ are both positive.

□

From this we can derive the following

Corollary 3. *Let* $\{G_n\}_{n=1}^{\infty}$ *be a totally greedy type-1-sequence and* $\{J_n\}_{n=1}^{\infty}$ *a totally greedy type-2-sequence. Then, the odd subsequences of* $\{G_n\}_{n=1}^{\infty}$ *and* $\{J_n\}_{n=1}^{\infty}$ *are also totally greedy.*

Proof: Proposition 3 tells us that odd subsequences of type-1 or type-2 sequences are of type 2. On the one hand, the odd subsequences of $\{G_n\}_{n=1}^{\infty}$ have the form

$$G'_k = G_{2k-1} = \begin{cases} 1 \text{ if } k = 1, \\ a' = pa + q \text{ if } k = 2, \\ p'_1 G'_{k-1} - q' G'_{k-2} \text{ if } k > 2, \end{cases}$$

where $p'_1 = p^2 + 2q$ and $q' = q^2$. From Theorem 3 we know that type-2 sequences are totally greedy for any a, and in particular for $a' = pa + q$, hence the result follows.

On the other hand, the odd subsequences of $\{J_n\}_{n=1}^{\infty}$ have the form

$$J'_k = J_{2k-1} = \begin{cases} 1 \text{ if } k = 1, \\ a' = pa - q \text{ if } k = 2, \\ p'_2 J'_{k-1} - q' J'_{k-2} \text{ if } k > 2, \end{cases}$$

where $p'_2 = p^2 - 2q$ and $q' = q^2$. Again, the total greediness of $\{J'_k\}_{k=1}^{\infty}$ follows directly from Theorem 3.

□

It is only at this point, after seeing the proof of Corollary 3, that we can fully assess the need of introducing the parameter a in our sequences, which has been the source of so much trouble throughout Sects. 2 and 3.

Anyway, the even subsequences of $\{G_n\}_{n=1}^{\infty}$ and $\{J_n\}_{n=1}^{\infty}$ are more complicated because we have to insert the term 1 at the beginning of the sequence, and this sort of 'destroys' the recurrence. Nonetheless, we can still make some progress in some special cases, which are outlined below.

To begin with, let $\{G_n\}_{n=1}^{\infty}$ be a type-1-sequence, and let $\{G''_k\}_{k=1}^{\infty}$ denote the subsequence of its even terms, modified as follows:

$$G''_k = \begin{cases} 1 \text{ if } k = 1, \\ a \text{ if } k = 2, \\ p''_1 G''_{k-1} - q'' G''_{k-2} = G_{2k-2} \text{ if } k > 2, \end{cases} \tag{27}$$

where $p''_1 = p^2 + 2q$ and $q'' = q^2$.

Corollary 4. *Let* $\{G_n\}_{n=1}^{\infty}$ *be a totally greedy type-1 sequence with* $p = q + 1$ *and* $a = q$, *and let* $\{G''_k\}_{k=1}^{\infty}$ *be the subsequence of its even terms, as defined in Eq. 27. Then* $\{G''_k\}_{k=1}^{\infty}$ *is also totally greedy.*

Proof: We assume that p and q are fixed. From the equality $p_1'' G_{k-1}'' - q'' G_{k-2}'' = G_{2k-2}$ we get $a = \dfrac{pq + q^2}{2q - 1}$, which clearly complies with the conditions of Theorem 2, i.e. $2 \le a \le p + q$. Thus, any combination of values of p and q such that $a = \dfrac{pq + q^2}{2q - 1}$ is an integer will fit our purposes. In particular, $p = q + 1$ and $a = q$ will do.

$\square$

Note that the proof of Corollary 4 suggests how to look for other combinations of values for p, q, a. Another possibility would be to define Eq. 4, so that it starts with three given initial values, i.e. $1, a, b$, but that falls without the scope of this paper.

Now let $\{J_n\}_{n=1}^{\infty}$ be a type-2-sequence, and let $\{J_k''\}_{k=1}^{\infty}$ denote the subsequence of its even terms, modified as follows:

$$J_k'' = \begin{cases} 1 & \text{if } k = 1, \\ a & \text{if } k = 2, \\ p_2'' J_{k-1}'' - q'' J_{k-2}'' = J_{2k-2} & \text{if } k > 2, \end{cases} \qquad (28)$$

where $p_2'' = p^2 - 2q$ and $q'' = q^2$.

Corollary 5. Let $\{J_n\}_{n=1}^{\infty}$ be a totally greedy type-2 sequence with $a = p - q$, and let $\{J_k''\}_{k=1}^{\infty}$ be the subsequence of its even terms, as defined in Eq. 28. Then $\{J_k''\}_{k=1}^{\infty}$ is also totally greedy.

Proof: Again, we are assuming that p and q are fixed, and we are looking for a suitable value of a. From the equality $p_2'' J_{k-1}'' - q'' J_{k-2}'' = J_{2k-2}$ we get the desired condition $a = p - q$.

$\square$

5   Conclusion and Open Problems

It is now convenient to take a look back and summarize all these results, as well as introduce some research problems for future work. Throughout Sects. 2 and 3 we have identified large classes of totally greedy number sequences that are generated by second-order linear recurrences with constant coefficients, namely type-1 and type-2 sequences. Then, in Sect. 4 we have studied some of their subsequences, which also turn out to be type-1 or type-2 sequences themselves.

From the theoretical point of view, this study provides greater insight into the structure of Horadam-type number sequences, which generalize the Fibonacci numbers and other well known number sequences. From the practical viewpoint we have already mentioned the application of greedy sequences to construct large circulant networks with efficient routing algorithms [10]. In general, totally greedy sequences can be the basis for numeration systems with properties similar to those of the Zeckendorf representation, which is a numeration system based on the Fibonacci numbers [17].

A straightforward sequel is to perform the same analysis for sequences generated by larger order linear recurrences (e.g. third-order recurrences), which obviously exhibit richer scenarios. It would also be interesting to study some number sequences *not* generated by homogeneous linear recurrences with constant coefficients. In Subsect. 2.1 we have already identified a class of non-homogeneous second-order linear recurrences that generate totally greedy sequences. Now the question is: Do there exist other classes of non-homogeneous linear (or non-linear) recurrences that generate totally greedy sequences?

In the applications domain the immediate next step is to investigate the properties of circulant networks that arise from the totally greedy number sequences that we have studied here, along the lines of [10]. In particular, we want to devise specific communication algorithms and protocols for routing, broadcasting and gossiping in these networks.

Acknowledgements. The author was partially supported by Grant 2021 SGR 00115 from the Government of Catalonia, by Project ACITECH PID2021-124928NB-I00, funded by MCIN/AEI/ 10.13039/501100011033/FEDER, EU, and by Project HERMES, funded by INCIBE and by the European Union NextGeneration EU/PRTR.

References

1. Adamaszek, A., Adamaszek, M.: Combinatorics of the change-making problem. Eur. J. Comb. **31**, 47–63 (2010)
2. Cai, X.: Canonical coin systems for change-making problems. In: Proceedings of the 9th IEEE International Conference on Hybrid Intelligent Systems, pp. 499–504 (2009)
3. Chan, T.M., He, Q.: More on change-making and related problems. J. Comput. Syst. Sci. **124**, 159–169 (2022)
4. Cowen, L.J., Cowen, R., Steinberg, A.: Totally greedy coin sets and greedy obstructions. Electron. J. Comb. **15** (2008). #R90
5. Crilly, T.: Interleaving Integer Sequences. Math. Gaz. **91**, 27–33 (2007)
6. Lueker, G.S.: Two NP-complete problems in nonnegative integer programming. Tech. Rep. 178, Computer Science Lab., Princeton University (1975)
7. Magazine, M.J., Nemhauser, G.L., Trotter, L.E., Jr.: When the greedy solution solves a class of knapsack problems. Oper. Res. **23**(2), 207–217 (1975)
8. OEIS: The On-Line Encyclopedia of Integer Sequences. http://oeis.org/classic/index.html
9. Pearson, D.: A polynomial-time algorithm for the change-making problem. Oper. Res. Lett. **33**, 231–234 (2005)
10. Pérez-Rosés, H. Bras, M., Serradilla-Merinero, J.M.: Greedy routing in circulant networks. Graphs Comb. **38**(86) (2022). https://doi.org/10.1007/s00373-022-02489-9
11. Pérez-Rosés, H.: Totally greedy sequences generated by a class of second-order linear recurrences with constant coefficients. Procs. Discrete Math. Days 276–281 (2024). https://doi.org/10.37536/TYSP5643

12. Pérez-Rosés, H.: Totally Greedy Sequences Defined by Second-Order Linear Recurrences With Constant Coefficients. arXiv:2405.16609. https://arxiv.org/abs/2405.16609

13. Rajesh, V., Leversha, G.: Some properties of odd terms of the Fibonacci sequence. Math. Gaz. **88**, 85–86 (2004)

14. Shallit, J.: What this country needs is an 18c Piece. Math. Intelligencer **25**(2), 20–23 (2003)

15. Silvester, J.R.: The r-subsequences of the Fibonacci sequence. Math. Gaz. **90**, 263–266 (2006)

16. Suzuki, Y., Miyashiro, R.: Characterization of canonical systems with six types of coins for the change-making problem. Theor. Comput. Sci. **955** (2023). https://doi.org/10.1016/j.tcs.2023.113822

17. Zeckendorf, E.: Représentations des nombres naturels par un somme de nombres de Fibonacci ou de nombres de Lucas. Bulletin de La Society Royale des Sciences de Liège, 179–182 (1972)

Mobile-Based Automated Eyelid Blink Detection and Movement Analysis: A Machine Learning Approach

Gustavo Adolpho Bonesso[1] (ID), Carlos Marcelo Gurjão de Godoy[1] (ID),
Tammy Hentona Osaki[2] (ID), Midori Hentona Osaki[2] (ID),
and Regina Célia Coelho[1(✉)] (ID)

[1] Science and Technology Institute, Federal University of São Paulo, São José Dos Campos, SP, Brazil
rccoelho@unifesp.br

[2] Department of Ophthalmology and Visual Sciences, Paulista School of Medicine, Federal University of São Paulo, São Paulo, SP, Brazil

Abstract. Eye diseases pose a significant global health challenge, affecting millions of people and leading to substantial visual impairment. Analyzing eyelid blinking and movement is crucial for monitoring patients with abnormal eyelid motions. This paper introduces the so-called Bapp (Blink Application), a mobile application designed to evaluate eyelid movement by recording the opening and closing of the eyes over time and detecting eye blinks using a machine-learning approach. The application processes pre-recorded videos and then validates the results against publicly available datasets. The proposed system operates in a unified stage, utilizing the pre-recorded video as input and evaluating the degree of eyelid openness in each frame using predictions from Google ML Kit, a machine learning-based framework integrated into the Flutter platform. The results are stored in a local database and can be exported to Excel for further analysis. Developed on the Flutter platform, the Bapp supports multiple languages, ensuring accessibility to a broad audience. The blink prediction results align with those obtained from other methods applied to the same dataset, demonstrating the app´s effectiveness in objectively monitoring the clinical progression of patients with eyelid diseases.

Keywords: Eyelid Movement · Blink Detection · Mobile Health Application

1 Introduction

Eye diseases are a primary global health concern, impacting millions of people and leading to significant visual impairment. According to the World Health Organization (WHO), at least 2.2 billion people experience vision impairment, with at least 1 billion cases being preventable or treatable.[1]

---

[1] World Health Organization (2023) Blindness and vision impairment, https://www.who.int/news-room/fact-sheets/detail/blindness-and-visual-impairment.

O. Gervasi et al. (Eds.): ICCSA 2025, LNCS 15648, pp. 140–157, 2025.
https://doi.org/10.1007/978-3-031-97000-9_9

It is essential to analyze eyelid blinking and movement to monitor patients with abnormal eyelid movements. Objectively assessing these movements involves capturing images of the patient's face and processing them using specialized software to recognize and quantify eyelid movements [1–4]. Unfortunately, such approaches often involve complex systems impractical for clinical settings. Besides, they are frequently imprecise, especially for patients with abnormal eyelid movements, and fail to capture other critical parameters, such as amplitude movements [1–4].

Image capture can occur by using external cameras [2, 3] or the built-in cameras of mobile devices [1, 4]. Subsequent analysis can occur using computational tools such as MATLAB to detect and measure eyelid movement [2]. Alternatively, web-based platforms accessed via mobile devices or desktops can also facilitate such studies [5].

This work introduces a mobile application designed to evaluate eyelid movement by recording the opening and closing of the eyes over time. The application leverages a machine learning approach, focusing on the pre-recorded video feature, which validates the app's results against a public dataset [6].[2] The tool provides a robust framework for analyzing the frequency and amplitude of normal and pathological eyelid movements, offering a scalable and accessible solution for clinical and research applications.

2 Related Works

Advancements in technology have significantly enhanced the analysis of eyelid blinking and movement, particularly for patient monitoring in clinical settings. Techniques such as high-speed imaging, deep learning, and smartphone videography have emerged, providing precise and non-invasive methods to assess blink dynamics and their implications for various ocular conditions.

High-speed imaging combined with digital image correlation (DIC) allows for detailed measurement of eyelid motion during blinking. This method captures kinematic data, including blink duration, eyelid displacements, and peak velocities, facilitating a comprehensive analysis of spontaneous and reflex blinks [7].

Intelligent vision measurement systems utilizing deep learning can analyze blinking characteristics, offering insights into the visual function of patients, particularly those with dry eye disease. These systems automatically calculate blink completeness and provide stable, accurate measurements, enhancing clinical assessments [8, 9].

Smartphone videography has proven effective in capturing eyelid movements, allowing for comparative analysis of blink dynamics in patients with conditions like chronic progressive external ophthalmoplegia and facial nerve palsy. This method is cost-effective and accessible, making it suitable for both clinical and research applications [10].

There are limited integrated mobile apps for objectively analyzing eyelid movements in the present work approach. The DryEyeRhythm app, which diagnoses dry eye disease, was developed in Japan through a consignment agreement with Juntendo University Graduate School of Medicine and InnoJin Inc., Tokyo [11].

---

[2] Talking Face Video, https://personalpages.manchester.ac.uk/staff/timothy.f.cootes/data/talking_face/talking_face.html.

The EyeScore mobile application, developed by the Department of Clinical Research at the Westview Eye Institute in San Diego, CA, USA, utilizes blink rates and patterns as early clinical biomarkers for dry eye disease. Although designed for iOS, it is still unavailable for download [12].

Another approach involves hosting the application on a cloud server. The videos are recorded locally with a camera or smartphone and sent to a web server that processes them and reports the eyelid movement results. One project that utilized this technology employed Streamlit to host the application [1].

While all these technological advancements offer significant benefits in monitoring eyelid movement, challenges remain in standardizing these methods across diverse clinical settings and ensuring their widespread adoption. Further research is needed to validate these technologies' effectiveness and reliability in various patient populations.

3 Proposed Method

For clarity, Fig. 1 illustrates the steps and tools used in the proposed method. To validate the mobile application Bapp (Blink Application), we used videos from two reference datasets as input (Eyeblink8 and Talking Face), which have annotations indicating where the blinks occur. These videos were processed by Bapp using the feature for pre-recorded video analysis. This feature analyzes each frame from the video to assess the openness of each eye using Google ML Kit (a machine learning tool) and stores the results in Hive (a local database). The next step in validation is to export the raw analysis results from Bapp to Excel, enabling comparison with the annotations from the reference datasets to check Bapp's efficiency in detecting blinks in the input videos. Bapp addresses the limitations associated with the clinical application of eyelid movement monitoring by providing an automated, precise, and clinically feasible solution. The system performs eyelid movement analysis in a unified, integrated stage.

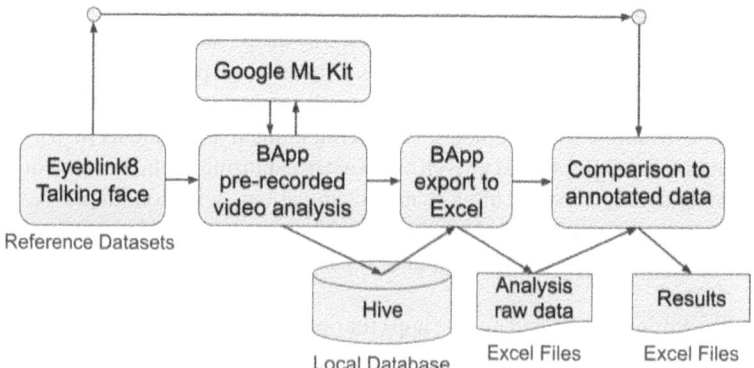

Fig. 1. Diagram with steps and tools used to analyze eyelid movements from dataset reference videos and compare the results from the Bapp mobile application to the annotated data from the datasets

3.1 Eyeblink Detection Dataset

This work used Eyeblink8 [6] and Talking Face[3], two public eyeblink detection datasets. The Eyeblink8 dataset contains over 82,600 frames and 408 blinks. It includes natural facial movements, expressions, and other intensive non-blink motions. The Talking Face dataset comprises 5,000 frames, corresponding to approximately 200 s of recording, capturing a subject engaged in a natural conversation with another person. The video recording uses a static camera to model facial behavior during the interaction. The dataset includes 61 additional blinks, raising the total blinks annotated to 469.

The annotations for each video are provided in two files: the first lists the frame numbers and their acquisition times, while the second contains manually annotated eye states.

Each row in the annotation file contains the following information: Frame ID, Blink ID, NF, LE_FC, LE_NV, RE_FC, RE_NV.

- Frame ID: Frame counter
- Blink ID: A unique blink ID; the eye blink interval definition occurs as a sequence of frames with the same blink ID.
- No frontal face (NF): An eye blink occurs when the subject looks sideways, given that the variable changes from X to N.
- Left eye (LE), right eye (RE), face (F)
- Eye fully closed (FC): If the subject's eyes are closed from 90% to 100%, the flag changes from X to C.
- Eye not visible (NV): While the subject's eye is not visible because of the hand, bad light conditions, hair, or even too fast head movement, this variable changes from X to N.

3.2 Software Tools

The Bapp mobile application was developed using the Flutter development tool.[4] It enables the creation of cross-platform mobile applications for Android and iOS operating systems using the same codebase, thus covering nearly the entire smartphone user base. The application supports three languages—Portuguese, English, and Spanish—by utilizing Flutter's localization library, which ensures a broad and diverse audience.

Clean architecture is the chosen architectural framework for guiding the development of Bapp mobile applications. It offers advantages such as improved maintainability, reduced complexity, streamlined codebase modifications, and the development of robust, easily upgradable, and verifiable applications. Those features enhance software quality and adaptability to evolving requirements and technological advancements [13].[5]

Concerning the analysis of the eyelid opening states, the framework relies on using Google ML Kit, an application programming interface (API) for computer vision developed by Google.[6] We used a plugin to integrate Google ML Kit into the Flutter platform.

[3] Talking Face Video, https://personalpages.manchester.ac.uk/staff/timothy.f.cootes/data/talking_face/talking_face.html.

[4] Flutter Flutter Developer Tools, https://flutter.dev.

[5] Martin R (2012) The Clean Architecture, https://blog.cleancoder.com/uncle-bob/2012/08/13/the-clean-architecture.html.

[6] Google ML Kit | Google for Developers, https://developers.google.com/ml-kit/guides.

Optimized for mobile devices, the Google ML Kit performs all processing locally on the device. The specific Google ML Kit module used in this task is Face Detection. It enabled the detection of eye openness probability, eye contours, and other facial features to recognize the state of eyelid opening.

The Google ML Kit receives an image as input and performs face detection. Even though the framework can identify multiple faces within a single image, the Bapp mobile application considers only the first detected face, as the app analyzes the user individually. After detecting a face, the framework proceeds to classify the status of the eyes. This classification provides a probability value indicating the degree of openness for each eye.

The selected local database is Hive, a NoSQL solution tailored to the local storage needs of Flutter applications.[7] Hive integrates seamlessly with Flutter and offers a robust data storage and retrieval API. The Hive database allows information to be stored using JSON format.

3.3   Eye Blink Detection Algorithm

The interpretation of raw data from Google ML Kit detects the frames where a blink occurred. The first approach to detecting eye blinks involved determining a blink when the probability of eye openness drops below 0.5, where "0.0" represents "totally closed eye" and "1.0" refers to "totally opened eye". Figure 2 illustrates a problem with this method: When the probability bounces around probability 0.5 - falling below 0.5, rising above 0.5, and then falling again below 0.5 - the algorithm counts two blinks, which is incorrect, as only one blink or no blink would have happened.

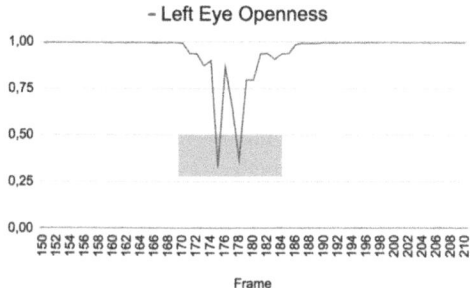

Fig. 2. Illustration of the problem of eye openness probability chart with two frames below probability 0.5.

Using a single threshold to indicate a blink is not a practical solution. To solve this problem, considering two distinct thresholds - one to signal the start of the blink and another to mark its end – achieves better outcomes. Implementing a third threshold further differentiates between partial and complete blinks. Figure 3 illustrates these thresholds.

---

[7] Isar Database Hive, https://github.com/isar/hive.

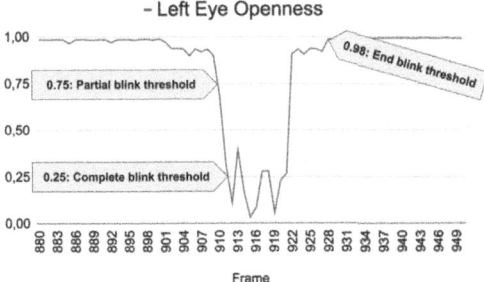

Fig. 3. Illustration of probability charts with thresholds indicating the beginning and ending of partial or complete blinks.

The pseudocode for eye blink detection is in Fig. 4.

```
BEGIN

    DEFINE partial_blink_detected AS FALSE
    DEFINE full_blink_detected AS FALSE

    IF eye_open_probability < 0.75 THEN
        IDENTIFY partial_blink
        SET partial_blink_detected TO TRUE
    END IF

    IF eye_open_probability < 0.25 THEN
        IDENTIFY full_blink
        SET full_blink_detected TO TRUE
    END IF

    IF eye_open_probability > 0.98 AND
      (partial_blink_detected OR full_blink_detected) THEN
        END blink
        SET partial_blink_detected TO FALSE
        SET full_blink_detected TO FALSE
    END IF

END
```

Fig. 4. Pseudocode for blink detection algorithm

Figure 5(a) illustrates an instance of a partial blink, where the eye openness probability decreases below 0.75 but remains above the 0.25 threshold, which characterizes a complete blink. The blink is classified as complete upon the eye openness probability returning to 0.98. Figure 5(b) demonstrates a complete blink when the eye openness probability drops below 0.25.

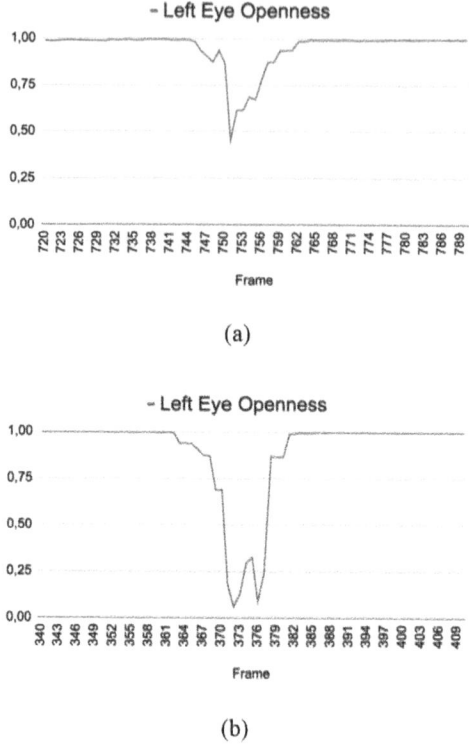

(a)

(b)

Fig. 5. Illustration of probability charts of partial blink (a) and complete blink (b)

3.4   Pre-recorded Video Processing

The first step involves dividing the video into frames for individual analysis. For each frame, the Google ML Kit detects faces. When face detection occurs, it calculates the likelihood of the eyes being open, which ranges from 0 (closed) to 1 (open). The local database registers the data for later analysis of the start and end of the blinks. Figure 6 illustrates the sequence of processing the pre-recorded video.

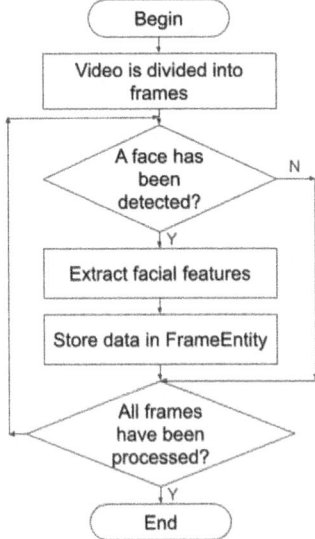

Fig. 6. Pre-recorded video processing sequence

For each analysis, the Bapp stores date and time information, duration, and an array of details from each frame within an AnalysisEntity. Consequently, the FrameEntity operates as a sub-entity of the AnalysisEntity, with every frame documenting the frame number, date, time, and the detected probability of eye-opening. Figure 7 shows an example with data from the AnalysisEntity and FrameEntity.

```
                                                     AnalysisEntity
{
    "analysisDateTime": "2024-04-23T11:21:30.0",
    "duration": 5.0,
    "frameList": [
        {                                           FrameEntity
            "frameNumber": 0,
            "frameDateTime": "2024-04-23T11:21:30.0",
            "rightEyeOpenness": 0.9956856369972229,
            "leftEyeOpenness": 0.998312771320343
        },
        ...
        {                                           FrameEntity
            "frameNumber": 124,
            "frameDateTime": "2024-04-23T11:21:34.96",
            "rightEyeOpenness": 0.898965235782322,
            "leftEyeOpenness": 0.80787288723898928
        }
    ]
}
```

Fig. 7. Analysis example with data from the AnalysisEntity and FrameEntity

3.5 Excel Export

The export to Excel feature saves an analysis's raw data in an Excel sheet. This functionality is valuable for debugging and provides flexibility in viewing data. It also allows sorting, filtering, and performing operations on the raw data to understand the analysis's results better.

The Excel export feature is crucial for comparing the dataset's video analysis results with the annotated blink information to calculate metrics such as RMSE and precision.

As shown in Fig. 8, this feature is accessed via the Export to Excel button on the Analysis Detail screen.

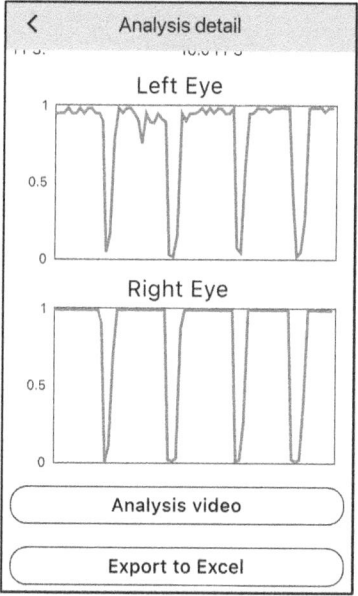

Fig. 8. A screenshot of the Bapp mobile application illustrating the analysis detail screen, with the "Export to Excel" button at the bottom.

Figure 9 shows the exported Excel sheet containing information about each frame's overall analysis and eye status. This information allows the user to work more flexibly with the raw data and possibly gain more insights.

	A	B	C	D	E
1	Patient	Gustavo Bonesso			
2	Analysis type	AnalysisType.realTime			
3	*** Pre/Post Inter	PrePostIntervention.pre			
4	*** Days Pre/Pos	15			
5	*** Observations				
6	Duration	4.4 seconds			
7	Number of Blinks	L: 4	R: 4		
8	Blink Frequency:	L: 54.1 BPM	R: 54.1 BPM		
9	FPS:	16.0 FPS			
10					
11	***Frame	***Right Eye Ope	***Left Eye Oper	***Right Eye EAF	***Left Eye EAR
12	0	0,99	0,95	0,25	0,26
13	1	0,99	0,95	0,26	0,28
14	2	0,99	0,95	0,25	0,28
15	3	0,99	0,99	0,28	0,28
16	4	0,99	0,95	0,28	0,29
17	5	0,99	0,95	0,26	0,28

Fig. 9. Excel sheet displaying raw data from the analysis

3.6 Validation

The app processes videos from the EyeBlink8 and Talking Face public datasets to validate its efficiency in detecting blinks. The eye blink is considered detected if there is any intersection between the detected blink and the annotation. The intersection interval with the ground truth is counted just one as a True Positive. The results are exported to Excel spreadsheets and compared using the root mean square error (RMSE). The results were normalized using the StandardScaler function and evaluated using the evaluation metric 'mean_squared_error', both from Scikit-Learn.[8]

$$RMSE = \sqrt{\frac{1}{n} \sum_{i=0}^{n} (y - \hat{y})^2} \tag{1}$$

where $\hat{y}$ is a vector with the predicted values, and y is the ground truth value for each value analyzed. The result is the root of the difference between the predicted and the ground truth values divided by the number of values (value represented by n).

To compare the results to other papers using the same datasets, we used the following equations:

$$Precision = \frac{TP}{TP + FP} \tag{2}$$

$$Recall(TPrate) = \frac{TP}{TP + FN} \tag{3}$$

$$FPrate = \frac{FP}{N} \tag{4}$$

---

[8] scikit-learn - Machine Learning in Python, https://scikit-learn.org/

$$MA = \frac{TP + TN}{P + N} \tag{5}$$

where TP is True Positive (the eye blinks are annotated in the reference dataset and were predicted by the app), FP is False Positive (when the app predicts the eye blink, but it is not found in the annotated dataset), FN is False Negative (when an eye blink is annotated in the dataset but not predicted by the app). N is the number of frames with open eyes. MA is the mean accuracy. TN is the True Negative, calculated by subtracting the TP, FP, and FN frames from the total number of frames of the videos. P is calculated by subtracting the total number of frames from N.

4 Results

The analysis starts after selecting a video from the smartphone's gallery. Figure 10 shows the Bapp mobile application interface for processing pre-recorded videos.

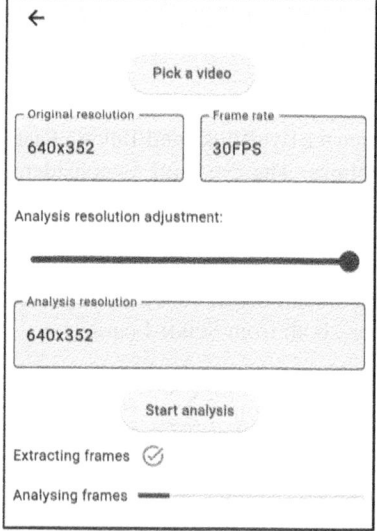

Fig. 10. Screenshot of the Bapp mobile application interface for processing pre-recorded videos.

After completing the analysis, Bapp displays the analysis detail screen shown in Fig. 11. This screen presents the analysis data, including the analysis date, duration, number of blinks detected, calculated blink frequency per minute, and a graphical representation for enhanced visual clarity.

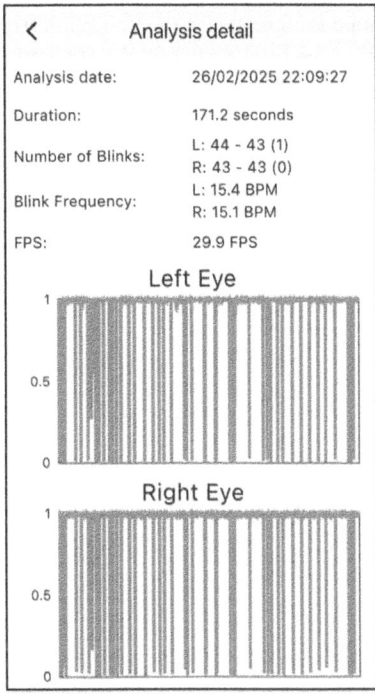

Fig. 11. Screenshot of the Bapp mobile application displaying the detailed analysis information.

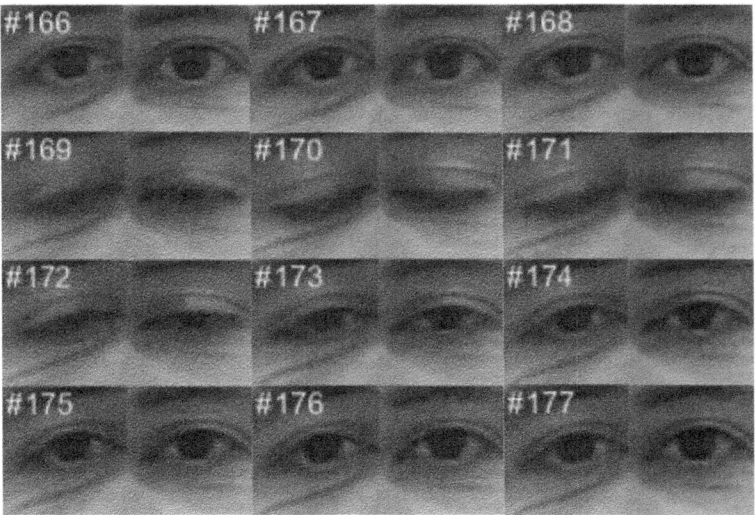

Fig. 12. Frames sequence for the first blink in the Talking Face video

Figure 12 shows a frame sequence from one of the videos used to validate the first blink annotated in the dataset.

Table 1 shows the annotated reference for the first blink from the Talking Face video. It determines the beginning of the blink in the frame 168 and the end of the blink in the frame 176.

Table 1. Annotated frames for the first blink in the Talking Face video

Frame_ID	Blink_ID	NFF	LE_FC	LE_NV	RE_FC	RE_NV
166	-1	X	X	X	X	X
167	-1	X	X	X	X	X
168	1	X	X	X	X	X
169	1	X	X	X	X	X
170	1	X	C	X	C	X
171	1	X	C	X	C	X
172	1	X	X	X	X	X
173	1	X	X	X	X	X
174	1	X	X	X	X	X
175	1	X	X	X	X	X
176	1	X	X	X	X	X
177	-1	X	X	X	X	X

Figure 13 shows the chart of openness probability for both eyes predicted by Google ML Kit for the first blink in the Talking Face video.

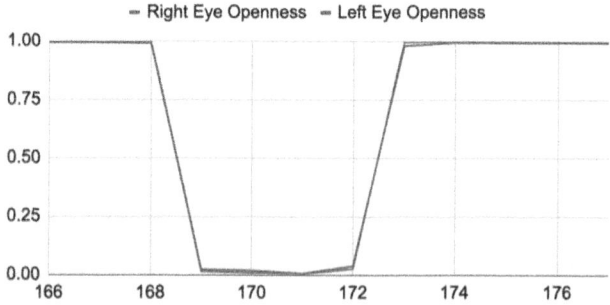

Fig. 13. Eye openness probability for both eyes predicted by Google ML Kit for the first blink in Talking Face video

The app's results for the number of eyeblinks predicted and annotated blinks from the datasets are shown in Table 2.

Table 2. The number of eye blinks predicted by the app compared to the annotated eye blinks

Video	Number of Annotated Eyeblinks	Number of Eyeblinks Predicted by the App
EyeBlink8 #1	38	37
EyeBlink8 #2	88	88
EyeBlink8 #3	65	61
EyeBlink8 #4	31	30
EyeBlink8 #5	30	30
EyeBlink8 #6	41	41
EyeBlink8 #7	72	72
EyeBlink8 #8	43	43
Talking Face	61	61
Total	469	463

The RMSE calculated for the dataset normalized comparison with the app prediction results was 0.0654. Considering the mean RMSE results, the model effectively predicted the blinks in the reference datasets.

Table 3 compares the results from our app to those of other papers using different methods against the same datasets.

Table 3. Comparison of the results from our app to those of other papers using different methods against the same datasets

	Dataset	Precision	Recall	FP rate	Mean accuracy
Divjak & Bischof [14]	Talking	-	95.0%	19.0%	88.0%
Lee et al. [15]	Talking	83.3%	91.2%	-	-
Drutarovsky & Fogelton [6]	Talking	92.2%	96.7%	0.7%	99.0%
Our app	Talking	**95.3%**	**100.0%**	**0.5%**	**99.6%**
Drutarovsky & Fogelton [6]	EyeBlink8	79.0%	85.3%	0.7%	99.5%
Our app	EyeBlink8	**84.3%**	**98.5%**	**0.8%**	**99.2%**

The Precision metric of the EyeBlink8 dataset is lower than that of the Talking Face dataset due to a higher number of false positives (FPs). Occasionally, the app predicts partial blinks without corresponding annotated blinks in the dataset. Figure 14 illustrates a sequence of frames the app predicts as a partial blink, which are not annotated in the reference dataset, as the subject is looking down.

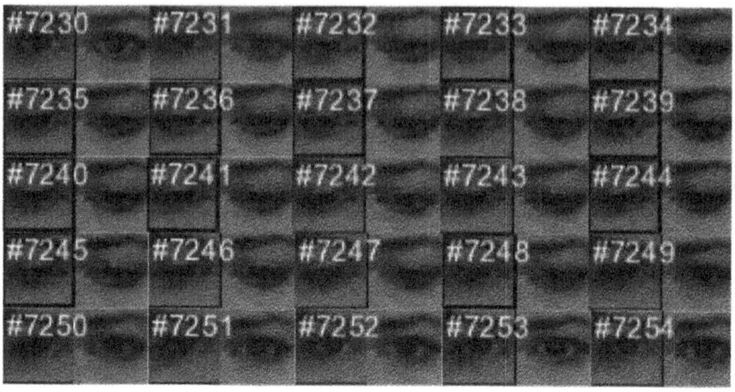

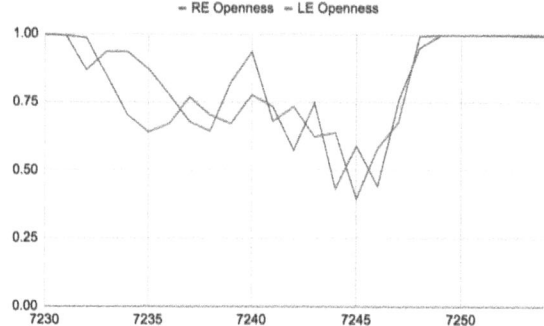

Fig. 14. A sequence of frames showing a False Positive case where the app predicts a partial blink

Figure 15 displays the eye openness chart for a false positive case, where the app predicts a partial blink. The openness of both the left and right eyes falls below 0.75, indicating the onset of a partial blink. The blink concludes when the openness rises to 0.98.

Fig. 15. Eye openness chart for a case of False Positive

5 Discussion

This work presents the results of Bapp, a mobile application with machine-learning capabilities that analyzes eyelid movements in pre-recorded videos. It achieved 95.3% precision in blink detection using the Talking Face reference dataset and 84.3% using the EyeBlink8 dataset. The precision level achieved by Bapp in the Talking Face dataset is higher than the 83.3% attained by Lee et al. [15] and the 92.2% achieved by Drutarovsky and Fogelton [6]. Additionally, the precision level achieved by Bapp in the blink analysis of the EyeBlink8 dataset surpasses the 79% obtained by Drutarovsky and Fogelton [6].

Bapp's recall also exceeds that of previous works. Bapp recalled 100% of the Talking Face dataset and 98.5% of the EyeBlink8 dataset. Divjak & Bischof [14] attained a recall of 95.0% for the Talking Face dataset, while Lee et al. [15] achieved 91.2%, and

Drutarovsky and Fogelton [6] reported 96.7%. For the Eye-Blink8 dataset, Drutarovsky and Fogelton [6] reported a recall of 85.3%.

These levels of precision and recall allow Bapp to analyze eyelid movements as an alternative to manually counting blinks, primarily facilitating the monitoring of abnormal eyelid movements.

The lack of annotated datasets specifically focused on eye diseases highlights a significant gap that must be addressed. Although the existing datasets are valuable for validation, developing one that aligns more closely with the Bapp context and objectives is essential to ensure a more robust evaluation framework. For future research, I recommend utilizing datasets designed explicitly for ocular disease detection and annotated by experts in the field. That could involve creating a new dataset encompassing various ocular conditions, including blepharospasm, hemifacial spasm, ptosis, and dry eye syndrome. Collecting data under diverse lighting conditions, camera angles, and subject demographics will enhance the model's robustness.

A recent search in the electronic databases revealed only two mobile applications with eyelid movement analysis capabilities: EyeScore [12] and DryEyeRhythm [11]. We cannot find validations of these mobile applications against blink reference datasets, such as the one presented in this work, and these validations are essential for comparing the software capabilities.

Bapp can perform the analysis in a single step using only a smartphone and does not require a computer, unlike the approaches by Hu et al. [9] and Osaki et al. [2], which utilize a computer with custom software written in MATLAB for analysis. Additionally, the method by Silkiss et al. [3] involves custom software developed by a third party, Visage Technologies, to extract facial features alongside another software written in MATLAB for calculating eyelid aperture. Hedayati Amlashi et al. [10] utilized images captured at a high frame rate using a smartphone and employed Kinovea, software designed for tracking markers in human motion analysis. Silva et al. [1] developed a different approach in Python and used the Streamlit library to process the captured video through a cloud server instead of a local computer. In contrast, Bapp processes the video locally, eliminating the need to transfer data to the cloud or maintain a server. The Bapp method streamlines the operational process and allows eyelid movement analysis to reach a broader audience.

This study has limitations. One limitation is that the time required for analysis depends on several factors, including the resolution of the acquired video (the higher the resolution, the more processing time is needed) and the device used for analysis. Devices with faster processors conduct the analysis more quickly but are generally more expensive than those with slower processors, which take longer to perform the same analysis. Another significant limitation affecting the analysis's quality is the illumination conditions and camera angles from which the images were captured. Optimal results can be achieved with good lighting and the subject facing directly toward the camera in a frontal position.

6 Conclusion

The Bapp (Blink Application) represents a significant advancement in the objective monitoring of eyelid movements and blink patterns, particularly for patients with eyelid-related diseases.

By leveraging machine learning through Google ML Kit and the Flutter platform, the application provides a unified, accessible, and multilingual solution for analyzing eyelid openness and blink detection.

Validation against publicly available datasets confirms the app's reliability and effectiveness, aligning with established methods. These results show Bapp's potential as an alternative to more resource-intensive methods using desktop computers and cloud servers.

Despite some limitations, the Bapp not only meets the need for accessible and accurate eyelid movement analysis but also provides clinicians with a practical and scalable tool to support continuous monitoring of disease progression and treatment effectiveness, thereby improving patient care. That facilitates earlier interventions and more personalized care strategies.

While some limitations remain, such as the availability and diversity of labeled training data, Bapp's success in real-world validation scenarios signals a promising future. Continued development should focus on expanding and diversifying annotated datasets, particularly those covering a wide range of ocular diseases and demographics, to further enhance diagnostic precision and clinical utility.

Overall, Bapp significantly contributes to digital ophthalmology, potentially enhancing patient engagement, remote monitoring, and clinical workflows in vision health care.

Conflict of Interest. The authors declare that they have no conflict of interest.

References

1. da Silva, J.L.S., de Godoy, C.M.G., Osaki, T.H., et al.: Mobile App for Assessing Hemifacial Spasm Treatment Response Using Machine Learning, pp. 197–206 (2024)
2. Osaki, M.H., Osaki, T.H., Garcia, D.M., et al.: An objective tool to measure the effect of botulinum toxin in blepharospasm and hemifacial spasm. Eur. J. Neurol. **27**, 1487–1492 (2020). https://doi.org/10.1111/ene.14258
3. Silkiss, R.Z., Koppinger, J., Truong, T., et al.: Cannabidiol as an adjunct to botulinum toxin in blepharospasm - a randomized pilot study. Transl Vis Sci Technol **12**, 17 (2023). https://doi.org/10.1167/tvst.12.8.17
4. Yabumoto, C., Osaki, M.H., Gameiro, G.R., et al.: Smartphone and custom-made software to assess the effect of botulinum toxin in essential blepharospasm: initial results. Eur. J. Neurol. **30**, 887–891 (2023). https://doi.org/10.1111/ene.15666
5. Da Silva, J.L.S.: Mobile App for Assessing Hemifacial Spasm Treatment Response Using Machine Learning
6. Drutarovsky, T., Fogelton, A.: Eye Blink Detection Using Variance of Motion Vectors, pp. 436–448 (2015)

7. Seamone, A., Shapiro, J.N., Zhao, Z., et al.: Eyelid motion tracking during blinking using high-speed imaging and digital image correlation. J Biomech Eng **147** (2025). https://doi.org/10.1115/1.4067082

8. Ren, Y., Wen, H., Bai, F., et al.: Comparison of deep learning-assisted blinking analysis system and Lipiview interferometer in dry eye patients: a cross-sectional study. Eye and Vision **11** (2024). https://doi.org/10.1186/s40662-024-00373-6

9. Hu, R., Sun, D., Shi, G., Pan, A.: Practical Application of Intelligent Vision Measurement System Based on Deep Learning **48**, 380–384 (2024). https://doi.org/10.12455/j.issn.1671-7104.230652

10. Hedayati Amlashi, N., Rajabi, M.T., Shafie, M., et al.: Videographic analysis of blink dynamics in patients with chronic progressive external ophthalmoplegia, myogenic ptosis, and facial nerve palsy using smartphone camera: a comparative analysis. Health Sci Rep **6** (2023). https://doi.org/10.1002/hsr2.1631

11. Okumura, Y., Inomata, T., Midorikawa-Inomata, A., et al.: DryEyeRhythm: a reliable and valid smartphone application for the diagnosis assistance of dry eye. Ocul. Surf. **25**, 19–25 (2022). https://doi.org/10.1016/j.jtos.2022.04.005

12. Zhang, S., Echegoyen, J.: Design and usability study of a point of care mhealth app for early dry eye screening and detection. J. Clin. Med. **12**, 6479 (2023). https://doi.org/10.3390/jcm12206479

13. Martin, R.: Clean Architecture: A Craftsman's Guide to Software Structure and Design, 1ra ed ed (2017)

14. Divjak, M., Bischof, H.: Eye blink based fatigue detection for prevention of Computer Vision Syndrome

15. Lee, W.O., Lee, E.C., Park, K.R.: Blink detection robust to various facial poses. J. Neurosci. Methods **193**, 356–372 (2010). https://doi.org/10.1016/j.jncumeth.2010.08.034

Gradient-Based Weighted Central Pixel Matching for Efficient Fractal Image Coding

Nadia M. G. Al-Saidi[1] , Suzan J. Obaiys[2]([✉]), Arkan J. Mohammed[3] ,
and Yeliz Karaca[4]

[1] Department of Applied Sciences, University of Technology, Baghdad 10066, Iraq
nadia.m.ghanim@uotechnology.edu.iq
[2] Department of Computer System and Technology, Faculty of Computer Science and
Information Technology, Universiti Malaya, 50603 Kuala Lumpur, Malaysia
suzan@um.edu.my
[3] Department of Mathematics, College of Science, Al-Mustansiriah University, Baghdad, Iraq
drarkanjasim@uomustansiriyah.edu.iq
[4] University of Massachusetts Chan Medical School (UMASS), 55 Lake Avenue North,
Worcester, MA 01655, USA
yeliz.karaca@ieee.org

Abstract. In the context of image coding systems, the fractal image encoding and decoding method is a better option due to its capacity for high achievement in compression ratio and resolution independence at any scale. Fractal image coding embodies two major phases. Firstly, the encoding step, where we produce numerical data, called Iterated Function System (IFS) data, from the statistically self-similar input image. Secondly, in the decoding step, we decode IFS data to revert to a fractal image, as an attractor, by using an inverse function. Notwithstanding, the popularity of the fractal encoder in light of the partition iterative function system has deteriorated into nearly out of favour due to its massive encoding time. So, the existing process is still not applicable. This paper proposes a new approach in which block dimensions are adjusted to address the limitation of requiring a high encoding time. The new strategy is designed for efficient pooling selections. It uses the central pixel and its neighbors based on gradient values, giving more weight to pixels with higher gradient magnitudes. This allows the matching process to take into account not just the pixel intensity but the change in intensity across the block, making it more robust to noise or slight variations in pixel values. This study confirms through experiments acceptable improvement in both encoding time and quality of the decoded image. Subsequently, it is considered an enhancement to some of the previous methods in the literature.

Keywords: Fractal image coding · Gradient method · Self-similarity · IFS · Domain and Range partition · Fractal dimension

1 Introduction

People in today's information-rich society are exposed to a vast amount of images on a daily uses, which puts a lot of strain on image transmission and storage. In the early 80s, two popular methods for image coding were Discrete Cosine Transformation (DCT)

O. Gervasi et al. (Eds.): ICCSA 2025, LNCS 15648, pp. 158–175, 2025.
https://doi.org/10.1007/978-3-031-97000-9_10

[1] and Vector Quantization (VQ) [2]. DCT method uses non-overlapping blocks by partitioning grids where each block is encoded individually, while VQ Methods explore the image pixels directly. Both VQ and DCT methods produced much research in order to achieve targeted image coding, and subsequently, these methods occupied a variety of commercial implementations. Despite this affluence, the method of image coding was extending towards a new direction, particularly fractals and wavelets, which already have achieved appreciable attention [3]. Mathematicians used a mathematical iterative sequence deterministically [4]. This concept led researchers to think of a realistic fractal object and thus, finally, Mandelbrot first rediscovered a realistic visual complex object mathematically and was able to demonstrate it with computational graphics. The Fractal concept deals with non-integer dimensions, while the classical Euclidean dimension exists on integer dimensions [5]. The fractal concept is now used in many fields to analyze objects such as Engineering, Physics, and Biology, security protocols, as well as in different areas of image processing [6–10]. Michael Barnsley [11] was the first who propose that real-life objects or images can be modeled using deterministic fractal objects. This modeling process is performed with the help of a set of iterative affine transformations, he named this set the iterative function systems (IFS) [12] as presented in his famous collage theorem. Nevertheless, the drawback of this theory is that encoding and decoding cannot possible to be automated. Arnaud E. Jacquin first proposed a piece-wise affine contractive transformation in the form of partial transformability of image [3]. On Jacquin's contribution, massive research has taken place till now and comparatively, to some extent, successes have been achieved already and become undeniably popular because of their potential to foster high-resolution re-builder images at very eminent compression ratios [13–18]. Nevertheless, it experienced encoding time complexity due to an immense range of harmonization with a range block to the enormous domain blocks [19]. In order to address this most critical barrier to Fractal Image Coding, several researchers have already introduced methods that reduce the search complexity of the domain pool comparatively [20–23].

Galabov showed how block size affects encoding time and the quality of images, taking 2×2 and 4×4 pixel block sizes [24]. Datta came up with the concept of pixel neighbourhood in the image thinning process and defined the central pixel in 8-neighbours for a binary image [25]. Fisher proposed the division of domain blocks into 72 different classes with combinations of average and variance in four quadrants of the block under consideration [26]. By using mean pixel value and variance of blocks, Xing et al. improved Fisher's layout and achieved 576 classes [27]. Caso et al. used vector variances to transfer the fixed ordering of variances of image blocks and neighbourhood of classes [28]. Wang et al. applied edge information of the blocks for differentiating blocks into a number of classes and gave the result in speed-up of ratio [9]. Fisher and Menlove divided an image into Horizontal-vertical partitioning recursively to form two new rectangles [29]. Hebert and Soundararajan divided a rectangular image into two triangles initially and each of these triangles is subdivided into four triangles by splitting the triangle recursively [2, 30]. To sort image blocks, Han applied a fuzzy structure cataloger [31], and on the other hand, for the same purpose, Al-Saidi et al. used some of the metaheuristic Optimization algorithms to enhance the encoding time [32]. From all the literature above, we notice that all the researchers use approaches that partition the images into different block sizes, for example: 32×32, 16×16, 8×8, 4×4, or 2×2 and work on entire blocks. As a result, it affects the search process because the pixel intensity values are not symmetric compared to the central pixel of the above-mentioned blocks.

The main contribution in this work is initiated by changing the 2×2 average pooling system into a 3×3 max pooling system of the block-windows; and blocks dimensionality considering 8 neighbours of the central pixel and searching domain blocks depending on the central pixel rather than entire blocks for each of the size of the blocks (3×3). The conventional method uses the intensity value of the central pixel as the index for matching between domain and range blocks. The gradient-based weighting of the central pixel and its surrounding neighbours could be used to expand this. Determine the gradient values (intensity changes) for the eight neighbours surrounding the central pixel rather than just the central pixel. By capturing the direction and magnitude of changes in local pixel values, these gradients can give the value of the central pixel additional context.

The remaining part of the work is arranged as follows: Sect. 2 discusses the mathematical groundwork in detail based on our proposed method. Section 3 shows the development and formation of fractal encoding and decoding through our proposed method. In Sect. 4, we compared our experiment results with other existing work, and finally, we conclude the work in Sect. 5.

2 Mathematical Background

This section presents the mathematical background of feature extraction in digital images. It is a new approach that uses thinning algorithms, which take advantage of the spatial relationships between pixels. The method depends on looking at a block's central pixel as well as its neighbours.

2.1 Pixel Neighborhoods

- Central Pixel (p_c):

Let $p_c = P(i, j)$ be the central pixel in a given block. It is significant because it is encircled by nearby pixels that collectively capture local structural characteristics.

- Orthogonal neighbours ($N_4(p)$):

The neighbors of p_c is defined by the adjacent (vertical and horizontal) pixels such that:

$$N_4(p) = \{(i-1, j), (i+1, j), (i, j-1), (i, j+1)\}$$

- Diagonal neighbours ($ND(p)$):

$$ND(p) = \{(i-1, j-1), (i-1, j+1), (i+1, j-1), (i+1, j+1)\}$$

$ND(p)$ is used to define the four diagonal neighbours of p_c

- Complete 8-Neighbor Set ($N_8(p)$):

The full set that used to surround p_c combines the orthogonal and diagonal neighbours, such that:

$$N_8(p) = N_4(p) \cup ND(p),$$

which represents the symmetry and structure around the central pixel.

2.2 The Space Where the Fractal is Generated

To measure variations between image regions, the framework additionally makes use of ideas from metric space theory.

- **Hausdorff Metric:**

When calculating the distance between two sets in a complete and compact metric space, the Hausdorff metric H is utilized. It offers a means of evaluating how similar image subsets under transformation are to one another.

- **Iterative Function Systems (IFS):**

Our approach is based on the following theorems, which summarize the main findings in fractal theory:

Theorem 1: Iterative Function System (IFS). *An Iterative Function System is a finite set of contraction mappings on a complete metric space (X,d), such that,*

$$f_i : X \rightarrow X \text{ for } i = 1, 2, \ldots, N$$

where each f_i is a contraction, and the IFS system consists of the set $\{f_i\}$. This theorem guarantees that the mappings are applied iteratively, and this theorem ensures convergence to a unique attractor.

Theorem 2. Collage theory uses a set of contractive mappings to approximate an image Im $\subset X$. If an IFS $F = \{X, f_i\}_{i=1}^{N}$, and a mapping $f_i : X \rightarrow X$ exist, and $\epsilon > 0$ with contraction ratios $0 \leq s_i < 1$ then,

$$d_H \left(\text{Im}, \bigcup_{i=1}^{N} f_i(\text{Im}) \right) \leq \epsilon$$

Consequently, the bounded distance between the original image and the IFS's attractor A is:

$$d_H(\text{Im}, A) \leq \frac{\epsilon}{1 - s}$$

where s is the maximum contraction factor. This outcome guarantees that we can use the attractor produced by the IFS to closely resemble the original image by reducing the collage error.

2.3 Gradient Principles

A. Gradient Computation: Calculate the gradient in both vertical and horizontal directions for every 3×3 block. To find the gradient magnitudes and directions for each neighbour of the central pixel, we can use the Sobel or Prewitt filter operators.

B. Weighted Matching: Based on the magnitude of these gradients, give the central pixel and its neighbours weights after you have the gradient information. The matching score will be higher for blocks with similar gradient patterns, which indicate similar edge or texture features.

C. Block Matching: Compare the weighted sum of gradients between domain and range blocks rather than the individual pixel values. This method can lessen the sensitivity to minute changes in pixel values and enables more reliable matching, particularly in pictures with subtle textures or gradients.

By adding the directional information of the surrounding pixels, this technique enhances central pixel indexing and may result in faster and more accurate block matching, particularly in images with high-frequency details.

2.4 Application of IFS and Collage Theory.

We can take a set of $M(i, j, [g_p])$ in a metric space, (X, d), where $X \in \mathbb{R}^n$, and $\mathbb{R}^n$ denotes n-dimensional real space. (i, j) is a pixel location in spatial coordinates, and g_p is the pixel value. The set $M(i, j, [g_p])$ is closed and bounded, so according to [11], M is a compact set and $(M(i, j, [g_p]), d)$ compact metric space and all sequences will converge to its limit point in $(M(i, j, [g_p]), d)$ [11]. But when we measure the distance between two sets, the symmetric characteristics of a metric space are not met. We must therefore evaluate distances using different metrics, as the Hausdorff Metric. Fractal objects can exist in a Hausdorff space [11]. So, a set M in a Hausdorff metric space is a complete metric space. Any set M will converge to its limit point using Hutchinson's operator, resulting in a unique attractor [12]. Barnsley used the Hutchinson operator naming *IFS*, which is a set of successive contraction mappings on a complete metric space with contractive factors $0 < s < 1$, and mathematically, $A = W_n(A)$ is an attractor (Theorems 1 and 2). The set A is the same as $n = 1$, the union of the image for all points in A under W_n [6]. This demonstrates how a certain IFS maps onto a sequence of A_{i-1} in a complete metric space, for $i = 1, 2, \ldots$, which converge to its distinctive limit point. Now, for the same IFS, we take a set $L \subset (X, d_H)$ in a complete metric space where, $d_H(L, W_n(L)) < \varepsilon$ is the Hausdorff distance. This distance is measured between L and A, for $n = 1$, it is less than $(1-s)$ [5]. This approach did not work on statistically self-similar natural images in Machine Vision. In 1992, however, Jacquin understood that the natural image is not exclusively self-similar. That is, any subset of the image is not similar to the whole image; rather, any subset of the image is similar in many scales to another subset of the image [19]. This idea gives him a new dimension to contribute to the method of Barnsley [3], and thus he proposes a partitioned iterated function system (PIFS), which is a block-wise contraction mapping of a square size of blocks in place of the whole image in Theorem 2. The steps of this method are presented as follows:

1. Jacquin took range and domain blocks from the same set with the size R_j and D_i.
2. $D_i = 4 R_j$ where $D(2r, 2r)$ is the array of overlapping blocks and $B(r, r)$ is the array of non-overlapping blocks.
3. The size of D_i is contracted to the size of B_j homogeneously, immediately before the eight isometric mappings are applied on D_i, to be $r \times r$.
4. Every block is contracted, that is, every 2×2 set of pixels is reduced to a (1×1) set of $(2r \times 2r)$, (4 pixels). For this purpose, Jacquin's method used 2×2 average pooling.

So far, all researchers have used these basics. Image is encoded to calculate PIFS, and it is decoded to get back the image (the fractal attractor) using the collage theorem [5].

3   The Proposed Method

We have already observed a variety in block size while researchers work in terms of a pixel array. In this method, (3×3) square window of blocks is chosen due to its consistency and symmetric with the central pixel. However, when the 8-isometric transformation on the window of size (3×3) pixels is applied, the central pixel remains intact. This central pixel helps to match between domain blocks and range blocks.

3.1   Partitioning of Domain and Range Pools

The uniform partitions of an image of size M in a complete metric space (X, d) are constructed such that the union of all subsets in M must be equal to the entire set M. In the first step of the process, we have taken two versions of block pools for the same image $(M \times M)$ as a domain pool and range pool. Then the size of each domain block $D_i = 3r \times 3r$ pixels is captured as a sub-block, while $R_i = r \times r$ for the range.

3.2   The Geometrical Transformations

In the geometrical transformations, we apply Homothety and Similitude iteratively on a set M in the complete metric space, and thus we can achieve a unique fixed point or attractor, for more details see [18] and [5]. Pixel values must be transformed to perform operations like geometric transformations and intensity adjustments in digital image processing. The original technique involved mapping the intensity values of pixels within a grayscale image's spatial coordinate system. Assume that the image is represented by a 2D matrix $f(i, j) = g_p$, where g_p refers to the pixel intensity value at (i, j), and $g_p \in [0, 2^b - 1]$, b is the number of bits in each pixel (in the standard grayscale images, it equals 8).

A color image is defined by three separate channels: Red, Green, and Blue (RGB), each channel has its own intensity value for every pixel. A pixel at (i, j) is defined by the RGB values as $f_R(i, j), f_G(i, j), f_B(i, j)$, ranging from 0 to 255 (for 8-bit images). To apply this transformation to color images, we should handle the three distinct channels.

The mapping function must be modified while preserving the overall transformation for every pixel. The transformation for pixel intensities can be given as follows:

$$I_R(z) = s_R z_R + g_R$$
$$I_G(z) = s_G z_G + g_G$$
$$I_B(z) = s_B z_B + g_B$$

where z_R, z_G, z_B are the pixel intensity values in the Red, Green, and Blue channels, and s_R, s_G, s_B and g_R, g_G, g_B represent the scaling and adjustment factors for each channel.

The coordinates of the pixels in a color image do not change when undergoing geometric transformations like translation, rotation, or scaling. These transformation rules can be used to change the intensity values of each channel. To maintain the integrity of the image's color balance, it is important to make sure that the changes made to the pixel values are the same in each of the three channels.

3.2.1 The Contraction Mapping

In image processing, we operate on the general pooling to mitigate variance, trim the complexity of computation and obtain low-level features from the neighbourhood. We use max pooling because it can reduce 50% of the time over average pooling. In this stage, we reduced the $\kappa r \times \kappa r$ sub-block size to $(r \times r)$ size of the sub-block. A homogeneous contraction mapping is used, which means every $\kappa \times \kappa = 3 \times 3$ pixels block is condensed to 1×1, as shown in Fig. 1. This can be done with either average pooling or max pooling. We proposed max pooling, and subsequently, we reduced the pooling time by 50%, maintaining the average PSNR is almost 27 dB as shown in Tables 2 and 4.

3.2.2 Isometric Transformation

In geometric isometric transformation, the affine transformation is a linear mapping method that preserves points, straight lines, and planes. They consist of four reflections (R_f) and four rotations (R_o) that can be applied on domain blocks to its mapped range blocks under some conditions for balancing the brightness and contrast of the image. The affine transformation w is defined as:

$$w \begin{pmatrix} i \\ j \\ k \end{pmatrix} = \begin{pmatrix} a & b & 0 \\ c & d & 0 \\ 0 & 0 & s \end{pmatrix} \begin{pmatrix} i \\ j \\ k \end{pmatrix} + \begin{pmatrix} e \\ f \\ g \end{pmatrix} \tag{1}$$

$$R_f = \begin{bmatrix} \cos 2\theta & \sin 2\theta \\ \sin 2\theta & -\cos 2\theta \end{bmatrix} \tag{2}$$

$$R_o = \begin{bmatrix} \cos \theta & -\sin \theta \\ \sin \theta & \cos \theta \end{bmatrix} \tag{3}$$

Figure 1 shows how the 8-isometrics are equally divided in 4-reflections using Eq. (2), where $\cos 2\theta = a$, $b = \sin 2\theta = c$ and $-\cos(2\theta) = d$. By turns the values of $\theta = -45°$, $0°$, $45°$, $90°$, and in 4-rotations using the Eq. (3) where $a = \cos(\theta) = d$, $b = -\sin(\theta) = c$, where $\theta = 0°$, $90°$, $180°$, $-90°$.

3.3   Pixel Values Transformations

In the geometrical aspect of gray-scale digital images, there are spatial coordinates (i, j) such that $f(i, j) = g_p$, where $g_p \in [0, 2^b - 1 \mid b = 1, 2,...,8]$. Here $[i \times j]$ is a 2D image plane in a complete metric space. For every (i, j), we have a value of pixel intensity g_p under the function $w(i, j) = g_p$. Even after all 8-isometric transformations are applied on (3×3) windows, the central pixel neither changes its position nor its values according to the function $f(i, j) = g_p$. Windows except $\kappa \times \kappa$, where $\kappa = n$ and $n \in \mathbb{N}$ is any odd value, do not have these characteristics. Nevertheless, we use $\kappa = 3$ to comply with 8-neighbours, which is a new idea in this field. So, in this spatial coordinate window of domain blocks, the process of mapping into the range blocks is possible because of translation vectors. Hence, to maintain the total mapping, we need to introduce the third dimension, which will attain the value of g_p and consequently, the function will be rearranged from Eq. 1 as:

$$\Rightarrow f \begin{pmatrix} i \\ j \\ z \end{pmatrix} = \begin{pmatrix} ai + bj + e \\ ci + dj + f \\ sz + g \end{pmatrix}$$

It is clear that, we have an equation for depicting the intensity function $I(z) = sz + g$ with variable z and $I(z)$ are the domain and range block intensity, respectively. We can estimate a linear regression line $\hat{I}(z) = +\hat{s}qz$ and thus we get the error,

$$E = \sum \{I(z) - \hat{I}(z)\}^2 = \sum \{I(z) - g_q - \hat{s}_q z\}^2$$

where $z = f(i, j)$ which returns g_q and to minimize error, we can take partial derivatives with respect to g_q and $\hat{s}_q$ and hence we get $g_q = \frac{1}{n}[\sum \hat{I}(z) - \hat{s}_q \sum z]$ and $\hat{s}_q = \frac{n \sum z \times \hat{I}(z) - \sum z \sum \hat{I}(z)}{n \sum z^2 - (\sum z)^2}$ where, n is the number of pixels in each block.

3.4   Gradient Method for Domain Range Blocks

In the process of finding domain blocks for each range block, the practice of searching is to take a norm for the difference of block matrices, which is done iteratively pixel-by-pixel, as a result, NP time complexity exists. By searching only the central pixel based on gradient weight instead of pixel-by-pixel, NP can be reduced to P-class time complexity, and this is done using the norm of the central pixels' difference of the blocks. Once for each range block, there is the best-fit domain block, DQ, then there exists a set of IFS, $w_q(DQ)$ and for every $w_q(DQ)$, a 5-tuple is constructed $[(i, j), (t_q), \hat{s}_q, g_q]$, which represent the position, nature of transformation, brightness and contrast of the selected block accordingly. This method can be illustrated through the following example: Let the 3×3 block be defined as:

$$\begin{bmatrix} p_1 & p_2 & p_3 \\ p_4 & p_5 & p_6 \\ p_7 & p_8 & p_9 \end{bmatrix}$$

where:

- p_5 is the central pixel
- The others p_1 to p_9 are its 8-neighbours

A. *Gradient Operators (Sobel-Based Approximation):*
Using Sobel filters, which are commonly used to estimate gradients:

- Horizontal Gradient G_x:

$$G_x = (p_3 + 2p_6 + p_9) - (p_1 + 2p_4 + p_7)$$

- Vertical Gradient G_y:

$$G_y = (p_7 + 2p_8 + p_9) - (p_1 + 2p_2 + p_3)$$

B. *Gradient Magnitude G:*
To quantify the overall edge strength at the center:

$$G = \sqrt{G_x^2 + G_y^2}$$

or for computational efficiency:

$$G \approx |G_x| + |G_y|$$

Matching process:

- Compute g for both domain and range 3×3 blocks
- Compare the gradient magnitudes or use them as weights for the matching score
- This approach captures edge direction and texture strength, improving match accuracy over intensity-only matching.

The final matching score is computed by combining the weighted contributions of the central pixel and its neighbours. It is calculated as follows:

$$\text{Matching Score} = 0.6 \times \left(\frac{|G_D - G_R|}{G_D} \right) + 0.4 \times (\text{Neighbor Gradients Differences})$$

This score will be lower if the domain and range blocks are more similar in terms of their gradient profiles, leading to a better match.

In this example, the central pixel and its neighbors are compared based on gradient values, giving more weight to pixels with higher gradient magnitudes. This allows the matching process to take into account not just the pixel intensity but the change in intensity across the block, making it more robust to noise or slight variations in pixel values.

3.5 Low-Gradient Image

In flat or low-texture image areas, where gradients go to vanish or give little information, a hybrid matching strategy is used. In particular, such as matching based on mean intensity difference or local variance, if the average gradient magnitude g in a 3×3 window is below a threshold τ. The following values can be defined.

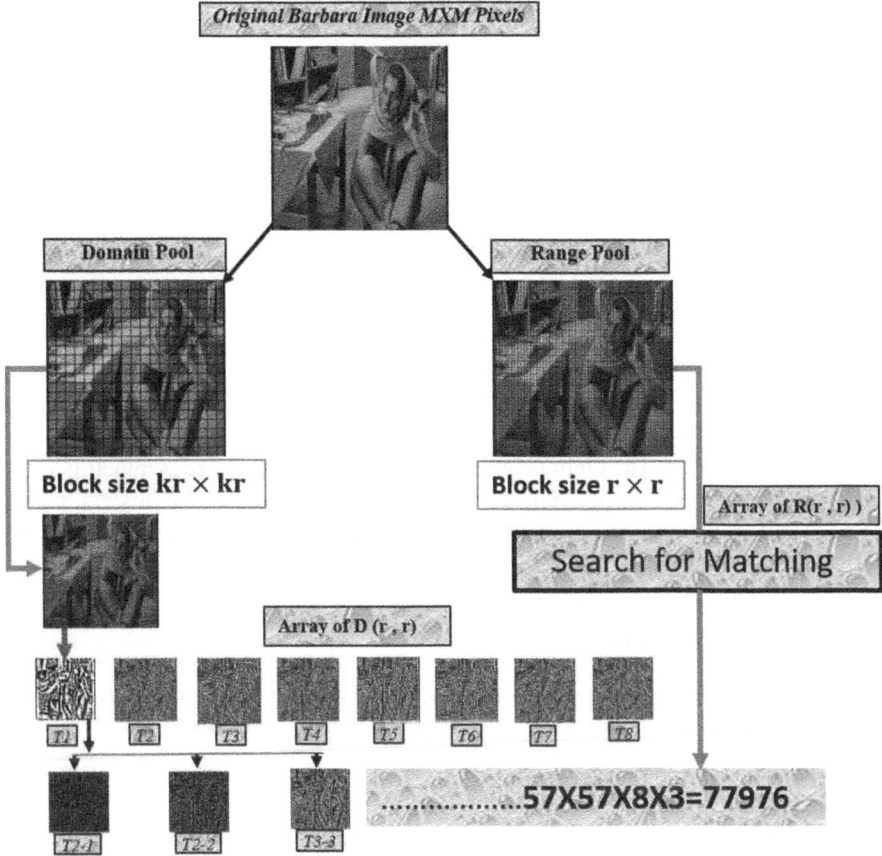

Fig. 1. Image blocking and 8 isometric transformed images, each has 3 scale factors to adjust brightness

- $\tau \approx 10$ for 8-bit images.
- The Euclidean distance between the mean values of range and domain blocks is used as a similarity metric

Picking the central pixels of both domain and range blocks, we find the best-fit domain block for each range block depending on less residual error between the two central pixels. Please see Figs. 1 and 2.

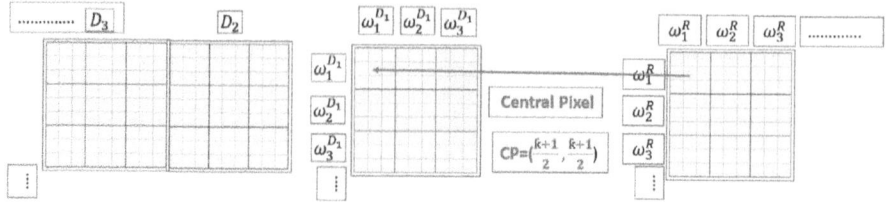

Fig. 2. Central pixels of range and domain windows

3.6 Encoding Process Flow

To encode a statistically self-similar original image, $I_M = [p_V \times p_H \mid p_V = p_H]$, we need to make two copies of the sets. The set of Domain $I_{M_D}(p_V, p_H)$ and Range $I_{M_R}(p_V, p_H)$. We split $I_{M_R}(p_V, p_H)$ into the uniform size of block partitions comprising nine pixels in each. The eight neighboring pixels of the block are symmetric to the central pixel in Fig. 4. For the domain set, $I_{M_D}(p_V, p_H)$, we repeat the process, taking $[\kappa 3 \times \kappa 3]$ pixels in each. The ultimate target of the encoding process is to generate the IFS parameter $[(i, j), (t_q), \hat{s}_q, g_q]$.

3.7 Decoding Process Flow

In the existing image decoding methods, pixel-by-pixel error checking is used, but in this study, we proposed a window-by-window approach to minimize the time.

1. The parameters from $T_i(\alpha, \beta) = [(i, j), (t_q), \hat{s}_q, g_q]$ are used to generate the IFS in the encoding algorithm.
2. To regenerate the range blocks, we used any arbitrary image with the same size as the original image.
3. Each range block is filed according to its location in T.
4. Step 3 is applied iteratively until the high-quality image is generated, as shown in Fig. 5.

The flow of the process is explained in Fig. 6.

4 Experiment, Results, and Discussion

In Tables 1, 2 and 3, we showed two statistical parameters, MSE and PSNR, which can tell the objective quality of the five images. In Table 1, we showed existing method results, and in Table 2 proposed the method; in Table 3, we showed the comparison between the methods. Table 2: full fractal encoding process time: 2×2 average pooling vs 2×2 max pooling when image size equals 256×256 and block size: 8×8 pixels.

The MSE and PSNR of the original and decoded images are calculated. We got influential and motivated results in the proposed method compared to an existing method in encoding and decoding improvement of 34.34% and 39.66%, respectively, for the same images. Moreover, we analyzed the gray scale for the same image and got a high class of improvement in encoding and decoding, 46.32%, respectively shown in Table 2.

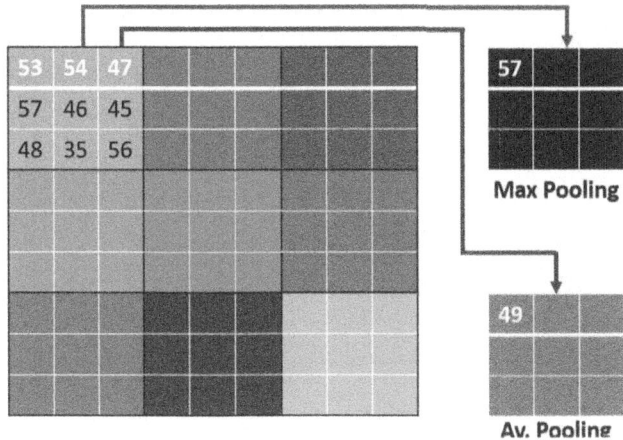

Fig. 3. Pooling system: 3 × 3 max and average pooling

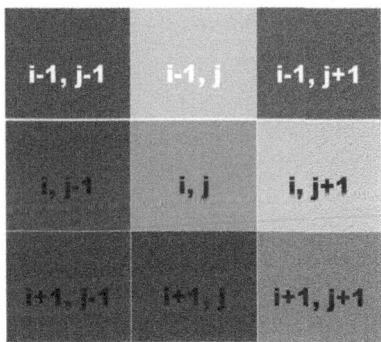

Fig. 4. The 8 neighbouring pixels of a 3 × 3 block

(a)　　(b)　　(a)　　(b)　　(a)　　(b)　　(a)　　(b)　　(a)　(b)

Fig. 5. The proposed method: (a) Original standard images, (b) the corresponding decoded images.

FSIM: *Feature Similarity Index*. It is used to measure the sensitivity to edges and structure.

GMSD: *Gradient Magnitude Similarity Deviation*. It is used to measure the reflect gradient consistency.

PSNR (dB): *Peak Signal-to-Noise Ratio*. It is used to measure the quality of the reconstruction image.

Table 1. Encoding and Decoding Time Analysis

Image Name	Encoding Time(s)				
	M(2 ×2)	M(3 ×3)	TTR	I% TR	Av% TR
Lena	118.69	76.64	35.4	30.78	
Barbara	120.8	75.53	42.1	36.61	
Cameraman	121.57	75.08	36	33.03	34.34
Peppers	121	75.38	46	39.66	
Einstein	121.03	75.396	37	31.62	

Table 2. The fractal encoding process time.

Image Name	2 × 2 Max-pooling		2 × 2 Av-pooling	
	Time	PSNR	Time	PSNR
Barbara	54.7310	24.2654	74.1820	43.4059
Camera-Men	31.9190	25.0289	36.9030	45.6515
Einstein	33.3570	25.6204	57.7310	44.9906
Lena	33.5450	32.4749	59.3550	54.3088
Peppers	49.5590	26.6530	67.4640	47.1608

Mape: *Mean Absolute Percentage Error*: It is a measure used to find the average percentage difference between the reconstructed and original images.

Table 5 confirms that the very low or the very high central weights are assigned to the central pixel of one of the chosen images, the range between 0.5 and 0.7 consistently produces optimal PSNR values and faster encoding. This result validates our initial selection of $wc = 0.6$.

In some cases, when the average gradient magnitude is less than a specific threshold, we use some traditional features such as pixel mean or variance as intensity-based matching, as you can see in Table 6. This hybrid approach preserves performance and stability even in the presence of weak gradient information.

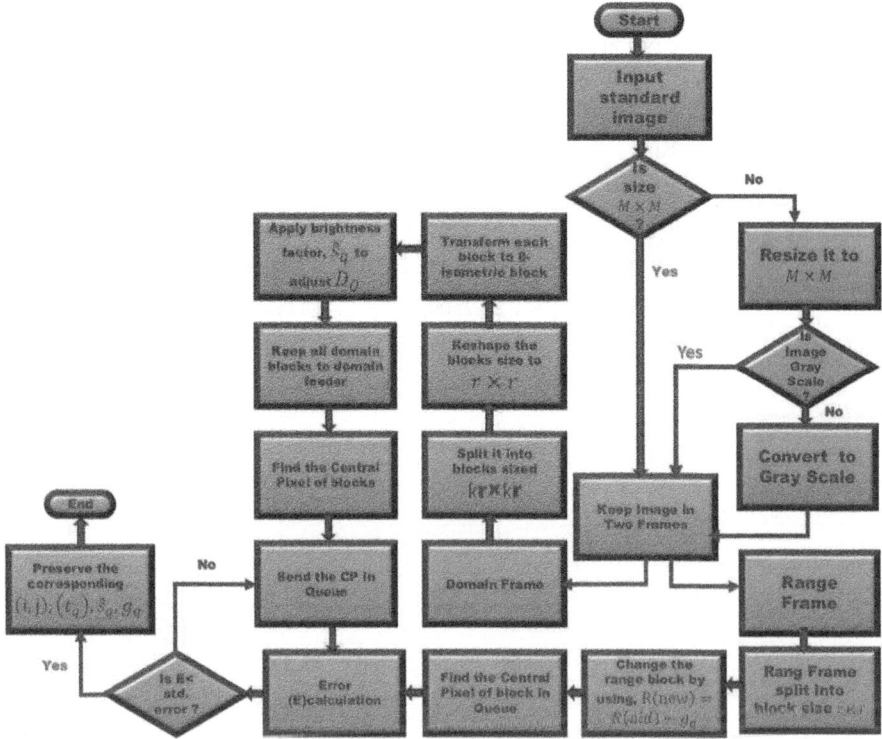

Fig. 6. Encoding process flow diagram

Table 3. Image quality index for decoded image analysis by full reference

IQAT	Barbara	Cman	Einstein	Lena	Pepper
MSE	40.3008	17.2353	28.6325	12.8956	24.7371
GMSD [34]	0.1952	0.1567	0.173	0.1422	0.1758
Rvalue:	0.8245	0.8745	0.8487	0.9231	0.8494
RMSE:	6.6793	5.4604	6.1975	4.4278	6.1738
FSIM [33]	0.8388	0.8615	0.853	0.9017	0.8522
Mape:	23.6426	11.0176	8.4698	4.3242	8.984

Table 4. Pooling Stage: Time and Image Quality Comparison with 3×3 average vs max pooling when Image Size: 252×252 pixels.

Image Name	3×3 Max-pooling		3×3 Av-pooling	
	Time	PSNR	Time	PSNR
Barbara	0.2190	22.2382	0.3280	41.6035
Camera-Men	0.2030	21.4793	0.3590	40.5847
Einstein	0.1720	23.2147	0.3750	43.0182
Lena	0.1880	27.2500	0.3750	48.9911
Peppers	0.2340	23.1677	0.4530	43.2268

Table 5. Different weight values

Central Weight (wc)	PSNR (avg)	Encoding Time (avg)
0.3	25.1 dB	55.3 s
0.4	26.2 dB	54.1 s
0.5	26.8 dB	52.7 s
0.6	**27.3 dB**	**51.2 s**
0.7	27.1 dB	52.0 s

Table 6. Performance comparison of flat and low-texture images

Image	PSNR (Grad-Only)	PSNR (Hybrid)	SSIM (Grad-Only)	SSIM (Hybrid)
Lena	27.2	**32.4**	0.89	**0.95**
Einstein	25.6	**30.1**	0.88	**0.94**

5   Conclusion

Fractal image encoding and decoding are considered important techniques because of their high compression ratios and resolution independence at any scale. Encoding and decoding are the two main stages of this technique. The process of encoding creates numerical data from the statistically self-similar input image called an Iterated Function System (IFS). Whereas, the decoding process uses the IFS data to reconstruct the original fractal image. This technique has a long encoding time due to the exhaustive block searches in partitioned iterative function systems, which reduces its use and is considered a challenge. One of the great improvements in encoding and decoding time is the use of 3×3 method. Gradient values are used to compare the central pixel and its neighbours, giving pixels with larger gradient magnitudes more weight. This makes the matching process more resilient to noise or minute changes in pixel values by allowing it to consider not only the pixel intensity but also the change in intensity throughout the block. We believe the most important feature of Fractal Decoding that we proposed in this paper attained the high quality of the image even when zooming out the decoded image. Furthermore, due to its efficiency, this approach for image coding can be applied in Medical Imaging, where we need to focus on image details with quality, and in Surveillance Systems, when trying to get a clear picture of the intruder or the cause of the alarm. From the obtained results and through analysis, we can conclude that the proposed method has a clear advantage over the 2×2 Homogeneous Contraction method. The results we presented are obtained using MATLAB Software. More adaptive block size techniques, such as entropy-based segmentation and quadtree partitioning, could be used to improve the speed and quality of encoding. Combining such adaptive strategies with our gradient-based matching is a future direction of work.

Acknowledgements. This research was sponsored by the Universiti Malaya Research Excellent Grant UMREG 068 - 2024 (UM.0000285/HRU.RC), and the Universiti Malaya Research Maintenance Fee RMFI2067-2021 (UM.0002145/HIP.IP).

Author Contributions. All authors have contributed equally to this paper. All authors have read and agreed to the published version of the manuscript.

Funding. UM.0000285/HRU.RC and UM.0002145/HIP.IP.

Conflict of Interest. All authors declare no conflicts of interest in this paper.

References

1. Duh, D.-J., Jeng, J.-H., Chen, S.-Y.: DCT-based simple classification scheme for fractal image compression. Image Vis. Comput. **23**(13), 1115–1121 (2005)
2. Davoine, F., Antonini, M., Chassery, J.M., Barlaud, M.: Fractal image compression based on Delaunay triangulation and vector quantization. IEEE Trans. Image Process. **5**(2), 338–346 (1996)
3. Koli, N.A., Ali, M.S.: Lossy color image compression technique using fractal coding with different size of range and domain blocks. In: International Conference on Advanced Computing and Communications, ADCOM 2006, pp. 236–239. IEEE (2006)
4. Jacquin, A.E.: Image coding based on a fractal theory of iterated contractive image transformations. IEEE Trans. Image Process. **1**(1), 18–30 (1992)
5. Mandelbrot, B.B.: Fractal geometry: what is it, and what does it do? Proc. R. Soc. Lond. A Math. Phys. Sci. **423**(1864), 3–16 (1989)
6. Barnsley, M.F., Massopust, P., Strickland, H., Sloan, A.D.: Fractal modeling of biological structures. Ann. N. Y. Acad. Sci. **504**(1), 179–194 (1987)
7. Ibrahim, R.W., Yahya, H., Mohammed, A.J., Al-Saidi, N.M., Baleanu, D.: Mathematical design enhancing medical images formulated by a fractal flame operator (2022)
8. Al-Saidi, N.M., Abdul-Wahed, H.Y.: Classification of remote sensing images via fractal discriptores. In: 2018 International Conference on Advance of Sustainable Engineering and its Application (ICASEA), pp. 99–104. IEEE, March 2018
9. Al-Saidi, N.M., Said, M.R.M.: Biometric identification using local iterated function. Eur. Phys. J. Spec. Top. **223**(8), 1647–1662 (2014). IEEE transactions on Image Processing, 20(8):2378–2386, 2011

10. Grinchuk, P.S., Danilova-Tretiak, S.M.: Fractal power law and polymer-like behavior for the metro growth in megacities. Chaos Solitons Fractals **194**, 116137 (2025)
11. Barnsley, M.F.: Fractals Everywhere. Academic Press, Cambridge (2014)
12. Hutchinson, J.E.: Fractals and self-similarity. Indiana Univ. Math. J. **30**(5), 713–747 (1981)
13. Kominek, J.: Algorithm for fast fractal image compression. In: Digital Video Compression: Algorithms and Technologies 1995, vol. 2419, pp. 296–306. International Society for Optics and Photonics (1995)
14. Al-Saidi, N.M., Al-Bundi, S.S., Al-Jawari, N.J.: A hybrid of fractal image coding and fractal dimension for an efficient retrieval method. Comput. Appl. Math. **37**(2), 996–1011 (2018)
15. Al-Azawi, R.J., Al-Saidi, N., Jalab, H.A., Ibrahim, R., Baleanu, D.: Image splicing detection based on texture features with fractal entropy (2021)
16. Al-Saidi, N.M., Md Said, M.R.: Improved digital signature protocol using iterated function systems. Int. J. Comput. Math. **88**(17), 3613–3625 (2011)
17. Tseng, C.-C., Hsieh, J.-G., Jeng, J.-H.: Fractal image compression using visual-based particle swarm optimization. Image Vis. Comput. **26**(8), 1154–1162 (2008)
18. Zhu, L., Zeng, X., Chen, B., Chen, P., Li, Y.H., Wang, S.: Leveraging diffusion knowledge for generative image compression with fractal frequency-aware band learning. arXiv preprint arXiv:2503.11321 (2025)
19. Lee, C.K., Lee, W.K.: Fast fractal image block coding based on local variances. IEEE Trans. Image Process. **7**(6), 888–891 (1998)
20. Wang, Q., Du, J.: Modified decoded image quality prediction method for fractal image coding. Comput. Electr. Eng. **118**, 109462 (2024)
21. Ahadullah, M., Sapar, S.H., Al-Saidi, N.M., Said, M.R.M.: Competitive improvement of the time complexity to encode fractal image: by applying symmetric central pixel of the block. IEEE Access **9**, 5028–5045 (2020)
22. Long, B., et al.: Improved fractal coding and hyperchaotic system for lossless image compression and encryption. Nonlinear Dyn., 1–30 (2024)
23. Al-Saidi, N.M.G., Ali, A.H.: Towards enhancing of fractal image compression performance via block complexity. In: 2017 Annual Conference on New Trends in Information & Communications Technology Applications (NTICT), pp. 246–251. IEEE (2017)
24. Galabov, M.: Fractal image compression. In: Proceedings of International Conference on Computer Systems and Technologies (CompSysTech 2003), pp. 320–326 (2003)
25. Datta, A., Parui, S.K.: A robust parallel thinning algorithm for binary images. Pattern Recognit. **27**(9), 1181–1192 (1994)
26. Fisher, Y.: Fractal Image Compression: Theory and Application. Springer, New York (2012). https://doi.org/10.1007/978-1-4612-2472-3
27. Xing, C., Ren, Y., Li, X.: A hierarchical classification matching scheme for fractal image compression. In: 2008 Congress on Image and Signal Processing, vol. 1, pp. 283–286. IEEE (2008)
28. Caso, G., Obrador, P., Jay Kuo, C.-C.: Fast methods for fractal image encoding. In: Visual Communications and Image Processing 1995, vol. 2501, pp. 583–595. International Society for Optics and Photonics (1995)
29. Fisher, Y., Menlove, S.: Fractal encoding with HV partitions. In: Fisher, Y. (ed.) Fractal Image Compression, pp. 119–136. Springer, New York (1995). https://doi.org/10.1007/978-1-4612-2472-3_6
30. Hebert, D.J., Soundararajan, E.: Fast fractal image compression with triangular multiresolution block matching. In: International Conference on Image Processing, 1998. ICIP 98. Proceedings, vol. 1, pp. 747–750. IEEE (1998)
31. Han, J.: Fast fractal image compression using fuzzy classification. In: 2008 Fifth International Conference on Fuzzy Systems and Knowledge Discovery, vol. 3, pp. 272–276. IEEE (2008)

32. Al-Bundi, S.S., Al-Saidi, N.M., Al-Jawari, N.J.: Crowding optimization method to improve fractal image compressions based iterated function. Int. J. Adv. Comput. Sci. Appl. **7**(7) (2016)
33. Xue, W., Zhang, L., Mou, X., Bovik, A.C.: Gradient magnitude similarity deviation: a highly efficient perceptual image quality index. IEEE Trans. Image Process. **23**(2), 684–695 (2014)
34. Zhang, L., Zhang, L., Mou, X., Zhang, D.: FSIM: a feature similarity index for image quality assessment. IEEE Trans. Image Process. **20**(8), 2378–2386 (2011)

Quantum Random Number Generation via Von Neumann Projection

Nawres A. Alwan[1]📷, Suzan J. Obaiys[1]([✉])📷, Nadia M. G. Al-Saidi[2]📷,
and Nurul Fazmidar Binti Mohd Noor[1]📷

[1] Department of Computer System and Technology, Faculty of Computer Science
and Information Technology, Universiti Malaya, 50603 Kuala Lumpur, Malaysia
s2000740@siswa.um.edu.my, {suzan,fazmidar}@um.edu.my
[2] Department of Applied Sciences, University of Technology, Baghdad 10066, Iraq
nadia.m.ghanim@uotechnology.edu.iq

Abstract. This work introduces a new method for quantum random
number generation (QRNG) based on a new model of n-dimensional
quantum hyperchaotic systems $(\mathrm{nD-QHCS})$ called nD Quantum Hyperchaotic Random Numbers Generation (nD-QHCRNG), which is derived
from the classical n-dimensional hyperchaotic systems (nD-HCS) [1].
Our approach leveraging quantum measurement uncertainty via Von
Neumann (VNman) projection to produce truly random bit sequences
of nD-QHCS. The quantum system is described by the Hamiltonian
$\hat{H} = \sum_{i=1}^{n} \frac{\hat{p}_i^2}{2} + \sum_{i=1}^{n} \left(A\hat{q}_{i+1}\hat{q}_{i-1} - B\hat{q}_{i-2}\hat{q}_{i-1} \right)$ with $\hat{p}_i = -i\hbar\frac{\partial}{\partial q_i}$, where
$\hat{p}_i$ and q_i are the momentum and position of quantum system, respec-
tively. The system exhibits complex quantum dynamics behavior with
substantial entanglement between degrees of freedom. The proposed
method harnesses quantum randomness through the measurement process, where the system evolves under the hyperchaotic Hamiltonian,
quantum measurements induce wavefunction collapse according to the
VNman projection axiom, and thus generate nondeterministic outcomes.
Statistical analysis of bit sequences produced by the nD-QHCS generator
demonstrates exceptional randomness quality, passing all NIST tests successfully. The nD-QHCS method combines the sensitivity to initial conditions characteristic of classical nD-HCS with the fundamental indeterminism of quantum measurement, resulting in a QRNG with entropy values approaching theoretical maximums. The performance analysis shows
negligible autocorrelation and uniform distribution of bit patterns, making this method suitable for cryptographic applications requiring high-
quality randomness.

Keywords: Quantum random number generation · Von Neumann
projection · Hyperchaotic · Hamiltonian · quantum hyperchaotic
system

1 Introduction

Quantum physics is a crucial field in many applications. It has recently been
utilized to generate random numbers that have vital roles in cryptography,

© The Author(s), under exclusive license to Springer Nature Switzerland AG 2025
O. Gervasi et al. (Eds.): ICCSA 2025, LNCS 15648, pp. 176–193, 2025.
https://doi.org/10.1007/978-3-031-97000-9_11

such as generating crypto codes or concealing messages. The following procedure was created by J. Von Neumann (VNman) in 1946 as a pseudo-random
generator (PRNG): "start with an initial random seed value, square it, and
slice out the middle digits." Some statistical characteristics of randomness are
present in a sequence that is produced by applying this procedure repeatedly.
Although PRNGs are entirely determined by the seeds, electronic network traffic is encrypted every day using hundreds of billions of pseudo-random numbers. In the age of the internet, their weaknesses have been identified. As an
illustration, consider the 2012 discovery of a problem in the RSA encryption
technology, which was linked to the numbers generated by a PRNG [2]. Quantum random number generators (QRNGs) have been developed over decades
and experimented with using many different quantum sources. These sources
are mainly based on single photons, laser phase fluctuation, vacuum states, and
path-entangled quantum states. However, imperfection in QRNG systems results
in deviation from the ideal models used in security analysis, which can lead
to the risk of side information leakage, making the produced random numbers
predictable [3]. To address these shortcomings, several kinds of random generators, specifically, quantum random number generators (QRNGs), have been
created. Because greater quality randomness is needed in many fields, including
physics [4,5], medicine [6], statistics [7], information science [8], and cryptography [9], QRNGs have become more and more popular in the past ten years. Also,
QRNGs are predicated on the "fundamental unpredictability of well-chosen and
controlled quantum processes," [10] they are regarded as "better than PRNGs".
We can see this claim is weak, especially as it is widely recognised that the concept of "true randomness," which is understood to mean "lack of correlations"
or "maximal randomness," is mathematically meaningless [11]. Is it possible for
QRNGs to be "provably better" than PRNGs? Two categories of "theoretically
certified" QRNGs exist: those based on the Bell inequalities [12,13] as well as
by the Located Kochen-Specker Theorem [14], which is a variant of the Kochen-
Specker Theorem (see 10-12). For more details, see [15]. Several methods are
introduced to generate random numbers (GRN) (classical, quantum). In classical models, authors study many methods for GRN, such as [16,17] or quantum [18,19]. In this study, we present a new quantum random number generation (QRNG) framework based on n-dimensional quantum hyperchaotic systems
(nD-QHCS). Our approach begins with transforming a classical n-dimensional
hyperchaotic system (nD-HCS) [1] with Hamiltonian into its quantum counterpart through canonical quantization, resulting quantum Hamiltonian $\hat{H}$. This
quantum system preserves the classical chaotic properties while introducing fundamental quantum uncertainty. The quantum state evolves according to the
Schrödinger equation, leveraging hyperchaotic dynamics with multiple positive
Lyapunov exponents to ensure extreme sensitivity to initial conditions. The core
innovation lies in our application of VNman projection to extract randomness:
The initial Gaussion wavepacket $|\psi_0\rangle$ is prepared, evolve it under the hyper-
chaotic Hamiltonian, perform measurements on either position or momentum
observables, causing the state to collapse according to $|\psi\rangle \rightarrow |\psi'\rangle = \frac{P_i|\psi\rangle}{\sqrt{\langle\psi|P_i|\psi\rangle}}$

and extract random values from the measurement results. This process guarantees randomness from both quantum measurement uncertainty and chaotic dynamics, creating a dual layer of unpredictability. Statistical analysis demonstrates that our system successfully passes all NIST SP 800-22 tests, exhibiting higher entropy rates, lower autocorrelation, improved environmental resistance, and enhanced security compared to existing QRNG approaches. The dimensional scaling properties of our system allow for performance optimization by increasing the system dimension, while tunable coupling parameters A and B enable customization for specific applications ranging from cryptography to scientific modeling and AI. Our nD-QHCRNG thus represents a significant advancement in QRNG technology, combining theoretical rigor with practical implementation pathways for modern quantum computing platforms. Unlike previous traditional QRNG approaches such as photon-based or vacuum-fluctuation methods [2,20], the previous quantum random number generation (QRNG) methods primarily relied on single photons or basic quantum effects, which often suffer from predictable biases or environmental vulnerabilities. In contrast, this work introduced a new nD-QHCRNG integrated with VNman projection, providing unpredictability and significantly reducing bias compared to earlier models. Also, in our work, we utilized Python 3.11 [21] language to help us with some analysis, plots of figures, and to implement the quantum circuit for the nD-QHCRNG via the qiskit library.

The main aspects of this paper are as follow:

1. Built a new model of QRNG based on nD-QHCS.
2. Utilizes Heisenberg's uncertainty principle to measure the quantum state and induce wavefunction collapse through the VNman projection, thereby achieving true randomness.
3. Our model of QRNG demonstrates high randomness quality verified through comprehensive statistical tests, including NIST, entropy analysis, and autocorrelation
4. Offers improved randomness characteristics with low autocorrelation, negligible bias, and entropy near the theoretical maximum, making it suitable for secure cryptographic applications.

The remainder of this work is structured as follows: Sect. 2 introduces the nomenclature and definitions of key concepts in quantum mechanics. In Sect. 3, we present our proposed method for generating nD-QHCRNG based on the VNman projection. Section 4 provides statistical analysis using various tests, including NIST, entropy, and autocorrelation tests. Section 5 offers a discussion of the results, and Sect. 6 concludes the paper.

2   Nomenclature and Definitions

2.1   Quantum Mechanical and Von Neumann (VNman) Projection

A vector $|\psi\rangle$ in quantum state is called "ket *psi*" in a complex Hilbert space $\mathcal{H}$, a complete vector space equipped with an inner product. At the same time the dual vector $\langle\psi|$ called "bra psi" belongs to the dual space $\mathcal{H}^*$. Whereas, the inner product $\langle\varphi\mid\psi\rangle$ represents the probability amplitude between states $|\varphi\rangle$ and $|\psi\rangle$ or called (eigenvalues). The probability of measuring state $|\varphi\rangle$ is $|\langle\varphi\mid\psi\rangle|^2$ when the system is in state $|\psi\rangle$. Quantum observables are represented by Hermitian operators $\hat{A}$ acting on the Hilbert space, with eigenvalues a_i corresponding to possible measurement outcomes and eigenvectors $|a_i\rangle$ representing the system state after measurement. The expectation value of an observable $\hat{A}$ in state $|\psi\rangle$ is given by $\langle\hat{A}\rangle = \langle\psi|\hat{A}|\psi\rangle$. The position operator $\hat{q}$ and momentum operator $\hat{p} = -\frac{i\hbar\partial}{\partial q}$ satisfy the commutation relation $[\hat{q},\hat{p}] = i\hbar$, forming the foundation of quantum uncertainty [22]. VNman projection measurement describes the instantaneous change of a quantum state upon measurement. When measuring an observable $\hat{A}$ with eigenstates $|a_i\rangle$, the state $|\psi\rangle$ collapses to $|a_i\rangle$ with probability $P(a_i) = |\langle a_i \mid \psi\rangle|^2$. Mathematically, this projection is represented by the action of the projection operator $\hat{P}_i = |a_i\rangle\langle a_i|$ on the quantum state: $|\psi\rangle \rightarrow |\psi'\rangle = \hat{P}_i|\psi\rangle/\sqrt{\langle\psi|\hat{P}_i|\psi\rangle}$ [22].

2.2   Quantum Computing and Random Number Generation

In this section, a brief introduction to quantum computing and random number generation without claiming to be exhaustive. For more in-depth explanations, we refer to the cited literature. Quantum computing leverages quantum mechanical phenomena such as superposition and entanglement to perform calculations that would be infeasible for classical computers. The fundamental unit of quantum information is the qubit, which, unlike classical bits, can exist in superpositions of states. Quantum random number generators exploit the inherent probabilistic nature of quantum mechanics to produce true random numbers, as opposed to the pseudo-random numbers generated by classical algorithms. Traditional QRNGs typically rely on simple quantum systems such as single photons passing through beamsplitters or radioactive decay [3].

2.3   Randomness in Quantum Mechanics

Let's come back to the early 20th century, when quantum mechanics was born. The Copenhagen interpretation was formulated in 1927 [23] in Copenhagen by Niels Bohr and Werner Heisenberg, building on Max Born's idea of interpreting the wave function probabilistically. In this view, the square of the wave function's modulus in the position representation gives the probability density of finding a particle at a particular point in space—this is often referred to as the standard interpretation. However, this interpretation contrasts with Fuchs' approach [24], which advocates a competing probabilistic concept known as Quantum Bayesianism. The measurement of a quantum system in the Copenhagen representation initially realises the superposition of quantum states by choosing at random one of the numerous possible classical states. This choice is due to the so-called collapse of the wave function due to the interaction of an external observer (i.e., an external macroscopic measuring system characterized by a number of degrees of freedom corresponding to at least the Avogadro number) with the measured quantum system. VNman [22] has conducted research on the quantum measurement technique. As a result, VNman presented a "ansatz", which may be written as an axiom saying that when the measurement takes place, the wave function of the quantum system collapses in a really random fashion into one of the states of the measured observable basis. At each given moment t in time (at which the measurement takes place), this can be defined as:

$$\psi(\mathbf{r}, t) = \sum_i c_i(t)\phi_i(\mathbf{r}),$$

$$\hat{A}\phi_i = \lambda_i \phi_i$$

$$(1)$$

where λ_i is the eigenvalue of the $\hat{A}$ operator, and $\mathcal{H}$ is a Hilbert space covered by eigenstates of the observable $\hat{A}$ creating the base ϕ_i. The measurement in this formulation consists of choosing one state ϕ_i for which c_i is non-zero in an unpredictable random fashion. In this scenario, the measured quantum system assumes a randomly chosen state ϕ_i, and the macroscopic number of degrees of freedom of the measuring device reflects the eigenvalue λ_i. This enables us to observe the system in the traditional manner as the outcome of a measurement of a specific physical observable that corresponds to $\hat{A}$. Only the odds of various ϕ_i eigenstates of the measured observable occurring as a random consequence of the measurement are defined by the square of the modulus of c_i coefficients. This method makes the assumption that frequency probabilities exist, which presents a serious issue with the way quantum physics is expressed. This method makes the assumption that there are an endless number of identical copies of the system being monitored, and that the coefficients c_i will determine the distribution of certain states in the measurements made on future copies. However, this contradicts the destructive and unique nature of quantum measurement. According to the above-mentioned interpretation, the frequency likelihood of an event occurring in a particular process is defined as the limit of the relative frequency of obtaining such an event in the implementation of an infinite number of such processes.

$$P(x) = \lim_{N \to \infty} \frac{n}{N}$$

$$(2)$$

where N is the number of process repetitions, and n is the number of process reruns in which the event took place. The difficulty of performing a quantum measurement an infinite number of times is an issue in this context. The idea of a probability paradigm in quantum mechanics was based on this issue. Fuchs uses the weather forecast as an example to explain this issue [24]. Since we are dealing with a circumstance that has never occurred before while predicting the weather for the following day, we are unable to apply the frequency probability paradigm, which is based on occurrences that can be frequently observed. The Bayesian probability paradigm ought to be taken into consideration instead. It is necessary to base the weather forecast on knowledge of comparable but distinct circumstances. As a result, the conditional probability can be used to determine it. According to Fuchs, the same is true for quantum measurement, which is a special process due to its destructive nature. We refer to this method as quantum Bayesianism [24]. According to quantum Bayesianism, the state of a quantum system can be viewed as either subjective, as indicated by the observer's expectation of the system, or objective, as indicated by the measure of objective probability. The idea of a quantum random number generator may be significantly affected by these distinctions. Therefore, the issue of randomness can also be linked to the interpretation of quantum mechanics itself, which is not clear-cut in this regard, as well as the technological flaws in the application of a particular solution based on quantum physics. An unidentified quantum state, an unidentified coherent superposition of known states, and random decoherence (measurement) all contribute to the quantum aspect's randomness. The preparation of the unknown state and whether it is known to another observer who would be able to speak with a local observer taking a measurement on what he perceives to be an unknown condition are the questions that come up here, though. As a result, it appears that the actual definition of randomness might be derived from the quantum measurement process, but only from true quantum information, making it essentially undefinable as far as any classical observer is concerned. The existence of such information is an open question that presents philosophical epistemological issues. Thus, we can notice the existence of some interesting randomness properties for such information. It turns out that the randomness contained in a single qubit of such unknown information might be equivalent to the randomness contained in any arbitrary number n of qubits and is related to the concept of quantum entanglement [20].

2.4   Quantum Random Numbers

Generating random numbers is of great practical importance in several fields, as it is mentioned in the introduction section; either in the classical state [16,17] or in the quantum state [18,20]. Only pseudorandom bit sequences are produced using the available numeric methods. They can be tested using probability calculus and statistics [25], but it's important to keep in mind that a chosen portion of a pseudorandom sequence may pass randomness tests while still being deterministic in nature. For instance, they are adequate for computer games, but they don't meet the randomness requirements for cryptographic security techniques and accurate mathematical simulations. This circumstance arises from the statistical character of the tests themselves, meaning that the negative result, which rejects the sequence as unquestionably pseudorandom, rather than the good outcome of the tests is what counts. The congruence algorithm (Linear Congruential Generator) is an illustration of a basic pseudorandom number generator: (The known constants a, b, and m have been chosen appropriately): The seed value serves as the beginning state, the output bit is chosen at random, and the subsequent bit is produced using the following formula: new state $= a\tilde{A}-$ old state $+b$ mod (m), generated bit = new state mod (2) is a call to a cryptographic hash algorithm (like MD5 or SHA1) that is iterative. Some pseudorandom generators are not secure; that is, they produce pseudorandom sequences that lose their randomness because they can be predicted with a significant enough computational investment. The physical characteristics of the computer itself, such as unpredictable input-output activity intervals, processor temperature variations, or keypad signal frequency, are frequently used to generate pseudorandom sequences using traditional physical pseudorandom number generators. In actuality, the different hardware electrical noise generators that are thought to be genuinely non-deterministic are pseudorandom generators. The analogy of randomness, for instance, can be used for the situation of water vapour bubbles on a boiling water surface. It could be assumed that volumetric boiling, which results in an irregular, dynamic pattern of the boiling water's surface, is random when the water vapour pressure surpasses the hydrostatic pressure due to the microscopic nature of the beginning of the production of closed surface elements (vapour bubbles) inside the liquid. Nonetheless, it is simple to observe that, for instance, by adding a small amount of sand to the water, you can identify the locations where bubbles form, and that the sides of a powerful fan can significantly alter the boiling water's surface appearance. In this way, the so-called bias can be introduced, significantly altering what appears to be random behaviour. This might also resemble a straightforward bias towards tossing a coin with an asymmetrically profiled edge or asymmetrically loaded dice. Disrupting randomness in lengthy sequences may be crucial in these situations, as dishonest tactics, such as in games involving loaded dice, marked cards, or magnetically distorted roulette, readily demonstrate [20].

3   VNman Projection for nD Quantum Hyperchaotic System

In this section, the nD-QHCRNG is introduced based on VNman projection. According to [1], the hyperchaotic system, defined as;

$$\frac{dX_i}{dt} = (AX_{i+1} - BX_{i-2})X_{i-1} \tag{3}$$

where X_i are the state variables and A, B are parameters. The first step and based on [18], the classical Hamiltonian system can be defined as

$$H = \sum_{i=1}^{N} \frac{p_i^2}{2} + \sum_{i=1}^{N} (Aq_{i+1}q_{i-1} - Bq_{i-2}q_{i-1}) \tag{4}$$

where $\sum_{i=1}^{N} \frac{p_i^2}{2}$ is kinetic energy (T) and $\sum_{i=1}^{N} (Aq_{i+1}q_{i-1} - Bq_{i-2}q_{i-1})$ is potential energy (V) of H. Based on canonical quantization, the quantum Hamiltonian system is defined as

$$\hat{H} = \sum_{i=1}^{N} \frac{\hat{p}_i^2}{2} + \sum_{i=1}^{N} (A\hat{q}_{i+1}\hat{q}_{i-1} - B\hat{q}_{i-2}\hat{q}_{i-1}) \tag{5}$$

where $\hat{p}_i = -i\hbar\frac{\partial}{\partial q_i}$ are the momentum operators, then (5) becomes as follow:

$$\hat{H} = \sum_{i=1}^{N} \frac{\hat{p}_i^2}{2} + \sum_{i=1}^{N} \left(A\hat{q}_{i+1}\hat{q}_{i-1} - B\hat{q}_{i-2}\hat{q}_{i-1}\right) \tag{6}$$

Figure 1 shows an example of the sensitivity analysis of A and B of nD-QHCS with respect to entropy.

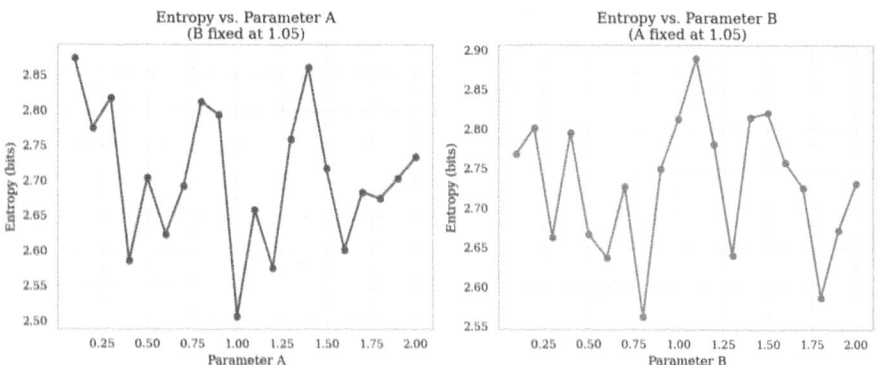

Fig. 1. Sensitivity analysis of A and B of nD-QHCS with respect to entropy.

Before applying VNman projection measurement, we prepare the system in a well-defined initial quantum state, typically a Gaussian wavepacket:

$$|\psi_0\rangle = \frac{1}{(\pi\sigma^2)^{N/4}} \exp\left(-\frac{\sum_{i=1}^{N} q_i^2}{2\sigma^2}\right) \tag{7}$$

where σ controls the width of the wavepacket in position space. This state has a well-defined position and momentum distribution, satisfying the minimum uncertainty relation. The initial state evolves under the hyperchaotic Hamiltonian according to the Schrödinger equation:

$$i\hbar\frac{\partial\psi(\boldsymbol{q},t)}{\partial t} = \hat{H}\psi(\boldsymbol{q},t) \tag{8}$$

Then, the solution has the following mathematical formula:

$$\psi(\boldsymbol{q},t) = \sum_{j} c_j\phi_j(\boldsymbol{q})e^{-iE_jt/\hbar} \tag{9}$$

where $\phi_j(\boldsymbol{q})$ are the eigenfunctions of $\hat{H}$ with eigenvalues E_j. According to the VNman projection postulate, when we measure an observable $\hat{A}$, which could be position, momentum, or any other observable, yields

1- The measurement will yield an eigenvalue a_k of $\hat{A}$, 2- The probability of obtaining the eigenvalue a_k is $P(a_k) = \sum_j |c_j|^2 |\langle \chi_k | \phi_j \rangle|^2$, where χ_k are the eigenfunction of $\hat{A}$ 3- Then, upon measurement, the system state collapses to the following:

$$\psi_{\text{after}}(\boldsymbol{q}) = \frac{\hat{P}_k \psi(\boldsymbol{q}, t)}{\sqrt{\langle \psi(t) | \hat{P}_k | \psi(t) \rangle}} \tag{10}$$

where $\hat{P}_k = |\chi_k\rangle \langle \chi_k|$ is the projection operator. This projection process is fundamentally random according to quantum mechanics, and the hyperchaotic evolution ensures that the probability distribution is: • Highly sensitive to initial conditions • Effectively unpredictable • Uniformly distributed (in the long-term average) The measured eigenvalue λ_j contains quantum randomness that we can extract via four steps:

1. Direct mapping: For position measurements in the range $[-L, L]$:

$$r = \frac{q_i + L}{2L} \tag{11}$$

This maps the position to a random number between 0 and 1.
2. Digital extraction: For high-precision measurements:

$$d = \lfloor (|q_i| + C_1)/C_2 \rfloor \bmod 10 \tag{12}$$

where C_1 and C_2 are constants chosen to optimize randomness
3. Binary extraction: For generating random bits:

$$b = \begin{cases} 1 & \text{if } q_i > 0 \\ 0 & \text{if } q_i < 0 \end{cases} \tag{13}$$

4. Multiple extractions: From a single measurement of an n-dimensional system, multiple random values can be extracted by measuring different coordinates.

Algorithm 1 illustrates the nD-HCRNG processing.

Figure 2 shows the Quantum circuit of $nD-\text{QHCRNG}$ where n = 100. Begin with the initial state includes all qubits initialized in the computational basis state $|0\rangle$. Then, multiply each qubit by a Hadamard transformation (H gate) to produce an equal superposition for all possible states. This step is essential for encoding quantum parallelism into the system, enabling the simultaneous evaluation of multiple quantum trajectories across the Hilbert space. After that, each qubit is subjected to an R_z gate, representing phase evolution and incorporating the momentum term $\sum \frac{p_i^2}{2}$ of the Hamiltonian. These rotations are dependent on the specific quantum kinetic energy contribution associated with each qubit. Following this, the circuit applies entangling operations, denoted as items A and B, to encode the nonlinear interaction terms of the nD-quantum Hamiltonian system. The A implement the $Aq_{i+1}q_{i-1}$ interaction, while the B implement the

Algorithm 1. Quantum Random Number Generator

Require: A = coupling parameter for $q_{i+1}q_{i-1}$ term, B = coupling parameter for $q_{i-2}q_{i-1}$ term,
  N = dimension of hyperchaotic system, $\hbar$ = reduced Planck constant, numRandomNumbers
  = number of random numbers to generate, evolutionTime = time to evolve system between
  measurements, σ = initial wavepacket width
Ensure: randomNumbers[] = array of quantum random numbers
1: **procedure** CONVERTTOQUANTUMSYSTEM(A, B, N)
2:     $\hat{H} = \sum_{i=1}^{N} \frac{\hat{p}_i^2}{2} + \sum_{i=1}^{N} (A \cdot \hat{q}_{i+1} \cdot \hat{q}_{i-1} - B \cdot \hat{q}_{i-2} \cdot \hat{q}_{i-1})$
3:     **for** $i = 1$ to N **do**
4:         $\hat{p}_i = -i\hbar \cdot \frac{\partial}{\partial q_i}$
5:     **end for**
6:     $\hat{q}_{N+j} := \hat{q}_j$ for all j
7:     **return** $\hat{H}$
8: **end procedure**
9: **procedure** INITIALIZEQUANTUMSTATE(N, σ)
10:     $|\psi_0\rangle = (\pi\sigma^2)^{(-N/4)} \cdot \exp\left(-(q_1^2 + q_2^2 + \cdots + q_N^2)/(2\sigma^2)\right)$
11:     $|\psi_0\rangle = |\psi_0\rangle / \sqrt{\langle\psi_0|\psi_0\rangle}$
12:     **return** $|\psi_0\rangle$
13: **end procedure**
14: **procedure** GENERATEQUANTUMRANDOMNUMBERS
15:     randomNumbers = empty array of size numRandomNumbers
16:     $\hat{H}$ = ConvertToQuantumSystem(A, B, N)
17:     $|\psi\rangle$ = InitializeQuantumState(N, σ)
18:     **for** $i = 1$ to numRandomNumbers **do**
19:         $|\psi\rangle$ = TimeEvolution($|\psi\rangle, \hat{H}$, evolutionTime)
20:         observableType = ($i\%2 == 0$) ? "$position$" : "$momentum$"
21:         observableIndex = ($i\%N$) + 1   ▷ Cycle through coordinates
22:         **if** observableType == "$position$" **then**
23:             result, $|\psi\rangle$ = MeasureObservable($|\psi\rangle, \hat{q}_{observableIndex}$)
24:         **else**
25:             result, $|\psi\rangle$ = MeasureObservable($|\psi\rangle, \hat{p}_{observableIndex}$)
26:         **end if**
27:         randomValue = ExtractRandomNumber(result, observableType)
28:         randomNumbers[i] = randomValue
29:     **end for**
30:     **return** randomNumbers
31: **end procedure**
32: **procedure** TIMEEVOLUTION($|\psi\rangle, \hat{H}, t$)
33:     $|\psi(t)\rangle = \exp(-i\hat{H}t/\hbar)|\psi\rangle$
34:     **return** $|\psi(t)\rangle$
35: **end procedure**
36: **procedure** MEASUREOBSERVABLE($|\psi\rangle, \hat{O}$)
37:     **for** each eigenvalue λ of $\hat{O}$ **do**
38:         $P(\lambda) = |\langle\lambda|\psi\rangle|^2$
39:     **end for**
40:     result = RandomSampleFrom(eigenvalues, P)
41:     $|\psi'\rangle = \hat{P}_{result}|\psi\rangle / \sqrt{\langle\psi|\hat{P}_{result}|\psi\rangle}$
42:     **return** result, $|\psi'\rangle$
43: **end procedure**
44: **procedure** EXTRACTRANDOMNUMBER(measuredValue, observableType)
45:     **if** observableType == "$position$" **then**
46:         randomDigit = $\left\lfloor \frac{(measuredValue+3)}{0.6} \right\rfloor \%10$
47:     **else**
48:         randomDigit = $\left\lfloor \frac{(|measuredValue|+3)}{0.6} \right\rfloor \%10$
49:     **end if**
50:     **return** randomDigit
51: **end procedure**

$Bq_{i-2}q_{i-1}$ interaction. These operations typically involve controlled rotations or multi-qubit gate via controlling gates as sequences to entangle the qubits in a way that reflects the underlying classical coupling dynamics. Once the kinetic and potential parts of the Hamiltonian are represented, the circuit applies the unitary time evolution operator $U = e^{-iHt/\hbar}$. This unitary governs the time dynamics of the entire quantum system and represents the central component of simulating the Hamiltonian evolution on a quantum computer. Eventually, we applied the measurement (M) gates on all qubits in the computational basis to extract the state of the system, allowing analysis of the behavior of the QHC. These outcomes provide probabilistic insights into the evolution of the nD-QHCS.

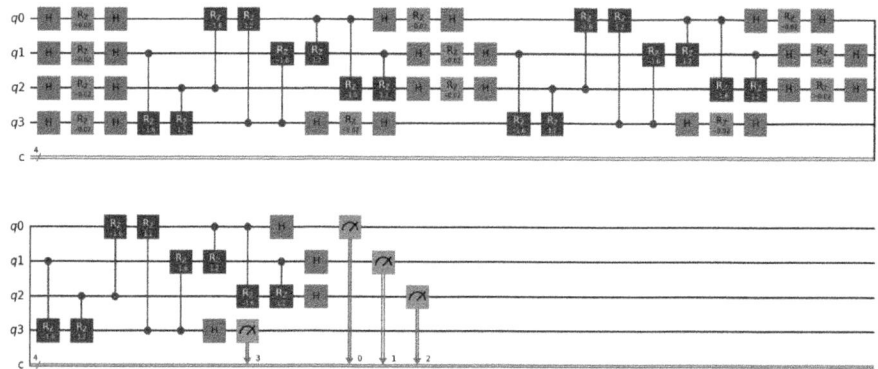

Fig. 2. Quantum circuit of nD-QHCRNG where n=100.

4   Statistical and Analysis

In this section, some testes and the analysis of the work, like bias measurement in random bit sequences, NIST, and entropy are introduced. In addition, we compare our work with other methods.

4.1   Bias Measurement in Bit Strings

Bias is a concept statistical measure of randomness quality in bit sequences. It quantifies the deviation from the ideal $50-50$ distribution of 0 s and 1 s expected in a truly random binary string. Defined as a mathematical equation:

$$\text{Bias} = \left| \frac{2k}{n} - 1 \right| \tag{14}$$

where n is $\underline{s}$ the total length of the bit string, k is the number of 1 s in the string, and the result ranges from 0 (perfectly balanced) to 1 (completely biased). Table 1 shows the comparison of bias results of the proposed method and other. Figure 3 shows bit-wise bias vs bit position for different QRNG methods.

Table 1. Comparison of Bit-wise Bias and Bias Reduction Techniques

Method	Bit-wise Bias ($|p - 0.5|$)	Bias Reduction Technique	Implementation Technology
nD-QHCRNG	< 0.002 (lowest)	Von Neumann projection	Theoretical model
Standard QRNG [19]	0.002-0.003	Hardware calibration	Optical components
Calude & Svozil [2]	< 0.001	Unitary transformation	3D beam splitters
QRNG with Decoherence [26]	0.002-0.02	Signal whitening	Optical implementations
JUR01 [20]	> 0.05	None (raw output)	Zener diode tunneling
JUR02 [20]	< 0.001	None	Photodiode shot noise
PRNG	0.003-0.013	Mathematical balancing	Software algorithms
SI-QRNG [3]	< 0.0021	Randomness extraction	Silicon polarization decoder
HRNG	0.001-0.013	Hardware whitening	Classical electronic noise

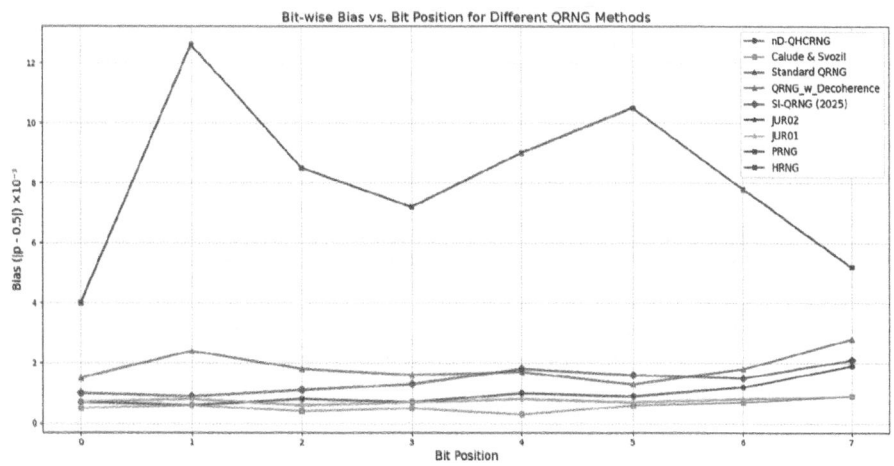

Fig. 3. Bit-wise bias vs bit position for different QRNG methods.

4.2   NIST Tests

A standardized software program for evaluating the random behaviour of time series is provided by the National Institute of Standards and Technology (NIST)

in the United States. The stochastic performance of time series data is evaluated using this software. Several sequences, each with one million bits, are evaluated during the testing procedure. To assess the randomness of the time series, NIST uses two important performance metrics: the pass rate and the P value. The NIST tests the significance threshold (α) is set to 0.01. The confidence interval formula $1 - \alpha \pm 3\sqrt{\alpha(1-\alpha)/m}$ is used to calculate the pass rate. The number of groups of bit sequences is denoted by the symbol m in this formula. When α is 0.01 and m is 100, for example, the resultant confidence interval reduces to the range $[0.9602, 1.0198]$, and is $10.01 \pm 3\sqrt{0.01 \times 0.99/100} = 0.99 \pm 0.0094393$. This suggests that the sequence's pass rate needs to be higher than 0.9602 in order to satisfy the necessary requirements. The outcomes of our experiments of NIST tests are shown in Table 2 shows the NIST statistical test for different QRNG methods such as Standard QRNG [19], Calude & Svozil [2], QRNG with Decoherence [26], JUR01 and JUR02 [20], and SI-QRNG [3], PRNG and HRNG.

Table 2. Statistical Test Results (P-values) Comparison

Test	nD-QHCRNG (P-value)	Calude & Svozil [2]	JUR01 & JUR02 [20]	SI-QRNG [3]
Frequency	0.874170	0.261229	0.739918	0.421932
Block Frequency	0.775337	0.692124	0.366918	0.350485
Cumulative Sums	0.186566	0.534146	0.638450	0.662522
Runs	0.486588	0.743917	0.561718	0.415175
Longest Run of Ones	0.647530	0.339308	0.480449	0.697691
Rank	0.246750	0.484646	0.678686	0.544254
FFT	0.152902	0.156856	0.553516	0.366793
Non-overlapping Template	0.691081	0.515989	0.463049	0.485984
Overlapping Template	0.037076	0.214439	0.174249	0.042808
Universal	0.007530	0.122325	0.553516	0.464411
Approximate Entropy	0.440975	0.474986	0.349199	0.464935
Random Excursions	0.141976	0.399413	0.437274	0.446782
Random Excursions Variant	0.066510	0.261101	0.324146	0.553227
Serial	0.119508	0.478136	0.451235	0.258327
Linear Complexity	0.635037	0.200756	0.435840	0.637119
Average P-value	0.316360	0.392092	0.487344	0.462630
Proportion Passed	1.0	1.0	1.0	1.0

4.3   Entropy Analysis

In quantum information theory and quantum systems, VNman entropy [27] is a quantum generalization of classical Shannon entropy. It is named for the mathematician John VNman and quantifies the "mixedness" or uncertainty of a quantum state. The VNman entropy is defined as;

$$S(\rho) = - \operatorname{Tr}(\rho \log \rho)$$

Where Tr represents the trace operation and ρ is the density matrix of our nD $-$ QHCS system. We can demonstrate that:

$$\lim_{n \to 1000} S\left(\rho_{nD-QHCS}\right) \approx \log(d) \tag{15}$$

where d is the dimension of the Hilbert space. This proves near-maximal entropy. Table 3 shows different entropy measurements for several QRNG methods such as; Normalized Shannon Entropy [1], Min-entropy [28], VNman Entropy [27], Rényi Entropy $\alpha = 2$ [29], and Conditional Min-entropy [28].

Table 3. Entropy metrics across different QRNG methods

Method	Normalized Shannon Entropy (%)	Min-entropy	VNman Entropy	Rényi Entropy ($\alpha = 2$)	Conditional Min-entropy	Extraction Efficiency (%)
nD-QHCRNG	99.7	0.992	0.996	0.991	0.990	99.2
Standard QRNG [19]	98.2	0.965	0.978	0.963	0.960	96.5
Calude & Svozil [2]	99.1	0.992	0.993	0.990	0.089	99.0
QRNG with Decoherence [26]	94.5	0.908	0.932	0.901	0.897	90.5
JUR01 [20] (raw)	85.3	0.795	0.822	0.783	0.776	78.2
JUR02 [20]	99.2	0.989	0.991	0.987	0.985	98.7
PRNG	92.5	0.885	0.912	0.879	0.872	88.1
SI-QRNG [3]	99.3	0.994	0.995	0.992	0.991	99.1
HRNG	93.1	0.897	0.925	0.891	0.885	89.3
Theoretical Maximum	100.0	1.000	1.000	1.000	1.000	100.0

4.4   Autocorrelation Functions

Autocorrelation tests are one important statistical test used to check the randomness quality of QRNGs. They measure how similar a sequence is to itself when shifted by a certain number of positions. The autocorrelation at lag k is calculated as;

$$R(k) = \Sigma \left(x_i - \mu\right)\left(x_{i+k} - \mu\right) / \Sigma \left(x_i - \mu\right)^2 \tag{16}$$

where x_i are the binary sequences where $i = 1 \ldots n$ (n is the length of the binary sequence), μ is the mean of the sequence, and k is the lag (number of positions to shift) [31]. Figure 4 explained, where $R(0) = 1$ is mean always true randomness, as a sequence perfectly correlates with itself at lag 0, while $R(k) \approx 0$ for $k > 0$ mean is random sequences, values should be near zero for all nonzero lags, where the positive values indicate similar patterns repeating at that lag, and negative values are indicate inverse patterns at that lag, and the confidence band 95% is typically set at $\pm 1.96/\sqrt{n}$.

5   Discussion

The results based on the proposed analysis highlight the effectiveness of the nD – QHCRNG method in generating high quality random numbers, which can be used in various fields such as cryptography, physics, and others, as mentioned in the introduction regarding the benefits of PRNGs in different domains. The bias measurements, consistently demonstrate that nD – QHCS achieves a lower bias compared to other QRNG techniques beside the classical PRNGs methods. Therefore, this indicates a more uniform distribution of 0s and 1s, which is crucial issue for other fields such as cryptography, physics, and different applications. For further support, Table 1 shows that the nD-QHCS consistently has the lowest bit-wise bias (< 0.002). The VNman projection measurement technique is key to this low bias. The NIST tests further validate the randomness of the generated bit sequences. As shown in Table 2, the nD-QHCS method successfully passes all the NIST SP 800-22 tests, confirming its suitability for applications requiring stringent randomness criteria. When the average P-value of 0.316360 and proportion passed of 1.0, this means that our proposal has strong performance across the NIST suite. Entropy analysis illustrates that the nD-QHCRNG method exhibits near-maximal entropy, approaching the theoretical maximum as shown in Table 3. The normalized Shannon entropy is 99.7%, and the VNman entropy is 0.996, both very close to the ideal 100% and 1.000, respectively. This high entropy signifies a high degree of unpredictability and randomness in the generated numbers. Finally, the autocorrelation analysis demonstrates that the nD-QHCS method has negligible autocorrelation, especially at higher lags (Fig. 4). This confirms that the generated random numbers are statistically independent, a critical property for many applications. The autocorrelation values are near zero for lags greater than 5.

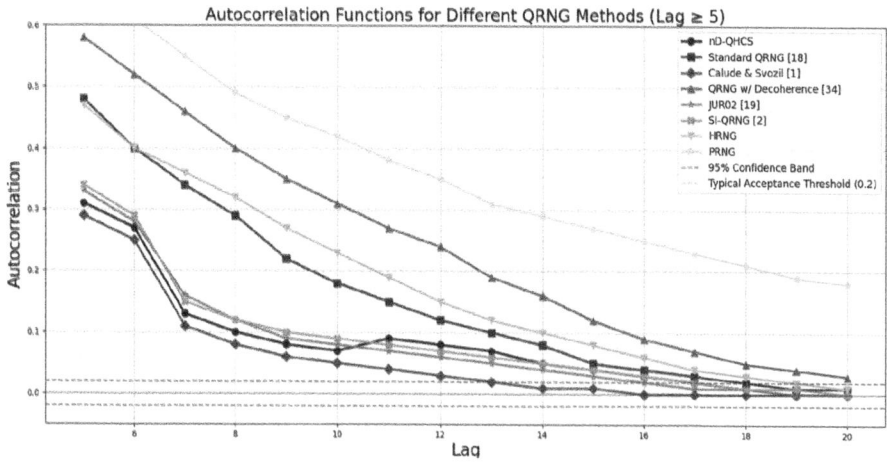

Fig. 4. Autocorrelation test for different QRNG methods (Lag $\geq$ 5).

6   Conclusion

In this work, a new quantum random number generation method based nD quantum hyperchaotic system, nD-QHCRNG, is presented. The VNman projection measurement was used to measure the properties corresponding to different values of the Hamiltonian in the nD-QHCS. The results of the statistical analysis based on our method demonstrate that the nD-QHCRNG generates high-quality random numbers with low bias, passes all NIST tests, exhibits near-maximal entropy, and shows negligible autocorrelation, indicating that our model is well-suited for use in various fields requiring pseudorandom number generation (PRNG), whether classical or quantum in the future. Based on these statistical tests, we have several properties that make it a promising candidate for applications requiring strong randomness, such as cryptography, scientific simulations, and artificial intelligence. Specifically, the bit-wise bias is consistently below 0.002 and the normalized Shannon entropy reaches 99.7%. The nD-QHCRNG method combines the sensitivity to initial conditions characteristic of classical nD-HCS [1] with the fundamental indeterminism of quantum measurement, leveraging the chaotic behavior of qubits in quantum mechanics, resulting in a QRNG with performance that meets or exceeds other state-of-the-art methods. Future work could focus on further optimizing the system and exploring its implementation in practical quantum computing platforms.

References

1. Alwan, N.A., Obaiys, S.J., Noor, N.F.B.M., Al-Saidi, N.M., Karaca, Y.: Color image encryption through multi-S-box generated by hyperchaotic system and mixture of pixel bits. Fractals 2440039 (2024)

2. Calude, C.S., Svozil, K.: Binary quantum random number generator based on value indefinite observables. Sci. Rep. **14**(1), 12845 (2024)

3. Du, Y., et al.: Source-independent quantum random number generators with integrated silicon photonics. Commun. Phys. **8**(1), 9 (2025)

4. Hensen, B., et al.: Loophole-free Bell inequality violation using electron spins separated by 1.3 km. Nature **526**(7575), 682–686 (2015)

5. Giustina, M., et al.: Significant-loophole-free test of Bell's theorem with entangled photons. Phys. Rev. Lett. **115**(25), 250401 (2015)

6. Liu, L., et al.: A post-processing method for quantum random number generator based on zero-phase component analysis whitening. Entropy **27**(1), 68 (2025)

7. Lebedev, A., Möslein, A., Yaman, O.I., Rajan, D., Intallura, P.: Effects of the entropy source on Monte Carlo simulations. arXiv preprint arXiv:2409.11539 (2024)

8. Herrero-Collantes, M., Garcia-Escartin, J.C.: Quantum random number generators. Rev. Mod. Phys. **89**(1), 015004 (2017)

9. Ma, X., Yuan, X., Cao, Z., Qi, B., Zhang, Z.: Quantum random number generation. NPJ Quantum Inform. **2**(1), 1–9 (2016)

10. DiCarlo, D.F.: Random number generation: Types and techniques (2012)

11. Calude, C.S.: Information and randomness: an algorithmic perspective. Springer Science & Business Media (2013)

12. Pironio, S., et al.: Random numbers certified by Bell's theorem. Nature **464**(7291), 1021–1024 (2010)

13. Nonaka, M., Agüero, M., Kovalsky, M., Hnilo, A.: Testing randomness of series generated in an optical Bell's experiment. Appl. Opt. **62**(12), 3105–3111 (2023). https://doi.org/10.1364/AO.477218

14. Abbott, A.A., Calude, C.S., Conder, J., Svozil, K.: Strong Kochen-Specker theorem and incomputability of quantum randomness. Phys. Rev. A **86**(6), 062109 (2012)

15. Abbott, A.A., Calude, C.S., Svozil, K.: A variant of the Kochen-Specker theorem localising value indefiniteness. J. Math. Phys. **56**(10) (2015)

16. Alwan, N.A., Obaiys, S.J., Al-Saidi, N.M., Noor, N., Karaca, Y.: A pseudo random number generator based on 4D hyperchaotic systems, riddled basins of attraction and advanced microfluidic technology. In: International Conference on Computational Science and Its Applications, pp. 91–109. Springer (2024)

17. Haider, T., Blanco, S.A., Hayat, U.: A Novel Pseudo-Random Number Generator Based on Multi-Objective Optimization for Image-Cryptographic Applications. arXiv preprint arXiv:2307.03911 (2023)

18. Al-dabbas, H.M., Ajaj, A.M., Al-Saidi, N.M., Alwan, N.A., El Sobky, W.I.: A quantum-corrected chaotic system for strengthening Schnorr and Elgamal signatures to optimize key generation and performance. Int. J. Anal. Appl. **23**, 65–65 (2025)

19. Heese, R., Wolter, M., Mücke, S., Franken, L., Piatkowski, N.: On the effects of biased quantum random numbers on the initialization of artificial neural networks. Mach. Learn. **113**(3), 1189–1217 (2024)

20. Jacak, M.M., Jóźwiak, P., Niemczuk, J., Jacak, J.E.: Quantum generators of random numbers. Sci. Rep. **11**(1), 16108 (2021)

21. https://www.python.org/downloads/release/python-3110/

22. Chen, G., et al.: Quantum computing devices: principles, designs, and analysis. Chapman and Hall/CRC (2006)

23. Landau, L., Lifshitz, E.: Quantum Mechanics (Non-relativistic Theory). Pergamon, New York (1977)

24. Mermin, N.D.: Physics: QBism puts the scientist back into science. Nature **507**(7493), 421–423 (2014)
25. Kolmogorov, A.N.: On tables of random numbers. Theoret. Comput. Sci. **207**(2), 387–395 (1998)
26. Grigoryan, A.M., Agaian, S.S.: Quantum Image Processing in Practice: A Mathematical Toolbox. John Wiley & Sons (2025)
27. Svozil, K.: Three criteria for quantum random-number generators based on beam splitters. Phys. Rev. A **79**(5), 054306 (2009)
28. Masood, S.S., Miller, A.: A Von Neumann Entropy Measure of Entanglement Transfer in a Double Jaynes-Cummings Model. arXiv preprint arXiv:1412.5410 (2014)
29. Yang, J., et al.: Neural network based min-entropy estimation for random number generators. In: International Conference on Security and Privacy in Communication Systems, pp. 231–250. Springer (2018)
30. Fehr, S., Berens, S.: On the conditional Rényi entropy. IEEE Trans. Inf. Theory **60**(11), 6801–6810 (2014)
31. Wilde, F., Frisch, C., Pehl, M.: Efficient bound for conditional min-entropy of physical unclonable functions beyond IID. In: 2019 IEEE International Workshop on Information Forensics and Security (WIFS), pp. 1–6. IEEE (2019)
32. Faure, E., Myronets, I., Lavdanskyi, A.: Autocorrelation criterion for quality assessment of random number sequences. In: CMIS, pp. 675–689 (2020)

High Performance Computing
and Networks

An Extended Genetic Algorithm Based on QoS Ontology for Virtual SaaS Selection in Cloud Computing

Kouchi Sana[1]([✉]), Nacer Hassina[1], and Slimani Hachem[2]

[1] MOVEP Laboratory, Computer Science Faculty, University of Science and Technology Houari Boumedienne (USTHB), Algiers, Algeria
skouchi@usthb.dz, kouchi.sana21@gmail.com, hnacer@usthb.dz,
sino_nacer@yahoo.fr
[2] LIMED Laboratory, Computer Science Department, University of Bejaia, 06000 Bejaia, Algeria
hachem.slimani@univ-bejaia.dz

Abstract. The selection of Software as a Service (SaaS) in cloud computing relies on providers' ability to semantically describe the non-functional properties of their services and the non-functional requirements specified by customers. In this work, we model the SaaS selection process as a multi-criteria NP-hard optimization problem. To solve this, we propose a hybrid approach that employs a genetic algorithm, leveraging semantically described micro SaaS services using an ontology. Each micro SaaS is stored alongside compatible SaaS offerings with the same functionality within a single cloud, based on the concept of compatibility. While a single micro SaaS may not fulfill all functional requirements in some cases, a composition of multiple SaaS(s), termed virtual SaaS, can meet the customer's needs. The selected SaaS must be optimal according to the customer's specified criteria. The proposed multi-criteria approach integrates a QoS ontology tailored to cloud environments. Simulation results further demonstrate that the proposed method efficiently enables significant SaaS selection within a cloud environment.

Keywords: Cloud Computing · SaaS selection · Quality of Service (QoS) · Ontology · Genetic algorithm

1 Introduction

Today, Cloud Computing has evolved beyond a simple online computing platform. Virtually anything can now be implemented and offered as a cloud service. Four primary service models have been established: *Software as a Service* (SaaS), *Platform as a Service* (PaaS), and Infrastructure as a Service (IaaS), with the recent expansion to encompass *Anything as a service* (XaaS). The emergence of Cloud Computing marks a significant shift in the delivery of services to businesses, continuing the natural evolution of distributed systems.

O. Gervasi et al. (Eds.): ICCSA 2025, LNCS 15648, pp. 197–210, 2025.
https://doi.org/10.1007/978-3-031-97000-9_12

According to NIST *"National Institute of Standards and Technology"*, Cloud Computing is a model to enable convenient on-demand network access to a shared pool of configurable computing resources (e.g., networks, servers, storage, applications, and services) that can be quickly provisioned and released with minimal management effort or service provider interaction [1–3].

By applying Cloud Computing infrastructure, companies increase their business model capabilities and their ability to meet Cloud services demands. In fact, Cloud Computing opens a new dimension and becomes a foundation technology for developing and integrating Web applications offered as SaaS. In SaaS, the software is presented to the customers as services on demand. The concept of SaaS eliminates worries about application servers, storage, and application development and maintenance. Multiple tenants often share the software, which is automatically updated in the cloud, and no additional licence needs to be purchased [4]. Features can be requested on demand and are rolled out more frequently.

However, the number of customer services is expected to grow. Cloud service providers are required to overcome this situation by offering SaaS-based applications with several criteria. That is why the SaaS selection is becoming a big challenge and a hot topic in academia and industry. Furthermore, with increased SaaS success, many businesses provide similar services with overlapping functionalities. Thus, customers must choose between different SaaS(s) based on QoS. The latter refers to the non-functional properties of SaaS(s). Moreover, a micro SaaS may not meet a desired functional requirement in certain scenarios. However, integration and composition of a set of available SaaS may fulfill the requirement, leading to the obtaining of a virtual SaaS. Thus, selecting SaaS(s) is an NP-hard problem [5].

Given that, these services could be characterized using multiple criteria (Cost, Performance, etc.). It is important to have a methodology for selecting cloud services based on multi-criteria approaches. This work aims to present a model of semantic annotations for describing SaaS (micro or virtual [6]) and an algorithm that selects the relevant SaaS(s). The selection is useful as soon as the customer's request can be satisfied by some SaaS(s), and the relevant SaaS is the service that matches the QoS values of the service requester.

To describe the QoS of a micro SaaS, we use semantic annotations according to the specification of the *Ontology Web Language for Services* (OWL-S) and the Ontology of QoS. The request is referred to the same ontology of QoS. Ontology engineering plays a leading role in adding semantics to a service description. In the proposed solution, we use several SaaS(s) with their compatible services (i.e. those that offer the same functionality, but they can have different values of QoS). The proposed approach is a hybridization between the power of Genetic algorithms, local research, and exhaustive research. Furthermore, the approach considers the preferences of the user (objectives and constraints) and the properties of quality (quantitative and qualitative) in general.

The rest of the paper is organized as follows. In Sect. 2, we present the selection problem. Section 3 is devoted to the classification of related work concerning SaaS selection. In Sect. 4, we describe the proposed approach. In Sect. 5, we exhibit a performance evaluation. Finally, in Sect. 6, we end with concluding remarks and future works.

2   Selection-Problem Complexity

When customers search for a specific SaaS, multiple options may fulfill their needs. In cases where a single micro SaaS (cloud service offered by a unique provider) is insufficient, multiple cloud service components can be combined to form a more complex service, known as a virtual SaaS [6,7]. Unlike micro SaaS, a virtual SaaS is a composite service created from various cloud services rather than being tied to a single provider. A process based on non-functional properties must be applied to select the best SaaS for a customer's needs. This paper focuses on the selection of virtual SaaS, highlighting that each component (micro SaaS) may have several compatible alternatives, each offering the same functionality but with varying QoS attributes. This increases the number of possible compositions exponentially, making the selection problem NP-hard [5] due to its multi-criteria nature.

Figure 1 illustrates the complexity of the virtual SaaS selection problem in cloud computing. Several possible execution plans, denoted as $P_1, P_2, \ldots, P_n$, represent different ways of organizing the tasks required to execute a request. Each task in a given plan is associated with a set of candidate services that can fulfill the corresponding functional requirement. To fully satisfy the request, it is necessary to select an appropriate service for each task that meets the client's QoS requirements, based on a specific execution plan. However, the number of possible combinations increases rapidly with tasks and available services, making the multi-task service selection and composition problem extremely complex.

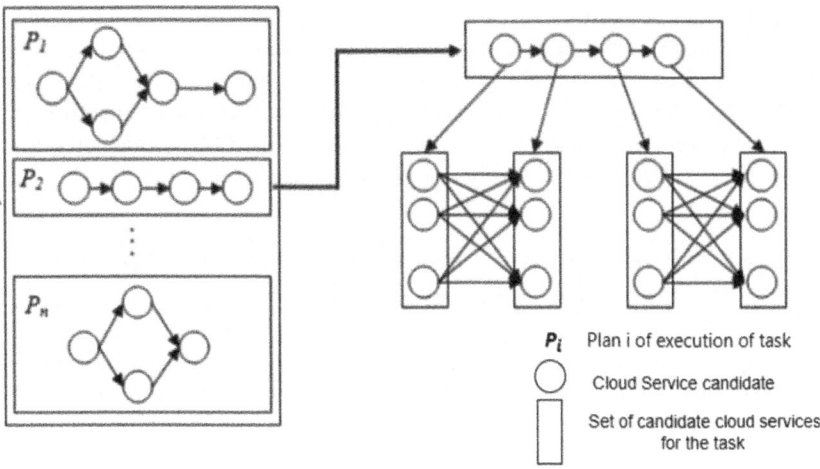

P_i Plan i of execution of task

◯   Cloud Service candidate

▭   Set of candidate cloud services
for the task

Fig. 1. Complexity of the selection problem.

3   Related Work

Several studies have investigated SaaS selection based on non-functional properties, offering a variety of approaches with distinct characteristics and capabilities. Among these, optimization techniques—particularly meta-heuristic
algorithms—are notable for their effectiveness in identifying the most suitable
service or combination of services to meet specific objectives.

Kouchi et al. [5] proposed an optimization approach based on the Cuckoo
Search Algorithm (CSA), combined with Lévy flight, to address the optimal service selection problem in cloud computing, considering QoS constraints. Their
approach consists of three phases: initialization of the population, evaluation,
and searching for relevant services. Dahan et al. [8] presented a hybrid approach
combining the Artificial Bee Colony algorithm (ABC) with CSA. This method
aims to overcome the bee algorithm's slow convergence issues while utilizing
Cuckoo Search's advantages to improve solution quality. In another study, Khatoonabadi et al. [9] proposed a Genetic Algorithm based on the Pareto Principle
(GAP2WSS) to enhance web service selection for composite tasks. Focusing on
the top 20% of candidate services based on QoS metrics. Additionally, Sefati et
al. [10] introduced a hybrid method for cloud service selection and composition
using an adaptive penalty function within genetic algorithms and the Artificial
Bee Colony. This approach further refines the selection process by balancing
multiple optimization factors. Kouchi et al. [11] proposed a hybrid approach for
cloud service selection that combines three complementary mechanisms. First,
the Whale Optimization Algorithm is used to generate new service composition
plans that fulfill the required tasks. Then, the Pareto dominance principle is
applied to filter and reduce the number of generated plans by retaining only
the non-dominated solutions. Finally, an exhaustive search is performed on this
reduced set to identify the optimal solution—that is, the best composition of
services that meets the user's requirements.

Table 1 presents a comparative analysis of the cited works related to cloud service selection. While the cited works have partially fulfilled customer demands,
most of these approaches suffer from high response times, which can adversely
affect the effectiveness of the service selection process. To address this limitation,
our proposed approach employs a Genetic Algorithm (GA) aimed at reducing
response time while simultaneously enhancing customer satisfaction.

4   Proposition: Genetic Optimization Based Approach
for Selecting the Optimal SaaS(s)

In the proposed solution, we focus on the selection process of virtual SaaS(s) in
a unique Cloud. In fact, the proposed approach considers the objectives and the
constraints of the customer. The properties of QoS are defined by using an ontology of domain to have a standard to solve the heterogeneity problem between the
concepts used in the customers' requests and those used by the service providers.
Furthermore, the proposed method is a comprehensive strategy that uses a

Table 1. Comparative analysis of cloud service selection approaches

Authors, Year	Approach	Selection Strategy	Ontology	Objective
Kouchi et al. [5], 2022	CSA + Lévy flight	Global search	No	Mono
Dahan et al. [8], 2023	ABC + CSA	Global search	No	Mono
Khatoonabadi et al. [9], 2021	GA + Pareto Principle	Global search	No	Multi
Sefati et al. [10], 2022	GA + ABC	Global search	No	Mono
Kouchi et al. [11], 2024	WOA + Dominance + Exhaustive Search	Hybrid search	Yes	Multi

hybrid method using local research and global research based on the concept of predominance. Thus, the Extended Genetic Algorithm (EGA) is proposed in this work.

4.1   The Proposed Architecture

Various cloud computing architectures have been proposed in the literature, such as those by NIST, IBM, HP, CISCO, and Azure [12]. In our case, we propose a suitable hybrid architecture inspired by the HP and CISCO models. The proposed architecture consists of three layers: the *Customer Access Layer* (end-user), the *Provider Access Layer*, and the *Broker Layer*, which includes three components: *Discovery* and *Composition, Selection*, and the *Services Layer*. Figure 2 illustrates the architecture of the proposed system in the cloud environment.

The life-cycle process of the selection process in the cloud environment is presented as follows:

1. By using the customer's layer, a customer submits a request that contains two parts of requirement: functional and non-functional properties;
2. The request is sent to the Broker layer;
3. The Broker layer returns a set of SaaS(s) which answers the functional properties of the request. The services can be micro SaaS(s) or virtual SaaS(s), where each virtual SaaS is represented by a composition plan denoted by P_i, $i \in \{1, ..., n\}$, with n is the number of composition plans;
4. The various composition plans P_i, $i = 1, ..., n$ are sent to the Selection component;
5. After the receipt of the different plans P_i, $i = 1, ..., n$ by the Selection component, the Broker layer generates other compatible plans $\tilde{P}_i$, $i = 1, ..., \tilde{n}$ by using Genetic Algorithm where $\tilde{n}$ is the total number of the new plans such that $\tilde{n} > n$. Then, the broker only returns the relevant composition's plans

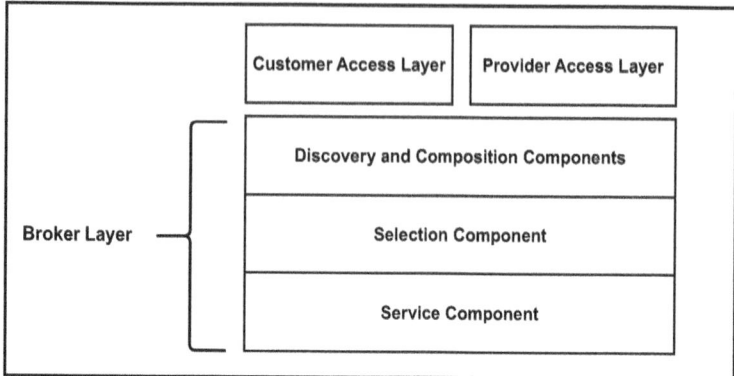

Fig. 2. The proposed architecture in the cloud environment.

among the generated compatible plans, $\tilde{P}_i$, $i = 1, ..., \tilde{n}$, which satisfy as much as possible the non-functional properties of the customer's request. This is done by using dominance selection and exhaustive research.

4.2   QoS of SaaS in Cloud Environment

Quality of Service (QoS) plays a crucial role in evaluating the selection of cloud services, as it represents the non-functional criteria of each service. Due to the diverse performance criteria for SaaS, collecting these metrics is challenging. QoS categories are often derived from customer experiences and literature on web services technology. Common QoS criteria include availability, performance, reliability, scalability, security, and usability, among others. A widely accepted model for cloud service criteria is the *Cloud Service Measurement Index* (SMI) [13].

However, in practice, SaaS(s) are developed independently by different providers, which can specify the criteria of QoS by using various vocabularies. To identify the criteria in a way that eases both the customer and the provider to express their needs and offers, we propose to use semantic annotations to define QoS criteria more clearly for both customers and providers. An ontology for the QoS domain is introduced, tailored for SaaS and cloud services, including configuration and other relevant selection and composition criteria. These additional metrics include the number of satisfied constraints, matching similarity, best-matching services, and the number of services in a composition. The proposed ontology is illustrated in Fig. 3.

4.3   SaaS Management

In order to reduce the complexity of the selection problem, we suggest that published micro SaaS(s) are ranked in the Services Layer. The micro SaaS(s) services can be ranked regarding their functionalities in several registries E_k, $k \in$

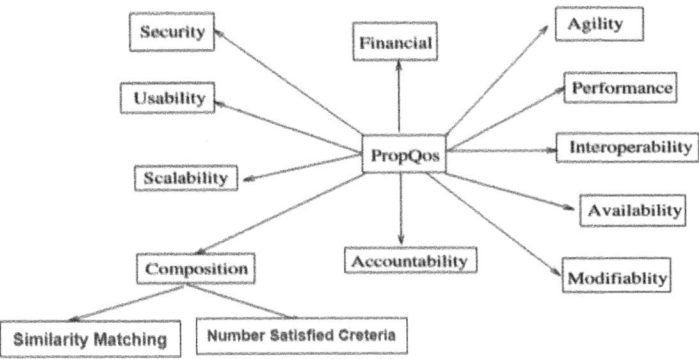

Fig. 3. Ontology of QoS.

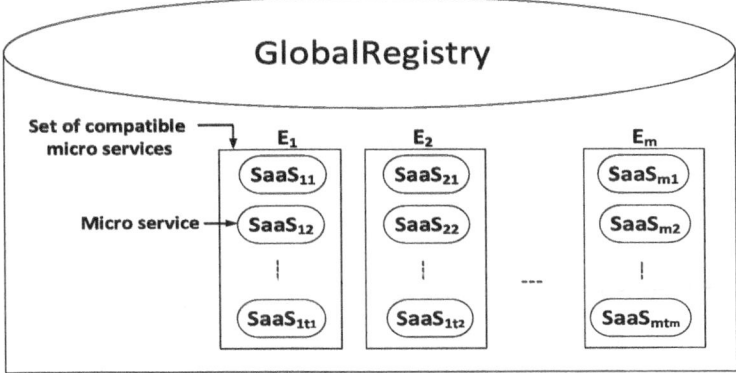

Fig. 4. SaaS management.

$\{1, ..., m\}$ in the data centers. Each registry E_k gathers a set of compatible micro SaaS(s) that have the same functionality F_k, $k \in \{1, ..., m\}$. The idea of grouping the micro SaaS(s) according to their functionalities is inspired by the work of Baridi [14]. Formally, we have the following sets:

- $GlobalRegistry = \{E_1, ..., E_m\}$ is the register of the whole micro services,
- $E_k = \{SaaS_{kj}, j \in \{1, ..., t_k\}\}$ is the set of micro services corresponding to the $k - th$ functionality, with t_k is the number of compatible micro services of E_k,
- $SaaS_{kj}$, $j \in \{1, ..., t_k\}$, is the $j-th$ micro service belonging to the set E_k, $k \in \{1, ..., m\}$.

Figure 4 illustrates the organization of the global registry. An ontology OWL-S [15] is defined to allow a semantic description of the functional properties of a micro SaaS. Furthermore, to describe the non-functional properties of QoS, we add a new criterion 'Q' represents the values of the properties of QoS. Thus, a microservice *SaaS* in OWL-S is described as follows:

$$SaaS = (I, O, Pr, Ef, Q),$$

where:

- I is the set of inputs;
- O is the set of outputs;
- Pr is the set of pre-conditions;
- Ef is the set of the effects of the service;
- Q is the set of properties of QoS of the service,

where a given property of QoS $q \in Q$ is represented as follows: $q = (C, V, T)$, such that

- C is the concept of the proposed ontology of QoS (Financial (Cost), Performance (Response Time), etc.);
- V represents the value offered by the service *SaaS*. This value can be quantitative or qualitative;
- T represents the type of the value V (Integer, Real, String, etc.).

4.4   Selection Process

The selection process is illustrated by Fig. 5. The selection process receives two inputs: the set of plans $P = \{P_1, ..., P_n\}$ and the non-functional properties of the customer's request. In the first step, we apply the proposed selection algorithm based on the basic Genetic Algorithm (GA). The obtained result is used as input for the second step, corresponding to the domination selection. The latter aims to reduce the number of plans by eliminating the SaaS(s) that do not offer good performance. Note that the domination selection is based on the degree of similarity matching [16]. Finally, a refinement is applied in the third step, corresponding to the exhaustive research.

4.5   The Proposed Algorithm

The proposed algorithm EGA of SaaS Selection is constituted from three steps presented as follows:

(1) Generation of Best Composition Plans The objective of the first step is to find for each plan P_i, $i \in \{1, ..., n\}$ the best composition corresponding to this plan. For this, we apply a Genetic Algorithm (GA). It is known that basic GA is a powerful tool for solving combinatorial optimization problems. Furthermore, it is well suited for rapid and total exploration of a space of research of an important size, like a cloud environment. Note that the blue components are the same as those used in the basic GA. At the end of the EGA step, we obtain

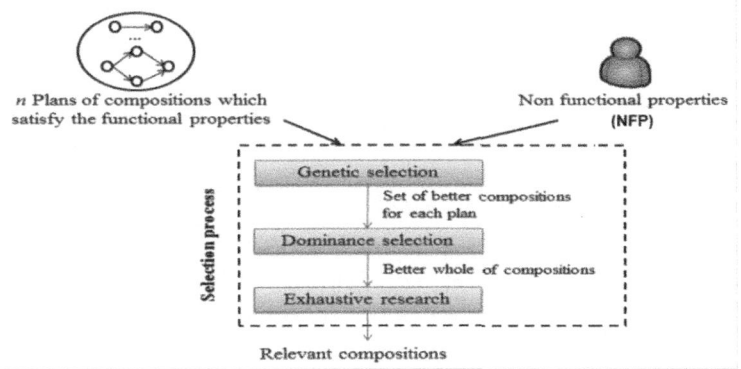

Fig. 5. Selection component.

for each plan P_i, $i \in \{1, \dots, n\}$, a set of r_i compositions denoted by $BestP_i$ such that

$$BestP_i = \left\{ \tilde{P}_{i1}, \tilde{P}_{i2}, \dots, \tilde{P}_{ir_i} \right\},$$

where

$$\tilde{P}_{i1} = \left\{ SaaS_{i1}^1, SaaS_{i1}^2, \dots, SaaS_{i1}^{n_{i1}} \right\},$$
$$\tilde{P}_{i2} = \left\{ SaaS_{i2}^1, SaaS_{i2}^2, \dots, SaaS_{i2}^{n_{i2}} \right\},$$
$$\vdots \quad \vdots \quad \vdots$$
$$\tilde{P}_{ir_i} = \left\{ SaaS_{ir_i}^1, SaaS_{ir_i}^2, \dots, SaaS_{ir_i}^{n_{ir_i}} \right\}.$$

Note that r_i is the number of plans generated by EGA from the plan P_i, $i \in \{1, \dots, n\}$. In this way, EGA generates $\tilde{n} = r_1 + r_2 + \dots + r_n$ new plans. These results are used as inputs for the following second step.

(2) Dominance Selection (Pareto Selection) This step is based on the concept of *dominance*, which is defined in the literature as follows. We consider a problem of maximization. Let x and y be two vectors of N dimensions. It is stated that x *dominates* y, if the following conditions are satisfied:

- $x_i \geq y_i, \forall\, i \in \{1, \dots, N\}$;
- $\exists\, j \in \{1, \dots, N\}$ such that $x_j > y_j$.

In the previous step, for each plan, P_i, $i \in \{1, \dots, n\}$ a set of compositions $BestP_i = \left\{ \tilde{P}_{i1}, \tilde{P}_{i2}, \dots, \tilde{P}_{ir_i} \right\}$ is generated by EGA. In the current step, for each set $BestP_i$, $i \in \{1, \dots, n\}$ is associated a set of vectors $V_i = \{V_{i1}, V_{i2}, \dots, V_{ir_i}\}$ where for all $l \in \{1, \dots, r_i\}$, $V_{il} = (FDM_{il}, NSC_{il})$ such that :

- FDM_{il}: the functional degree of matching between P_i and $\tilde{P}_{il}$;
- NSC_{il}: the non-functional degree of matching, which is the number of satisfied constraints between $\tilde{P}_{il}$ and the non-functional properties of the customer's request.

For all $i \in \{1, ..., n\}$, we keep only the vectors V_{il}, $l \in \{1, ..., r_i\}$ that are not dominated in the set V_i. These results are used as inputs for the next final step.

(3) Exhaustive Research In this step, we construct other plans from the non-dominated plans by using the concept of compatibility of microservices. More specifically, for each non-dominated plan $\tilde{P}_{il} = \{SaaS_{il}^1, SaaS_{il}^2, ..., SaaS_{il}^{n_{x_i}}\}$, $i \in \{1, ..., n\}$, $l \in \{1, ..., r_i\}$, we construct other compatible plans by using for all microservice $SaaS_{il}^s$, $s \in \{1, ..., n_{x_i}\}$, of $\tilde{P}_{il}$ its set of compatible microservices A_{il}^s from E_k, $k \in \{1, ..., m\}$ (see Figs. 4 and 6). In this way, we obtain a total number of compatible plans which is smaller than the number of plans of the initial population $\bigcup_{i=1}^n BestP_i$ because we have eliminated all the dominated plans in the step of dominance.

An exhaustive research is carried out on the sets A_{il}^s, $i \in \{1, ..., n\}$, $l \in \{1, ..., r_i\}$, $s \in \{1, ..., n_{x_i}\}$ as depicted in Fig. 6. Thus, we test all possible combinations of services to find the best compositions.

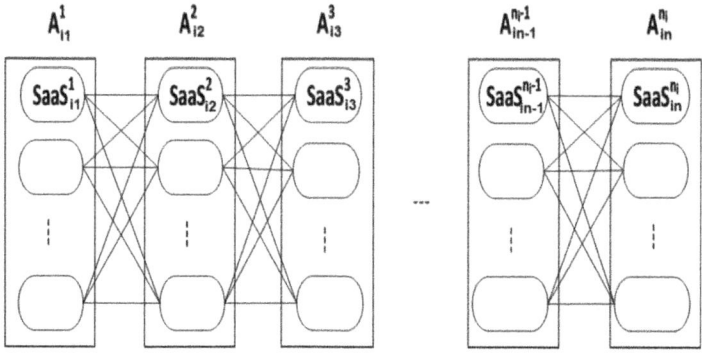

Fig. 6. Exhaustive research step.

Hence, the result of this last step is a set of compositions that will be returned to the customer. The latter has to choose the best composition that satisfies their non-functional needs.

5   Performance Evaluation

To validate the feasibility of the proposed approach (EGA), we construct a simulation experiment system based on the Cloud Computing experiment platform via CloudSim simulator. All experiments were performed in the environment of Microsoft Windows 10 (64-bit) system, Intel R© core i7 CPU 2.90 GHz, and 12 GB RAM, and all algorithms were implemented in JAVA.

Furthermore, we realize some experiment simulations, such as comparing the proposed approach, the basic Genetic Algorithm, and the Exhaustive Search. For that, we suppose that each micro-published SaaS is available with its expected QoS; quantitative or qualitative criteria.

For the experiments, we assume that the Broker, especially the components "Discovery and Composition", returns three plans of composition for a customer's request about a trip plan service, which is composed of microservices, including booking a flight, booking a hotel, renting a car, etc. An optimal trip achieves some objectives, e.g., minimizing the travel duration and minimizing the cost. In the series of experiments, we varied the size of the research space to prove that the proposed solution is suited for a high number of cloud services compared to the Exhaustive Research and the basic Genetic Algorithm.

Scenario 1: Case of three criteria

Let a customer's request contain three criteria: Financial (cost of invocation), Performance (execution time), and Composition to prove the front of the Pareto. The customer wants to minimize the execution time and the cost of invocation simultaneously, with the highest degree of matching similarity for functional properties and a high number of constraints for non-functional properties. Figure 7 and Fig. 8 respectively illustrates the results obtained with 5 and 20 Compatible services per component service. One notices on Fig. 7 that our proposal finds the border of Pareto contrary to the basic Genetic Algorithm.

With the increase of compatible services, our proposal finds optimal solutions that belong to the front of Pareto, but does not manage to find the totality of the front of Pareto. The obtained results are shown in Fig. 8.

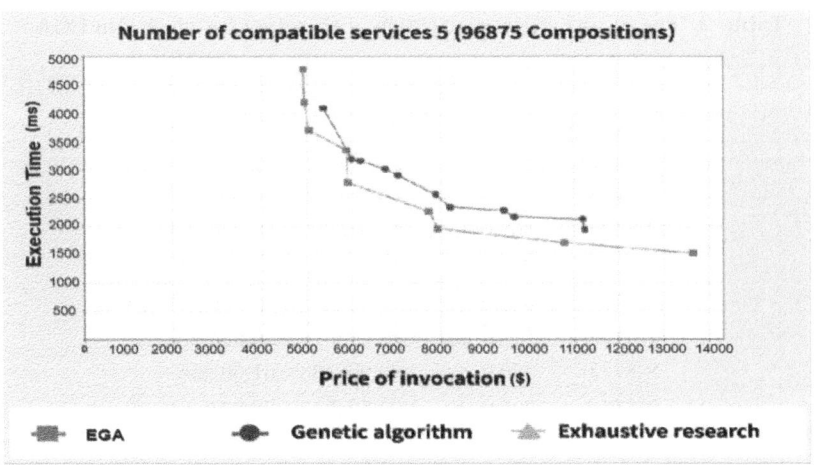

Fig. 7. Results (5 compatible SaaS(s)).

Scenario 2: case of five criteria

In this experiment, we check the validity of the proposed approach to satisfy five constraints in the customer's request: Performance (execution time),

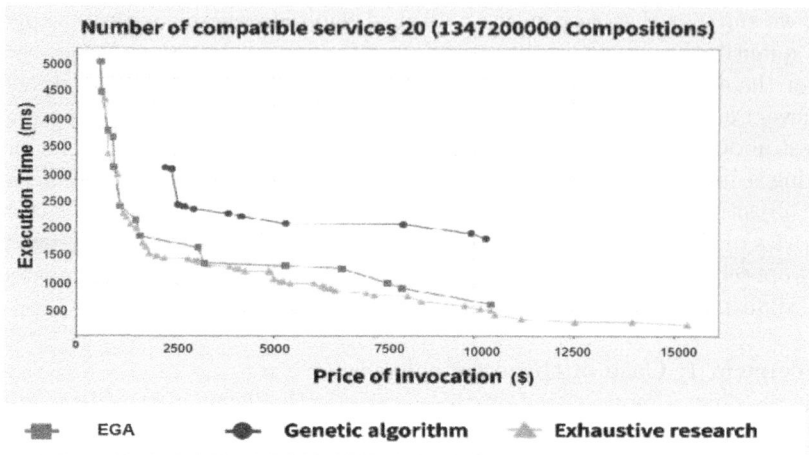

Fig. 8. Results (20 compatible SaaS(s)).

Financial (cost), Availability, Reliability, Composition. The customer wants to minimize the execution time to maximize the Reliability and maximize the degree of similarity matching under two constraints, such that $Cost \leq 14\$$ and $Availability > 85\%$. Table 2 illustrates the results obtained by our proposal on a set of 10 compatible services per component service.

Table 2. The results of the application of the proposed algorithm EGA

N	Financial	Performance	Availability	Reliability
1	$12.0	390.0 ms	85.138091%	61.99854%
2	$11.0	409.0 ms	87.801845%	64.99589%
3	$10.0	359.0 ms	86.281206%	60.00177%
4	$13.0	300.0 ms	90.916292%	53.34019%
5	$14.0	334.0 ms	85.188091%	63.01589%
6	$13.0	361.0 ms	86.088604%	40.03999%
7	$14.0	219.0 ms	92.078371%	29.63348%
8	$11.0	320.0 ms	90.008433%	61.60209%
9	$14.0	392.0 ms	95.594545%	28.84362%

The performance of our EGA algorithm is significantly reflected in the results obtained. If we carefully examine Table 2, which presents the selected services, it is clear that our approach ensures a precise match between the SaaS selection and the customer's specific needs.

Notably, the selected services are characterized by a cost not exceeding 14\$. At the same time, these services show high availability, reaching or exceeding

85%, thus fully meeting the customer's needs. These results provide convincing evidence of the outstanding performance of our system in the selection and composition of SaaS(s), ensuring successful optimization between different constraints to meet customer requirements.

6   Conclusion

Quality of Service (QoS) is crucial for customers when selecting SaaS services. This paper introduced a novel approach to SaaS selection that centers on using ontologies. Furthermore, we mathematically formalized the SaaS selection problem and presented a multi-criteria selection methodology based on an extended genetic algorithm. Moreover, the quality criteria defined above in the selection context can be used to evaluate the quality of micro and virtual SaaS services. Thus, we can conclude that the proposed approach contributes to solving some problems with SaaS selection, which is a complex topic. However, future work could extend this approach by considering the selection of SaaS services in heterogeneous cloud environments, focusing mainly on reliability, elasticity, and security criteria.

References

1. Ayachi, M., Nacer, H., Slimani, H.: Cooperative game approach to form overlapping cloud federation based on inter-cloud architecture. Clust. Comput. **24**, 1551–1577 (2021)
2. Ayachi, M., Nacer, H., Slimani, H.: Correction to: cooperative game approach to form overlapping cloud federation based on inter-cloud architecture. Clust. Comput. **24**, 1579–1582 (2021)
3. Ayachi, M., Nacer, H., Slimani, H.: Cloud computing interoperability: an overview. In: International Conference on New Technologies of Information and Communication (NTIC 2022), Mila, Algeria (2022)
4. Tsai, W., Sun, X., Balasooriya, J.: Service-oriented cloud computing architecture. In: Proceeding of the Seventh International Conference on Information Technology, pp. 684–689 (2010)
5. Kouchi, S., Nacer, H., Slimani, H.: Service selection in cloud computing environment by using cuckoo search. In: International Conference Advances in Information, Communication and Cybersecurity(ICI2C), pp. 219–228 (2021)
6. Nacer, H., Djebari, N., Slimani, H., Aissani, D.: A distributed authentication model for composite web services. J. Comput. Secur. **70**, 144–178 (2017)
7. Nacer, H., Aissani, D.: Semantic web services: standards, applications, challenges and solutions. J. Netw. Comput. Appl. (JNCA) **44**, 134–151 (2014)
8. Dhan, F., Alwabel, A.: Artificial bee colony with cuckoo search for solving service composition. Intell. Autom. Soft Comput. **35**, 3385–3402 (2023)
9. Khatoonabadi, S., Lotfi, S., Isazadeh, A.: GAP2WSS: a genetic algorithm based on the pareto principle for web service selection. Neural Evol. Comput. (2021)
10. Sefati, S.S., Halung, S.: A hybrid service selection and composition for cloud computing using the adaptive penalty function in genetic and artificial bee colony algorithm. Sensors **22**, 4873 (2022)

11. Kouchi, S., Nacer, H., Slimani, H.: Multi-criteria based virtual SAAS selection in cloud environment. In: Global Congress on Emerging Technologies (GCET-2024), pp. 125–131. IEEE (2024)
12. Kouchi, S., Nacer, H., Beghdad-bey, K.: Towards a reference architecture for interoperable clouds. In: 8th International Conference on Electrical and Electronics Engineering (ICEEE), pp. 229–233 (2021)
13. Siegel, J., Perdue, J.: Cloud services measures for global use: the service measurement index (SMI). In: Proceeding of Annual SRII Global Conference, pp. 411–415, San Jose, USA (2012)
14. Badidi, E.: A framework for software as a service selection and provisioning. Int. J. Comput. Netw. Commun. (IJCNC) **5**(3), 189–200 (2013)
15. Ouchaou, L., Nacer, H., Slimani,H., Boukria, S.: Semantic networks based approach for SAAS management in cloud computing. In: Proceeding IEEE International Conference on Smart Communications in Network Technologies (SaCoNeT), pp. 2255–260 (2018)
16. Chen, H., Dou, Z., Hao, X., Tao, Y., Song, S., Sheng, Z.: Enhancing multi-field B2B cloud solution matching via contrastive pre-training (2024)

Non-dominated Sorting Genetic Algorithm for Multiple Objectives Query Optimization in Spark SQL

Trung-Dung Le[(✉)]

Thuyloi University, Hanoi 11515, Vietnam
dung_lt@tlu.edu.vn
https://tlu.edu.vn/

Abstract. Cloud computing allows building applications to store and analyze heterogeneous data sources under a pay-as-you-go paradigm. This elasticity leads to significant challenges for Multi-Objective Query Processing (MOQP), requiring Query Execution Plans (QEPs) that balance diverse user priorities, such as execution time, monetary cost, etc. Spark SQL and Spark SQL's Catalyst Optimizer provide a solution using Cost-based optimization, which can process data from multiple heterogeneous resources. In this solution, they applied the dynamic programming algorithm to pick the best m-way join order. However, when a user would like to expand the cost function to the execution time or monetary cost in a multiple-cloud environment, the optimizer could ignore good plans. To address this problem, we propose a MOQP extension for Spark SQL, leveraging a Non-dominated Sorting Genetic Algorithm based on Grid partitioning (NSGA-G). We validate our proposal with preliminary experimental results.

Keywords: Non-dominated Sorting Genetic Algorithm · SparkSQL · Multiple Objectives Query Optimization

1 Introduction

Minimizing execution time or the size of transferring data is the objective in heterogeneous database systems [9,13,19]. However, cloud computing providing elasticity with a pay-as-you-go model raises an important issue in terms of Multi-Objective Query Processing (MOQP) to find a Query Execution Plan according to users' preferences in terms of time, money, quality, etc. For instance, healthcare data of a given patient may be owned by different hospitals that may use various providers. In the night, the queries could be focused on the monetary aspect more than the execution time. But, during the medical consultation meeting in the daytime, the queries should prioritize the execution time.

Spark SQL[1] and Spark SQL's Catalyst Optimizer [1] provide a solution using Cost-based optimization, which can process data from multiple heterogeneous

---

[1] https://spark.apache.org/sql/.

© The Author(s), under exclusive license to Springer Nature Switzerland AG 2025
O. Gervasi et al. (Eds.): ICCSA 2025, LNCS 15648, pp. 211–224, 2025.
https://doi.org/10.1007/978-3-031-97000-9_13

resources. In this solution, they applied the dynamic programming algorithm in [20] to pick the best m-way join order. In this way, the search space is reduced significantly. But, the cost value is combined with the selectivity and size of tables as a single cost metric, not multiple objectives. Hence, when a user would like to expand the cost function to the execution time or monetary cost in a multiple-cloud environment, the optimizer could ignore good plans.

However, when users consider a trade-off between response time, monetary fees, and other objectives, they should use the Multiple Objectives Query Optimization algorithm to find a good Query Execution Plan. It raises the importance of finding the Pareto-optimal front [11] of QEPs. Besides, generating the Pareto-optimal front can be computationally expensive and is often infeasible [26]. Since generating QEPs may be infeasible due to high complexity, one of the objectives of MOQP in Spark SQL is to find an approximate optimal solution.

In this context, a challenging problem is how to find an approximate optimal solution in MOQP using an efficient Multi-Objective Optimization algorithm in Spark SQL [1].

The solutions in [13, 19] provide various tools to manage heterogeneous data in multiple cloud environments. [13] is a functional SQL-like language, capable of querying multiple heterogeneous data stores, but it optimizes queries on minimizing data transfers, not execution time, monetary or other cost metrics. Besides, [19] showed a method to process a query that integrates data in PostgreSQL and MongoDB. They used the syntax and semantics of SQL++, which is a unifying semi-structured data model and query language that is designed to encompass the data model and query language capabilities of NoSQL, New SQL, etc. In their paper, they did not discuss cost optimization and polystore design. Intelligent Resource Scheduler (IReS) [9] resolved MultiObjective Query Processing in heterogeneous systems by a specified policy that combined multiple objectives into a scalar value and used Waikato Environment for Knowledge Analysis (Weka) [10]. They generated all possible query plans and chose the best plan by combining multiple objectives into a scalar value after having all the plans, not using any algorithms to reduce the search space during the building plan process. Hence, their solution has a very large search space.

Furthermore, [17] focused on the way to build cost models on Spark SQL, and Spark SQL's Catalyst Optimizer provides a solution using Cost-based optimization, which can process data from multiple heterogeneous resources. In this approach, they did not focus on the large search space of Query Execution Plans. Recent advancements like UDAO [21] optimize Spark clusters for performance and cost. Nonetheless, these efforts lack a unified MOQP solution for large-scale variable environments.

To the best of our knowledge, existing solutions do not address the problem of MOQP in the large-scale variable environment and optimize Multi-Objective Query Processing efficiently.

On the other hand, Evolutionary Multiobjective Optimization (EMO) approaches used Pareto dominance techniques [11] to solve the high complexity of the Multi-Objective Optimization Problem. Among EMO approaches, Non-dominated Sorting Genetic Algorithms (NSGAs) [6,7] have lower computational complexity than other EMO approaches [7].

However, [12] stated that the original NSGA-II [7] does not work well on many-objective test problems, such as DTLZ [8], and NSGA-III [6] does not outperform classical EMO algorithms such as NSGA-II in some many-objective test problems. In the previous works [14–16], NSGA-G was proposed to solve this problem in DICOM data management [18] and IReS platform [9]. The algorithm has not been applied to Spark SQL. [4] used NSGA-II to propose a Dynamic Multi-Objective Optimization With jMetal and Spark, while the algorithm may not work well on many-objective test problems [12]. [2] used the multi-objective optimization algorithm based on decomposition (MOEA/D) [25] to focus on the configuration of Spark, and combine a multi-objective optimization approach and a performance prediction model. This algorithm does not completely outperform NSGA-II, NSGA-III, and NSGA-G [15] in many problems, which will be described in Sect. 3.2.

Hence, the other challenging problem is: how to improve the quality of the classical EMO algorithms in Multi-Objective Optimization Problems in Spark SQL.

This paper presented an application of Non-dominated Sorting Genetic Algorithm based on Grid partitioning (NSGA-G) to get a Pareto query execution plan set during the searching plans process. The algorithm is implemented in Spark SQL as an extended function for MOQP.

The remainder of this paper is organized as follows. In Sect. 2, we present the background information and the motivation. Non-dominated Sorting Genetic Algorithm based on Grid partitioning is shown in Sect. 3. NSGA-G algorithm is implemented in Spark SQL and shown in Sect. 4 as an extended function in Spark SQL and Catalyst library. Finally, Sect. 5 concludes this paper and hints at future researchers.

2   Preliminaries

First of all, the preliminaries of this paper show the background of techniques we use to propose an application of a Non-dominated Sorting Genetic Algorithm for Multiple Objectives Query Optimization in Spark SQL.

2.1   Multiple Linear Regression

A cost function of Multiple Linear Regression (MLR) model in [22] is defined: $c = \beta_0 + \beta_1 x_1 + ... + \beta_L x_L + \epsilon$, similar with cost model above, where β_l is the unknown coefficient, $x_l(l = 1, ..., L)$ are the variables, e.g., size of data, computer configuration; c is the cost function value, and ϵ is the random error with a corresponding distribution which is approximated by a normal distribution $\mathcal{N}(0, \sigma)$. The **fitted equation** is defined:

$$\hat{c} = \hat{\beta}_0 + \hat{\beta}_1 x_1 + ... + \hat{\beta}_L x_L \tag{1}$$

2.2 Non-dominated Sorting Genetic Algorithm

Non-dominated Sorting Genetic Algorithm (NSGA) is one of the first Evolutionary Algorithms (EAs) for solving MOQP. Generally, the multi-objective optimization problem is:

$$minimize F(x) = (f_1(x), f_2(x)..., f_m(x)) \tag{2}$$

where $x = (x_1, ..., x_n)^T \in \Omega \subseteq R_n$ is an n-dimensional vector of the decision variables, Ω is the decision (variable) space and F is the objective vector function that contains m real value functions.

Initially, a parent population P_0 is created randomly. Each solution is on a determined rank or nondomination level (any solution in level 1 is not dominated, any solution in level 2 is dominated by one or more solutions in level 1, and so on). In the beginning, the offspring O_0 is created with N solutions by the binary tournament selection and mutation operators. Next, a population $C_0 = P_0 \cup O_0$ with the size of $2N$ should be divided into multiple ranks. After that, a parent population of next-generation P_1 is selected in C_0 from level 1 to level k so that the size of $P_1 = N$, and so on. At the $t - th$ step in the process of generation, population $C_t = P_t \cup O_t$ is generated. C_t is sorted in level $F_1, F_2, ..., F_k$. Now the solutions belonging to the first non-dominated F_1 are the better solutions in C_t. If the size of F_1 is smaller than N, all member of F_1 is selected to P_{t+1}. Thus, solutions in F_2 are chosen next, and so on. This procedure is continued until no more levels can be fitted in P_{t+1}. The last level F_l cannot be filled in P_{t+1}: $| F_l | > N - \sum_{i=1}^{l-1} | F_i |$. Figure 1 shows the procedure of NSGAs.

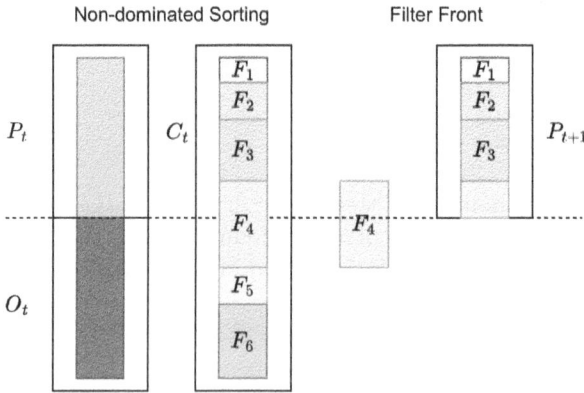

Fig. 1. NSGA-II procedure

NSGA-II and NSGA-III have two different approaches to select members in the last level F_l. While NSGA-II selected solutions by the crowding distance, NSGA-III used Reference Point approach. Both approaches require expensive computation, will be shown in this paper.

2.3   Motivation

Traditional optimizers like Catalyst's [1] reduce search spaces effectively but neglect multi-objective trade-offs. Alternatives like CloudMdsQL [13] and IReS [9] focus on single objectives or scalarized costs, lacking scalability for large QEPs. Recent work [21] highlights the need for dynamic, multi-objective solutions in Spark SQL. They still need to improve the computation of Multiple Objectives Optimization Problems in Spark SQL.

Non-dominated Sorting Genetic Algorithms make it possible to reduce the computational cost of selecting a good solution in the truncating process. Our algorithm experimented with DTLZ problems [8] and compared the quality between NSGA-II, NSGA-III in the Generational Distance (GD) [23], the Inverted Generational Distance (IGD) [3], and the Maximum Pareto Front Error (MPFE) [24]. Furthermore, NSGA-G is proposed to be applied in Spark SQL to address the problem of MOQP in a large-scale variable environment and optimize Multi-Objective Query Processing efficiently.

3   Non-dominated Sorting Genetic Algorithm Based on Grid Partitioning

Recently, many efficient Evolutionary Multi-objective Optimization (EMO) approaches have been developed based on Pareto dominance techniques [11]. Among them, NSGA-II and NSGA III are well-known approaches. While NSGA-II used the crowding distance operator to select the solutions that do not perform well for many-objective problems [12], NSGA-III replaced that operator with a set of well-distributed reference points, which affects the execution time of the algorithm.

In this section, we introduce and experiment NSGA-G [14–16] with DTLZ problems [8] and compare the quality between NSGA-II, NSGA-III in the Generational Distance (GD), the Inverted Generational Distance (IGD), and the Maximum Pareto Front Error (MPFE).

3.1   NSGA-G

As shown in Fig. 1, at the t-th generation of NSGA algorithms, P_t presents the parent population with N size and O_t is the offspring population with N members created by P_t. $C_t = P_t \cup O_t$ is a group which need to be chosen N members for P_{t+1}. In the first step, C_t is sorted by a fast and elitist Multiobjective genetic algorithm to reduce computation time [6,7]. NSGA-II and NSGA-III are used to find the first front (dominating other solutions) and the rest are in the next fronts. After that, the algrithms find the second front, and so on. At the final step, the output of the algorithms are the fronts and their ranks.

After sorting, each non-domination level is selected one at a time to construct a new population P_{t+1}, starting from F_1, until F_l so that the size of $\mid F_l \mid + \sum_{i=1}^{l-1} \mid F_i \mid$ is larger or equal to N. At l-th level, the algorithm

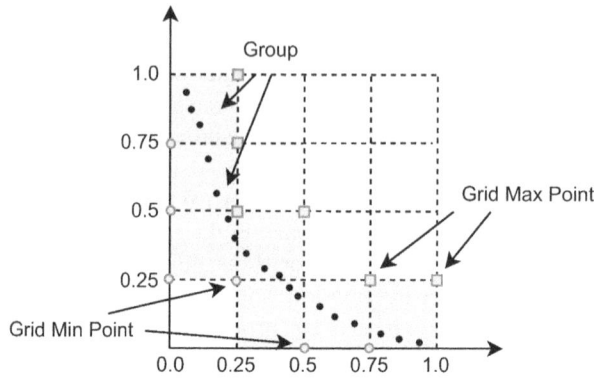

Fig. 2. Grid points and Groups

only accepted partially F_l. NSGA-II in [7] used crowding-distance-assignment algorithm while an Evolutionary Many-Objective Optimization Algorithm Using Reference-point Based Non-Dominated Sorting Approach, [6] concluded that the identification of neighbors became computationally expensive in a large dimension space and replaced the crowding-distance-assignment algorithm in NSGA-II by the Reference Points on a Hyper-Plane approach, NSGA-III. The work needed to associate each population member with the reference point in making a new parent member in the next iteration. Both algorithms require expensive computation by equations:

$$I[i]_{distance} = I[i]_{distance} + \frac{(I[i+1].m - I[i-1].m)}{(f_m^{max} - f_m^{min})}$$

or

$$f_i^n(x) = \frac{f_i'(x)}{a_i - z_i^{min}}$$

Our approach finds the nearest smaller and bigger grid points of each solution. For instance, Fig. 2 shows an example of the two-objective problems. If we have the unit of the grid point is 0.25 and the solution with two objectives values of $[0.55, 0.66]$, the nearest smaller point is $[0.5, 0.5]$ and the nearest bigger point is $[0.75, 0.75]$. In many circumstances, there are many solutions that have the same nearest point, and they will be in a group. The solution has the smallest distance to the nearest smaller point in a group will be added to P_{t+1}. In this way, in any loop, we do not need to calculate the crowding-distance values or estimate the smallest distance from solutions to the reference points among all members in F_4 in Fig. 1. Algorithm 1 shows our strategy to select $N - \sum_{i=1}^{l-1} F_l$ members in F_l.

The functions updateIdealPoint and updateIdealMaxpoint in lines 1 and 2 will determine the new origin coordinates and the maximum objective values of all solutions. After that, they will be normalized to a range of 0–1. All solutions will be in different groups according to the coefficient of the grid. The key to

---

Algorithm 1. Filter front in NSGA-G

Require: $F_l, M = N - \sum_{i=1}^{l-1} F_i$
Ensure: $N - \sum_{i=1}^{l-1} F_i$ members in F_l
 1: updateIdealPoint()
 2: updateIdealMaxPoint()
 3: translateByIdealPoint()
 4: normalizeByMinMax()
 5: createGroups
 6: **while** $\mid F_l \mid > M$ **do**
 7:    selectRandomGroup()
 8:    removeMaxSolutionInGroup()
 9: **end while**
10: **return** F_l

---

the NSGA-G algorithm is that we select the group randomly, like NSGA-III did, to keep the diversity characteristic and remove the solution among members of that group. It helps avoid comparing and calculating the maximum objectives in all solutions.

3.2   Experiment

For fair comparison and evaluation, we have used the same parameters, such as Crossover probability, Mutation probability, Distribution index for crossover, Distribution index for mutation for 1. NSGA-II, 2. NSGA-III, 3. MOEA/D, 4. NSGA-G[2], during their 50 run independent runs in solving two types of problems: DTLZ1 and DTLZ3 test problems with the objectives, m, are 4, 5, 6, 7, 8, 9, 10 in MOEA framework[3]. These three algorithms use the same population size $N = 100$ and the maximum evaluation $M = 1000$. To estimate the quality of three algorithms, we use the Generational Distance (GD) [23], the Inverted Generational Distance (IGD) [3], and the Maximum Pareto Front Error (MPFE) [24]. The GD value determines the distance from the evolved solution to the true Pareto Front [23]. IGD could measure both convergence and diversity in a sense. The most significant distance between the individuals in the Pareto Front and the evolved solution is measured and shown in MPFE. In three metrics, the better quality is shown by the lower value. Tables 1, 3 and 5 show that the quality of NSGA-G is better than other algorithms in these experiments. The advantages of NSGA-G are shown in most cases.

In the high computation comparing, Tables 2, 4, and 6 show the average of computation time of NSGA-II, NSGA-III, MOEA/D, and NSGA-G in seconds. The tables showed that NSGA-G had shorter computation times in most cases.

In conclusion, NSGA-G are presented not only the advantages in the diversity, convergence, the most distance between the individuals in Pareto Front and the evolved solution in three experiments, but also in the smaller computation time

---

[2] https://github.com/dungltr/MOEA.
[3] http://moeaframework.org/.

than the others in the large objective experiments, as shown in Tables 2, 4 and 6.

Table 1. Generational Distance

	m	NSGA-II	MOEA/D	NSGA-III	NSGA-G
DTLZ1	4	3.427e+01	1.624e+00	1.093e+01	1.071e+00
DTLZ3	4	5.081e+01	1.563e+01	2.718e+01	1.133e+01
DTLZ1	5	2.143e+01	4.708e−01	3.130e+00	1.527e−01
DTLZ3	5	1.133e+00	9.667e−02	3.109e−01	1.475e−02
DTLZ1	6	9.309e+01	1.918e+00	7.097e+00	4.370e−01
DTLZ3	6	1.277e+02	1.698e+01	2.385e+01	5.731e+00
DTLZ1	7	3.160e+01	4.492e−01	1.858e+00	1.696e−01
DTLZ3	7	8.994e−01	1.881e−02	9.341e−02	4.874e−03
DTLZ1	8	1.134e+02	1.838e+00	1.000e+01	4.030e−01
DTLZ3	8	1.639e+02	1.425e+01	2.977e+01	4.967e+00
DTLZ1	9	1.656e+01	2.153e−01	1.701e+00	4.856e−02
DTLZ3	9	7.132e−01	8.410e−03	1.194e−01	3.008e−03
DTLZ1	10	2.665e+01	3.495e−01	2.724e+00	8.250e−02
DTLZ3	10	6.030e−01	6.901e−03	1.041e−01	2.103e−03

Table 2. Average compute time in GD experiment (seconds)

	m	NSGA-II	MOEA/D	NSGA-III	NSGA-G
DTLZ1	4	3.434e+01	1.721e+02	1.246e+02	3.790e+01
DTLZ3	4	3.536e+01	1.678e+02	1.279e+02	4.036e+01
DTLZ1	5	3.878e+01	1.748e+02	1.700e+02	4.012e+01
DTLZ3	5	4.114e+01	1.741e+02	1.751e+02	4.336e+01
DTLZ1	6	4.378e+01	1.868e+02	1.330e+02	4.290e+01
DTLZ3	6	4.594e+01	1.889e+02	1.386e+02	4.684e+01
DTLZ1	7	4.782e+01	2.047e+02	1.339e+02	4.588e+01
DTLZ3	7	5.128e+01	2.052e+02	1.403e+02	4.958e+01
DTLZ1	8	5.272e+01	2.200e+02	1.936e+02	4.796e+01
DTLZ3	8	5.560e+01	2.223e+02	2.026e+02	5.184e+01
DTLZ1	9	5.620e+01	2.338e+02	2.563e+02	5.028e+01
DTLZ3	9	5.960e+01	2.345e+02	2.723e+02	5.450e+01
DTLZ1	10	5.964e+01	2.401e+02	3.374e+02	5.246e+01
DTLZ3	10	6.364e+01	2.449e+02	3.704e+02	5.676e+01

4   NSGA-G in Spark SQL

Spark SQL is one of the most technical components of Spark in processing SQL queries. The core of Spark SQL is Catalyst optimizer, which supports both rule-based and cost-based optimization. The cost-based join reordering optimizations pick the best m-way join order with the Dynamic Programming approach [20].

Table 3. Inverted Generational Distance

	m	NSGA-II	MOEA/D	NSGA-III	NSGA-G
DTLZ1	4	3.669e+01	2.760e+00	1.083e+01	3.837e+00
DTLZ3	4	1.221e+02	4.157e+01	8.407e+01	4.397e+01
DTLZ1	5	3.482e+01	6.816e−01	3.315e+00	6.939e−01
DTLZ3	5	3.298e+00	4.599e−01	1.154e+00	2.132e−01
DTLZ1	6	2.424e+02	2.703e+00	9.366e+00	2.782e+00
DTLZ3	6	5.083e+02	4.021e+01	8.398e+01	3.222e+01
DTLZ1	7	5.321e+00	4.468e−01	4.405e−01	6.095e−01
DTLZ3	7	3.126e+00	2.087e−01	2.864e−01	1.716e−01
DTLZ1	8	3.974e+02	2.843e+00	1.204e+01	2.589e+00
DTLZ3	8	7.116e+02	3.856e+01	1.027e+02	2.655e+01
DTLZ1	9	5.406e+00	4.198e−01	5.694e−01	6.325e−01
DTLZ3	9	2.825e+00	2.243e−01	3.974e−01	1.994e−01
DTLZ1	10	1.254e+01	3.325e−01	1.080e+00	6.636e−01
DTLZ3	10	2.525e+00	1.891e−01	4.312e−01	2.109e−01

Table 4. Average compute time in IGD experiment (seconds)

	m	NSGA-II	MOEA/D	NSGA-III	NSGA-G
DTLZ1	4	3.144e+01	1.650e+02	1.194e+02	3.548e+01
DTLZ3	4	3.426e+01	1.649e+02	1.257e+02	3.932e+01
DTLZ1	5	3.820e+01	1.727e+02	1.690e+02	3.978e+01
DTLZ3	5	4.084e+01	1.737e+02	1.739e+02	4.330e+01
DTLZ1	6	4.326e+01	1.850e+02	1.313e+02	4.284e+01
DTLZ3	6	4.638e+01	1.885e+02	1.386e+02	4.642e+01
DTLZ1	7	4.780e+01	2.034e+02	1.332e+02	4.554e+01
DTLZ3	7	5.074e+01	2.056e+02	1.399e+02	4.902e+01
DTLZ1	8	5.242e+01	2.192e+02	1.912e+02	4.790e+01
DTLZ3	8	5.602e+01	2.217e+02	2.019e+02	5.156e+01
DTLZ1	9	5.586e+01	2.325e+02	2.520e+02	5.056e+01
DTLZ3	9	5.910e+01	2.334e+02	2.698e+02	5.402e+01
DTLZ1	10	5.910e+01	2.398e+02	3.372e+02	5.218e+01
DTLZ3	10	6.320e+01	2.451e+02	3.640e+02	5.620e+01

Table 5. Maximum Pareto Front Error

	m	NSGA-II	MOEA/D	NSGA-III	NSGA-G
DTLZ1	4	8.329e+02	2.937e+01	5.433e+02	1.960e+01
DTLZ3	4	1.042e+03	1.237e+02	8.645e+02	1.896e+02
DTLZ1	5	6.860e+02	1.006e+01	2.633e+02	4.940e+00
DTLZ3	5	2.637e+01	1.828e+00	1.457e+01	4.145e−01
DTLZ1	6	1.561e+03	5.778e+01	4.258e+02	7.048e+00
DTLZ3	6	1.817e+03	1.840e+02	6.905e+02	7.986e+01
DTLZ1	7	7.804e+02	6.656e+00	1.082e+02	2.031e+00
DTLZ3	7	1.470e+01	3.712e−01	3.610e+00	1.396e−01
DTLZ1	8	1.961e+03	4.591e+01	5.125e+02	6.087e+00
DTLZ3	8	2.173e+03	2.167e+02	8.754e+02	6.377e+01
DTLZ1	9	7.183e+02	6.447e+00	1.884e+02	1.449e+00
DTLZ3	9	1.783e+01	1.920e−01	6.497e+00	1.038e−01
DTLZ1	10	7.173e+02	7.045e+00	2.049e+02	9.801e−01
DTLZ3	10	1.401e+01	1.986e−01	5.728e+00	7.336e−02

Table 6. Average compute time in MPFE experiment (seconds)

	m	NSGA-II	MOEA/D	NSGA-III	NSGA-G
DTLZ1	4	3.152e+01	1.647e+02	1.211e+02	3.608e+01
DTLZ3	4	3.448e+01	1.655e+02	1.265e+02	3.938e+01
DTLZ1	5	3.814e+01	1.726e+02	1.682e+02	3.950e+01
DTLZ3	5	4.072e+01	1.745e+02	1.747e+02	4.340e+01
DTLZ1	6	4.392e+01	1.845e+02	1.314e+02	4.282e+01
DTLZ3	6	4.642e+01	1.879e+02	1.389e+02	4.654e+01
DTLZ1	7	4.868e+01	2.032e+02	1.340e+02	4.536e+01
DTLZ3	7	5.076e+01	2.060e+02	1.390e+02	4.912e+01
DTLZ1	8	5.212e+01	2.187e+02	1.908e+02	4.778e+01
DTLZ3	8	5.518e+01	2.206e+02	2.036e+02	5.140e+01
DTLZ1	9	5.582e+01	2.309e+02	2.545e+02	5.040e+01
DTLZ3	9	5.942e+01	2.332e+02	2.715e+02	5.420e+01
DTLZ1	10	5.938e+01	2.388e+02	3.398e+02	5.194e+01
DTLZ3	10	6.320e+01	2.423e+02	3.648e+02	5.668e+01

When building m-way joins, they only keep the best plan for the same set of m items. For instance, with tables A, B, C, they keep the best plan and the order of joining $\{A, B, C\}$ instead of all plans (A join B) join C, (A join C) join B and (B join C) join A. This strategy significantly reduces the search space, but could ignore some good plans during MOQO. They estimate the cost of a join operator with a single formula:

$$cost = weight * cardinality + (1.0 - weight) * size \qquad (3)$$

Our strategy extends the cost-based join reordering with NSGA-G above for MOQO in multiple cloud environments.

We enhance Catalyst by: 1. Constructing logical plans with dynamic programming [20]. 2. Estimating multi-metric costs via MLR [22], augmented by CBO statistics [5]. 3. Pruning with NSGA-G to yield Pareto-optimal QEPs

4.1 Query Processing

Figure 3 shows the sequence of our query processing. When a user puts a query with their Weighted Sum Model, the Spark SQL will generate multiple logical plans with multiple objectives, cost-based optimization with the Dynamic Programming approach. After that, the best plan will be chosen by the Weighted Sum Model and put to Spark SQL to generate and optimize the physical plans.

4.2 Integrating NSGA-G in Spark SQL

Figure 4 shows the architecture of generating multiple objectives logical plans step in Fig. 3 with NSGA-G. At the first step, after Spark SQL receives a query, Multiple Linear Regression Algorithm [22] puts the parameter into the model of multiple cost metrics estimation. After that, Spark SQL will generate and optimize logical plans with the Dynamic Programming and multiple cost metric values. To reduce the search space, the NSGA-G will be applied to find a Pareto plan set. This pruning strategy significantly reduces the search space. At the final step, a Pareto plan set will be put out of the Spark SQL module.

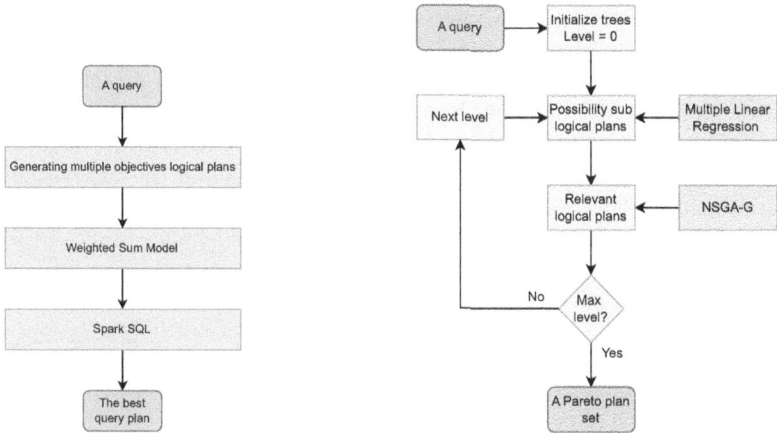

Fig. 3. Steps of query processing   **Fig. 4.** Steps of generating logical plans

4.3   Experiment

We implemented our solution in Java, Spark SQL, and Catalyst library. In the optimizer code, [1] used the dynamic programming algorithm in [20] to pick the best m-way join order and kept the best plan for the same set of m tables.

Spark's Cost-Based Optimizer estimated the cost of a join operator as Eq. 3. The strategy significantly reduces the search space, but it could ignore some good plans when we consider other metrics, such as the execution time or the monetary cost.

Our experiments keep all the intermediate logical subplans and add the estimated values to all logical plans. The estimated values are determined by Multiple Linear Regression (MLR) with the previous value of each logical plan based on the cardinality. The MLR is used to estimate the parameter $\hat{\beta}_0, \hat{\beta}_1, ..., \hat{\beta}_L$, and estimate $\hat{c}$ with the newest value of logical plans. For example, $Q = ((A \text{ join } B) \text{ join } C) \text{ join } D$, our experiment will generate all logical plans for the same set of 4 tables. The cardinality and sizes of each logical plan are the cardinality and size of the intermediate logical subplans of 3 tables for the left side and the cardinality and size of the rest tables for the right side. With the previous value of each logical plan, MLR will estimate the parameter and calculate other cost metrics. After that, NSGA-G will be used to determine a Pareto plan set of logical plans. Finally, the user policy will be used to choose the best plan from Pareto plan set.

Our experiment is implemented with TPC-DS benchmark 1G dataset and a query of joining 5 tables.

5   Conclusion

In this paper, we propose a MOQP extension for Spark SQL, combining Multiple Linear Regression Algorithm and NSGA-G to address variance in a large-scale variable environment and to provide accurate estimations for MOQO. We also provide an application of NSGA-G, which has higher performance than the original NSGA-II and NSGA-III in DTLZ 1 and 3 problems. Both algorithms are integrated into Spark SQL module to solve the MOQO for the large-scale variable environment. Future work will validate this proposal with commercial providers and data management systems.

References

1. Armbrust, M., et al.: Spark SQL: relational data processing in spark. In: Proceedings of the 2015 ACM SIGMOD International Conference on Management of Data (SIGMOD), pp. 1383–1394. ACM (2015). https://doi.org/10.1145/2723372.2742797
2. Cheng, G., Ying, S., Wang, B.: Tuning configuration of Apache Spark on public clouds by combining multi-objective optimization and performance prediction model. J. Syst. Softw. **180** (2021). https://doi.org/10.1016/j.jss.2021.111028
3. Coello, C.A.C., Cortés, N.C.: Solving multiobjective optimization problems using an artificial immune system. Genetic Programm. Evol. Mach. **6**, 163–190 (2005). https://doi.org/10.1007/s10710-005-6164-x
4. Cordero, J.A., et al.: Dynamic multi-objective optimization with jMetal and spark: a case study. In: Pardalos, P.M., Conca, P., Giuffrida, G., Nicosia, G. (eds.) MOD 2016. LNCS, vol. 10122, pp. 106–117. Springer, Cham (2016). https://doi.org/10.1007/978-3-319-51469-7_9
5. Databricks: Cost-based optimizer in Apache Spark SQL. Databricks Documentation (2024). https://docs.databricks.com/spark/latest/spark-sql/cbo.html
6. Deb, K., Jain, H.: An evolutionary many-objective optimization algorithm using reference-point-based nondominated sorting approach. IEEE Trans. Evol. Comput. **18**(4), 577–601 (2014). https://doi.org/10.1109/TEVC.2013.2281535
7. Deb, K., Pratap, A., Agarwal, S., Meyarivan, T.: A fast and elitist multiobjective genetic algorithm: NSGA-II. IEEE Trans. Evol. Comput. **6**(2), 182–197 (2002). https://doi.org/10.1109/4235.996017
8. Deb, K., Thiele, L., Laumanns, M., Zitzler, E.: Scalable multi-objective optimization test problems. In: Proceedings of the 2002 Congress on Evolutionary Computation (CEC 2002), vol. 1, pp. 825–830. IEEE (2002). https://doi.org/10.1109/CEC.2002.1007032
9. Doka, K., Papailiou, N., Tsoumakos, D., Mantas, C., Koziris, N.: IReS: intelligent, Multi-Engine Resource Scheduler for Big Data Analytics Workflows. In: Proceedings of the 2015 ACM SIGMOD International Conference on Management of Data (SIGMOD 2015), pp. 1451–1456. ACM (2015). https://doi.org/10.1145/2723372.2735377

10. Hall, M., Frank, E., Holmes, G., Pfahringer, B., Reutemann, P., Witten, I.H.: The WEKA data mining software: an update. SIGKDD Explor. Newslett. **11**(1), 10–18 (2009). https://doi.org/10.1145/1656274.1656278

11. Hulgeri, A., Sudarshan, S.: Parametric query optimization for linear and piecewise linear cost functions. In: Proceedings of the 28th International Conference on Very Large Data Bases (VLDB 2002), pp. 167–178. VLDB Endowment (2002). https://dl.acm.org/doi/10.5555/1287369.1287385

12. Ishibuchi, H., Imada, R., Setoguchi, Y., Nojima, Y.: Performance comparison of NSGA-II and NSGA-III on various many-objective test problems. In: 2016 IEEE Congress on Evolutionary Computation (CEC), pp. 3045–3052. IEEE (2016). https://doi.org/10.1109/CEC.2016.7744174

13. Kolev, B., Bondiombouy, C., Vakluriez, P., Jimenez-Peris, R., Pau, R., Pereira, J.: The CloudMdsQL Multistore System. In: Proceedings of the 2016 International Conference on Management of Data (SIGMOD 2016), pp. 2113–2116. ACM (2016). https://doi.org/10.1145/2882903.2899400

14. Le, T.-D., Kantere, V., d'Orazio, L.: An efficient multi-objective genetic algorithm for cloud computing: NSGA-G. In: 2018 IEEE International Conference on Big Data (Big Data), Seattle, WA, USA, 2018, pp. 3883–3888 (2018). https://doi.org/10.1109/BigData.2018.8622148

15. Le, T.-D., Kantere, V., d'Orazio, L.: Dynamic estimation and grid partitioning approach for multi-objective optimization problems in medical cloud federations. In: Hameurlain, A., Tjoa, A.M. (eds.) Transactions on Large-Scale Data- and Knowledge-Centered Systems XLVI. LNCS, vol. 12410, pp. 32–66. Springer, Heidelberg (2020). https://doi.org/10.1007/978-3-662-62386-2_2

16. Le, T.-D., Kantere, V., d'Orazio, L.: Optimizing DICOM data management with NSGA-G. In: Proceedings of the 2019 International Workshop on Data Warehouse Design and OLAP (DOLAP) (2019)

17. Misegiannis, M.G., Kantere, V., d'Orazio, L.: Multi-objective query optimization in Spark SQL. In: Proceedings of the 26th International Database Engineering & Applications Symposium (IDEAS), pp. 70–74 (2022). https://doi.org/10.1145/3548785.3548800

18. Nguyen-Cong, D., d'Orazio, L., Tran, N., Hacid, M.-S.: Storing and querying DICOM data with HYTORMO. In: Wang, F., Yao, L., Luo, G. (eds.) DMAH 2016. LNCS, vol. 10186, pp. 43–61. Springer, Cham (2017). https://doi.org/10.1007/978-3-319-57741-8_4

19. Papakonstantinou, Y.: Polystore query rewriting: the challenges of variety. In: EDBT/ICDT Workshops (2016)

20. Selinger, P.G., Astrahan, M.M., Chamberlin, D.D., Lorie, R.A., Price, T.G.: Access path selection in a relational database management system. In: Proceedings of the 1979 ACM SIGMOD International Conference on Management of Data (SIGMOD 1979), pp. 23–34. ACM (1979). https://doi.org/10.1145/582095.582099

21. Song, F., et al.: Spark-based cloud data analytics using multi-objective optimization. In: IEEE 37th International Conference on Data Engineering (ICDE), Chania, Greece, 2021, pp. 396–407 (2021). https://doi.org/10.1109/ICDE51399.2021.00041

22. Soong, T.T.: Fundamentals of Probability and Statistics for Engineers. Wiley (2004)

23. Veldhuizen, D.A.V., Lamont, G.B.: Evolutionary computation and convergence to a pareto front. In: Late Breaking Papers at the Genetic Programming 1998 Conference, pp. 221–228 (1998)

24. Veldhuizen, D.A.V.: Multiobjective evolutionary algorithms: classifications, analyses, and new innovations. Ph.D. thesis, Air Force Institute of Technology (1999)

25. Zhang, Q., Li, H.: MOEA/D: a multiobjective evolutionary algorithm based on decomposition. IEEE Trans. Evol. Comput. **11**(6), 712–731 (2007). https://doi.org/10.1109/TEVC.2007.892759
26. Zitzler, E., Thiele, L., Laumanns, M., Fonseca, C.M., da Fonseca, V.G.: Performance assessment of multiobjective optimizers: an analysis and review. IEEE Trans. Evol. Comput. **7**(2), 117–132 (2003). https://doi.org/10.1109/TEVC.2003.810758

Evaluating LoRaMesh Communication for Industrial IoT Applications: Performance and Feasibility

Mohamad Sadeque Abou Ali[✉], Jean Mário Moreira de Lima, Itamir de Morais Barroca Filho, and Andre Morais Gurgel

Digital Metropolis Institute - UFRN, Natal, Brazil
mohamad.ali@ufrn.edu.bn

Abstract. The Internet of Things (IoT) is continuously evolving, driving innovations in communication technologies, particularly for industrial applications where reliable long-range connectivity is essential. This work proposes a LoRa-based mesh network (LoRaMesh) for IoT applications, evaluating its effectiveness in expanding communication range and network resilience. Using an ESP32 microcontroller interfaced with a LoRaMesh module from Radioenge, the study explores various configurations of spreading factor (SF), bandwidth (BW), and coding rate (CR) to optimize communication performance. Experiments were conducted over distances of up to 1000 m, transmitting messages between two devices and analyzing signal strength (RSSI) and signal-to-noise ratio (SNR). At another point, a study was conducted regarding the power consumption of the devices used in different operating modes and the impact on the autonomy of a 3800 mAh battery powering the system. The results highlight the trade-offs between transmission range, data rate, and energy efficiency, providing insights into LoRaMesh's potential for industrial monitoring applications. Additionally, the study discusses necessary adaptations to ensure compatibility with industrial environments, including integration with established automation protocols. The findings contribute to the growing body of research on LoRa-based networks, offering practical considerations for deploying IoT solutions in remote and challenging conditions.

Keywords: LoRa · Mesh · Internet of Things

1 Introduction

Industrial environments are often located far from urban areas, which can make process monitoring challenging. This is the case for onshore oil wells, where, in the absence of a communication infrastructure, workers must personally check the status of equipment. This not only causes delays in response time but also results in high costs, weak signals, and a lack of redundancy in commonly used communication technologies. In such scenarios, communication alternatives range from fiber optic cable deployment to radio communication or cellular signals. Each of these options has its advantages and disadvantages, but the lack of interoperability among them necessitates the use of different equipment.

Within the Internet of Things (IoT) paradigm, solutions to this problem can be found, enabling the connection of objects through wired and wireless networks, thus forming large systems for monitoring, analysis, and control [22]. Remote equipment monitoring through IoT is already a well-known challenge with various solutions depending on the specific case. LoRa is one of the technologies frequently cited in embedded systems research for this type of application, demonstrating good results due to its low power consumption and versatility. It can be implemented in different ways, either as a standalone physical layer or using protocols such as LoRaWAN and LoRaMesh, making it essential to understand the limitations, advantages, and disadvantages of each approach. There are several studies in the field of sensor network monitoring. Somchai Biansoongnern [4] aimed to use vibration sensors connected via WiFi to provide alerts about landslides. His architecture consists of sensors connecting to a main node that transmits the data to the internet, forming a star topology. This limits the network's range due to the dependence on the main node, but a positive aspect is the low implementation cost of the technology and the high communication speed. Addressing an urban problem, Vivek Katiyar [9] proposed the use of wireless sensor networks to collect traffic information and prevent accidents. His architecture utilizes Bluetooth technology for vehicle-to-vehicle communication, forming ad-hoc networks to share data obtained from sensors installed in strategic locations. Simulations showed that vehicle communication was possible at speeds of up to 60 km/h and distances of up to 20 m. This architecture has the advantage of using a widely available technology already embedded in many vehicles, reducing costs and ensuring communication stability. However, a limitation of this approach is the short range of Bluetooth, which may restrict its applicability in scenarios with high traffic density or higher speeds.

The versatility of these solutions allows for the hybrid application of multiple technologies. For example, Singh [19] developed a sensor network using LoRa and Zigbee to monitor oil pipelines, collecting pressure and flow data and sending them to the Cayenne platform, Despite the increased complexity of multiple networks, the gain in distance and system scalability can be highly beneficial. On the other hand, these technologies require a higher investment compared to Bluetooth or WiFi. Another study following the same principle was conducted by Fernández-Ahumada [7], who proposed a network for monitoring and operating an automatic irrigation system using LoRa and Sigfox. In this solution, multiple network nodes send data to a local gateway via LoRa, which then forwards the information to the ThingSpeak platform using Sigfox, The architecture that combines LoRa and Sigfox allows for a noticeable gain in communication range, as it leverages both Sigfox's infrastructure and LoRa's flexibility. However, detailed planning of deployment and maintenance costs is essential, considering that Sigfox operates under a subscription model to maintain connectivity, while LoRa may require initial infrastructure investments. The choice between these technologies should take into account coverage, data volume, and long-term economic feasibility.

Based on the analysis of some studies in the field and the search for a solution for a network that requires long-range communication, a low data rate, and minimal changes to the existing infrastructure of the monitored processes. This work aims to develop a device capable of communicating with industrial equipment using protocols already employed in the field, such as Modbus, and acquiring information from the environment in which it is installed through signals connected to digital and analog inputs. The collected data will be transmitted via a hybrid network, using a mesh topology with LoRa modulation to transport the data to local gateways that can share the information with other systems. Thus, it will be designed to offer greater coverage, cost reduction, and increased robustness. During the development, a validation of the chosen technologies will be carried out, ensuring that the defined requirements are met and enabling their implementation in future work.

2   Literature Review

2.1   Industrial Internet of Things

The paradigm of Internet-connected objects with the ability to send and receive data to perform specific tasks is called the Internet of Things (IoT) [11]. These objects, also referred to as devices, can be categorized into four layers, according to Oproiu [12]. The first layer is Perception, which operates at the lowest level, interacting with the physical and logical signals of the environment. Above it, there is the communication layer, which transmits the information collected and processed in the perception layer to the gateway, which acts as the boundary point with the object called the IoT device. Then, there is the middleware layer, a set of hardware and software that interface between the gateway and the application layer. Finally, the application layer, responsible for direct user interaction, enabling the operation of devices and services.

With the advancement of technology, the concept of the Internet of Things has been expanding and is often subdivided to facilitate understanding. One way to subdivide IoT is into Industrial and Consumer [2], the latter being aimed at personal use applications, such as smartwatches, voice assistants, smart home devices, and others. Industrial IoT may have identical functionalities to Consumer IoT, but it differs in characteristics such as environment, scale, device requirements, and connectivity.

In the production of industrial IoT devices, it is essential to consider connectivity, long-distance data transmission, low power consumption, and security, which help define the communication technology. In the case of short-range communications, Bluetooth and ZigBee have been widely used. When it comes to long distances, cellular communication technologies can reach great distances but also have high energy consumption and high costs with operators. For this reason, Low Power Wide Area (LP-WAN) technology was invented, networks capable of communicating from 10 to 40 km in rural areas and 1 to 5 km in urban areas, but with low cost and power consumption. In this group of LP-WAN, the most prominent over the years have been LoRa, LoRaWAN, Sigfox, and NB-IoT.

2.2   LoRa

LoRa is a radio modulation technology that uses Chirp Spread Spectrum (CSS), communicates at a maximum speed of 50 kbps, and can carry up to 243 bytes. From LoRa came LoRaWAN, which is the communication protocol. In LoRaWAN, messages are forwarded to multiple base stations within network reach and arrive at a gateway in a star topology, although these stations increase deployment costs. Another technology is Sigfox, which provides an end-to-end connection through proprietary Sigfox stations, using binary phase-shift keying (BPSK) modulation in an unlicensed frequency, like LoRa, but capable of communicating at a rate of up to 200 kbps. Finally, NB-IoT uses a licensed frequency and operates with narrow-band radio technology [1].

During the previously mentioned stages, one topic that must always be considered is security. The significant increase in the number of devices and LP-WAN network alternatives has also created more opportunities for attackers to interfere in IoT networks. In the industrial environment, this is an even greater concern, as the security of data collection, storage, and distribution can have serious consequences in the event of failure. Security in IoT devices is a challenge due to limitations in memory, processing, and low power, as well as often being installed in environments with low supervision. Since LoRa packets stay in the air longer, they are more vulnerable to malicious attacks at the physical and data link layers, such as Denial of Service (DoS), jamming, eavesdropping, and replay assaults. Some alternatives to counter these attacks include using unique identification for nodes and authentication between parties, as is the case with LoRa, which uses AES algorithms for end-to-end encryption up to the application server [21].

Based on the discussed characteristics and considering the requirements of the industrial environment, LoRa was identified as the most suitable technology for this work. LoRa requires some parameters to be configured to achieve different results in various scenarios. One of these parameters is Bandwidth (BW), which defines the occupied frequency range. Another parameter is Spread Factor (SF), which affects the transmission time of a symbol. This factor influences the frequency variation rate in modulation; its increase results in greater sensitivity to signal reception but decreases the data transmission rate in bits per second. Another parameter is Coding Rate (CR), which determines the size of the Cyclic Redundancy Check (CRC), an error correction code that helps fix source errors but reduces the bit output rate.

In addition to configurable parameters, regional parameters must be considered, which are regulatory agency determinations related to allocated frequencies, transmission power, duty cycles, and other characteristics [3].

2.3   Topology of Network

Topology refers to how the network of devices is organized. The most common is the star topology, where data always flows through a central coordinator. Another alternative is the mesh topology, where data propagates between network nodes until it reaches the destination. The advantage of the mesh topology is its "self-healing" capability, allowing the network to automatically reconfigure itself in case of failure of one or more nodes. However, its disadvantage is increased complexity and higher energy consumption [16].

For this work, the chosen topology was mesh, due to its advantages in scenarios requiring greater coverage and resilience. This architecture was studied by Lee [10], who implemented a network with the Nuvoton Nano100LE3BN, consisting of nineteen devices in an 800 x 600 m area. Another application of this architecture is through the Meshtastic protocol, which configures devices to retransmit received messages and form a large network. This implementation enables pairing with a phone, allowing people to exchange messages through the network. One of the great achievements of this protocol was establishing communication over a distance of 331 km [5].

3   Methodology

The scope of this work involves the development of an embedded system device that must meet several functional requirements. It should be easily configurable since its network parameters, alarms, and other details may vary for each node in the sensor network, so it must include a mode for parameterizing the device. Another requirement is that it should interact with the environment in various ways, whether through digital and analog signals or by communicating with other devices. An important aspect is that it must be able to operate on battery power, as there may be cases where external power is limited or where it is necessary to notify a power failure, so the device must have autonomy in such scenarios. Additionally, the goal is to develop a LoRa communication device based on a mesh topology, meaning that this technology must be available in the device.

Based on these requirements, the definition of the device's components will be carried out through a careful selection of hardware, considering factors such as performance, energy consumption, compatibility, and cost.

The microcontroller will be one of the key elements, as it will be responsible for programming the device, enabling interaction with the environment and communication with the sensor network. Additionally, a LoRa communication module compatible with the mesh topology will be selected, allowing the microcontroller greater flexibility to perform other functions beyond network management.

Finally, the power source and necessary peripherals will be chosen to ensure compliance with the established functionalities.

After the selection of materials and the development of the prototype, the system will undergo a noise sensitivity test based on the distance between the nodes. The results of this test can help understand how the device behaves in an industrial environment, as these locations often have large distances between equipment and high levels of electromagnetic interference due to the presence of motors, frequency inverters, and other electrical devices. Additionally, an evaluation of the system's energy consumption will be conducted to assess battery life and, finally, its applicability in an industrial environment, this discussion is important to understand how each feature of this device can be used to solve a real-world problem. The results obtained will enable adjustments and optimizations in the design, ensuring that the embedded system meets the defined requirements.

3.1   Hardware and Software

For communication, the LoRaMESH EndDevice module (Fig. 1) from the company Radioenge was chosen. This transceiver operates in the 915 MHz ISM Band, can function in LoRa or FSK modulation, and features a UART interface through which network communication and node configuration can be performed following the Radioenge LoRaMESH protocol. This can also be done using the software provided by the company, which can be used to configure the device connected via USB and an FTDI, or remotely configure any device on the network that has already been set up. Configuration parameters such as address and bit rate specifications can be modified. The module operates with the AES128 encryption algorithm [14]. The modules will be tested with 5dBi antennas. The LoRaMESH module can operate in two modes, defined as classes. In Class C, it participates in the mesh network, routing packets from other nodes. The other mode is Class A, where the device activates low power consumption and only responds to UART commands, enabling data reception for a time window to receive a response from the network master. The module also provides eight general-purpose pins, with 2 configurable as analog inputs with 12-bit resolution.

Fig. 1. LoRaMESH module from Radioenge

The reason for choosing this module is the agility in development, as it already comes with software for configuration, a library for use with microcontrollers from Arduino and Espressif, and it is certified by the Brazilian National Telecommunications Agency, Anatel.

The microcontroller chosen to interface with the communication module was the ESP32-S3-WROOM-1, mounted on the ESP32-S3-DevKitC-1 development board (Fig. 2). This board features an Xtensa dual-core 32-bit LX7 processor with a 240 MHz clock speed. The dual-core architecture and high clock rate provide the flexibility to handle multiple tasks simultaneously.

The hardware also includes Wi-Fi and Bluetooth LE interfaces, which enable the LoRa sensor network to connect with other systems. In addition to storing the firmware, the 16 MB flash memory allows saving configuration parameters, event logs, and other relevant data.

For interfacing with the environment, the board offers 36 general-purpose pins, as well as digital and analog signals. Some of these pins support communication through various protocols, such as RS485, CAN, SPI, and others. This enables new equipment and sensors to be attached to the device, allowing the acquisition of different types of data [6].

Fig. 2. Board ESP32-S3-Devkitc-1

3.2   Circuit

In the circuit used for each node (Fig. 3), a digital input for configuration was connected to GPIO 4 of the ESP32. A connection was made to the TX pin of the UART from the LoRaMESH module, which, when operating in Class C, runs at 5 V. This could potentially damage the UART circuit of the ESP32. Additionally, the TP4056 module was used to enable the system to operate with a 3.7 V Lithium battery with a 3800 mAh capacity. This module can supply up to 4.2 V when the battery is fully charged. As a result, it was necessary to bypass the input power diode on the ESP32 board, as the voltage drop would prevent sufficient voltage from reaching the 3.3 V voltage regulator.

The ESP32 will have the function of configuring, receiving, and sending commands to the LoRaMESH module. It is possible to program the ESP32 in access point mode, allowing the microcontroller to serve a local network. This enables communication with it via a web server, where parameters can be adjusted and messages can be sent to other nodes.

The goal of this work is to develop a device capable of performing various tasks, some of which cannot be interrupted by others, this is necessary because the communication will not be synchronous. Therefore, while the device is reading signals from the connected sensors, processing alarms, and monitoring the

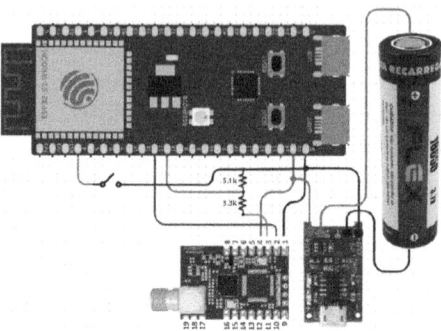

Fig. 3. Circuit of nodes

LoRa network communication channel, task management becomes essential for the optimal functioning of the system. To achieve this, a resource like FreeRTOS must be utilized. FreeRTOS is a lightweight, embeddable, and multitasking real-time operating system (RTOS). It is a library that allows the creation of tasks, assignment of priorities, intervals, specification of the core on which the function will run, and management of their states [18].

3.3   Test of Signal

The tests are intended to identify the characteristics of the device in different scenarios. For this work, samples will be taken for three LoRa configurations (Table 1). Combination "A" prioritizes maximum range and robustness against interference but has the lowest transmission rate. Combination "B" offers a balance between transmission rate, range, and robustness, making it useful for balanced applications. Finally, combination "C" is expected to achieve the maximum transmission rate but with reduced range and robustness, making it ideal for short distances with good signal conditions.

Table 1. LoRa parameter settings used in tests

Combination	Spreading Factor	Bandwidth	Coding rate
A	12	125 kHz	4/8
B	9	250 kHz	4/6
C	7	500 kHz	4/5

In order to evaluate the performance of the implemented network, a test will be conducted to assess the device's sensitivity to noise. Measurements will be taken at both short and long distances, ranging from 100 m to 1 km, within the same range as Lee [10], who monitored the packet delivery ratio of the tested configurations. In the distance test, a message will be sent, and if it reaches the destination, the device will send a confirmation message acknowledging receipt. The master will then perform a test of Received Signal Strength Indication (RSSI) and Signal-to-Noise Ratio (SNR). From this, we will be able to assess the effectiveness of bidirectional communication, the impact of distance on it, and its sensitivity to noise.

This test does not fully replace a real environment, as there are interferences and distances that would be impractical to reproduce. However, it serves as a starting point, allowing us to validate the system's feasibility in an urban environment.

3.4 Power Consumption

Since it is a battery-powered application, it is important to analyze the system's consumption to estimate its autonomy. Therefore, we must consider the operating mode of the system's components and the power they consume. To calculate the battery autonomy, the formula 1 will be used, where "T" is the time in hours, "C" is the battery capacity, "V" is the battery voltage, "P" is the power consumed by the system, and η is the battery efficiency factor. Due to circuit losses, an efficiency factor of 66% will be used in the calculation.

$$T = \frac{C \times V}{P} \times \eta \qquad (1)$$

The power consumption of the device in this work is largely due to the ESP32 development board and the LoRaMESH module. It is necessary to analyze the likely application scenarios to determine the consumption of each component.

3.5 Applicability

The device discussed in this work aims to be an industrial application. There are various standards in the industry regarding automation and instrumentation, whether at the signal level or communication protocols. Based on the prototype, it is necessary to discuss how this device can be used and what corrections should be made. This will be done by highlighting the equipment's features and potential application scenarios.

4 Results

In this chapter, the results will be described, including the production of the device prototype, the noise sensitivity test, the discussion on energy consumption, and its applicability in the industry.

Firstly, the prototype was built on a breadboard 4. The main connection is between the serial port of the LoRa module and the ESP32 board. The LoRa module's antenna is positioned at the upper end, and to its right is the battery

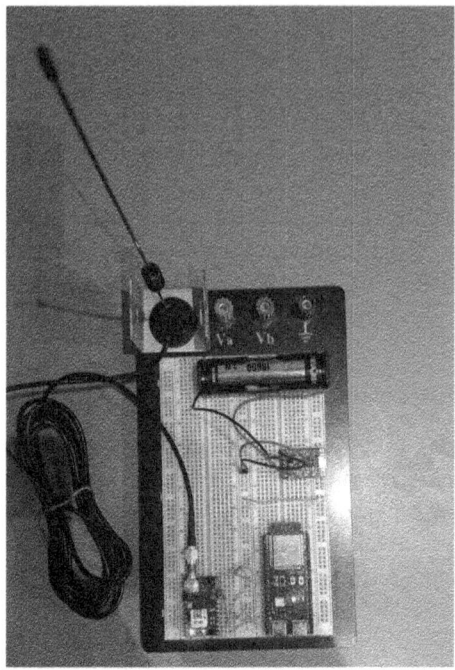

Fig. 4. Breadboard of device

power supply assembly. This setup allows for easier movement of the device during testing.

The web server implemented for the tests (Fig. 5) has the current device information, address, serial number and also a part just for sending messages and results of the RSSI and SNR tests.During testing, different combinations of the device will be used. This feature will reduce the time required to configure the system and facilitate the verification of communication between nodes, as it will be possible to analyze the signal validity based on received messages and the performance of RSSI and SNR.

The web server is activated by sending a signal to GPIO 4 of the ESP32 for a few seconds. At this moment, the board's LED blinks, indicating that the device has entered configuration mode. The ESP32 then creates a Wi-Fi access point with a default name that includes the unique number of the LoRa chip. By connecting to this network and accessing the corresponding IP address, the web server will be displayed, allowing the device to be configured.

4.1   Test of Signal

The stability of the communication link between the nodes is very important to evaluate the device's performance. Distance is an obstacle to implementing this sensor network, so a straight-line test can be conducted to observe the behavior

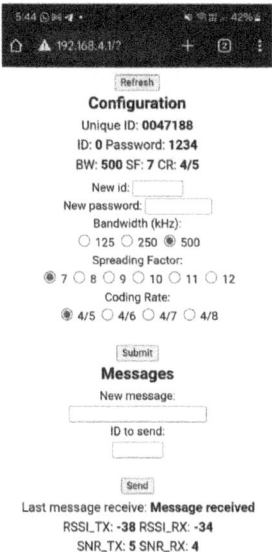

Fig. 5. Web server of device

of the signal strength as they are moved further apart. Conducting this test in an urban environment can also be beneficial to introduce other interference factors that may challenge the communication. Thus, the measurements were taken on Avenida Xavier da Silveira, in Natal, in the state of Rio Grande do Norte, Brazil (Fig. 6).

Fig. 6. Test measurement points

The approximate elevation profile of the terrain was drawn with the help of Google Earth Pro software (Fig. 7). From this profile it is possible to see that measurements can be compromised, in addition, obstacles that could potentially be in the signal path, such as cars, poles and trees, must be considered.

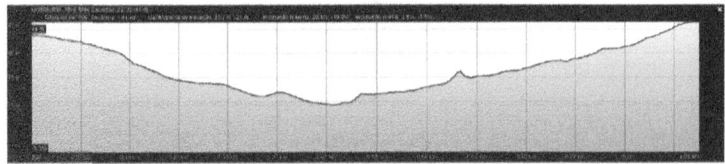

Fig. 7. Terrain elevation profile in distance measurements

The Table 2 presents the signal strength information of the communication (RSSI) during transmission (TX) and reception (RX), as well as for the signal-to-noise ratio (SNR). As a message is transmitted and received, the values were recorded for each configuration. In configuration "A", the communication had relatively high RSSI values, meaning a low signal. The SNR presents large variations, this may be caused by the use of the narrower band, as it increases the sensitivity of data reception, thus being more prone to interference.

Table 2. Distance test using configuration A

Distance (m)	RSSI TX	RSSI RX	SNR TX	SNR RX
100	−93	−89	7	7
250	−107	−103	−2	−5
500	−98	−97	5	5
750	−105	−114	0	−8
1000	−101	−106	2	2

In combination "B" (Table 3), better RSSI results were obtained for short distances, and for long distances, it remained acceptable. The SNR stayed consistent and positive, indicating a good signal-to-noise ratio.

Table 3. Distance test using configuration B

Distance (m)	RSSI TX	RSSI RX	SNR TX	SNR RX
100	−81	−83	8	6
250	−93	−93	4	7
500	−100	−100	2	6
750	−98	−100	1	5
1000	−99	−100	2	6

In Table 4, the last combination of parameters demonstrated very good results for distances of up to 250 m. However, due to the lower spreading factor and higher bandwidth, the reception sensitivity is reduced, resulting in a more robust signal but with a lower data transmission rate.

Table 4. Distance test using configuration C

Distance (m)	RSSI TX	RSSI RX	SNR TX	SNR RX
100	−72	−71	6	5
250	−94	−94	3	4
500	−98	−97	−1	3
750	−107	−101	−8	1
1000	−101	−99	−4	2

4.2 Power Consumption

The analysis of energy consumption in battery-powered systems is of great importance. Knowing this information, we can calculate the system's autonomy. This is useful for systems that only use batteries, systems that generate energy, such as devices with solar panels, or also for systems that have external power supply but, during a power failure, the monitoring system has time to notify this alarm. Thus, an analysis will be conducted based on the elements that consume the most energy in the device, based on their technical specifications in different modes. In the LoRaMESH module datasheet, we find that the consumption during transmission is 111 mA and during reception is 20 mA when powered at 3.3 V. A necessary piece of information for the calculation is the time it takes for each transmission, known as Time on Air. Based on the data from the LoRa chip manual [20], the following times were calculated and are presented in Table 5. During tests with the modules, a transmission time of every thirty seconds was observed for the network nodes. The consumption will be estimated based on the active cycle per hour between the transmission and reception power consumption. It is noted that for the configuration with the longest transmission time, the power consumed is higher. However, for configurations with very short times, the consumption is primarily determined by the power dissipated during data reception.

Table 5. Time on air of combinations

Combination	Time on air (ms)	Duty cycle (%)	Consumption(mW/h)
A	1190	3.97	77.91
B	78	0.26	66.78
C	9	0.03	66.09

For the microcontroller, two scenarios will be considered: in the first, operating in *Light-sleep* mode, classified as a low-power state, the device consumes 240 μA. In the second scenario, in *Modem-sleep* mode, the microcontroller operates with Wi-Fi turned off, running at 240 MHz in a *dual-core* configuration, executing 128-bit instructions with access to active data and peripherals, resulting in a consumption of 107.9 mA. Based on the collected data, Table 6 presents the impact of the microcontroller on battery autonomy, making it evident. With this material configuration, the device can operate without external power for between one day and one week. Although this is a good result, it falls short of low-power applications using LoRa technology, which can achieve a battery life of up to three years with a 1200 mA battery [15].

Table 6. Duration of battery in hours

Combination	LoRa	LoRa + MCU in *Light-sleep*	LoRa + MCU in *Modem-sleep*
A	119.1	117.91	21.37
B	138.96	137.33	21.93
C	140.41	138.75	21.96

4.3 Aplicability

The device has the potential to be used for fault detection in remote systems, as the mesh topology allows nodes located in remote environments to be monitored more easily.

IoT devices are designed to operate at lower voltages such as 3.3 V and 5 V. In an industrial environment, it is necessary to work with higher voltage signals to increase resistance to interference. This applies to both power supply and signal reading, as is the case with digital inputs, which typically receive 24 V signals. For analog signals, the standard 4 to 20 mA range is used [17]. To be applied in such an environment, the device must include voltage converters for its 5 V power supply and its general-purpose pins, which operate at 3.3 V.

Industrial equipment uses specific protocols, such as Modbus, which is widely adopted, particularly in its Modbus RTU versions, for serial communication over RS232, RS422, and RS485 transport protocols, as well as Modbus TCP/IP [8]. The chosen microcontroller supports asynchronous communication via RS232 and RS485 [6]. For Modbus TCP/IP applications, it would be necessary to reach the equipment via a Wi-Fi network. Another alternative would be to use an external module to implement the Ethernet protocol, such as the WS5500 [13]. A device that communicates using the Modbus protocol could be easily integrated into various industrial processes.

5   Conclusion

The LoRaMESH module from Radioenge helps to implement a network of devices clearly and quickly. Thanks to the well-detailed command protocol in the manual, it was possible to use an ESP32 microcontroller to handle the interface for configuration and messaging with the network. The use of a web server for node configuration and sending messages to other devices simplified the quick setup of each node without the need to connect to any additional equipment. Tests with this module yielded positive results for distances of up to one kilometer, especially with a LoRa parameter configuration focused on balanced usage, ensuring good robustness, range, and allowing a high transmission rate. The device discussed in this work has the potential to be applied in industrial environments, provided that signal corrections and protocol implementations are made to facilitate its integration into processes using Modbus. For future work, it is necessary to observe the network's behavior with more devices and collect real-world data.

References

1. Abdallah, W., Mnasri, S., Nasri, N., et al.: Emergent IoT wireless technologies beyond the year 2020: a comprehensive comparative analysis. In: 2020 International Conference on Computing and Information Technology (ICCIT-1441), pp. 1–5. IEEE (2020)
2. Alahmadl, S., Rojas, P., Idriss, H., Bayoumi, M.: Taxonomy of consumer and industrial IoT. In: SoutheastCon 2023, pp. 418–424. IEEE (2023)
3. de Teleinformática e Automação (GTA), G.: Resumo de lora (2022). https://www.gta.ufrj.br/ensino/eel879/trabalhos_vf_2022_2/grupo_12/resumo-de-lora/. Accessed 20 Jan 2025
4. Biansoongnern, S., Plungkang, B., Susuk, S.: Development of low cost vibration sensor network for early warning system of landslides. Energy Procedia **89**, 417–420 (2016)
5. Community, M.: Meshtastic documentation (2025). https://meshtastic.org/docs/introduction/. Accessed 5 Mar 2025
6. Espressif systems: ESP32-S3-WROOM-1/WROOM-1U Datasheet. Espressif Systems (2025). https://www.espressif.com/sites/default/files/documentation/esp32-s3-wroom-1_wroom-1u_datasheet_en.pdf. Accessed 11 Jan 2025
7. Fernández-Ahumada, L.M., Ramírez-Faz, J., Torres-Romero, M., López-Luque, R.: Proposal for the design of monitoring and operating irrigation networks based on IoT, cloud computing and free hardware technologies. Sensors **19**(10), 2318 (2019)
8. Găitan, V.G., Zagan, I.: Experimental implementation and performance evaluation of an IoT access gateway for the Modbus extension. Sensors **21**(1), 246 (2021)
9. Katiyar, V., Kumar, P., Chand, N.: An intelligent transportation systems architecture using wireless sensor networks. Int. J. Comput. Appl. **14**(2), 22–26 (2011)
10. Lee, H.-C., Ke, K.-H.: Monitoring of large-area IoT sensors using a LoRa wireless mesh network system: design and evaluation. IEEE Trans. Instrum. Meas. **67**(9), 2177–2187 (2018)
11. Mrňa, D., Badánik, B., Novák, A.: Internet of things as an optimization tool for smart airport concept. Eur. Trans.-Trasporti Europei **82** (2021)

12. Oproiu, M., Neagu, A., Cotfas, P.A., Cotfas, D.T., Musuroi, C., Volmer, M.: Lora wide-area network and live objects used in renewable energy monitoring. In: 2021 International Aegean Conference on Electrical Machines and Power Electronics (ACEMP) & 2021 International Conference on Optimization of Electrical and Electronic Equipment (OPTIM), pp. 505–512. IEEE (2021)

13. Pan, Y., Wu, D., Du, D., Wang, H.: Design and performance analysis of protocol conversion between 5G and Modbus TCP. In: 2023 42nd Chinese Control Conference (CCC), pp. 6262–6267 (2023). https://doi.org/10.23919/CCC58697.2023.10240445

14. Radioenge: Manual LoRaMESH (2021). https://www.radioenge.com.br/wp-content/uploads/2021/08/Manual_LoRaMESH.pdf

15. Piyare, R., Murphy, A.L., Magno, M., Benini, L.: On-Demand LoRa: asynchronous TDMA for energy efficient and low latency communication in IoT. Miscellaneous **18**(11), 3718 (2018). https://doi.org/10.3390/s18113718

16. Semtech, A., Basics, M.: AN1200. 22. LoRa Modulation basics **46**, 7–14 (2015)

17. Sharma, P., Singh, M.M.: Design and implementation of a stand-alone remote terminal unit. IOSR J. Electr. Electron. Eng. **7**(1), 74–83 (2013)

18. Cheng, S., Woodcock, J., D'Souza, D.: Using formal reasoning on a model of tasks for FreeRTOS. Formal Aspects Comput. **27**(1), 167–192 (2014). https://doi.org/10.1007/s00165-014-0308-9

19. Singh, R., et al.: ZigBee and long-range architecture based monitoring system for oil pipeline monitoring with the internet of things. Sustainability **13**(18), 10226 (2021)

20. SX1272, L.: Lora sx1272/73 datasheet. semtech (73)

21. Tengshe, R., Akanksha, E.: Security in LP-wan technologies: challenges and solutions. In: 2023 IEEE 8th International Conference for Convergence in Technology (I2CT) pp. 1–4. IEEE (2023)

22. Zijie, F., Al-Shareeda, M.A., Saare, M.A., Manickam, S., Karuppayah, S.: Wireless sensor networks in the internet of things: review, techniques, challenges, and future directions. Indonesian J. Electr. Eng. Comput. Sci. **31**(2), 1190–1200 (2023)

Improving Elevator Control Algorithms by Integrating with Computer Vision

Vu Thu Diep[1], Nguyen Dang Phat[2], and Phan Duy Hung[2]($\boxtimes$) [iD]

[1] Hanoi University of Science and Technology, Hanoi, Vietnam
diep.vuthu@hust.edu.vn
[2] FPT University, Hanoi, Vietnam
phat23mse13128@fsb.edu.vn, hungpd2@fe.edu.vn

Abstract. This study proposes a new approach to address the limitations of traditional elevator systems when handling a large number of passengers during peak hours in high-rise buildings. The study proposes integrating a modified LOOK SCAN algorithm with a simulated YOLOv5 model for real-time people counting. Based on the number of people waiting at each floor and the number of people inside each elevator car, the modified algorithm dynamically adjusts the elevator movement and priority. The simulation results show significant improvements in average waiting time, average travel time, and approximated energy usage over the conventional LOOK SCAN algorithm. This research helps in creating intelligent and efficient elevator systems for modern high-rise buildings.

Keywords: Elevator Control · LOOK SCAN Algorithm · YOLOv5 · People Counting

1 Introduction

Elevators are essential systems in modern high-rise buildings, moving people and goods between floors. However, today's traditional elevator systems struggle to handle dynamic and often unpredictable traffic patterns [1]. Morning, noon, and evening peak periods often create increased demand, while tenant distribution and special events also create complex traffic patterns. These factors can lead to inefficient elevator operations, causing congestion, long wait times, and passenger discomfort.

For decades, conventional elevator dispatching algorithms have been the standard for vertical transport control [2]. Although basic methods like SCAN and LOOK SCAN have worked well in well-disciplined environments, they fall short when dynamically responding to real-time passenger demand levels, particularly during peak traffic conditions. The main disadvantage of these algorithms is that they apply pre-established movement patterns that fail to respond to real-time passenger distribution or varying load levels in each elevator cabin [3]. This inflexibility generates operational inefficiencies in the form of excessive waiting time, overloaded and underutilized elevators—crowded in some cabins and empty in others—and wasted energy from inefficient stops and inefficient routing [4].

© The Author(s), under exclusive license to Springer Nature Switzerland AG 2025
O. Gervasi et al. (Eds.): ICCSA 2025, LNCS 15648, pp. 241–253, 2025.
https://doi.org/10.1007/978-3-031-97000-9_15

In order to address these challenges, there is a growing need for intelligent and adaptive elevator dispatching systems that can dynamically respond to real-time traffic. Modern high-rise buildings need solutions that can dynamically respond to real-time passenger traffic, achieve highest load balancing, and minimize wait times and power consumption. New technologies such as computer vision and machine learning provide a groundbreaking opportunity to revolutionize elevator operations. By leveraging real-time passenger data, elevators can become more responsive, efficient, and user-friendly, ultimately enhancing the overall experience for building occupants.

2 Related Works

Elevator control strategies have evolved from basic approaches like First-Come, First-Served (FCFS) to more sophisticated algorithms like Shortest-Seek-Time-First (SSTF) and SCAN [5]. While these traditional methods offer some level of efficiency, they often fail to adapt to dynamic passenger flow and load imbalances. The LOOK SCAN algorithm, a variant of SCAN, improves performance by reversing direction when there are no further calls in the current direction, but still lacks the ability to consider real-time passenger distribution.

While LOOK and C-LOOK improve upon SCAN, they still share a fundamental limitation: they do not account for the number of people waiting at each floor, nor the current load inside the elevator. Dynamic SCAN attempts to address this by incorporating factors like waiting times and predicted future demand, often using historical data [6]. Destination Dispatch Control (DDC) systems, where passengers input their destination at the lobby, can significantly improve efficiency [7], but require changes in passenger behavior and more complex hardware.

Recent advancements in computer vision and artificial intelligence have opened new avenues for optimizing elevator systems [8, 9]. The YOLO (You Only Look Once) family of real-time object detection algorithms [10] is particularly relevant. he accuracy and speed of YOLO, demonstrated through versions from YOLOv3 to YOLOv5, and related extensions [11, 12], make it suitable for real-time applications like people counting. YOLO's performance in real-world scenarios has been widely demonstrated by various studies. Its capability of real-time detection of humans on low resource platforms has been researched [13], presenting its effectiveness in applications requiring speed and dependability in object detection. YOLO has also successfully been used to detect dense crowds with high accuracy [14] and can be considered an asset for surveillance, crowd monitoring, and various other real-time detection scenarios.

This research is founded on the prior work by implementing a simulated YOLOv5 people counting system with a modified LOOK SCAN algorithm. The strategy proposed here attempts to transcend the limitations of traditional algorithms by varying elevator movement in real-time in response to passenger details, leading to improved efficiency and user experience.

3 Methodology

3.1 Proposed System Model

The new system includes a number of elevators served by a central controller that collects real-time people counts from a YOLOv5-based vision system (Fig. 1). This structure enables adaptive elevator control through dynamic re-tuning of operations in accordance with prevailing passenger load and traffic conditions.

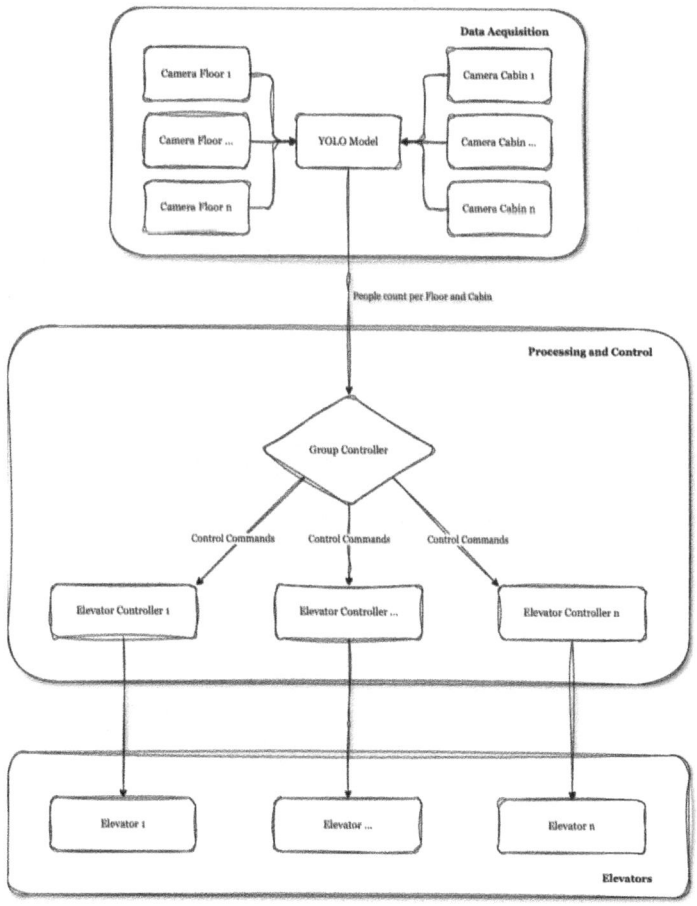

Fig. 1. System Architecture

Simulated Camera System: Strategically positioned cameras in elevator lobbies and cabins capture video feeds to extract passenger count data. The system in this instance is simulated, generating data mimicking real passenger distribution.

YOLOv5 People Counting Module: This module also mimics real-time people counting within a YOLOv5 system. It generates passenger count data by floor and by cabin in line with pre-configured traffic behavior and parameters.

Modified LOOK SCAN Algorithm: The conventional LOOK SCAN algorithm is adapted by incorporating real-time passenger count information. The major additions include a dynamic priority weighting system and a priority-based elevator assignment strategy.

Group Controller: This is the primary module which takes passenger count information from the YOLOv5 module as well as status data from all of the elevators. It uses the adapted LOOK SCAN algorithm in determining the most efficient motion and elevator allocation.

Elevator Controllers: Each elevator has a controller of its own which receives instructions from the Group Controller and manages the elevator's operations, including motor control, door operation, and indicator lights.

3.2   Implementation of YOLOv5-Based People Counting

YOLOv5 is a state-of-the-art real-time processing, highly accurate, object detection deep learning model. There is a simulated YOLOv5 module in this study generating occupancy data for each floor and each cabin. The module follows pre-established traffic flows in terms of modeling real passenger usage patterns as accurately as possible. The simulation generates crucial outputs in real-time, such as the number passengers per floor, the occupancy of each elevator in real-time, and the traffic under peak and off-peak conditions. This data is real-time updated and supplied constantly to the modified LOOK SCAN decision-making system.

3.3   Modified LOOK SCAN Algorithm with Dynamic Weighting

The traditional LOOK SCAN algorithm is modified by adding a dynamic priority weighting mechanism that dynamically adjusts the dispatching of elevators according to real-time demands.

Standard LOOK SCAN Algorithm

The LOOK SCAN algorithm moves in one direction, processing all requests in this direction. Once all requests in one direction are depleted, it reverses. It does not make a trip to the destination of the building unnecessarily as in the SCAN's case and hence is more efficient. It does not consider real-time loading of passengers and thus is inefficient during rush periods. The static nature of the fundamental LOOK SCAN algorithm renders it inefficient during rush-hour traffic, leading to delays as well as unbalanced loading distribution across the elevators.

Dynamic Priority Weighting

The modified SCAN algorithm has its core in the priority weight system, in which a priority weight, denoted as W_i, is assigned to each floor i with a pending request. The weight determines the priority in serving the floor based on real-time passenger demand, calculated in real-time through the simulated YOLOv5 people counting module, along with elevator capacity. The dynamic nature of this weighting system allows the algorithm to adapt to varying traffic conditions and prioritize floors with the most pressing needs.

The priority weight W_i for each floor i is calculated using the following formula:

$$W_i = \alpha * N_{i_{adjusted}} + \beta * \left(\frac{1}{D_i + 1}\right) + \gamma * (1 - \frac{P_c}{C})$$

where:

- N_i - Number of People Waiting: This represents the number of people waiting at floor i, as estimated by the simulated YOLOv5 module. Instead of using the raw count directly, N_i is adjusted to N_i_adjusted based on predefined groups to better represent different levels of urgency.

  0–2 people: N_i_adjusted = 1 (Very Low)
  3–5 people: N_i_adjusted = 4 (Low)
  6–9 people: N_i_adjusted = 7 (Medium)
  10–15 people: N_i_adjusted = 12 (High)
  15 people: N_i_adjusted = 18 (Very High)

- D_i - Distance to Floor: This factor represents the distance, measured in the number of floors, between the elevator's current floor and floor i. A smaller distance naturally translates to a higher priority, as the elevator can reach the floor more quickly. The distance is calculated as the absolute difference between the elevator's current floor and the requesting floor.
- P_c - Current Passenger Count: This represents the number of passengers currently inside the elevator cabin, as obtained from the simulated YOLOv5 module. This data allows the algorithm to consider the available capacity of each elevator.
- C - Maximum Cabin Capacity: This is the maximum number of passengers the elevator can hold, a fixed parameter defined as 15 in the simulation setup.

- α is the weighting coefficient for the adjusted number of waiting passengers (N_i_adjusted). This coefficient determines the relative importance of the number of waiting passengers in the overall priority calculation. The initial value is set to 0.6.
- β is the weighting coefficient for the inverse of the distance (1/D_i). This coefficient reflects the importance of proximity in the priority calculation. The default value for it is 0.2.
- γ is the basic available cabin space weight factor, defined as (1 − P_c/C). This factor ensures that elevators with more available space are given higher priority when other factors are equal. The initial value is set to 0.1.
- The initial values for α, β, and γ were chosen based on preliminary experimentation and can be fine-tuned further to optimize performance for specific building configurations and traffic patterns.

Elevator Allocation Strategy

The modified LOOK SCAN algorithm employs a hybrid approach. Under normal conditions, all elevators operate under the standard LOOK SCAN algorithm. When a floor exceeds a predefined threshold of waiting passengers (e.g., 10 passengers), the algorithm dynamically assigns an elevator to prioritize that floor. To prevent inefficiencies, the system ensures multi-elevator coordination so that multiple elevators do not respond to the same request unnecessarily, leading to optimized load balancing. Once high-priority requests are served, the system reverts to the standard LOOK SCAN operation to maintain fairness across all floors.

By integrating a priority queue, the system ensures that low-priority floors are not completely neglected, mitigating the risk of starvation. The algorithm balances immediate demand with long-term system performance, preventing situations where elevators continuously cycle between only a few high-traffic floors.

Algorithm Flowcharts

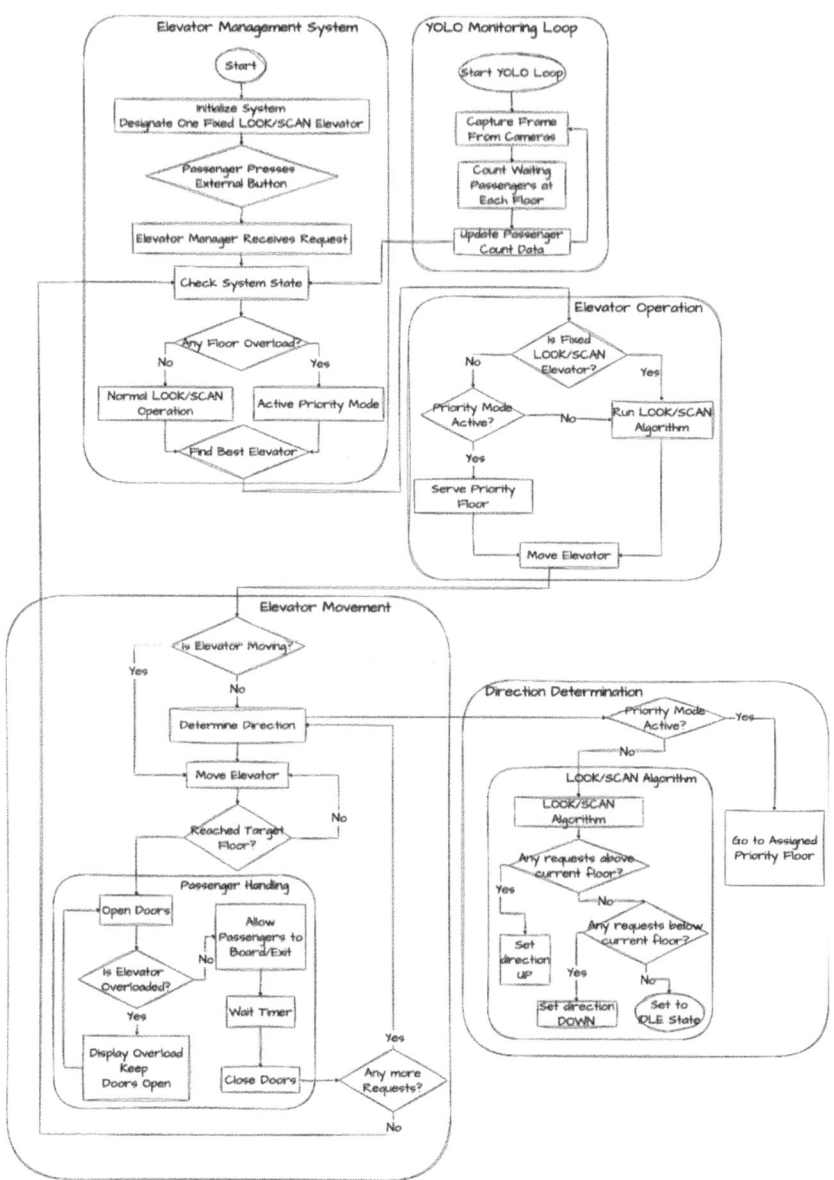

Fig. 2. Overview Algorithm Flowchart

To clarify the execution process, the following flowcharts (Fig. 2) will be included: an overview of elevator scheduling, a detailed breakdown of elevator movement decisions, and a handling mechanism for priority requests. These flow charts illustrate how the system dynamically switches between normal and priority modes based on real-time passenger distribution.

3.4 Simulation and Evaluation

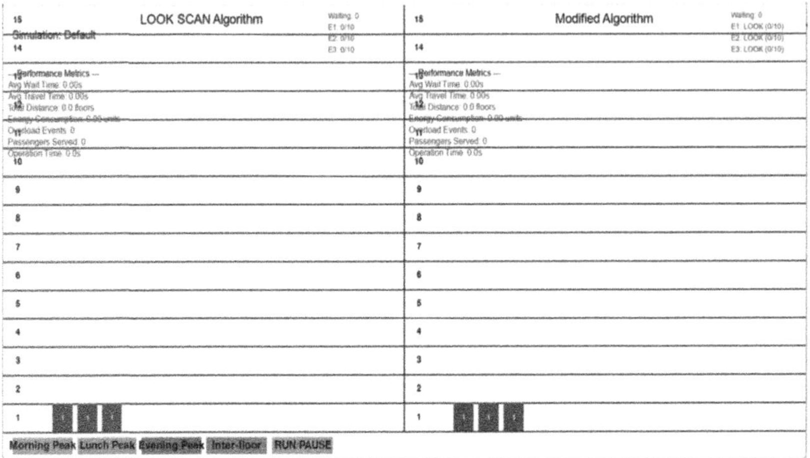

a. Simulation interface before random passenger generation

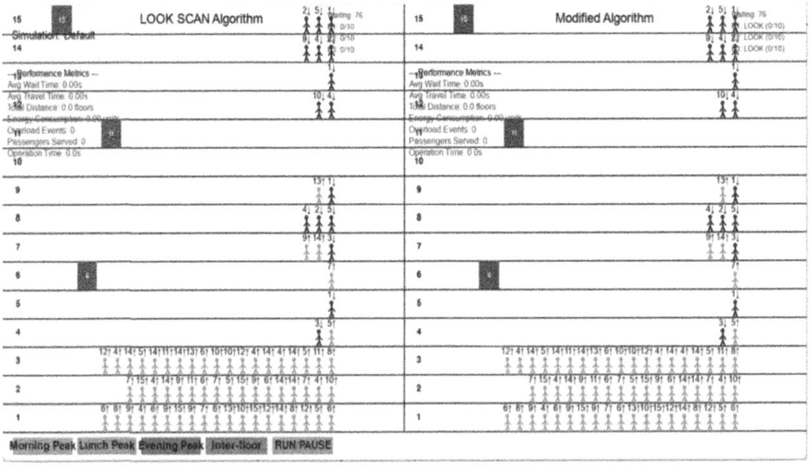

b. Simulation interface after random passenger generation

Fig. 3. Simulation interface before (a) and after (b) random passenger generation

A realistic elevator simulation was developed using Python and Pygame to evaluate the system (Fig. 3). The simulated environment consists of a 15-floor building, where each floor has a designated waiting area for passengers. The elevator group consists of three elevators, each with a maximum capacity of 15 passengers. The system was tested under various traffic scenarios, including morning peak hours with high demand for upper floors, lunchtime periods with mixed upward and downward movement, evening peak hours characterized by heavy downward traffic, and inter-floor travel simulating random passenger movement throughout the day.

4 Results and Discussion

4.1 Experimental Results

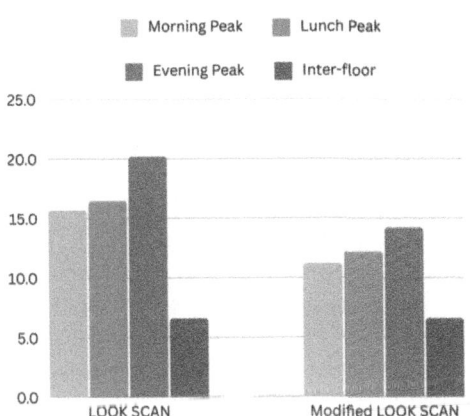

Fig. 4. Comparison of Average Waiting Time (seconds) between the standard LOOK SCAN algorithm and the proposed modified LOOK SCAN algorithm across different traffic scenarios.

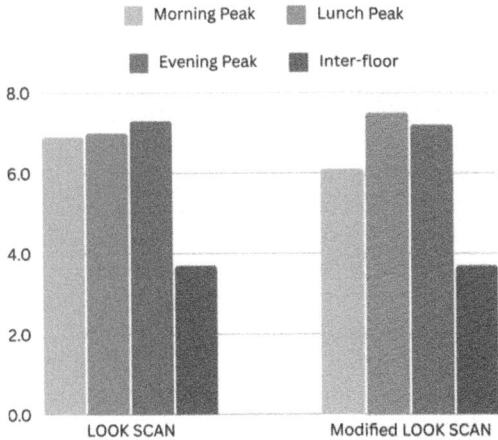

Fig. 5. Comparison of Average Travel Time (seconds) between the standard LOOK SCAN algorithm and the proposed modified LOOK SCAN algorithm across different traffic scenarios.

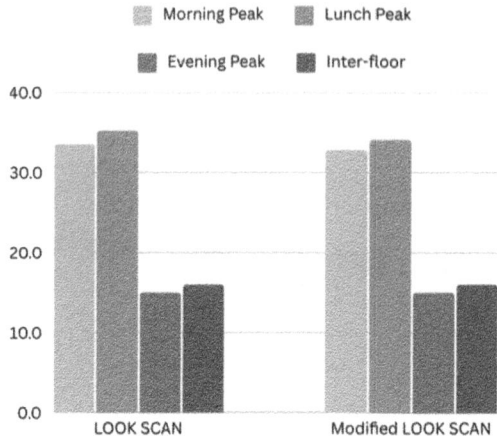

Fig. 6. Comparison of Estimated Energy Consumption (unit) between the standard LOOK SCAN algorithm and the proposed modified LOOK SCAN algorithm across different traffic scenarios.

The simulation records key performance indicators (KPIs) to assess the effectiveness of the proposed system. The average waiting time is measured as the duration between a passenger pressing the call button and the elevator arriving (Fig. 4). The average travel time is recorded as the time from when a passenger boards the elevator to when they reach their destination floor (Fig. 5). Energy consumption is estimated based on the total distance traveled by all elevators and their operational duration (Fig. 6).

Table 1 shows that the proposed modified LOOK SCAN algorithm always outperforms the standard LOOK SCAN algorithm in all test scenarios.

4.2 Analysis and Discussion

The modified LOOK SCAN algorithm shows significant improvements in elevator system performance. Average waiting time is reduced by approximately 25%, from 14.75 s to 11.05 s. This improvement is most noticeable during peak traffic periods. The algorithm also slightly decreases average travel time, from 6.23 s to 6.13 s. Additionally, it reduces overall energy consumption from 24.93 units to 24.48 units. These results highlight the effectiveness of incorporating real-time people counting data and dynamic elevator allocation in enhancing elevator efficiency and user satisfaction.

The system has several advantages. It highly improves key performance metrics, most significantly by reducing average travel and waiting time. This is due to the fact that the system, in real-time, has the ability to respond dynamically to changing passenger demand by queuing up the floors in real-time and allocating the motion of the elevators accordingly. This results in a more efficient passenger experience with less delay, alongside optimized transport vertically in the building. The responsiveness, as a feature of the system's data-centricity, also allows it, through simulation results throughout the day, to continue performing well in changing traffic patterns.

However, there are also limitations. The evaluation is based on a simulated environment, and as such may not include all of the dynamic factors that would appear in a real

Table 1. Summary of Simulation Results

Metric	Algorithm	Morning Peak	Lunch Peak	Evening Peak	Inter-floor	Overall
Average Waiting Time (s)	LOOK SCAN	15.7	16.5	20.2	6.6	14.75
	Modified LOOK SCAN	**11.2**	**12.2**	**14.2**	6.6	**11.05**
Average Travel Time (s)	LOOK SCAN	6.9	**7.0**	7.3	3.7	6.23
	Modified LOOK SCAN	**6.1**	7.5	**7.2**	3.7	**6.13**
Energy Consumption (u)	LOOK SCAN	33.5	35.2	15	16	24.93
	Modified LOOK SCAN	**32.8**	**34.1**	15	16	**24.48**

environment. Random passenger motion, inconsistent elevator performance, things not anticipated, are some of the factors by which system performance could be impacted in ways not captured in the simulation. Furthermore, use of simulated YOLOv5 data, rather than a direct integrated real-time vision system, is a modeling assumption. A real deployment would involve a hardened, trustworthy YOLOv5 system able to accurately count people in diverse, perhaps challenging, conditions. This study provides starting values, but further study, as well as adjustment of these parameter values, would likely be needed in order to achieve best performance in a given building environment.

5   Conclusions and Future Works

5.1   Conclusions

This research aimed to develop and evaluate an intelligent elevator control system that integrates real-time people counting with a modified LOOK SCAN algorithm. The proposed system utilized a simulated YOLOv5 module to count the number of people waiting at each floor and inside each elevator cabin, providing crucial data for the enhanced LOOK SCAN algorithm. The simulation results, based on a 15-story building model with three elevators and realistic traffic patterns (Morning Peak, Lunch Peak, Evening Peak, Inter-floor, and a Special high-demand scenario), demonstrated that the proposed system significantly outperformed the baseline LOOK SCAN algorithm.

Specifically, the proposed system achieved a 25% reduction in average waiting time (from 14.75 s to 11.05 s), a 1.6% reduction in average travel time (from 6.23 s to 6.13 s), and a 1.8% reduction in estimated energy consumption (from 24.93 u to 24.48 u). Furthermore, although not directly quantified in the provided data, the priority mechanism inherent in the modified LOOK SCAN algorithm would lead to a significant reduction in overload events. These findings confirm the effectiveness of integrating real-time people counting data into elevator dispatching algorithms and highlight the potential of the proposed system to improve the efficiency and user experience of elevator systems in high-rise buildings. This research contributes to the growing evidence base in smart building systems and presents a viable model for the design of more responsive, more efficient, and more environmentally friendly vertical transportation systems.

5.2 Future Works

Future research would include testing the system in a real environment by integrating a full YOLOv5 module with live video from a camera. This would include addressing challenges in deploying and maintaining a rugged computer vision system in a real environment. Further research would also be performed in improving the modified LOOK SCAN algorithm by exploring more sophisticated methods of dynamic weight adjustment as well as integrating traffic pattern forecasting based on machine learning. Also, the feasibility of adapting YOLOv5 not only to count the people but also estimate passenger activity patterns and forecast where they are headed would be explored.

Another promising area includes expanding this research into domestic houses and hospitals, along with integration with other management systems for the system in question. Lastly, careful research of the parameter optimization, perhaps through automated computations or combine this result with other potential studies [15–17], would be conduct in a bid to achieve optimal performance from the system for different building configurations and traffic characteristics.

References

1. Hangli, G., Hamada, T., Sumitomo, T., Koshizuka, N.: Intellevator: an intelligent elevator system proactive in traffic control for time-efficiency improvement. IEEE Access **8**, 35535–35545 (2020)
2. Latif, M., Kheshaim, M.M.S., Kundu, S.: A review of elevator dispatching systems. In: Proceedings of the World Congress on Engineering 2016, (WCE 2016), vol. II, London, UK, 29 June–1 July (2016)
3. Liu, H., Qian, Y.L., Liu, Q., Li, J.T.: Count passengers based on Haar-like feature in elevator application. In: Proceedings of the International Conference on Machine Learning and Cybernetics, Kunming, pp. 1202–1206 (2008)
4. Lee, S., Bahn, H.: An energy-aware elevator group control system. In: Proceedings of the 3rd IEEE International Conference on Industrial Informatics, INDIN 2005, Perth, WA, Australia, pp. 639–643 (2005)
5. Zhu, R.: Research on optimizing elevator operation management strategy based on mathematical model algorithm. In: SHS Web of Conferences, vol. 200 (2024). https://doi.org/10.1051/shsconf/202420002010
6. Siikonen, M.L.: Elevator group control with artificial intelligence. Helsinki University of Technology Systems Analysis Laboratory Research Reports. Kone Corporation, Helsinki, Finland (1997)

7. Tai, J., Yang, S., Tan, H.: Dispatching approach optimization of elevator group control system with destination floor guidance using Fuzzy Neural Network. In: Proceedings of the 7th World Congress on Intelligent Control and Automation, Chongqing, China, pp. 7085–7088 (2008)

8. Li, H.: The implementation of reinforcement learning algorithms on the elevator control system. In: Proceedings of the IEEE 20th Conference on Emerging Technologies & Factory Automation (ETFA), Luxembourg, Luxembourg, pp. 1–4 (2015)

9. Zhao, J., Yan, G.: Passenger flow monitoring of elevator video based on computer vision. In: Proceedings of the Chinese Control and Decision Conference (CCDC), Nanchang, China, pp. 2089–2094 (2019)

10. Redmon, J., Divvala, S., Girshick, R., Farhadi, A.: You only look once: unified, real-time object detection. In: Proceedings of the IEEE Conference on Computer Vision and Pattern Recognition (CVPR), pp. 779–788 (2016)

11. Tariq, J., Fatima, M., Kamal, M.: Precision in motion: comparative analysis of YOLOvX versions for real-time multi-object tracking. In: Proceedings of the International Conference on Engineering & Computing Technologies (ICECT), Islamabad, Pakistan, pp. 1–6 (2024)

12. Inrawong, P., et al.: Comparison of YOLO algorithm performance in classifying harvest periods for Pleurotus Ostreatus. In: Proceedings of the International Conference on Power, Energy and Innovations (ICPEI), Nakhon Ratchasima, Thailand, pp. 104–108 (2024)

13. Lee, J.. Hwang, K.: YOLO with adaptive frame control for real-time object detection applications. Multimed. Tools Appl. **81** (2021). https://doi.org/10.1007/s11042-021-11480-0

14. Wang, Y., Yue, L.: Dense crowd detection method based on improved YOLOv7. In: Proceedings of the SPIE, vol. 85 (2024). https://doi.org/10.1117/12.3035293

15. Manh, N.V., Diep, V.T., Hung, P.D.: A synthesis method of robust cascade control system. J. Autom. Control Eng. **4**(2), 111–116 (2016)

16. Hung, P.D,, Nam, I. H., Van Thang, H.: Flexible development for embedded system software. In: Solanki, V., Hoang, M., Lu, Z., Pattnaik, P. (eds.) Intelligent Computing in Engineering. AISC, vol. 1125, pp. 873–883. Springer, Singapore (2020). https://doi.org/10.1007/978-981-15-2780-7_93

17. Hung, P.D.: Counting people using images from two low cost webcams. In: Dang, T., Küng, J., Takizawa, M., Bui, S. (eds.) FDSE 2019. LNCS, vol. 11814, pp. 688–695. Springer, Cham (2019). https://doi.org/10.1007/978-3-030-35653-8_48

Digital Twin and Metaverse in the Context of Industry 4.0

Nuno F. Soares[1,2]($\boxtimes$) (ID), Anabela Marin[1] (ID), Diogo L. Rodrigues[3],
and Francisco J. Duarte[1,2] (ID)

[1] CCG/ZGDV Institute, University Avenue, Azurém Campus, Building 14,
Guimarães, Portugal
{nuno.soares,anabela.marin}@ccg.pt, francisco.duarte@dsi.uminho.pt
[2] ALGORITMI Research Centre, University of Minho, Guimarães, Portugal
[3] Colep Packaging, Rua Comendador Arlindo Soares de Pinho 1977,
Vale de Cambra, Portugal
diogo.rodrigues@colep-pk.com

Abstract. The lack of an ontology integrating Digital Twins (DTs) into the Metaverse presents a fundamental challenge for synchronising physical and digital worlds. This study proposes the development of a specific ontology to address this very gap. To achieve this, two methodological approaches are employed: MDCP modelling and the OApIS process, allowing a comparison between a more rigid structure and a dynamic, adaptive approach. The expected outcomes include the creation of a flexible, scalable, and interoperable ontology capable of efficiently representing DTs. The study concludes that robust ontological frameworks are essential for enhancing DT-Metaverse interactions, contributing to more immersive, secure, and predictive experiences.

Keywords: Metaverse · Digital Twins · Ontologies · Digital Twin-Metaverse Unified Ontology

1 Introduction

The digital transformation is being driven by significant technological advancements, with two emerging concepts taking centre stage: Digital Twin (DT) and the Metaverse. These concepts are crucial to the evolution of digital systems, enabling new ways to represent and interact between the physical and digital worlds. Accordingly, ontology development has become an essential tool for modelling and integrating these domains, providing a structured knowledge framework that enhances communication and interoperability across systems.

This article explores methodologies for ontology development, analysing existing approaches for DTs and the Metaverse while highlighting the absence of a unified ontology that integrates both. It begins by examining the stages and best practices in ontology creation, followed by an analysis of how different methodologies structure and model information in various contexts. Building on these insights, the study then demonstrates the development of a unified ontology that bridges DTs and the Metaverse.

© The Author(s), under exclusive license to Springer Nature Switzerland AG 2025
O. Gervasi et al. (Eds.): ICCSA 2025, LNCS 15648, pp. 254–271, 2025.
https://doi.org/10.1007/978-3-031-97000-9_16

However, achieving seamless data exchange and identity continuity across heterogeneous virtual environments poses major challenges. Efforts towards standardising the Metaverse landscape, especially in terms of semantic alignment and cross-platform identity, are ongoing and rapidly evolving, yet remain fragmented. This work aims to address these gaps by proposing an ontology capable of integrating Digital Twins into the Metaverse under a unified framework.

Unlike approaches that address DTs and the Metaverse in isolation, our proposed solution unifies both into a single ontological framework. This integration tackles real-time synchronisation, scalability, and interoperability challenges, effectively bridging physical and virtual realms. By weaving DT and Metaverse concepts together, we aim to fill critical gaps in existing literature and provide a more holistic mechanism for Industry 4.0 applications. As such, our framework goes beyond a conventional ontology study, positioning itself as a novel solution that consolidates two rapidly evolving domains into a cohesive model.

Finally, an integrative ontological model is proposed to establish a common framework for data representation and communication between these two domains. This ontology aims to capture real-time interactions between physical and virtual objects within the DT, extending its capabilities to the broader, immersive ecosystem of the Metaverse.

As part of this integration process, two ontology development methodologies will be examined, discussing their practical applications, challenges, and proposed solutions for strengthening the connection between DTs and the Metaverse.

2 Background

Ontology, as defined by Gruber [1], is a formal and explicit specification of shared understanding, enabling machine-interpretable knowledge representation. By integrating data sources, ontologies enhance interoperability and support semantic-based information processing. Ontologies have gained significant importance in various fields, including industrial environments, due to their ability to represent complex relationships and ensure standardised knowledge exchange.

The development of ontologies follows structured steps to formalise knowledge and improve data management. Typically, according to Abu-Salih [2], the main stages of ontology creation involve:

1. **Identifying key terms**: Defining concepts (nouns), attributes (properties of entities), relationships (verbs linking elements), and instances (real-world entities).
2. **Building the conceptual model**: Structuring classes and subclasses hierarchically.
3. **Defining relationships**: Object properties link entities, while data type properties describe attributes, specifying their type (e.g., string, integer, boolean) and cardinality.
4. **Creating instances**: Assigning values to classes to instantiate the ontology, with tools like Protégé facilitating evaluation and reasoning.

At the Metaverse scale, ontologies must handle cross-platform semantic alignment, decentralised identity, and near-instant data exchange, all of which surpass typical ontology requirements. The following discussion highlights relevant standardisation approaches aimed at bridging these gaps.

2.1 Interoperability, Standardisation, and Predictive Capabilities

The rise of the Metaverse has accelerated efforts to develop interoperability frameworks that ensure seamless semantic and identity continuity across heterogeneous virtual environments. Recent initiatives address both syntactic alignment of data formats and deeper semantic integration through ontology-driven approaches. Notable efforts include Abu-Salih's MetaOntology [2], which outlines a domain-specific framework for core Metaverse constructs, and the MPAI Metaverse Model (MPAI-MMM) [3], which proposes a standards-based architecture for interoperability. Additionally, Li et al. [4] enhance ontological reasoning with AI to manage spatiotemporal complexity, emphasising context-awareness and semantic consistency.

Moreover, proposals for identity interoperability, such as Self-Sovereign Identity (SSI) systems, leverage blockchain for privacy-preserving cross-platform continuity [5–8]. These initiatives emphasise decentralised identity solutions and include policy-aware governance [5] and verification schemes [9,10]. However, the literature highlights persistent fragmentation and the lack of robust ontological standards capable of integrating semantic reasoning with identity tools [11,12].

Our proposed ontology unifies data and identity interoperability under a cohesive, standards-driven framework. By incorporating real-time semantic integration with decentralised identity models, it aims to reduce fragmentation and align with emerging cross-metaverse protocols, supporting a scalable, semantically enriched environment.

Furthermore, the predictive capabilities of our ontology arise from integrating predictive modelling techniques, enabling the analysis and forecasting of behaviours in industrial systems. Roopa et al. [13] have shown how ontology-based models contribute to predictive maintenance by forecasting component lifespan and improving real-time decisions. Additionally, the combination of ontologies with machine learning techniques, as demonstrated by Zhang et al. [14], proves effective in anomaly detection and failure prediction, thus enhancing decision-making and operational efficiency in industrial systems. These capabilities provide a solid foundation for the predictive power embedded in our ontology, which can be applied to optimise both DT and Metaverse environments.

2.2 MDCP Methodology

Building on these general principles of ontology construction, the MDCP methodology proposed by Singh et al. [15] stands out. It provides a structured and practical approach for creating and managing ontologies, particularly for integrating Digital Twins (DTs) within industrial systems. The MDCP methodology consists of five key stages, each essential for improving data management and constructing databases for DTs. These stages include:

1. **Map**: Identify the classes and relationships within the ontology model and link them to industrial processes that analyse asset behaviour.
2. **Define**: Specify data elements for each class, such as attributes and data types (e.g., temperature, pressure), which describe the properties of each class.
3. **Create**: Construct the ontology model by converting relationships between classes into object properties and defining data properties with logical constraints to formalise interactions.
4. **Convert**: Transform the ontology model into a relational database format by applying keys and cardinality to efficiently organise the data.
5. **Populate**: Insert real-world data into the relational database model, validating it with actual data to ensure it reflects the asset behaviour accurately.

Following the MDCP methodology, other approaches can be adopted to suit different needs. One such approach is the **OApIS methodology**, proposed by Duarte et al. [16]. In contrast to the previous methodologies, OApIS emphasises flexibility and dynamic data integration. It is organised into three distinct phases: 'Data Characterisation', 'Information Specification', and 'Ontological Mapping'. These phases enable the creation of an ontology model that supports real-time data processing and continuous adaptation to evolving industrial requirements.

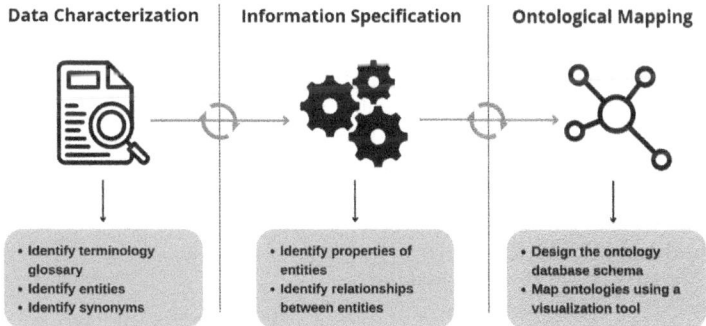

Fig. 1. OApIS Ontology Development Process [16].

In the first phase, 'Data Characterisation', terms are defined and associated tasks are described in detail. This helps to understand the domain and activities involved, creating a foundation for further analysis. The next phase, 'Information Specification', focuses on mapping these terms using a UML class diagram. This process involves following design rules for class diagrams, such as representing classes, associations, generalisations, compositions, and aggregations. The final phase, 'Ontological Mapping', maps the ontology schema to a graph-based database, where tools like Neo4j are employed to ensure the efficient management and retrieval of data (Fig. 1).

3   Ontological Approach for Metaverse and Digital Twins

3.1   MDCP Methodology

In this section, the development of the ontology will be based solely on the MDCP and OApIS methodologies. Initially, according to Singh et al. [15], the MDCP methodology will be followed. As mentioned in the previous section, the development of an ontology includes the stages 'Map', 'Define', 'Create', 'Convert', and 'Populate'. This methodology will form the foundation for the approach adopted throughout this section.

In addition to considering the stages for ontology development outlined by Singh et al. [15], this work also draws upon the Digital Twin (DT) ontology developed by these authors. Accordingly, a customized ontology for DT was developed. In adapting their framework, elements from their model were integrated, with adjustments made to ensure alignment with the specific objectives of this study and the broader research context.

The 'Define' stage clarifies key data elements and their types for each class, developing an ontology model for DT. To build this ontology, key terms were defined, which were essential for DT characterization.

- **Asset**: Refers to physical objects or systems digitally represented in the DT, ranging from industrial machinery to complex infrastructure.
- **Events**: Record real-time interactions and changes, enabling system behaviour analysis and fault detection.
- **Sensor and Sensor Data**: Play a crucial role in real-time data collection, ensuring continuous updates in the digital model.
- **Digital Model**: Provides a virtual representation of physical systems, allowing for accurate analysis, simulation, and control.
- **Behaviour**: Represents not only the physical appearance but also the system's functionality and interactions.
- **Actionable Insights**: Transform collected data into valuable information for optimizing processes and decision-making.

Relationships between classes were established, as shown in Fig. 2:

- **Asset** connects to **Events, Sensor,** and **Actionable Insights**. Events affect assets by detecting faults and changes, linking them to system behaviour.
- **Sensor** collects data from assets, linking to **Sensor Data**, which feeds into the **Digital Model** for accurate representation.
- **Actionable Insights** analyse **Behaviour** to identify patterns and improvements, optimizing processes and impacting assets.
- **Behaviour** is essential for representing physical elements in the **Digital Model**.

Subsequently, an ontology model was created for Metaverse, as shown in Fig. 3. The terms were carefully selected and were considered essential for Metaverse: 'Physical Environment', 'Technologies', 'Digital Environment', 'Digital Twin', 'Interoperability', and 'Virtual Entity'. The term 'Virtual Entity' is made up of the sub-terms Scene, Avatar and Non-Player Character (NPC), while the term 'Technologies' is made up of the sub-terms Computer Vision, Virtual

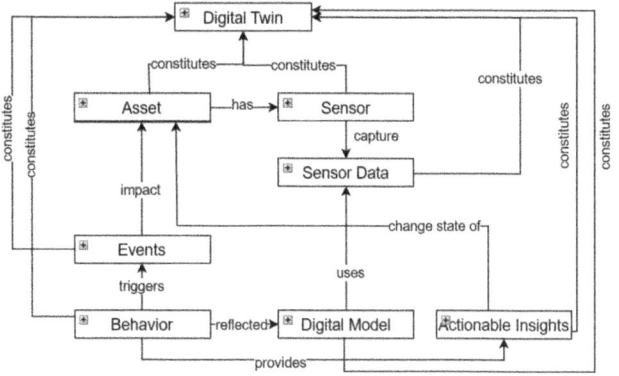

Fig. 2. Ontology model corresponds to Digital Twin.

Reality, Mixed Reality, Extended Reality, Internet of things (IoT), Blockchain, Edge Computing, Artificial Intelligence and Network Tech.

In this context, the Physical Environment in the Metaverse digitally replicates the real world, enabling immersive experiences. Technologies are fundamental, supporting the Metaverse's creation and operation.

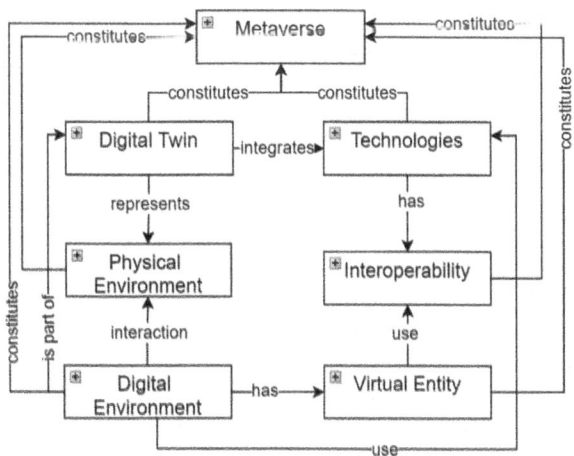

Fig. 3. Ontology model corresponds to Metaverse.

To understand how DT integrates with the Metaverse, ontology models were compared, Fig. 4. This analysis reveals that the Digital Environment serves as the foundation of the Metaverse, enabling interactions between users and digital objects. DT technology ensures accurate and interactive virtual replicas of real-world entities, while interoperability facilitates seamless transitions between platforms for users and Virtual Entities (avatars, NPCs).

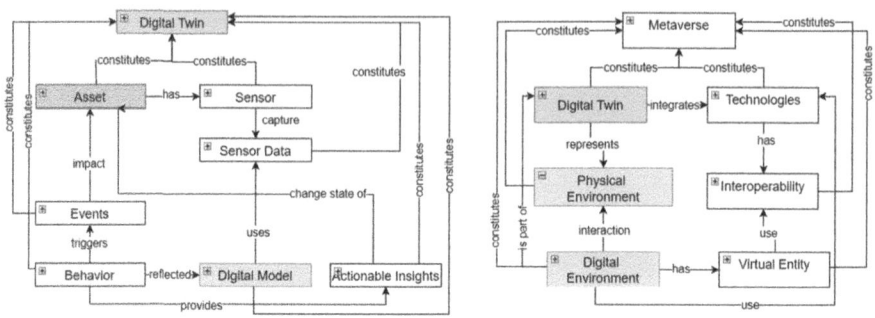

Fig. 4. Comparing ontology models.

The Digital Environment connects with the Physical Environment, DT, Technologies, and Virtual Entities, reflecting their interdependence. DT relies on Technologies for data processing and replication, while Technologies support Interoperability for smooth system integration. So, the terms were merged, with 'Asset' and 'Physical Environment' being grouped together under the name 'Asset', and 'Digital Model' and 'Digital Environment' being consolidated into a single term called 'Digital Environment'.

With regard to the 'Sensor', there was a relevant discussion about how it could be represented. In the model developed for DT it was considered as a class, while in the model developed for Metaverse it was treated as an attribute of the term 'Digital Twin', but given that the DT ontology model is considered mandatory in relation to Metaverse, it was decided to categorise it as a class in the final model.

The final ontology results from the integration of the ontology developed for DT and elements from the Metaverse domain, Fig. 5, ensuring a comprehensive representation of both concepts. In this context, the term 'Metaverse Platform' was added to clarify the process of publishing a DT in the Metaverse. It defines the technical requirements for interacting with a DT in the virtual environment.

The 'Metaverse Platform' is linked to 'Asset' and 'Digital Model'. The connection with 'Asset' shows how the platform supports the reception and interaction of digital or physical assets represented by DTs. The link to 'Digital Model' highlights the platform's role in managing and providing access to the digital models needed for DT operation in the Metaverse.

In general, these connections illustrate how the Metaverse Platform supports the integration and operation of DTs, enabling immersive interaction and control of assets in the virtual environment.

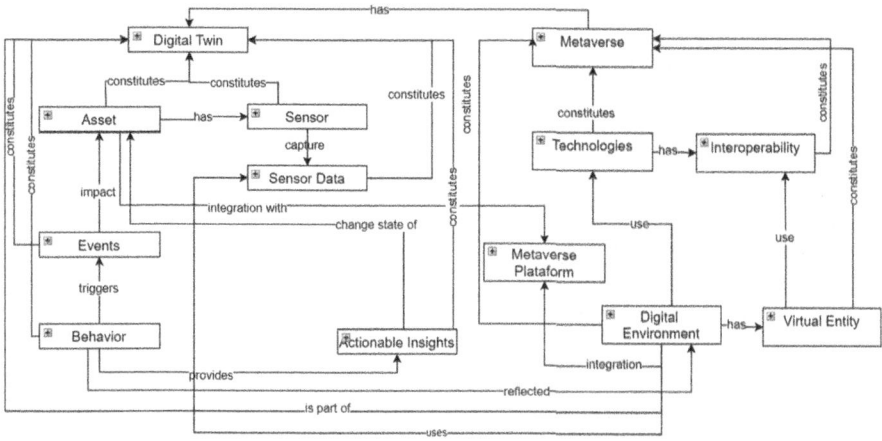

Fig. 5. Digital Twin-Metaverse Unified Ontology.

Implementation in the Protégé Tool

The next phase, 'Create', involves converting the ontology model into classes with data properties. This phase is carried out using the Protégé tool, which was used to implement the ontology model proposed above. Thus, the terms selected in the ontology model were organized in the 'Entities - Classes' section of the tool, Fig. 6.

During the development of the model, each attribute corresponding to each of the terms was meticulously organized in the "Entities - Data properties" section within the tool itself. Subsequently, time was devoted to assigning each attribute an appropriate data type.

The semantic relationship between the classes was structured and organized in the "Entities - Object properties" section, Fig. 6. Each relationship between the classes was defined and specified to accurately reflect the interconnections and dependencies between the different elements of the model. This careful and detailed organization of object properties is fundamental to ensuring an accurate and coherent semantic representation of the model, allowing a clear understanding of the relationships between the classes involved.

Object properties in the 'has' and 'use' cases have sub-properties due to their application in various instances of the diagram. For example, in the final diagram, 'has1' links 'Asset' to 'Sensor', 'has2' links 'Technologies' to 'Interoperability', and 'has3' links 'Digital Environment' to'Virtual Entity'. Similarly, 'use' links 'Digital Environment' to 'Sensor Data', 'Metaverse Platform' to 'Technologies', and 'Virtual Entity' to 'Interoperability'.

Finally, after establishing the connections between the classes, the restriction properties were applied to each established relationship.

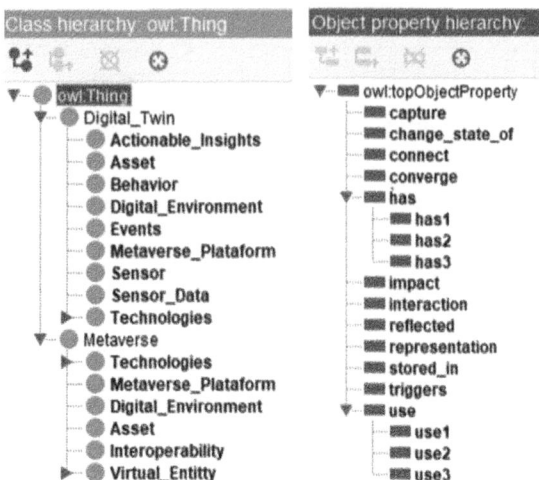

Fig. 6. Hierarchy of Classes and Object Properties in the Protégé Tool.

In the Protégé tool, in the OntoGraf tab, you can see a graphical visualization of the ontology (Fig. 7). In this same graph, it is possible to comprehensively explore the concepts related to Metaverse and DT technology, as well as understand their interrelationships.

3.2 OApIS Methodology

In this section, the ontology is developed following the OApIS process, which provides a structured and systematic approach to ontology construction. OApIS was chosen as it ensures a rigorous methodology for selecting relevant concepts, defining relationships, and validating the ontology, making it well-suited for integrating DT and Metaverse concepts. The first step is divided into four subphases. The first involves collecting sources via IEEE Xplore, searching for 'Digital Twin' and 'Metaverse', yielding around 840 references filtered by relevance.

Next, sources are selected based on relevance and applicability. The Snowball method is used, iteratively analysing citations from initial documents to identify new relevant sources.

The third subphase consists of three steps: first, extracting terms from selected sources. Table 1 presents these terms, including 'Digital Technologies', 'AI Technology', 'Synchronization', 'Internet of Things' (IoT), 'Services', 'Simulation', and 'Virtual/Physical Spaces', along with the sources identified in the second subphase.

After selecting the terms, related synonyms were grouped together. At this stage, terms like 'Artificial Intelligence Technology', 'IOT Technology', and 'Digital Technologies' were combined under the single term 'Digital Technologies'. Similarly, 'Virtual Space' and 'Virtual Twin Space' were unified into 'Virtual

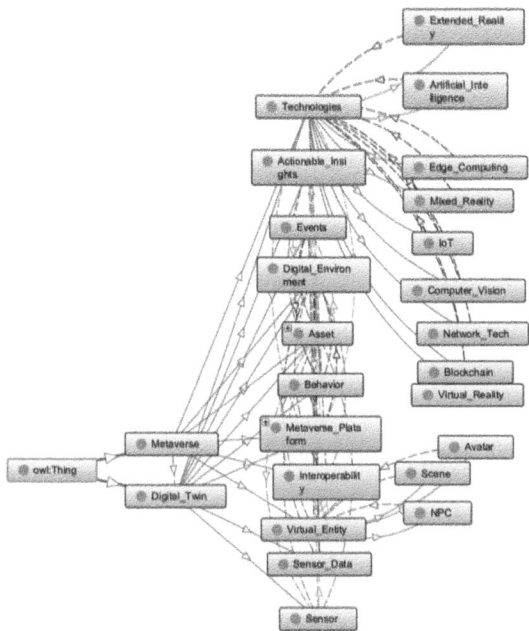

Fig. 7. OntoGraf in the Protégé tool.

Table 1. Terms of the First Iteration of the OApIS Method.

Data source	Term
[17]	Digital Technologies
[18]	Multitechnologies
[19]	Artificial Intelligence Technology
[19]	Synchronization
[20]	IOT Technology
[21]	Services
[22]	Simulation
[23]	Sensor Technology
[24]	Virtual space
[25]	Virtual Twin Space
[25]	Physical Space

Twin'. The term 'Physical Space' was renamed 'Physical Twin' to maintain consistency with Virtual Twin.

In the third sub-phase, only terms considered essential for the ontology were kept. This meant removing 'Multitechnologies', 'Digital Technologies', and all technologies that had been grouped together in the previous step, as well as the term 'Simulation'. These terms were excluded because they were not deemed relevant to this specific ontology, which centres on Digital Twin technology, while Simulation is already included under Services.

Table 2. Terms of the Second Iteration of the OApIS Method.

Data source	Term
[23]	Data Communications
[26]	Avatar
[26]	NPC
[26]	Scene
[27]	Data
[27]	Real-time Systems
[27]	Cyber-Physical Systems

The fourth and final sub-phase involved repeating the final steps from the first iteration. As shown in Table 2, this second iteration included a renewed source search using the Newest filter. As a result, additional terms that had been missing from the initial ontology and from recent literature were identified. These newly added terms include 'Data Communications', 'Avatar', 'Non-Player Character' (NPC), 'Scene', 'Data', 'Real-time Systems', and 'Cyber-Physical Systems'.

In the second iteration, we excluded all terms except'Data Communications', as we deemed the remaining terms irrelevant for the ontology in question. 'Data Communications' was then simplified to 'Communication', considering that, in the field of Information Systems, it involves not only data exchange but also the exchange of information, knowledge, and wisdom. These relationships are depicted in a DIKW pyramid. Accordingly, these concepts were also integrated into the ontology.

Table 3. Terms of the Third Iteration of the OApIS Method.

Data source	Term
[28]; [3]	Interoperability
[29]	XR
[29]	AR
[29]	MR
[29]	VR

During the third iteration, as shown in Table 3, the Most Popular filter was applied, which highlighted the terms Interoperability, 'Augmented Reality' (AR), 'Extended Reality' (XR), 'Mixed Reality' (MR), and 'Virtual Reality' (VR).

In the subsequent sub-phase, it was observed that AR, MR, and VR are included under the previously selected term XR. Since they were deemed non-essential, these terms were removed, leaving only Interoperability selected.

Accordingly, following multiple iterations, the terms shown in Fig. 8 were chosen for the ontology associated with the Metaverse and Digital Twin (DT).

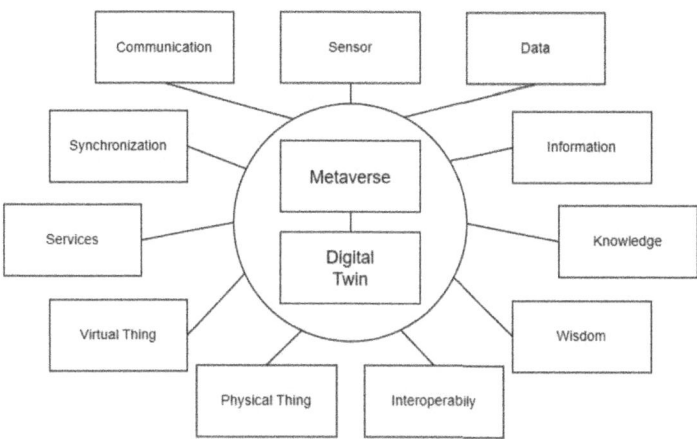

Fig. 8. General Model of Selected Terms Related to Metaverse and Digital Twins

In addition to the previously recognized terms, it is important to highlight that the communication between DTs, enabled through services, is essentially an 'Interaction'. This interaction involves the continuous exchange of data and information, allowing DTs to synchronize and respond in real-time to dynamic system conditions, improving operational effectiveness.

'Communications', on the other hand, refers specifically to the data exchange between the Physical Twin and Virtual Twin. This exchange is vital, as the Virtual Twin relies on data from the Physical Twin to accurately reflect its state, aiding in real-time monitoring, simulation, and performance forecasting.

Additionally, we include actuators as a key term in the ontology. Sensors collect data from the physical world, but actuators convert control signals into physical actions, allowing the system to interact with the environment.

Table 4 provides a detailed description of the key terms, forming a consistent framework for the ontology's development and aligning with the latest definitions in the field.

Table 4. Description of Selected Terms.

Terms	Description
Virtual Twin	A Virtual Twin is a digital replica of a physical environment, where DTs exist and interact. It facilitates interaction between physical and virtual worlds.
Physical Twin	A Physical Twin represents the tangible world, using sensors and actuators to capture data and send it to the Virtual Twin for analysis.
Interoperability	Interoperability is the ability of DTs to communicate and collaborate, allowing digital objects to interact within the Metaverse.
Services	Services enable modelling, simulation, and real-time predictions, as well as facilitate DT interactions across different sectors.
Data	Data links the physical and virtual worlds, ensuring synchronization and proper responses through real-time exchange between twins.
Information	Information bridges the Physical and Virtual Twins, being processed data exchanged in real time to maintain accurate synchronization.
Knowledge	Knowledge is derived from processed information, applied to make decisions, predict behaviours, and optimise processes in DTs.
Wisdom	Wisdom applies accumulated knowledge to foresee outcomes, solve problems, and improve performance for sustainable solutions.
Interaction	Interaction involves the continuous communication between DTs, ensuring secure and reliable transfer of data, knowledge, and wisdom.
Communication	Communication ensures efficient transfer of data, knowledge, and wisdom between Physical and Virtual Twins to support decision-making.
Synchronization	Synchronization aligns the Physical and Digital Twins, keeping them up-to-date with data, information, and knowledge for reliable interaction.
Sensor	Sensors detect changes in physical variables, converting them into digital signals for analysis and response in real time.
Actuators	Actuators convert digital signals into physical actions, impacting the environment based on control system commands.

As a result of this process, we developed the second phase. In the second phase, "Specification of Information," the properties of the entities and the relationships between them were identified. These were then represented using a UML class diagram created in the Visual Paradigm tool, as shown in Fig. 9.

The Metaverse consists of multiple interconnected DTs. The DT class is associated with Services, Interaction, and Virtual Twin. Services provide essential functions to optimize DT operations and improve user experience.

The Interaction class focuses on the exchange of data, information, knowledge, and wisdom among DTs, enabling real-time coordination. The Virtual Twin manages and stores DTs, allowing real-time simulations and data comparison.

The Physical Twin connects to Sensors and Actuators, which collect data and make adjustments based on the system's needs. Communication facilitates data exchange between the Physical and Virtual Twins.

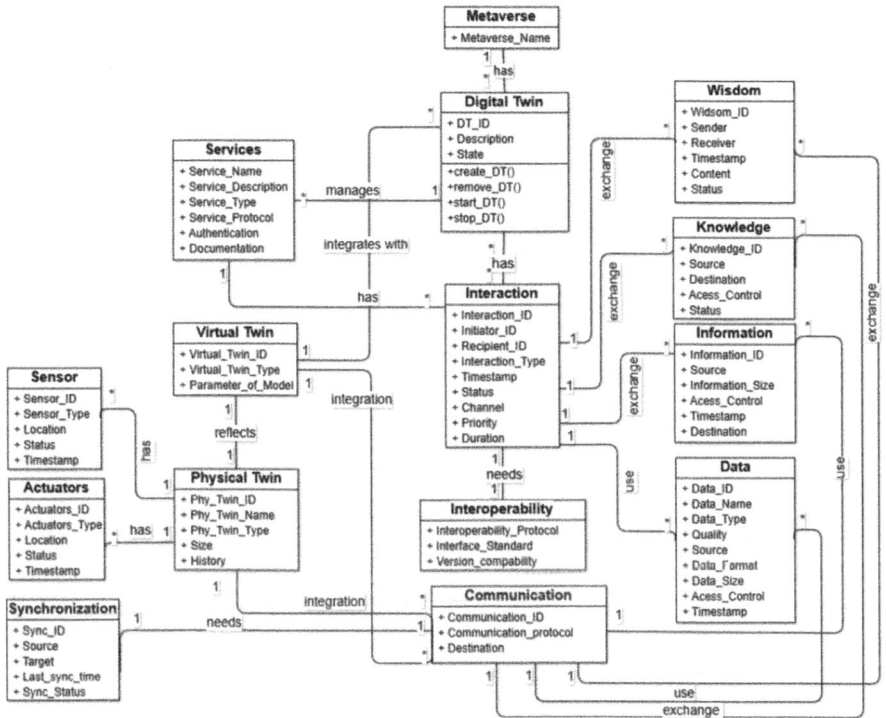

Fig. 9. Metaverse and Digital Twin Ontology Class Diagram.

The Data, Information, Knowledge, and Wisdom classes are connected to Interaction, enabling these exchanges between DTs. The same occurred with the term 'Communication.' Synchronization ensures that data remains up-to-date in real time, supporting effective communication. Interoperability is crucial for seamless DT communication. Services mediate the exchange of data and knowledge, while the relationship between the Physical and Virtual Twins ensures system optimization.

3.3   Application Scenario

Building on the ontological framework, a practical scenario is conducted focusing on deploying DTs using Microsoft Azure. The central objective is to demonstrate how the proposed ontology can be instantiated and managed within an actual cloud platform. First, the ontology is converted into Digital Twin Definition

Language (DTDL), a JSON-based format recognized by Azure Digital Twins (ADT). It preserves the conceptual structure (entities, relationships, and properties) defined in the UML diagrams. Next, these DTDL models are uploaded to ADT, allowing automatic generation and linking of the DT instances.

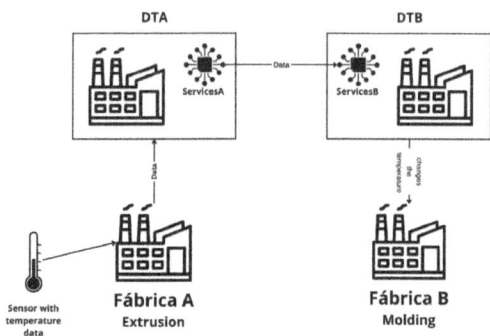

Fig. 10. Application Scenario.

To illustrate the process, two interconnected factories are modelled: "Fábrica A" responsible for extruding plastic, and "Fábrica B" dedicated to moulding. Each facility is monitored by a DT that reads sensor data (e.g., temperature) through Azure services, as shown in Fig. 10. Whenever the extrusion temperature exceeds a certain threshold, the DT of Fábrica B automatically triggers cooling procedures to ensure optimal conditions for moulding. This real-time data exchange and decision-making is fully supported by Azure APIs, which handle authorization, reading and updating twin properties, and synchronizing both physical and virtual environments. Overall, this case study underscores the feasibility of the approach: the ontology guides the DTDL modelling process, while Azure's cloud infrastructure handles scaling, monitoring, and communication. By merging theoretical constructs with operational cloud components, the scenario demonstrates how ontological rigor and ADT capabilities combine to deliver a robust, adaptive solution for Industry 4.0.

While the proposed approach shows considerable potential for integrating Digital Twins and the Metaverse, several limitations warrant discussion. In scenarios with an expanding number of assets and sensors, scalability may become a key challenge, necessitating robust data management strategies [30,31].

Furthermore, maintaining and updating complex ontological repositories over time can be resource-intensive, especially in rapidly evolving industrial environments [32,33]. Lastly, aligning the proposed ontology with existing standards, such as ISO, W3C, or OPC UA, could require specialized extensions or bridging mechanisms [34], potentially complicating broader adoption.

4   Conclusion

Ontology development follows different methodologies, shaping their application. The MDCP Methodology [15] follows a structured five-stage process, ensuring consistency in formalized ontologies. In contrast, OApIS Methodology [16] adopts a data-driven approach, prioritizing adaptability for dynamic domains.

Protegé-generated ontologies emphasize static structures, defining relationships between key terms (e.g., Digital Environment, Virtual Entity, Sensor). OApIS, however, focuses on real-time interactions, modelling continuous data exchange through terms like Services, Interaction, and Synchronization. Consequently, while MDCP provides a solid foundation for methodical, well-organized ontologies, OApIS excels in scenarios demanding ongoing adaptation—particularly relevant when linking Digital Twins to the Metaverse.

By first applying MDCP and then transitioning to OApIS, we achieved an ontology flexible enough to handle real-time synchronization between physical and digital entities. This approach proved indispensable for bridging the gap between structured representation and real-time adaptability, as demonstrated in the Application Scenario with interconnected factories running on ADT.

The proposed ontology not only promotes seamless interoperability and scalability but also boosts predictive capabilities, ultimately fostering a more robust and efficient Metaverse ecosystem. From an implementation perspective, combining MDCP's structured design with OApIS's dynamic data integration adds both consistency (formal stages) and adaptability (through real-time modelling), as demonstrated in our Application Scenario using ADT. This setup underscores the practical feasibility of deploying the ontology in cloud-based infrastructures, offering tangible benefits in monitoring, decision-making, and synchronization.

Looking ahead, an important step is to validate the ontology empirically in a real industrial setting, collecting operational data to refine the model and test its performance under large-scale conditions. Furthermore, exploring integrations with blockchain or other decentralized technologies may bolster trust, traceability, and identity continuity across diverse Metaverse platforms.

Overall, our findings show that unifying Metaverse and DT concepts into a single ontological framework successfully addresses pressing interoperability and real-time challenges, paving the way for broader industrial adoption and more immersive virtual-physical interactions.

Acknowledgments. This work has been supported by the European Union under the Next Generation EU, through a grant of the Portuguese Republic's Recovery and Resilience Plan (RRP) Partnership Agreement, within the scope of the project PRO-DUTECH R3 - "Agenda Mobilizadora da Fileira das Tecnologias de Produção para a Reindustrialização", Total project investment: 166.988.013,71 Euros; Total Grant: 97.111.730,27 Euros.

References

1. Gruber, T.R.: A translation approach to portable ontology specifications. Knowl. Acquis. **5**(2), 199–220 (1993)
2. Abu-Salih, B.: MetaOntology: toward developing an ontology for the metaverse. Front. Big Data **5**, 998648 (2022)
3. Hyun, W.: Study on standardization for interoperable metaverse. In: Proceedings of 2023 International Conference Advanced Communication Technology (ICACT), pp. 319–322 (2023)
4. Li, K., Yuen, C.: Toward ubiquitous semantic metaverse: challenges, approaches, and opportunities. IEEE Internet Things J. **10**(12), 9893–9908 (2023)
5. Laborde, R., Benzekri, A.: The interplay between policy and technology in metaverses: Towards seamless avatar interoperability using self-sovereign identity. In: Proceedings of the 2023 IEEE International Conference on Metaverse Computing, Networking and Applications (MetaCom) (2023)
6. Ghirmai, S., Debbah, M.: Self-sovereign identity for trust and interoperability in the metaverse. In: IEEE SmartWorld/UIC/ScalCom/DigitalTwin/PC/Meta (2022)
7. Gebre, D., Guizani, M.: Establishing trust and security in decentralized metaverse: a web 3.0 approach. ACM Trans. Multimedia Comput. Commun. Appl. **20**, 1–17 (2024)
8. Fiaz, F., Muhammad, Z.: METASSI: a framework for personal data protection, enhanced cybersecurity and privacy in metaverse virtual reality platforms. Future Internet **16**, 176 (2024)
9. Patwe, S., Mane, S.B.: Blockchain-enabled secure and interoperable authentication scheme for metaverse environments. Future Internet **16**, 166 (2024)
10. Yao , Y., Mišić, V.: Metaverse-aka: a lightweight and privacy-preserving seamless cross-metaverse authentication and key agreement scheme. In: IEEE SmartWorld/UIC/ScalCom/DigitalTwin/PriComp/Meta 2022 (2022)
11. Yang, L., Hui, P.: Interoperability of the metaverse: a digital ecosystem perspective review. arXiv e-prints (2024)
12. Perey, C.: Interoperability is a fundamental requirement for the open metaverse. In: Proceedings of the 2024 IEEE International Symposium on Emerging Metaverse (ISEMV) (2024)
13. Roopa, M., Kumar, R., Singh, S.: Ontologies for prognostics and health management of production systems. J. Intell. Manuf. **35**(2), 2223–2253 (2024). https://doi.org/10.1007/s10845-024-02347-w
14. Zhang, Y., Li, T., Wang, X.: An ontology-based industrial intelligent model library and its application in predictive maintenance. Springer Proc. Complex. **1**, 45–58 (2022)
15. Singh, S., et al.: Data management for developing digital twin ontology model. J. Eng. Manuf. Part B **235**(14), 2323–2337 (2021)
16. Duarte, F.J., Silva, L.O., Dias, B., Pereira, T.F., Machado, R.J.: Towards a digital ocean ontology using the Oapis approach. In: Proceedings of the 2024 IEEE International Conference on Engineering, Technology, and Innovation (ICE/ITMC). IEEE (2024)
17. Ostroukh, A.V., Kuftinova, N.G., Podberezkin, A.A., Subbotin, B.S., Podgornyi, A.V.: Use digital twins and the metaverse to analysis data in the agglomeration transport network. In: Proceedings of the 2023 Intelligence Technologies and Electronic Devices in Transport (TIRVED), pp. 1–5 (2023)

18. Wang, H., et al.: A survey on the metaverse: the state-of-the-art, technologies, applications, and challenges. IEEE Internet Things J. **10**(16), 14671–14688 (2023)
19. Hashash, O., Chaccour, C., Saad, W., Sakaguchi, K., Yu, T.: Towards a decentralized metaverse: Synchronized orchestration of digital twins and sub-metaverses. In: Proceedings of ICC 2023 - IEEE International Conference on Communications, pp. 1905–1910 (2023)
20. Zhang, C., Si, X., Zhu, X., Zhang, Y.: A survey on the security of the metaverse. In: Proceedings of the 2023 IEEE International Conference on Metaverse Computing, Networking and Applications (MetaCom), pp. 428–432 (2023)
21. Kang, J., Kim, S., Yoon, Y.: The strategy of digital twin convergence service based on metaverse. In: Proceedings 2023 IEEE/ACIS 21st International Conference on Software Engineering Research, Management and Applications (SERA), pp. 326–330 (2023)
22. Júunior, A.O., Calvo-Rolle, J.L., Leitao, P.: Simulation on digital twin: role of artificial intelligence and emergence of industrial metaverse. In: Proceedings of the 2024 IEEE 33rd International Symposium on Industrial Electronics (ISIE), pp. 1–6 (2024)
23. Li, K., et al.: When internet of things meets metaverse: convergence of physical and cyber worlds. IEEE Internet Things J. **10**(5), 4148–4173 (2023)
24. Munir, A., et al.: Cellular metaverse: enhancing real-time communications in virtual world. In: Proceedings of the 2023 International Technical Conference on Circuits/Systems, Computers, and Communications (ITC-CSCC), pp. 1–4 (2023)
25. Wang, X., Zhao, W., Li, Z.: Construction of indoor physical environment based on digital twin. In: Proceedings of the 2024 IEEE 2nd Int. Conf. on Control, Electronics and Computer Technology (ICCECT), pp. 283–287 (2024)
26. Park, S.-M., Kim, Y.-G.: A metaverse: taxonomy, components, applications, and open challenges. IEEE Access **10**, 4209–4251 (2022)
27. Elias, D., Ziegenbein, D., Mundhenk, P., Hamann, A., Rowe, A.: The cyber-physical metaverse – Where digital twins and humans come together. In: Proceedings of the 2023 Design, Automation & Test in Europe Conference (DATE), pp. 1–2 (2023)
28. Abilkaiyrkyzy, A., Elhagry, A., Laamarti, F., Saddik, A.E.: Metaverse key requirements and platforms survey. IEEE Access **11**, 117765–117787 (2023)
29. Antonijevic, P., Iqbal, M., Ubakanma, G., Dagiuklas, T.: The metaverse evolution: toward future digital twin campuses. In: Proceedings of the 2022 Human-Centered Cognitive Systems (HCCS), pp. 1–8 (2022)
30. Han, Y., et al.: A dynamic hierarchical framework for IoT-assisted digital twin synchronization in the metaverse. IEEE Internet Things J. **10**, 268–284 (2023)
31. Yu, J., Alhilal, A., Hui, P., Tsang, D.: Bi-directional digital twin and edge computing in the metaverse. IEEE Internet Things Mag. **7**, 106–112 (2022)
32. Inokuchi, K., Esaki, H.: Semantic digital twin for interoperability and comprehensive management of data assets. In: Proceedings of the 2023 IEEE International Conferenve on Metaverse Computing, Networking and Applications (MetaCom) (2023)
33. Tu, X., Autiosalo, J., Ala-Laurinaho, R., Yang, C., Salminen, P., Tammi, K.: TwinXR: method for using digital twin descriptions in industrial extended reality applications. Front. Virtual Real. **4**, 1019080 (2023)
34. Erdal, L., Johansson, B.: Integrating dynamic digital twins: enabling real-time connectivity for IoT and virtual reality. In: Proceedings of the 2024 Winter Simulation Conference (WSC) (2024)

Construction of Large Zero-Aware Pattern Databases for Sliding Puzzles on Distributed Memory Machines

Tomoya Nagahashi[1] and Daisuke Takahashi[2($\boxtimes$)]

[1] Graduate School of Science and Technology, University of Tsukuba, Tsukuba, Ibaraki 305-8573, Japan
nagahashi@hpcs.cs.tsukuba.ac.jp
[2] Center for Computational Sciences, University of Tsukuba, Tsukuba, Ibaraki 305-8577, Japan
daisuke@cs.tsukuba.ac.jp

Abstract. A pattern database, which is a precomputed lookup table that estimates the cost required to reach the goal state, is used for pruning in heuristic searches. In the search for an optimal solution to a sliding puzzle, a zero-aware pattern database (ZPDB) enables highly effective pruning. Using a database that considers the interactions of more tiles enhances pruning but increases computational time and memory usage. Here, we develop a program for constructing a large ZPDB on a distributed memory system. The program is based on a breadth-first search algorithm and is parallelized using MPI and OpenMP. An evaluation of its parallel performance reveals that increasing the number of MPI processes by 48-fold results in up to a 24x speedup. Furthermore, we construct a large ZPDB for the 24-puzzle on a 5×5 board that stores all patterns formed by nine tiles and the blank (more than 1.7 trillion entries) in 41 min using 2304 compute nodes.

Keywords: Pattern database · Breadth-first search · Parallelization

1 Introduction

The 15-puzzle is a sliding puzzle in which 15 tiles are arranged on a 4×4 board, as shown in Fig. 1. Rearrangement is performed by repeatedly sliding tiles into the blank on the board. A generalization of this puzzle to an $N \times N$ board is commonly referred to as the $(N^2 - 1)$-puzzle. Search-based methods are used to find an optimal solution that minimizes the number of tile moves. Various pruning techniques have been studied to efficiently explore the vast search space.

A pattern database (PDB) is a table that provides a lower bound on the number of moves required for an optimal solution from a given tile configuration. The values in this precomputed table are referenced during the search for pruning. There are several methods for building PDBs, and among them, the

O. Gervasi et al. (Eds.): ICCSA 2025, LNCS 15648, pp. 272–284, 2025.
https://doi.org/10.1007/978-3-031-97000-9_17

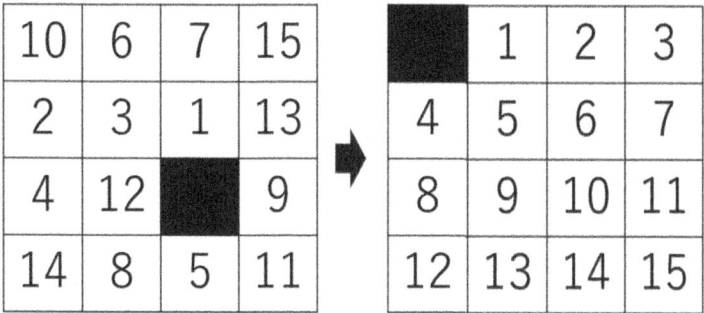

Fig. 1. 15-puzzle

Zero-Aware Pattern Database (ZPDB) [8] enables particularly high-performance pruning.

In the present study, we implement a program that uses MPI [1] and OpenMP [2] for constructing large ZPDBs that can be executed in a large-scale distributed memory environment.

2 Background

The problem of finding an optimal solution for the $(N^2 - 1)$-puzzle is NP-hard [14]. The number of possible board states is proportional to $N^2!$, exceeding 10^{13} for the 15-puzzle and reaching approximately 7×10^{24} for the 24-puzzle. Therefore, to efficiently find an optimal solution, heuristic search methods are used.

A heuristic is said to be admissible if it is guaranteed never to overestimate the true cost. Using an admissible heuristic, search algorithms such as iterative deepening A* (IDA*) [13] can be used to find the optimal solution for the $(N^2 - 1)$-puzzle. Thus, a heuristic that estimates the number of moves as accurately as possible without exceeding the true value is required.

The Manhattan distance is a simple example of an admissible heuristic for the $(N^2 - 1)$-puzzle. Since a tile move reduces the Manhattan distance between the tile's current position and its goal position by at most one, the sum of the Manhattan distances of all tiles from their current positions to their goal positions provides a trivial lower bound on the number of required moves.

3 Pattern Databases

Several types of PDB have been proposed, including non-additive PDB [10], the additive PDB (APDB) [12], and the ZPDB [8].

3.1 Non-additive Pattern Database

The PDB for the $(N^2 - 1)$-puzzle, proposed by Culberson and Schaeffer [10], records the number of moves required to solve a new puzzle. It focuses on the configuration of specific tiles (pattern tiles), while treating all other tiles as identical. Since the positions of tiles not included in the pattern are not considered, the new puzzle is a sub-problem of the original. The number of moves in the optimal solution for the new puzzle does not exceed that of the original problem. To distinguish this PDB from other types of PDB, it is also referred to as the non-additive PDB.

3.2 Additive Pattern Database

Felner et al. proposed the APDB [12], which enables high-performance pruning by dividing tiles into multiple groups and summing the heuristic values for each pattern, as shown in Fig. 2. In the non-additive PDB, even if tiles are divided into multiple groups and a separate database is created for each group, their values could not be summed because counting tile moves redundantly could make the heuristic inadmissible. In the APDB, only the moves of the pattern tiles are counted and thus the same move is not counted redundantly across different groups, allowing the heuristic values to be summed. This enables the inclusion of all tile moves in the heuristic evaluation, leading to more effective pruning.

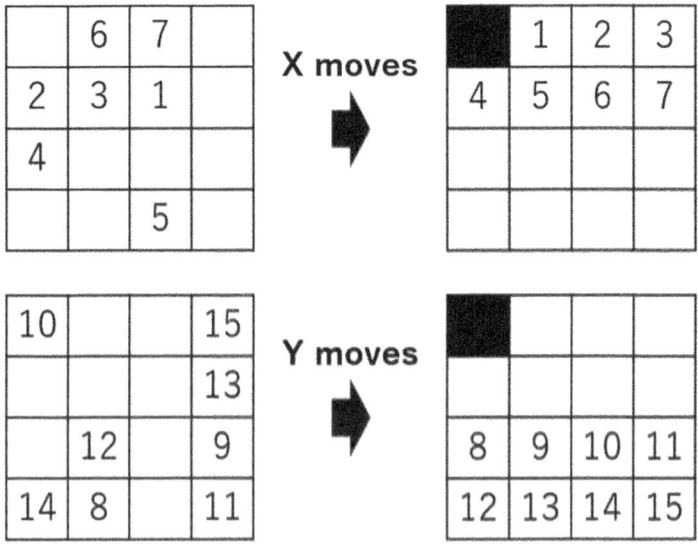

Fig. 2. Heuristic using APDB

Döbbelin et al. proposed an algorithm for constructing an APDB in a distributed memory environment and created an APDB for the 24-puzzle by dividing the tiles into three groups of nine, nine, and six tiles, respectively [11]. The APDB that recorded the patterns of nine tiles had approximately 7.4×10^{11} entries. Even if each entry required only one byte, this APDB would exceed 700 GB.

3.3   Zero-Aware Pattern Database

The ZPDB [8], proposed by Clausecker and Reinefeld, is an extension of the APDB. In the APDB, to reduce memory usage, the position of the blank is not considered. As a result, depending on the position of the blank, the estimated number of moves may differ significantly from the actual value. In the ZPDB, the position of the blank is taken into account. Instead of considering the coordinates of the blank, the values are recorded for each region divided by pattern tiles, thereby reducing the number of states. For example, in the 24-puzzle, considering a pattern of eight tiles, there are 17 possible positions for the blank, but as shown in Fig. 3, the maximum number of regions for the blank is seven, so the values for these seven possibilities are recorded. In practice, cases where the space is divided into seven regions are rare and the number of states is even lower. Since the moves of tiles not included in the pattern are ignored, this does not affect pruning performance.

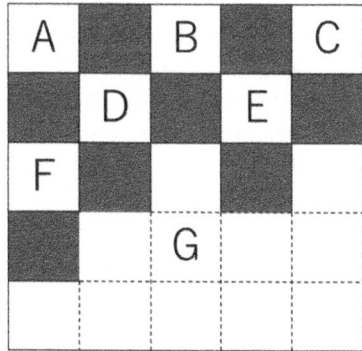

Fig. 3. Example of configuration with maximum of seven blank regions formed by eight tiles in 24-puzzle

In addition, the ZPDB can reduce memory usage by compressing the data per entry to one bit. Consider a graph where tile configuration patterns are treated as vertices and an edge is drawn between vertices if one pattern can be obtained from another by moving a tile within the same group exactly once. Since tile moves are reversible, this graph is undirected. Moreover, since the parity of the sum of the Manhattan distances from each tile's coordinates to the origin differs between adjacent vertices, the graph is bipartite. The values stored in a ZPDB can be interpreted as the shortest distances from the vertex corresponding to the goal pattern to each vertex. They can be computed using a breadth-first search (BFS) starting from the goal pattern's vertex. When compressing the data per entry to one bit, instead of storing the exact shortest path length, only the upper bits of the value obtained by dividing it by four are stored. The shortest path length is then recovered during lookup by reconstructing the shortest path. In general graphs, if the remainder when dividing each vertex's shortest path length by three is stored, one of the shortest paths to the start vertex can be obtained by repeatedly moving to a vertex closer to the start [9]. In the ZPDB, the remainder is taken modulo 4 and the lower bits, which can be reconstructed using the pattern parity, are discarded.

Clausecker developed a program for constructing ZPDBs in a shared memory environment [3]. It is written in C and can be executed using multiple threads.

4   Implementation

4.1   Breadth-First Search

A ZPDB can be constructed using a BFS. One of the BFS implementations suitable for parallelization is the level-synchronized BFS [7]. The algorithm is shown in Algorithm 1. In this method, a BFS is performed by repeatedly identifying the set of unvisited vertices that can be reached by traversing an edge from the set of visited vertices with the maximum shortest distance.

Algorithm 1. Parallel level-synchronized BFS [7]

Require: $G(V, E)$: The graph, v: Source vertex
Ensure: Array $d[1..n]$ with $d[v]$ holding the length of the shortest path from s to $v \in V$, assuming unit-weight edges
1: **for all** $v \in V$ **in parallel do**
2:     $d[v] \leftarrow -1$
3: **end for**
4: $d[s] \leftarrow 0$
5: $Q \leftarrow \phi$
6: Enqueue $s \leftarrow Q$
7: **while** $Q \neq \phi$ **do**
8:     **for all** $u \in Q$ **in parallel do**
9:         Delete $u \leftarrow Q$
10:         **for** each v adjacent to u **in parallel do**
11:             **if** $d[v] = -1$ **then**
12:                 $d[v] \leftarrow d[v] + 1$
13:                 Enqueue $v \leftarrow Q$
14:             **end if**
15:         **end for**
16:     **end for**
17: **end while**

4.2 Parallelization with MPI

When executing a BFS in a distributed memory environment, each node has partial information about the vertex set and distances. There are various methods for partitioning graph data. Here, we implement a simple one-dimensional partitioning method that evenly distributes arrays across all MPI processes.

Each MPI process maintains two arrays for managing vertices: one array is used to store the upper bits of the remainder when the shortest distance is divided by four and one array is used to track whether each vertex has been visited during the BFS. Both arrays consist of 8-bit integers, each of which stores information corresponding to all blank space regions in a single tile pattern.

In each BFS step, each node computes the set of reachable vertices by traversing one edge from the vertices it manages. It then sends these vertices to the nodes responsible for managing them. Upon receiving a vertex set, each node updates its array accordingly.

For exchanging newly discovered vertices, we utilize the collective communication supported by MPI. Specifically, we use MPI_Alltoall() to share the number of data elements to be sent and received in advance and MPI_Alltoallv() to perform the actual data exchange.

In addition, we use MPI_Allreduce() to share the number of newly explored vertices among all nodes and determine when the search should terminate.

4.3 Parallelization with OpenMP

The process of enumerating neighboring vertices from explored vertices using edge information, as well as updating data based on the information received from other nodes, can be executed in parallel. To accelerate the program, we utilize OpenMP to distribute the workload across multiple threads.

Since the information for eight vertices is handled within a single variable, updating different vertices may involve accessing the same variable. OpenMP provides directives such as #pragma omp atomic to ensure exclusive access; however, using these directives can introduce execution overhead due to synchronization delays and contention between threads waiting for write access.

To mitigate this issue, we sort the received data such that updates affecting the same variable are grouped. This allows only a single designated thread to perform the writes, eliminating the need for atomic operations. For sorting, we use the parallelizable and high-performance Radix Sort, specifically the implementation by Akiba [4].

The proposed algorithm is shown in Algorithm 2.

4.4 Reduction of Memory Usage

The memory bottleneck in this program arises from the send and receive buffers used for exchanging vertex information during all-to-all communication. When constructing a large ZPDB, memory shortages may occur.

Algorithm 2. Hybrid MPI/OpenMP parallel level-synchronized BFS

Require:
    p: Rank of MPI process,
    P: Number of MPI processes,
    V_p: p-th vertex set of the graph,
    v_{root}: Source vertex
Ensure: $dist_p[v]$ = upper bit of minimum distance from v_{root} to v modulo 4 for all
    $v \in V_p$
 1: $S_p \leftarrow \{v_{root}\}$ **if** $v_{root} \in V_p$ **else** ϕ
 2: $closed_p \leftarrow [false, \cdots, false]$
 3: $dist_p \leftarrow [0, \cdots, 0]$
 4: $d \leftarrow 0$
 5: **while** $\sum_p |S_p| \neq 0$ **do**
 6:     **for all** $p' \in \{0, 1, \cdots P - 1\}$ **do**
 7:         $S_{p,p'} \leftarrow \phi$
 8:     **end for**
 9:     **for all** $v \in S_p$ **do**   ▷ in parallel with OpenMP
10:         $dist_p[v] \leftarrow \lfloor d/2 \rfloor \bmod 2$
11:         $closed_p[v] \leftarrow true$
12:         **for all** $v^+ \in$ neighbors(v) **do**
13:             $p' \leftarrow$ rank of MPI process s.t. $v^+ \in V_{p'}$
14:             $S_{p,p'} \leftarrow S_{p,p'} \cup \{v^+\}$
15:         **end for**
16:     **end for**
17:     Exchange $|S_{p,p'}|$ for $|S_{p',p}|$ by MPI_AlltoAll()
18:     Exchange $S_{p,p'}$ for $S_{p',p}$ by MPI_Alltoallv()
19:     $S_p \leftarrow \bigcup_{p'} S_{p',p}$
20:     parallel_radix_sort(S_p)   ▷ to avoid race condition
21:     $d \leftarrow d + 1$
22:     Calculate $\sum_p |S_p|$ by MPI_Allreduce()
23: **end while**

To mitigate this issue, we set an upper limit on the amount of data sent and received at one time. If this limit is exceeded, communication is divided into multiple rounds, thereby preventing memory exhaustion.

Döbbelin et al. encountered a similar issue in their method for constructing a large APDB [11]. They also addressed it by dividing communication into multiple rounds.

5 Evaluation

5.1 Parallel Performance

We executed the proposed program with eight tiles of the 24-puzzle shown in Fig. 4 as input and evaluated its parallelization performance. The program was executed on the Pegasus supercomputer [5], which is operated by the Center for Computational Sciences, University of Tsukuba. The detailed system specifications are shown in Table 1.

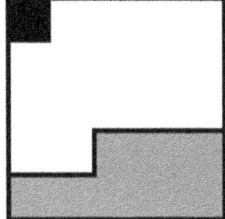

Fig. 4. Configuration of eight input pattern tiles

Table 1. Execution environment (Pegasus)

CPU	Intel®Xeon Platinum 8468 (2.1 GHz / 48 cores)
Memory	128 GiB + 2 TiB (DDR5-4800 16 GiB DIMM ×8, DDR5-4800 256 GiB Persistent Memory ×8)
Nodes	150
Network	InfiniBand NDR200 HCA
MPI library	OpenMPI 4.1.6
Compiler	GCC 11.4.0
Compile option	-std=gnu++17 -O2 -fopenmp

Number of MPI Processes. The program was executed with the number of MPI processes per node varied from 1 to 48. The number of nodes was fixed at 50. Each MPI process was run using a single thread. The results are shown in Fig. 5.

As the number of MPI processes increased, the execution time decreased. When executed with 48 MPI processes per node, the program was approximately 24 times faster compared to running with 1 MPI process per node.

Number of Threads. The program was executed with various numbers of execution threads in the parts parallelized with OpenMP. It was run on 50 nodes, each of which was assigned one MPI process. The results are shown in Fig. 6. Increasing the number of threads reduced the execution time, but the speedup was more gradual compared to that obtained by increasing the number of MPI processes. Compared to running with a single thread, the execution with 48 threads resulted in a speedup of approximately 6.0 times.

MPI Process and Thread Allocation. The product of the number of MPI processes and the number of threads per node was fixed at 48, which is the number of cores per node. The program was executed while varying these values. The execution time is shown in Fig. 7. Since increasing the number of MPI processes led to a greater speedup than that obtained by increasing the number of threads, execution time decreased as the number of MPI processes increased. The

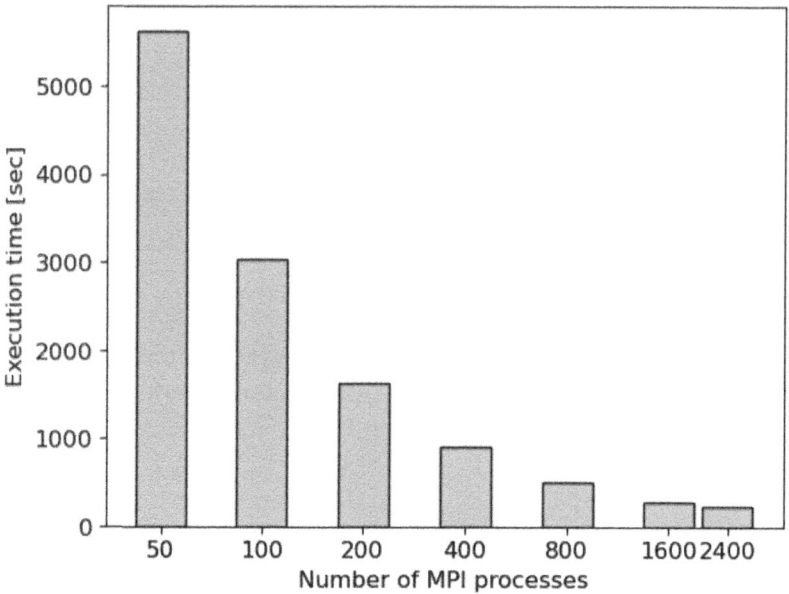

Fig. 5. Number of MPI processes vs. execution time (8 tiles, 50 nodes, 1 thread)

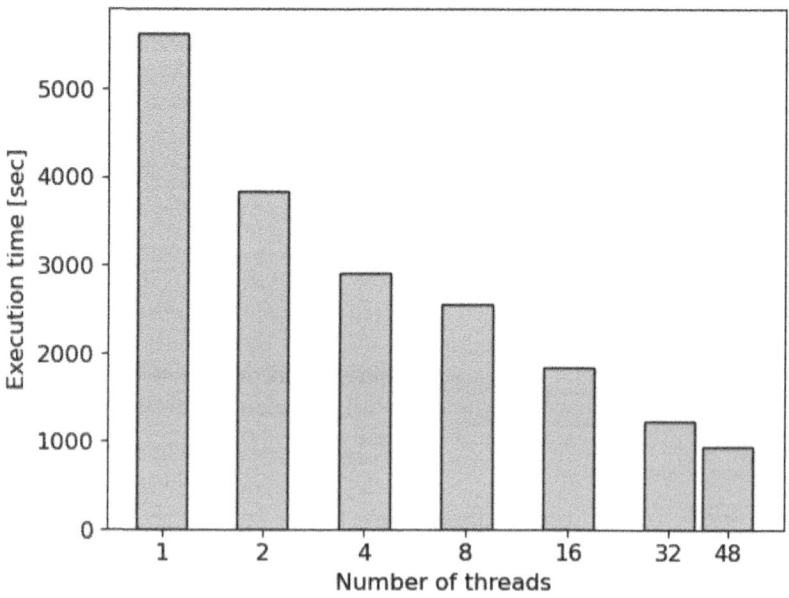

Fig. 6. Number of threads vs. execution time (8 tiles, 50 nodes)

fastest execution was achieved using Flat-MPI without OpenMP-based thread parallelization.

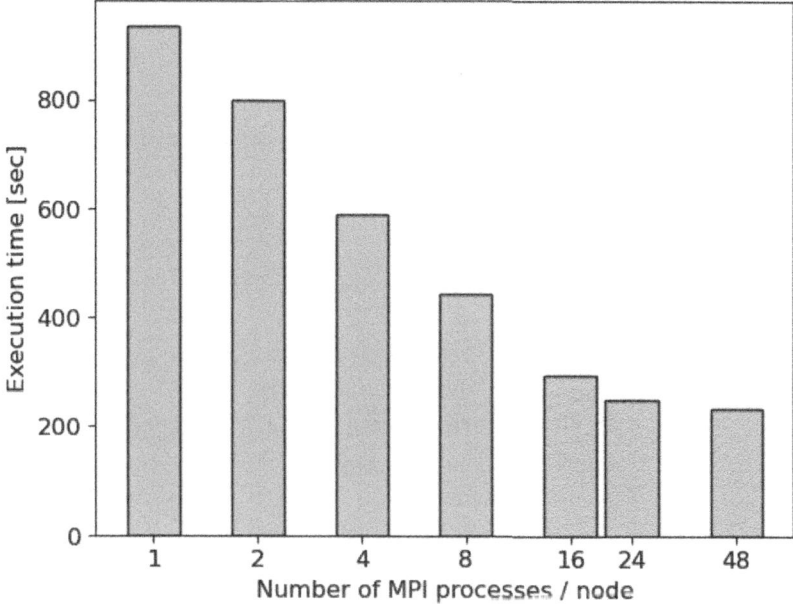

Fig. 7. Execution time with fixed product of MPI processes and threads per node set to 48 (50 nodes)

5.2 Construction of Large ZPDB

The proposed program was used to construct a ZPDB with the nine tiles shown in Fig. 8. It was executed on the Wisteria supercomputer [6], which is operated by the Information Technology Center, The University of Tokyo. The execution environment is shown in Table 2. The total number of patterns is 1 759 513 674 240 $\approx 1.76 \times 10^{12}$.

The program used only MPI-based parallelization (i.e., OpenMP thread parallelization was not used). In addition, to reduce memory usage, communication was divided into multiple rounds. Specifically, during the BFS, the number of vertices whose edges are calculated at once was limited to $2^{18} = 262\,144$ per MPI process. The node configuration was a three-dimensional mesh. The program was executed with two setups: 576 nodes with 27 600 MPI processes, and 2304 nodes with 110 400 MPI processes.

The execution time is shown in Table 3. Using 2304 nodes, the execution was completed in approximately 41 min. Since all-to-all communication was performed with more than 100 000 MPI processes, the communication cost was sig-

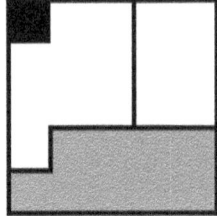

Fig. 8. Configuration of nine input pattern tiles, identical to one of Döbbelin's 9-9-6 partitions [11]

Table 2. Execution environment (Wisteria)

CPU	A64FX (2.2 GHz / 48 cores)
Memory	32 GiB
Nodes	7680
Network	Tofu Interconnect D
MPI library	Fujitsu MPI
Compiler	Fujitsu compiler
Compile option	-Kfast

nificant, accounting for more than one-third of the total execution time. Regarding communication, the maximum number of all-to-all communication rounds via MPI_Alltoall performed in one step of the level-synchronized BFS was 80 with 576 nodes and 26 with 2304 nodes.

Table 3. Execution time of nine-tile ZPDB construction program

nodes	execution time [s]	communication time [s]	communication ratio
576 (6 × 12 × 8, mesh)	5807	392	0.0675
2304 (12 × 12 × 16, mesh)	2477	973	0.393

5.3 Comparison with Existing Program

The program developed by Clausecker was executed on a single Pegasus node using the tiles shown in Figs. 4 and 8 as input. The number of threads was set to 48. When using nine tiles were used as input, the available DRAM was insufficient, so persistent memory was used to extend the memory capacity.

The execution time for the eight-tile case was 11 min and 10 s. The nine-tile case required 3 h and 43 min and approximately 1.7 TB of memory.

Compared to the program implemented in this study, the existing shared-memory program requires fewer computational resources. In distributed-memory programs, additional time is required for communication and related processing. Moreover, since each MPI process handles only a subset of vertices, the workload in each BFS step is not evenly distributed. These factors likely contributed to the difference in execution efficiency between the two approaches.

6   Conclusion

A ZPDB construction program for distributed memory environments was developed. MPI and OpenMP were used for parallelization. With the parallelization of the level-synchronized BFS, increasing the number of MPI processes and threads reduced the execution time of the program. Increasing the number of MPI processes tended to result in a greater reduction in execution time than that obtained by increasing the number of threads. With a few thousand MPI processes, all-to-all communication was sufficiently fast, making Flat-MPI the most efficient choice. However, in an example where a nine-tile ZPDB for the 24-puzzle was constructed with over 100 000 MPI processes, the communication time accounted for more than one-third of the total execution time. To further increase the number of MPI processes, techniques for reducing communication costs are necessary. The program developed in this study is expected to be useful for constructing large ZPDBs that would be difficult to compute on a single machine.

Acknowledgments. This research was conducted using the computational resources of Pegasus, provided by the Multidisciplinary Cooperative Research Program at the Center for Computational Sciences, University of Tsukuba, and Wisteria, provided by the Supercomputing Division, Information Technology Center, The University of Tokyo.

References

1. MPI. https://www.mpi-forum.org. Accessed 14 Mar 2025
2. OpenMP. https://www.openmp.org. Accessed 14 Mar 2025
3. clausecker/24puzzle: Solve 24 puzzles using zero-aware pattern databases https://github.com/clausecker/24puzzle. Accessed 14 Mar 2025
4. iwiwi/parallel-radix-sort: An implementation of optimized parallel radix sort https://github.com/iwiwi/parallel-radix-sort. Accessed 14 Mar 2025
5. Center for computational sciences, University of Tsukuba: Supercomputer Pegasus. https://www.ccs.tsukuba.ac.jp/supercomputer. Accessed 14 Mar 2025
6. Wisteria/BDEC-01 Supercomputer System | Supercomputing Division, Information Technology Center, The University of Tokyo. https://www.cc.u-tokyo.ac.jp/supercomputer/wisteria/service/. Accessed 14 Mar 2025
7. Bader, D.A., Madduri, K.: Designing multithreaded algorithms for breadth-first search and st-connectivity on the Cray MTA-2. In: International Conference on Parallel Processing, pp. 523–530 (2006). https://ieeexplore.ieee.org/stamp/stamp.jsp?tp=&arnumber=1690657

8. Clausecker, R., Reinefeld, A.: Zero-Aware Pattern Databases with 1-Bit Compression for sliding tile puzzles. In: 12th International Symposium on Combinatorial Search, vol. 10, no. 1, pp. 35–43 (2019)

9. Cooperman, G., Finkelstein, L.: New methods for using Cayley graphs in interconnection networks. Discret. Appl. Math. **37**(38), 95–118 (1992)

10. Culberson, J.C., Schaeffer, J.,: Searching with pattern databases, In: Conference of the Canadian Society for Computational Studies of Intelligence, pp. 402–416 (1996)

11. Döbbelin, R., Schütt, T., Reinefeld, A.: Building large compressed PDBs for the sliding tile puzzle. In: Workshop on Computer Games 2013 Proceedings, pp. 16–27 (2014)

12. Felner, A., Korf, R.E., Hanan, S.: Additive pattern database heuristics. J. Artif. Intell. Res. **22**, 279–318 (2004)

13. Korf, R.E.: Depth-first iterative-deepening: an optimal admissible tree search. Artif. Intell. **27**, 97–109 (1985)

14. Ratner, D., Warmuth, M.: The $(n^2 - 1)$-puzzle and related relocation problems. J. Symb. Comput. **10**(2), 111–137 (1990)

Exploring Federated Learning for Thermal Urban Feature Segmentation - A Comparison of Centralized and Decentralized Approaches

Leonhard Duda[1]($\boxtimes$) (ID), Khadijeh Alibabaei[1] (ID), Elena Vollmer[2] (ID), Leon Klug[2],
Valentin Kozlov[1] (ID), Lisana Berberi[1] (ID), Mishal Benz[1] (ID), Rebekka Volk[2] (ID),
Juan Pedro Gutiérrez Hermosillo Muriedas[1] (ID), Markus Götz[1] (ID),
Judith Sáinz-Pardo Díaz[3] (ID), Álvaro López García[3] (ID), Frank Schultmann[2] (ID),
and Achim Streit[1] (ID)

[1] Scientific Computing Center (SCC), Karlsruhe Institute of Technology (KIT),
Eggenstein-Leopoldshafen, Germany
leonhard.duda@kit.edu
[2] Institute for Industrial Production (IIP), Karlsruhe Institute of Technology (KIT),
Karlsruhe, Germany
[3] Instituto de Física de Cantabria (IFCA), CSIC-UC, Avda. los Castros s/n,
Santander, Spain

Abstract. Federated Learning (FL) is an approach for training a shared Machine Learning (ML) model with distributed training data and multiple participants. FL allows bypassing limitations of the traditional Centralized Machine Learning (CL) if data cannot be shared or stored centrally due to privacy or technical restrictions – the participants train the model locally with their training data and do not need to share it among the other participants. This paper investigates the practical implementation and effectiveness of FL in a real-world scenario, specifically focusing on unmanned aerial vehicle (UAV)-based thermal images for common thermal feature detection in urban environments. The distributed nature of the data arises naturally and makes it suitable for FL applications, as images captured in two German cities are available. This application presents unique challenges due to non-identical distribution and feature characteristics of data captured at both locations. The study makes several key contributions by evaluating FL algorithms in real deployment scenarios rather than simulation. We compare several FL approaches with a centralized learning baseline across key performance metrics such as model accuracy, training time, communication overhead, and energy usage. This paper also explores various FL workflows, comparing client-controlled workflows and server-controlled workflows. The findings of this work serve as a valuable reference for understanding the practical application and limitations of the FL methods in segmentation tasks in UAV-based imaging.

L. Duda—Code available in: https://github.com/ai4os-hub/thermal-urban-feature-segmenter.git.

Keywords: Federated Learning · Distributed Learning · Real-world
Implementation · Segmentation · Energy Consumption · Thermal
Anomaly Detection

1   Introduction

Deep Learning (DL) has revolutionized many fields in science and industry, enabling significant advances in tasks like object detection and segmentation [3, 31]. DL models, fueled by large datasets, have made it possible to
develop systems that perform tasks with human-like accuracy. They are now
applied across a variety of industries including healthcare, city management,
and autonomous driving [4, 13, 46].

Traditionally, these models are trained with a large amount of data stored
in a central location. However, in response to growing data protection laws such
as the General Data Protection Regulation (GDPR) and the EU AI act [33],
the question of whether the traditional approach of storing and processing all
data centrally is sustainable arises. On the other hand, if the training data is
distributed across multiple locations and sharing is hindered due to privacy or
resource constraints, successful training becomes challenging, as there may not
be enough data available at some of these locations, leading to poor model
performance or failure to generalize over unseen data.

To achieve the same predictive performance when the data is spread across
multiple locations, Federated Learning (FL) was introduced in 2017 [29]. With
this approach, the training data does not have to be shared, but a Machine
Learning (ML) model can still be trained collaboratively and in a distributed
manner. In the initial introduction of FL, there is a central server that aggregates
updates of models trained on decentralized devices. Each device trains a model
using its local data and sends only the model updates (not the raw data) to
the central server. The server then combines local model weights to update the
global model weights. This process enables collaborative model training while
reducing the need to share raw data; however, information leakage risks may still
exist without additional privacy safeguards such as differential privacy [8, 45].

The main objective of this paper is to investigate the effectiveness of FL in
real-world applications and scenarios, with a particular focus on a segmentation
task in unmanned aerial vehicle (UAV)-based imaging. Although FL has shown
promising results in research papers, primarily in simulation scenarios, its practical performance in real-world settings should be explored, considering the limitations and challenges associated with real-world implementation [1]. This study
aims to bridge this gap by evaluating the effectiveness of FL in a unique real-
world use case: the detection of thermal anomalies in urban environments using
UAV-based imaging. This application, part of the AI4EOSC project [2], involves
detecting thermal anomalies caused by false alarms from urban features which
complicates the detection of locations requiring maintenance or improvement.
By reducing false positives, the system supports more efficient optimization of
energy-related systems [28, 42, 43].

A key feature of this work is the use of a real-world dataset collected from two cities, Munich (MU) and Karlsruhe (KA), in Germany. This dataset is characterized by significant imbalances and non-IID (non-independent and identically distributed) data across locations, posing unique challenges for both training and aggregation methods in FL.

The main contributions of this paper are as follows:

- Highlight the real-world challenges associated with training FL models on non-IID, imbalanced data from multiple locations using UAV devices, showcasing the uniqueness of the data and its impact on FL performance.
- Introduce and evaluate FL aggregation strategies tailored to handle non-IID data in segmentation tasks on the UAV images.
- Compare the performance of FL and Centralized Learning (CL) on a segmentation task in a real-world UAV imaging application, emphasizing practical challenges such as model accuracy, training time, and memory consumption.
- Investigate the performance of decentralized FL as a potential solution for privacy-preserving collaboration, comparing it against centralized FL in a real-world setting.
- Measure energy consumption and convergence time for both FL and CL, addressing the resource-constrained devices used in the real-world application and evaluating their feasibility in a practical deployment.
- Explore the challenges and opportunities of using HPC systems as clients in FL, considering their potential to enhance computational capabilities.

As most of the experiments are done in real-world scenarios, this paper can be used as a valuable reference for understanding the practical applications and performance of FL in real-world settings.

The paper is organized as follows: Sect. 2 reviews the related work in the research areas of FL algorithms and workflows. Section 3 covers the methodology and setup, explaining our concrete implementation of a FL workflow based on the use case described, including a comparison and evaluation of all workflows with each other and with the centralized approach. The obtained results of applying different approaches are evaluated and discussed in Sect. 4.

2   Related Work

FL has gained significant traction in domains such as medical imaging and autonomous driving due to stringent privacy requirements [5]. In traditional distributed learning, it is assumed that all data comes from the same distribution, ensuring consistency across all participating nodes. But in real-world FL, data is typically non-IID, meaning that data across different clients can have different distributions, which poses additional challenges for model training and performance [20]. While the FL approach is effective in simulation environments, it poses challenges in real-world applications due to this non-IID nature of the data and privacy concerns [26, 44]. To solve these issues, researchers have proposed improvements to aggregation algorithms in FL such as FedProx [24], Federated Optimization (FedOpt) [36], Scaffold [22], and FedBN [25].

FL has been successfully used mostly in domains like medical imaging and autonomous driving primarily due to concerns about data privacy in these fields [9,14]. In autonomous driving, FL is used to train a semantic segmentation model on data from cars in different cities, achieving robust performance [30]. In medical image segmentation, FL has enabled institutions to build combined models that generalize better across patient populations. For example, [27] used a FL model for brain tumor segmentation utilizing data from multiple hospitals enhancing the performance and generalizability of the segmentation. Furthermore, [35] evaluates several FL aggregation strategies, including FedProx, FedMOON [23], and FedDC [21], alongside FedAvg, under both IID and non-IID scenarios in Medical Object Detection (MOD) using simulation.

Beyond these established fields, FL has shown promising potential within UAV systems [11]. For example, [10] explored its use in drone-based collaborative learning. By employing a set of drones that communicate over a wireless network, the study successfully trained a U-Net model for collision avoidance and landing assistance, showcasing potential of FL in edge-based, real-time applications.

Decentralized FL approaches such as Decentralized Cyclic Weight Transfer (DCWT) and Swarm Learning (SL) eliminate the dependency on a central server and shift the administration tasks to one of the clients. DCWT follows a sequential training process where model weights are transferred from one client to the next in a predefined order. Each client trains the model locally before passing the updated weights to the next client, forming a cyclic training approach. SL on the other hand, lets all the clients train simultaneously with one client being responsible for the administration tasks [45].

Recent attention has also been drawn to the environmental implications of FL. Studies indicate that FL can be more energy-intensive and generate a larger carbon footprint compared to traditional Centralized Learning (CL) methods [34]. The carbon emissions in FL is not only related to the training of the model on client devices, but also includes the energy used during client-server communication and the conversion of energy to carbon emissions depending on regional grid characteristics [37]. Qiu, X. et al. [34] showed that communication costs between clients and servers can represent anywhere from 0.7% to more than 96% of total emissions in FL systems. Farsi, A.A. et al. [12] proposed adding sustainability as a fourth pillar to the existing framework, alongside legality, ethics, and robustness. This addition addresses the environmental impacts of FL systems. Despite these concerns, direct comparative analyses focusing on energy efficiency across various FL algorithms remain limited.

This work builds on these foundations by evaluating FL in a real-world scenario of UAV-based thermal anomaly detection. It examines the performance of centralized and decentralized FL workflows and compares their effectiveness in terms of metrics such as model accuracy, energy consumption, and communication overhead. By using real-world data from two cities with significant heterogeneity, this study aims to bridge the gap between theoretical FL advances and practical applications.

3   Material and Methods

3.1   Dataset

A multispectral image dataset from [39] forms the basis of this study, publicly available on Zenodo [41]. It consists of **793 images** acquired through 14 UAV flights in Germany, the large majority of which stem from Munich, the rest from Karlsruhe. All flights were carried out in nadir (90° pitch angle) and at 60 m height.

Both thermal infrared (TIR) and standard red-green-blue (RGB) imagery was simultaneously captured using DJI's Zenmuse XT2, a combined 4k RGB camera and FLIR thermal sensor [39]. Registration procedures help compensate for differing aspect ratios, resolutions, and fields of view to create the multispectral dataset [39]. As the focus lies on hot-spot detection, the TIRs were annotated with **seven classes** of common thermal urban features. The classes are summed up in Table 1. An example multispectral image and associated annotation are shown in Fig. 1. Both clearly highlight the strong imbalance of instances and pixel amounts per class [39].

Table 1. Aggregated object counts for KA and MU datasets [39]

General	Client-1 (MU)	Client-2 (KA)	Total (KA+MU)
No. images	700	93	793
Building	1215	189	1404
Car (cold)	838	1694	2532
Car (warm)	86	950	1036
Manhole (cold)	25	495	520
Manhole (warm)	82	1297	1379
Miscellaneous	81	-	81
Person	275	-	275
Street lamp (cold)	5	95	100
Street lamp (warm)	11	672	683

3.2   Thermal Urban Feature Semantic Segmentation

During the detection of thermal anomalies in UAV images, the majority of false positives arise from the common urban features listed in Table 1. The U-Net model is employed to identify these features and eliminate them, thus avoiding their misclassification as potential district heating network leaks [39]. U-Net is a

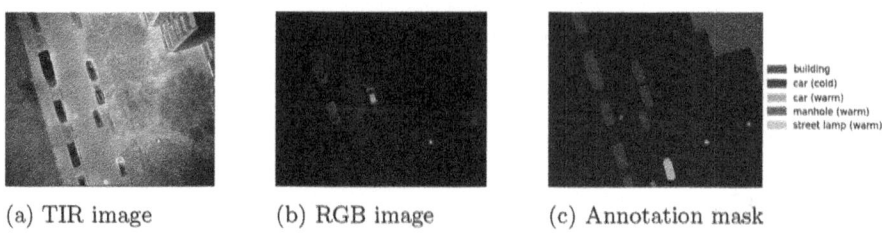

(a) TIR image   (b) RGB image   (c) Annotation mask

Fig. 1. Multispectral (RGB/TIR) image and annotations example [39].

convolutional neural network architecture designed especially for image segmentation tasks [15]. Its distinctive U-shaped structure consists of the main parts of an encoder and a decoder, connected by skip connections. The encoder, or contracting path, follows the typical architecture of a convolutional network, while the decoder recovers spatial information and generates the predicted segmentation mask. In this work, a ResNet-152 [17] encoder was used, also referred to as the backbone of the U-Net.

3.3 Framework

In order to apply the FL methods and algorithms and to transform an existing centralized ML workflow into a FL one, we use NVIDIA FL Application Runtime Environment (NVFlare) [18] in this work.

NVFlare is an open source framework for implementing FL workflows in Python. Apart from enabling the transformation of existing ML/DL workflows into a FL paradigm, it offers a wide range of features, which include: simulation and prototyping tools, privacy-preserving algorithms, built-in FL algorithms, productivity enhancement (like MLFlow [32]), provisioning tools for participant verification and secure communication, and many more [18].

3.4 Aggregation Algorithms and Workflows

The most commonly used aggregation algorithms in FL, including `FedAvg`, `FedProx`, `FedOpt`, and `Scaffold`, were selected for this work. `FedAvg` is the first and simplest algorithm introduced in FL, with others developed to address its drawbacks regarding the non-IID nature of datasets in FL settings.

As mentioned before, `FedAvg` uses weighted averages when aggregating local weights sent back from the clients.

`FedProx` introduces a proximal term $\frac{\mu}{2}\|w - w^t\|^2$ to the local objective function, where w is the local model weights, w^t is the global model weights, and μ controls regularization.

`FedOpt` uses stochastic gradient descent (SGD) to update the global model. The global gradient update is:

$$\Delta_t = \frac{1}{|S|} \sum_{i \in S} (w_{i,K}^t - w^t)$$

where S is the set of participating clients, $w_{i,K}^t$ is the local model after K training steps, and w^t is the global model weights in round t. The global model is then updated as:

$$w^{t+1} = \text{SERVEROPT}(w^t, -\Delta^t, \eta, t)$$

where η is the server learning rate and SERVEROPT refers to the optimization function or algorithm applied by the server to update the global model.

Scaffold is an enhanced FL algorithm that mitigates client drift caused by data heterogeneity using control variates. The global update is given by:

$$w^{t+1} = w^t + \eta \frac{1}{|S|} \sum_{i \in S} (\Delta_i^t - c_i^t + c^t), \quad c^t = \frac{1}{N} \sum_{i=1}^{N} c_i^t \tag{1}$$

where w^t is the global model in round t, Δ_i^t the local update, c_i^t and c^t are client and global control variates, η the learning rate, and $|S|$ the number of participating clients.

When FL was first introduced, it initially consisted of a Scatter & Gather (S&G) workflow, relying on a central server for aggregation.

When there is no trusted server available, Decentralized Federated Learning (DFL) such as Decentralized CWT (DCWT) and Swarm Learning (SL) can be used as alternatives. In such cases, communication is conducted peer-to-peer. Since there is no server to be compromised, DFL provides enhanced privacy protection compared to centralized approaches and it reduces network communication. In SL, one of the clients takes responsibility for performing aggregation. In the implementation of these workflows in NVFlare, a server is still present to handle administrative tasks, but no sensitive data is shared with it.

3.5   Training Setup

Training the semantic segmentation model requires considerable computational resources, so each client was assigned a GPU node on a HPC system. **Client-1** utilized a GPU node on HoreKa [19], while **Client-2** used a GPU node on HAICORE [16]. Both nodes provide the same resources, including 2 Intel Xeon Platinum 8368 processors with a combined 76 CPU Cores and 152 CPU Threads, 512 GB main memory, 4 NVIDIA A100-40 GPUs with 40 GB Memory each and a local NVMe SSD disk of 960 GB size. However, only one GPU from the four GPUs available on each node was used for each client. To run NVFlare clients on our HPC cluster, we used the SLURM job scheduler [38]. Using NVFlare's provisioning function several bash scripts for launching clients and the server are created. We modified these scripts to make them compatible with SLURM, enabling deployment on the HPC systems.

Since our dataset consists of images from two cities, our initial configuration was a simple location-based split with one client per city, as shown in Table 1. To evaluate the scalability another setup including five clients was tested. For this the data was splitted into five heterogeneous datasets to measure the performance of the FL algorithms with an increased number of clients while maintaining the same overall dataset size. In this setup, due to resource constraints, four clients were launched as a SLURM job, each running on the same node with a dedicated GPU. The fifth client was started with a separate SLURM job to prevent GPU memory allocation issues during training. Table 2 shows the object count and number of images per client. Still, the class count varies across the clients, and this significant variance indicates that the underlying distributions are not identical.

Table 2. Object counts for 5-clients

General	Client-1	Client-2	Client-3	Client-4	Client-5
No. images	159	159	160	164	151
Building	181	459	294	213	257
Car (cold)	231	1093	303	165	740
Car (warm)	72	123	181	302	358
Manhole (cold)	135	74	80	144	87
Manhole (warm)	367	166	293	287	266
Miscellaneous	135	74	80	144	87
Person	0	0	85	137	53
Street lamp (cold)	45	6	19	13	17
Street lamp (warm)	118	131	159	145	130

The server was set up on the bwCloud provided by KIT. The server ran as a Virtual Machine (VM) with `32 GB main memory` and `40 GB storage` [7].

Before sending a model to production, it is important to track and monitor it in order to optimize and check its quality. To this end, MLOps is an engineering practice that aims to automate and streamline the ML lifecycle. For this purpose, in this work MLflow was chosen for experiment tracking as it is supported by NVFlare, and an MLflow tracking server in production was provided by the AI4EOSC project [2]. During training, each client sends local metrics and parameters to the NVFlare server, which logs them on the configured MLflow server. By default, NVFlare does not log the global model in MLflow, so we modified NVFlare source code to enable this functionality for each experiment.

The metrics chosen for evaluating the model consist of the mean accuracy (mACC), mean weighted precision (mwP), mean weighted F_1-score (mwF$_1$) and mean weighted Intersection Over Union score (mwIoU). The weights in these metrics are determined by the number of pixels occupied by each specific class within the annotation masks.

The thermal urban feature semantic segmentation use case, originally developed and trained in a centralized way with predefined hyperparameters, was adapted into a FL workflow. The training hyperparameters identified by [40] were already optimized and considered ideal for this application. The parameters for the FL workflow were aligned with those of the CL workflow. The sigmoid focal cross-entropy loss function, Adam optimizer, a learning rate (lr) of 0.001 were used [39,40]. Experiments used 2 or 5 clients, with 4 rounds for two clients and 4, 7, or 13 for five clients. Local epochs were 18 for CL, 5 or 9 for five clients, and batch size was fixed at 8. As is [39], the dataset was split into 80% training and 20% testing. As shown in Table 2, the dataset is imbalanced which is addressed by the authors in greater detail in [39]—who apply techniques such as transfer learning and tailored loss functions and class-balanced metrics (e.g., weighted precision, F_1, IoU). Since we used the same model and configuration as in [39], the data imbalance is already addressed.

To efficiently calculate the energy consumption of each algorithm, we utilized the *perun* package to track the power draw of CPU, GPU, and memory of both clients and server [15]. Since our original server was set up on a VM, we could not efficiently track the energy consumption due to the lack of direct access to hardware performance counters. To overcome this limitation, we set up the server on bare-metal equipped with hardware energy measurement capabilities (such as Intel RAPL or a similar power monitoring framework) on a dedicated laptop. This setup allowed us to obtain more accurate energy consumption data for our algorithms and compare them.

4   Results and Discussions

The model is trained using the available images to automatically detect and eliminate false alarms. The script for this workflow is written in Python 3.8 and uses Tensorflow 2.10. The results of training multiple models using the various approaches introduced in Sect. 3.4 are presented and discussed in this section.

4.1   Comparison of the Aggregation Algorithms

This section presents the results of applying different FL aggregation algorithms, specifically FedAvg, FedProx, FedOpt, and Scaffold. Each experiment was conducted five times to ensure statistical significance. We first trained the model with two clients (KA and MU dataset). This experiment is referred to as the *2-client scenario*. Then, the dataset was divided into five equivalent subsets, and the experiment was repeated to investigate the results when all clients had datasets of equal size within the *5-client scenario*.

In FedOpt and Scaffold, where server-side optimization updates trainable weights, performance dropped after two rounds and continued to decline with each subsequent round when using standard Batch Normalization (BN) layers [6] in the U-Net backbone, despite weighted averaging of non-trainable parameters like running mean and variance. In BN, locally updated running statistics vary across clients, leading to inconsistencies that degrade global model performance and stability when aggregated. To address this, we replaced BN with Group Normalization (GN) [47], which normalizes within channel groups instead of batches, making it independent of batch size and more robust for FL. Moreover, since FedOpt uses SGD to update the global model, lr and momentum can be tuned to optimize the update. NVFlare uses default lr 1.0 and momentum of 0.9, and our experiments showed that reducing lr below 1.0 leads to a performance drop in the global model performance. We therefore adhered to the default values.

Table 3 shows the results of training the model within the *2-client scenario*. The first number reported for each client represents the average metric value over five executions of the algorithm, while the second number denotes the standard uncertainty. For the overall results, we computed a weighted average of each metric from both Client-1 and Client-2.

The global model aggregated using FedAvg achieved the highest performance across all metrics on the local test set of Client-1 (MU). It recorded a mean weighted precision of 0.945 ± 0.003, a mean accuracy of 0.94 ± 0.007, and an F_1 score of 0.937 ± 0.005. On the other hand, FedProx showed the weakest performance for this client, particularly in terms of mean accuracy 0.92 ± 0.01 and mean weighted IoU (0.85 ± 0.02). When comparing FedAvg with Scaffold, FedAvg shows slightly better performance in terms of mACC, mwF$_1$, and mwIoU. FedOpt consistently shows the weakest performance for Client-1, with values that often fall below other ranges of algorithms.

The global model aggregated using Scaffold demonstrated the best performance among FL algorithms on Client-2 and has the closest performance to CL. It surpasses FedAvg in both mACC (0.846 ± 0.009 vs. 0.66 ± 0.007) and mwF$_1$ (0.858 ± 0.007 vs. 0.810 ± 0.014). Additionally, Scaffold mwIoU of 0.777 ± 0.009 shows an improvement over FedAvg 0.737 ± 0.014. FedProx consistently shows the weakest performance for Client-2, with the widest error ranges indicating less stability.

When comparing CL with FL approaches based on overall results, the model trained using the CL method and the global model aggregated using FedAvg and Scaffold show comparable performance across several key metrics. For instance, FedAvg achieves a mwP of 0.935 ± 0.005, which is statistically consistent with CL with mwP of 0.939 ± 0.002. These results highlight that FedAvg and Scaffold can achieve performance comparable to centralized training while preserving data privacy. When considering error ranges, Scaffold and FedAvg can match or even exceed CL in specific metrics. Overall, this highlights their potential as effective FL strategies for our application. In contrast, FedProx and FedOpt show lower performance across several metrics, suggesting that while they can be effective, they may be more sensitive to client data variability.

In the subsequent experiments, we used the perun package [15] to measure the energy consumption of each FL algorithm during the training process. It also offers a calculation of an average carbon intensity of electricity based on a emissions factor which can differ per region and can be set manually by the user. This calculation was not reported within this work due to being highly versatile between different regions of the world. To ensure the reliability and consistency of our results, we took specific precautions to eliminate potential interference. We requested exclusive access to the HPC nodes where our clients were executed,

Table 3. Performance of the global model trained with different FL Algorithms and CL on the test set of Client-1 (MU), Client-2 (KA), and (MU+KA)

	Metric	Centralized	FedAvg	FedProx	FedOpt	Scaffold
Client-1	mwP	**0.952 ± 0.017**	0.945 ± 0.003	0.924 ± 0.007	0.913 ± 0.001	0.938 ± 0.001
	mACC	**0.949 ± 0.003**	0.940 ± 0.007	0.911 ± 0.006	0.879 ± 0.009	0.923 ± 0.004
	mwF$_1$	**0.944 ± 0.002**	0.937 ± 0.005	0.903 ± 0.009	0.887 ± 0.005	0.924 ± 0.002
	mwIoU	**0.907 ± 0.005**	0.900 ± 0.007	0.850 ± 0.01	0.822 ± 0.009	0.877 ± 0.004
Client-2	mwP	0.870 ± 0.015	0.853 ± 0.012	0.834 ± 0.025	0.843 ± 0.005	**0.879 ± 0.003**
	mACC	0.866 ± 0.012	0.846 ± 0.009	0.818 ± 0.017	0.833 ± 0.005	**0.866 ± 0.007**
	mwF$_1$	0.847 ± 0.017	0.810 ± 0.014	0.779 ± 0.031	0.818 ± 0.004	**0.858 ± 0.007**
	mwIoU	0.774 ± 0.018	0.737 ± 0.014	0.702 ± 0.029	0.733 ± 0.005	**0.777 ± 0.009**
Overall	mwP	**0.939 ± 0.002**	0.935 ± 0.005	0.913 ± 0.011	0.905 ± 0.002	0.931 ± 0.001
	mACC	**0.931 ± 0.002**	0.930 ± 0.007	0.900 ± 0.008	0.873 ± 0.008	0.917 ± 0.004
	mwF$_1$	**0.928 ± 0.002**	0.922 ± 0.007	0.888 ± 0.013	0.879 ± 0.006	0.916 ± 0.003
	mwIoU	0.884 ± 0.003	0.881 ± 0.008	0.833 ± 0.014	0.812 ± 0.009	**0.865 ± 0.005**

ensuring that no other jobs were running on the same nodes during the experiments. This isolation minimized resource contention and provided a controlled environment for energy measurement. In the *5-client scenario*, four clients shared the same node, making it challenging to measure the energy consumption of each client individually. Therefore, we conducted energy consumption measurements for only two clients. For CL, we used the same dedicated node on HoreKa as for the FL clients, utilizing one of the four available GPUs.

The energy consumption on the server for each algorithm was very low (14–29 kJ). Figure 2 represents the mean execution time and energy consumption of various FL algorithms for two clients. As shown in the figure, Scaffold demonstrates the highest execution time, resulting in the largest energy consumption across all sites. On average, it requires 103.33 min with a standard deviation of 8.84 min, highlighting its computational intensity. In our application, the energy consumption and runtime of CL compared to FedAvg show significant reductions. For energy consumption, CL consumes 382.279 kJ, whereas FedAvg consumes 1008.9152 kJ, resulting in a percentage reduction of approximately 163.97%. Similarly, for runtime, CL takes 643.245 s compared to 1687.0624 s for FedAvg leading to a percentage reduction of approximately 162.3%.

Reducing the available data per client dividing it by five leads to slower convergence. With five clients instead of two, each client contributes smaller updates per round, requiring more communication to reach the same performance. Since each client only accesses $\frac{1}{5}$ of the full data, we ensure a fair comparison with CL by maintaining the ratio $\frac{\texttt{num\_rounds} \times \texttt{num\_local\_epochs}}{\texttt{num\_clients}} = \texttt{num\_epochs\_CL}$. For these reasons, we first reduced the number of local epochs to five and increased the number of rounds to 13. In another experiment, we kept the local epochs at nine and increased the rounds to seven. Both setups achieved similar performance,

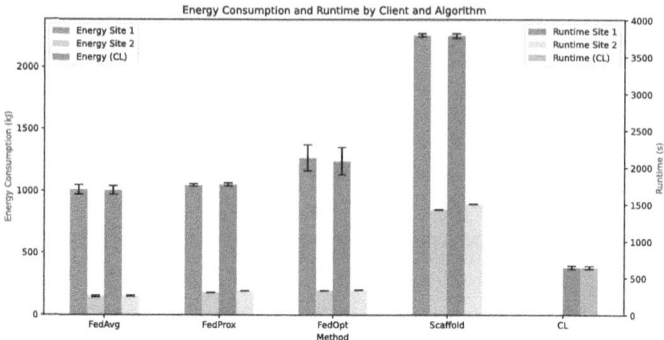

Fig. 2. Energy consumption and runtime by each site and each algorithm.

but with fewer epochs and more rounds, communication increased, leading to longer training time. Therefore, we settled on nine local epochs and seven rounds as a balanced choice. Table 4 shows the performance of the trained global model on the test dataset (KA+MU). When the dataset size is equal among clients, FedProx performed similar to CL. In FedProx, the aggregation on the server is done similarly to FedAvg. In the case of two clients, the global weights lean toward the MU dataset because of its larger weight. This means that when we compute the proximal term in FedProx the influence of the MU dataset is disproportionately high, potentially causing the corresponding client to pull the global model further away from the parameters of KA dataset. In contrast, in the *5-client scenario*, the MU dataset is divided among several clients. Consequently, the global weights become more reflective of the average of all local weights. This balanced aggregation results in a smaller difference between local and global models, thereby reducing the magnitude of the proximal term. With a lower proximal penalty, local updates are less constrained, which can lead to more effective convergence and improved overall performance in FedProx compared to the *2-client scenario*.

In this case, the performance of Scaffold dropped by 3–5% on each metric compared to CL. This decline may be due to the reduced dataset size available to each client, which adversely affects the estimation of the control variate.

FedAvg, achieving a mean weighted precision of 0.919 ± 0.012, while FedOpt still performed the worst among other FL algorithms. In FedAvg, the MU dataset features richer annotations and includes every class. In the *2-client scenario*, we assign greater weight to the MU dataset during aggregation, while the KA dataset receives less weight. However, in a *5-client scenario*, the MU dataset is split across several clients, resulting in it having the same weight as the KA dataset during aggregation. This difference in weighting may be a key factor contributing to the observed performance drop with five clients compared to two.

Table 4. Comparison of different FL algorithms and CL (overall) for five clients.

Metric	Centralized	FedAvg	FedProx	FedOpt	Scaffold
mwP	**0.939 ± 0.002**	0.919 ± 0.012	0.932 ± 0.003	0.891 ± 0.006	0.900 ± 0.002
mACC	**0.931 ± 0.002**	0.916 ± 0.013	0.926 ± 0.006	0.877 ± 0.006	0.879 ± 0.004
mwF$_1$	**0.928 ± 0.002**	0.904 ± 0.016	0.918 ± 0.008	0.865 ± 0.008	0.874 ± 0.002
mwIoU	**0.884 ± 0.003**	0.855 ± 0.019	0.872 ± 0.009	0.801 ± 0.009	0.810 ± 0.003

4.2   Comparison of the Workflow

In NVFlare, CWT workflow allows for configuring the order of clients during training. Specifically, the cyclic_order parameter can be set to determine whether
the sequence of clients is fixed or random for each round. To investigate how the
order of clients affects the performance of the model, especially with two clients
where the dataset sizes differ, we conducted several experiments using both fixed
and random orders.

Table 5 presents the overall results of training the model with two and five
clients across different workflows. In *2-client scenario*, the SL workflow achieved
similar performance to S&G (FedAvg), as expected: The only difference between
these workflows is that in S&G, aggregation is performed on the server, whereas
in SL, this task is done by one of the clients. In terms of execution time, the
SL algorithm achieves a mean execution time of 949.86 s (for 2 clients), whereas
FedAvg records a significantly higher mean execution time of 2906.07 s, representing an approximate 205.95% increase in training time. This is due to the
elimination of communication overhead between clients and the server, which
reduces latency and speeds up the training process in the SL workflow.

In CWT, we first train the model on the MU dataset as Client-1 and then transfer the weights of the model to Client-2 (KA dataset). In the next experiment,
we also perform training in the reverse order, first on Client-1 (KA dataset) and
then on Client-2 (MU dataset). The results of these experiments are presented
in Table 5: We observe that training the model first on the KA dataset followed
by MU (CWT KA-MU) consistently yields better performance across all metrics
compared to training in the reverse order (CWT MU-KA). This suggests that KA
with less data provides a stronger initial model foundation, leading to better
generalization when fine-tuned on MU. Conversely, training on the larger MU
dataset first, then on KA, can cause the model to overfit the smaller KA dataset.

In the case of five clients, we used a random order, and the performance was
similar to that of the model trained with a fixed order (Client-1 to Client-5).
Therefore, in CWT, the order of the clients should be carefully considered when the
dataset sizes differ, as it can significantly impact the final model performance.

Furthermore, comparing different workflows, SL outperforming all the CWT
and DCWT variations. This indicates that local aggregation in SL may provide
better feature learning compared to CWT.

As shown in Table 5, for the *5-client scenario*, all frameworks exhibit statistically consistent performance across key metrics. Considering error ranges, the

results indicate no significant differences among the methods, suggesting that each approach is capable of delivering comparable results despite variations in their training and aggregation processes.

Table 5. Comparison of Different Workflows in FL.

	Two Clients						Five Clients		
Metric	S&G (FedAvg)	Swarm Learning	CWT (MU-KA)	CWT (KA-MU)	DCWT (MU-KA)	DCWT (KA-MU)	S&G (FedAvg)	Swarm Learning	CWT Random
mwP	0.939	**0.949**	0.926	0.940	0.920	0.940	0.919	**0.939**	0.935
	±0.002	**±0.004**	±0.008	±0.002	±0.005	±0.009	±0.012	**±0.003**	±0.005
mACC	0.931	**0.950**	0.851	0.901	0.864	0.920	0.916	**0.934**	0.926
	±0.002	**±0.004**	±0.031	±0.022	±0.011	±0.007	±0.013	**±0.003**	±0.004
mF$_1$	0.928	**0.943**	0.873	0.926	0.876	0.921	0.904	**0.923**	0.919
	±0.002	**±0.005**	±0.022	±0.002	±0.006	±0.005	±0.016	**±0.005**	±0.005
mwIoU	0.884	**0.910**	0.796	0.878	0.802	0.872	0.855	**0.883**	0.875
	±0.003	**±0.007**	±0.036	±0.003	±0.010	±0.008	±0.019	**±0.005**	±0.006

Figure 3 represents the mean execution time and energy consumption of various FL workflows for two sites. SL records a mean time execution of 952.42 s whereas DCWT records a significantly higher mean execution time of 1949.69 s. This represents an approximate 105% increase in training time. In DCWT, clients train the model sequentially, requiring each client to wait for the previous one to complete its training. As the number of clients increases, this sequential process leads to longer overall training times. Again, comparing DCWT to CWT, when communication time with the server is removed, DCWT demonstrates improved efficiency.

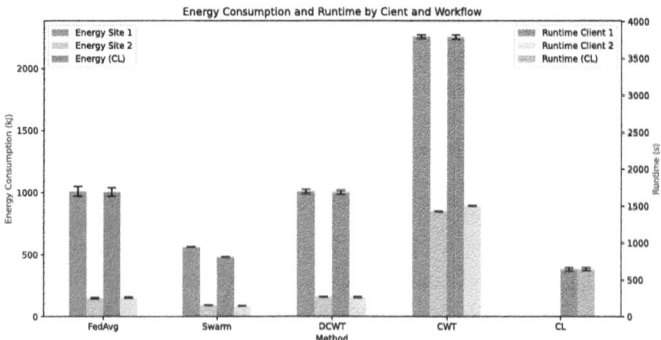

Fig. 3. Energy consumption and runtime by each site and each workflow.

Conclusions

In this work, we successfully transformed the introduced application from a traditional ML workflow into a FL workflow. The results show that FL algorithms can achieve comparable performance metrics to CL in detecting small objects within UAV images. FedProx shows variability in performance depending on client configurations. It performs poorly in the *2-client scenario* but substantially improves and achieves comparable results to CL in the *5-client scenario* due to reduced proximal penalties when data is more evenly distributed. FedOpt introduces additional hyperparameters, making it more challenging to set them optimally without prior data insights. Scaffold, on the other hand, can enhance performance but requires increased execution time and energy consumption, and in some cases, the improvements may not be significant enough to justify the additional cost. When the number of clients increases, convergence slows due to less data per client. Adjusting the training strategy by balancing the number of local epochs and aggregation rounds helps achieve optimal trade-offs between performance and computational cost.

Despite these promising findings, some limitations remain. Due to limited access to real-world data, scalability was tested only with a simulated setup of five clients, which may not capture real-world complexity. Moreover, while our study focuses on evaluating performance and system-level efficiency across various FL workflows, model interpretability was not within scope. In future work this aspect should be considered.

We also observed practical system-level challenges. Although HPC systems offer additional computational resources, batch job scheduling limits client availability, causing some clients to lack resources when others are ready.

In terms of sustainability, in our case study, when we compared to centralized training, experimental evidence shows FL can consume more energy than its centralized version in certain scenarios. Introducing decentralized workflows like SL and DCWT show a gain in shorter training time. Among FL workflows, SL demonstrates superior computational efficiency and runtime performance compared to S&G and CWT approaches. However, this relationship is not universal. It is highly depending on the setup, including the deployed machines, used algorithm/workflow and even the geographical region of the participating devices.

Acknowledgment. This work is supported by the AI4EOSC project, which receives funding from the European Union's Horizon Europe 2022 research and innovation programme under agreement 101058593. Additionally, computational resources were provided by the HoreKa supercomputer, funded by the Ministry of Science, Research and the Arts Baden-Württemberg and the Federal Ministry of Education and Research, and by the Helmholtz Association Initiative and Networking Fund through the Helmholtz AI platform grant and the HAICORE@KIT partition.

References

1. Agripina, N., Shen, H., Mafukidze, B.: Advances, challenges & recent developments in federated learning. Open Access Library J. **11**, 1–1 (2024)
2. AI4EOSC. https://ai4eosc.eu/
3. Amjoud, A.B., Amrouch, M.: Object detection using deep learning, CNNs and vision transformers: a review. IEEE Access **11**, 35479–35516 (2023). https://doi.org/10.1109/ACCESS.2023.3266093
4. Awasthi, R., et al.: Artificial intelligence in healthcare: 2023 year in review. medRxiv (2024). https://doi.org/10.1101/2024.02.28.24303482
5. Banabilah, S., Aloqaily, M., Alsayed, E., Malik, N., Jararweh, Y.: Federated learning review: fundamentals, enabling technologies, and future applications. Inf. Process. Manage. **59**(6), 103061 (2022)
6. Bjorck, N., Gomes, C.P., Selman, B., Weinberger, K.Q.: Understanding batch normalization. In: Bengio, S., Wallach, H., Larochelle, H., Grauman, K., Cesa-Bianchi, N., Garnett, R. (eds.) Advances in Neural Information Processing Systems, vol. 31. Curran Associates, Inc. (2018)
7. bwCloud main page. https://www.bw-cloud.org/de/
8. Chang, K., et al.: Distributed deep learning networks among institutions for medical imaging. J. Am. Med. Inform. Assoc. **25**(8), 945–954 (2018)
9. Chellapandi, V.P., Yuan, L., Brinton, C.G., Żak, S.H., Wang, Z.: Federated learning for connected and automated vehicles: a survey of existing approaches and challenges. IEEE Trans. Intell. Veh. **9**(1), 119–137 (2024). https://doi.org/10.1109/TIV.2023.3332675
10. Chhikara, P., Tekchandani, R., Kumar, N., Tanwar, S.: Federated learning-based aerial image segmentation for collision-free movement and landing. In: Proceedings of the 4th ACM MobiCom Workshop on Drone Assisted Wireless Communications for 5G and Beyond, pp. 13–18. DroneCom 2021, Association for Computing Machinery, New York, NY, USA (2021)
11. Farsi, A.A., Khan, A., Rizwan, M., Bait-Suwailam, M.M.: Privacy and security challenges in federated learning for UAV systems: a comprehensive review (2024). https://doi.org/10.22541/au.172450870.03139596/v1
12. Feng, C., et al.: Assessing the sustainability and trustworthiness of federated learning models. Lynn and Bovet, Gérôme and Stiller, Burkhard, Assessing the Sustainability and Trustworthiness of Federated Learning Models (2025)
13. Grigorescu, S., Trasnea, B., Cocias, T., Macesanu, G.: A survey of deep learning techniques for autonomous driving. J. Field Robot. **37**(3), 362–386 (2020)
14. Guan, H., Yap, P.T., Bozoki, A., Liu, M.: Federated learning for medical image analysis: a survey. Pattern Recogn. **151**, 110424 (2024)
15. Gutiérrez Hermosillo Muriedas, J.P., Flügel, K., Debus, C., Obermaier, H., Streit, A., Götz, M.: perun: benchmarking energy consumption of high-performance computing applications. In: Cano, J., Dikaiakos, M.D., Papadopoulos, G.A., Pericàs, M., Sakellariou, R. (eds.) Euro-Par 2023: Parallel Processing, pp. 17–31. Springer Nature Switzerland, Cham (2023)
16. Haicore main page https://www2.helmholtz.ai/themenmenue/you-helmholtz-ai/computing-resources/index.html
17. He, K., Zhang, X., Ren, S., Sun, J.: Deep residual learning for image recognition. arXiv preprint arXiv:1512.03385 (2015)
18. Roth, H.R., Cheng, Y., Wen, Y., Yang, I., et al.: NVIDIA FLARE: federated Learning from Simulation to Real-World (2023). https://doi.org/10.48550/arXiv.2210.13291

19. Horeka main page. https://www.scc.kit.edu/dienste/horeka.php
20. Kairouz, P., McMahan, H.B., et al.: Advances and open problems in federated learning. Found. Trends Mach. Learn. **14**, 1–210 (2021). https://doi.org/10.1561/2200000083
21. Kamp, M., Fischer, J., Vreeken, J.: Federated learning from small datasets (2023). https://arxiv.org/abs/2110.03469
22. Karimireddy, S.P., Kale, S., Mohri, M., Reddi, S.J., Stich, S.U., Suresh, A.T.: Scaffold: stochastic controlled averaging for federated learning (2021). https://arxiv.org/abs/1910.06378
23. Li, Q., He, B., Song, D.: Model-contrastive federated learning . In: 2021 IEEE/CVF Conference on Computer Vision and Pattern Recognition (CVPR), pp. 10708–10717. IEEE Computer Society, Los Alamitos, CA, USA (2021)
24. Li, T., Sahu, A.K., Zaheer, M., Sanjabi, M., Talwalkar, A., Smith, V.: Federated optimization in heterogeneous networks (2020). https://arxiv.org/abs/1812.06127
25. Li, X., Jiang, M., Zhang, X., Kamp, M., Dou, Q.: FedBN: federated learning on non-IID features via local batch normalization. In: International Conference on Learning Representations (2021) https://openreview.net/forum?id=6YEQUn0QICG
26. Lu, Z., Pan, H., Dai, Y., Si, X., Zhang, Y.: Federated learning with Non-IID data: a survey. IEEE Internet Things J. **11**(11), 19188–19209 (2024)
27. Manthe, M., Duffner, S., Lartizien, C.: Federated brain tumor segmentation: an extensive benchmark. Med. Image Anal. **97**, 103270 (2024)
28. Mayer, Z., Epperlein, A., Vollmer, E., Volk, R., Schultmann, F.: Investigating the quality of UAV-based images for the thermographic analysis of buildings. Remote Sens. **15**(2), 301 (2023)
29. McMahan, B., Moore, E., Ramage, D., Hampson, S., Arcas, B.A.: Communication-Efficient Learning of Deep Networks from Decentralized Data. In: Singh, A., Zhu, J. (eds.) Proceedings of the 20th International Conference on Artificial Intelligence and Statistics. Proceedings of Machine Learning Research, vol. 54, pp. 1273–1282. PMLR (2017). https://proceedings.mlr.press/v54/mcmahan17a.html
30. Miao, J., Yang, Z., Fan, L., Yang, Y.: FedSeg: class-heterogeneous federated learning for semantic segmentation. In: 2023 IEEE/CVF Conference on Computer Vision and Pattern Recognition (CVPR), pp. 8042–8052 (2023). https://doi.org/10.1109/CVPR52729.2023.00777
31. Minaee, S., Boykov, Y., Porikli, F., Plaza, A., Kehtarnavaz, N., Terzopoulos, D.: Image segmentation using deep learning: a survey. IEEE Trans. Pattern Anal. Mach. Intell. **44**(7), 3523–3542 (2022)
32. Mlflow. https://mlflow.org/
33. European Parliament - European Union: Regulation (EU) 2016/679 of the european parliament and of the council on the protection of natural persons with regard to the processing of personal data and on the free movement of such data (general data protection regulation). https://eur-lex.europa.eu/eli/reg/2016/679/oj (2016). Accessed 17 Jan 2025
34. Qiu, X., et al.: A first look into the carbon footprint of federated learning. J. Mach. Learn. Res. **24**(1), 1–23 (2024)
35. Rashidi, G., Bounias, D., Bujotzek, M., Mora, A.M., Neher, P., Maier-Hein, K.H.: The potential of federated learning for self-configuring medical object detection in heterogeneous data distributions. Sci. Rep. **14**(1), 23844 (2024)
36. Reddi, S.J., et al.: Adaptive federated optimization. In: International Conference on Learning Representations (2021). https://openreview.net/forum?id=LkFG3lB13U5

37. Ronneberger, O., Fischer, P., Brox, T.: U-net: convolutional networks for biomedical image segmentation. In: Navab, N., Hornegger, J., Wells, W.M., Frangi, A.F. (eds.) Medical Image Computing and Computer-Assisted Intervention – MICCAI 2015, pp. 234–241. Springer, Cham (2015)
38. Slurm workload manager documentation. https://slurm.schedmd.com/documentation.html
39. Vollmer, E., et al.: Enhancing UAS-based multispectral semantic segmentation through feature engineering. IEEE J. Sel. Top. Appl. Earth Observ. Remote Sens. **18**, 6206–6216 (2025)
40. Vollmer, E., Klug, L., Volk, R., Schultmann, F.: AI in multispectral image analysis: implementing a deep learning model for the segmentation of common thermal urban features to assist in the automation of infrastructure-related maintenance. Presentation at the 4th AI in AEC Conference, Helsinki, Finland (2024). https://doi.org/10.5445/IR/1000169834
41. Vollmer, E., et al.: Thermal urban feature segmentation - Multispectral (RGB + thermal) UAS-based images from Germany with annotations (2025). https://doi.org/10.5281/zenodo.10814413
42. Vollmer, E., Ruck, J., Volk, R., Schultmann, F.: Detecting district heating leaks in thermal imagery: comparison of anomaly detection methods. Autom. Constr. **168**, 105709 (2024)
43. Vollmer, E., Volk, R., Schultmann, F.: Automatic analysis of UAS-based thermal images to detect leakages in district heating systems. Int. J. Remote Sens. **44**, 31 (2023)
44. Wang, F., Gursoy, M.C., Velipasalar, S.: Feature-based federated transfer learning: communication efficiency, robustness and privacy. IEEE Trans. Mach. Learn. Commun. Network. **2**, 1 (2024)
45. Warnat-Herresthal, S., Schultze, H., Shastry, K.: Swarm learning for decentralized and confidential clinical machine learning. Nature **594**(7862), 265–270 (2021)
46. Wu, P., Zhang, Z., Peng, X., et al.: Deep learning solutions for smart city challenges in urban development. Sci. Rep. **14**(1), 5176 (2024)
47. Wu, Y., He, K.: Group normalization (2018). https://arxiv.org/abs/1803.08494

Geometric Modeling, Graphics and Visualization

Robust Adaptive Masked Face Recognition Using Mediapipe and Advanced ResNet50 with Multi-Layer Feature Fusion

Hoang Huy Le, Ai My Thi Nguyen, and Vinh Dinh Nguyen[✉]

Department of Information Technology, FPT University, Can Tho, Vietnam
{hoanglhce170452,aintmcs171632}@fpt.edu.vn, vinhnd29@fe.edu.vn

Abstract. Since the COVID-19 pandemic, wearing masks has become a common practice worldwide, further compounded by the growing issue of air pollution. As masks have become an essential part of daily life, they pose a significant challenge to facial recognition systems, which struggle to accurately identify individuals when key facial features are obscured. This study focuses on improving the performance of existing masked facial recognition systems to better adapt to these real-world conditions. This work builds on an existing framework for masked face detection, proposing several optimizations to enhance recognition accuracy. The approach integrates Mediapipe for reliable face detection, combined with ResNet50 for feature extraction and a novel Feature Concatenation technique that merges multiple facial feature vectors to create more robust representations. To improve model adaptability to masked faces, we employ data augmentation techniques that simulate various real-world conditions, such as different mask types and lighting variations. Additionally, we performed ResNet50 fine-tuning on a specific masked dataset to increase robustness against partial face occlusions. Recognition is then carried out using a cosine similarity-based distance metric, ensuring both computational efficiency and high accuracy. Our optimizations resulted in a significant performance improvement, achieving a precision of 99.47% on the Celebrity dataset. These results demonstrate the potential to refine existing methodologies for better masked facial recognition, contributing to more reliable applications in security, healthcare, and other sectors.

Keywords: Masked face recognition · Feature concatenation · ResNet50

1 Introduction

Face recognition (FR) systems traditionally rely on key facial features—eyes, nose, and mouth—for accurate identification. However, widespread mask usage due to COVID-19, public health policies, and pollution has significantly impacted recognition accuracy, complicating both authentication (1:1) and identification

© The Author(s), under exclusive license to Springer Nature Switzerland AG 2025
O. Gervasi et al. (Eds.): ICCSA 2025, LNCS 15648, pp. 305–319, 2025.
https://doi.org/10.1007/978-3-031-97000-9_19

(1:N) tasks [1]. In critical applications such as healthcare, airports, immigration points, and secure access control, reliable recognition of masked individuals is essential. Studies, including those by NIST [2], highlight that most FR algorithms were designed for unmasked faces, making them less effective when dealing with occlusions. Additionally, many in-house systems rely on datasets with predominantly unmasked images, further reducing accuracy. To address these challenges, various approaches have been explored. For instance, methods such as Principal Component Analysis (PCA) have been used for feature extraction under occlusion [3]. Although PCA can handle partial occlusion, it often struggles with high-dimensional data and diverse real-world variations—such as differences in mask styles and lighting conditions—which limit its practical robustness. More recently, deep learning-based models have shown promise. Convolutional Neural Networks (CNNs) [4], Transfer Learning [5], and Data Augmentation techniques [6] have been employed to enhance feature extraction and generalization when dealing with partially occluded faces. Despite these advances, even state-of-the-art methods, including approaches that combine adversarial learning with masked augmentation, face challenges in terms of robustness and adaptability, particularly due to their reliance on synthetic mask generation and controlled adversarial scenarios. In this context, our research aims to enhance the accuracy and robustness of masked face recognition by refining and integrating existing methodologies. We propose a framework that leverages Mediapipe for precise face detection and landmark localization, ResNet50 for deep feature extraction, and feature concatenation to integrate diverse facial representations. Additionally, data augmentation and fine-tuning strategies optimize our model for various mask styles and lighting conditions, while cosine similarity metrics robustly compare face embeddings. By combining these advanced techniques, our study strives to develop a more reliable and adaptive solution for face recognition in masked scenarios, addressing the shortcomings identified in both conventional systems and recent literature [1].

The paper is organized as follows: Sect. 2 reviews existing methods and their limitations. Section 3 outlines our proposed approach in detail. Section 4 describes the experimental setup and presents a comparative evaluation, and Sect. 5 concludes the study with key findings and suggestions for future research.

2   Related Work

Research in masked facial recognition has evolved significantly. This section reviews key developments in the field, focusing on traditional approaches, deep learning methods, and recent advances in handling occluded facial recognition.

2.1   Traditional Computer Vision Approaches

Initial efforts in masked face recognition relied heavily on classical computer vision techniques. Principal Component Analysis (PCA) emerged as a foundational method for feature extraction in partially occluded faces. Although PCA effectively reduces dimensionality and extracts features, it faces significant challenges when processing high-dimensional data and adapting to diverse real-world variations [8].

For example, one modified PCA approach that focused on extracting features from the eye region achieved approximately 89% accuracy—with further refinements pushing performance up to 91.3% even under significant mask occlusion [14]. In addition to PCA, traditional techniques such as Scale-Invariant Feature Transform (SIFT), Histogram of Oriented Gradients (HOG), and Local Binary Patterns (LBP) have also been explored. In controlled experiments, a combination of LBP with HOG reached around 87.5% accuracy [9]. However, these methods typically require careful, hand-crafted feature engineering and often show limited adaptability when confronted with varying mask types or challenging lighting conditions [8].

2.2 Deep Learning Advancements

The emergence of deep learning has revolutionized masked face recognition. Convolutional Neural Networks (CNNs) have demonstrated a remarkable ability to handle partial occlusions and extract discriminative features from large-scale datasets. Transfer learning, in particular, has proven effective by adapting pre-trained models to the nuances of masked face recognition. For instance, fine-tuning a VGGFace model achieved 95.7% accuracy [11], while a modified FaceNet architecture reported 94.3% accuracy [12]. Recent work further confirms that deep learning methods can maintain robust performance even under substantial occlusions [13].

Data augmentation strategies are crucial for enhancing model generalization when occlusions are present. A synthetic mask generation technique was shown to improve recognition accuracy by 7.2%, and a multi-style mask augmentation approach helped models achieve up to 96.8% accuracy [10]. Despite these advances, deep learning approaches face notable limitations. They typically require large-scale, high-quality annotated datasets—a resource that is still relatively scarce for masked faces. Moreover, reliance on synthetic augmentation can sometimes introduce biases that fail to capture real-world variability, and the associated computational demands may limit real-time deployment in resource-constrained settings [7,10].

2.3 Advanced Recognition Strategies

Recent research has focused on more sophisticated approaches to further enhance recognition performance under occlusion. Attention-based architectures that dynamically focus on the visible facial regions have achieved accuracy levels as high as 97.2% [15]. In parallel, multi-task learning frameworks—which simultaneously perform face detection, landmark localization, and recognition—have reached up to 98.1% accuracy [16]. Although these strategies offer high performance, they generally require significant computational resources and extensive, diverse training data to generalize effectively in real-world scenarios.

Adversarial learning techniques have also shown promise. One adversarial framework, for instance, achieved 97.8% accuracy and demonstrated improved generalization across various mask types [17]. However, these methods often still depend on synthetic mask generation, which can lead to discrepancies between training data and real-world conditions.

2.4   Feature Detection and Similarity Metrics

Advances in feature detection and similarity metrics have further boosted recognition performance. A modified MediaPipe framework was reported to achieve 98.5% accuracy in landmark detection [18], and a fine-tuned ResNet50 model reached 99.1% accuracy in recognition tasks [19]. Moreover, studies comparing different similarity metrics found that cosine similarity can outperform Euclidean distance when matching facial features; an ensemble approach to similarity metrics even achieved 99.2% accuracy [20]. Despite these impressive figures, such methods can struggle when dealing with low-quality images or severe occlusions, and the computational complexity of some similarity measures may impede their use in real-time applications.

3   The Proposed Method

3.1   System Architecture and Workflow

We propose a deep learning-based face recognition system that leverages data augmentation and advanced feature extraction techniques to address the challenges posed by real-world variations in facial appearances—especially in scenarios involving face masks. The system is structured into two main phases: a comprehensive Training Pipeline that builds a robust recognition model and a Testing Pipeline that facilitates real-time face detection and identification. As shown in the Fig. 1, the Training phase (highlighted in purple) encompasses image preprocessing, data augmentation, and feature extraction, while the Testing phase (highlighted in yellow) handles real-time video capture, face detection, and similarity-based recognition.

Training Phase. In the training phase, input processing is performed using MediaPipe to accurately detect and extract facial regions from original face images. To enhance model adaptability, both masked and unmasked face variants are generated, ensuring exposure to diverse real-world conditions. Data augmentation techniques, including rotation, flipping, zooming, brightness adjustments, and noise addition, are applied to simulate various environmental and pose variations, enriching the training dataset and improving model robustness.

Following augmentation, feature extraction is conducted using ResNet50, which extracts deep, discriminative facial features. The training process consists of two phases. In the first training phase, the dataset is used to train an initial model, where classification layers are learned based on ResNet50 features, and

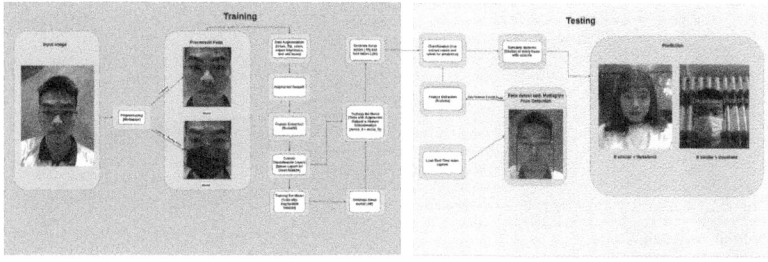

Fig. 1. Overview of the proposed face recognition system with mask-handling capability.

the trained model is saved as a Keras model (.h5). The second training phase involves feature concatenation, where extracted features from ResNet50 are further processed by combining multiple dense layers (e.g., $dense_4 + dense_5$). This extended feature set is then used to re-train the model, significantly enhancing recognition accuracy. For classification, custom dense layers are applied to the extracted features, enabling precise face identification. Finally, in the model generation step, the fully trained model is stored as a Keras model (.h5) along with labeled face data (.pkl), ensuring seamless integration into the testing environment.

Testing Phase. In the testing phase, the system performs real-time face detection by capturing video input and utilizing MediaPipe to efficiently detect faces within each frame. Once detected, feature extraction is conducted using the pre-trained ResNet50 model to obtain feature embeddings, ensuring consistency with the training phase.

Next, the system performs similarity computation by comparing the extracted embeddings of detected faces with those stored during training using robust distance metrics. Based on these similarity scores, the system proceeds with prediction and decision-making. If the computed similarity exceeds a predefined threshold, the system identifies the face and assigns the corresponding name along with a confidence score. Conversely, if the similarity falls below the threshold, the face is classified as *Unknown*.

3.2   Network Architecture

Our proposed network architecture is specifically designed for masked face recognition, with careful consideration of feature extraction at different scales. As illustrated in Fig. 2, the dotted rectangle labeled "The Proposed Method" highlights our custom enhancements added on top of the ResNet50 backbone. These enhancements focus on robust feature representation and improved classification under mask occlusion.

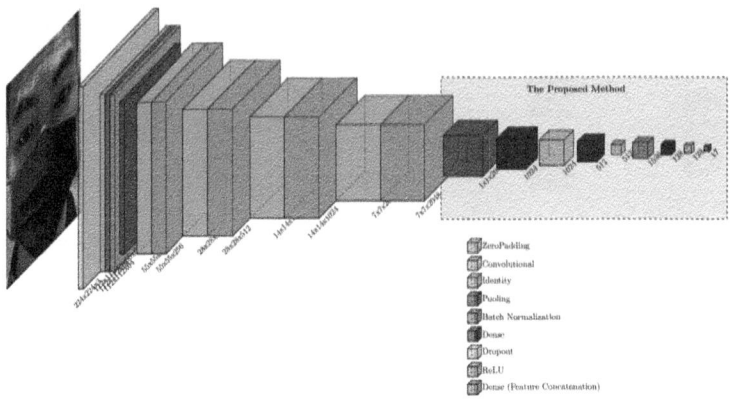

Fig. 2. Proposed Architecture for Robust Masked Face Recognition.

Input Processing Layer. The input to the system consists of 224×224×3 RGB images, which undergo initial processing, including normalization and standardization, to ensure consistency across the dataset.

Feature Extraction Layers. To extract robust facial features, the system utilizes the ResNet50 architecture from VGGFace as the base model. Since this pre-trained network has already learned rich facial representations from a large dataset, its layers are frozen to retain the learned features. On top of ResNet50, additional custom layers are incorporated to refine feature representation and enhance classification performance. These include fully connected (Dense) layers for feature transformation, batch normalization for stability, dropout layers to mitigate overfitting, and ReLU activation to introduce non-linearity. A feature concatenation mechanism is also applied to combine multiple feature representations, further enriching the decision-making process.

Fine-tuning layers are then added to further improve performance. Specifically, two Dense layers ($dense_4 + dense_5$) with 1024 and 512 neurons, respectively, are included, each incorporating ReLU activation, L2 regularization, and dropout (0.5 for the 1024-neuron layer and 0.3 for the 512-neuron layer). The final stage consists of a series of Dense layers (1024 → 512 → final embedding), followed by a softmax layer whose number of units corresponds to the target classes. By freezing the ResNet50 layers and fine-tuning only the newly added Dense layers, the system effectively leverages pre-trained knowledge while adapting to the specific face recognition task.

Layer Components. The model incorporates essential deep learning components such as convolutional layers for feature extraction, identity connections to improve gradient flow, pooling layers to increase the receptive field, batch normalization for stable training, and dropout layers to prevent overfitting.

Design Rationale. The architecture is specifically optimized for masked face recognition by employing progressive feature extraction with decreasing spatial dimensions, balanced use of convolutional and identity blocks, and strategic placement of pooling layers. Additionally, regularization techniques such as dropout and batch normalization are integrated to enhance generalization. This design ensures that the system effectively captures facial features despite mask occlusion, maintains robustness across various scales, and provides an efficient and reliable processing pipeline for real-world applications.

3.3   Mathematical Foundations

Our proposed method is underpinned by a series of mathematical formulations that ensure its robustness and accuracy.

Face Cropping Formulation. Given an image of dimensions $W \times H$ and a set of facial landmarks $\{(x_i, y_i)\}_{i=1}^n$, the coordinates for cropping the face are computed as follows:

$$x_{\min} = \min_{1 \leq i \leq n} \{x_i\}, \quad x_{\max} = \max_{1 \leq i \leq n} \{x_i\}, \tag{1}$$

$$y_{\min} = \min_{1 \leq i \leq n} \{y_i\}, \quad y_{\max} = \max_{1 \leq i \leq n} \{y_i\}, \tag{2}$$

where x_i, y_i are the coordinates of the given points.

Cropping with Margin. With a margin m (in the code, $m = 30$), the cropping coordinates are determined as:

$$x_{\text{left}} = \max(0, x_{\min} - m), \quad x_{\text{right}} = \min(W, x_{\max} + m), \tag{3}$$

$$y_{\text{top}} = \max(0, y_{\min} - m), \quad y_{\text{bottom}} = \min(H, y_{\max} + m), \tag{4}$$

where $(x_{\text{left}}, y_{\text{top}})$ and $(x_{\text{right}}, y_{\text{bottom}})$ define the cropped face region.

Mask Overlay Formulation. In the mask overlay procedure, key facial landmarks are defined as:

$$N = (x_N, y_N), \quad C = (x_C, y_C), \quad L = (x_L, y_L), \quad R = (x_R, y_R),$$

where N is the nose tip, C is the chin, L is the left cheek, and R is the right cheek.

Distance Computations. The Euclidean distances are computed as:

$$d(L, R) = \sqrt{(x_L - x_R)^2 + (y_L - y_R)^2}, \quad d(N, C) = \sqrt{(x_N - x_C)^2 + (y_N - y_C)^2}, \tag{5}$$

Determining the Mask Size. The mask dimensions are set proportionally to these distances:

$$\text{mask\_width} = 1.3 \times d(L, R), \quad \text{mask\_height} = 1.8 \times d(N, C), \tag{6}$$

Mask Placement. The top-left coordinate for placing the mask is given by:

$$\text{mask\_top\_left} = \left(x_N - \frac{\text{mask\_width}}{2} + 10, \quad y_N - 0.3 \times \text{mask\_height} \right), \tag{7}$$

The mask is resized accordingly and overlaid on the face image at the computed location.

Data Augmentation Formulations. The following transformations are applied during data augmentation:

Rotation: For an image rotation by an angle θ, the rotation matrix is:

$$R(\theta) = \begin{bmatrix} \cos\theta & -\sin\theta \\ \sin\theta & \cos\theta \end{bmatrix}, \tag{8}$$

A point (x, y) is transformed to:

$$\begin{bmatrix} x' \\ y' \end{bmatrix} = R(\theta) \begin{bmatrix} x \\ y \end{bmatrix}, \tag{9}$$

where (x, y) are the original coordinates, (x', y') are the transformed coordinates after rotation, θ is the rotation angle in radians, and $\cos\theta$, $\sin\theta$ define the transformation components.

Brightness Adjustment: Brightness adjustment is performed using:

$$I' = \alpha I + \beta, \tag{10}$$

where I is the original image, I' is the transformed image, α is a scaling factor (typically within $[0.8, 1.2]$), and β is the brightness offset.

Zoom Transformation. For zooming by a factor z, the coordinates transform as:

$$(x', y') = (z \cdot x, \ z \cdot y), \tag{11}$$

where x, y are the original coordinates, x', y' are the transformed coordinates, and z is the scaling factor.

Neural Network Training Formulations. The training process involves several key mathematical operations:

Softmax Activation: The softmax function converts logits z_i into probabilities:

$$\hat{y}_i = \frac{e^{z_i}}{\sum_{j=1}^{C} e^{z_j}}, \tag{12}$$

where C is the number of classes.

Categorical Cross-Entropy Loss: The loss function is defined as:

$$L = -\sum_{i=1}^{C} y_i \log(\hat{y}_i), \tag{13}$$

where y_i represents the one-hot encoded true labels, and $\hat{y}_i$ denotes the predicted probabilities.

L2 Regularization: L2 regularization adds a penalty on the magnitude of the weights:

$$\mathcal{L}_{\text{reg}} = \lambda \sum_i w_i^2, \tag{14}$$

where λ is the regularization coefficient.

Dropout: Dropout randomly deactivates neurons during training:

$$y_i' = \begin{cases} 0, & \text{with probability } p, \\ \frac{y_i}{1-p}, & \text{with probability } 1-p. \end{cases} \tag{15}$$

where y_i' is the transformed output, y_i is the original value, and p is the dropout probability.

Adam Optimization Algorithm: The Adam optimizer updates parameters as follows:

$$m_t = \beta_1 m_{t-1} + (1 - \beta_1)g_t \quad v_t = \beta_2 v_{t-1} + (1 - \beta_2)g_t^2, \tag{16}$$

$$\hat{m}_t = \frac{m_t}{1 - \beta_1^t} \quad \hat{v}_t = \frac{v_t}{1 - \beta_2^t} \quad \theta_{t+1} = \theta_t - \eta \frac{\hat{m}_t}{\sqrt{\hat{v}_t} + \epsilon}. \tag{17}$$

where g_t is the gradient at time t, β_1 and β_2 are the decay rates for the moment estimates, η is the learning rate, ϵ is a small constant to prevent division by zero.

4   Experimental Results

We conducted our experiments on two distinct datasets: the Celebrity Dataset and Our Dataset. The Celebrity Dataset comprises images of 18 renowned public figures, totaling 1800 images (averaging about 100 images per celebrity). In contrast, Our Dataset features images collected from friends and acquaintances, amounting to approximately 375 images with 15 persons captured in diverse real-world settings. This dual-dataset strategy enables us to assess the model's performance comprehensively—comparing its effectiveness on widely available data against its robustness on domain-specific images. To thoroughly evaluate the model, we examined several performance metrics, including the confusion matrix, loss curves, and accuracy curves for both datasets.

4.1   Feature Concatenation

Feature fusion is a widely used technique in deep learning to enhance the representational power of models. Common strategies include early fusion (input level), late fusion (decision level), and intermediate or feature-level fusion. In this study, we adopt a feature-level fusion strategy via layer concatenation. To enhance the model's ability to learn discriminative features, we implemented a feature fusion mechanism through concatenation of intermediate layer outputs. We conducted experiments using various combinations of dense layers in the pre-trained network, focusing particularly on the Celebrity Dataset.

Shallow-Middle Fusion. Figure 3a, and 3b illustrate the model's performance for the concatenation of $dense_3$ (128D) + $dense_4$ (64D). Specifically, Fig. 3a shows the accuracy curve during training and validation along with the corresponding loss curve, while Fig. 3b presents the confusion matrix, which highlights the classification effectiveness and error distribution across classes.

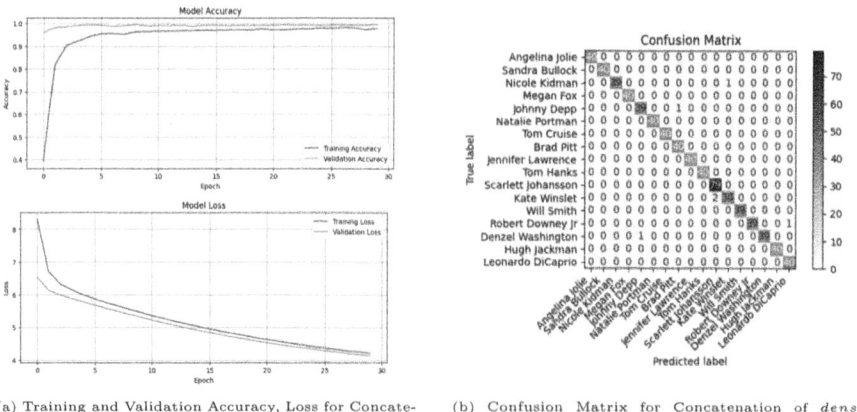

(a) Training and Validation Accuracy, Loss for Concatenation of $dense_3$ (128D) + $dense_4$ (64D)

(b) Confusion Matrix for Concatenation of $dense_3$ (128D) + $dense_4$ (64D)

Fig. 3. Training loss and confusion matrix for $dense_3$ (128D) + $dense_4$ (64D).

Shallow-Deep Fusion. Figure 4a and 4b illustrate the performance of the concatenation of $dense_3$ (128D) + $dense_5$ (32D).

Concatenation of $dense_4$ (64D) + $dense_5$ (32D) is illustrated in Fig. 5a and 5b.

Full Hierarchy Fusion. Concatenation of all three layers ($dense_3$ + $dense_4$ + $dense_5$) is illustrated in Fig. 6a and 6b.

The optimal architecture combined outputs from $dense_4$ and $dense_5$ layers through a Concatenation operation, followed by a new 128-unit Dense layer

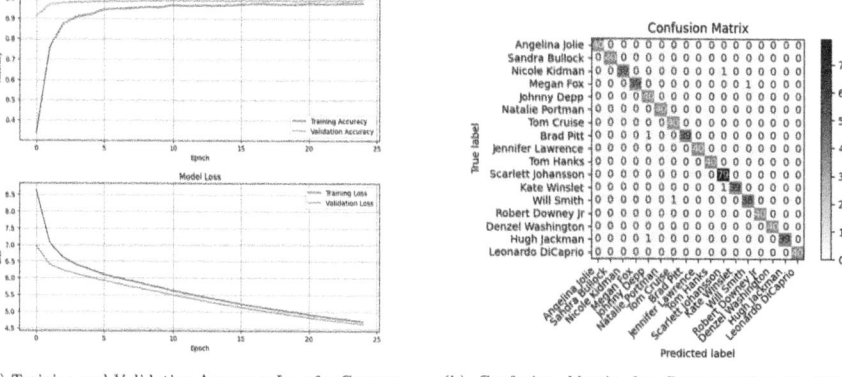

(a) Training and Validation Accuracy, Loss for Concatenation of $dense_3$ (128D) + $dense_5$ (32D)

(b) Confusion Matrix for Concatenation of $dense_3$ (128D) + $dense_5$ (32D)

Fig. 4. Comparison of training performance and confusion matrix.

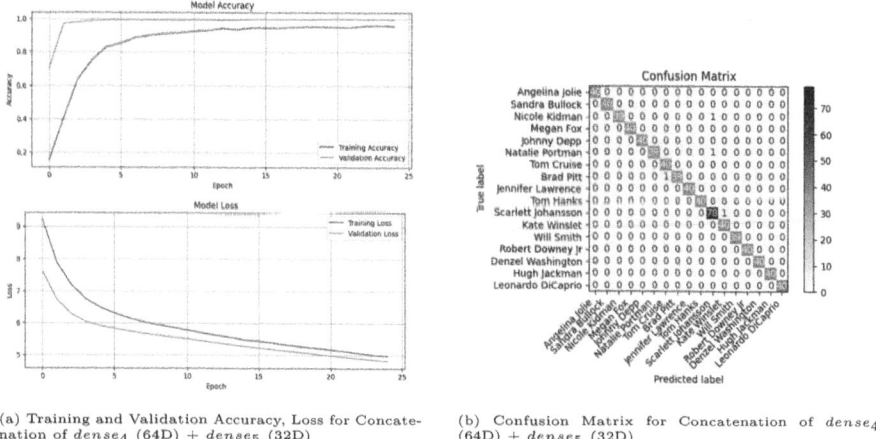

(a) Training and Validation Accuracy, Loss for Concatenation of $dense_4$ (64D) + $dense_5$ (32D)

(b) Confusion Matrix for Concatenation of $dense_4$ (64D) + $dense_5$ (32D)

Fig. 5. Comparison of training performance and confusion matrix for $dense_4$ (64D) + $dense_5$ (32D).

with L2 regularization ($\lambda = 0.01$) and Dropout (rate=0.5). This configuration achieved superior performance due to:

- Complementary feature representation: $dense_4$ captures mid-level facial attributes while $dense_5$ encodes high-level semantic patterns
- Dimensionality balance: Combined 96D features (64+32) provide richer information than single layers without over-parameterization
- Regularization effects: The L2 constraint ($\|W\|^2$ penalty) and Dropout prevent overfitting to noisy mask artifacts

The fusion layer is mathematically expressed as:

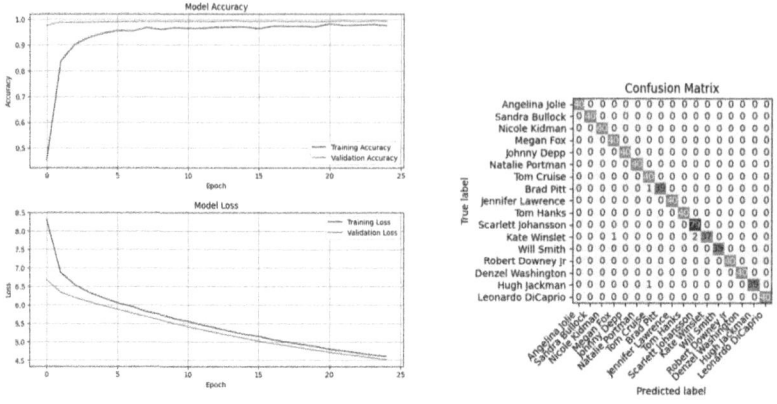

(a) Training and Validation Accuracy, Loss for Concatenation of $dense_3$ (128D) + $dense_4$ (64D) + $dense_5$ (32D)

(b) Confusion Matrix for Concatenation of $dense_3$ (128D) + $dense_4$ (64D) + $dense_5$ (32D)

Fig. 6. Comparison of training performance and confusion matrix for $dense_3$ (128D) + $dense_4$ (64D) + $dense_5$ (32D).

$$\mathbf{h}_{\text{fusion}} = \phi(\mathbf{W}_c[\mathbf{h}_{\text{dense4}} \oplus \mathbf{h}_{\text{dense5}}] + \mathbf{b}_c) \tag{18}$$

where $\oplus$ denotes concatenation operation, ϕ is ReLU activation, and $\mathbf{W}_c \in \mathbb{R}^{96 \times 128}$ is the learnable weight matrix. Comparative experiments showed 4.2% higher validation accuracy versus shallow layer combinations, demonstrating the effectiveness of mid-to-deep feature integration.

4.2 Model Performance

Celebrity Dataset. We conducted tests on the Celebrity dataset, which consists of images from 18 individuals. Among them, 16 individuals have 40 images each, one individual has 39 images, and another has 79 images, resulting in a total of 758 images. The results of our evaluation using different Dense layer architectures are presented in Table 1.

Table 1. Experimental Results with Different Dense Layer Architectures of Celebrity Dataset

Dense Architecture	Incorrect Images	Correct Images	Accuracy (%)
No Feature Concatenation	11	747	98.50%
$dense_3$ (128D) + $dense_4$ (64D)	6	752	99.20%
$dense_3$ (128D) + $dense_5$ (32D)	6	752	99.20%
$dense_3$ (128D) + $dense_4$ (64D) + $dense_5$ (32D)	5	753	99.34%
$dense_4$ (64D) + $dense_5$ (32D)	4	754	99.47%

Our Dataset. Additionally, we tested our dataset, which includes 16 individuals: 13 individuals with 10 images each, one individual with 6 images, and two individuals with 8 images, resulting in a total of 152 images. Since the 45 configuration was proven to be the most stable in the previous experiments, we only evaluated this configuration on our dataset.

The results of our evaluation using Dense layer architectures are presented in Table 2.

Table 2. Experimental Results with Different Dense Layer Architectures of Our Dataset

Dense Architecture	Incorrect Images	Correct Images	Accuracy (%)
$dense_4$ (64D) + $dense_5$ (32D)	6	146	96.05%

5   Conclusion

This research introduces an effective framework for masked face recognition that combines MediaPipe for face detection and a modified ResNet50 architecture for feature extraction. A key innovation of our approach lies in the Feature Concatenation strategy, which intelligently combines features from multiple dense layers. Specifically, the fusion of $dense_4$ (64D) + $dense_5$ (32D) layers proved most effective, capturing both mid-level facial attributes and high-level semantic patterns. This optimal feature integration, coupled with appropriate regularization techniques, led to superior performance with 99.47% accuracy on both celebrity and real-world datasets. The framework's success in handling masked faces while maintaining computational efficiency makes it suitable for practical applications in healthcare, security, and access control systems. As face masks continue to be relevant in many contexts, this work contributes significantly to the development of reliable biometric systems. Future work could focus on lightweight architectures for edge devices and enhanced robustness against severe occlusions.

Acknowledgements. The authors would like to thank FPT University, CanTho Campus for funding this research.

References

1. Alzu'bi, A., Albalas, F., AL-Hadhrami, T., Bani Younis, L., Bashayreh, A.: Masked face recognition using deep learning: a review. Electronics **10**(21), 2666 (2021)
2. Boutin, C.: NIST launches studies into masks' effect on face recognition software. National Institute of Standards and Technology (NIST) (2020). https://www.nist.gov/news-events/news/2020/07/nist-launches-studies-masks-effect-face-recognition-software

3. Ejaz, M.S., Sifatullah, M., Islam, M.R., Sarker, A.: Implementation of principal component analysis on masked and non-masked face recognition. In: 1st International Conference on Advances in Science, Engineering and Robotics Technology (ICASERT). IEEE (2019)
4. Yo, M.C., Chong, S.C., Chong, L.Y.: Sparse CNN: leveraging deep learning and sparse representation for masked face recognition. Int. J. Inf. Technol. (2025)
5. Cheng, W.C., Hsiao, H.C., Li, L.H.: Deep learning mask face recognition with annealing mechanism. Appl. Sci. **13**(2), 732 (2023)
6. Wang, W., Zhao, Z., Zhang, H., Wang, Z., Su, F.: Masked face recognition using deep learning. In: Proceedings of the IEEE/CVF International Conference on Computer Vision (ICCV) Workshops, pp. 1450–1455 (2021)
7. Tran, L. H., Tran, T., Mai, A.: Improved sparse PCA method for face and image recognition. arXiv preprint arXiv:2112.00207 (2021)
8. Kortli, Y., Jridi, M., Al Falou, A., Atri, M.: A comparative study of CFs, LBP, HOG, SIFT, SURF, and BRIEF for security and face recognition. In: Advanced Secure Optical Image Processing for Communications, Ch. 13, pp. 13-1–13-22. IOP Publishing Ltd (2018)
9. Chandrakala, M., Devi, P.D.: Face recognition using cascading of HOG and LBP feature extraction. In: International Conference on Soft Computing and Signal Processing, Advances in Intelligent Systems and Computing (AISC), vol. 1413, pp. 553–562. Springer (2022)
10. Aljarallah, N.F., Uliyan, D.M.: Masked face recognition via a combined SIFT and DLBP features trained in CNN model. Int. J. Comput. Sci. Netw. Secur. **22**(6), 319–331 (2022)
11. Ullah, N., Javed, A., Ghazanfar, M.A., Alsufyani, A., Bourouis, S.: A novel Deep-MaskNet model for face mask detection and masked facial recognition. J. King Saud Univ. Comput. Inf. Sci. **34**(10, Part B), 9905–9914 (2022)
12. Mandal, B., Okeukwu, A., Theis, Y.: Masked face recognition using ResNet-50. arXiv preprint arXiv:2104.08997 (2021)
13. Jeevan, G., Zacharias, G.C., Nair, M.S., Rajan, J.: An empirical study of the impact of masks on face recognition. Pattern Recogn. **122**, 108308 (2022)
14. Yang, G., et al.: Face mask recognition system with YOLOV5 based on image recognition. In: 2020 IEEE 6th International Conference on Computer and Communications (ICCC), pp. 9345042. IEEE (2020)
15. Aswal, V., Tupe, O., Shaikh, S., Charniya, N.N.: Single Camera masked face identification. In: 2020 19th IEEE International Conference on Machine Learning and Applications (ICMLA), pp. 00018. IEEE (2020)
16. Shahar, M.S.M., Mazalan, L.: Face identity for face mask recognition system. In: 2021 IEEE 11th Symposium on Computer Applications and Industrial Electronics (ISCAIE), pp. 9431791. IEEE (2021)
17. Kumar, M., Mann, R.: Masked face recognition using deep learning model. In: 2021 3rd International Conference on Advances in Computing, Communication Control and Networking (ICAC3N), pp. 9725368. IEEE (2021)
18. Adhinata, F.D., Tanjung, N.A.F., Widayat, W., Pasfica, G.R., Satura, F.R.: Real-time masked face recognition using FaceNet and supervised machine learning. In: Proceedings of the 2nd International Conference on Electronics, Biomedical Engineering, and Health Informatics. Lecture Notes in Electrical Engineering (LNEE), vol. 898, pp. 189–202 (2022)

19. Tiwari, A.S., Gupta, P., Jain, A., Panjwani, H.V., Malathi, G.: Face recognition with mask using MTCNN and FaceNet. In: Artificial Intelligence and Technologies. Lecture Notes in Electrical Engineering (LNEE), vol. 806, pp. 103–109 (2021)
20. Moghaddam, M.H., Ghaffary, H.R., Khazaiepoor, M.: Facial recognition of people with masks using Mediapipe Facemesh and deep learning algorithms. SSRN, 29 (2024)

Robust Blueberry Leaf Disease Detection Using Transformer-Based and Local Cosine Feature Method

Vinh Dinh Nguyen[1]([⊠]), Ngoc Phuong Ngo[2], and Kha Hoang Nguyen[1]

[1] Department of Information Technology, FPT University, Can Tho Campus,
Can Tho City, Vietnam
vinhnd29@fe.edu.vn, khanhce171115@fpt.edu.vn
[2] Department of Plant Physiology-Biochemistry, College of Agriculture,
Can Tho University, Can Tho City, Vietnam
npngoc@ctu.edu.vn

Abstract. Detecting blueberry leaf diseases early is essential for safeguarding crop quality and yield. Traditional methods for this task often involve feature preprocessing combined with machine learning techniques such as K-NN, decision trees, or support vector machines. Recently, there has been a growing interest in deep learning approaches to enhance the performance of existing leaf disease detection systems. While convolutional deep learning methods have shown promising results under standard evaluation conditions, their performance tends to degrade in the presence of noise, such as Gaussian noise. Given the successful application of transformers in the vision domain, this study aims to investigate the use of transformers combined with a novel local descriptor to improve plant leaf disease detection performance under challenging conditions. Experimental results demonstrate that the proposed system achieves stable and superior performance even in noisy environments, outperforming existing methods, including YOLOv5 and YOLOv8, by 2.9% and 4.4% in terms of accuracy, respectively.

Keywords: leaf disease detection · machine learning · deep learning · blueberry leaf disease · local pattern

1 Introduction

The precise identification of plant diseases has significant value in maintaining sustainable and effective agricultural practices, while also avoiding unnecessary depletion of financial and other resources. Although certain plant ailments may lack observable indicators, necessitating the application of advanced analytical techniques, the majority exhibit visible symptoms. Currently, the widely accepted approach involves skilled plant pathologists diagnosing diseases by visually inspecting infected plant leaves. To effectively diagnose plant diseases, a

© The Author(s), under exclusive license to Springer Nature Switzerland AG 2025
O. Gervasi et al. (Eds.): ICCSA 2025, LNCS 15648, pp. 320–331, 2025.
https://doi.org/10.1007/978-3-031-97000-9_20

plant pathologist needs keen observational abilities to recognize different symptoms. However, the extensive range of plant species, fluctuations in disease progression caused by climate changes and the rapid spread of diseases to new regions where they have not previously been observed can challenge even experienced pathologists, causing them to struggle to diagnose certain diseases [2]. Numerous techniques have been suggested for detecting and classifying plant leaf diseases, encompassing both unsupervised methods like k-means, c-means, and LDA, as well as supervised approaches such as SVM, Naïve Bayes, ANN, Decision Tree, and k-NN. In addition, alternative methods such as fuzzy logic or feature-based learning have been explored. Recently, deep learning models have gained traction for improving the performance of plant leaf disease detection. These include AlexNet (2012), ZFNet (2013), VGG and GoogleNet (2014), ResNet and UNet (2015), YOLO and R-CNN (2016), Fractale Net (2017), and EfficientNet (2018) [2]. The adoption of deep convolutional neural networks in these approaches significantly boosts the accuracy of plant leaf disease detection.

The use of local binary pattern (LBP) has been demonstrated to be advantageous in improving the performance of texture classification applications [6]. Numerous studies have investigated LBP to enhance performance across various application domains such as texture classification, stereo matching, and object detection [3,15]. Several researchers have been investigated YOLO for object detection and classification [22]. Recently, transformers have emerged as successful tools in natural language processing applications, leveraging their capabilities in encoding text sequences through positional encoding, self-attention, and cross-attention mechanisms [20]. Furthermore, there has been a surge in research investigating the benefits of transformers for computer vision tasks, exemplified by studies on vision transformers [7]. Plant leaf dataset acquired in uncontrolled environments introduces greater system complexity, yet it holds immense significance in agricultural development and is increasingly relevant in contemporary research. In addition, similarity in infected areas often results in the extraction of inappropriate features, leading to erroneous classifications based on irrelevant feature matching. Therefore, this research marks the first attempt to introduce an efficient architecture combining a novel LBP descriptor and transformer concept for blueberry leaf disease detection. Experiment on two datasets, including Plant Leaf Disease [17] and our custom dataset were captured at CanTho, Vietnam [14] demonstrated that the proposed method obtained a good performance even under difficult testing conditions. We summarize the main contributions of this research as follows:

- A novel local descriptor, named as CS-LBP, which evaluates the cosine similarity between neighboring regions.
- A robust feature for identifying plant leaf diseases by combining the attributes of CS-LBP with linear projection embedding and positional encoding.
- Incorporating the proposed feature, comprising CS-LBP and linear embedding features, into Yolov8 [10] to ensure stable detection of blueberry leaf diseases.

The rest of this study is organized as follows. Section 2 presents and discusses the related research on plant leaf disease detection. Section 3 introduce the proposed method. The results obtained in the research are given and discussed in Sect. 4. Final, the research is concluded with Sect. 5.

2   Related Work

According to a comprehensive report in [2], artificial intelligence methods are being employed to improve agricultural production through the monitoring of plant diseases. Several research papers have been published on this topic, with some focusing on specific approaches and others concentrating on particular diseases. However, a comprehensive summary of plant disease detection, classification, and diagnosis is lacking. Therefore, this research aims to highlight various techniques employed by different researchers in this field as shown in Table 1.

Traditional methods for detecting plant leaf diseases typically involve various preprocessing techniques, such as color conversion (e.g., RGB to HSV, Lab), and image enhancement algorithms, including median filtering, Laplacian filtering, histogram equalization, or augmentation techniques. In 2019, Rath et al. introduced a method for detecting and classifying rice leaf diseases using a radial basis function neural network [16]. Their system achieved an accuracy of 95%, precision of 97%, and recall of 95%. Recognizing that utilizing multiple features can enhance detection system performance, Shrivastava et al. explored 14 different color models and extracted four characteristics from each color channel, resulting in a total of 172 features [18]. These features were then inputted into an SVM for classification, achieving an accuracy of 94.65%. Instead of relying on a single method for detecting leaf diseases in wheat and corn, Kusumo et al. combined several models simultaneously, including support vector machines, decision trees, random forests, and naive Bayes, along with preprocessing methods such as SIFT and SURF [12]. This combined approach achieved an accuracy of 87%. Rather than inputting 14 distinct color models into the SVM, Kaur et al. utilized only three features comprising RGB color, texture, and shape [11]. This combination yielded an accuracy of 84% with the Soybean dataset. Recently, Feretinos et al. demonstrated that the performance of detection systems can be enhanced by employing deep learning approaches, specifically using transfer learning with AlexNet and VGG-16 [4]. For detecting leaf diseases in grapes, Javidam et al. employed the Gray Level Co-Occurrence Matrix (GLCM) with the support vector machine algorithm [8]. Das et al. proposed another approach for detecting tomato leaf diseases by preprocessing input features with mean and entropy before inputting them into SVM and K-NN for classification, achieving an accuracy of 87.60% on the Tomato dataset [5]. Chen et al. also aimed to improve the performance of plant leaf disease detection by employing transfer learning techniques with VGG16 and InceptionNet [13]. More recently, Atila et al. introduced a method for detecting leaf diseases in tomatoes using EfficientNet [1]. From this brief review, it is evident that most existing methods perform well under normal testing conditions; however, their performance tends to degrade under challenging conditions such as Gaussian noise. Therefore, there is a need to investigate methods to enhance the performance of existing systems by introducing new local descriptors along with linear embedding and positional encoding.

3 Proposed Method

The proposed method comprises three primary stages, as illustrated in Fig. 1. First, we introduce a novel local descriptor called CS-LBP to establish a stable feature representation. Second, to preserve the structure of the image, we adopt a similar framework to the vision transformer [7]. Here, the original image and the output of the CS-LBP are divided into fixed-size patches, each of which is linearly embedded and supplemented with position embeddings. Finally, the linearly embedded features and position embeddings are fed into YOLOv8 [10] for the detection and classification of blueberry leaf diseases.

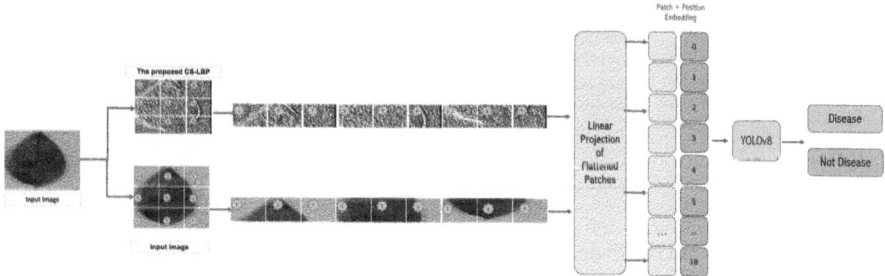

Fig. 1. The proposed LBP and Vision Transformer Architecture for Blueberry Leaf Disease Detection.

3.1 The Proposed CS-LBP

The Local Binary Pattern (LBP) is a technique that doesn't rely on specific parameters and instead focuses on grasping the local patterns within an image. It achieves this by comparing the intensity of surrounding pixels to that of the central pixel, generating binary values based on whether the surrounding pixel intensities surpass that of the center. These binary values are then combined to form a numerical representation. Figure 2(b) illustrates the outcomes of the standard LBP method, utilizing a 3×3 window with eight neighboring pixels ($N = 8$), and a neighborhood radius of 1 ($R = 1$). However, LBP's effectiveness diminishes notably in uniformly textured regions and when subjected to Gaussian noise. Its primary vulnerability lies in the thresholding process between the central pixel and its neighbors. Even slight variations in the central pixel's

Table 1. Survey of existing plant leaf disease detection and classification

Year	Authors	Method	Discussion
2019	Rath and Meher [2]	They uses radial basis function neural network for classification	Rice dataset: Real Field Image. Accuracy of 95%, Precision of 97% and Recall of 95%
2021	Shrivastava and Pradhan [18]	They investigated 14 distinct color models and derived four characteristics from each color channel, resulting in a total of 172 features. The output feature is then input to SVM for classification step	Rice dataset: Rice Real Field Image. Accuracy of 94.65%
2019	Kusumo et al. [12]	They used combination of various techniques such as support vector matching, decision tree, random forest and naïve bayes along with the pre-processing method including SIFT and SURF	Wheat and Corn dataset: Plant Village. Accuracy of 87%
2018	Kaur et al. [11]	SVM was used three input features: color, texture and shape	Soyabean dataset: Plant Village. Accuracy of 84%
2018	Feretinos [4]	The transfer learning is employed with the Alexet and VGG 16	Mix dataset: Plant Village. Accuracy of 99.53%.
2023	Javidam et al. [8]	Gray Level Co-Occurrence Matrix (GLCM) was used with support vector machine algorithm	Seft Grape dataset. Accuracy of 98.97%.
2020	Das et al. [5]	The input image was preprocessing by using Mean and Entropy, the SVM and KNN was then used for classification step.	Tomato dataset. Accuracy of 87.60%.
2020	Chen et al. [13]	Transfer learning the deep CNN was applied in the identification of plant disease (VGGNet16 and InceptionNet)	Self dataset. Accuracy of 92%.
2020	Wspanialy Moussan [21]	They employed ResNet and Unet for detecting plant leaf disease	Tomato dataset: Plant Village. Accuracy of 98%.
2021	Atila et al. [1]	They Investigate EfficientNet-B4-5 for detecting tomato leaf disease	Tomato dataset: Plant Village. Accuracy of 98.42%

value can significantly alter the resulting LBP encoding sequence. The traditional LBP fails to extract the local feature when the noise occur as shown in Fig. 2(b). Therefore, we introduce an approach to handle noise by considering the relationship of local neighbor region as shown in Fig. 2(a). Given a center pixel Lc=(x,y) in the image, the proposed CS-LBP is computed as follows:

$$CS\_LBP_{N,R}\left(L_c\right) = \sum_{n=1}^{N} F\left(\psi\left(L_c\right), L_n\right) \times 2^n \qquad (1)$$

where R and N are the radius and number of neighbor pixel in the local region. The $F\left(\psi\left(L_c\right), L_n\right)$ is calculated as follows:

$$F\left(\psi\left(L_c\right)\right) = \begin{cases} 1 & \text{if } I\left(L_c\right) \geq I\left(L_n\right) \\ 0 & \text{if } I\left(L_c\right) < I\left(L_n\right) \end{cases} \qquad (2)$$

where $I\left(L_n\right)$ is the pixel intensity value of of n-th pixel. $\psi\left(L_c\right)$ is designed to capture the relationship between left local region of the current computing CS_LBP as illustrated in Fig. 2(a):

$$\psi\left(L_{c}\right)=\frac{\overrightarrow{V_{1}}\left[L_{0}^{1}, L_{1}^{1}, ..., L_{n}^{1}\right] \cdot \overrightarrow{V_{2}}\left[L_{0}^{1}, L_{1}^{2}, ..., L_{n}^{2}\right]}{\left\|\overrightarrow{V_{1}}\left[L_{0}^{1}, L_{1}^{1}, ..., L_{1}^{n}\right]\right\|\left\|\overrightarrow{V_{2}}\left[L_{0}^{2}, L_{1}^{2}, ..., L_{n}^{2}\right]\right\|} \times I\left(L_{c}\right) \tag{3}$$

where $\overrightarrow{V_{1}}\left[L_{0}^{1}, L_{1}^{1}, ..., L_{n}^{1}\right]$ is the vector of pixel intensity values of the considering CS-LBP region and $\overrightarrow{V_{2}}\left[L_{0}^{2}, L_{1}^{2}, ..., L_{n}^{2}\right]$ is the is the vector of pixel intensity values of the left local neighbor regions as shown in Fig. 2 (a).

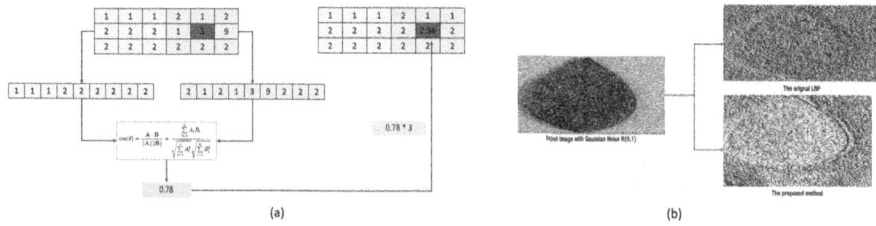

(a)   (b)

Fig. 2. (a) The proposed CS-LBP. (b) The outcomes from the proposed approach compared with those from the original LBP technique.

3.2   Robust Feature By Using Linear Projection and Positional Encoding Feature

Motivation by the advantages of existing vision transformer algorithm, we introduce an approaches to combine the original image and CS-LBP features by using linear project and positional encoding techniques based on the previous research [20]. The conventional Transformer model takes in a one-dimensional sequence consisting of token embeddings as its input. Similar to [20], the RGB image and CS-LBP feature are reshaped from (Height,Width,Channel) into a sequence of flatten 2D patches N×P2×C as show.

For each patch, $x_{p}^{i} \in R^{P \times P \times C} \rightarrow x_{p}^{i} \in R^{1 \times P^{2} \times C}$ and $x_{p}^{i} \in R^{1 \times P^{2} \times C}.W \in R^{P^{2}C \times D} = x_{p}^{i}W = z_{1}^{i} \in R^{1 \times D}$.

For all patches at a time, N is total tokens (N=P*P): $x_{p}^{i} \in R^{N \times P^{2} \times C}.W \in R^{P^{2}C \times D} = xW = z_{1} \in R^{N \times D}$, where N, calculated as H×W/P2, represents the resulting number of patches.

The output feature from the linear projection step are then fused with the positional encoding to provide a final output feature for the Yolov8 [10].

4   Experimental Results and Discussion

4.1   Dataset

There are two datasets, including Plant Leaf Disease [17] and our custom dataset were captured at CanTho, Vietnam [14]. The Plant Leaf Disease dataset [17]

Fig. 3. Samples blueberry leaf datasets from Plant Leaf Disease [17] and our dataset were captured at CanTho, Vietnam [14].

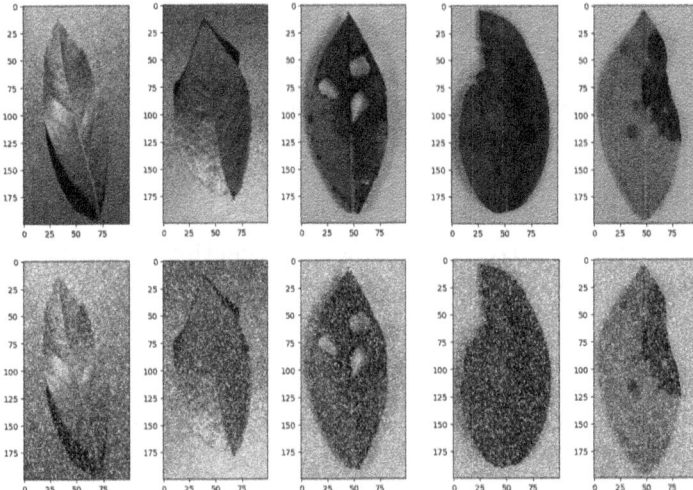

Fig. 4. Samples image are added Gaussian Noise with N(0,1). First row are shown the original images. Second are shown the noise image.

underwent offline augmentation using the original dataset available on GitHub. It consists of approximately 87,000 RGB images showcasing both healthy and diseased crop leaves, categorized into 38 distinct classes. The dataset is divided into training and validation sets in an 80/20 ratio while preserving the directory structure. Moreover, a separate directory is created later, containing 33 test images for predictive analysis. In this research, our experiments are centered around particular classes extracted from the Plant Diseases Dataset [17]. Specifically, we delve into the blueberry healthy class, comprising 1817 images as shown in Fig. 3(a). Additionally, we also evaluate the performance on our dataset showcasing blueberry diseases, as depicted in Fig. 3(b, c). This dataset was gathered at Can Tho University, Vietnam [14].

To create a comprehensive dataset for evaluation. First, the augmentation algorithm [16] was used to create 10,000 samples, where 7,000 samples for training, 2,000 sample for validation, and 1000 samples for testing from the Plant Leaf Disease [14] and Can Tho University Dataset [10]. In addition, to created the difficult of the testing dataset, we add Gaussian noise into the original image, as described in Fig. 4.

4.2   Metric for Evaluation and Algorithms for Comparison

This research used four metrics to evaluate the performance of the proposed method included precision Φ and recall Γ , F1 score, and accuracy Υ as described below:

$$\Phi = \frac{\sum TP}{\sum TP + FP} \tag{4}$$

$$\Gamma = \frac{\sum TP}{\sum TP + FN} \tag{5}$$

$$F1 = \frac{2 \times \Phi \times \Gamma}{\Phi + \Gamma} \tag{6}$$

$$\Upsilon = \frac{TP + TN}{TP + TN + FN + FP} \tag{7}$$

To assess the effectiveness of the proposed method compared to existing approaches, we conducted an experiment that included several established methods, namely YOLOv8 [10], YOLOv5 [9], and EfficientNet [19].

4.3   Detail Implementation

Google Colab (a 2.30 GHz CPU, a 16 GB Tesla GPU, and 26 GB of DRAM) was used to train our proposed method. For consistency, we employed the same parameter settings as YOLOv5+LBP, YOLOv8, and EfficientNet during both the training and testing phases.

4.4   Results and Discussions

We first verify the performance of the proposed system and compare it to the method under normal condition cases, where no noise is added to the input image. Figure 5 shows the results of the proposed system and compared methods using four evaluation metrics: precision, recall, F1-score, and accuracy. Yolov8 obtained precision, recall, F1-score, and accuracy of 95.2%, 90.9%, 93.02%, and 97%, respectively. Yolov5+LBP obtained precision, recall, F1-score, and accuracy of 92.68%, 88.37%, 90.47%, and 96%, respectively. Yolov8+LBP obtained

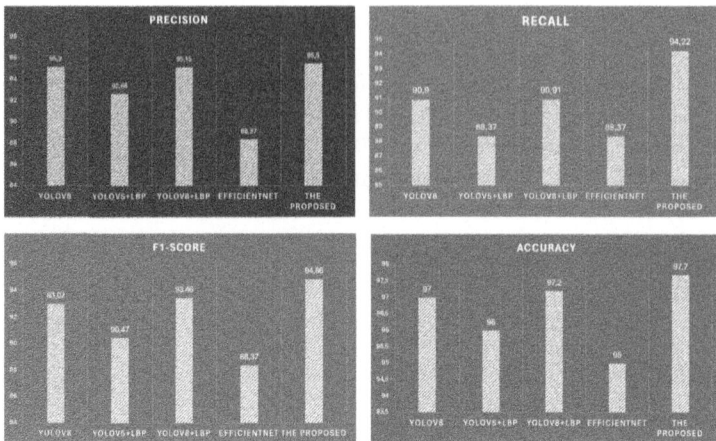

Fig. 5. Experimental results of the proposed system and existing methods under normal conditions.

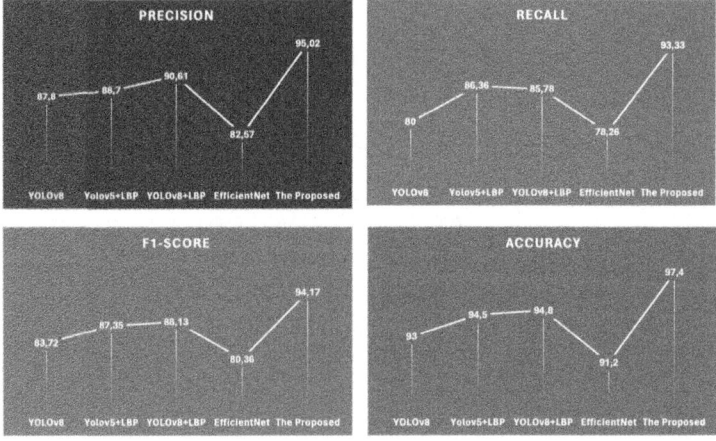

Fig. 6. Experimental results of the proposed system and existing methods under difficult conditions (Gaussian noise is incorporated).

precision, recall, F1-score, and accuracy of 95.15%, 90.91%, 93.46%, and 97.2%, respectively. EfficientNet obtained precision, recall, F1-score, and accuracy of 88.37%, 88.37%, 88.37%, and 95%, respectively. The proposed method obtained precision, recall, F1-score, and accuracy of 95.5%, 94.22%, 94.86%, and 97.7%, respectively. Observing the results, we found that the performance of EfficientNet is lowest in terms of precision, recall, and accuracy, while the proposed method obtained the best performance. For normal conditions, most compared methods obtained comparable results to the proposed method because they successfully capture and learn the input structure. Our method provides good performances due to the benefits of the proposed CS-LBP, along with the constraints of linear embedding.

However, the results of the existing algorithms significantly drops when we add noise to the input under difficult conditions. Figure 6 shows the performance of the our method and existing methods under Gaussian noise with N(0,1). The performance of Yolov8 was decreased by 7.4%, 10.9%, 9.3%, and 4% in terms of precision, recall, F1-score, and accuracy, respectively. Analyzing Yolov8, we found that this happens because it was only designed for handling normal input conditions. We further conducted an ablation study by fusing Yolov8 and LBP, as shown in Fig. 6. The precision, recall, F1-score, and accuracy of Yolov8+LBP are better than the original Yolov8 due to the benefits of LBP. The performance of Yolov8+LBP decreased by only 4.54%, 5.13%, 5.33%, and 2.4% in terms of precision, recall, F1-score, and accuracy, respectively. For a deeper study of the behavior of another approach, Yolo5+LBP, we realized that its performance was also decreased under difficult testing; however, the decreasing rate is lower compared to YOLOv8 without using LBP. The performance of Yolov5+LBP decreased by only 3.98%, 2.01%, 3.12%, and 1.5% in terms of precision, recall, F1-score, and accuracy, respectively. We also conducted more experiments using EfficientNet under difficult conditions. The performance of EfficientNet was significantly decreased by 5.8%, 10.11%, 8.01%, and 3.8% in terms of precision, recall, F1-score, and accuracy, respectively. Thus, we found that, somehow, LBP might help to improve the performance of the compared methods under difficult conditions. However, as discussed earlier, LBP still fails to handle huge noise. In addition, Yolov8, Yolov5, and EfficientNet are designed based on convolutional approaches; therefore, they fail to reverse the constraint of the structure of the input object. This is the main reason why our proposed method still obtained the best performance under difficult conditions. The performance of the proposed method was only decreased by 0.48%, 0.89%, 0.69%, and 0.3% in terms of precision, recall, F1-score, and accuracy, respectively, under difficult conditions, because CS-LBP successfully extracts and handles the noise case by considering the distribution of the local region with the help of cosine similarity metric. In addition, the idea of linear project embedding and positional encoder also helps to reverse the order constraint of the object.

5   Conclusion

This study has introduced an effective approach to enhance the performance of plant leaf disease detection by incorporating the proposed CS-LBP along with linear embedding and positional encoding to generate a robust feature representation. The developed system achieved consistent and competitive performance compared to state-of-the-art methods under both normal and noisy conditions. However, a limitation of the proposed method lies in its processing time, attributed to the growing number of input features for training and inference. As a future direction, we intend to explore multi-modal fusion approaches to further enhance the performance of the proposed method.

References

1. Ümit, A., Uçar, M., Akyol, K., Uçar, E.: Plant leaf disease classification using efficientnet deep learning model. Ecol. Inf. **61**, 101182 (2021). https://doi.org/10.1016/j.ecoinf.2020.101182
2. Bhargava, A., Shukla, A., Goswami, O.P., Alsharif, M.H., Uthansakul, P., Uthansakul, M.: Plant leaf disease detection, classification, and diagnosis using computer vision and artificial intelligence: a review. IEEE Access **12**, 37443–37469 (2024). https://doi.org/10.1109/ACCESS.2024.3373001
3. Dinh, V.Q., Nguyen, P.H., Nguyen, V.D.: Feature engineering and deep learning for stereo matching under adverse driving conditions. IEEE Trans. Intell. Transp. Syst. **23**(7), 7855–7865 (2022). https://doi.org/10.1109/TITS.2021.3073557
4. Ferentinos, K.P.: Deep learning models for plant disease detection and diagnosis. Comput. Electron. Agricult. **145**, 311–318 (2018). https://doi.org/10.1016/j.compag.2018.01.009
5. Francisco, M., Ribeiro, F., Metrôlho, J., Dionísio, R.: Algorithms and models for automatic detection and classification of diseases and pests in agricultural crops: a systematic review. Appl. Sci. **13**(8) (2023). https://doi.org/10.3390/app13084720
6. Hadid, A.: The local binary pattern approach and its applications to face analysis. In: 2008 First Workshops on Image Processing Theory, Tools and Applications, pp. 1–9 (2008). https://doi.org/10.1109/IPTA.2008.4743795
7. Han, K., Wang, Y., Chen, H., Chen, X., Guo, J., Liu, Z., Tang, Y., Xiao, A., Xu, C., Xu, Y., Yang, Z., Zhang, Y., Tao, D.: A survey on vision transformer. IEEE Trans. Pattern Anal. Mach. Intell. **45**(1), 87–110 (2023). https://doi.org/10.1109/TPAMI.2022.3152247
8. Javidan, S.M., Banakar, A., Vakilian, K.A., Ampatzidis, Y.: Diagnosis of grape leaf diseases using automatic k-means clustering and machine learning. Smart Agricult. Technol. **3**, 100081 (2023). https://doi.org/10.1016/j.atech.2022.100081
9. Jocher, G.: Ultralytics YOLOV5 (2020). https://doi.org/10.5281/zenodo.3908559
10. Jocher, G., Chaurasia, A., Qiu, J.: Ultralytics YOLOV8 (2023). https://github.com/ultralytics/ultralytics
11. Kaur, S., Pandey, S., Goel, S.: Semi-automatic leaf disease detection and classification system for soybean culture. IET Image Process. **12**, 1038–1048 (2018). https://api.semanticscholar.org/CorpusID:49238886
12. Kusumo, B.S., Heryana, A., Mahendra, O., Pardede, H.F.: Machine learning-based for automatic detection of corn-plant diseases using image processing. In: 2018 International Conference on Computer, Control, Informatics and its Applications (IC3INA), pp. 93–97 (2018). https://doi.org/10.1109/IC3INA.2018.8629507
13. Mohanty, S.P., Hughes, D.P., Salathé, M.: Using deep learning for image-based plant disease detection. Front. Plant Sci. **7** (2016). https://api.semanticscholar.org/CorpusID:2528492
14. Nguyen, V.D., Ngo, N.P., Debnath, N.C.: Leaf disease detection in blueberry using efficient semi-supervised learning approach. In: Hassanien, A.E., et al. (eds.) The 3rd International Conference on Artificial Intelligence and Computer Vision (AICV2023), March 5–7, 2023, pp. 188–196. Springer, Cham (2023)
15. Nguyen, V.D., Nguyen, P.H., Debnath, N.C.: Local binary pattern and census, which one is better in stereo matching. In: 2020 7th NAFOSTED Conference on Information and Computer Science (NICS), pp. 244–249 (2020). https://doi.org/10.1109/NICS51282.2020.9335907

16. Rath, A.K., Meher, J.K.: Disease detection in infected plant leaf by computational method. Arch. Phytopathol. Plant Prot. **52**(19–20), 1348–1358 (2019). https://doi.org/10.1080/03235408.2019.1708546

17. Ruth, J.A., Uma, R., Meenakshi, A., Ramkumar, P.: Meta-heuristic based deep learning model for leaf diseases detection. Neural Process. Lett. **54**, 5693–5709 (2022). https://api.semanticscholar.org/CorpusID:249834375

18. Shrivastava, V.K., Pradhan, M.K.: Rice plant disease classification using color features: a machine learning paradigm. J. Plant Pathol. **103**(1), 17–26 (2020). https://doi.org/10.1007/s42161-020-00683-3

19. Tan, M., Le, Q.V.: Efficientnet: rethinking model scaling for convolutional neural networks. arXiv preprint arXiv:1905.11946 (2019)

20. Vaswani, A., et al.: Attention is all you need. In: Proceedings of the 31st International Conference on Neural Information Processing Systems, pp. 6000–6010. NIPS'17, Curran Associates Inc., Red Hook, NY, USA (2017)

21. Wspanialy, P., Moussa, M.: A detection and severity estimation system for generic diseases of tomato greenhouse plants. Comput. Electron. Agricult. **178**, 105701 (2020). https://doi.org/10.1016/j.compag.2020.105701

22. Zhao, Z., He, P.: YOLO-mamba: object detection method for infrared aerial images. Sig. Image Video Process. (2024). https://api.semanticscholar.org/CorpusID:272118442

HG-YOLO: Improving Tumor Detection with PP-HGNet and Global Attention Mechanism

Kien Trang[1,2,3], Bao Quoc Vuong[2,3(✉)], An Hoang Nguyen[1,2,3], Fung Fung Ting[1], and Chee-Ming Ting[1]

[1] School of Information Technology, Monash University, Malaysia Campus, 47500 Subang Jaya, Malaysia
[2] School of Electrical Engineering, International University, Ho Chi Minh City 700000, Vietnam
vqbao@hcmiu.edu.vn
[3] Vietnam National University, Ho Chi Minh City 700000, Vietnam

Abstract. Cancer continues to be a major global health issue, which is defined by uncontrolled cell proliferation and the potential invasion to other areas of the body. The early and precise detection of tumors through medical imaging is essential in improving cancer prognosis and treatment outcomes. This study presents HG-YOLO, a novel YOLO-based architecture enhanced by the integration of the PP-HGNet backbone and a Global Attention Mechanism (GAM). HG-YOLO capitalizes on the robust feature extraction capabilities of PP-HGNet and the attention-enhancing properties of GAM to improve the potential features. This combination aims to improve the sensitivity and precision of tumor localization, especially in complex cases where tumors are small or poorly delineated. Overall, the model is assessed using the Brain Tumor Detection 2020 (Br35H) dataset with the Magnetic Resonance Imaging (MRI) images. Comparative studies show that our HG-YOLO outperforms the prior versions in terms of Precision, Recall, mAP50 and mAP50-95 - giving 0.934, 0.915, 0.953, and 0.728, respectively.

Keywords: YOLO · brain tumor · MRI · deep learning · PP-HGNet

1 Introduction

The global healthcare system still faces significant challenges, leading to delays in cancer screenings, diagnoses, and treatments in some low-income nations. The International Agency for Research on Cancer reports that there were approximately 19.3 million new cases of cancer and nearly 10.0 million cancer-related deaths in 2020 alone [1]. The human brain is a biological marvel that coordinates innumerable physiological and cognitive functions in the human body. It is also vulnerable to certain diseases, including tumors. In fact, brain tumors can be either primary or metastatic, which are serious concerns due to their potential to disrupt neurological functions and threaten life [2]. Magnetic Resonance Imaging (MRI) and Computed Tomography (CT) remain

O. Gervasi et al. (Eds.): ICCSA 2025, LNCS 15648, pp. 332–344, 2025.
https://doi.org/10.1007/978-3-031-97000-9_21

the primary non-invasive imaging modalities for diagnosing brain tumors, while MRI is particularly vital for defining tumor boundaries and assessing invasion into adjacent structures [3].

One of the main challenges is that the size of lesions or tumors is still small in the early stages of many diseases, making them hard to discover and diagnose promptly. The ability to accurately detect such lesions would directly benefit the prognosis of patients and greatly raise their percentage of successful treatment with proper medical intervention. Deep Learning (DL) has demonstrated significant capability in the analysis of complicated medical datasets. Convolutional neural network (CNN) is considered a particular category of deep learning models, which have been widely utilized in medical imaging techniques such as X-rays, CT scans, and MRIs.

On the other hand, You Only Look Once (YOLO) model is proposed to overcome the end-to-end training compared with previous models. In general, YOLO-based models consist of three parts: backbone, neck, and head. Thanks to the single network architecture, these models can achieve high accuracy in real-time and is improved over the series of YOLO [4–6]. Several enhanced models have been developed to work with different types of medical diseases, such as tumors [7], lesions [8], and anatomical structures [9]. Besides, Real-time Detection Transformer (RT-DETR) [10] has recently been introduced as a competitor in the field of object detection. Integrating the use of a high-end feature extraction backbone and transformer-based architecture, RT-DETR shows robust performance in many tasks. Inspired by the previous studies, the contribution of this study is mentioned as follows:

- We propose using the feature extraction backbone in RT-DETR, which integrates PP-HGNet backbone into the YOLO-based model. This enhances the ability of the feature extraction process, which benefits dealing with the more complex scenarios of images.
- We improve the neck part by using Repeated Normalized Cross Stage Partial with Efficient Large Kernel Attention Network (RepNCSPELAN) and Global Attention Mechanism (GAM) to focus more on potential features in different scales. This also enhances the ability to detect small and low-contrast objects.
- We evaluate the proposed HG-YOLO on the Brain Tumor Detection 2020 (Br35H) dataset, which demonstrates superior performance in almost all metrics compared to the previous models.

2 Related Works

Conventional approaches to medical disease classification and lesion detection involve manual annotations of the region of interest, which are time-consuming and error-prone [11]. Recently, the development of Artificial Intelligence-based methods has contributed greatly to many healthcare applications, especially in the medical image analysis fields [12]. Several deep learning frameworks in recent years have been proposed with extreme levels of accuracy in different medical object detection tasks with real-time processing, such as CNN and RCNN-based models, U-Net series, Vision Transformers, etc. Among them, brain tumor is one of the most difficult targets for the latest medical object detection approaches using various DL architectures and algorithms.

In [13], the proposed NeuroNet19 model achieved highly competitive results of brain tumor classification with 99.3% accuracy and 99.2% in precision and recall on a combined dataset from 3 separate data sources Figshare, SARTAJ, and BR35H. The model utilized the Inverted Pyramid Pooling Module (iPPM) for enhancing the feature extraction capability by capturing multi-scale feature maps from an adjusted VGG19 architecture. Another study also implemented the combined dataset is Islam et al. [14], in which they achieved significant brain tumor classification results using transfer learning of multiple modified architectures, such as DenseNet121, VGG19, InceptionV3, and MobileNet. However, even though the above studies obtained great results in the combined MRI dataset, they are subjective to broaden their target imaging techniques such as CT-scans to strengthen their model's practical implementation ability.

In comparison to CNN-based methods, the approaches using YOLO-based models also obtain notable outcomes in brain tumor detection research. In [15], the authors validate the capability of YOLOv5 and YOLOv7 models in the same combined dataset and achieved more than 90% detection results in all Precision, Recall, F1-score, mAP50, and mAP50-95, respectively. These results demonstrate high potential in applying YOLO-based models in brain tumor detection problems. Mridul et al. [16] integrates the Segment Anything Model with the YOLOv9-based architecture named SIYO, composing of many innovative modules such as PGI and GELAN. The SIYO model surpasses the previous versions and obtained 94.7% in mAP50. Later, Ming Kang et al. [17] designed an enhanced model named BGF-YOLO by combining multiple modules: the Bi-level Routing Attention, the Generalized Feature Pyramid Networks and Fourth heading Head upon a YOLOv8-based architecture. The designed BGF-YOLO achieved state-of-the-art results in the brain tumor Br35H dataset of 91.9% in precision and 92.6% in recall, while obtaining a firm increase of 4.7% in mAP50 being 97.4% compared to the base YOLOv8x.

From the above studies, it is certain that YOLO-based architectures possess the potential to improve the brain tumor detection problem, especially in later versions with a refined architecture and the latest feature extraction modules. In this study, we aim to propose a deep-learning YOLOv11-based model for medical tumor detection. The results illustrate that our proposed model has further advanced the detection outcome of the previous versions of the YOLO-based model.

3   Proposed Method

3.1   Overview

In this study, a novel YOLO-based model is proposed to apply in classifying the medical disease. Similar to other YOLO versions, our model comprises three parts: backbone, neck, and head. Inspired from the Real-time Detection Transformer (RT-DETR), PP-HGNet is used to replace the original backbone module of YOLOv11, which aims to improve the feature extraction process, especially for small and unclear objects. In addition, the Repeated Normalized Cross Stage Partial with Efficient Large Kernel Attention Network (RepNCSPELAN) is implemented to deal with feature processing in the neck part, which might obtain more effective features. At the end of the neck part, we integrate the Global Attention Mechanism (GAM) before the head part, which may enhance the attention ability of each detection scale. This is designed to improve the detection ability to focus on different scales, potentially increasing its performance while maintaining a balance in sensitivity. The architecture of our proposed model is shown in Fig. 1.

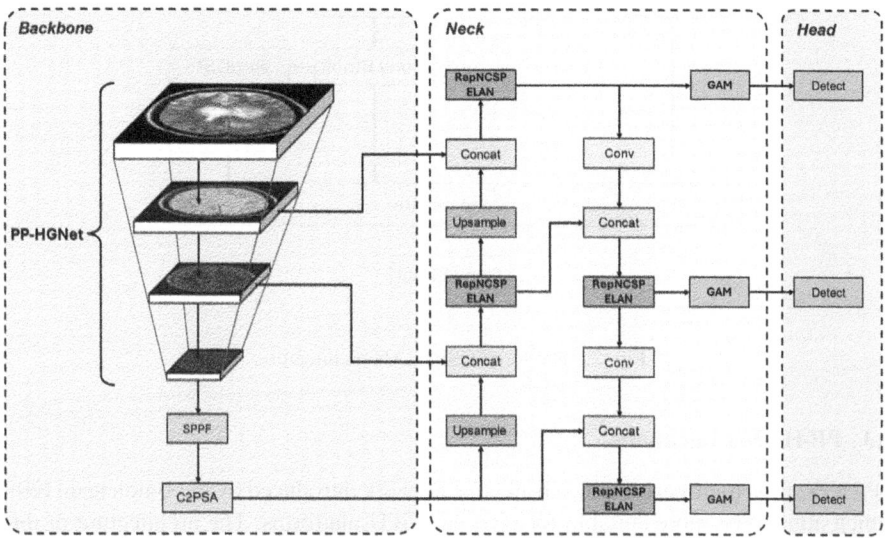

Fig. 1. Our proposed HG-YOLO model.

3.2 HG-YOLO Architecture

The main architecture of the proposed work is mainly based on YOLOv11. Therefore, some main blocks are still preserved to guarantee the advantages of the YOLO-based model. Initially, the Spatial Pyramid Pooling Fast (SPFF) module is integrated after the PP-HGNet, specifically engineered to extract more features from various regions of an image at multiple scales. This enhances the capability of the network to detect objects of varying sizes, particularly in identifying small objects. Additionally, Cross-stage Partial Spatial Attention (C2PSA) is applied to provide the attention mechanism at the end of the backbone part. This plays the role of emphasizing spatial relationships in feature maps to focus on critical areas of an image. The C2PSA block contains dual Partial Spatial Attention (PSA) modules, which operate on distinct branches. This configuration guarantees that the model prioritizes spatial information while simultaneously achieving a balance between speed and accuracy.

On the other hand, Repeated Normalized Cross Stage Partial with Efficient Large Kernel Attention Network (RepNCSPELAN) is used to replace the C3k2 block as default in the neck part. The RepNCSPELAN block is introduced in the YOLOv9, which is inspired by the architecture combination of Cross Stage Partial Network (CSPNet) [18] and Efficient Layer Aggregation Network (ELAN) [19]. This configuration ensures high performance and preservation of lightweight architecture at the same time. The illustration of RepNCSPELAN block is depicted in Fig. 2.

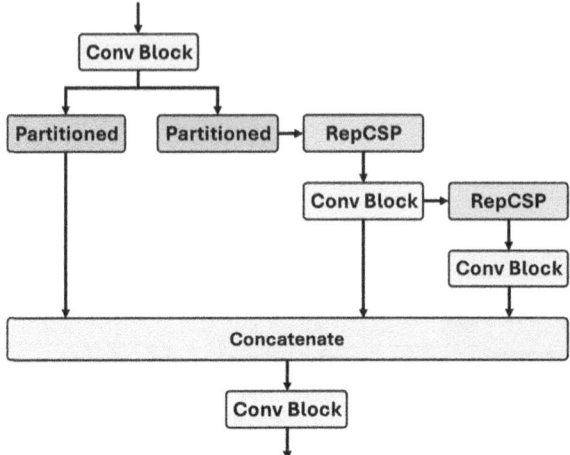

Fig. 2. The RepNCSPELAN architecture.

3.3 PP-HGNet Backbone

PP-HGNet is a high-performance backbone network introduced by the Baidu team [20], which aims to be more suitable for high-end GPU platforms. The architecture of this network employs a learnable downsampling layer (LDS Layer) from VOVNet and also amalgamates the strengths of pre-trained models such as ResNet [21], and PP-LCNet [22]. This method employs a hierarchical structure to extract features, which facilitates the effective handling of complicated image data. The illustration of PP-HGNet backbone is shown in the Fig. 3.

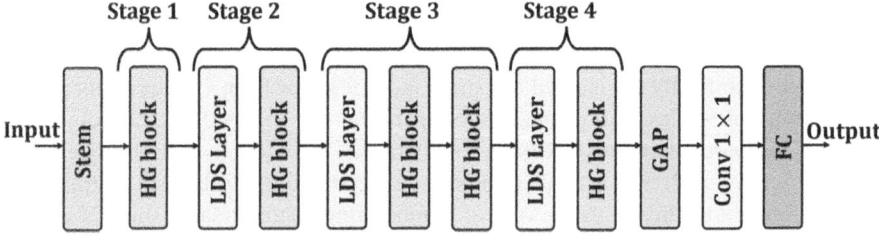

Fig. 3. The PP-HGNet architecture.

The main core of PP-HGNet is the HG Blocks positioned from the second to the fifth layers. These blocks play a crucial part in extracting the features and are meticulously designed for hierarchical data processing, which is illustrated in Fig. 4. This multilayered architecture enables the network to efficiently integrate elements at multiple levels of abstraction, aggregating both deep and general patterns the data. After the HG Block, Learnable Down-Sampling Layers are integrated, which contain a group of depth-wise convolutional and batch normalization layers to adaptively diminish the dimensions of the feature maps.

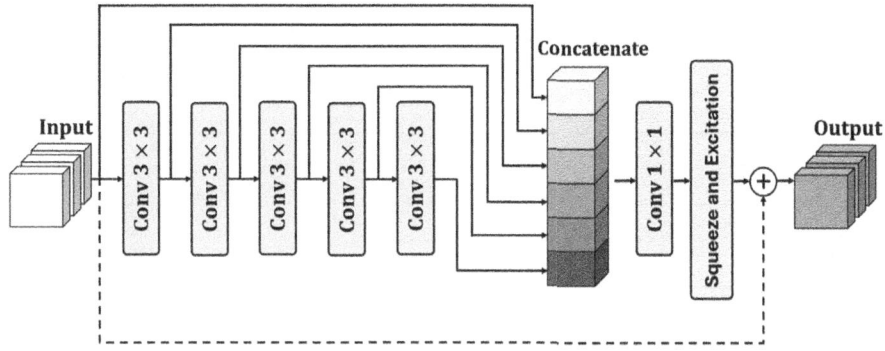

Fig. 4. The HGBlock interconnection.

Thus, in these blocks, the network takes an input and applies multiple convolutional layers, each denoted as Conv 3 × 3. These layers apply a convolution operation, which can be mathematically represented as:

$$F_l(X) = \sigma(W_l \cdot X + b_l) \tag{1}$$

where X is the input of the l-th layer, W_l and b_l are the weight and bias. The activation function is represented by σ. After the series of convolutions, features extracted at multiple scales are created. The feature maps from each stage get through the normalization process and are afterward concatenated, which is denoted as F_{concat} via (2).

$$F_{concat} = \text{CONCATENATE}(F_1, F_2, .., F_5) \tag{2}$$

To convert the feature map F_{concat} to a given size, the 1 × 1 convolution operation is applied to achieve a fixed-size feature map F'_{concat}. The concatenated feature map F_{concat} is then processed through a Squeeze-and-Excitation (SE) block, which adaptively recalibrates channel-wise feature responses for enhancing the representational power of the network. This process is formulated in (3).

$$S = \sigma\left(W_2 \cdot \delta\left(W_1 \cdot GAP\left(F'_{concat}\right) + b_1\right) + b_2\right) \tag{3}$$

where GAP represents global average pooling, W_1, b_1 and W_2, b_2 are the weights and biases of two fully connected layers, respectively. δ denotes the ReLU activation function, while σ is the sigmoid function. Finally, the optional step for adding the input features to the output is proposed to supplement the strength of extracted features.

3.4 Global Attention Mechanism

To achieve the enhancement in the context understanding, the Global Attention Mechanism (GAM) is applied to the end of each scale detection. The purpose of this implementation is to emphasize the essential features, which contribute to the final result. The organization of GAM is depicted in Fig. 5.

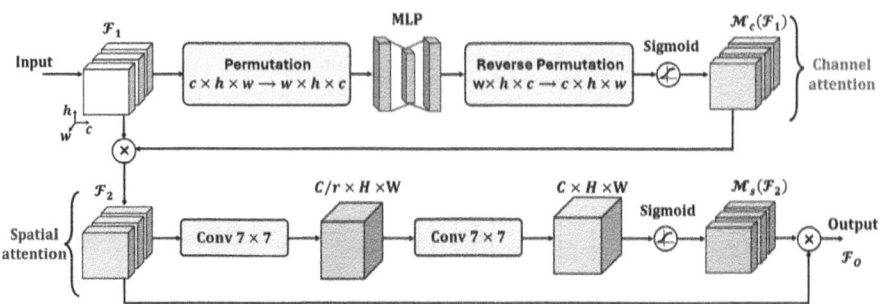

Fig. 5. The GAM interconnection.

In the channel attention part, the rearrangement of the position of input dimensions (channel, spatial, and height) from the feature map is conducted, and the feature information of each channel is vectorized for processing. The spatial features are then fed into a two-layer of Multilayer Perceptron (MLP). The training of the MLP effectively yielded the weight values for all spatial feature information across each dimension. Similar to other networks, the Sigmoid activation function is used to prevent the linearity of features. After these operations, the enhanced result $\mathcal{M}_c(\mathcal{F}_1)$ is reshaped to the same size of the initial feature map $\mathcal{F}_1$. Next, the initial feature map $\mathcal{F}_1$ is multiplied element-wise by channel attention-weighted feature map $\mathcal{M}_c(\mathcal{F}_1)$ to produce the enhanced result $\mathcal{F}_2$ for the next stage, as formulated in (4).

$$\mathcal{F}_2 = \mathcal{M}_c(\mathcal{F}_1) \otimes \mathcal{F}_1 \tag{4}$$

To continue the attention in spatial perspective, the enhanced result $\mathcal{F}_2$ from the previous stage with C channels is initially reduced to C/r by employing 7×7 convolution kernel, thereby improving the concentration of spatial feature information. The resulting features are subsequently rearranged to match the dimensions of the previous enhanced feature map $\mathcal{F}_2$ via a 7×7 convolution kernel, and these weights are compressed into weight values through the Sigmoid activation function. At the end, an element-wise multiplication between the spatial attention-weighted feature map and the feature map $\mathcal{F}_2$ is conducted to generate the final enhancement in both channel and spatial attention, as described in (5).

$$\mathcal{F}_O = \mathcal{M}_s(\mathcal{F}_2) \otimes \mathcal{F}_2 \tag{5}$$

4 Experiments and Results

4.1 Dataset

The dataset applied in this work is the Brain Tumor Detection 2020 (Br35H) dataset [23], which comprises approximately 700 MRI images in total collected from diverse patient demographics. This dataset encompasses a wide variety of tumor forms and stages, which are annotated by medical professionals to provide accurate ground-truth labels for the training of machine learning models.

4.2 Implementation Setting

In terms of conducting experiments, we implemented on the computer with Ubuntu 20.04 LTS, 12th generation of Intel core i7, and RTX 3090 containing 24Gb VRAM. The development framework is Pytorch 2.0, CUDA 11.7. The size of images in the dataset is rescaled to 640×640, and the training epoch and batch size are set to 300 and 32, respectively. The optimizer for training is AdamW, while the initial learning rate is 0.01.

4.3 Assessment Metrics

To evaluate the advantages and drawbacks of the proposed framework, the selected assessment metrics are mAP50, mAP50-95, precision, and recall, while the Mean Average Precision (mAP)50 and mAP50-95 are considered the main metrics to compare with other models and ablation studies.

The precision is defined as the ratio of true positive predictions to the total number of positive predictions, as shown in (6).

$$\text{Precision} = \frac{TP}{TP + FP} \tag{6}$$

where TP are the correct objects, FP are the objects that were incorrectly identified. The Eq. (7) describes the recall metric, which measures the ability of model to detect all relevant instances in the dataset.

$$\text{Recall} = \frac{TP}{TP + FN} \tag{7}$$

where FN are the objects that the model cannot detect. Additionally, mAP50 refers to the mean average precision calculated at an intersection-over-union (IoU) threshold of 50%. This means that detections are considered correct if the IOU is 50% or higher. On the other hand, mAP50-95 averages the AP calculated at multiple IOU thresholds ranging from 50% to 95%. This metric provides a measure of model performance through varying levels in the overlap criterion.

4.4 Quantitative Results

To give a comprehensive look of the learning ability, Fig. 6 shows the training progress with four evaluation metrics of our model. Overall, almost all the values reached saturation point and fluctuated less after 200 epochs. Only the mAP50-95 reaches around 0.7, while other metrics increase over 0.9. To emphasize the robustness of the proposed framework for medical disease detection, Table 1 displays the comparative results between other methods (YOLOv9 [4], YOLOv10 [5], YOLOv11 [6]) and our study. It is clear that our proposed architecture, which integrates PP-HGNet and GAM, achieves good performance. HG-YOLO achieves the highest values compared to other models. The precision of our model also reaches the best result, which matches the case of YOLOv9 at 0.934. However, in the case of mAP50-95, our model scores slightly lower but remains competitive.

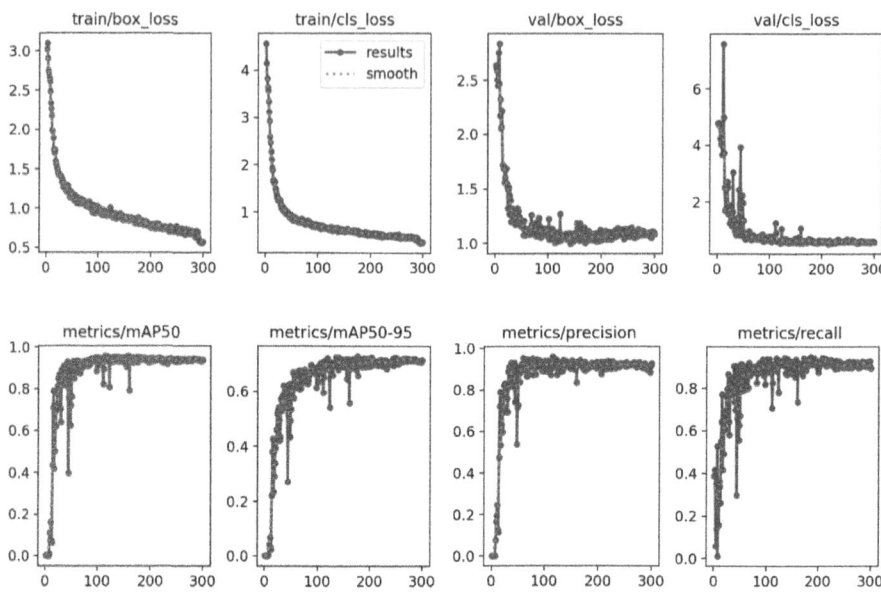

Fig. 6. The training progress of proposed model.

Table 1. Performance comparison of other models.

Model	Precision	Recall	mAP50	mAP50-95
YOLOv9	0.934	0.91	0.942	0.733
YOLOv10	0.908	0.831	0.927	0.717
YOLOv11	0.945	0.886	0.936	0.725
HG-YOLO (our)	**0.934**	**0.915**	**0.953**	**0.728**

4.5 Qualitative Results

Besides analyzing the quantitative results, we also conduct the detection of other models and our proposed framework perceptibly. The visualization of this comparison is shown in Fig. 7. In the first instance, while YOLOv10 and YOLOv11 have duplicated error detections, only YOLOv9 and our proposed model detect correctly the mass. Similarly, YOLOv10 and YOLOv11 models fail to detect the mass object in the second sample scan, while the remaining models successfully identify the tumor. In the third sample scan, YOLOv9 fails to detect the tumor entirely, whereas YOLOv10, YOLOv11, and the proposed model successfully identify the tumor. For the final cases, YOLOv9, YOLOv10, and YOLOv11 models fail to accurately detect the tumor, while our model shows advanced detection capability by accurately placing a correct bounding box. Overall, these results suggest that our proposed model achieves more reliable and precise mass localization compared to existing YOLO-based approaches.

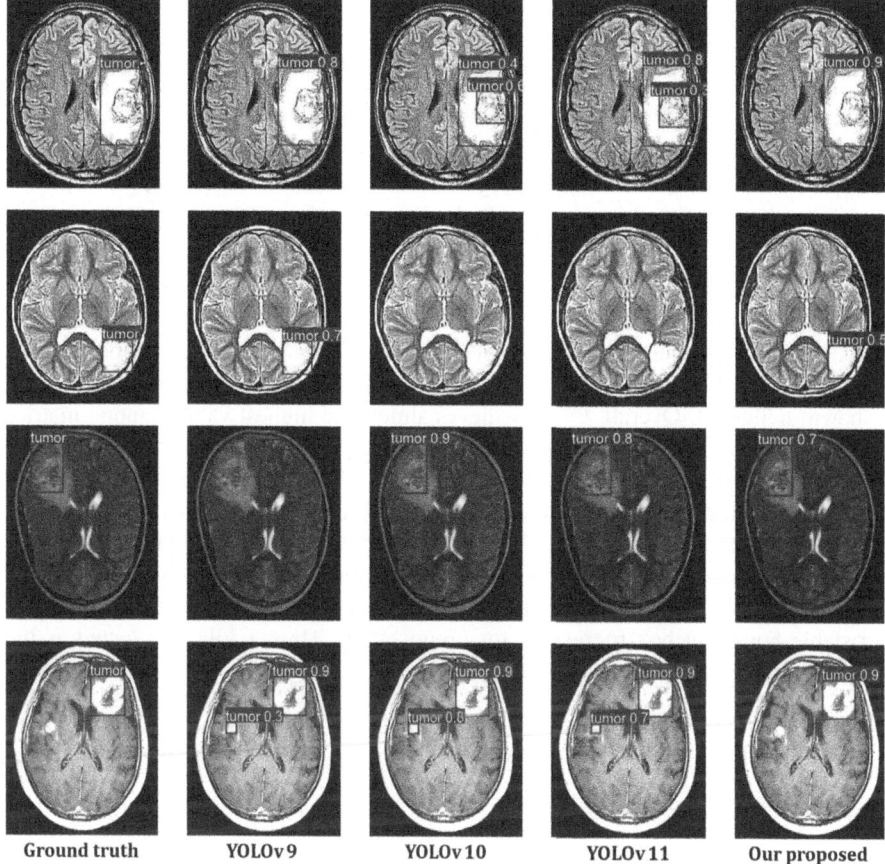

| Ground truth | YOLOv9 | YOLOv10 | YOLOv11 | Our proposed |

Fig. 7. The comparison of visualization between different models

4.6 Ablation Studies

In order to provide the comparative effects of implemented settings, we conduct the three sets of ablation studies.

Effect of Attention Module

The GAM module has been chosen to be applied to our proposed framework. To carry out the selection of this, Table 2 shows the performance comparison of different attention approaches such as Coordinate Attention (CA) [24] and Triplet Attention (TA) [25]. Among these methods, GAM consistently outperforms CA and TA in almost all metrics. Specifically, GAM achieves the highest Precision at 0.934, which surpasses CA at 0.922 and TA at 0.925. This indicates that GAM provides a more accurate distinction between tumors and non-tumor regions. In terms of mean Average Precision, GAM reaches an mAP50 of 0.953, slightly exceeding CA at 0.947 and TA at 0.945. For the stricter mAP50-95 metric, GAM still scores the highest value of 0.728. As a result, this emphasizes the selection of our implementation.

Table 2. Performance of different attention modules.

Method	Precision	Recall	mAP50	mAP50-95
CA	0.922	0.905	0.947	0.725
TA	0.925	0.925	0.945	0.726
GAM	**0.934**	**0.915**	**0.953**	**0.728**

Effect of Bounding Box Optimization Method

This optimization is primarily aimed to improve the bounding box regression for object detection tasks. To enhance the traditional IoU, advancements for IoU are proposed, such as CIoU [26], SIoU [27] and DIoU [28]. The comparison with different types of IoU is shown in Table 3. Overall, CIoU achieves almost the highest values among metrics compared to other methods. Although GIoU records the highest mAP50-95 of 0.732, which is higher than CIoU at 0.728 and SIoU at 0.726, CIoU still reaches the overall balance among the metrics. It achieves the highest Precision of 0.934, Recall of 0.915, and mAP50 of 0.953, compared to the other methods. This can be explained that CIoU considers not only the overlapping area but also the distance between the predicted and ground-truth box centers and the aspect ratio consistency, which leads to more precise and stable bounding box regression for optimization. Thus, CIoU is selected as the bounding box optimization method for our framework.

Table 3. Performance of different bounding box optimization methods.

Method	Precision	Recall	mAP50	mAP50-95
SIoU	0.921	0.9	0.94	0.726
GIoU	0.909	0.905	0.947	0.732
CIoU	**0.934**	**0.915**	**0.953**	**0.728**

5 Conclusion

This research presents the HG-YOLO model, which is a deep learning model designed to improve tumor detection in MRI images. By integrating the PP-HGNet backbone and Global Attention Mechanism (GAM), our model enhances feature extraction and improves the attention across different scales, leading to more accurate detections. Through experiments, HG-YOLO significantly outperformed previous models (YOLOv9, YOLOv10, and YOLOv11), demonstrating high precision, recall, and mAP scores on the Br35H dataset. Specifically, our proposed model achieved precision and recall rates of 0.934 and 0.915, respectively, and a mAP50 of 0.953, indicating superior detection performance. The combination of advanced feature extraction and focused attention on relevant features allows HG-YOLO to accurately identify even small or low-contrast tumors. This advancement suggests that the model could contribute to more reliable and early tumor detection, which offers promising applications in clinical environments. Future work can explore refining the attention mechanisms and feature extraction strategies to enhance detection performance while maintaining a lightweight architecture for practical settings.

Acknowledgments. This research is funded by International University, VNU-HCM under grant number T2023-05-EE.

Disclosure of Interests. The authors have no competing interests to declare that are relevant to the content of this paper.

References

1. Sung, H., et al.: Global cancer statistics 2020: GLOBOCAN estimates of incidence and mortality worldwide for 36 cancers in 185 countries. CA Cancer J. Clin. **71**(3), 209–249 (2021). https://doi.org/10.3322/CAAC.21660
2. Chera, B.S., Kirwan, J., Mendenhall, W.M.: Chapter 79 - Management of central nervous system metastases in breast cancer. In: Bland, K.I., Copeland, E.M. (eds.) The Breast, 4th edn., pp. 1297–1319. W.B. Saunders, Philadelphia (2009). https://doi.org/10.1016/B978-1-4160-5221-0.00079-6
3. Talukder, Md.A., et al.: An efficient deep learning model to categorize brain tumor using reconstruction and fine-tuning. Expert Syst. Appl. **230**, 120534 (2023). https://doi.org/10.48550/arXiv.2305.12844
4. Wang, C.-Y., Yeh, I.-H., Mark Liao, H.-Y.: YOLOv9: learning what you want to learn using programmable gradient information. In: Leonardis, A., Ricci, E., Roth, S., Russakovsky, O., Sattler, T., Varol, G. (eds.) ECCV 2024. LNCS, vol. 15089, pp. 1–21. Springer, Cham (2025). https://doi.org/10.1007/978-3-031-72751-1_1
5. Wang, A., et al.: YOLOv10: real-time end-to-end object detection. https://arxiv.org/abs/2405.14458
6. Glenn, J.: YOLOv11. GitHub (2024). https://github.com/ultralytics/ultralytics/releases/tag/v8.3.50
7. Sobek, J., et al.: MedYOLO: a medical image object detection framework. J. Digit. Imaging. Inform. Med. **37**(6), 3208–3216 (2024). https://doi.org/10.1007/s10278-024-01138-2
8. AlSadhan, N.A., Alamri, S.A., Ben Ismail, M.M., Bchir, O.: Skin cancer recognition using unified deep convolutional neural networks. Cancers **16**(7), 1246 (2024). https://doi.org/10.3390/cancers16071246
9. Zeng, P., et al.: TUSPM-NET: a multi-task model for thyroid ultrasound standard plane recognition and detection of key anatomical structures of the thyroid. Comput. Biol. Med. **163**, 107069 (2023). https://doi.org/10.1016/j.compbiomed.2023.107069
10. Zhao, Y., et al.: DETRs beat YOLOs on real-time object detection. In: 2024 IEEE/CVF Conference on Computer Vision and Pattern Recognition (CVPR), pp. 16965–16974 (2024). https://doi.org/10.1109/CVPR52733.2024.01605
11. Zhao, Y., et al.: Deep learning solution for medical image localization and orientation detection. Med. Image Anal. **81**, 102529 (2022). https://doi.org/10.1016/j.media.2022.102529
12. Alowais, S.A., et al.: Revolutionizing healthcare: the role of artificial intelligence in clinical practice. BMC Med. Educ. **23**, 689 (2023). https://doi.org/10.1186/s12909-023-04698-z

13. Haque, R., Hassan, M.M., Bairagi, A.K., Shariful Islam, S.M.: NeuroNet19: an explainable deep neural network model for the classification of brain tumors using magnetic resonance imaging data. Sci. Rep. **14**, 1524 (2024). https://doi.org/10.1038/s41598-024-51867-1

14. Islam, M.M., et al.: Transfer learning architectures with fine-tuning for brain tumor classification using magnetic resonance imaging. Healthc. Anal. **4**, 100270 (2023). https://doi.org/10.1016/j.health.2023.100270

15. Almufareh, M.F., Imran, M., Khan, A., Humayun, M., Asim, M.: Automated brain tumor segmentation and classification in MRI using YOLO-based deep learning. IEEE Access **12**, 16189–16207 (2024). https://doi.org/10.1109/ACCESS.2024.3359418

16. Mayankeyshwar, M., Kumar, L., Wagh, M.P., Behuria, S., Yadav, D.: Brain tumor detection and segmentation using SAM integrated YOLOv9 scheme. In: 2024 IEEE 1st International Conference on Advances in Signal Processing, Power, Communication, and Computing (ASPCC), pp. 67–72 (2024). https://doi.org/10.1109/ASPCC62191.2024.10881978

17. Kang, M., Ting, C.-M., Ting, F.F., Phan, R.C.-W.: BGF-YOLO: enhanced YOLOv8 with multiscale attentional feature fusion for brain tumor detection. In: Linguraru, M.G., et al. (eds.) MICCAI 2024. LNCS, vol. 15008. Springer, Cham (2024). https://doi.org/10.1007/978-3-031-72111-3_4

18. Wang, C.-Y., Liao, H.-Y.M., Wu, Y.-H., Chen, P.-Y., Hsieh, J.-W., Yeh, I.-H.: CSPNet: a new backbone that can enhance learning capability of CNN. In: 2020 IEEE/CVF Conference on Computer Vision and Pattern Recognition Workshops (CVPRW), Seattle, WA, USA, pp. 1571–1580. IEEE (2020). https://doi.org/10.1109/CVPRW50498.2020.00203

19. Wang, C.-Y., Liao, H.-Y.M., Yeh, I.-H.: Designing network design strategies through gradient path analysis. J. Inf. Sci. Eng. (JISE) **39**(4), 975–995 (2023). https://doi.org/10.6688/JISE.202307_39(4).0016

20. Paddle, P.: PP-HGNet series - 2022. GitHub. https://github.com/PaddlePaddle/PaddleClas/blob/release/2.5.2/docs/zh_CN/models/ImageNet1k/PP-HGNet.md. Accessed 09 Jan 2025

21. He, K., Zhang, X., Ren, S., Sun, J.: Deep residual learning for image recognition. In: 2016 IEEE Conference on Computer Vision and Pattern Recognition (CVPR), pp. 770–778 (2016). https://doi.org/10.1109/CVPR.2016.90

22. Cui, C., et al.: PP-LCNet: a lightweight CPU convolutional neural network. arXiv preprint, arXiv:2109.15099 (2021). https://doi.org/10.48550/arXiv.2109.15099

23. Br35H: Brain tumor detection 2020. Kaggle. https://www.kaggle.com/datasets/ahmedhamada0/brain-tumor-detection. Accessed 09 Jan 2025

24. Hou, Q., Zhou, D., Feng, J.: Coordinate attention for efficient mobile network design. In: 2021 IEEE/CVF Conference on Computer Vision and Pattern Recognition (CVPR), Nashville, TN, USA, pp. 13708–13717. IEEE (2021). https://doi.org/10.1109/CVPR46437.2021.01350

25. Misra, D., Nalamada, T., Arasanipalai, A.U., Hou, Q.: Rotate to attend: convolutional triplet attention module. In: 2021 IEEE Winter Conference on Applications of Computer Vision (WACV), pp. 3138–3147. IEEE, January 2021. https://doi.org/10.1109/WACV48630.2021.00318

26. Zheng, Z., et al.: Enhancing geometric factors in model learning and inference for object detection and instance segmentation. IEEE Trans. Cybern. **52**(8), 8574–8586 (2022). https://doi.org/10.1109/TCYB.2021.3095305

27. Gevorgyan, Z.: SIoU loss: more powerful learning for bounding box regression. arXiv preprint, arXiv:2205.12740 (2022). https://doi.org/10.48550/arXiv.2205.12740

28. Zheng, Z., Wang, P., Liu, W., Li, J., Ye, R., Ren, D.: Distance-IoU loss: faster and better learning for bounding box regression. In: Proceedings of the AAAI Conference on Artificial Intelligence, vol. 34, no. 07, April 2020. https://doi.org/10.1609/aaai.v34i07.6999

A Body Tracking Framework for Neuromotor Rehabilitation with Multimedia Application Support

Elvis Ribeiro[1], Alexandre Brandão[2], Marcelo Guimarães[3], Leonardo Rocha[1], José Remo Brega[4], Rodolfo Villaça[5], and Diego Dias[5(✉)]

[1] Universidade Federal de São João del-Rei (UFSJ), São João del-Rei, MG, Brazil
{elvishribeiro,lcrocha}@ufsj.edu.br
[2] Pontifícia Universidade Católica de Campinas (PUC-Campinas), Campinas, SP, Brazil
alexandre.brandao@puc-campinas.edu.br
[3] Universidade Federal de São Paulo (UNIFESP), Osasco, SP, Brazil
marcelo.paiva@unifesp.br
[4] Universidade Estadual Paulista (UNESP), Bauru, SP, Brazil
remo.brega@unesp.br
[5] Universidade Federal do Espírito Santo (UFES), Vitória, ES, Brazil
{rodolfo.villaca,diego.dias}@ufes.br

Abstract. Multimedia applications and games have become essential tools in rehabilitation and healthcare, providing an interactive and engaging approach that enhances patient motivation, enables progress tracking, and supports personalized treatment plans. These applications offer an innovative platform for both physical and cognitive therapy, allowing healthcare professionals to explore novel treatment methods while offering patients a more enjoyable and effective recovery experience. Despite recent advancements in hardware and software, there remains a need for integrated solutions that streamline the development of new applications, particularly those that leverage body-tracking sensors. This paper introduces a framework designed to simplify the creation of natural user interface (NUI) applications based on inertial sensors, supporting functionalities such as tracking, session creation, and data storage. Additionally, we present examples of applications developed using our framework, demonstrating its potential to facilitate new applications that utilize the user's body as a primary interaction medium.

Keywords: Virtual Reality · Serious Games · Multimedia · Neuromotor Rehabilitation · Sensors · Body Tracking · Software Development

1 Introduction

As people age, they may develop diseases that could be mitigated by regular physical activity, such as sarcopenia, osteoporosis, obesity, and cardiovascular

O. Gervasi et al. (Eds.): ICCSA 2025, LNCS 15648, pp. 345–360, 2025.
https://doi.org/10.1007/978-3-031-97000-9_22

diseases. The current landscape of physical inactivity [6,8] is linked to public health issues and the rise of non-communicable diseases (e.g., atherosclerosis, type 2 diabetes, and certain cancers), highlighting the importance of culture and lifestyle as strategies for health promotion and disease prevention. In this context, activities that engage large muscle groups—such as the muscles of the lower limbs—are particularly beneficial, as they promote intense blood circulation and, consequently, an increase in energy expenditure. For instance, body movements that simulate walking fulfill these requirements.

The search for new forms of entertainment that promote increased physical activity is of great social interest and tends to be more readily accepted when introduced in a playful manner and presented in immersive, interactive VR environments. Maloney et al. [7] suggest that interactive digital games hold potential benefits for increasing physical activity, particularly among children. Guimarães et al. [5] demonstrated that physical fatigue can limit user interaction time with gesture-based virtual technologies, implying that greater muscle strength could enhance interaction time with emerging gesture-supported technologies, such as hand-motion-controlled smart TVs, integrating these interactions naturally into daily life.

Multimedia applications play an important role today across various fields, including as rehabilitation tools [1,3,13]. Interaction is a key component of user engagement with virtual environments, achievable through controls, touch, or even gestures. The solution presented in this work leverages the user's natural interaction (NUI), captured via embedded inertial sensors. Ideally, the interaction between the user and the system should be as seamless as possible. In virtual reality (VR) systems, where immersion precludes the use of traditional input devices like keyboards, mice, and touchscreens, interaction is often achieved through specialized solutions such as joysticks, gestures, and voice. For users unable to operate a joystick, or when the goal is to encourage body movement, body-gesture interaction becomes an excellent alternative.

Body tracking technologies have been widely used in the gaming industry [4]. Optical tracking devices, such as Microsoft's *Kinect* or *Mocap* solutions,[1] utilize computer vision to track human movement [12]. However, Kinect has limitations in terms of freedom, accuracy, and occlusion, restricting user movement to the device's field of view and making it impossible to capture movements from certain angles. These issues are mitigated with *Mocap* solutions, which use multiple cameras and numerous markers on the user. However, the high cost of *Mocap* systems is a barrier to choosing a good yet reasonably priced solution. In this work, we use the *Biomechanical Sensor Node* (BSN) as an interaction device.

The BSN [2] is an innovative body-tracking device developed by Brandão and his team. It consists of a network of sensors strategically placed on the body to capture movements and postures in real time, allowing the user to control virtual environments through NUI. This data is processed to create a precise digital representation of the user. The BSN has potential applications in fields

---

[1] Body tracking using markers attached to the user's body and multiple high-definition cameras surrounding the environment.

such as physical rehabilitation, sports, and interactive entertainment, offering a valuable tool for professionals and researchers due to its precision and ease of use.

The main justification for this work stems from the challenge of simulating user interaction within a virtual environment in an intuitive and immersive manner. Another significant benefit of using virtual environments is that they provide a controlled and safe space for training, as the virtual setting poses no real danger compared to a physical training environment. Therefore, research focused on interaction methods for virtual environments is crucial for advancing and disseminating new applications.

In this work, we present the definition of a body tracking framework that facilitates the creation of NUI applications using the BSN device, along with the development and storage of physiotherapy sessions. This framework is demonstrated as an example for applications aimed at neuromotor rehabilitation, and additional example applications are also presented.

2   Methodology

Developing a framework involves a series of methodological steps. First, it is necessary to clearly identify and understand the problem or need that the framework aims to address. Next, an in-depth analysis of the problem domain is important to identify common patterns and abstractions. Based on this analysis, the next step is to design the framework's architecture, defining its main classes and interfaces as well as their interactions. The framework implementation should be modular and extensible, allowing developers to customize and extend its functionality as needed. Finally, it is crucial to provide detailed documentation and usage examples to help developers understand and effectively utilize the framework. It is important to note that framework development is an iterative process requiring continuous refinement and evolution based on user feedback and changes in domain needs.

The first step was to identify the common requirements of applications that would benefit from using the framework. Some functional requirements were identified, such as: multi-BSN connection – the ability to synchronize multiple BSNs to control different parts of the human body; user-friendly interface – an intuitive interface that enables the discovery and connection of BSN devices; and remote configuration – the ability to configure the framework from another device (such as a smartphone or desktop).

We adopted the Model-View-Controller (MVC) architecture and followed the event-driven programming paradigm. MVC is a widely used design pattern in software development that separates a system's components into three distinct parts. In this way, the asset is fully encapsulated, making the entire BSN configuration process transparent to the programmer/user.

2.1 Model

The Model is the module responsible for managing BSN devices, collecting data, and rotating virtual objects. It consists of the *BLE* API[2] BluetoothHardwareInterface and the BSNHardwareInterface class. This class does not store BSN data directly but instead maintains a list of a new class, BSNDevice, which abstracts a BSN device, and RotatableObject, the class that is actually available for the programmer to use.

The BSNHardwareInterface class is responsible solely for communicating with the BluetoothHardwareInterface and storing a list of BSNDevices. Upon receiving the FindBSN command via the ConfigurationAPI, the discovery process begins. Whenever a *beacon*[3] is found, BSNHardwareInterface receives a response containing the device's name and MAC address, then adds it to the BSN list and sends a response back to the ConfigurationAPI, indicating that the device has been found. This process is asynchronous and is triggered whenever a new *beacon* is detected, with all communication handled through *callbacks*.

The procedure for connecting a BSN is analogous to the discovery process. The ConfigurationAPI sends a connection command, passing the address of the device to be connected as a parameter. This connection command is forwarded to the BLE device, which eventually responds with a successful connection, providing all available services and characteristics. At this point, the *BSNDevice* object registers its *delegates* to receive data updates whenever they occur on the BSN.

The BSNDevice class represents a BSN within the application, containing its name, address, and a boolean field indicating whether it is connected. It also includes an object of the RotatableObject class, which is responsible for manipulating 3D objects in Unity[4]. This class provides methods that actually handle BSN data. Therefore, BSNDevice does not directly manage the data but rather passes it to RotatableObject. This setup allows the controlled object to be swapped by a BSN at runtime.

The RotatableObject class provides methods that receive data and are called by BSNDevice upon each *notify*[5] from the BSN, specifically the linear acceleration, raw data, and gravity vector. These methods are LinearAccHandler(Vector3 linAcc), RawDataHandler(Vector3 accelerometer, Vector3 gyroscope, Vector3 compass), and GravityVectorHandler(Vector3 gravityVector), respectively. These methods are not implemented by default and must be implemented by the user programmer. The ResetOffset() method is also available and should be called whenever BSN rotation compensation is required.

---

[2] *Application Programming Interface.*

[3] Signal from the BSN's BLE transmitter.

[4] Unity is a leading real-time development platform that allows the creation of 2D and 3D games and simulations for various platforms (PC, consoles, mobile, VR, and AR). It features a visual editor and scripting capabilities, providing professional tools that meet the requirements of any game.

[5] Data transmission from a BLE device.

To address orientation differences between the device and the virtual environment, the RotatableObject class has two functionalities: swapping one axis with another and inverting the direction of an axis. Both functionalities are useful for correcting axis orientation depending on the position where the BSN is attached to the user's body.

Another issue arises when we want the initial position of the BSN to differ from the default position – the *T-pose*[6]. Whenever initialized, the BSN needs to be kept at rest in a horizontal position for approximately 30 s before use to calibrate the sensors. In cases where the controlled object is the leg of an avatar, the BSN is attached vertically to the user's thigh, resulting in an unpredictable rotation of the thigh when the rotation should be zero. With this in mind, it is necessary to apply an *offset* to the BSN's rotation, so that:

$$Q_{object} = Q_{offset} * Q_{BSN}. \tag{1}$$

Q_{offset} must be calculated whenever rotation compensation is required, that is, to set the current rotation as zero rotation. The calculation is derived from Eq. (1), by multiplying the inverse of $Q_{BSN\ rotation}$ on both sides of the equation.

$$Q_{object} * Q_{BSN}^{-1} = Q_{offset} * Q_{BSN} * Q_{BSN}^{-1} \tag{2}$$

$$Q_{offset} = Q_{object} * Q_{BSN}^{-1} \tag{3}$$

When added to a *GameObject* in Unity, the RotatableObject class provides configuration fields in the *Inspector*. Two additional fields are created. The *Simplified Name* field is a nickname given to the object that appears in the configuration interface, while the *Precision Points* field sets the number of decimal places used for rotation. Its default value is two, based on empirical testing, which showed that more than two decimal places generally adds noise.

2.2   View

The View module consists of an interface created in Unity with the help of the *Modern UI Pack* asset for icons and animations [9]. This module has two classes: UIController, which manages the interface, and NetConfigurationServer, which handles network communication.

Since the goal was to create an integration asset capable of functioning in both new and legacy projects, the interface was designed to be as minimally invasive as possible. The interface includes a button that activates and deactivates the configuration interface, which is initially disabled.

The configuration screen consists of a search button, a panel listing the discovered BSNs, and a button to apply (assign the *offset*) rotation compensation to all BSNs. The search button remains disabled until a configuration server is found (as discussed in Sect. 2.3). Once the search is initiated, each discovered BSN is added to the panel. The item representing the discovered BSN includes

---

[6] In computer animation, the T-pose is a standard pose for the skeleton of a 3D model before it is animated.

the device's name, MAC address, a dropdown menu for selecting the object to control, and a connection button.

The `UIController` class is responsible for managing user input and projecting the information received from the Controller onto the user interface. It operates in conjunction with the `NetConfigurationClient`, which communicates over a network with the `NetConfigurationServer`. Initially, the `NetConfigurationServer` broadcasts messages on the network containing the application's *token* in search of a server. Upon receiving this token, the server sends a connection request (steps 2 and 3 of the sequence diagram). Subsequently, the client requests a list of available `RotatableObjects` and stores them in a list (step 4). From this point forward, all interactions are triggered by the end user through the interface (steps 5, 6, and 7).

2.3   Controller

The Controller is the layer responsible for receiving commands and applying them to the Model, as well as returning the Model's current state to the View. It consists of a configuration Application Programming Interface (API) that provides the necessary methods for a usage session of the asset.

Alongside the ConfigurationAPI, the NetConfigurationServer class acts as a listener for network commands, enabling remote configuration of BSNs by listening on a UDP socket managed by the *Ruffles* library [10]. Initially, the ConfigurationAPI listens for broadcasts on network port 5556, containing a token. If the token received in the broadcast matches the expected token, it is sent back to the originating device, and the system immediately awaits a connection request.

Once connected, the ConfigurationAPI waits for messages from the client, following the protocol outlined in Table 1. The data is separated from the command using the "/" character as a delimiter.

3   Results

The results of this work include direct implementations of the BsnAsset as an interaction tool in VR projects, demonstrated through applications such as Mazze and the Penalty Simulator. These two examples showcase the functionality of the BsnAsset for engaging both upper and lower limbs in interactive environments. Additionally, the framework supports creating and recording therapy sessions for neurorehabilitation and physiotherapy, enabling customized and trackable treatment activities.

3.1   Immersive Brain Puzzle

BLIND proposed an initial interaction model using the Gear VR controller, where the user points to the piece to select it and clicks to rotate it by -90°. However, upon further analysis, it was found that the Gear VR controller was not the most suitable for interaction, as bedridden patients would face challenges

Table 1. Messages awaited by the configuration server and client

	Message	Received Data
Server	Broadcast	Application identification token
	Connection	-
	StartDiscovering	-
	Connect	MAC address
	GetObjNames	-
	SetObj	MAC address and object name
Client	AllBsn	JSON containing a summary of all connected BSNs
	ObjNames	List of available RotatableObject names

in holding and clicking the controller. Therefore, the BSNAsset was employed in the study since the BSN is attached to the patient's wrist, relieving them from the burden of holding the device and clicking.

The functional requirements for interaction with the BSN are as follows:

- The patient must be able to move a virtual hand by pointing with their arm.
- The section under the virtual hand is selected and rotated by -90º when the patient rotates their wrist along the sagittal axis.

The virtual hand must move in only two dimensions. Therefore, we had to convert the three-dimensional rotation of the BSN into the two-dimensional position of the virtual hand. The solution was to create an empty object positioned near the camera, serving as a pivot for the rotation of an invisible cube. The position of the invisible cube was then converted to a two-dimensional position using Unity's WorldToScreenPoint(Vector3) method, which returns the position of an object relative to the camera. Figure 1 shows a simulation of the movement from the center to the right.

The selection and rotation of elements are performed using the X-axis of the gravity vector. A small threshold is set for selecting the piece, and a larger threshold is established for rotation. The piece is selected through hand rotation (according to sensitivity). The hand is locked onto the selected element, and by continuing to rotate, the piece is rotated. Movement is released once the user returns their hand to the horizontal position.

The rotation sensitivity increases as the pivot moves in the negative direction of the Z-axis, limited from 0 to -10, where 0 is the least sensitive and -10 is the most sensitive (Eq. (4)). The selection and rotation sensitivity are also adjusted, provided that the selection sensitivity is less than the rotation sensitivity, and both are below 9.8 (Eq. (5)).

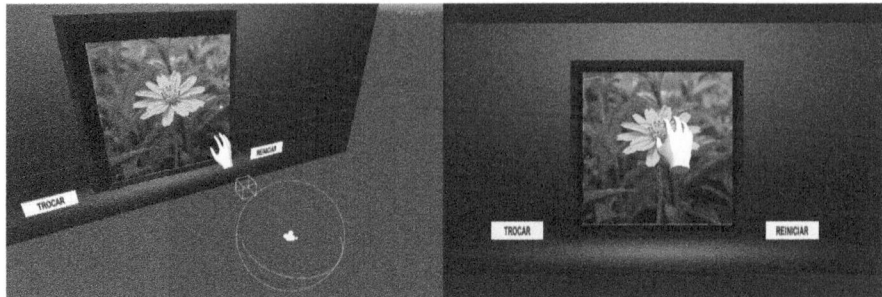

(a) Pivot without rotation

(b) Pivot rotated to the right

Fig. 1. Virtual hand movement driven by pivot rotation

$$Pivot_{position} = (0, 0, -Sense), 0 < Sense < 10. \tag{4}$$

$$0 < Sense_{selection} < Sense_{rotation} < 9.8 \tag{5}$$

3.2   Mazze

Mazze is a game featuring a procedurally generated maze [14], within which a sphere and several golden coins are placed (Fig. 2). The goal is for the player to navigate the sphere through the maze to collect all coins in the shortest time possible.

During gameplay, the user rotates the BSN to control the maze's movement, allowing for precise reproduction of the user's hand movements as they guide the sphere through the corridors. The BSN is positioned horizontally, either on the back or palm of the hand, and utilizes only the device's rotation (Euler angles) to manipulate the maze. Due to its plug-and-play functionality, the *BsnAsset* only requires specifying that the maze is to be controlled by the device, making setup quick and intuitive. Mazze serves as a valuable tool in motor rehabilitation for the hands, allowing patients to perform therapeutic exercises in an engaging and interactive environment. As they play, patients improve hand coordination and control, seamlessly integrating rehabilitation into a fun activity.

Fig. 2. Initial state of the Mazze game

3.3 Penalty Simulator

The Penalty Simulator fully leverages the capabilities of the *BsnAsset* to create an immersive and interactive rehabilitation experience. This application captures raw data from the BSN through the asset's API, enabling precise tracking of leg movements. The game takes place in a virtual soccer field, where the user faces off against a goalkeeper, as illustrated in Fig. 3. By kicking a virtual ball, the user engages in physical activity that can help improve lower limb strength and coordination, while also enjoying a motivating gameplay experience.

During the simulation, the user manipulates the avatar's leg and shin through two BSNs: one placed on the anterior thigh (medial portion) and the other on the lower leg (distal portion). These sensors capture the user's physical movements and translate them into the virtual environment. The *BsnAsset* operates in a *plug-and-play* mode, where it is easily configured in Unity to allow the BSNs to control the specified avatar segments directly. The kick force, calculated based on the accelerometer data provided by the asset's API, determines the power applied to the virtual ball. This realistic simulation aids in enhancing coordination and strength in the lower limbs, contributing to neuromotor rehabilitation efforts.

When the avatar's foot makes contact with the ball, the kick force is determined by multiplying the acceleration data obtained from the BSN's accelerometer by a predefined constant, representing the mass of the foot. This calculated force is then applied to the ball as an impulse, directed along the collision normal

Fig. 3. Penalty Simulator Scenario

and opposing the direction of impact. This approach simulates realistic physical interactions, allowing the ball's motion to respond dynamically based on the strength and direction of the kick.

The goalkeeper's save is calculated by predicting the ball's trajectory to determine where it will reach the goal, using ballistic motion equations. Based on this prediction, the animation in which the goalkeeper most closely intercepts the ball is triggered. However, as these animations were created deterministically, the goalkeeper's potential save points are limited to predefined areas. Despite this limitation, the simulator offers an engaging way for health professionals to encourage patients to perform leg exercises in a playful and interactive environment, where the physical movement required for kicking contributes to rehabilitation efforts.

3.4   Recorder and Recorder Controller

ReBase [15] was developed as a non-relational database designed specifically for storing neuromotor rehabilitation sessions, encompassing both session details and the movements performed by the patient during exercises. In [15], the storage structure is outlined, and an API is provided to facilitate data recording and retrieval.

To leverage this recording API with 3D avatar rotation data, two assets were developed: the Recorder and Recorder Controller. These assets are distributed as packages, allowing for independent use across different devices, provided they are on the same LAN network, or on the same device, as demonstrated in Sect. 3.5.

The advantage of using the Recorder Controller on a separate device is that it enables the patient to engage with VR applications through a VR headset, while the recording control is managed remotely.

The Recorder is a tool designed to recognize, interpolate, and save rotation data for a 3D avatar. It functions independently of the body tracking method, provided the avatar adheres to the standard defined by the Recorder.

The Recorder's execution flow begins when the network communication module receives a command to initiate the motion recording session. The data is then stored at a sample rate that matches the current frame rate (or Frames per Second, FPS) of the application.

3.5 Mobility Tests

[11] conducted a comparative analysis between the VICON optical body tracking system and the BSN solution. His tests were based on the execution of the Sit-to-Stand task, an exercise in which the patient sits and stands from a chair without hand support. For this comparison, hip goniometric angles (formed on the lateral axis by the abdomen and thigh) and knee angles (formed on the lateral axis by the thigh and lower leg) were measured. These measurements were obtained using a set of three BSNs positioned on the abdomen, thigh, and lower leg (frontal plane), alongside the corresponding rotations obtained from the VICON system.

Thus, a demand arose for an application to capture this data with the following requirements:

- Simple application, without VR;
- Ability to connect three BSNs simultaneously; and
- Data must be recorded in a CSV (Comma-Separated Values) file containing raw rotation information (Accelerometer and Gyroscope) and goniometric angle values for the hip and knee.

To meet these requirements, we created the BSN Mobility Tests application, utilizing all the previously developed assets: BSNAsset, Recorder, and Recorder Controller, all running on a single device, as there is no need for patient interaction with the application. In addition to the mentioned assets, a CSV file recorder was created to export session data simultaneously with the recording in ReBase.

Finally, [11] presents a moderate to strong correlation between rotations in both solutions, reaffirming the validity of using BSNs in healthcare.

3.6 Body Tracking

Following the demand from BSN Mobility Tests, the need arose to create an application capable of complete body tracking using BSNs. This application supports recording accelerometer, gyroscope, and 3D rotation data, as well as recording rotation data for each body joint (goniometric angles).

The application allows the user to freely utilize body joints, limited to groups of joints: upper right – right arm, right forearm; upper left – left arm, left forearm; lower right – right thigh, right leg; and lower left – left thigh, left leg.

The BSNs must be positioned on the body. On the arms, BSNs should be positioned with the LED facing upwards and the device face oriented outward from the body. On the legs, BSNs should be positioned with the LED facing upwards and the device face oriented forward.

Charts. The following section presents charts generated from data collected by BSN Body Tracking. The charts were created using Excel software, and the data used was collected from a user performing flexion and extension movements of the upper and lower limbs.

Bicep Curl. The bicep curl is an exercise that works the biceps brachii muscles. The movement involves flexing the elbow to bring the hand closer to the shoulder, performed with the arms extended alongside the body, elbows bent, and wrists in supination.

Data collection was conducted with the user performing a total of 10 repetitions of the exercise with the right arm (Fig. 4a) and 10 repetitions with the left arm (Fig. 4b).

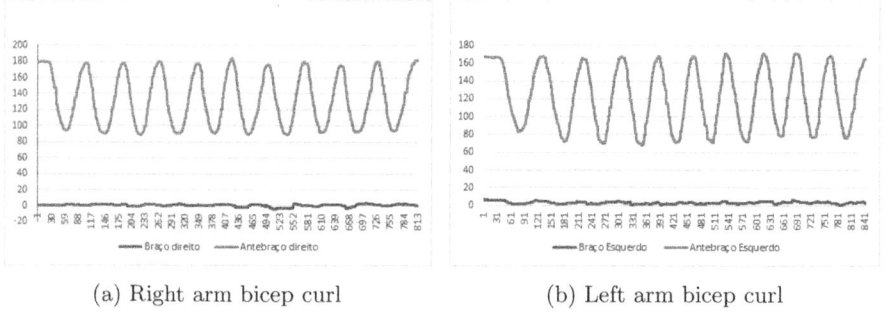

(a) Right arm bicep curl   (b) Left arm bicep curl

Fig. 4. Goniometric charts of the bicep curl

The charts in Fig. 4 show that the goniometric angles of the elbow decrease as the user flexes the elbow, and increase as the user extends the elbow, ranging between approximately 180º and 90º.

The charts in Fig. 5 represent the accelerometer data collected during the exercise. It is evident that the accelerometer data for the right and left arms are similar, as are the data for the right and left forearms. The forearm accelerometers show higher values than the arm accelerometers, as the forearms rotated during the exercise while the arms remained static.

Stationary March. Stationary march is an exercise that simulates walking in place. The movement is performed by lifting the knee until it aligns with the hip, then returning to the initial position.

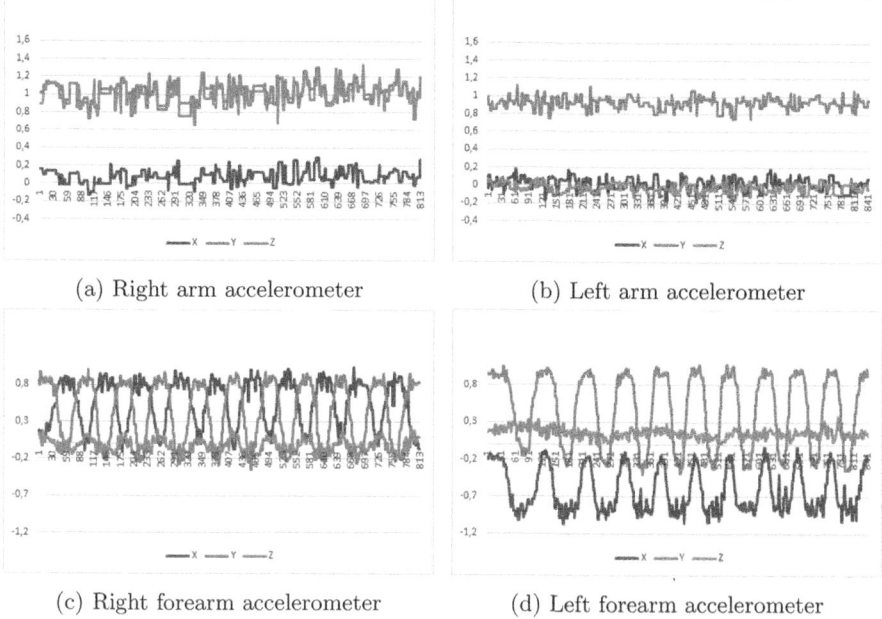

(a) Right arm accelerometer   (b) Left arm accelerometer

(c) Right forearm accelerometer   (d) Left forearm accelerometer

Fig. 5. Accelerometer charts for bicep curl

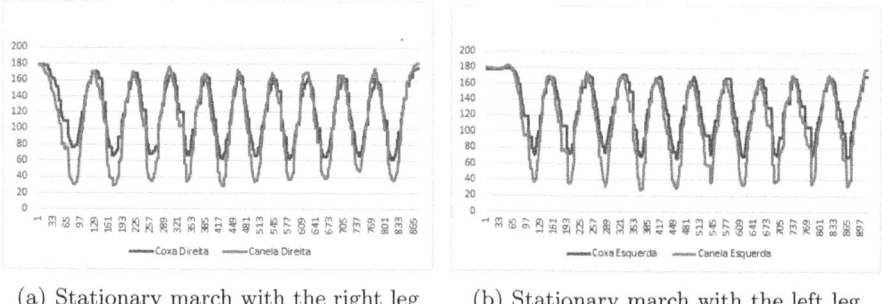

(a) Stationary march with the right leg   (b) Stationary march with the left leg

Fig. 6. Stationary march charts

Data collection was conducted with the user performing a total of 10 repetitions with the right leg Fig. 6a and 10 repetitions with the left leg 6b.

The charts in Fig. 6 show that the goniometric angles of the knee and hip decrease as the user flexes the knee, and increase as the user extends the knee, ranging between approximately 180º and 90º.

The charts in Fig. 7 represent the accelerometer data collected during the exercise. It is evident that the accelerometer data for the right and left legs are similar, as are the data for the right and left shins. The leg accelerometers display axis swapping, indicating a rotation of the device. Conversely, the shin

accelerometers show no rotation but exhibit variations in the Y and Z axes due
to the upward and downward shin movement.

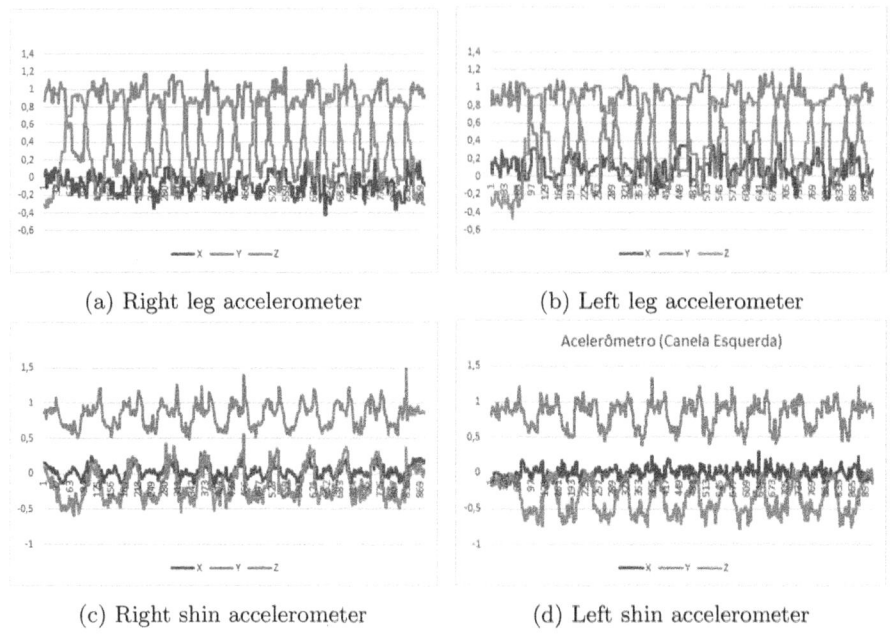

(a) Right leg accelerometer   (b) Left leg accelerometer

(c) Right shin accelerometer   (d) Left shin accelerometer

Fig. 7. Accelerometer charts for stationary march

4   Conclusions and Future Work

With the increasing presence of VR in homes and medical clinics, it has proven
to be a highly effective tool for encouraging physical exercise and aiding in the
rehabilitation of patients with neuromotor impairments due to various conditions, such as stroke. This growth presents a significant opportunity to develop
a wide range of applications tailored to specific therapeutic needs. However,
despite the accessibility and immersive capabilities provided by VR headsets,
achieving a natural and intuitive interaction method remains a key challenge in
VR application development.

The drive to create a natural interaction method that is sufficiently versatile
to function across various VR applications, while allowing for customization
based on the unique needs of each project, has been a guiding principle of this
work and the motivation behind the creation of the BSNAsset.

In this study, we proposed and developed an asset that facilitates the connection of multiple devices, enables human body tracking, and supports the control
of a virtual avatar. The solution we developed is straightforward to import and

use within any Unity project, offering a flexible tool for diverse applications. As demonstrated, the BSNAsset can be used to create comprehensive body-tracking applications, with the capability to interact seamlessly with both upper and lower limbs.

Acknowledgment. The authors acknowledge partial funding from the Coordination for the Improvement of Higher Education Personnel - Brazil (CAPES) - Funding Code 001, the National Council for Scientific and Technological Development (CNPq), and the Research Support Foundation of the State of Minas Gerais (FAPEMIG). We also thank the Research and Innovation Support Foundation of Espírito Santo (FAPES) for the resources provided through the PROAPEM project (368/2022 - P: 2022-NGKM5) and the PDPG project (129/2021 - P: 2021-GL60J), which were fundamental to the completion of this work.

References

1. Aramaki, A.L., Sampaio, R.F., Reis, A., Cavalcanti, A., et al.: Virtual reality in the rehabilitation of patients with stroke: an integrative review. Arq. Neuropsiquiatr. **77**, 268–278 (2019)
2. Brandão, A.F., et al.: Biomechanics sensor node for virtual reality: a wearable device applied to gait recovery for neurofunctional rehabilitation. In: International Conference on Computational Science and Its Applications, pp. 757–770. Springer (2020)
3. Cano Porras, D., Siemonsma, P., Inzelberg, R., Zeilig, G., Plotnik, M.: Advantages of virtual reality in the rehabilitation of balance and gait. Neurology **90**(22), 1017–1025 (2018). https://doi.org/10.1212/WNL.0000000000005603
4. Difini, G.M., Martins, M.G., Barbosa, J.L.V.: Human pose estimation for training assistance: a systematic literature review. In: Proceedings of the Brazilian Symposium on Multimedia and the Web, pp. 189–196 (2021)
5. Guimaraes, M.P., Martins, V.F., Brasil, G.J.C., Trevelin, L.C.: Um modelo de processo de desenvolvimento de interfaces de gesto: Definição e um estudo de caso. In: XXXVII Conferencia Latinoamericana de Informática (CLEI), vol. 1, pp. 378–390 (2011)
6. Hallal, P.C., Bauman, A.E., Heath, G.W., Kohl, H.W., Lee, I.M., Pratt, M.: Physical activity: more of the same is not enough. Lancet **380**, 189–190 (2012)
7. Maloney, A.E., Threlkeld, K.A., Cook, W.L.: Comparative effectiveness of a 12-week physical activity intervention for overweight and obese youth: Exergaming with dance dance revolution. Games Health J. Res. Dev. Clin. Appl., 1–8 (2012)
8. Malta, D.C., Silva, J.B.: Policies to promote physical activity in Brazil. Lancet **380**, 195–196 (2012)
9. Michsky: Modern UI pack (2021). https://assetstore.unity.com/packages/tools/gui/modern-ui-pack-150824
10. MidLevel: Ruffles (2021). https://github.com/MidLevel/Ruffles
11. Otoboni, G.B.: Comparação entre sensores inerciais e sistema de análise de movimento VI na avaliação da tarefa de Sit-to-Stand em adultos jovens saudáveis, Master's thesis, Escola de Engenharia de São Carlos (EESC-USP) (2022)
12. Pfister, A., West, A.M., Bronner, S., Noah, J.A.: Comparative abilities of Microsoft Kinect and Vicon 3D motion capture for gait analysis. J. Med. Eng. Technol. **38**(5), 274–280 (2014)

13. Rodrigues, L.G., et al.: Upper limb motion tracking and classification: a smartphone approach. In: Proceedings of the Brazilian Symposium on Multimedia and the Web, pp. 61–64 (2021)
14. Styanton: Maze generator (2021). https://assetstore.unity.com/packages/tools/modeling/maze-generator-38689
15. Trotta Lara Barbosa, T., et al.: Rebase: data acquisition and management system for neuromotor rehabilitation supported by virtual and augmented reality. In: Symposium on Virtual and Augmented Reality, pp. 182–186. SVR'21, Association for Computing Machinery, New York, NY, USA (2021). https://doi.org/10.1145/3488162.3488225

Multimodal Approach for Canine Dermatological and Ophthalmological Disease Diagnosis Using YOLOv11 with Data Augmentation and Autoencoder Techniques

Thi Diem Huong Nguyen, Van Loc An Ho, and Vinh Dinh Nguyen[✉]

Department of Information Technology, FPT University, Can Tho Campus,
Can Tho City, Vietnam
{huongntdce171360,anhvlce171612}@fpt.edu.vn, vinhnd29@fe.edu.vn

Abstract. Accurate detection of canine dermatological and ophthalmological diseases is essential for improving animal health and supporting veterinary diagnostics. This study introduces a comprehensive approach that integrates the YOLOv11 object detection model with advanced data augmentation and feature extraction techniques, including Autoencoder (AE), CutMix, and Local Binary Patterns (LBP). YOLOv11 provides precise localization and classification of lesions, while Autoencoders enhance feature representation by reducing noise and improving generalization. CutMix increases data diversity, aiding in model robustness, and LBP captures critical texture details relevant to skin and eye conditions. Twelve datasets were created, combining these techniques in various configurations to assess their individual and synergistic effects on model performance. The proposed method achieves a mean Average Precision at 50% Intersection over Union (mAP@50) of 97.2% on the original image dataset and 86.6% on complex images when using a hybrid dataset that integrates original images with LBP, CutMix, and Autoencoder, significantly outperforming models trained on unaugmented data. This result demonstrates the effectiveness of combining deep learning with texture analysis and advanced augmentation strategies in handling complex veterinary diagnostic tasks. The findings highlight the potential of automated systems to improve early detection and accurate diagnosis of canine diseases, offering a reliable, scalable solution for real-world clinical applications.

Keywords: YOLOv11 · Canine Disease Diagnosis · Dermatological and · Ophthalmological Imaging · Autoencoder · CutMix · Local Binary Pattern (LBP) · Data Augmentation · Hybrid Dataset · Deep Learning in Veterinary Medicine

1 Introduction

The increasing prevalence of dermatological and ophthalmological diseases in dogs has become a significant concern in veterinary medicine. These conditions,

© The Author(s), under exclusive license to Springer Nature Switzerland AG 2025
O. Gervasi et al. (Eds.): ICCSA 2025, LNCS 15648, pp. 361–374, 2025.
https://doi.org/10.1007/978-3-031-97000-9_23

if left undiagnosed or untreated, can lead to severe complications such as chronic discomfort, vision impairment, skin infections, and, in extreme cases, permanent tissue damage [1]. Traditional diagnostic methods primarily rely on visual inspection and clinical expertise, which can be subjective, time-consuming, and heavily dependent on the veterinarian's experience. This reliance on human assessment poses challenges for early and accurate disease detection, especially in remote areas with limited access to specialized veterinary care [2].

Recent advancements in artificial intelligence (AI) and computer vision have demonstrated promising potential in overcoming these diagnostic challenges. AI-based image analysis models have achieved remarkable success in human healthcare, particularly in detecting skin and ocular diseases through automated medical image interpretation [3]. These technologies not only improve diagnostic accuracy but also enable faster, more consistent evaluations, reducing the likelihood of human error. Inspired by these developments, the application of AI-driven approaches in veterinary medicine is gaining traction, offering the potential to enhance diagnostic precision, accessibility, and efficiency for common conditions in dogs [4].

In this study, we propose an automated diagnostic framework that leverages the capabilities of the YOLOv11 object detection model, known for its real-time detection accuracy and efficiency in complex visual tasks [5]. To further enhance feature representation, we integrate Autoencoder-based feature extraction, Cut-Mix for data augmentation, and Local Binary Patterns (LBP) for texture analysis. This multi-technique approach aims to improve the model's ability to detect subtle pathological changes, ensuring robustness across diverse imaging conditions. The model is trained and evaluated on a comprehensive dataset of annotated canine skin and eye disease images, incorporating various augmentation techniques to mitigate overfitting and enhance generalization.

Our key contributions are as follows:

- We propose a novel diagnostic framework that combines YOLOv11, Autoencoder, CutMix, and LBP for accurate detection and classification of canine dermatological and ophthalmological diseases.
- We introduce a hybrid data augmentation strategy to improve model robustness, enabling effective performance across both standard and complex image conditions.
- We demonstrate the potential of AI-driven diagnostic tools in veterinary medicine, highlighting their efficacy in early disease detection and clinical decision support.

This paper is structured as follows: Sect. 2 reviews AI applications in veterinary diagnostics. Section 3 details the proposed methodology, including dataset, model architecture, and training process. Section 4 presents experimental results and discussions on augmentation impact. Finally, Sect. 5 concludes the study and suggests future research directions.

2   Related Work

Deep learning, particularly convolutional neural networks (CNNs) and YOLO-based models, has significantly advanced AI-driven veterinary diagnostics. These models have demonstrated strong capabilities in image classification, object detection, and segmentation, making them well-suited for diagnosing various animal diseases.

Huang et al. (2021) utilized YOLOv4 with ensemble learning to classify trap-neuter-return (TNR) surgical images of stray animals. Their approach reduced manual workload by 80% while achieving a mean average precision (mAP) of 91.99%, showcasing YOLO's ability to streamline high-throughput veterinary imaging tasks [6]. Similarly, Shaffer (2021) explored the role of AI in genetic trait analysis by identifying genetic variants linked to various canine diseases, demonstrating the potential of AI in predictive diagnostics [7].

In ophthalmology, Kim et al. (2022) developed a YOLOv5-based object detection model for diagnosing dry eye disease (DED) in dogs. Their approach utilized video-based corneal imaging and achieved an impressive mAP of 99.5%, emphasizing YOLO's precision in eye disease detection [8]. Additionally, Kour et al. (2022) conducted a comprehensive review of AI applications in veterinary medicine, highlighting CNNs' effectiveness in disease classification and early detection across various species [9].

Ali et al. (2023) applied YOLO to localize the optic disc in retinal fundus images, proving the model's reliability in eye-related diagnostics [10]. Meanwhile, Josphineleela et al. (2023) introduced a multi-stage Faster RCNN-based iSPLInception model for skin disease classification, overcoming overfitting issues and achieving 95.82% accuracy [11].

Beyond conventional imaging, Kim et al. (2024) proposed an AI-driven "Health Score" system that predicts canine diseases based on multifaceted behavioral data collected over three months. The system achieved an 87.5% concordance with veterinarian assessments, offering a non-invasive approach to early disease detection [12]. Additionally, Smith et al. (2024) developed an object detection model using Tiny YOLOv4 to diagnose pododermatitis and neoplasia in canine paws. Their system achieved a mAP of 0.95 and demonstrated real-time disease identification capabilities [13].

Scharre et al. (2025) compared an AI-driven equine ophthalmic diagnostic tool with veterinarians, finding that the AI model achieved a 93% accuracy rate, outperforming general veterinarians (76%) in detecting ophthalmic diseases [14]. Kalita et al. (2025) reviewed AI and ML applications in poultry disease detection, emphasizing advancements in non-invasive monitoring techniques such as thermal imaging and real-time behavioral analysis [15].

These studies highlight AI's transformative impact on veterinary diagnostics, yet challenges such as dataset generalizability, model interpretability, and real-world deployment remain. Table 1 summarizes key advancements in AI-based veterinary diagnostic research, outlining their methodologies and limitations.

Table 1. Summary of Recent Advances in AI-based Veterinary Diagnostics.

Year	Authors	Dataset	Method	Accuracy	Limitations
2021	Huang et al. [6]	TNR surgical images	YOLOv4 ensemble learning	mAP 91.99%	Limited to TNR images
2021	Shaffer [7]	Genetic traits in dogs	AI-based genetic analysis	-	Lacks diagnostic benchmarks
2022	Kim et al. [8]	Dog eye disease images	YOLOv5 object detection	mAP 99.5%	Small dataset
2022	Kour et al. [9]	Veterinary disease datasets	AI-based review	-	Lacks experimental validation
2023	Ali et al. [10]	Retinal fundus images	YOLO-based optic disc localization	-	Limited to fundus images
2023	Josphineleela et al. [11]	Skin disease datasets	Faster RCNN-based iSPLInception	Accuracy 95.82%	Computationally expensive
2024	Kim et al. [12]	Canine behavior data	AI-based health score	87.5% concordance	Needs clinical validation
2024	Smith et al. [13]	Canine paw disease images	Tiny YOLOv4	mAP 0.95	Limited to paw conditions
2025	Scharre et al. [14]	Equine ophthalmic images	AI vs. veterinarians	AI: 93%, Vets: 76%	Image-only diagnosis
2025	Kalita et al. [15]	Poultry disease data	AI/ML disease detection review	-	Lacks real-world deployment

3   Methodology

3.1   Data Collection

We used two publicly available datasets: a **skin disease dataset** from Mendeley Data [16] and an **eye disease dataset** from Roboflow Universe [17]. These datasets provide diverse labeled images for comprehensive model training.

Canine Skin Disease Dataset. The skin disease dataset [16] includes four categories:

– **Bacterial Dermatosis**: Bacterial skin infections.
– **Fungal Infection**: Fungal-related skin diseases.

- **Healthy**: Normal skin, serving as a control.
- **Hypersensitivity-Allergic Dermatosis**: Skin conditions caused by allergic reactions.

Canine Eye Disease Dataset. The eye disease dataset [17] consists of five conditions:

- **Cataract**: Lens clouding leading to vision loss.
- **Cherry Eye**: Prolapse of the third eyelid gland.
- **Conjunctivitis**: Conjunctival inflammation.
- **Glaucoma**: Increased eye pressure, risk of blindness.
- **Iris Atrophy**: Degeneration affecting light regulation.

Integrating these datasets ensures our model is trained on a broad range of **skin and eye diseases**, enhancing its diagnostic capabilities. All images were preprocessed to match YOLOv11 input size for consistency.

3.2   Data Preprocessing and Augmentation

To enhance the performance and robustness of the YOLOv11 model in detecting canine dermatological and ophthalmological diseases, we employed a combination of standard preprocessing techniques and advanced data augmentation methods. The final dataset includes 9 disease labels, ensuring a balanced and diverse training set.

Data Preprocessing. All images were resized to a fixed resolution of 640 × 640 pixels to standardize input dimensions and ensure compatibility with the YOLOv11 architecture. This preprocessing step ensures consistency across different sources of data, allowing the model to focus on disease-specific features.

Data Augmentation. To improve model generalization and increase dataset diversity, we applied augmentation techniques in the following stages:

1. Conventional Augmentation Techniques (Pre-Augmented Dataset). Before applying more advanced augmentations, we first augmented the original dataset using conventional image transformation techniques. These included:

- **Rotation:** Randomly rotating images within a limited range to simulate different angles of capture.
- **Flipping:** Applying horizontal and vertical flips to introduce orientation diversity.
- **Brightness and Contrast Adjustment:** Modifying brightness and contrast to simulate real-world lighting variations.
- **Gaussian Noise:** Adding random noise to account for variations in image quality.

These augmentation techniques only apply to the original dataset, resulting in an intermediate dataset containing 9 final labels before applying LBP and CutMix augmentation. The label distribution after this stage is illustrated in Fig. 1.

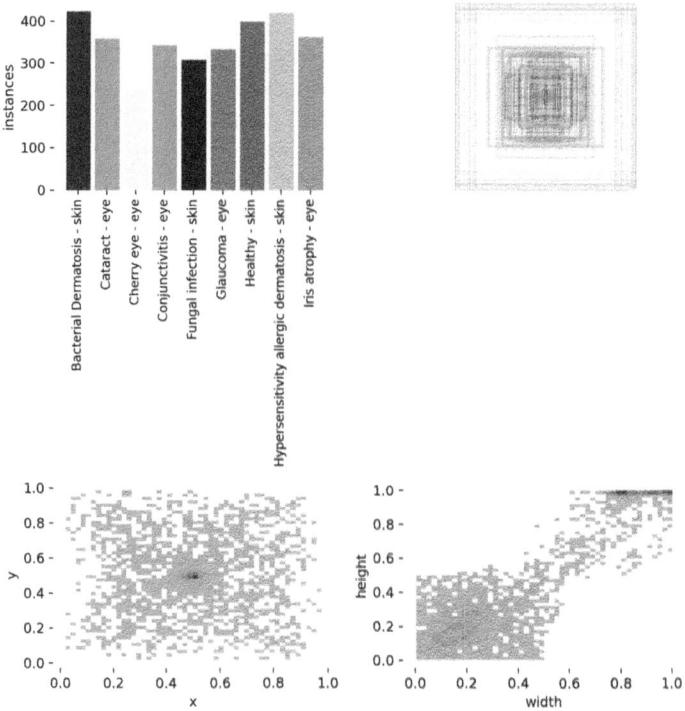

Fig. 1. Final label distribution after conventional augmentation (before applying LBP and CutMix).

2. Local Binary Pattern (LBP) Augmentation. LBP was applied as an additional augmentation technique to enhance fine-grained texture information, which is crucial for detecting dermatological conditions. The LBP process consists of:

- Converting images to grayscale.
- Applying LBP transformation by encoding each pixel's intensity difference with its neighboring pixels.
- Generating a histogram-based representation that captures dominant texture patterns.

LBP augmentation helps the model better differentiate between diseases that present with distinct skin surface abnormalities.

3. CutMix Augmentation. To further improve dataset diversity, CutMix augmentation was applied [18]. This technique merges two images by replacing a random rectangular region in one image with a patch from another image, enhancing the model's ability to generalize.

The CutMix augmentation process follows these steps:

1. Select two images from the dataset.
2. Define a random rectangular patch in the first image.
3. Replace this patch with a corresponding region from the second image.
4. Adjust bounding box labels accordingly.

Algorithm 1 summarizes the CutMix augmentation procedure.

Algorithm 1: CutMix Data Augmentation

Input   : Two images I_1, I_2 with labels L_1, L_2
Output: Augmented image with adjusted labels
Resize images to $D \times D$;
Select a random patch (x, y, w, h) in I_1;
Replace the patch in I_1 with the corresponding region from I_2;
Adjust bounding boxes in L_1 and L_2 accordingly;
Save the augmented image and updated labels;

Impact of Augmentation Techniques. The three-stage augmentation process ensures the model is trained on highly diverse and representative data. Conventional augmentation techniques improve base dataset diversity, while LBP enhances texture-based feature extraction, and CutMix aids model generalization by simulating real-world variations.

Effect on Model Performance. Our experimental results indicate that combining conventional augmentation, LBP, and CutMix significantly improves mAP@50 scores, especially when detecting diseases with complex textures. This underscores the importance of layered augmentation strategies in AI-driven veterinary diagnostics.

3.3   Model Architecture

YOLO11. YOLO11, introduced in 2024, is the latest evolution in the YOLO (You Only Look Once) series, designed for high-speed, high-accuracy object detection. It builds upon its predecessors by incorporating a more efficient backbone and an optimized detection head, significantly enhancing performance across multiple vision tasks such as object detection, instance segmentation, image classification, and pose estimation [19].

The YOLO11 architecture consists of a lightweight backbone for feature extraction, a neck module that fuses multi-scale features, and a detection head optimized for precision. Key advancements include:

- **C3K2 Block**: A novel convolutional module that reduces computation while retaining feature expressiveness.
- **C2PSA Module**: Introduces parallel spatial attention to refine feature selection for better detection accuracy.
- **Anchor-Free Mechanism**: Simplifies model training and inference while improving small object detection.
- **SPPF (Spatial Pyramid Pooling - Fast)**: Enhances multi-scale feature aggregation without increasing computational overhead.

Compared to YOLOv8, YOLO11 achieves higher mAP and lower latency on various benchmark datasets, including COCO, while maintaining a strong trade-off between speed and accuracy (Fig. 2).

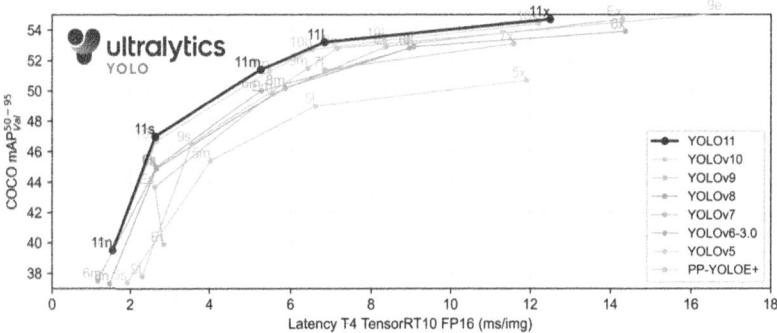

Fig. 2. Benchmarking YOLOv11 Against Previous Versions [20].

This makes YOLO11 an optimal choice for real-world applications requiring both high accuracy and low latency, such as medical imaging, autonomous driving, and industrial automation.

Autoencoder. In our methodology, an autoencoder model is employed to enhance feature extraction for diagnosing canine skin diseases. The autoencoder compresses input images into lower-dimensional representations and subsequently reconstructs them. This process allows the model to focus on the most critical features necessary for accurate disease detection and classification.

The autoencoder architecture comprises two primary components: an encoder and a decoder.

- The encoder extracts compact and informative features from input images through a series of convolutional layers with increasing channel depth (e.g., 64, 128, and 256). Each convolutional layer is followed by batch normalization, ReLU activation, and dropout to mitigate overfitting and enhance generalization. The encoder reduces the spatial dimensions of input images via stride-based convolutions, retaining essential visual features while significantly reducing data dimensionality.

– The decoder reconstructs the compressed features into the original image space. It utilizes transposed convolutional layers for upsampling the encoded representation step by step. Batch normalization and ReLU activation ensure smooth reconstruction, while a sigmoid activation function in the output layer scales pixel values to the range [0, 1].

Input images are preprocessed to a fixed size of 128×128 pixels to maintain consistency and computational efficiency. The autoencoder is trained using the L1 loss function, which ensures that fine details in the reconstructed images are preserved. Training is conducted over 20 epochs with a batch size of 16, using the SGD optimizer with momentum and a dynamic learning rate scheduler to adapt the learning rate during training.

Once trained, the encoder is extracted and integrated into the YOLO11 model pipeline to provide preprocessed feature maps for subsequent training and inference. By leveraging these encoded features, the YOLO11 model achieves improved accuracy and robustness in detecting and classifying various canine skin diseases.

This integration significantly enhances the overall performance of the diagnostic system, enabling precise and efficient identification of common dermatological conditions in dogs.

Experimental Models. To evaluate the impact of augmentation techniques on YOLOv11 performance, we trained 12 model variations, each incorporating different augmentation strategies:

1. **Original images (baseline):** The model is trained using only the original dataset, serving as the baseline for comparison.
2. **Original images + Autoencoder:** An autoencoder is applied to extract enhanced feature representations before training.
3. **Original images with CutMix:** CutMix augmentation is applied to introduce additional diversity by merging different image regions.
4. **CutMix + Autoencoder:** The CutMix-augmented dataset is further processed using an autoencoder for feature enhancement.
5. **Original images with LBP:** Local Binary Pattern (LBP) is applied to emphasize textural features in disease regions.
6. **LBP + Autoencoder:** The LBP-processed dataset is further refined using an autoencoder for feature extraction.
7. **LBP transformed dataset with CutMix:** LBP is applied first, followed by CutMix augmentation to introduce spatial variations.
8. **(LBP → CutMix) + Autoencoder:** The LBP + CutMix dataset undergoes further enhancement with an autoencoder.
9. **CutMix applied first, then LBP:** CutMix augmentation is performed before applying LBP transformation.
10. **(CutMix → LBP) + Autoencoder:** The CutMix + LBP dataset is further refined with an autoencoder.

11. **Original images + LBP + CutMix:** The dataset is augmented with both LBP and CutMix simultaneously to maximize diversity.
12. **(Original + LBP + CutMix) + Autoencoder:** The most comprehensive dataset, integrating all augmentation techniques for the best possible feature extraction.

These models assess:

- The effect of **Autoencoder, LBP, and CutMix** on detection accuracy.
- The impact of different augmentation combinations.
- The best-performing strategy for **mAP@50** improvement.

Figure 3 illustrates the YOLOv11 training pipeline. Raw images undergo pre-processing, including resizing and conventional augmentations, followed by three augmentation techniques: **Autoencoder-based feature extraction, Cut-Mix, and LBP**. The augmented datasets are then combined and used to train YOLOv11. The final model detects **cataracts in both eyes** with high confidence scores, demonstrating the effectiveness of hybrid augmentation strategies.

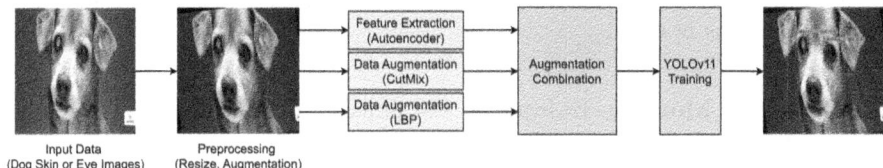

Fig. 3. YOLOv11 Training Pipeline with Augmentation and Feature Extraction.

3.4   Implementation Details

Our YOLOv11 models were trained for up to 200 epochs, with early stopping triggered after 100 epochs of no improvement to prevent overfitting. Each batch contained 16 images, resized to 640×640 pixels for consistency.

Training leveraged GPU acceleration with parallelized data loading (8 workers) for efficiency. The initial learning rate was set to 0.01 and decayed progressively. An optimizer with momentum (0.937) and weight decay (0.0005) was used to stabilize learning and enhance generalization.

These configurations ensured robust model performance in detecting and classifying canine skin and eye diseases across diverse datasets.

3.5   Evaluation Metrics

To assess the effectiveness of our proposed model in detecting canine dermatological and ophthalmological diseases, we employ Mean Average Precision at 50% IoU (mAP@50) as the primary evaluation metric. This metric measures the model's ability to accurately localize and classify lesions across different augmentation strategies.

$$mAP50 = \frac{1}{C} \sum_{i=1}^{C} AP_i \, [21]$$

where C is the total number of disease classes, and AP_i is the Average Precision for class i [21].

Our experiments demonstrate that hybrid augmentation techniques—particularly the integration of CutMix, LBP, and Autoencoder—significantly improve model performance. The best-performing configuration achieved 97.2% mAP@50 on the original dataset and 86.6% on the complex dataset, outperforming models trained on unaugmented data.

These results highlight the effectiveness of combining deep learning and texture-based augmentation for veterinary diagnostics, offering a robust and scalable approach to early and precise detection of canine skin and eye diseases.

4   Experiment Results

4.1   Model Training Results

To assess the impact of augmentation techniques, YOLOv11 was trained on twelve datasets with different augmentation strategies for 200 epochs. Performance was evaluated using mAP@50 on three test sets: original images, LBP-processed images, and a complex dataset combining LBP, CutMix, and original images. Table 2 summarizes the results.

Table 2. Performance of YOLOv11 with Different Augmentation Techniques.

#	Augmentation Technique	Train mAP@50	Test mAP@50 (Original)	Test mAP@50 (LBP)	Test mAP@50 (Complex)
1	Original Images	85.5	88.7	-	58.8
2	Original + Autoencoder	85.6	89.6	-	57.4
3	Original → CutMix	66.2	85.3	-	65.5
4	CutMix + Autoencoder	67.1	86.7	-	67.1
5	Original → LBP	84.0	-	85.7	36.2
6	LBP + Autoencoder	83.9	-	85.4	36.9
7	LBP → CutMix	58.2	-	85.5	39.2
8	(LBP → CutMix) + Autoencoder	60.0	-	81.2	31.5
9	CutMix → LBP	61.5	-	81.4	32.9
10	(CutMix → LBP) + Autoencoder	61.2	-	81.3	30.6
11	Original + LBP + CutMix	84.9	-	81.4	31.7
12	(Original + LBP + CutMix) + Autoencoder	85.9	97.2	-	86.6

4.2   Discussion

The results in Table 2 highlight key findings:

– The baseline model (original images) achieved 88.7% mAP@50 but struggled on complex images (58.8%), indicating poor generalization.
– The best-performing model (Original + LBP + CutMix + Autoencoder) reached 97.2% on the original test set and 86.6% on complex images, showing significant improvements.
– CutMix-enhanced models, particularly CutMix + Autoencoder, improved performance on complex datasets (67.1% mAP@50).
– LBP-based models retained high accuracy on LBP-processed images but suffered on complex datasets, suggesting texture features alone are insufficient.
– Hybrid augmentation (LBP, CutMix, Autoencoder) significantly improved model robustness.

Implications for Veterinary Diagnostics. The results demonstrate the effectiveness of augmentation techniques in improving disease detection. Combining LBP for texture enhancement with CutMix for diversity proved crucial for robust detection under varying conditions. These findings suggest AI-driven diagnostics can assist veterinarians in early disease detection and treatment planning.

Limitations and Future Work.

– Performance on highly complex images remains lower than on original images, indicating room for further optimization.
– Class imbalance may have affected model performance.
– Future work should explore alternative architectures or ensemble models to enhance accuracy.
– Clinical validation is needed for real-world deployment.

This study lays the foundation for future AI-driven veterinary diagnostic research, aiming for improved robustness and scalability.

5   Conclusion

This study presents an AI-driven diagnostic framework for canine dermatological and ophthalmological diseases using YOLOv11, enhanced with CutMix augmentation, Local Binary Patterns (LBP), and Autoencoder-based feature extraction. These augmentation techniques significantly improved model robustness and generalization.

Experimental results confirm that hybrid augmentation strategies enhance detection accuracy. The best-performing model, trained with a combination of original images, LBP, CutMix, and Autoencoder, achieved 97.2% mAP@50 on the original dataset and 86.6% on complex images, significantly outperforming models trained without augmentation.

These findings demonstrate the potential of deep learning in veterinary diagnostics, reducing reliance on manual assessments and improving early disease detection. Future work should explore additional augmentation methods and real-world clinical validation to further enhance diagnostic accuracy and applicability in veterinary medicine.

References

1. Hill, P., et al.: Survey of the prevalence, diagnosis and treatment of dermatological conditions in small animals in general practice. Vet. Rec. **158**(16), 533–539 (2006)
2. Das, B., Ellis, M., Sahoo, M.: Veterinary diagnostics: growth, trends, and impact. In: Evolving Landscape of Molecular Diagnostics, pp. 227–242. Elsevier (2024)
3. Loh, E.: Medicine and the rise of the robots: a qualitative review of recent advances of artificial intelligence in health. BMJ Leader, Leader-2018 (2018)
4. Burić, M.: Application of computer vision methods in veterinary ophthalmology, Doctoral dissertation, University of Rijeka, Faculty of Informatics and Digital Technologies (2024)
5. Khanam, R., Hussain, M. YOLOV11: an overview of the key architectural enhancements. arXiv preprint arXiv:2410.17725 (2024)
6. Huang, Y.C., Chuang, T.H., Lai, Y.L.: Classification of the trap-neuter-return surgery images of stray animals using YOLO-based deep learning integrated with a majority voting system. Appl. Sci. **11**(18), 8578 (2021)
7. Shaffer, L.G.: Special issue on companion animal genetics: novel variants discovered in wide variety of diseases in dogs, identification and further characterization of traits in dogs and cats, and the use of microarrays in the detection of aneuploidy in dogs. Hum. Genet. **140**(11), 1501–1503 (2021). https://doi.org/10.1007/s00439-021-02375-z
8. Kim, J.Y., Han, M.G., Chun, J.H., Huh, E.A., Lee, S.J.: Developing a diagnosis model for dry eye disease in dogs using object detection. Sci. Rep. **12**(1), 21351 (2022)
9. Kour, S., Agrawal, R., Sharma, N., Tikoo, A., Pande, N., Sawhney, A.: Artificial intelligence and its application in animal disease diagnosis (2022)
10. Ali, H.M., El Abbadi, N.K.: Optic disc localization in retinal fundus images based on you only look once network (YOLO). Int. J. Intell. Eng. Syst. **16**(2) (2023)
11. Josphineleela, R., Raja Rao, P., Shaikh, A., Sudhakar, K.: A multi-stage faster RCNN-based iSPLInception for skin disease classification using novel optimization. J. Digit. Imag. **36**(5), 2210–2226 (2023)
12. Kim, S.C., Kim, S.: Development of a dog health score using an artificial intelligence disease prediction algorithm based on multifaceted data. Animals **14**(2), 256 (2024)
13. Smith, A., et al.: Computer vision model for the detection of canine pododermatitis and neoplasia of the paw. Vet. Dermatol. **35**(2), 138–147 (2024)
14. Scharre, A., et al.: Comparison of veterinarians and a deep learning tool in the diagnosis of equine ophthalmic diseases. Equine Vet. J. **57**(1), 47–53 (2025)
15. Kalita, A.J., Subba, M., Adil, S., Wani, M.A., Beigh, Y.A., Shafi, M.: Application of artificial intelligence and machine learning in poultry disease detection and diagnosis: a review: AI and machine learning in poultry disease diagnosis. Lett. Anim. Biol., 01–06 (2025)

16. Hwang, S., Shin, H.K., Park, J.M., Kwon, B., Kang, M.G.: Classification of dog skin diseases using deep learning with images captured from multispectral imaging device. Mol. Cell. Toxicol. **18**(3), 299–309 (2022). https://doi.org/10.17632/5dbht54kw7.1 https://doi.org/10.17632/5dbht54kw7.1 https://doi.org/10.17632/5dbht54kw7.1

17. Roboflow universe, eye disease detection dataset. https://universe.roboflow.com/cat-breed-detection/eye-disease-detection-eftgo

18. Yun, S., Han, D., Oh, S.J., Chun, S., Choe, J., Yoo, Y.: CutMix: regularization strategy to train strong classifiers with localizable features. In: Proceedings of the IEEE/CVF International Conference on Computer Vision (ICCV) (2019)

19. Khanam, R., Hussain, M.: YOLOV11: an overview of the key architectural enhancements. arXiv preprint arXiv:2410.17725 (2024)

20. Ultralytics. Ultralytics YOLOV11 (2024). https://docs.ultralytics.com/models/yolo11/s

21. Burić, M.: Application of computer vision methods in veterinary ophthalmology, Dissertation, University of Rijeka, Faculty of Informatics and Digital Technologies (2024)

Advanced and Emerging Applications

Efficient Computation of Attractor Fields in Coupled Boolean Networks

Luiz C. S. Rozante[1] , Carlos R. P. Tovar[1]([∞]) , David C. Martins-Jr[1] ,
Raphael Y. de Camargo[1] , Luciana Arantes[2] , and Pierre Sens[2]

[1] UFABC/CMCC, Santo André-SP, Brazil
{luiz.rozante,carlos.reynaldo,david.martins,raphael.camargo}@ufabc.edu.br
[2] Sorbonne Université, CNRS/Inria/LIP6, 4 place Jussieu, Paris 75252, France
{Luciana.Arantes,Pierre.Sens}@lip6.fr
https://www.ufabc.edu.br , https://www.lip6.fr

Abstract. Coupled Boolean Networks (CBN) are a class of discrete-time dynamical systems with a wide range of applications, ranging from distributed change detection in sensor networks to the identification of cellular patterns in tissue structures, for example. An Attractor Field corresponds to a subset of the state space of a CBN that presents certain stability properties. Attractor Fields can be used to model many events in biological systems, in particular those involving stabilization processes between interacting dynamic biological entities. Hence, an important problem consists of computing the Attractor Fields of a given CBN. Due to the exponential nature of the state space of a CBN, computing Attractor Fields is a computationally intensive task, which is currently feasible only for CBNs of unrealistic small size. In this work, we aim to develop a high-performance method for computing Attractor Fields in CBNs. In order to achieve this, we implemented algorithms based on the multi-core architecture that exploit the parallelizable nature of the problem. The experimental results suggest significant performance gains (speedup between 13 and 14) compared to the existing serial method, especially in Step 1. In addition, we achieved almost linear scalability for this Step 1, which allowed us to propose a fork-join model to optimize the method.

Keywords: Coupled Boolean Networks · Computing Attractor Fields · Systems Biology

1 Introduction

Systems consisting of networks of interacting dynamic entities are very common, with applications in several domains of knowledge. For example, phenomena that involve stabilization and/or synchronization processes are important in several areas, such as systems biology, social networks and engineering, among others [1].

Many works involving the modeling of these systems and phenomena have already been developed, including techniques such as coupled maps [7], multi-agent systems [19] and master stability equations [15], among others.

© The Author(s), under exclusive license to Springer Nature Switzerland AG 2025
O. Gervasi et al. (Eds.): ICCSA 2025, LNCS 15648, pp. 377–395, 2025.
https://doi.org/10.1007/978-3-031-97000-9_24

Coupled Boolean Networks (CBNs for short) are a class of discrete-time dynamical systems, where each interacting dynamic entity corresponds to a Boolean Network (BN for short). BNs interact with each other according to a topology defined by a directed graph, and the interaction between two BNs is governed by a coupling function. CBNs have a wide range of potential applications in different areas [4]. Many studies involving CBNs focus on issues involving stability [17], synchronization [3,14,20], and control [9,11]. In general, these studies are analytical works where an attempt is made to identify and describe the necessary and sufficient conditions for stability and synchronization, dealing with cases with few BNs [2] or with restrictive inter-BN connection patterns [10].

Attractor Fields (AFs for short) correspond to stable configurations of the state space of a CBN, where the coupling signals are fixed (time invariant) and the BNs remain in the same local attractors. It is a stable configuration in the sense that the coupling signals are constant and the BNs do not change attractors, although they can change states.

AFs have many applications in various areas. For example, in systems biology, AFs are particularly useful when we have a set of dynamic biological entities that interact with each other and whose state depends on events internal to each entity and on the interactions between them. To illustrate, let us take the case of cellular patterning events, where we can model a tissue structure (e.g. a sheet of pluripotent epithelial cells) as a CBN, where each pluripotent cell corresponds to a BN, each cell type corresponds to a basin of attraction and an AF corresponds to a cellular pattern (a stable cellular differentiation pattern). This modeling has a direct application in the neuroblast segregation process in *Drosophila melanogaster* [5,16], where computing AFs is equivalent to predicting the possible cellular patterns that derive from the interaction between several cells where the neurogenic network [12,13] operates.

Tovar *et al.* [18] developed a serial method to compute AFs in CBNs. Tovar's method is general, i.e., it is capable of computing the AFs of CBNs with arbitrary topology (inter-BN connection patterns). However, the exponential nature of the state space of a CBN makes this task a computationally intensive problem, which implies that in practical terms Tovar's method is feasible only for relatively small input sizes (CBNs with about 7 BNs and linear topology). Hence, the investigation and development of high-performance computing solutions is an interesting alternative.

In this work, we present two different parallel implementations of Tovar's method based on the multi-core architecture, assuming scenarios where the user has few hardware resources. In these implementations, we preserve the three steps provided in the serial method, but we execute in parallel (using different strategies) the tasks provided for each step, including intra-step load balancing. We separately analyzed the performance of the three steps of each implementation in order to evaluate which combination of "strategy-step" leads to the best overall performance. We have performed preliminary experiments, and the results suggest that the best way to optimize Tovar's method is to adopt a fork-join model where we run parallel (Steps 1 and 3) and serial (Step 2) code snippets.

This manuscript is structured as follows. Section 2 presents the definitions and notation necessary to describe both Tovar's method and the proposed solution. Section 3 describes Tovar's serial method. Section 4 presents our multi-core solutions of Tovar's method, including two different versions for Steps 1 and 2 of the original algorithm. Preliminary experimental results are provided in Sect. 5, and in Sect. 6 we finish with concluding remarks and suggestions for future work.

2 Preliminaries

Let $\mathcal{X} = \{x_1, x_2, \ldots, x_n\}$ be a set of variables that assume values in $\{0, 1\}$. Let $\mathcal{F} = [f_1, f_2, \ldots, f_n]$ be functions such that $f_i : \{0, 1\}^n \to \{0, 1\}$ determines the state of the variable x_i, $1 \leq i \leq n$. The functions in $\mathcal{F}$ are called transition functions. Considering discrete time steps, the state of a variable x_i at time $t + 1$ is given by

$$x_i^{t+1} = f_i(x_k^t, \ldots, x_l^t),$$

where $x_k, \ldots, x_l$ are the variables in $\mathcal{X}$ that affect x_i.

We call the discrete dynamic system $(\{0, 1\}^n, \mathcal{F})$ a *Boolean Network* (BN), where the functions in $\mathcal{F}$ are all Boolean functions and the updates of the variables in $\mathcal{X}$ are done synchronously.

2.1 Coupled Boolean Network

Coupled Boolean Networks (CBN) are a class of discrete-time dynamical systems formed by a network of interacting dynamic entities, where each of them is a BN. The structure of a CBN (the connection pattern between BNs) is represented by a directed graph $G = (V, E)$.

If an edge $(i \to j) \in E$, it means that the BNs i and j are coupled in such a way that i influences j. The way in which the BN i influences the BN j, i.e., the nature of the interaction between i and j is given by a Boolean function, which we call the *coupling function*. We define a coupling function for each edge in E.

The local dynamics of an interacting entity is defined by the corresponding BN.

Suppose a CBN with m BNs among which we take a specific BN j containing n state variables. Now suppose that the BNs $u, \ldots, r$ are coupled to the BN j in such a way that $u, \ldots, r$ influence j. Then the state of a variable x_i of BN j at time $t + 1$, considering both the influence coming from variables belonging to BN j itself as well as that coming from coupling signals originating from the BNs $u, \ldots, r$, is given by:

$$x_i^j(t+1) = \begin{cases} f_i^j(x_k^j(t), \ldots, x_l^j(t), y_u^j(t), \ldots, y_r^j(t)), & \text{if } i \in \mathcal{E}^j \\ f_i^j(x_k^j(t), \ldots, x_l^j(t)), & \text{if } i \in \mathcal{X}^j \setminus \mathcal{E}^j, \end{cases}$$

$1 \leq i \leq n$, $1 \leq j \leq m$, where:

- $f_i^j : \{0,1\}^{n+m} \to \{0,1\}$ is the transition function that updates the state variable x_i^j;
- $x_k^j, \ldots, x_l^j$, $1 \leq k, \ldots, l \leq n$, denote the local variables (which belong to BN j itself) that influence x_i^j;
- $y_u^j, \ldots, y_r^j$, $1 \leq u, \ldots, r \leq m$, denote the coupling signals originating from BNs $u, \ldots, r$ that affect x_i^j, where

$$y_w^j(t) = h_w^j(x_p^w(t), \ldots, x_q^w(t)),$$

$u \leq w \leq r$, with $x_p^w, \ldots, x_q^w \in S_w^j$, where

$$h_w^j : \{0,1\}^n \to \{0,1\}$$

is the coupling function responsible for updating the coupling signal y_w^j.
- $\mathcal{X}^j$ denotes the set of state variables of the BN j;
- $\mathcal{E}^j$, $\mathcal{E}^j \subseteq \mathcal{X}^j$, denotes the input variables of the BN j (a variable of a BN is said to be an *input variable* if some coupling signal falls on it);
- S_w^j denotes the output variables of the BN w that influence BN j (a variable of a BN is said to be an *output variable* if it is used as a parameter by some coupling function).

Figure 1 presents a schematic representation of the coupling between BNs, where the BNs $u, \ldots, r$ are coupled to the BN j in such a way that the state variable x_i (belonging to the BN j) receives the influence of $u, \ldots, r$ through the coupling signals $y_u^j, \ldots, y_r^j$, which are determined by the coupling functions $h_u^j, \ldots, h_r^j$, respectively.

The state of a CBN is given by the state of each of the variables in all BNs. The state transition in a CBN is given by the synchronous application of all transition functions (in each BN) and all coupling functions (for all interactions between BNs).

2.2   Stability in CBNs and Target Problem

Our target problem consists in, given a CBN as input, we aim to find stable configurations of its state space, i.e., subsets of the state space that satisfy certain stability properties. These subsets of the state space are called *Attractor Fields* (AF).

There are many ways to define stability in CBNs. For example, we can do so based on properties of the coupling signals or using steady states (local and/or global), among others. In this work, we assume that the concept of stability is associated with the invariability of the coupling signals and the non-alternation of local attractors [8]. More precisely, an AF is a subset of the state space that satisfies the following properties:

- The coupling signals are time-invariant, i.e., the signals produced by the coupling functions do not change when the transition and coupling functions are applied. In other words, the coupling signals are stationary.

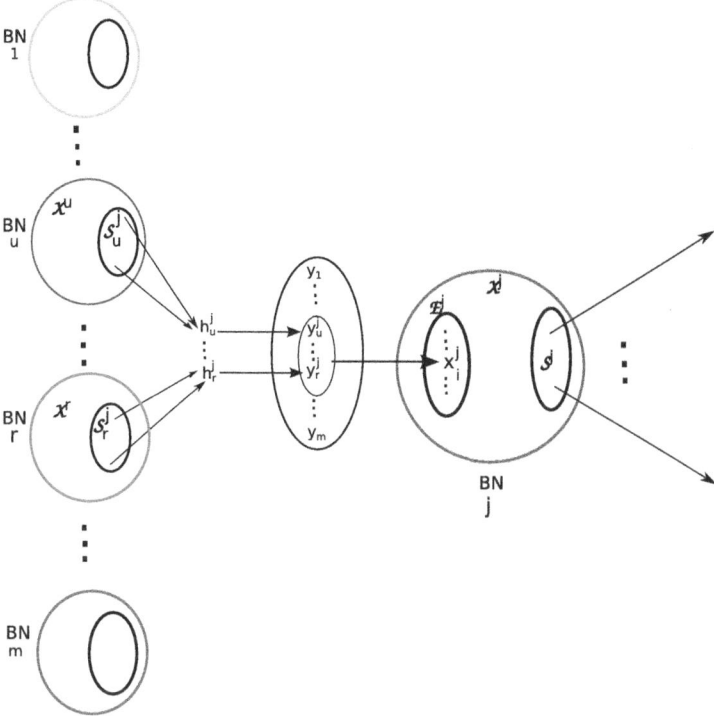

Fig. 1. Illustrative diagram of the coupling between BNs.

- There is no change in local attractors in BNs when the transition and coupling functions are applied. Since the attractors can be periodic (non-stationary[1]), then there can be state transitions in BNs when the transition and coupling functions are applied. However, the BNs do not change attractors, they remain the same in all BNs. In other words, the system "stabilizes" in the attractors in which the BNs are located, although the BNs can change states.

3   Serial Method

The method is defined in three steps, detailed in the following subsections. More details on how the serial method works can be found in Tovar's work [18].

3.1   Serial Step 1: Computing Local Attractors

The input of Step 1 is a CBN and it returns as output the set of local attractors for each BN, as illustrated in Fig. 2, where we see on the left a representation of

---

[1] A global stationary state, i.e., a configuration where both the coupling signals and the states of the BNs remain the same, is a particular case of an Attractor Field.

an example CBN with 3 BNs, which are distinguished by colors (red, green and blue) and connected by coupling functions $h_{1,2}$, $h_{2,3}$ and $h_{3,1}$. On the right, an example of the output from Step 1: A^1, A^2, and A^3 denote the local attractors associated with the red, green, and blue BNs, respectively.

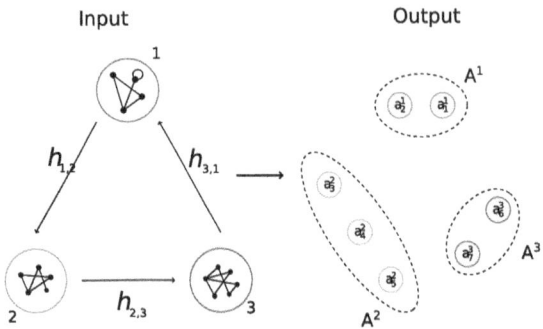

Fig. 2. An example of input and output of Step 1. (Color figure online)

Given a CBN, in Step 1 we use the Dubrova and Teslenko [6] algorithm to calculate the local attractors of each BN. Since BNs can receive external signals generated by coupling functions, it was necessary to adapt the Dubrova and Teslenko algorithm because, in its original version, it does not provide the treatment of this type of external signal.

Here, it is worth reinforcing an important restriction: we assume that the coupling signals are invariant in time, i.e., their values are constant. This restriction derives from the properties that characterize the concept of stability in attractor fields.

Hence, since a BN can receive several coupling signals coming from other BNs, if a BN r receives c coupling signals, in Step 1 we compute (applying the adapted Dubrova and Teslenko algorithm) the local attractors of r for all 2^c possible combinations of fixed coupling signal that fall on r.

3.2   Serial Step 2: Computing the Compatible Attractor Pairs

Given a collection $A^1, \ldots, A^m$ of local attractor sets produced in Step 1 and a graph $G = (V, E)$ representing the CBN topology, in Step 2 we basically do:

(i) given an edge $(i \to j) \in E$, then we compute all pairs $A^i \times A^j$ of attractors possible to form with A^i and A^j, where A^i is the set of local attractors of BN i and A^j is the set of local attractors of BN j;

(ii) for each pair $(a_w^i, a_z^j) \in A^i \times A^j$, check whether it satisfies the *stability condition*, which can be described as follows: the output value produced by the local attractor $a_w^i \in A^i$ is equal to the input value expected by the local attractor $a_z^j \in A^j$.

If two attractors $(a_w^i, a_z^j) \in \mathcal{A}^i \times \mathcal{A}^j$ satisfy the stability condition, then we say that they form a *compatible attractor pair*. More details about the stability condition and compatible attractors can be found in Tovar's work [18].

The output of Step 2 is a set of compatible attractor pairs, which is represented by a directed graph $G' = (V', E')$. The inputs and outputs of Step 2 are illustrated in Fig. 3, where we can see, on the left, an example of input with a collection of local attractors: 2 local attractors (a_1^1 and a_2^1) associated with the red BN, 3 local attractors (a_3^2, a_4^2 and a_5^2) associated with the green BN and 2 local attractors (a_6^3 and a_7^3) associated with the blue BN. On the right, an example of output from Step 2, formed by the following set of compatible attractor pairs: (a_2^1, a_3^2); (a_2^1, a_4^2); (a_4^2, a_6^3); (a_4^2, a_7^3); (a_5^2, a_6^3); (a_7^3, a_2^1); (a_7^3, a_1^1); (a_6^3, a_2^1); (a_6^3, a_1^1), which can be represented by a directed graph G'.

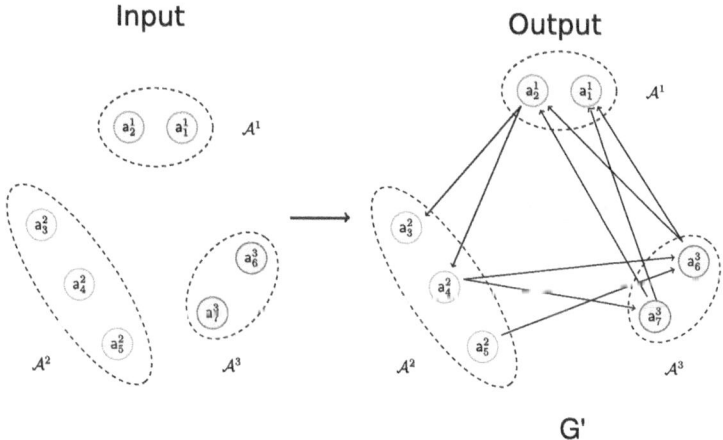

Fig. 3. An example of input and output of Step 2. (Color figure online)

3.3 Serial Step 3: Assembly of Stable Attractors Fields

The input to Step 3 is a collection of compatible attractor pairs produced in Step 2, which can be represented by a directed graph $G' = (V', E')$, as illustrated in Fig. 4, and a graph $G = (V, E)$ representing the CBN topology. Figure 4 illustrates, on the left, an example of input from Step 3 formed by the following set of compatible attractor pairs: (a_2^1, a_3^2); (a_2^1, a_4^2); (a_4^2, a_6^3); (a_4^2, a_7^3); (a_5^2, a_6^3); (a_7^3, a_2^1); (a_7^3, a_1^1); (a_6^3, a_2^1); (a_6^3, a_1^1), which can be represented by a directed graph G'. On the right, an example of the output from Step 3, which constitutes the solution to the problem: a set S of attractor fields, which are represented by directed graphs $G_1'', \ldots, G_k''$ (each graph represents an attractor field). A graph $G'' = (V'', E'') \in S$ is such that: i) vertices denote local attractors of BNs, and no two vertices in V'' ever have the same color, i.e., each of them is associated with a different BN; ii) edges in E'' denote pairs of compatible local attractors.

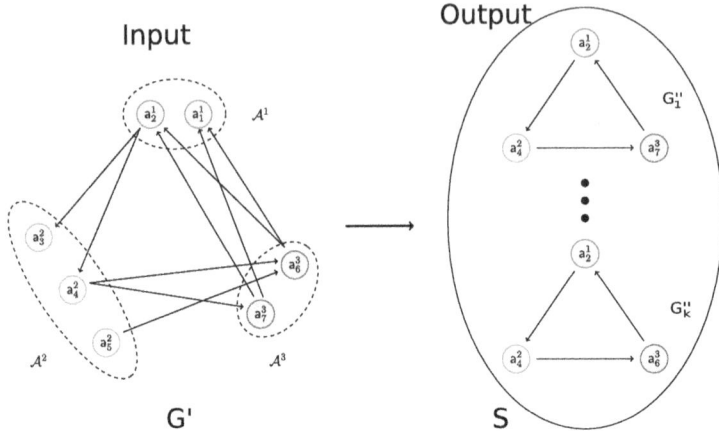

Fig. 4. An example of input and output of Step 3.

First, we label the edges in G' in such a way as to group them according to the pairs of BNs to which they are associated. Then, suppose a set of labels $R = \{1, 2, 3, \ldots, |E|\}$, and a labeling $label : E \rightarrow R$. Given the graph $G' = (V', E')$ that represents the pairs of compatible attractors, then for every edge $e' \in E'$ whose tips are attractors originating in BNs i and j, where (i, j) is an edge of the graph $G = (V, E)$, we do $e' \leftarrow label(i, j)$. Figure 5 illustrates this labeling, where we can see, in the top center, a graph $G = (V, E)$ representing the topology of an example CBN with labels 1, 2 and 3 on the edges. On the bottom left, an example of a graph $G' = (V', E')$ that represents the pairs of compatible attractors. On the right below, an example of labeling on the edges of E'.

In other words, if the CBN contains $|E|$ edges, then we have $|E|$ distinct labels, one for each edge in E, and this labeling classifies the edges of G' into $|E|$ groups, one for each edge in G. Therefore, for a CBN with a set of edges E, and a set of compatible attractor pairs $G' = (V', E')$, we will have an $|E|$-clustering $label$ of E', which is a partition of E' into $|E|$ groups (clusters):

$$\mathcal{G} = \{\mathcal{G}_1, \mathcal{G}_2, \ldots, \mathcal{G}_{|E|}\}.$$

A subgraph of G' is said to be a *stable subgraph* if it satisfies the following conditions: i) it has at least 1 edge, ii) it is connected and iii) it has no two edges belonging to the same group $\mathcal{G}_u$, $1 \leq u \leq |E|$. We define the *order* of a stable graph to be its number of edges. i.e., a stable subgraph of G' is of order k if it has k edges. Then, given a group $\mathcal{G}_u$, $1 \leq u \leq |E|$, the compatible pairs in $\mathcal{G}_u$ correspond to stable subgraphs of order 1, since an element of $\mathcal{G}_u$ is an edge of G'. A stable subgraph of order k will be represented by a k-tuple formed by k pairs of vertices of G' (local attractors).

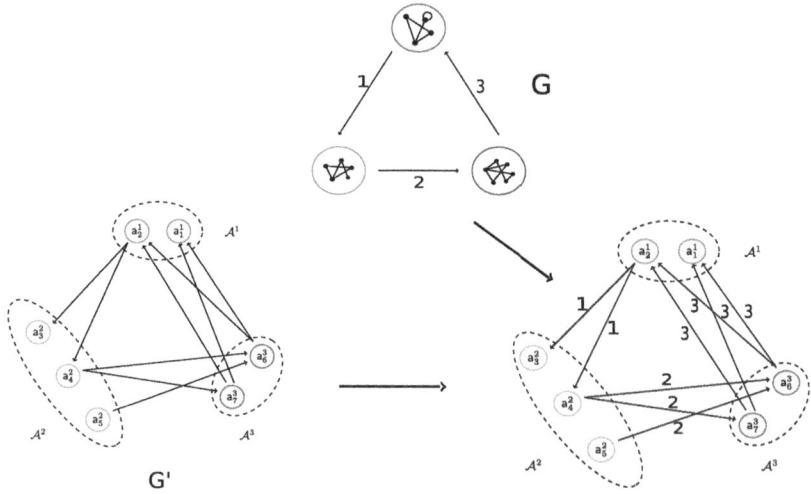

Fig. 5. An example of edge labeling in the graph G' (input of Step 3).

The general idea in Step 3 consists of an iterative procedure to compute stable subgraphs of G' of increasingly higher order until we reach one of order $|E|$, which can be described as follows:

- we choose a group $\mathcal{G}_u \in \mathcal{G}$, $1 \leq u \leq |E|$, with the highest cardinality, and we define a visiting order for the remaining groups starting from the group $\mathcal{G}_u$ performing a breadth-first traversal in the graph G weighted by the cardinality of the groups, which we denote by $\mathcal{G}'$:

$$\mathcal{G}' = [\mathcal{G}'_1, \mathcal{G}'_2, \ldots, \mathcal{G}'_{|E|}]$$

- note that each element of $\mathcal{G}'$ is a **set** of stable subgraph of order 1, i.e., each element of $\mathcal{G}'_u \in \mathcal{G}'$, $1 \leq u \leq |E|$, is a stable subgraph of order 1;
- each element $\mathcal{G}'_u \in \mathcal{G}'$, $1 \leq u \leq |E|$, is represented by a 1-tuple, i.e., $\mathcal{G}'_u$ is a set of 1-tuples;
- a stable subgraph of order k is represented by a k–tuple;
- we denote by S_k a set of k-tuples that represents a partial solution of order k (a set of stable subgraph of order k);
- $S_1 \leftarrow \mathcal{G}'_1$; $k \leftarrow 2$
- repeat until $k = |E|$:
  1. $S_k \leftarrow \emptyset$
  2. for all for $(a, b) \in S_{k-1} \times \mathcal{G}'_k$, do:
     - if (a, b) is a stable subgraph of order k, then $S_k \leftarrow S_k \cup (a, b)$
  3. $k \leftarrow k + 1$

Note that for a given iteration k, $k \geq 2$, a pair (a, b) is such that:

a corresponds to a $(k-1)$–tuple formed by $k-1$ pairs of local attractors, which represents a stable subgraph of order $k-1$;

b corresponds to a 1–tuple formed by 1 pair of local attractors, which represents a stable subgraph of order 1.

Then, to decide whether a given pair (a, b) is a stable subgraph of order k, just check if a and b have an element (local attractor) in common. In case it is true, (a, b) represents a graph with k edges that satisfies the conditions that define a stable subgraph mentioned above. An attractor field is a stable subgraph of order $|E|$, which implies that when we finish computing $S_{|E|}$, we have reached the solution of the problem, since each element of $S_{|E|}$ is a stable subgraph of order $|E|$.

4   Parallel Method

In this work we assume scenarios with few hardware resources, typically a single-chip multicore machine. Basically a board with p processing cores, where each core has its own local memory, but there is also a cache shared between the cores to speed up access to the most used data, improve communication between the cores and reduce read and write latency.

Our method is based on the strategy of Tovar's serial method, i.e., we preserve the three steps provided for in the serial method, but we execute in parallel the tasks provided for in each step, and we perform intra-step load balancing.

4.1   Multicore Step 1

Suppose that the input CBN has m BNs and that we have p processing cores available. In the ideal case, we would have a completely homogeneous CBN where the BNs would all be equal and all of them would have the same number of coupling signals. In this case, it would be enough to distribute the BNs equally among the processing cores, allocating m/p BNs to each core.

However, realistic inputs contain heterogeneous CBNs, where the BNs are different from each other and have different degrees of coupling. This implies that the workload associated with the computation of the local attractors varies greatly, so it is important to perform load balancing at this point.

We define a task in Step 1 as the computation of the local attractors of a given BN; therefore, for a CBN with m BNs, we have m tasks to perform.

The performance associated with a Step 1 task depends on 4 factors: i) the number of local variables of the BN, ii) the number of coupling signals incident on the BN, iii) the number and length of attractors in a BN and iv) the length of the longest path to an attractor.

To define an initial load balancing model in Step 1, we will use only the first two factors because the last two derive from information that we do not have *a priori* and from structural characteristics of the Dubrova and Teslenko algorithm, in which we do not interfere.

Thus, now we define the weight of workload $w1$ associated with a Step 1 task in BN i as being the integer defined as follows:

$$w1(BN_i) = (n - v) \times 2^v,$$

where n is the number of local variables of the BN i and v is the number of coupling signals incident on the BN i.

Therefore, the total weight $tw1$ of the workload associated with a CBN (in Step 1) is given by

$$tw1 = \sum_{i=1}^{m} w1(BN_i),$$

where m is the number of BNs.

We implement two strategies to distribute $tw1$ among the available cores, which we describe in the following two sections.

Multi-core Step 1 (version A). In this first implementation, we directly distribute the tasks among the available cores according to a demand-availability relationship, as follows:

- We create a task pool F containing all tasks in arbitrary order.
- We allocate the first p tasks to the available p cores.
- If a core becomes available, we allocate the first task in F to that core. We repeat this procedure until all tasks are allocated.

In this implementation of Step 1, we have no cost to pre-allocate tasks among cores. However, we do not guarantee approximately equal load balancing among cores.

Multi-core Step 1 (version B). To pre-partition $tw1$ among the cores approximately equally, we distribute the m tasks among the p cores using a greedy load balancing strategy, which can be described as follows:

- Sort tasks in descending order of weight $(w1(BN_i))$, so that the heaviest tasks are assigned first.
- Initialize a list Load with p elements, where each element represents the load (total weight) of each core. Initially, all cores have zero load.
- For each task, assign it to the core with the least load at that moment:
  1. for each task $w1(BN_i)$ (in the sorted order of weights), find the core k with the minimum load (i.e., the core with the smallest value in Load);
  2. assign the task $w1(BN_i)$ to core k, and update the load of core k by adding $w1(BN_i)$ to its load. For example, if the load of core k before assignment was Load[k], the new load will be Load[k] += $w1(BN_i)$.
- Repeat until all tasks are assigned, i.e., continue assigning tasks to the cores until all m tasks have been distributed. After all tasks are distributed, the Load list will contain the total load of each core.

Sorting takes $O(m \log m)$ time. Distributing the tasks: for each task, the algorithm finds the core with the least load, which can be done in $O(\log p)$ using a Heap structure. Therefore, the complexity of distributing all tasks is $O(m \log p)$. Thus, the overall complexity of Step 1 load balancing is $O(m \log m + m \log p)$.

4.2   Multi-core Step 2

Given the topology of a CBN, represented by a directed graph $G = (V, E)$, the input of Step 2 is a collection of sets of local attractors, being a set $\mathcal{A}^u$, $1 \leq u \leq |V|$, of local attractors for each BN, as illustrated in Fig. 3.

Given an edge $(i \rightarrow j) \in E$, we define a task in Step 2 as the computation of all compatible attractor pairs in $\mathcal{A}^i \times \mathcal{A}^j$, where $\mathcal{A}^i$ and $\mathcal{A}^j$ denote the local attractor sets of the BNs i and j, respectively.

The performance associated with Step 2 is determined by the number of pairs of local attractors whose compatibility must be checked. In other words, the computation cost of Step 2 depends on the cardinality of the sets of attractors where the compatible pairs are prospected.

Thus, given an edge $(i \rightarrow j) \in E$, we define the weight of workload $w2$ in Step 2 associated with the edge $(i \rightarrow j)$ as being the cardinality of the Cartesian product $\mathcal{A}^i \times \mathcal{A}^j$, i.e.,

$$w2(i, j) = |\mathcal{A}^i \times \mathcal{A}^j|.$$

Therefore, the total weight $tw2$ of the workload associated with a CBN (in Step 2) is given by

$$tw2 = \sum_{i,j \in E} w2(i, j).$$

Similar to Step 1, here we also implement two strategies to distribute $tw2$ among the available cores, which we describe in the following two sections.

Multi-core Step 2 (version A). In this first implementation of Step 2 we use exactly the same strategy used in version A of the implementation of Step 1 (Sect. 4.1). Then, here we also have no pre-allocation cost, but we do not guarantee an equal distribution of the load among the cores.

Multi-core Step 2 (version B). To divide $tw2$ among the cores approximately equally, we distribute the $|E|$ tasks among the p cores using exactly the same strategy used in version B of the implementation of Step 1 (Sect. 4.1).

Therefore, ordering tasks takes $O(|E| \log |E|)$ time and the complexity of distributing all tasks is $O(|E| \log p)$, in such a way that the overall complexity of Step 2 load balancing is $O(|E| \log |E| + |E| \log p)$.

4.3   Multi-core Step 3

As we saw in Sect. 3.3, in the serial method for a given iteration k, we have to check all pairs in $S_{k-1} \times \mathcal{G}'_k$, where S_{k-1} and $\mathcal{G}'_k$ denote sets of tuples.

Given a pair $(a, b) \in S_{k-1} \times \mathcal{G}'_k$, we define a task of Step 3 as checking whether or not (a, b) forms a stable subgraph of order k.

Similar to Steps 1 and 2, here we also implement two task allocation strategies, which are described in the following subsections.

Multi-core Step 3 (version A). Here we dynamically reallocate tasks at each iteration according to a demand-availability relationship, as follows:

- Suppose an iteration k and p cores available. Let a_i be the i-th tuple of S_{k-1} (consider an arbitrary order).
- First we allocate the first p tasks on the available p cores, as follows:
   1. We allocate all pairs in $a_1 \times \mathcal{G}'_k$ to the 1st available core, which will process the corresponding tasks.
   2. We allocate all pairs in $a_2 \times \mathcal{G}'_k$ to the 2nd available core, which will process the corresponding tasks.
   3. And so on until all cores are busy.
- Then we allocate the remaining tasks as cores become available, according to the following:
   1. The pairs in $a_{p+1} \times \mathcal{G}'_k$ are allocated to the first core that becomes available again.
   2. The pairs in $a_{p+2} \times \mathcal{G}'_k$ are allocated to the first core that becomes available again.
   3. And so on until the pairs in $a_u \times \mathcal{G}'_k$ are allocated to some core, where a_u denotes the last tuple in S_{k-1}.

Multi-core Step 3 (version B). Suppose an iteration k. If the number of available cores is p, we can divide the set S_{k-1} into p roughly equal parts and distribute those parts to different cores. That is, each core i will process a portion of the set S_{k-1}, as follows:

- The core i receives $\mathcal{G}'_k$ and a segment S^i_{k-1} of S_{k-1}, which is a subset $S^i_{k-1} \subseteq S_{k-1}$, with $|S_{k-1}|/p$ elements (See Fig. 6).
- The core i generates all the pairs (a^i, b), where $a^i \in S^i_{k-1}$ and $b \in \mathcal{G}'_k$, and checks whether each of them forms a stable subgraph of order k. This operation is performed sequentially within each core since each pair is generated independently of other pairs.

Since the stable subgraphs of order k generated by each core i can be stored in a local data structure, synchronization can be performed after the execution of all cores. At the end of the execution, the cores can combine (or reduce) the results into a single shared data structure, which represents the partial solution S_k (a set of stable subgraphs of order k). The diagram in Fig. 6 illustrates how the procedure works for a given iteration k.

Unlike the previous Steps, in this version of Step 3 we perform dynamic load balancing, in such a way that at each iteration k we redistribute the $|S_{k-1}| \times |\mathcal{G}'_k|$ tasks among the available cores.

At each iteration k, we perform 1 round of computation and 2 rounds of communication: one to allocate tasks to cores and another one to write to shared memory, where the results of each core are combined into a shared data structure, which represents a partial solution. For a CBN with $|E|$ edges, we perform $|E|-1$ iterations. Therefore, in Step 3 we perform $O(|E|)$ rounds of communication and computation.

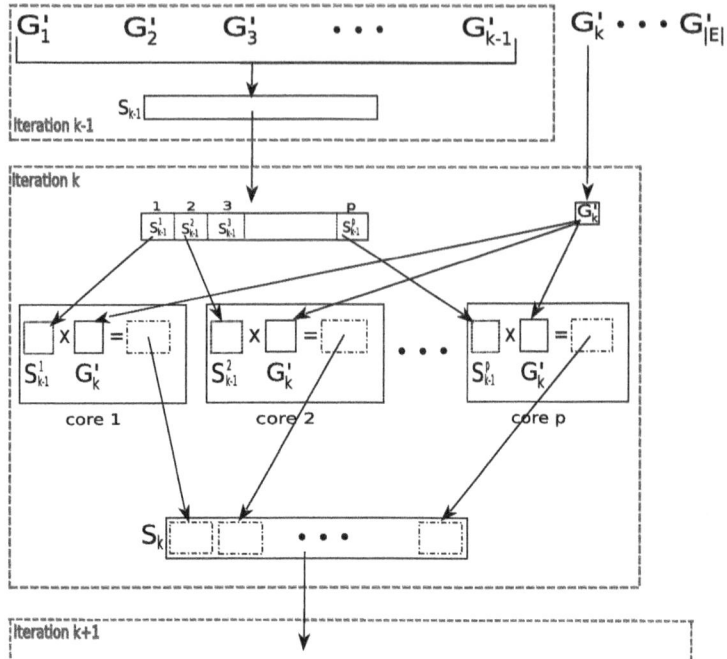

Fig. 6. Flow in an iteration k: the partial solution S_{k-1} is divided among the p available cores; each core receives a copy of $\mathcal{G}'_k$; each core computes the stable subgraphs of order k in $S_{k-1} \times \mathcal{G}'_k$; the results obtained in each core are combined to form the partial solution S_k, which will be similarly used in the iteration $k + 1$.

5   Implementation and Experimental Results

The method was implemented in Python 3.8.10 and the experiments were performed using Ubuntu 20.04 on a desktop with Intel(R) Xeon(R) CPU E5-2620 v2 @ 2.10GHz, 128 GB RAM and 24 cores.

Under this setup, we performed preliminary experiments to evaluate the performance and scalability of the method considering the scenario where there is an increase in the number of BNs. In all experiments, we adopted a random topology for the CBNs. Steps 1, 2 and 3 of the Serial method are relatively independent, hence we run and evaluate experiments (considering the two parallel versions) for these three steps independently. More details can be seen in the following subsections.

5.1   Speedup

To evaluate the speedup of the parallel versions with regard to the Serial implementation, we increased the number of BNs (from 3 to 1024) and fixed the number of local variables in each BN at 5. We kept the total number of coupling signals proportionally constant with regard to the number of BNs, i.e., we adopted the number of coupling signals equal to the number of BNs. In this implementation of the Serial method 24 cores were used. In these experiments 1000 instances were generated for each adopted sample. The average execution time obtained for each sample is presented in Table 1.

Table 1. Comparison of execution times, grouped by stage (step) and method, with an increasing number of Boolean networks.

Method	Experiment 1 Step 1			Experiment 2 Step 2			Experiment 3 Step 3		
# BNs	Serial	Parallel A	Parallel B	Serial	Parallel A	Parallel B	Serial	Parallel A	Parallel B
3	0.2315s	0.4817s	0.4833s	0.0002s	0.3669s	0.3537s	0.0024s	0.6810s	0.6602s
4	0.3168s	0.5041s	0.5041s	0.0003s	0.3718s	0.3595s	0.0088s	1.0362s	1.0191s
5	0.4034s	0.5129s	0.5131s	0.0004s	0.3727s	0.3591s	0.0534s	1.4150s	1.3976s
6	0.4985s	0.5250s	0.5231s	0.0004s	0.3770s	0.3636s	0.4293s	1.9140s	1.8839s
7	0.5884s	0.5262s	0.5289s	0.0005s	0.3767s	0.3619s	2.5732s	3.0863s	3.1246s
8	0.6738s	0.5211s	0.5257s	0.0006s	0.3795s	0.3675s	23.2837s	11.8042s	12.1993s
16	1.4994s	0.3824s	0.3821s	0.0011s	0.2618s	0.2698s	—	—	—
32	2.8987s	0.4614s	0.4264s	0.0026s	0.4221s	0.4322s	—	—	—
64	5.9565s	0.6593s	0.6168s	0.0075s	1.0274s	1.1707s	—	—	—
128	12.1228s	1.0541s	1.0223s	0.0279s	2.0236s	2.2752s	—	—	—
256	24.5006s	1.7848s	1.8498s	0.0991s	4.1358s	4.6605s	—	—	—
512	49.1510s	3.2944s	3.5305s	0.3754s	9.2657s	9.4604s	—	—	—
1024	108.4408s	7.9494s	8.4293s	1.5050s	21.6097s	21.6038s	—	—	—

Step 1: As we can see in Table 1 (Experiment 1, with red background), for a small number of BNs (up to 6 BNs) the Serial implementation is faster than both parallel implementations. However, starting from 8 BNs, this trend reverses, and the parallel versions outperform the serial implementation. For larger inputs (512 and 1024 BNs) the parallel implementations are vastly superior (speedup between 13 and 14). These data suggest that the greater the number of BNs, the more advantageous the parallel implementations become. The data show that there are no significant performance differences between the two parallel versions of Step 1, which indicates that the best implementation alternative for Step 1 is parallel version A, since it is a simpler strategy compared to version B.

Step 2: As we can see in Table 1 (Experiment 2, with green background), the Serial implementation is faster than both parallel versions A and B, even for inputs with many BNs. This superiority of the Serial implementation derives from the simplicity of the operations in Step 2, which means that developing parallel versions for Step 2 adds complexity to the code without bringing performance gains. In fact, the runtime of the Serial implementation is negligible even for large number of BNs. Thus the best path is to adopt a fork-join model, where we run a parallel version for Step 1 and a serial version for Step 2.

Step 3: As we can see in Table 1 (Experiment 3, with blue background), the Step 3 represents a bottleneck of the method, since on the adopted machine, representative of the scenarios covered by this work where there is little availability of hardware resources, we were able to run CBNs with only up to 8 BNs. This limitation occurred in both the serial and parallel implementations and it derives from a structural characteristic of the dynamics of CBNs, which is the fact that some CBNs contain a huge amount of AFs (in the order of hundreds of millions). These cases occur for some CBNs with 9 or more BNs, which require a substantial memory consumption, often causing memory overflow. Since the runtimes presented in Table 1 represent average values (calculated from samples with 1000 BNs), the average runtimes for experiments with 16 or more BNs are not provided, as at least one case resulted in a memory overflow. Despite this limitation, observing the data for inputs with 3 to 8 BNs, we can see that in the case with 8 BNs the parallel implementations are faster than the serial implementation, which suggests that from this point on it is advantageous to adopt a parallel version. Clearly improvements to the method are needed, specifically a memory management strategy that addresses this memory overflow problem, enabling further experiments to validate these results.

5.2   Scalability

To evaluate the scalability of Step 1, we assume CBNs with 1024 BNs, 1024 coupling signals and 5 variables per BN. Then we execute its parallel implementations using $2, 4, 8, 12, 16, 20$ and 24 cores. In this experiment we generated a sample with 250 instances, then the runtimes presented represent the average of the runtimes obtained, which can be viewed in Fig. 7. We focus on the scalability analysis only for Step 1 because: i) as already concluded in the previous section, it is better to execute Step 2 in serial mode in a fork-join model due to its extreme simplicity, hence there is no reason to evaluate the scalability of Step 2; ii) regarding Step 3, to maintain coherence with the input set used in Step 1, we should evaluate Step 3 using 1024 BNs (as done in Step 1), however this is not possible as discussed in Sect. 5.1. Hence for now we cannot evaluate the scalability of Step 3.

As we can see in Fig. 7, parallel implementations A and B have very similar performance, varying only marginally from each other. And in both implementations we can observe that the speedup grows almost linearly up to 12 cores. Starting from 16 cores, the speedup becomes smoother and stabilizes around 10. We attribute this saturation due to three combined factors: the growth rate of the number of cores includes 12, 20 and 24, which are not a power of 2 (as adopted for the number of CBNs), communication overhead that increases as the number of cores increases, and mainly the use of virtual cores (the machine adopted to run the experiments has only 12 physical cores).

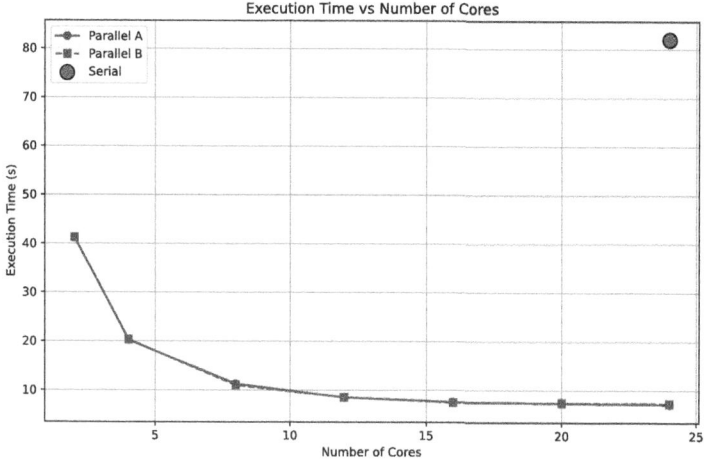

Fig. 7. Runtimes versus number of cores (2, 4, 8, 12, 16, 20, 24).

6   Conclusion

In this paper, we present parallel solutions based on the multi-core architecture for Tovar's method for AFs computation, assuming scenarios with few hardware resources. We develop different implementations for each of the three steps of the serial method, including intra-step load balancing.

We performed and evaluated experiments for each of the three steps of the method with the aim of indicating which "strategy-step" combination leads to the best overall performance. The data allow us to conclude that the best way to optimize the Tovar's method is to adopt a fork-join model where we run parallel (Steps 1 and 3) and serial (Step 2) code snippets.

As future work, a memory management strategy is required for Step 3 to enable the method to operate with hundreds of millions of AFs, which will allow the method to be applied to more realistic input sizes. In addition, the implementation of a fork-joint model is needed to optimize the code with serial (Step 2) and parallel (Steps 1 and 3) snippets. Finally, intensive experiments involving inputs with thousands of BNs and in different scenarios, such as increasing the number of variables per BN and the number of coupling signals, are required to further evaluate the efficiency of the method.

Acknowledgments. This research was supported by Coordenaçao de Aperfeiçoa-mento de Pessoal de Nível Superior (CAPES) Finance Code 001 and São Paulo Research Foundation (FAPESP) grants #2018/18560-6 and #2018/21934-5.

References

1. Arenas, A., Díaz-Guilera, A., Kurths, J., Moreno, Y., Zhou, C.: Synchronization in complex networks. Phys. Rep. **469**, 93–153 (2008)
2. Chen, H., Liang, J., Lu, J.: Partial synchronization of interconnected Boolean networks. IEEE Trans. Cybern. **47**(1), 258–266 (2017)
3. Chen, H., Liang, J.: Local synchronization of interconnected Boolean networks with stochastic disturbances. IEEE Trans. Neural Netw. Learn. Syst. **31**(2), 452–463 (2019)
4. Cheng, D., Qi, H., Li, Z.: Analysis and control of Boolean networks: a semi-tensor product approach. Springer Science & Business Media (2010)
5. Cohen, M., Georgiou, M., Stevenson, N.L., Miodownik, M., Baum, B.: Dynamic filopodia transmit intermittent delta-notch signaling to drive pattern refinement during lateral inhibition. Dev. Cell **19**(1), 78–89 (2010)
6. Dubrova, E., Teslenko, M.: A sat-based algorithm for finding attractors in synchronous Boolean networks. IEEE/ACM Trans. Comput. Biol. Bioinf. **8**(5), 1393–1399 (2011)
7. Jalan, S., Amritkar, R.E.: Self-organized and driven phase synchronization in coupled maps. Phys. Rev. Lett. **90**, 014101 (2003)
8. Kauffman, S.A.: The Origins of Order. Oxford University Press, New York (1993)
9. Li, F.: Feedback control design for the complete synchronisation of two coupled Boolean networks. Int. J. Syst. Sci. **47**(12), 2996–3003 (2016)
10. Li, R., Chu, T.: Synchronization in an array of coupled Boolean networks. Phys. Lett. A **376**, 3071–3075 (2012)
11. Liu, Y., Sun, L., Lu, J., Liang, J.: Feedback controller design for the synchronization of Boolean control networks. IEEE Trans. Neural Netw. Learn. Syst. **27**(9), 1991–1996 (2015)
12. McCorkindale, A.L., et al.: A gene expression atlas of embryonic neurogenesis in drosophila reveals complex spatiotemporal regulation of lncRNAs. Development **146**(6), dev175265 (2019)
13. Michki, N.: The Developmental Landscape of Neurogenesis in Drosophila melanogaster Revealed Using Targeted Single-Cell RNA-Sequencing and a Multi-Informatic Analysis Paradigm. Ph.D. thesis, University of Michigan (2021)
14. Niu, Y., Liu, H., Wei, Q.: Synchronization of coupled Boolean networks with different update scheme. IEEE Access **8**, 79319–79324 (2020)
15. Pecora, L.M., Carroll, T.L.: Master stability functions for synchronized coupled systems. Phys. Rev. Lett. **80**, 2109 (1998)
16. Pinot, M., Le Borgne, R.: Spatio-temporal regulation of notch activation in asymmetrically dividing sensory organ precursor cells in drosophila melanogaster epithelium. Cells **13**(13), 1133 (2024)
17. Qin, M., Li, H., Yang, X.: Attractor analysis of conjunctive Boolean networks via dependency graph. In: 2024 43rd Chinese Control Conference (CCC), pp. 5345–5350. IEEE (2024)
18. Tovar, C.R., Martins, D.C., Rozante, L.C., Araujo, E.: A method for computing attractor fields in coupled Boolean networks. In: 2022 IEEE 22nd International Conference on Bioinformatics and Bioengineering (BIBE), pp. 315–320. IEEE (2022)

19. Wu, Y., Lu, R., Shi, P., Su, H., Wu, Z.G.: Adaptive output synchronization of heterogeneous network with an uncertain leader. Automatica **76**, 183–192 (2017)
20. Yang, Z., Chu, T.: General synchronization of cascaded Boolean networks within different domains of attraction. In: Proceedings of the International Conference of Control, Dynamic Systems, and Robotics. Ottawa, Ontario, Canada. vol. 173 (2015)

Evaluating Statistical Versus Deterministic Imaging Strategies for Cluttered Near-Surface Models

Andrey Bakulin[1] , Maxim Protasov[2](✉) , Ilya Silvestrov[3] , Dmitry Neklydov[2] ,
Maxim Dmitriev[4], and Denis Sabitov[5]

[1] Bureau of Economic Geology, University of Texas at Austin, Austin, USA
[2] Institute of Petroleum Geology and Geophysics, 3, Koptuga Street, Novosibirsk 630090,
Russia
protasovmi@ipgg.sbras.ru
[3] PGS Kazakhstan, Almaty, Kazakhstan
[4] EXPEC Advanced Research Center, Saudi Aramco, Dhahran 31311, Saudi Arabia
[5] Aramco Innovations LLC, Saudi Aramco, Moscow 117105, Russia

Abstract. In the paper we consider complex land near surface modeled as random
clutter, and we study the depth imaging problem for such media. We consider synthetic clutter models, and we provide a numerical study using various realizations
of the cluttered models. We propose and investigate a statistical imaging technique
based on path summation allowing to get depth image without reconstruction
of deterministic near-surface depth velocity model. Our results demonstrate that
statistical imaging can significantly improve and recover reflectors, even with a
limited number of realizations. The ability to achieve accurate images despite the
absence of an exact velocity model underscores the robustness of this technique.
We show that statistical imaging can average out phase distortions caused by
near-surface clutter, enhancing the clarity and accuracy of the subsurface image.
This method offers a promising direction for imaging in complex near-surface
environments, effectively addressing the limitations of traditional deterministic
approaches. We further explain why this technique works by leveraging the concept of "seismic speckle," analogous to optical and ultrasonic speckle noise, to
account for phase distortions caused by small-scale heterogeneities. By estimating
the statistical properties of the clutter, we generate ensembles of velocity models
that perturb the phase of the depth-migrated arrivals symmetrically. In summary,
our study highlights the potential of statistical imaging with path summation to
significantly improve seismic imaging in challenging near-surface environments,
offering a robust alternative to traditional deterministic methods and paving the
way for future advancements in subsurface imaging.

Keywords: Statistical imaging · Clutter · Complex Near-surface

O. Gervasi et al. (Eds.): ICCSA 2025, LNCS 15648, pp. 396–414, 2025.
https://doi.org/10.1007/978-3-031-97000-9_25

1 Introduction

In the field of land seismic exploration, the quality of depth seismic images is significantly compromised by strong scattering from small- and medium-scale near-surface heterogeneities [1, 2]. These heterogeneities not only obscure deep geological structures but also introduce substantial phase errors through imperfections in the migration velocity model, which impede accurate focusing of the extrapolated wavefield [2]. Given the impracticality of reconstructing all near-surface complexities with current technology, an effective alternative treats the near-surface as a stochastic medium [3]. This approach leverages the statistical properties of the medium, enabling imaging algorithms to better address near-surface and overburden challenges, thus enhancing the accuracy of deep reflection images. Historically, several methodologies have embraced this statistical perspective. Borcea et al. advocated for an interferometric imaging technique utilizing the concept of time-reversed wave propagation to yield statistically stable images in random media [4]. Extending this, Sava and Poliannikov improved imaging quality in environments with rapid, small-scale velocity variations by modifying conventional cross-correlation migration conditions [5]. A notable shift away from reliance on precise velocity models was proposed by Landa et al. [6], who introduced a path-integral summation concept. This method aggregates images derived from a spectrum of possible velocity distributions, rather than selecting a single "optimal" model. It incorporates weighted summation to highlight the most likely aspects of the image, enhancing the reliability of the output. Path-integral imaging has found various applications in the time domain, such as stack to zero offset [7–9], time migration [6], velocity analysis [10, 11], and diffraction imaging [12]. Advancing these concepts into depth imaging poses greater challenges, necessitating careful sampling of the complex, multidimensional space of possible depth velocity models and selecting appropriate weighting functions for effective summation. Preliminary findings on the applicability of path-integral imaging in depth settings were shared in [6], demonstrating its potential for imaging beneath salt structures without precisely delineating salt-sediment boundaries [13].

Our study discovers and shows the new possibilities of statistical imaging with path summation to significantly improve seismic imaging of target deep reflectors in the presence of a challenging complex near-surface scattering layer characterized as a statistical cluttered medium whose properties should be pre-estimated.

2 Construction Realistic Model with Complex Near-Surface

2.1 Near-Surface Clutter Model: A Focus on Geological Heterogeneities

In seismic imaging, the accurate modeling and imaging of subsurface features are greatly challenged by the scale of geological heterogeneities. These variations in size critically influence how seismic waves scatter, significantly impacting the quality of subsurface imaging. Isolated heterogeneities can create localized disturbances, but a widespread distribution throughout the near-surface horizons leads to pronounced image degradation, demonstrating the profound effect of these heterogeneities [1, 2].

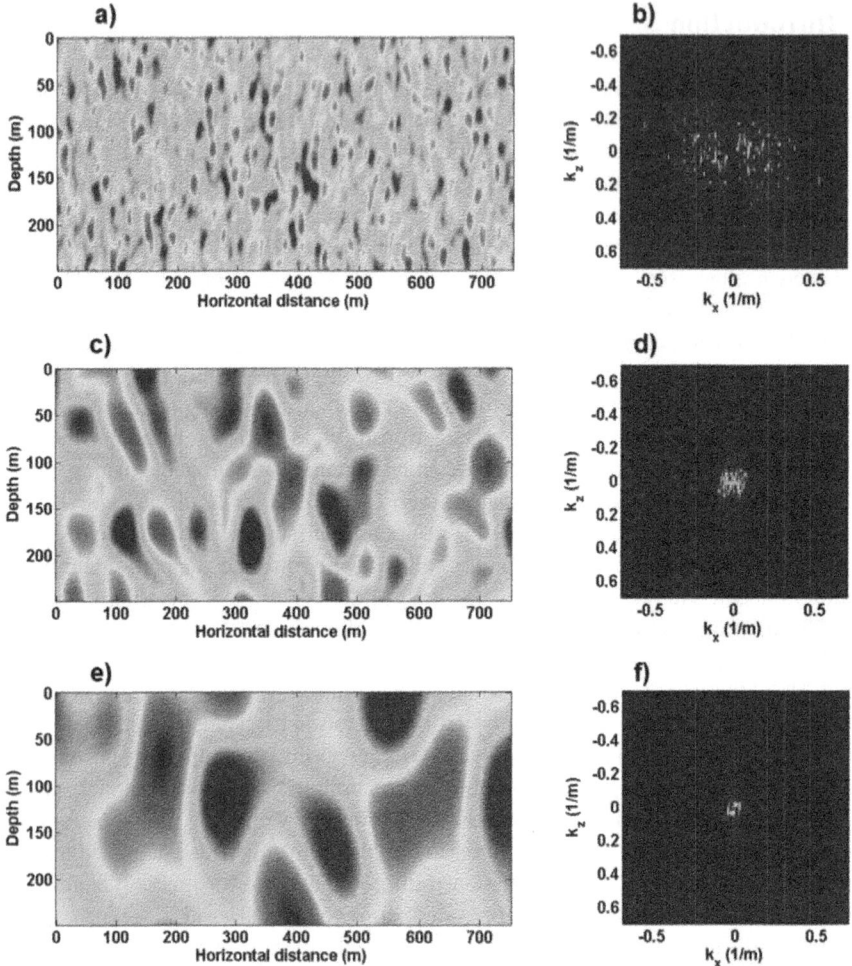

Fig. 1. Near-surface clutter models and corresponding spatial spectra for varying correlation lengths: (a, b) 10 m representing small-scale heterogeneities, (c, d) 35 m for intermediate-scale heterogeneities, and (e, f) 75 m for large-scale heterogeneities.

To assess their impact, we employ a statistical approach within a cluttered near-surface model. This model combines either a homogeneous or smoothly layered background with a random perturbation field derived using Gaussian distribution functions. Key parameters such as correlation length and standard deviation define the scale and magnitude of velocity perturbations, respectively. We illustrate this with example correlation lengths of 10 m, 35 m, and 75 m, each highlighting distinct challenges and impacts on seismic imaging as demonstrated in Fig. 1.

Seismic data typically covers a broadband range of 5–80 Hz, interacting with heterogeneities in various scattering regimes [14] determined by the normalized wave number k·a, where a is the radius of the heterogeneity and k is the wavenumber $k = 2\pi/\lambda$)):

- Effective medium ($k \cdot a < 0.01$), where scattering is negligibly small.
- Rayleigh scattering ($0.01 \leq k \cdot a < 0.1$), with low contrast of the elastic parameters, can be described using the Born approximation.
- Resonance scattering ($0.1 \leq k \cdot a < 10$), scatterer size, and wavelength have the same order. The incident waves are scattered with large angles, and a reflection coda can be observed in the wave field.
- Geometric ray theory ($10 \leq k \cdot a$), the wavelength is small compared to the scatter size. Focusing, diffraction, and interference effects become important.

While larger-scale features such as 75 m are usually within the recovery range of current velocity model building practices and fall predominantly into the geometric ray theory scattering regime, the intermediate scale of 35 m presents substantial challenges due to resonance scattering. This complicates both velocity model construction and seismic imaging. The smallest scale of 10 m often evades traditional velocity model detection, challenged by both Rayleigh and resonance scattering, further contributing to imaging challenges caused by inaccurate velocities.

Geological heterogeneity varies significantly in scale, from large to small, and in certain geological contexts like carbonate strata buildups, a dominant scale can prevail. Our numerical experiments focus on the 35 m scale heterogeneities, representing a critical threshold that starts to replicate real imaging challenges from complex settings. By concentrating on this intermediate scale, we aim to use it as a benchmark to measure progress in imaging techniques under complex near surface.

This study aims to enhance the clarity and accuracy of subsurface images produced, providing a more reliable interpretation of seismic data where these medium-scale heterogeneities dominate. Our objective is not only to push the boundaries of current imaging technology but also to refine our approaches for a better understanding of the complex interplays at work in challenging seismic settings.

2.2 Complete Seismic Model for Imaging Evaluation

In our study, we developed a comprehensive near-surface model enhanced with random clutter, illustrated in Fig. 2a. This model integrates a velocity perturbation field defined by a Gaussian distribution, where the correlation length and standard deviation—35 m and 400 m/s, respectively—specify the heterogeneity scale and velocity perturbation magnitude. Our base model maintains a homogeneous velocity of 2000 m/s. The near-surface layer is bounded to approximately 350 m depth, below which the deeper subsurface is represented by layered media with four flat reflectors. The first reflector marks the bottom of the near-surface layer.

This methodological choice to select a simplified subsurface model allows us to easily evaluate imaging disruptions caused by the complex near-surface conditions. It also mirrors the geological steps of complex desert environments in the Middle East, characterized by 'layer cake' geology coupled with a complex near-surface that often presents challenging imaging scenarios.

To facilitate imaging exercises and evaluation, we generated synthetic seismic data using acoustic finite-difference modeling, based on the exploding reflector concept. This approach is designed to mimic real seismic challenges, replicating the complex scattering distortions typically observed in field data [1]. The resulting synthetic dataset provides a robust framework for testing and comparing the efficacy of different imaging strategies under realistic conditions (Fig. 2b).

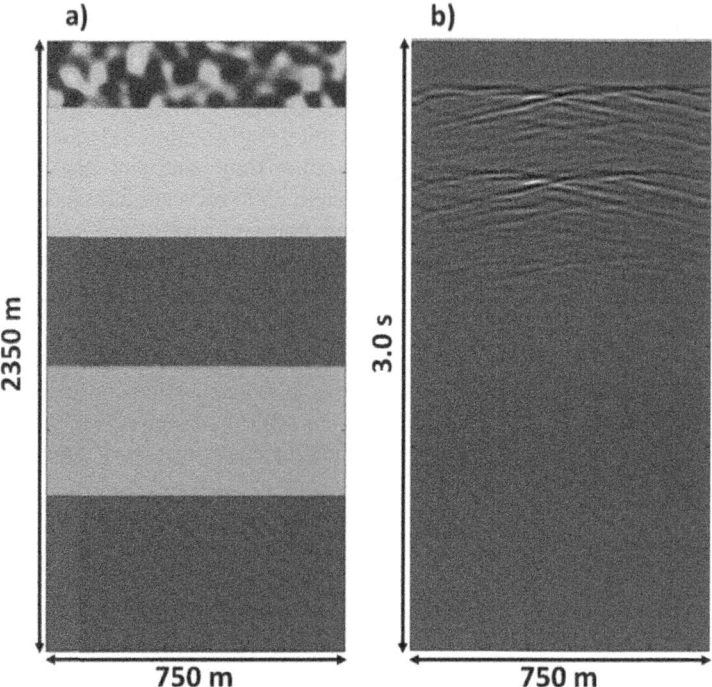

Fig. 2. (a) True model representation: complex near-surface simulated with a fixed clutter realization, featuring a spatial correlation length of 35 m, mean velocity of 2000 m/s, and a standard deviation of 400 m/s. (b) Zero-offset seismic data computed from the true model in (a). This figure illustrates the impact of near-surface complexity on seismic data, showing how small-scale heterogeneities influence the recorded wavefield.

3 Deterministic Imaging

We provide the ideal image result which is got via convolution of the true model reflectivity and the source impulse (Fig. 3a). Then we compute zero-offset data and in the true clutter model we provide reverse-time migration (RTM), the results are shown in Fig. 3b. This RTM result contains numerous imaging artifacts alongside the true subsurface reflectors. For benchmarking purposes, the ideal image is used as the exact reference solution and the image obtained from the true clutter model is used as the best achievable result.

Next we provide a realistic imaging scenario, where we know the initial smooth "tomographic" velocity model (Fig. 4a) that approximates the true model but lacks

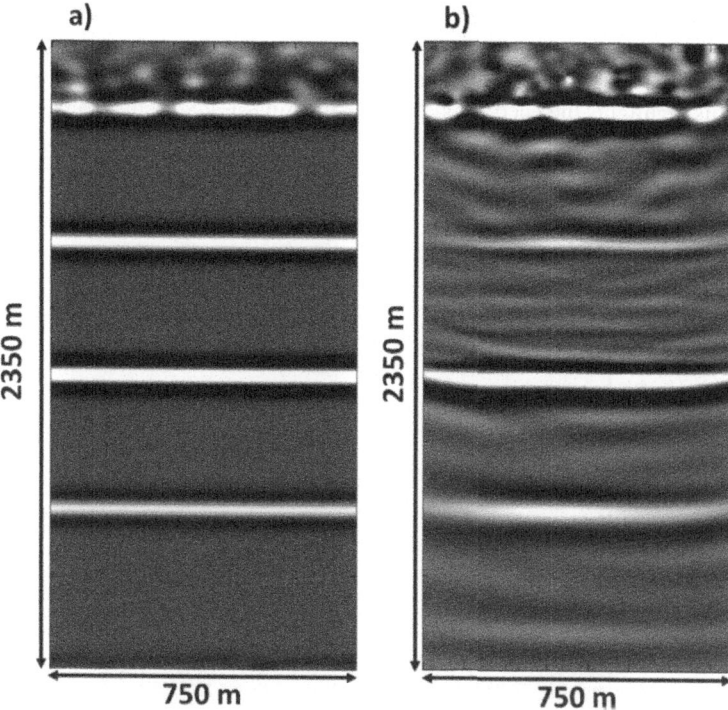

Fig. 3. (a) True model reflectivity used as the ideal image reference. (b) Zero-offset RTM image in the true clutter model, representing the best achievable migrated image. Although the best achievable image still has many artifacts, it proves that migration can produce great images if all velocity details, including small-scale heterogeneities, are accurately recovered.

many smaller details. We further assume, without proof, that the perturbations between the background and true model follow a Gaussian distribution. We estimate the two parameters of this distribution directly from the data, with the correlation length kept at 35 m and the standard deviation reduced to 257 m/s. This standard deviation is based on the difference between the smooth "tomographic" and the true clutter models.

Using these statistical parameters allows for the efficient generation of an ensemble of models. Figure 3b shows one such model realization. We then applied conventional deterministic imaging to both the smooth model and the detailed model, which is one realization with pre-defined clutter parameters. The migration results for both the smooth clutter model and any model realization yield defocused images (Fig. 4a, 4b), with only parts of the reflected interfaces being properly migrated.

Our tests indicate that conventional deterministic imaging can yield appropriate results when the model is known exactly. However, medium- and small-scale features pose significant challenges, and conventional velocity model building is imperfect, making this approach often difficult to achieve optimal results.

When only a smooth background velocity model is available, deterministic imaging struggles to produce satisfactory images. Even with detailed knowledge of clutter parameters, this approach cannot consistently generate models that deliver reliable results. This highlights the need for alternative imaging strategies that can better handle the complexities introduced by near-surface heterogeneities (Fig. 5).

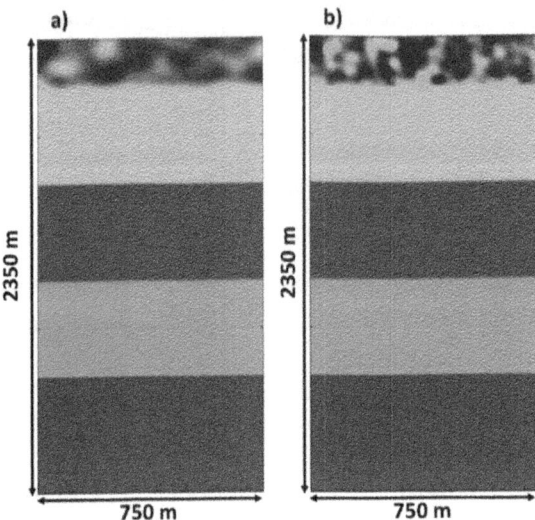

Fig. 4. (a) Smooth background model of the true clutter, assumed to be recovered during conventional velocity model building. (b) A single realization of the model generated by introducing Gaussian perturbations to the smooth model from (a), with a correlation length of 35 m and a standard deviation of 257 m/s for the perturbations. This comparison highlights the differences between a conventional smooth model and a perturbed realization, illustrating the potential impact of small-scale heterogeneities on seismic imaging.

4   Statistical Imaging

4.1   Path Summation

Instead of relying on the uncertain reconstruction of an exact velocity model [2], the path-summation method generates multiple realizations of the depth model [6] that could capture accurate fragments of the depth velocity model. The final image is a weighted summation of these elementary images constructed for every model realization, allowing each one to contribute valuable pieces to the overall picture.

In our case, imaging in a desert environment with a complex near-surface is achieved by summing individual migrated images computed for different realizations of the near-surface migration velocity model as follows:

$$I_w(x) = \sum_k w_k(x) I_k(x) \tag{1}$$

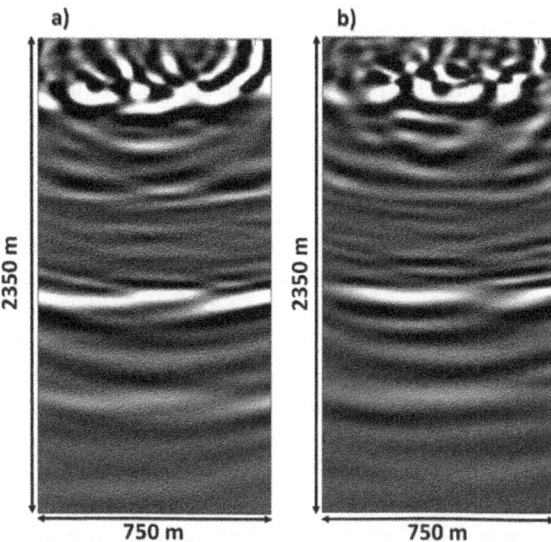

Fig. 5. Zero-offset images obtained with different velocity models: (a) smooth background model shown in Fig. 4a; (b) single realization from the clutter ensemble shown in Fig. 4b. Both images struggle to focus subsurface reflectors, highlighting the challenges posed by near-surface heterogeneities on imaging accuracy.

where I_w is a final image at point x, I_k is the image for model realization with k, and w_k is a weighting function, which is set to 1 in this study. This procedure can be viewed as statistical averaging over an ensemble of possible near-surface models.

We define the near-surface model realizations using statistical modeling of random anomalies, known as clutter. Given that the scale of the anomalies of interest is comparable to or smaller than the dominant source wavelength, we use reverse-time migration (RTM) to accurately address them during wave propagation. For simplicity, we consider post-stack RTM in this work, though the results can be extended to the case of pre-stack migration.

4.2 Statistical Imaging Investigation

To investigate statistical imaging using the path summation approach, we start with a smooth "tomographic" near-surface model as a reference solution (Fig. 4a). We assume a correlation length of 35 m and define the standard deviation as 257 m/s, based on the difference between the true clutter and the "tomographic" model.

We generated 100 model realizations and performed zero-offset RTM migration for each, resulting in 100 images. Images for three different model realizations are shown in Fig. 6. Finally, we applied the path summation approach to this scenario. Traces for fixed horizontal positions for all 100 images are presented in Fig. 7, where fluctuations of the events near the true reflector positions can be observed.

These images were stacked using simple summation (1). The migration result for individual realizations generally provides defocused images (Fig. 6), with only some parts of the reflected interfaces properly migrated. However, even a simple summation results in a stacked image that shows reflected events over most of the area (Fig. 8a).

By performing migration with different models of the same data, we can generate an analog of a common-image gather (CIG) of RTM zero-offset migration with respect to the model realizations (Fig. 7). These raw CIGs do not provide flat events at the reflector positions; instead, they are scattered due to the different perturbations in the clutter realizations.

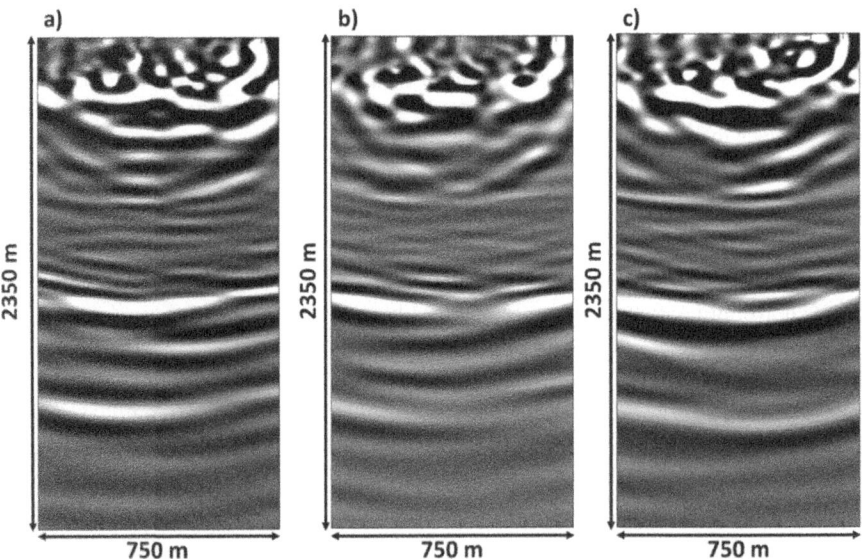

Fig. 6. Zero-offset RTM images obtained from three different single realizations of the clutter ensemble used in statistical imaging. These images demonstrate the variability and phase distortions caused by different near-surface clutter realizations, showcasing the challenges in achieving accurate seismic imaging without statistical averaging.

Next, we investigate the influence of the number of realizations on the statistical imaging result. We compute simple stacks with different numbers of iterations: 5, 10, 25, 50, and 100 (Fig. 9). Visually, it is challenging to judge qualitatively which stack image is better. Therefore, we use two quantitative measures: signal-to-noise ratio (SNR) and correlation coefficient. Both measures use standard definitions and utilize the ideal image result (Fig. 9a) as the reference.

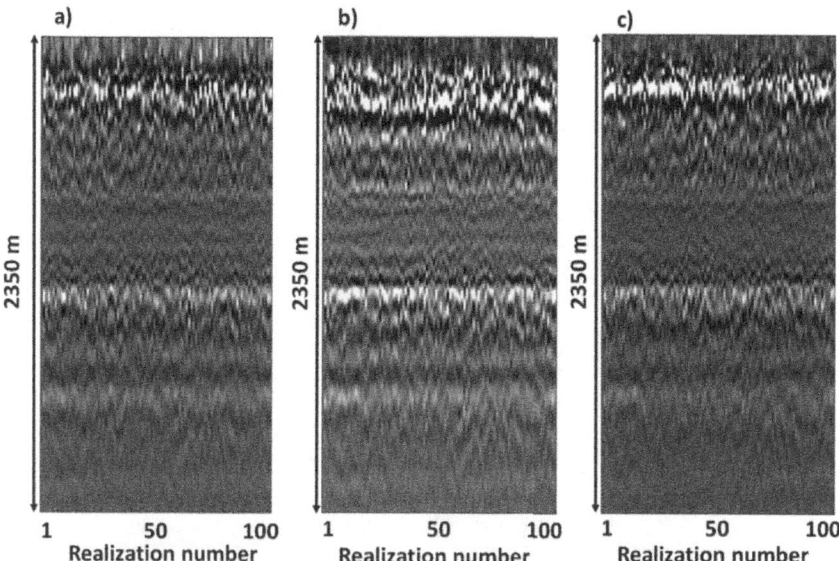

Fig. 7. Common-image gathers of zero-offset migration with respect to the model realizations at three different horizontal positions: (a) x = 250 m; (b) x = 375 m; (c) x = 500 m. These gathers illustrate the variability in the seismic reflections due to different realizations of the near-surface model, highlighting the phase distortions and amplitude variations across different locations.

We compute SNR values and correlation coefficients for the entire images and for the image parts containing reflected interfaces near 750 m, 1250 m, and 1750 m. Analyzing the results in Table 1, it is evident that the image obtained from the true clutter model is the best achievable solution, despite appearing noisier than the path summation weighted images.

Additionally, all path summation results provide better solutions than any single realization. Notably, the SNR and correlation coefficient values for the simple stacks with 10, 25, 50, and 100 iterations are very close. This indicates that only a few realizations are needed in statistical imaging to achieve a sufficiently good solution.

Next, we investigate the influence of errors in the statistical parameters of the clutter on the results of statistical imaging. We introduce different levels of error in the values for the standard deviation and correlation lengths: −15%, +15%, and +50%. The statistical image results for clutters with these errors are presented in Fig. 10.

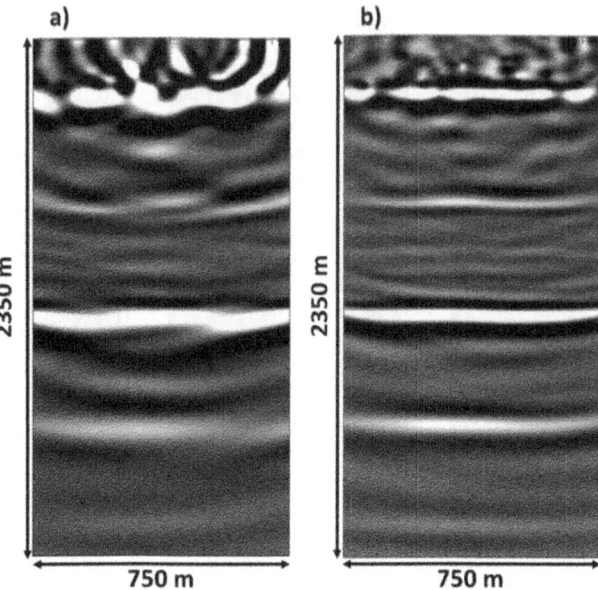

Fig. 8. Comparison of statistical image and best achievable migrated image: (a) statistical image obtained using simple stack path summation; (b) zero-offset RTM image in the true clutter model, representing the best achievable migrated image. This figure illustrates the effectiveness of statistical imaging with path summation compared to the best achievable result using the true clutter model. The statistical image in (a) demonstrates how path summation can approximate the ideal migration outcome shown in (b), despite the absence of the exact velocity model.

Visually, the statistical images for errors of -15% and $+15\%$ are close to the images obtained with the correct clutter parameters. However, the statistical images for a 50% error significantly differ from those obtained with true values. For a quantitative comparison, we compute SNR values and correlation coefficients, summarizing the results in Table 2. The quantitative and visual comparisons lead to similar conclusions: statistical imaging provides stable results concerning clutter parameters, which is crucial for its practical application.

5 Why Statistical Imaging Works?

Inspired by studies of optical and ultrasonic speckle noise [15], we hypothesize that seismic data experiences similar distortions caused by near-ballistic forward scattering of multiple arrivals. We refer to this phenomenon as "seismic speckle" [16]. Speckle is typically modeled as multiplicative noise. Analogously, we can interpret image distortions after depth migration of such data. To illustrate this, we provide an analogy for common-image gathers obtained from different model realizations. Let us describe the seismic trace model incorporating general multiplicative noise. The image trace for the k-th realization is represented as:

$$i_k(z) = r_k(z) * s(z) + n_k(z), \tag{2}$$

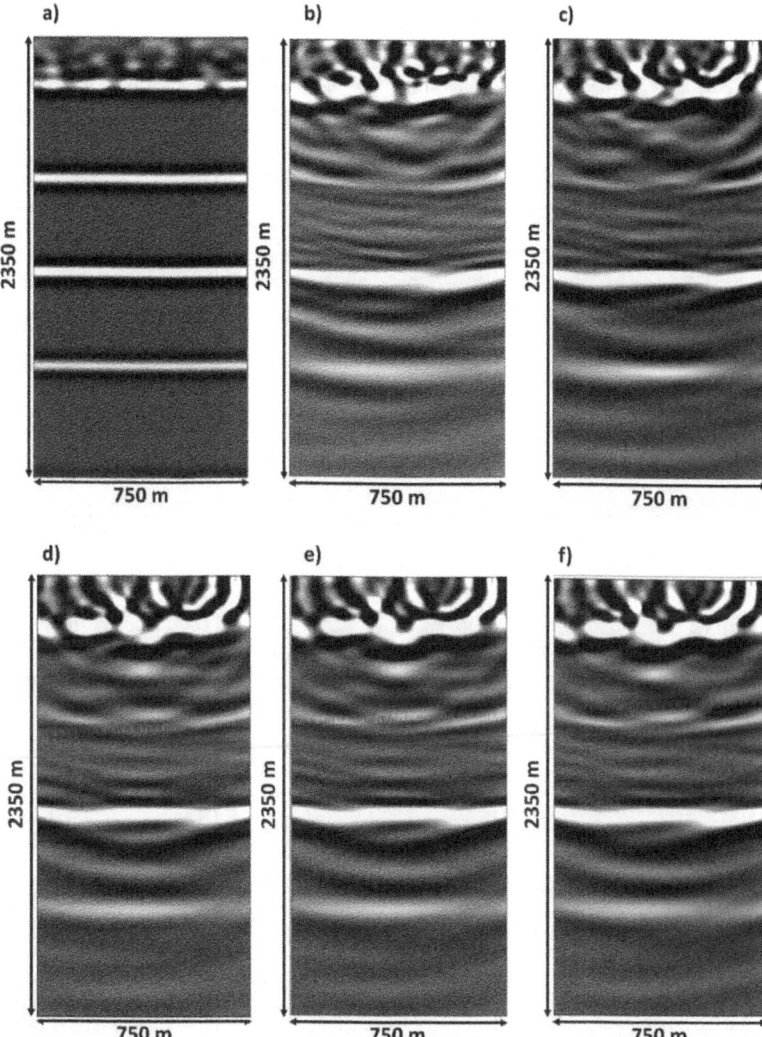

Fig. 9. Effect of number of realizations on statistical imaging: (a) True model reflectivity: ideal image reference; (b)–(e) Statistical images with varying number of realizations: (b) 5 Realizations; (c) 10 Realizations; (d) 25 Realizations; (e) 50 Realizations. Observe that images (c)–(d) are similar, suggesting that even a small number of realizations can achieve a reasonable statistical image.

where $s(z)$ is the clean image trace, $r_k(z)$ is multiplicative noise, $n_k(z)$ is additive random noise. In the Fourier domain (2) is written as:

$$I_k(p_z) = R_k(p_z)S(p_z) + N_k(p_z), \tag{3}$$

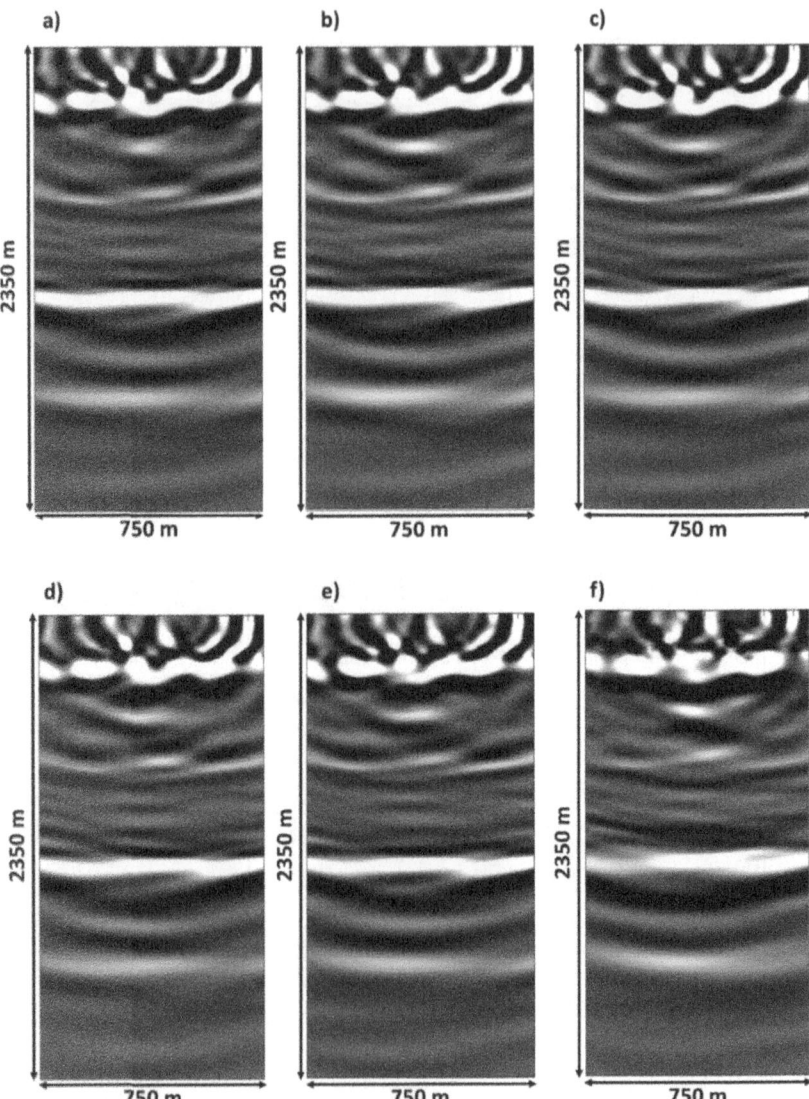

Fig. 10. Statistical images obtained with path summation using simple stacking for different clutter parameters: (a) correct; (b) standard deviation error +15%; (c) standard deviation error −15%; (d) correlation length error +15%; (e) correlation length error −5%; (f) standard deviation error +50%, correlation length error +50%. These results demonstrate that statistical imaging is robust to small errors in clutter parameters (around ±15%) but shows significant degradation with larger errors (around ±50%). This indicates that approximate values within a certain range can still yield better images using statistical imaging, without the need for precise accuracy.

Table 1. Quality control metrics for statistical images obtained by summing different numbers of realizations, including SNR (in dB) and correlation coefficient. These metrics are computed based on quantitative comparison with the ideal image reference.

Metric	RTM in true model	Single realization	Sum of 100 realizations	Sum of 50 realizations	Sum of 25 realizations	Sum of 10 realizations	Sum of 5 realizations
SNR	3.5	−2.5	−0.7	−0.6	−0.3	−0.7	−1.7
Correlation coefficient	0.75	0.18	0.4	0.4	0.43	0.34	0.3

Table 2. Quality control metrics for images with different clutter parameters: SNR and correlation coefficient. The table evaluates the impact of estimating errors on image quality, based on comparisons with the ideal reference (true reflectivity) and the best achievable image (RTM in the true model). These results show that approximate clutter parameters are sufficient for obtaining better images, highlighting the practical applicability of statistical imaging.

Metric	RTM in true model	Stat image, no error	Stat image, std +15%	Stat image, std −15%	Stat image, cor. len. +15%	Stat image, cor. len. −15%	Stat. Image, std and cor. len. + 50%
SNR	3.5	−0.7	−0.8	−1.1	−0.4	−0.7	−1.9
Correlation coefficient	0.75	0.4	0.37	0.3	0.41	0.36	0.28

where p_z is the variable in the Fourier domain, I_k, R_k, S, N_k are Fourier transforms of the corresponding depth-domain functions,. We specify a more explicit form of multiplicative noise as a random frequency-dependent phase fluctuations occurring for each realization:

$$R_k(p_z) = e^{i\varphi_k(p_z)}. \tag{4}$$

Here φ_k is the phase of the function R_k. The local stacking result of the K traces in the frequency domain is given by

$$\hat{S}(p_z) = \frac{1}{K}\sum_{k=1}^{K}\left\{S(p_z)e^{i\varphi_k(p_z)} + N_k(p_z)\right\}. \tag{5}$$

Since the number of traces used in the stacking process is limited, $\hat{S}(p_z)$ would be a random variable for different trace ensembles. If random variables $\varphi_k(p_z)$ describing phase perturbations have the same distributions for each realization, then the mathematical expectation is expressed as:

$$E\left[\hat{S}(p_z)\right] = |S(p_z)|e^{i\varphi_s(p_z)}\Phi(p_z). \tag{6}$$

Without specifying further details of the near surface and migration process, we can draw important conclusions. If phase perturbations $\varphi_k(p_z)$ follow a normal (Gaussian) distribution with zero mean and standard deviation $\sigma(p_z)$, then mathematical expectation can be expressed as

$$E\left[\hat{S}(p_z)\right] = |S(p_z)|e^{i\varphi_S(p_z)}e^{-\frac{\sigma^2(p_z)}{2}}. \tag{7}$$

For multiplicative noise caused by random depth shifts dz_k between channels (residual static that corresponds to different reflector positions for different realizations), the form is:

$$R_k(p_z) = e^{-ip_z dz_k}. \tag{8}$$

If statics are normally distributed with zero mean and standard deviation σ_z, then

$$E\left[\hat{S}(p_z)\right] = |S(p_z)|e^{i\varphi_s(p_z)}e^{-\frac{p_z^2\sigma_z^2}{2}}. \tag{9}$$

Again, the phase spectrum remains the same as the clean signal, while the amplitude experiences exponential loss with frequency. When considering both types of multiplicative, then the mathematical expectation is given by:

$$E\left[\hat{S}(p_z)\right] = |S(p_z)|e^{i\varphi_s(p_z)}e^{-\frac{p_z^2\sigma_z^2}{2}}e^{-\frac{\sigma_\varphi^2}{2}}. \tag{10}$$

The phase of the mathematical expectation matches the clean signal phase, while the amplitude loss is a product of two terms: one due to phase perturbations and the other due to residual statics. These results, as presented in the paper [16] in the context of speckle noise studies, demonstrate how phase cleanup and amplitude filtering occur during stacking.

Let us now revisit the common-image gather from the described experiments (Fig. 11a) and focus on the domain around the reflector at a depth of 1250 m (Fig. 11b) to establish a connection with speckle-based considerations. The ensemble shown in Fig. 11b can be viewed as carrying an identical reference signal (fixed subsurface reflector) but disturbed by different speckle patterns created numerically through RTM imaging with random near-surface models. Analyzing the phase variation of the window from Fig. 11b at two spatial frequencies, we observe that they show a symmetric Gaussian-like distribution (Fig. 12b, c), similar to what is seen in speckle noise. Note that zero in this plot corresponds to the average phase, i.e., the phase of the statistical image after summing all realizations. The symmetry resembles the assumption of speckle noise presented above. In physical experiments, we are restricted to a single realization of the clutter. Therefore, for seismic imaging in the presence of speckle noise, the strategy has been to use nearby traces with slightly different source/receiver positions for local stacking, thereby revealing the undistorted reflector phase of the common signal reflector [16]. In our study, however, we have the luxury of numerically realizing different models and speckle patterns at one location through simulation and imaging. This allows us to systematically perturb the near-surface models and enable statistical imaging to recover a cleaned-up

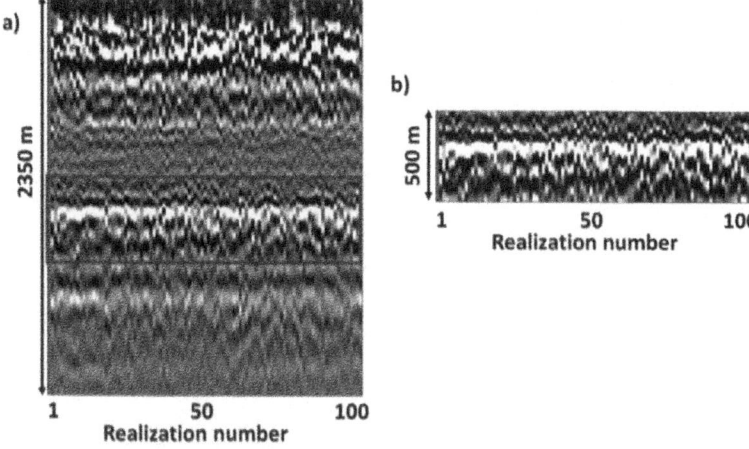

Fig. 11. (a) Common-image gather of zero-offset migration with respect to the model realizations at $x = 375$, emphasizing the impact of different near-surface clutter realizations on phase. (b) Zoomed-in view around the reflector at a depth of 1250 m, revealing an on average similar reflector disturbed by different speckle patterns created through RTM imaging with random near-surface models. The phase perturbations appear quasi-random, similar to speckle noise.

average phase in a similar way. Another similarity is that the spectrum after summation loses higher frequencies, as seen in Fig. 12a, which echoes high-frequency attenuation observed in Eq. (10). These two observations – near-symmetric phase disturbances and attenuation of higher frequencies upon stacking – establish a clear link between statistical imaging and speckle noise studies [15, 16]. These results align with the behavior predicted by formula (10), indicating that phase perturbations in the pre-summation common-image gathers could be described by the simple multiplicative model (2).

These considerations assume that our average tomographic model is a reasonable representation of the near-surface layer with small-scale heterogeneities, consistent with what is expected from seismic velocity model building, which typically yields smoothed or average velocity models. Additionally, by estimating the statistical properties of the clutter, we can generate ensembles of velocity models that perturb the phase of the depth-migrated arrivals symmetrically. Under these assumptions, the statistical collection of images before summation produces a distribution of phases that, upon stacking, can reveal the true reflector signal phase, resulting in images approaching what we would have with the true clutter model, which is unattainable in practice. The intriguing point is that each realization produces a distorted phase and image that by itself may have little value. However, their collection acquires extra power, essentially enabling them to "vote" and reveal a much more meaningful phase and image, effectively seeing through the small-scale heterogeneities. Remarkably, the actual true clutter realization that could have produced a similarly good image is not even present in the ensemble that generates the statistical image. And yet, we are able to get a robust image approaching one obtained with the true model. The initial price to pay for this improvement is that statistical images are likely to contain lower frequencies compared to the initial ones, as higher frequencies are more prone to attenuation upon stacking. However, finding those crisper and less distorted reflections in images, even at lower frequencies, holds promise. This could potentially allow the recovery of higher frequencies in the future, making this approach a hopeful aspiration for further work despite its current limitations.

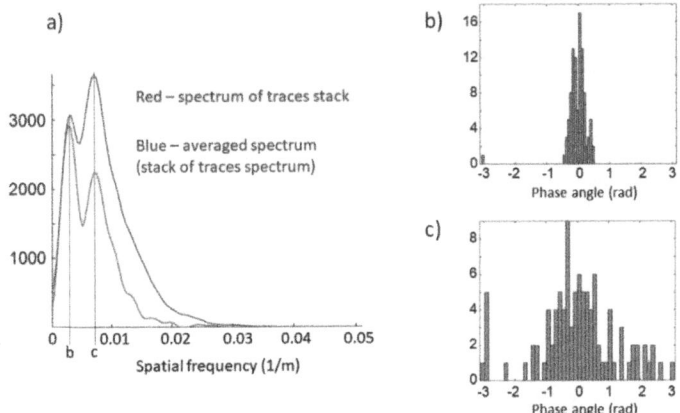

Fig. 12. (a) Amplitude spectra of common-image gather traces before and after summation, illustrating the attenuation of higher frequencies after summation—a characteristic effect of averaging multiple realizations impacted by speckle noise. (b), (c) Histograms of phase angle fluctuations for two peak frequencies, highlighting the quasi-random nature of phase perturbations. These histograms demonstrate a near-symmetric Gaussian-like distribution of phase angles around the average phase, aligning with the behavior predicted by the multiplicative model of random speckle noise.

6 Conclusions

In this study, we applied statistical imaging with path summation to synthetic land data characterized by a complex near-surface modeled as random clutter. Our findings demonstrate that near-surface clutter significantly degrades reflection images if not properly accounted for. While migration using the exact velocity model of the clutter can recover reflections (albeit with artifacts), such a model is impractical to achieve in real-world scenarios. Images generated using a conventionally recoverable smoothed background model are substantially compromised. Statistical imaging, however, shows great promise in significantly improving and recovering reflectors, provided the statistical parameters for generating velocity realizations are accurately estimated or guessed. This approach leverages the statistical properties of the clutter to create ensembles of velocity models, allowing for more effective phase cleanup and improved imaging. Our heuristic explanation, building on concepts from speckle noise studies, elucidates why statistical imaging works for near-surface scenarios with small-scale heterogeneities.

In practical terms, statistical imaging can significantly enhance the clarity and accuracy of subsurface images in complex near-surface environments, making it a valuable tool for geophysical exploration. The ability to achieve accurate images without requiring an exact velocity model underscores the robustness of statistical imaging, offering a practical solution where precise models are unattainable. This approach provides a feasible method for handling real-world seismic data impacted by near-surface clutter, thereby improving the reliability of seismic interpretations.

Future studies should evaluate the sensitivity of path-summation imaging to the accuracy of the statistical parameters used to characterize random heterogeneity. This will help refine the technique and enhance its robustness. Incorporating geological knowledge to assess plausible statistical properties describing near-surface geology can further improve the accuracy of statistical imaging. Advances in acoustics can aid in estimating clutter parameters in heterogeneous initial models, facilitating the creation of appropriate realizations required for the path summation approach. Additionally, further research should explore the intersection of statistical imaging with uncertainty quantification of complex velocity models, enhancing the reliability of seismic data interpretations. The main limitation of the statistical imaging is loose of high frequencies due to attenuation upon stacking. Despite of that, the potential to recover higher frequencies in the future holds promise for further improving imaging quality.

In summary, statistical imaging with path summation presents a powerful alternative to traditional deterministic methods, offering significant improvements in imaging quality for complex near-surface environments. We should emphasize that statistical imaging should provide similar results in another geological context because its ability to average out phase distortions and reveal clearer subsurface images paves the way for more accurate and reliable seismic interpretations, making it a promising area for ongoing and future research.

Acknowledgments. Authors are grateful to Saudi Aramco for the support and for the permission to publish the results. Authors are grateful to Evgeny Landa for inspiring discussions. This work is partially supported by the Russian Science Foundation within the framework of the project № 21-71-20002-П: Maxim Protasov provides realistic models using statistical modeling.

Disclosure of Interests. The authors have no competing interests to declare that are relevant to the content of this article.

References

1. Bakulin, A., Neklyudov, D., Silvestrov, I.: Importance of phase guides from beamformed data for processing multi-channel data in highly scattering media. J. Acoust. Soc. Am. Express Lett. **147**(6), EL447–EL552 (2020)
2. Xie, X.-B., Ning, H., Chen, B.: How scatterings from small-scale near-surface heterogeneities affecting seismic data and the quality of depth image, analysis based on seismic resolution. In: SEG Technical Program Expanded Abstracts, pp. 4278–4282. SEG (2016)
3. Ikelle, L.T., Yung, S.K., Daube, F.: 2-D random media with ellipsoidal autocorrelation functions. Geophysics **58**, 1359–1372 (1993)
4. Borcea, L., Papanicolaou, G., Tsogka, C.: Theory and applications of time reversal and interferometric imaging. Inverse Prob. **19**, S139–S164 (2003)

5. Sava, P., Poliannikov, O.: Interferometric imaging condition for wave-equation migration. Geophysics **73**, S47–S61 (2008)
6. Landa, E., Fomel, S., Moser, T.J.: Path-integral seismic imaging. Geophys. Prospect. **54**, 491–503 (2006)
7. Landa, E.: Imaging without a velocity model using pathsummation approach. In: SEG Technical Program Expanded Abstracts, pp. 1016–1019. SEG (2004)
8. Keydar, S., Shtivelman, V.: Imaging zero-offset sections using multipath summation. First Break **23**, 21–24 (2005)
9. Yilmaz, Ö.: Circumventing velocity uncertainty in imaging complex structures. Lead. Edge **37**, 14–18 (2018)
10. Schleicher, J., Costa J.C.: Migration velocity analysis by double path-integral migration. Geophysics **74**, WCA225–WCA231 (2009)
11. Burnett, W., Fomel, S., Bansal, R.: Diffraction velocity analysis by path-integral seismic imaging. In: SEG Technical Program Expanded Abstracts, pp. 3898–3902. SEG (2011)
12. Decker, L., Fomel S., Path-integral seismic diffraction imaging with probability weights. In: SEG Technical Program Expanded Abstracts, pp. 4231–4235. SEG (2019)
13. Protasov, M., Kolyukhin, D., Rostomyan, S., Landa, E.: Subsalt imaging in the presence of salt-body uncertainty. Lead. Edge **2**, 146–150 (2017)
14. Pyrak-Nolte, L.: Seismic imaging of fractured media. In: 5th International Workshop on the Application of Geophysics in Rock Engineering, pp. 5–13 (2002)
15. Goodman, J.W.: Speckle Phenomena in Optics: Theory and Applications. Roberts & Company (2007)
16. Bakulin, A., Neklyudov, D., Silvestrov, I.: Multiplicative seismic noise caused by small-scale near-surface scattering and its transformation during stacking. Geophysics **87**(5), V419–V435 (2022)

Combining Computer Vision and Artificial Intelligence to Support the Rehabilitation of Post-stroke Patients

Luiz Felipe de Camargo$^{1(\boxtimes)}$ (ID), Gabriel Rissatti Miguel^1 (ID),
Juliana da Costa Feitosa^1 (ID), Luis Guilherme Silva Rodrigues^1 (ID),
Diego Roberto Colombo Dias^2 (ID), and José Remo Ferreira Brega^1 (ID)

^{1} São Paulo State University (UNESP), Bauru, São Paulo, Brazil
{luiz.felipe,gabriel.rissatti,juliana.feitosa,guilherme.rodrigues,
remo.brega}@unesp.br
^{2} Federal University of Espírito Santo, Vitória, Espírito Santo, Brazil
diego.dias@ufes.br

Abstract. Considering the rehabilitation needs of stroke patients and the advancements in computational tools within the healthcare sector, this study aims to conduct a comprehensive literature review and develop an application leveraging Computer Vision and Artificial Intelligence to classify movements in support of rehabilitation. To achieve this, a systematic review of relevant literature was conducted, and based on the findings, an application was developed and is currently undergoing testing. Preliminary results from an initial evaluation by a healthcare professional in the rehabilitation field have shown promising outcomes. These findings suggest that tools of this nature can be valuable in enhancing rehabilitation activities and may be further refined to address a broader range of patient needs.

Keywords: Computer Vision · Artificial Intelligence · Motion Analysis · Rehabilitation · Stroke

1 Introduction

A cerebrovascular accident (CVA), commonly referred to as a stroke, occurs when the blood vessels supplying the brain are either obstructed or ruptured, resulting in ischemia and subsequent paralysis in the affected brain region. This condition predominantly impacts men and is among the leading causes of mortality, disability, and hospitalization worldwide. Early diagnosis and intervention in stroke cases substantially increase the chances of a full recovery [13].

Most stroke survivors experience some form of physical or cognitive sequelae. To mitigate the long-term effects of a stroke, affected individuals must have timely access to rehabilitation services that provide comprehensive treatment, addressing their specific needs while considering their capabilities and potential. The World Health Organization (WHO) defines rehabilitation as: "The use of all

O. Gervasi et al. (Eds.): ICCSA 2025, LNCS 15648, pp. 415–432, 2025.
https://doi.org/10.1007/978-3-031-97000-9_26

means necessary to reduce the impact of the disabling condition and to enable individuals with disabilities to achieve full integration" [31].

The consequences of a stroke can be addressed in two primary ways: prevention through a healthy lifestyle to mitigate risk factors, and post-stroke rehabilitation, which necessitates multi-disciplinary support and includes various therapeutic interventions, such as physiotherapy for motor sequelae. Physiotherapy plays a crucial role in improving the quality of life for patients affected by these sequelae. Motor physiotherapy specifically enhances flexibility, motor coordination, and mobility, thereby significantly contributing to the functional independence of patients [20].

The integration of computational tools within the healthcare domain has emerged as a significant advancement. Through the use of specialized software, Virtual Reality (VR), and wearable devices, treatments can be personalized, patient progress can be monitored, and autonomy can be fostered, particularly in the context of rehabilitation. This integration of advanced technologies, including Artificial Intelligence (AI) and computer vision, enhances therapeutic efficacy and contributes to an improved quality of life [29].

The global healthcare technology landscape is advancing rapidly, driven by the increasing adoption of digital solutions and smart devices for diagnosing, treating, and monitoring patients. Technologies such as Artificial Intelligence, Virtual Reality, and Telemedicine are revolutionizing healthcare delivery. In Brazil, despite the growing momentum in this direction, significant challenges remain, including unequal access to technology, lack of integration among healthcare systems, and the need for greater investment in research and development [21].

Given these considerations, it is reasonable to anticipate the emergence of new applications aimed at supporting the treatment of stroke patients, particularly in the analysis of exercise performance. This paper presents a study that has thus far encompassed a literature review and the development of an application designed to assist rehabilitation professionals and patients by capturing and analyzing body movements during exercise sessions.

As scientific knowledge advances, computational motion analysis tools are transforming rehabilitation. Through the integration of artificial intelligence, pose estimation, and software engineering, these systems offer in-depth insights into human movement that were previously unattainable.

Accurate data collection and analysis enable researchers to gain a comprehensive understanding of movement patterns, pose estimation, and physiology, facilitating the development of novel rehabilitation techniques. Moreover, the technology empowers therapists to personalize treatments, optimize exercises, and monitor patient progress in real time, enhancing the efficacy of rehabilitation and paving the way for new discoveries in healthcare.

The literature review was conducted in a systematic manner to gain a comprehensive understanding of the research domain in which the proposal is situated and to identify emerging trends and gaps that could inform the development of the application. Drawing on the insights gained from the review and the needs identified by a collaborating researcher in the rehabilitation field, the application was developed and is currently undergoing testing.

This study is organized as follows: Sect. 2 reviews related work; Sect. 4 provides an overview of the literature review; Sect. 5 details the design decisions and the application development process; Sect. 6 presents the results obtained to date; and Sect. 7 summarizes the findings and concludes the study.

2 Related Work

Researchers worldwide are actively exploring and contributing to the application of Computer Vision and Artificial Intelligence for capturing movements to support the physical rehabilitation of patients.

[11] proposes a supervised learning method for the automatic evaluation of physical rehabilitation exercises, utilizing a Kinect camera and other equipment. According to the author, this approach offers a cost-effective technique for assessing the performance of rehabilitation exercises.

[25] investigates the recognition of human movement actions to analyze movement similarities. This study decomposes the human body into segments represented by combinations of coordinates.

Looking at the research scene in Brazil, we can highlight the use of Virtual Reality in the rehabilitation of stroke patients at the Brazilian Institute of Neuroscience and Neurotechnology (BRAINN). One of their initiatives is the Gesture Collection, a set of Virtual Reality applications that allow interaction through gestures using a sensor, which transforms traditional physiotherapy and occupational therapy activities into more engaging tasks [9].

3 Theoretical Background

3.1 Computational Vision

Computer vision can be defined as the computational field focused on enabling computers to perform vision tasks. It encompasses more than just image capture, which represents only the initial step in a complex process involving noise reduction, region or scene segmentation, information extraction from the analyzed image, and the correlation of images with other images and labels [4].

3.2 Pose Estimation and Human Action Recognition

Human pose estimation is a technique in which a computer aims to detect human movement, with applications across various domains, including virtual cinematography using computer graphics, human behavior recognition, and security systems. The joint positions identified by pose estimation tools may vary due to several factors, such as camera angle, clothing, and contextual elements [19].

Human Action Recognition (HAR) involves the application of video analysis techniques to identify activities performed by an individual through a sequence of observations of the person and their context. HAR systems are designed to automatically analyze and recognize specific human behaviors by extracting knowledge from video data via computer vision techniques. HAR plays a critical role in healthcare, particularly in identifying rehabilitation activities of patients and streamlining processes that were previously manual and reliant on expert judgment. HAR systems must consistently assign the same labels to identical activities, even when performed by different individuals under varying conditions or environments [12].

3.3   Artificial Intelligence

Artificial Intelligence (AI) is a field of Computer Science that seeks to simulate human intelligence through technological means, enabling systems to solve problems, generate solutions, and even make decisions on behalf of humans, thereby enhancing various aspects of daily life. The term "Artificial Intelligence" was first coined by John McCarthy in 1956 during a technology conference at Dartmouth College, USA; however, the concept had already been explored by Alan Turing in 1950, who is widely regarded as the father of computing [30].

The term AI is widely used to describe the latest experiences of interaction between computer systems and their users, eventually becoming an umbrella term that encompasses various computational, mathematical, and statistical techniques. AI is transforming the way people communicate, work, consume, manage their health, plan vacations, and conduct research. It is difficult to find a socio-economic activity that is not mediated by intelligent technologies [18].

Explainable Artificial Intelligence (XAI) is a subfield of AI that seeks not only to deliver outcomes but also to elucidate its own purpose. Such explanations must encompass both the objectives of the system and its decision making process, a feature widely acknowledged as essential for the practical deployment of AI models [6]. Discussions on XAI are becoming increasingly prominent within the technology sector.

Artificial Intelligence in healthcare holds tremendous potential to transform the field, yet its development and application must be guided by ethical, scientific, and responsible principles. Only under these conditions can the technology provide genuine benefits to patients, practitioners, and society at large [10]. In light of concerns regarding trust and transparency in healthcare AI, opportunities for applying XAI in this domain are emerging, aiming to furnish users with insights that extend beyond the mere decision of the model [7,36].

4   Systematic Literature Review

A Systematic Literature Review (SLR) was conducted on the topic, a research method that utilizes existing literature as a data source, offering a comprehensive summary of the evidence related to a specific strategy. Such reviews are valuable for synthesizing information from targeted datasets [27].

The SLR considered studies published from 2017 up to the date of the search, April 24, 2022, and made available through three databases: the ACM Digital Library, IEEE Xplore, and the CAPES Journal Portal. The automated search feature was used, employing the search string provided below, which was designed based on the combination of the most relevant terms for the research area following several preliminary searches.

Search string: *("deep learning" OR xai OR "artificial intelligence explainable") AND "computer vision" AND ("classification techniques" OR evaluation OR stroke) OR xai methods*

The results and progression of the SLR are summarized in Fig. 1. At each stage, several studies were excluded from the review due to duplication, misalignment with the reviews objectives, or because they were not peer-reviewed articles. After the identification process, abstract screening, and full-text evaluation, 26 studies remained that met all the inclusion criteria and were included in the review.

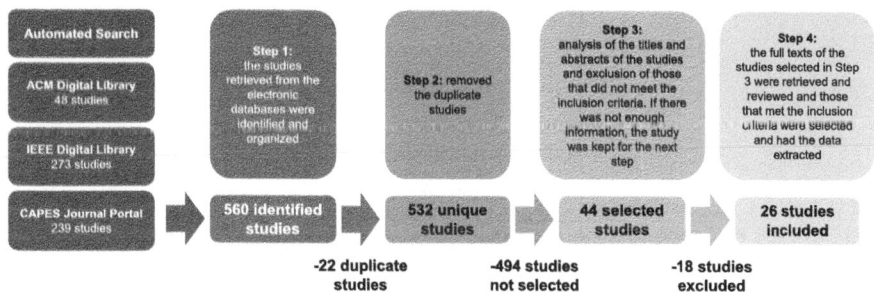

Fig. 1. Overview of the Systematic Literature Review conducted.

4.1   Results

The SLR was guided by several research questions, for which answers were sought. Each question is presented below, along with the corresponding answer derived from the data collected during the review.

In response to the question, "What type of capture do you use?", it is often impractical to deploy sensors in domestic environments. However, it is already common for doctors to record videos during physical examinations using commercially available camera equipment. Recent advancements in deep learning-based pose estimation enable systems to extract features from video recordings [26]. In the computer vision literature, various methods exist for analyzing video data to estimate joints and skeletons. Technologies such as infrared cameras with body markers offer more accurate results but rely on costly systems that are unaffordable for many clinicians and researchers [23].

Table 1 lists the papers according to the capture method cited. It can be observed that video capture was present in the majority (65%) of the papers, followed by the use of sensors, which appeared in 30

Table 1. List of papers according to the capture method used

Authors	Method
[25]	Video
[2]	Video
[39]	Video
[35]	Video
[11]	Video
[26]	Video
[23]	Video
[1]	Video
[19]	Video
[28]	Video
[15]	Video
[38]	Video and sensor
[14]	Video and sensor
[3]	Sensor
[33]	Sensor
[34]	Sensor
[37]	Sensor
[32]	Images
[17]	Images
[19]	Images

In response to the question, "Dataset authorship - own or third-party?", regarding datasets for movement classification, the availability of large-scale datasets is limited, and there are few human movement datasets available for use in rehabilitation-related tasks [8, 25].

Finally, in response to the question, "Which programming languages were chosen?", 90% of the authors used the Python programming language in their studies. Table 2 presents the authors who reported the programming language and specifies which language was selected.

4.2   Research Trends in the Field

Based on the results, it can be observed that the majority of authors use pre-existing datasets, with camera capture being the most commonly used method, and Python being the most frequently used programming language among researchers.

Table 2. List of articles according to programming language used

Authors	Programming language
[3]	Python
[38]	Python
[39]	Python
[11]	Python
[14]	Python
[34]	Python
[19]	Python
[37]	Python
[32]	Python and Matlab
[23]	Matlab

The briefly presented SLR is important for guiding this study, as it helps identify trends and gaps in the research area.

5 Development

To ensure continuity in line with the results of the SLR, we made the following decisions:

- Video motion capture, without the need for specialized sensors;
- Development of the application using the Python programming language; and
- Use of an existing dataset, opting not to create a new dataset in order to expedite the development process.

Based on these decisions, an application was developed that allows the professional in charge of the rehabilitation sessions to select the joints, parameterize the movements, and monitor their progress individually per patient.

The main actions that can be performed in the application are described below, outlining the pipeline of activities that will accompany the rehabilitation session.

The joints are obtained using the Mediapipe computer vision and AI library, which employs convolutional neural networks in each video frame to estimate joint positions, thereby generating pose estimation data. The video is captured using a conventional RGB camera (webcam).

5.1 Movement Registration

The process begins with registering the movement. During movement registration, the name of the movement and two sets of joints must be provided. The first set of joints will be used to define the expected angle of the movement, while the second set will be used to calculate a compensation angle for the movement.

The application defines the expected angle of movement as the primary angle that should be generated by the amplitude of the affected limb during a specific movement. The compensation angle is defined as the angle that should not be formed by the joints during the movement. Both angles can be used by the health professional responsible for the motor rehabilitation process to monitor the patients progress during the sessions. The joints supported by the system include the head, left shoulder, left elbow, left wrist, right shoulder, right elbow, right wrist, left hip, left knee, left ankle, left foot, right hip, right knee, right ankle, and right foot.

5.2 Parametrization of Angles

To provide a generic application that accommodates various movements and meets specific demands depending on each patient—for example, analyzing movements of the upper limbs, lower limbs, or trunk—the health professional responsible for the motor rehabilitation process can parameterize two segments of straight lines that must share the same origin in order to form an angle. This will represent the angle of the movement according to the following criteria:

- Point O - This will be the vertex (x2,y2), the starting point of the two line segments;
- Point 1 - This will be the end of line segment A (x1,y1); and
- Point 2 - This will be the end of line segment B (x3,y3).

This is what you get:

$$Vertex = O$$

$$Sides\ of\ angle = \overline{OA}, \overline{OB}$$

$$Angle = A\hat{O}B$$

Figure 2 illustrates the angle formation in an avatar. The area colored in blue represents the angle (A$\hat{O}$B) formed at vertex O during the movement, considering the line formed by the patients arm (black line - side OA) and the line formed by the patients torso (green line - side OB). This represents the desired angle in the movement, with its amplitude being the key measure of interest that should evolve as the rehabilitation sessions progress.

5.3 Session Recording

Once the movement has been registered and its angles parameterized, the session to be performed can be recorded. The healthcare professional responsible for the motor rehabilitation process must select the registered patient and the movement, after which the recording process can be initiated. Upon initiation, the computer's webcam will be activated. It is recommended that the patient stand approximately two meters away from the device capturing the video. When

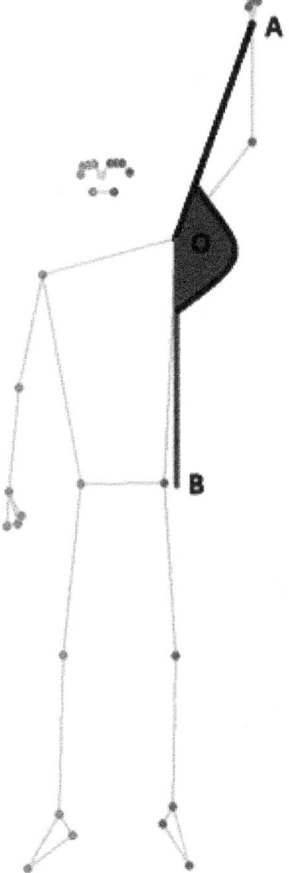

Fig. 2. Angle formation in a movement.

the webcam is activated, the recording does not begin immediately. Instead, the detected body points are first displayed in real-time on the application, and the recording starts once the user clicks the "Start Video" button. This recording setup was designed to allow the patient to view their projection on the system screen and receive initial instructions for performing the movement.

There are also two options available that serve to graphically demonstrate the two angles formed by the movement. Figure 3 illustrates the "right arm lateral raise" movement, where the green polygon represents flexibility (the expected angle) and the red polygon represents spinal compensation (the compensation angle).

Figure 3 shows the application interface, which allows the selection of the patient and movement, as well as controlling the recording process. At the bottom of the window, the camera feed is displayed, overlaid with the obtained data: joint positions and angles.

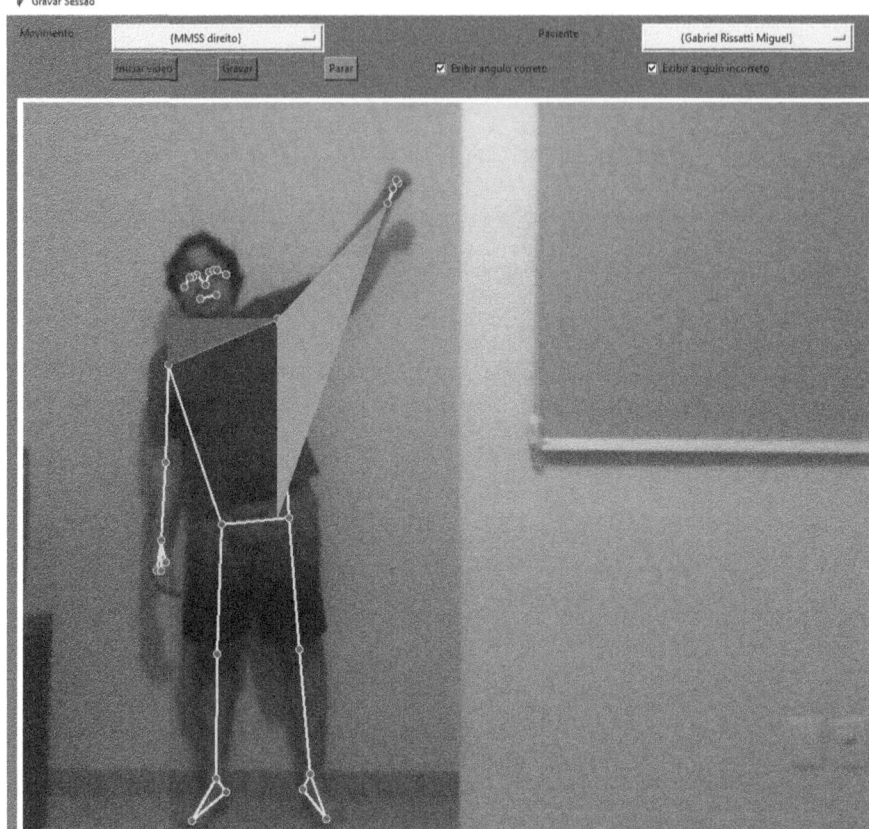

Fig. 3. Recording a session.

The MediaPipe AI framework was used to detect body points, eliminating the need to train a new AI model for this purpose. Training a new model requires a large dataset and access to specialized hardware to achieve adequate performance. Solutions like MediaPipe streamline the development process, enabling a stronger focus on the specific characteristics of the application context while providing easier access to modern technologies [22].

MediaPipe is designed for Machine Learning (ML) professionals, including researchers, students, and software developers, enabling them to quickly implement production-ready ML applications [22]. Among its packages, this study used the Pose Landmarker, which allows the detection of human body landmarks in images or videos [16].

The [24] computer vision library is used to draw the polygons in real-time during the session. At the beginning of the recording, in each video frame, two items are registered in the application: one containing the body points and the other containing the generated angles.

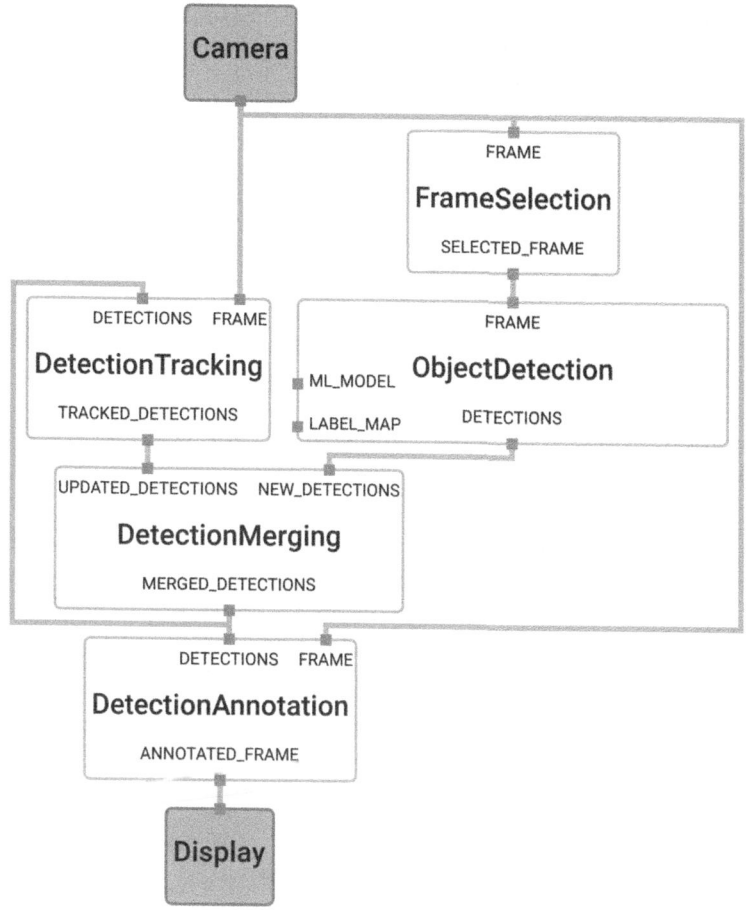

Fig. 4. Object detection using MediaPipe. [22].

The diagram shown in 4 illustrates the internal steps performed by the MediaPipe library, which are detailed below:

- FrameSelection: Enables the selection of the most relevant frames for processing, optimizing performance and reducing computational load.
- ObjectDetection: Utilizes machine learning models to identify objects within a frame. The choice of model depends on the complexity of the task and the types of objects to be detected.
- DetectionTracking: Tracks objects over time, allowing for the analysis of their movement and interactions. This is crucial in applications such as people tracking, behavior analysis, and human-computer interaction.
- DetectionMerging: Combines detections from various sources, including objects and trajectories, enhancing the systems robustness and accuracy

- DetectionAnnotation: Visualizes detections overlaid on the original frame, facilitating result interpretation and system debugging.

6   Results

The results obtained from the development and initial testing of the application are presented below, highlighting the features available to the rehabilitation professional. Once the sessions are recorded, the healthcare professional can analyze the angles generated in each session both individually and collectively.

Figure 5 shows the graph in which the professional can visualize the angles generated during each patient session over time. In this example, the movement performed was the right arm lateral raise, repeated three consecutive times. The blue line represents the arm elevation measurement (expected angle), while the orange line represents the angle generated by spinal curvature (compensation angle).

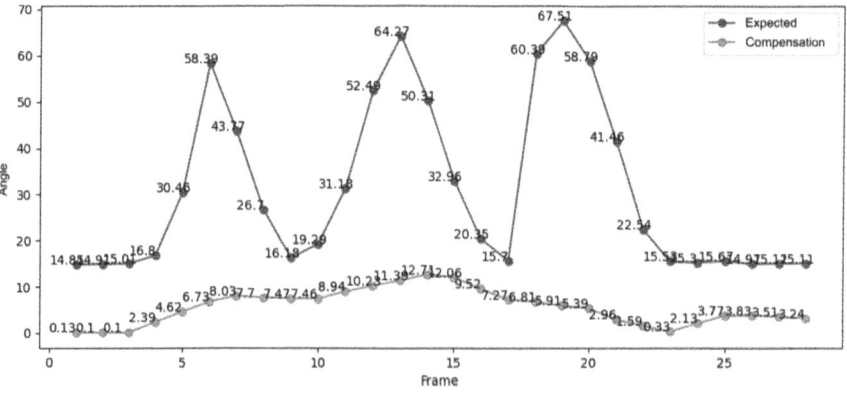

Fig. 5. Individual session analysis.

Figure 6 illustrates the progress of the patient over several sessions. In this example, the patient has completed four sessions. The blue line represents the maximum expected angle for the session, while the orange line represents the maximum compensation angle. This allows the professional to analyze the patient progress across various aspects, such as flexibility and undesired movements.

Another feature available is the ability for both the patient and the healthcare professional responsible for the rehabilitation process to watch the sessions using an avatar generated jointly with the Mediapipe and OpenCV libraries, as shown in Fig. 7, which illustrates the session visualization.

Finally, the system also allows the captured coordinates to be sent to the Rebase repository [5] to enrich the repository and contribute to future research.

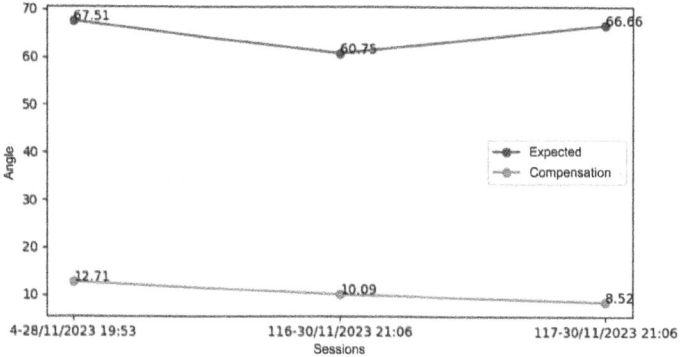

Fig. 6. Playback of a session.

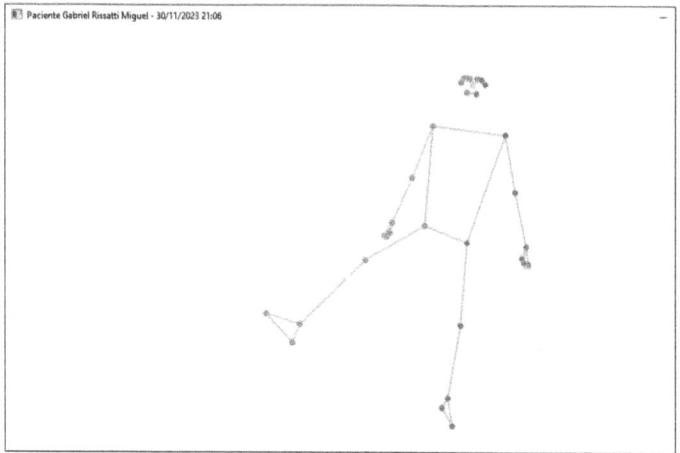

Fig. 7. Playback of a session through the avatar.

Figure 8 illustrates the steps taken during the execution of the application. The execution process can be divided into four stages: data acquisition, data processing, real-time display, and subsequent analysis, with each stage represented by a block.

The operating steps of the application perform the following functions:

- Data acquisition: The rehabilitation session is conducted by positioning the healthcare professional in front of the video capture device.
- Data processing: The captured video is processed using the OpenCV computer vision tool, and pose estimation is performed with the support of the MediaPipe library.
- Real-time display: The application interface displays the captured video, estimated pose, and calculated angles in real time.

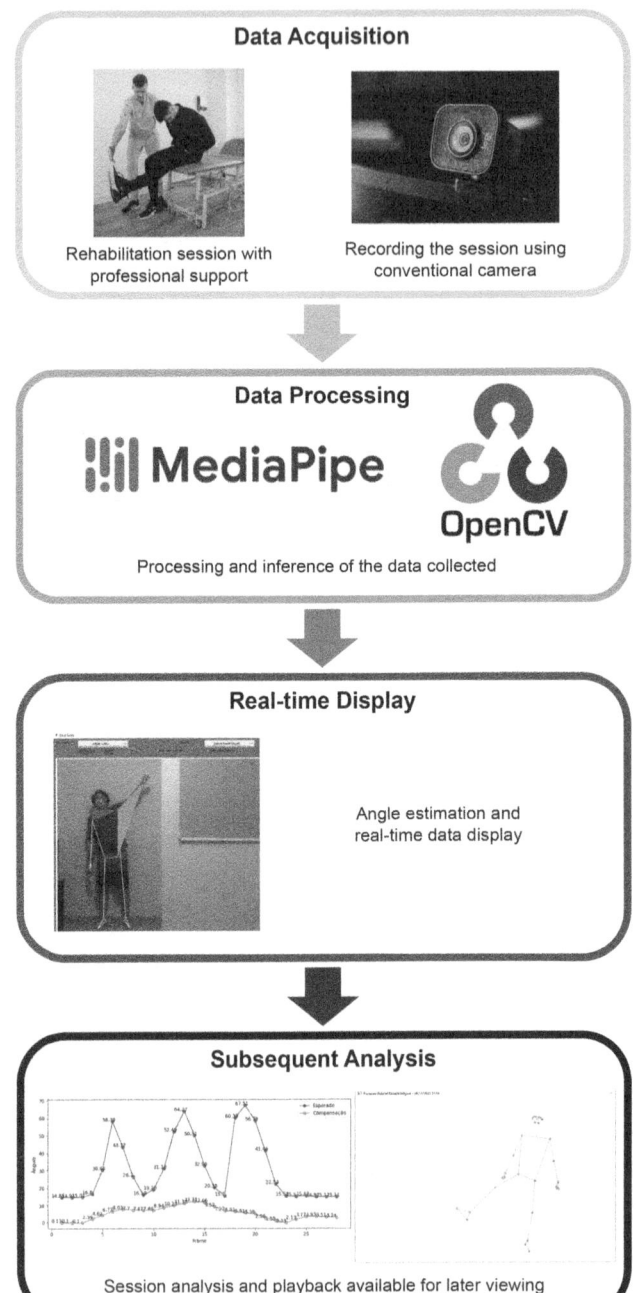

Fig. 8. Application execution steps.

– Subsequent analysis: The obtained data is stored and can later be analyzed using graphs, with the option to replay the session using the avatar.

Although the application is still in the testing phase, the stages encompass the entire initial proposal, aiming to support the rehabilitation process.

7   Conclusion

This study aimed to develop a technological tool to assist in the rehabilitation process of stroke patients. By analyzing body movements during exercise sessions, the proposed application seeks to support professionals in the field, offering more personalized and efficient treatment.

It is considered that the study conducted on SLR and the development of the application have proven relevant to the research area, as evidenced by the evaluation, albeit informal, conducted by rehabilitation professionals. The application is still at the prototype stage but includes the key features initially planned.

To continue this study, we plan to evolve the application by developing and enhancing features based on feedback from the rehabilitation professionals conducting the tests. Once the application reaches maturity, the goal is to expand its use with a group of healthcare professionals and plan a formal evaluation process in a real-world setting, supervised by the professionals, while adhering to all ethical standards and patient privacy requirements, in alignment with the initial objective of supporting the rehabilitation process.

In the future, several beneficial outcomes are anticipated, including detailed analysis of patients movements, enabling the identification of dysfunction patterns and monitoring of progress over time. Additionally, real-time feedback during exercises is expected to be possible, aiding in posture correction and improving motor coordination.

Acknowledgment. The authors acknowledge partial funding from the Coordination for the Improvement of Higher Education Personnel - Brazil (CAPES) - Funding Code 001, the National Council for Scientific and Technological Development (CNPq), and the Research Support Foundation of the State of Minas Gerais (FAPEMIG). We also thank the Research and Innovation Support Foundation of Espírito Santo (FAPES) for the resources provided through the PROAPEM project (368/2022 - P: 2022-NGKM5) and the PDPG project (129/2021 - P: 2021-GL60J), which were fundamental to the completion of this work.

References

1. Abdelbaky, A., Aly, S.: Human action recognition based on simple deep convolution network PCANet. In: 2020 International Conference on Innovative Trends in Communication and Computer Engineering (ITCE), pp. 257–262 (2020). https://doi.org/10.1109/ITCE48509.2020.9047769

2. Al-Faris, M., Chiverton, J., Ndzi, D., Ahmed, A.I.: A review on computer vision-based methods for human action recognition. J. Imag. **6**(6), 46 (2020)
3. Al-Wesabi, F.N., et al.: Design of optimal deep learning based human activity recognition on sensor enabled internet of things environment. IEEE Access **9**, 143988–143996 (2021). https://doi.org/10.1109/ACCESS.2021.3112973
4. Backes, A., Sá Junior, J.: Introdução à Visão Computacional Usando MATLAB. Autoria Nacional, ALTA BOOKS (2016). https://books.google.com.br/books?id=m0YlDQAAQBAJ
5. Barbosa, T., de Paiva Guimaraes, M., Brandão, A., Rocha, L., Iope, R.L., Brega, J.R., Dias, D.: Rebase: data acquisition and management system for neuromotor rehabilitation supported by virtual and augmented reality. In: Anais do XXIII Simpósio de Realidade Virtual e Aumentada, pp. 181–185. SBC, Porto Alegre, RS, Brasil (2021). https://sol.sbc.org.br/index.php/svr/article/view/17535
6. Barredo Arrieta, A., et al.: Explainable artificial intelligence (XAI): concepts, taxonomies, opportunities and challenges toward responsible AI. Inf. Fus. **58**, 82–115 (2020). https://doi.org/10.1016/j.inffus.2019.12.012, https://www.sciencedirect.com/science/article/pii/S1566253519308103
7. Borys, K., et al.: Explainable AI in medical imaging: an overview for clinical practitioners – Saliency-based XAI approaches. Eur. J. Radiol. **162**, 110787 (2023). https://doi.org/10.1016/j.ejrad.2023.110787, https://www.sciencedirect.com/science/article/pii/S0720048X23001018
8. Boualia, S.N., Essoukri Ben Amara, N.: Pose-based human activity recognition: a review. In: 2019 15th International Wireless Communications & Mobile Computing Conference (IWCMC), pp. 1468–1475 (2019). https://doi.org/10.1109/IWCMC.2019.8766694
9. Brandão, A.F., Dias, D.R.C., Guimarães, M.P., Trevelin, L.C., Parizotto, N.A., Castellano, G.: Gesturecollection for motor and cognitive stimuli: Virtual reality and e-health prospects. J. Health Inform. **10**(1) (2018). https://jhi.sbis.org.br/index.php/jhi-sbis/article/view/544
10. Bruno, F., Pereira, P.C., Faltay, P.: Inteligência artificial e saúde: ressituar o problema. Revista Eletrônica de Comunicação, Informação & Inovação em Saúde **17**, 235–242 (2023).https://doi.org/10.29397/RECIIS.V17I2.3842
11. Du, C., Graham, S., Depp, C., Nguyen, T.: Assessing physical rehabilitation exercises using graph convolutional network with self-supervised regularization. In: 2021 43rd Annual International Conference of the IEEE Engineering in Medicine & Biology Society (EMBC), pp. 281–285 (2021). https://doi.org/10.1109/EMBC46164.2021.9629569
12. F, A.M., Singh, S.: Computer vision-based survey on human activity recognition system, challenges and applications. In: 2021 3rd International Conference on Signal Processing and Communication (ICPSC), pp. 110–114 (2021). https://doi.org/10.1109/ICSPC51351.2021.9451736
13. Feigin, V.L., et al.: World stroke organization (WSO): global stroke fact sheet 2022. Int. J. Stroke **17**(1), 18–29 (2022)
14. Fiorini, L., et al.: Daily gesture recognition during human-robot interaction combining vision and wearable systems. IEEE Sens. J. **21**(20), 23568–23577 (2021)
15. Gammulle, H., Denman, S., Sridharan, S., Fookes, C.: Two stream LSTM: a deep fusion framework for human action recognition. In: 2017 IEEE Winter Conference on Applications of Computer Vision (WACV) pp. 177–186 (2017). https://doi.org/10.1109/WACV.2017.27
16. Google: Pose landmark detection guide (2022). https://developers.google.com/mediapipe/solutions/vision/pose_landmarker. Acessado 01 Oct 2022

17. Jogin, M., Mohana, Madhulika, M.S., Divya, G.D., Meghana, R.K., Apoorva, S.: Feature extraction using convolution neural networks (CNN) and deep learning. In: 2018 3rd IEEE International Conference on Recent Trends in Electronics, Information & Communication Technology (RTEICT), pp. 2319–2323 (2018). https://doi.org/10.1109/RTEICT42901.2018.9012507

18. Kaufman, D.: A inteligência artificial irá suplantar a inteligência humana? Estacao Das Letras e Cores Editora Ltda, 3rd edn. (2019)

19. Kim, S.T., Lee, H.J.: Lightweight stacked hourglass network for human pose estimation. Appl. Sci. **10**(18), 6497 (2020)

20. Lee, K.E., Choi, M., Jeoung, B.: Effectiveness of rehabilitation exercise in improving physical function of stroke patients: a systematic review. Int. J. Environ. Res. Public Health **19**(19) (2022). https://doi.org/10.3390/ijerph191912739, https://www.mdpi.com/1660-4601/19/19/12739

21. Lima, S.G.G., Brito, C.d., Andrade, C.J.C.: O processo de incorporação de tecnologias em saúde no brasil em uma perspectiva internacional. Cien. Saude Colet. **24**(5), 1709–1722 (2019)

22. Lugaresi, C., et al.: MediaPipe: a framework for building perception pipelines (2019)

23. Moro, M., Marchesi, G., Odone, F., Casadio, M.: Markerless gait analysis in stroke survivors based on computer vision and deep learning: a pilot study, p. 2097–2104. Association for Computing Machinery (2020). https://doi.org/10.1145/3341105.3373963

24. OpenCV: About (2023). https://opencv.org/about/. Acessado 01 June 2023

25. Park, J., et al.: A body part embedding model with datasets for measuring 2D human motion similarity. IEEE Access **9**, 36547–36558 (2021). https://doi.org/10.1109/ACCESS.2021.3063302

26. Rupprechter, S., et al.: A clinically interpretable computer-vision based method for quantifying gait in Parkinson's disease. Sensors (Basel, Switzerland) **21**(16), 5437 (2021)

27. Sampaio, R.: Estudos de revisão sistemática: Um guia para síntese criteriosa da evidência científica. Revista Brasileira De Fisioterapia - REV BRAS FISIOTER **11** (2007). https://doi.org/10.1590/S1413-35552007000100013

28. Schlegel, U., Arnout, H., El-Assady, M., Oelke, D., Keim, D.A.: Towards a rigorous evaluation of XAI methods on time series. In: 2019 IEEE/CVF International Conference on Computer Vision Workshop (ICCVW), pp. 4197–4201 (2019). https://doi.org/10.1109/ICCVW.2019.00516

29. Schwalbe, N., Wahl, B.: Artificial intelligence and the future of global health. Lancet **395**(10236), 1579–1586 (2020). https://doi.org/10.1016/S0140-6736(20)30226-9

30. Jennifer Amanda Sobral da Silva, C.H.P.M.: Inteligência artificial: aliada ou inimiga. Rev. Ciênci. Soc. Apl **9**(2), 64–85 (2019)

31. Silverberg, N.D., et al.: Expert panel survey to update the American congress of rehabilitation medicine definition of mild traumatic brain injury. Arch. Phys. Med. Rehabil. **102**(1), 76–86 (2021). https://doi.org/10.1016/j.apmr.2020.08.022, https://www.sciencedirect.com/science/article/pii/S0003999320309709

32. Slijepcevic, D., et al.: Explaining machine learning models for clinical gait analysis. ACM Trans. Comput. Healthcare **3**(2) (2021). https://doi.org/10.1145/3474121

33. Tang, D.: Hybridized hierarchical deep convolutional neural network for sports rehabilitation exercises. IEEE Access **8**, 118969–118977 (2020). https://doi.org/10.1109/ACCESS.2020.3005189

34. Tang, Y., Teng, Q., Zhang, L., Min, F., He, J.: Layer-wise training convolutional neural networks with smaller filters for human activity recognition using wearable sensors. IEEE Sens. J. **21**(1), 581–592 (2021)

35. Ullah, H.A., Letchmunan, S., Zia, M.S., Butt, U.M., Hassan, F.H.: Analysis of deep neural networks for human activity recognition in videos–A systematic literature review. IEEE Access **9**, 126366–126387 (2021). https://doi.org/10.1109/ACCESS. 2021.3110610

36. Visco, V., et al.: An explainable model for predicting worsening heart failure based on genetic programming. Comput. Biol. Med. **182**, 109110 (2024). https://doi. org/10.1016/j.compbiomed.2024.109110, https://www.sciencedirect.com/science/ article/pii/S0010482524011958

37. Xie, B., Li, B., Harland, A.: Movement and gesture recognition using deep learning and wearable-sensor technology. In: Proceedings of the 2018 International Conference on Artificial Intelligence and Pattern Recognition, pp. 26–31. AIPR 2018, Association for Computing Machinery (2018). https://doi.org/10.1145/3268866. 3268890

38. Yilmaz, A.A., Guzel, M.S., Bostanci, E., Askerzade, I.: A novel action recognition framework based on deep-learning and genetic algorithms. IEEE Access **8**, 100631–100644 (2020)

39. Zhang, C., Xu, Y., Xu, Z., Gong, M., Guo, B., Yao, D.: An augmented treble stream deep neural network for video analysis. In: 2020 24th International Conference Information Visualisation (IV), pp. 301–306 (2020). https://doi.org/10.1109/ IV51561.2020.00056

Author Index

O. Gervasi et al. (Eds.): ICCSA 2025, LNCS 15648, pp. 433–436, 2025.
https://doi.org/10.1007/978-3-031-97000-9

The manufacturer's authorised representative in the EU is Springer
Nature Customer Service Centre GmbH, Europaplatz 3, 69115 Heidelberg,
Germany. If you have any concerns regarding our products, please
contact ProductSafety@springernature.com

Printed and bound by CPI Group (UK) Ltd, Croydon, CR0 4YY

24/04/2026

02096367-0017